Romantic Art in Britain
Paintings and Drawings 1760-1860

Catalogue:
Frederick Cummings
Allen Staley

Essays:
Robert Rosenblum
Frederick Cummings
Allen Staley

The Detroit Institute of Arts
9 January-18 February 1968

Philadelphia Museum of Art
14 March-21 April 1968

Contents

The Detroit Institute of Arts   6
Philadelphia Museum of Art   7

Lenders to the Exhibition   8

Preface   9

British Art and the Continent, 1760-1860
by Robert Rosenblum   11

Romanticism in Britain, 1760-1860
by Frederick Cummings   17

British Landscape Painting, 1760-1860
by Allen Staley   25

Catalogue   31
Richard Wilson   32
Alexander Cozens   36
Sir Joshua Reynolds   38
Gavin Hamilton   44
George Stubbs   48
Paul Sandby   55
Thomas Gainsborough   57
Joseph Wright (Wright of Derby)   66
George Romney   73
Johann Zoffany   80
Alexander Runciman   85
John Singleton Copley   88
Benjamin West   97
Francis Towne   104
John Hamilton Mortimer   106
Philip James de Loutherbourg   111
James Barry   114

Angelica Kauffmann   119
John Henry Fuseli   121
Thomas Jones   128
Richard Cosway   130
William Hodges   131
Francis Wheatley   133
William Hamilton   136
John Brown   137
Master of the Giants   141
John Robert Cozens   142
Thomas Bewick   144
John Flaxman   146
James Gillray   151
Sir Henry Raeburn   153
Thomas Rowlandson   155
William Blake   157
George Morland   167
Robert Freebairn   169
George Samuel   171
Jacques-Laurent Agasse   172
Sir Thomas Lawrence   174
Thomas Barker (Barker of Bath)   179
James Ward   180
George Chinnery   184
Thomas Girtin   186
Joseph Mallord William Turner   189
John Constable   199
John Sell Cotman   209
Samuel Prout   212
David Cox   213
Sir David Wilkie   214
Benjamin Robert Haydon   223
William Mulready   226
William Etty   229

John Martin   232
William Henry Hunt   235
John Linnell   237
Francis Danby   240
Charles Robert Leslie   243
James Holland   245
Richard Parkes Bonington   246
Sir Edwin Landseer   251
Sir Francis Grant   255
John Frederick Lewis   256
Samuel Palmer   260
David Scott   268
William Dyce   270
Daniel Maclise   275
Theodore Von Holst   277
William Davis   278
Edward Lear   280
Augustus Leopold Egg   283
Richard Dadd   285
George Frederic Watts   288
John Ruskin   290
William Powell Frith   293
Ford Madox Brown   296
William Lindsay Windus   302
William Holman Hunt   304
Dante Gabriel Rossetti   309
Sir John Everett Millais   315
John William Inchbold   322
Frederic, Lord Leighton   323
Henry Wallis   326
John Brett   327
Arthur Hughes   330

Index by Artist   332

177 detail

Her Majesty Queen Elizabeth II
Mr. and Mrs. R. Kirk Askew, Jr.
Colonel Michael Barne
Professor and Mrs. I. R. C. Batchelor
Sir Alfred Beit, Bart.
Walter A. Brandt
The Duke of Buccleuch and Queensberry,
   K.T., G.C.V.O.
Richard Cavendish
Mrs. E. M. Clarke
Sir William H. Cooper, Bt.
Richard Page Croft
The Fyvie Trustees
The Viscountess Galway
Lawrence Gowing
Charles Handley-Read
Mr. and Mrs. A. M. Jaffé
Mr. and Mrs. Victor O. Jones
Dr. and Mrs. Sherman E. Lee
Leggatt Trustees
Mr. S. Bowes Lyon
Miss Veronica MacEwen
Mr. and Mrs. Thomas J. McCormick
Henry P. McIlhenny
Admiral of the Fleet the Earl Mountbatten of Burma,
   K.G., P.C., G.C.B., O.M., G.C.S.I., G.C.I.E.,
   G.C.V.O., D.S.O., F.R.S.
His Grace the Duke of Northumberland, K.G., T.D.
Mr. D. L. T. Oppé
Leona E. Prasse
Kerrison Preston
Charles J. Rosenbloom
Robert Rosenblum
Sir David Scott
Victor D. Spark
Mr. and Mrs. K. R. Thomson
Two anonymous lenders

Allen Memorial Art Museum, Oberlin College,
   Oberlin, Ohio
Amherst College
Art Association of Indianapolis,
   Herron Museum of Art
The Art Gallery and Museum, Brighton, England
Art Gallery of Ontario
The Art Institute of Chicago
The Art Museum, Princeton University
The Visitors of the Ashmolean Museum, Oxford
The Barber Institute of Fine Arts,
   Birmingham University
The Beinecke Rare Book and Manuscript Library,
   Yale University
Birmingham City Museum and Art Gallery
Bologna, Conservatorio di Musica "G. B. Martini"
Trustees of The British Museum
Brooks Memorial Art Gallery
Cincinnati Art Museum
City Art Gallery, Bristol
City of Manchester Art Galleries
City Museum and Art Gallery, Carlisle
The Cleveland Museum of Art
Courtauld Institute of Art
The Detroit Institute of Arts
Fitchburg Art Museum
Fogg Art Museum, Harvard University
The Gallery of Modern Art,
   The Huntington Hartford Collection
Hales Owen Grammar School
Hamburger Kunsthalle
Harris Museum & Art Gallery, Preston, England
Harvard College Library
H. M. Treasury and the National Trust
   (Collection of Lord Egremont, Petworth House)
The Iveagh Bequest, Kenwood, London
Leeds City Art Galleries
Leicester Museum and Art Gallery
Los Angeles County Museum of Art
The Metropolitan Museum of Art
The Montreal Museum of Fine Arts
The Pierpont Morgan Library
Museum of Art, Rhode Island School of Design
Museum of Fine Arts, Boston
National Gallery of Art, Rosenwald Collection
The National Gallery of Canada, Ottawa

National Gallery of Scotland
National Gallery of Victoria
National Museum of Antiquities of Scotland
National Portrait Gallery, London
Nelson Gallery—Atkins Museum
Nottingham Castle Museum
Philadelphia Museum of Art
Ponce Art Museum (The Luis A. Ferré Foundation)
The Philip H. & A. S. W. Rosenbach Foundation
Royal Academy of Arts, London
The Royal Borough of Kensington & Chelsea
Board of Commissioners, Royal Hospital, Chelsea
The Royal Society of Arts, London
Scottish National Portrait Gallery
Sheffield City Art Galleries
Smith College Museum of Art
J. B. Speed Art Museum, Louisville, Kentucky
The Trustees of The Tate Gallery, London
The Toledo Museum of Art, Toledo, Ohio
Vassar College Art Gallery
Victoria and Albert Museum, London
Wadsworth Atheneum, Hartford, Conn.
Walker Art Gallery, Liverpool
The Trustees of the Watts Gallery
Whitworth Art Gallery, University of Manchester
Worcester Art Museum
Worcester Public Library, Worcester, Mass.
Yale University Art Gallery

No foreign cultural manifestation is as well known in the United States as the literature of Great Britain; few schools of art have been more avidly collected by Americans, certain of its most famous pictures have even become synonymous with the word "art" for millions—yet, in our country, the extent of Great Britain's considerable achievement in the visual arts is still virtually unknown. The general image of lovely ladies and tumultuous landscapes has little relation to the facts of the vigorous and inventive school of painting that evolved in England between 1760 and 1860. This exhibition has as its point of departure, therefore, the desire to create as realistic a presentation as possible of one of Europe's most fascinating periods of art.

There have been countless exhibitions of English art in our country; one thinks of the magnificent exhibition of Turner, Bonington, and Constable held in Boston just after the Second War, or of "Masters of British Painting" held in New York, St. Louis, and San Francisco in 1956-1957, and "British Painting in the 18th Century" shown in Montreal, Ottawa, Toronto and Toledo in 1957-1958, or again of the recent exhibitions of Paul Mellon's astonishing collection of English art. Yet, while each to a degree contributed to our knowledge of British art, none of these attempted a methodical presentation of the complete span of English romantic art. Also, this country is second only to England for the importance of its public and private holdings of English art. Therefore, this exhibition has a twofold

aim: to create a more general awareness of what the artists of Great Britain were trying to achieve in what was probably that country's greatest period of pictorial creativity and, albeit of less importance, to point up the importance and the variety of American holdings in this area.

Given the exhibition's declared intention of creating in the United States a greater understanding of Britain, it seems fitting, even as it is a great honor, to have the exhibition come under the distinguished patronage of Her Majesty Queen Elizabeth II and of the President, Mr. Lyndon Baines Johnson. We are grateful to Her Majesty as well for having generously lent three works to the exhibition.

The cooperation that the organizers of the exhibition have received from their English colleagues in permitting most important loans to come to the United States for a considerable period of time and in facilitating the many practical details in connection with the loans cannot be adequately acknowledged. Particular thanks must go to The Tate Gallery and to Norman Reid, its Director, and Lawrence Gowing, formerly Keeper of British Art, whose initial support of the exhibition, which gave us the courage to attempt it, was even surpassed by their painstaking attention to all subsequent details. The British Museum was a generous lender as well; we appreciate the support that we have had from Mr. Edward Croft-Murray, Keeper of Prints and Drawings. The Victoria and Albert Museum has lent important treasures, Mr. Graham Reynolds, the Museum's Keeper of Prints & Drawings and Paintings, and Mr. Jonathan Mayne, the Deputy Keeper of Paintings, having constantly handled our many demands with dispatch and kindness. The loans from the Royal Collection have been expedited by Sir Anthony Blunt, Keeper of The Queen's Pictures, and Mr. Oliver Millar, Deputy Surveyor of The Queen's Pictures. Finally we should like to acknowledge our appreciation of the support we have had from Mr. Gabriel White, Director of Art of the Arts

Council of Great Britain, who kindly eased our approach to many of the British collections.

While the list of lenders is cited elsewhere, there are many people who have helped the two Museums and the two authors of the catalogue in a wide variety of ways, whether it be the sharing of academic knowledge or the handling of particularly difficult problems in connection with loans. The names are indeed numerous but from them the following should be cited: Keith Andrews, Keeper of Prints and Drawings, National Gallery of Scotland, Edinburgh; Sally Atkins, Witt Library, London; Mrs. Florence Barnes, Detroit; John Baskett, London; Jacob Bean, Curator of European Drawings, The Metropolitan Museum of Art; Mary G. Bennett, Keeper of British Art, Walker Art Gallery, Liverpool; Mary Lee Bennett, Assistant to the Curator of Drawings, Fogg Art Museum, Cambridge, Mass.; Linda Boyer, Department of Drawings, The Metropolitan Museum of Art; David S. Brooke, Curator, Art Gallery of Ontario; Humphrey Brooke, Secretary, Royal Academy of Arts, London; Peter Cannon Brookes, Keeper of Art, City Museum and Art Gallery, Birmingham; Charles E. Buckley, Director, City Art Museum of St. Louis; Martin Butlin, Assistant Keeper, The Tate Gallery; Professor Gian Carlo Cavalli, Director, Collezioni Comunali d'Arte, Comune di Bologna; Judith Cloake, Deputy Keeper, The Tate Gallery; Mary Delahoyd, Vassar College Art Gallery; Anne d'Harnoncourt, The Courtauld Institute of Art, London; Dr. Joseph W. Donohue, Jr., Princeton University; Louisa Dresser, Curator, Worcester Art Museum; Clive E. Driver, Director, The Philip H. & A. S. W. Rosenbach Foundation, Philadelphia; Rafael Fernandez, Assistant Curator of Prints and Drawings, The Art Institute of Chicago; Sir Ian Forbes-Leith, Bart.; Mrs. Robert Frank, London; Dr. Kenneth J. Garlick, The Barber Institute of Fine Arts, Birmingham; Eleanor M. Garvey, Assistant Curator of Prints and Graphic Arts, Houghton Library, Harvard University; John A. G. Gere, Deputy Keeper of Prints and Drawings, The British Museum; Helena Gibbon, Art Director, Harris Museum & Art Gallery,

Preston; Elizabeth Harrell, Assistant Curator and Registrar, Virginia Museum of Fine Arts, Richmond; John Harris, Curator of Drawings, Royal Institute of British Architects; Mr. D. Hart, Leighton House, London; Egbert Haverkamp-Begemann, Curator of Drawings and Prints, Yale University Art Gallery; John Hayes, Assistant Keeper, London Museum; Luke J. Herrmann, Assistant Keeper, Ashmolean Museum, Oxford; Frederick Hill, New York; Stephen B. Jareckie, Registrar, Worcester Art Museum; Dr. William McAllister Johnson, University of Toronto; Elizabeth Johnston, Keeper of Paintings, City Art Gallery, Manchester; Luigi A. Lauriola, First Secretary of the Legation, Italian Consulate, Detroit; Hugh Leggatt, London; Jeremy Maas, London; Hugh Macandrew, Assistant Keeper of Western Art, Ashmolean Museum, Oxford; Denis Mahon, London; Thomas J. McCormick, Director, Vassar College Art Gallery; Agnes Mongan, Associate Director and Curator of Drawings, Fogg Art Museum, Cambridge, Mass.; Benedict Nicolson, London; Armide Oppé, London; Dr. Stephen E. Ostrow, Chief Curator, Museum of Art, Rhode Island School of Design; Leslie Parris, Assistant Keeper, The Tate Gallery; William Plomer, Thos. Agnew & Sons, London; Leona E. Prasse, Associate Curator of Prints and Drawings, The Cleveland Museum of Art; Gert Schiff, Institute of Fine Arts, New York University; Hanson Schubart, Director, City Art Gallery, Bristol; Alan Shestack, Assistant Curator, National Gallery of Art, Washington, D. C.; Timothy Stevens, Walker Art Gallery, Liverpool; Miranda Strickland-Constable, Keeper, City Art Gallery, Leeds; Dr. John Sweetman, Keeper, Temple Newsam House, Leeds; Basil Taylor, Director, Paul Mellon Foundation for British Art, London; Colin E. Thompson, Keeper of Paintings, National Gallery of Scotland, Edinburgh; Professor Frank Anderson Trapp, Amherst College; Mr. P. O. Troutman, Curator, Courtauld Institute Galleries, London; Peter Ward-Jackson, Department of Prints and Drawings, Victoria and Albert Museum; Professor Ellis K. Waterhouse, Director, The Barber Institute of Fine Arts, Birmingham; Carl J. Weinhardt, Jr., Director, The Art Association of Indianapolis, Arnold Wilson, Curator of Art, City Art Gallery, Bristol; Marjorie G. Wynne, Research Librarian, The Beinecke Library, Yale University. The two Museums recognize with deep appreciation that the quality of the exhibition as it stands has been augmented by the assistance of not only these people but many other generously cooperative colleagues.

Creation of such a major international loan exhibition as "Romantic Art in Britain" requires months and even years of work. We were fortunate in having on the staffs of the Museums two such scholars of British art as Frederick Cummings, Assistant Director at Detroit, and Allen Staley, Assistant Curator of Painting and Sculpture at Philadelphia; their sound knowledge of the field has assured that their selection of the exhibits and their writings in the catalogue will bring about new insights into the artists even as different interpretations of the evolution of British painting will emerge. We are proud to have such colleagues.

Professor Robert Rosenblum of the Institute of Fine Arts at New York University has contributed a most welcome essay emphasizing the broader influence of English art on the continent, an influence which has only recently begun to be recognized properly.

Others on the staffs of the two Museums have played a significant role in the development of the exhibition. Mrs. May Brawley Hill and Mr. Charles Brownell assisted in clearing up numerous research problems. Miss Jane T. O'Brien achieved the admirable preparation of Dr. Staley's manuscript in Philadelphia and assiduously dealt as well with the myriad problems in connection with every aspect of the catalogue's proofreading; Miss Clara Janigian carried the responsibility of preparing Dr. Cummings' manuscript. Mrs. Susan Rossen of The Detroit Institute of Arts has also been of great assistance. The many research questions inevitably created constant challenges for the libraries of the Museums; Mrs. Marjorie L. Dixon and Mrs. Barbara S. Sevy in Philadelphia and Mr. Warren Peters and Miss Carol E. Selby in Detroit handled these problems with their characteristic enterprise. The Philadelphia Museum's Conservator, Mr. Theodor Siegl, made significant new discoveries in preparing the Museum's loans for the exhibition. The preparation of such an elaborate catalogue fraught with difficulties was easily handled by Mrs. Sarah J. Williams, Philadelphia's Editor of Publications, and her assistant, Miss Kristina Breidenbach. The Museums felt themselves fortunate to be working with such distinguished designers as Murphy Levy Wurman, Architects; the style of the catalogue complements the distinction of the art published in it. Mr. Eugene Feldman of the Falcon Press has solved the many printing problems with characteristic skill.

However, it is the lenders who have ultimately made the exhibition possible and our thanks to each of them is boundless. Lending works of art for such a length of time is difficult; it is our hope that the broader appreciation of British art that should come about because of their generous support of the exhibition will serve as some recompense for their being deprived of these treasures.

Evan H. Turner
Director
Philadelphia Museum of Art

Willis F. Woods
Director
The Detroit Institute of Arts

British Art and the Continent, 1760-1860

Robert Rosenblum

No respectable account of Western literature could give Britain anything but a major role in the hundred years, 1760 to 1860, bracketed by this exhibition; yet it is amazing how many times the history of the same century in Western art has been written as if Britain played only a peripheral, minor role in the international emergence of those new themes, styles, and anxieties which we loosely call romanticism. To be sure, some British artists of these years, like Hogarth before them, remained isolated from the continent; but others, like Fuseli, Loutherbourg, Angelica Kauffmann, Zoffany, and Agasse, were born and trained abroad and might justly be claimed, like the American colonials West and Copley, as belonging to other than British national histories. Moreover, the Channel was crossed with growing frequency, not only by British but by continental artists, so that no exclusively national history can ever offer more than an artificial fragment of the complex international whole. Indeed, keeping one's eye on both sides of the Channel can not only widen and correct our view of even the most insular of British islanders—a William Blake, for example—but can also make us realize, with increasing certainty, that from the 1760s on, Britain's contribution to establishing the conditions of modern art was fully as vital as that of any other European country.

Already in the first decade represented in the exhibition, the 1760s, two small sketches—Gavin Hamilton's *Priam Pleading With Achilles for the Body of Hector* (no. 11) and Benjamin West's

Agrippina with the Ashes of Germanicus (no. 49)—can serve to remind us of the generative role played by British artists in the initial formulation of that neoclassic mode which would finally come to dominate European art by the end of the century. With their choice of grave and heroic passages from Greco-Roman literature and history, whether Homer or Tacitus, and their archaeological efforts to reconstruct the costume and architecture appropriate to these historical scenes, such works, especially in engraved reproduction, helped to inflame throughout Europe that new romantic faith in, and longing for, the aesthetic and even the moral superiority of a long-lost classical world. That these British works of the 1760s had reformatory consequences of the international importance of Jacques-Louis David's neoclassicism is by now a well-known fact of art history; but it should be mentioned, too, that in the 1760s and 1770s, Britain also seems to have had priority in the logical counterpart to this encyclopedic recreation of antiquity, i.e., the accurate depiction of scenes from other historical periods, whether medieval or Renaissance. It was an attitude that continued well into the nineteenth century, as evidenced in this exhibition not only in modest terms by Bonington's and Cotman's Spanish Renaissance costume studies (nos. 133, 168), but also more ambitiously by Maclise's and Ford Madox Brown's projects for the competitions of the 1840s to redecorate the new Houses of Parliament with scenes culled from all pages of British history (nos. 193, 210). Indeed, the same search for fact extended quite as early to the illustration of contemporary history, particularly well represented here in the work of Copley, whose insistence upon documentary truth can not only take the guise, in the 1770s, of such hair-raising biography as *Watson and the Shark* (no. 44), which announces a multitude of later romantic collisions of man and beast, but in the 1780s, of such spectacular military events as the *Siege of Gibraltar* (nos. 45, 46), which presages that combination of journalistic horror and patriotic glory found in Antoine-Jean

Gros's Napoleonic history paintings.

Saturated with the idealist pretensions of the Royal Academy, masters like West and Copley consciously continued to quote venerable Renaissance and baroque sources as pictorial supports for their essentially modern vision of history, much as would later be the case with the history painting of David and his students. But other British artists, less ambitious and more provincial, could break these inherited molds of pictorial convention even more definitively in their search for empirical truth. One case in point is offered by Stubbs's *Lion Attacking a Horse* of 1770 (no. 14), which, while ultimately inspired by an antique marble of the same savage subject, brings this theme up to zoological date in a work whose fusion of a scrupulous knowledge of animal anatomy with a new empathy into the passions of wild beasts may well stand as the first in a long line of romantic paintings of animals in brutal combat that will culminate with Landseer and Delacroix. So used are we to measuring art-historical time by French standards that it may well come as a surprise to learn that a French copy of Stubbs's horse and lion at the Louvre, usually attributed to Géricault, must postdate the British work by about a half-century, yet another indication of the increasing evidence that French romanticism of the early nineteenth century is frequently dependent on themes and attitudes explored much earlier in Britain. The same priority is suggested more modestly in an astonishing Neapolitan window view by the Welsh painter, Thomas Jones (no. 72), who would seem to ignore the moribund landscape conventions of Poussin, Claude, the Dutch, and even of his own master, Richard Wilson, in favor of a fresh and loving record of vernacular domestic architecture, defined with cubic clarity by Mediterranean light. How easy it would be to locate this work in the wake of Corot's Roman landscapes of the 1820s, yet in fact, it is dated 1782. When the history of late eighteenth and early nineteenth century French landscape painting in Italy is finally written, Jones may well play the part of a pioneer, especially through his contact with his younger French contemporary, Pierre Henry de Valenciennes.

Even more compelling in his clear, unmitigated grasp of empirical experience is Joseph Wright of Derby, whose directness of observation is tellingly seen in the *Iron Forge* of 1772 (no. 28). As a document of an early pictorial interest in the still magical allure of the industrial revolution's dawn, it is not unique, for there are continental parallels in such other late eighteenth-century artists as the Swede Per Hilleström, the Fleming Léonard Defrance, and the Frenchman Louis Durameau. Yet especially by comparison with Durameau's view of a saltpeter factory, exhibited at the Salon of 1767 (a view which turns heavy industry into a rococo spectacle of sulfurous clouds and lilliputian figures), Wright's meticulous description of workers forging an iron bar strikes a note of photographic truth, a flash-bulb record of the incontrovertible facts of modern life that will form one of the major leitmotifs of mid-nineteenth-century painting both in Britain and on the continent.

What amounts, in such works, to a quiet pictorial revolution that will ultimately lead to the more programmatic realism of the 1840s and 1850s was accompanied, with seeming paradox, by its extreme opposite, a style of visionary fantasy. For what was so natural to the continental tradition—an indissoluble and harmonious marriage of the real and the ideal— was essentially foreign to British painting, despite the willful efforts of a Sir Joshua Reynolds to unite these two extremes. The precarious balance he achieved in works like *Lady Sarah Bunbury Sacrificing to the Graces* of 1765 (no. 6) could not be maintained for long. Thus, while such painters as Stubbs, Jones, Wright of Derby, and Hodges unpretentiously ignored this academic goal by insisting on an intensely wide-eyed and honest description of natural facts, others, more learned and ambitious, unbalanced

Reynolds' hopeful compromise in favor of the wildly unreal and abstract. Beginning in the 1770s, a strong demonic and fantastic strain could be felt in British painting, a current that was particularly stimulated by close study of Greco-Roman and Italian art, either in the original or in reproduction, and by readings in the most bizarre and imaginative pages of Western literature and legend, from Homer, Dante, Shakespeare, and Milton, to such newly explored medieval sources as the *Nibelungenlied* and the *Chanson de Roland.* Especially in the case of the Swiss-born Henry Fuseli, who was closely associated with Johann Jakob Bodmer, one of the Swiss ancestors of German romanticism, this current bears strong analogies to the passionate fervor of the *Sturm und Drang* movement of the 1770s for an art that would reject French reason and discipline in favor of the extravagantly heroic and sublime. It was, indeed, such a goal that haunted many late eighteenth-century British artists like John and Alexander Runciman, John Brown, Richard Cosway, James Barry, George Romney, John Mortimer, and Fuseli himself, artists who often spent years in Rome. There they participated, together with such other visitors from the Gothic North as the Dane Nicolai Abildgaard, in the formation of a stormy figural art that combined the anxieties of the new northern romantic spirit with an eclectic variety of Mediterranean sources, from antiquity itself through the *terribilità* of Michelangelo, the perverse grace of Parmigianino, and the grotesquerie of Salvator Rosa. With such works, whether executed in Italy or back in Britain, these artists first tapped some of the major veins associated with the romantic movement both in Britain and on the continent. Consider only *The Nightmare* and *The Madhouse* of Fuseli (nos. 66, 68), which turn the Age of Reason inside out and prophesy countless later continental inquiries into the dark side of the mind, from Goya to Géricault; the horrific inferno of Barry's *Satan Calling up His Legions* (no. 62), a Gustave Doré *avant la lettre;* or Romney's *John Howard Visiting a Prison* (no. 36), a scene

of human misery so much more benighted and disquieting than Gros's *Pesthouse at Jaffa.* So pervasive were these excursions into the macabre and the irrational that even British artists whose own personalities were considerably more balanced than, say, Barry's or Romney's, reflected, in more public ways, this precocious romanticism; witness only West's *Cadmus and the Dragon* (no. 52), with its repertory of Rosa-inspired horrors, or the same artist's *King Lear* (no. 51), with its raging, windswept fury.

Thanks to the increasing number of publications of continental art from all historical periods, some British artists could participate in these visionary currents without having crossed the Channel. The most conspicuous case in point is William Blake, whose esoteric style and symbolism have too often tempted historians to treat him as an isolated, hermetically sealed phenomenon. Yet Blake's art gains in intelligibility not only by being seen in connection with, and perhaps even as a culmination of, the anti-empirical currents of late eighteenth-century British art, but also as a counterpart to the work of the Danish-German master Asmus Jakob Carstens, a close contemporary of Blake's who lived out his short artistic career in Rome. There, like Blake in London, he pushed to further extremes the legacy of a Fuseli, a Barry, a Mortimer, sharing with the British poet-painter a compulsive need to invent strange private cosmologies that could replace stagnant religious beliefs and creating, like Blake, a Michelangelesque style of heroic figures that soared through flattened, abstract spaces. Both artists, too, were vehement in their hatred of the academic art establishment. Not only did they reject the techniques of oil-painting in favor of drawing, tempera, and watercolor, which they felt could counter the earthbound illusionism of the oil medium as practiced in the eighteenth century, but they held, in London and in Rome, privately-sponsored one-man exhibitions in which their unique geniuses were to be pitted against the official world.

So many are the rapports between Blake and Carstens that it is hard to realize that they could not, in fact, have known of each other. However, in the case of another northern romantic artist who may be fruitfully compared with Blake —the short-lived German painter Philipp Otto Runge—there may well be an actual point of contact (though hardly a decisive one), for a review of Blake's London exhibition of 1809 by Crabb Robinson was published in the Hamburg periodical *Vaterländisches Museum,* which was edited by Runge's friend Perth. Be that as it may, Runge's own version of romanticism, in which the artist, painfully severed from a decadent public tradition of religious art, tries to create his own mystical symbolism, again offers useful analogies to Blake's position. And Runge's style, too, suggests parallels with Blake's, especially in his *Tageszeiten,* a complex symbolic cycle of proto-Wagnerian ambition, in which, as in Blake, the flat, emblematic symmetries of pre-Renaissance art are resurrected as a means of evoking a lost pictorial world in which all forms are charged with transcendent meaning rather than being spiritless imitations of the randomness of perceived fact.

If Runge may not have known of Blake until the very last years of his short life, he, like all continental artists of his generation, was intensely aware of the work of one of Blake's friends and strongest artistic influences, John Flaxman, whose outline illustrations to Homer and Dante— represented here in preparatory drawings (nos. 87, 88)—were circulated in engraved form from the 1790s on all over the Western world. Chaste and unpretentious as they may seem to us today, these linear abstractions, conjuring up the pure dawn of Greek art or the visionary spaces of the *Inferno* or the *Paradiso,* provided a kind of visual primer for avant-garde artists throughout the continent, as well as in Britain; and given a list that includes David, Ingres, Runge and Goya (not to mention such lesser artists, among countless others, as Koch, Girodet, Scheffer), it would not be an exaggeration to say

that no British artist of any century exerted so wide and so varied an influence on European art as did Flaxman.

One reason for the pervasive effect of Flaxman's outlines on the continent was their ease of transmission; for as books of engravings, they could cross the Channel or be reprinted on the continent at a time when British and continental artists, and their works, were far less mobile. Indeed, beginning in 1793—the date of the first editions of Flaxman's outlines—the continent was closed to British travellers until the onset of the brief Peace of Amiens in March 1802, at which time Turner rushed to Switzerland, to be awed by Alpine thunderstorms; Flaxman visited Paris, to find nothing so beautiful there as a work that reflected his own Homeric outlines, Ingres's Prix de Rome painting, the *Ambassadors of Agamemnon;* and the President of the Royal Academy, Benjamin West, was honored by the French, who called him "the Vien of the Thames," referring to his role as a great artistic reformer, and who exhibited his *Death on a Pale Horse* at the Salon, a work whose immense Rubensian turmoil prophesies by decades the French equivalents of such scenes of full-scale terror as would be found in the art of a Delacroix or of lesser-known romantics like Louis Boulanger. But the reprise of the Napoleonic Wars in May 1803 again isolated British artists until the final demise of French imperial ambitions at Waterloo, an event which itself was later commemorated in widely varying ways by such British artists as James Ward (no. 111) and Benjamin Robert Haydon (no. 146).

From 1814 on, the dialogue between British and continental art became so agitated and vital that even the most nationalistic histories of French art or the most parochial ones of British art have not been able to ignore the constant Channel crossings of pictures, artists, and ideas. Anglo-French relations in the years 1815-1840 are particularly close on all levels of style, subject, and mood, as may be symbolized by the

fact that one work in the exhibition, the *View of the Doge's Palace, Venice* (no. 169), has been attributed both to the British painter Richard Parkes Bonington (who, as a student of Gros and an intimate friend of Delacroix, spent most of his brief career in France) and to the Baron Schwiter, a Parisian artist who frequented the same French romantic circles. In terms of history painting, the best-known cases of Anglo-French reciprocity in these years pertain to the two greatest masters of French romanticism, Géricault and Delacroix. The former left France in April 1820 to spend twenty months in Britain and arranged for his most ambitious painting, the *Raft of the Medusa,* to be shown there in a circulating exhibition; the latter, in the company of Bonington, paid a much shorter visit to London, from May to August 1825, and later, in 1828, exhibited at the British Institution two works —*Greece on the Ruins of Missolonghi* and *Marino Falieri*—that paid tribute to the inspiration of both the life and the work of a great British poet, Lord Byron. Such French romantic paintings, crowded with full-blooded figures and steeped in continental traditions of pictorial virtuosity, left almost unrealizable dreams for many British romantic artists, witness only David Scott's *Philoctetes* (no. 187), a Greek paraphrase of the heroic desperation of Géricault's shipwrecked figures, or William Etty's *Toilet of Venus* (no. 152), a reflection of the fleshy Venetian abundance and sensuality that came so much more naturally to Delacroix than to an Anglo-Saxon. In return, these French masters were stunned by the more naturalistic, unrhetorical aspects of British art, admiring as Géricault did, the animals of Ward and Landseer, the honest expressions of Wilkie's genre figures, the unvarnished truth of Constable's landscapes. The impact of this native strain of British empiricism upon French art is best known through the famous Paris Salon of 1824, where three landscapes by Constable (above all, the *Hay Wain,* which had earlier dazzled Géricault), not to mention landscapes by the Fielding brothers, Harding, and Bonington, startled French artists into a new search for pictorial techniques that could record the transient facts, the vivid sparkle of light, color, atmosphere. It was a goal that not only inspired Delacroix to retouch some of the foreground figures in his *Massacre at Chios* at the same Salon, but that left an intense impression on those French landscape painters of the Barbizon School who, like Constable himself, retreated from the growing ugliness and complexity of the nineteenth-century urban world to find their subjects in the simple, as yet unblighted beauty of the countryside. However, this classic textbook example of French indebtedness to British painting is only one of many complex interchanges of these years that demand further study. Anglomania in France extended to British literature, history, and tourism; and the Salon of 1824 included not only Thales Fielding's *Macbeth and the Witches* but a painting by Louis Daguerre (who was soon to be known as the pioneer of photography) of the *Ruins of the Chapel at Holyrood* which, as the Salon catalogue explained to a French audience, had served as the site for both Mary Stuart's wedding and the tomb of the Scottish royal family. Indeed, an inventory of pictures shown at the Parisian Salons from 1817 to 1840 would reveal an extraordinarily high proportion of British subjects, whether illustrations from Shakespeare, Milton, Byron, Scott; scenes from British history, like those by Paul Delaroche, who exhibited the *Death of Queen Elizabeth* (1827), the *Children of Edward IV* (1830), *Cromwell Opening the Coffin of Charles I* (1831); or views of British landscape and architecture. Moreover, the particularly gloomy, gothic, or visionary aura that Britain could evoke in the French romantic soul reached its climax in the enthusiastic reception of the sublime fantasies of John Martin, who in 1829 received a gold medal from Charles X and in the following year dedicated his *Fall of Nineveh* to the French King. Not only did Martin exhibit at the Salons of 1827-28 and 1834, but as Jean Seznec has demonstrated, his illustrations to the most cataclysmic pages of the Bible or Milton haunted

the extravagant recesses of the French romantic imagination, in the prints of Gustave Doré and the poetry of Hugo. One might remember, too, that another British romantic apocalypse, John Mortimer's *Death on a Pale Horse,* would later inspire Baudelaire.

Not only history and landscape painting, but also animal painting raise many unsolved problems of Anglo-French relations in these years. Looking at James Ward's *Marengo* of 1824 (no. 111) or his *Lioness and Heron* of 1816 (no. 110) offers many shocks of recognition which make one realize that the dialogue between British and French romantic animal painting goes beyond the better known case of Géricault, who copied three prints after Stubbs before his trip to London in 1820. Thus, the febrile emotion of Napoleon's charger, as interpreted by Ward, belongs to the same romantic realm of animal empathy so conspicuous in the quasi-human psychologies of Gros's military horses. Did Ward know Gros's work before his trip to Paris in 1825? As for the close-up ferocity of the disturbed lioness, the date, 1816, suggests that, as in the case of Stubbs, this uncommonly intense identification with the savagery of wild beasts precedes, rather than follows, the desperate combats of Delacroix's or Barye's painted and sculpted jungles. Even the work of Sir Edwin Landseer, too often considered as only the pictorial counterpart of British sentimentality toward animals, can be prophetic in terms of major French painting. Thus, the theme of *The Challenge* of about 1844 (no. 175), a drama enacted by noble stags in a chilly wilderness, was often to be adapted in the following decades by Courbet, who knew such works by Landseer through their reproduction in the *Magasin pittoresque* or their inclusion at the 1855 *Exposition Universelle* and who translated them into even more palpable snow, antlers, and wounded hides while, at the same time, maintaining their romantic empathy with animals in a wild state.

And there is also the question of portraiture.

To what degree, for example, did Sir Thomas Lawrence leave his mark on France, which, by 1825, he had visited three times? Already in the 1790s, in works like *Arthur Atherley as an Etonian* (no. 104), he had established a romantic portrait type of a standing figure emotionally wedded to an agitated landscape, a formula that is echoed throughout the portraiture of Gérard, Gros, Ingres, and Delacroix. And Lawrence's more official side, too, was well known in Paris, where, at the Salon of 1824, his portrait of the Duc de Richelieu was to be seen and where, in the following year, he himself was a visitor in the capacity of a state portraitist who had come to record King Charles X and the Dauphin.

Britain's artistic relations with France are so abundant and fruitful during these high years of romanticism that one tends to forget her rapports with other countries, especially of northern Europe. The art of Constable is a case in point; for if his acutely honest vision of nature has usually been grafted onto the history of French landscape painting, from Huet, Rousseau, and Dupré to the impressionists, it can be seen no less profitably in connection with some of the preoccupations of northern romantic landscape painters. In particular, his painted sketches of clouds of 1821-22 (no. 126) offer direct analogies, as Kurt Badt has demonstrated, to the fresh meteorological observation found in the cloud paintings of the Norwegian Johann Christian Clausen Dahl and the German Karl Blechen, and provide yet another example of that peculiarly romantic capacity to combine an almost scientific interest in the phenomena of nature with an intense privacy of feeling, whereby, in this case, these boundless, shifting clouds almost become, as in the poetry of the romantics, a symbol of personal freedom.

This fusion of objective fact and subjective experience is even more apparent in the work of Turner, whose vision of landscape once more evokes Northern rather than French parallels, especially with the art of his almost exact

117 detail

contemporary, the great German romantic painter Caspar David Friedrich. Again, as with Blake and Carstens, the community of feeling and intention here is not a question of specific influence but rather one of broad analogy. For both Turner and Friedrich managed to take a traditional repertory of seventeenth-century landscape styles, enrich these in turn with the new late eighteenth-century explorations of melancholic ruins and sublime expanses of sea, sky, earth, and mountain, and achieve a wholly original and overwhelming synthesis that could express the romantic metaphor of landscape as a mirror of the divine, a new secular religion that could find nature crushingly malevolent in its superhuman powers—witness only Turner's avalanche and fire (nos. 116, 120)—or awesomely mysterious in its immeasurable infinities. Although Turner's pictorial techniques finally attained an unprecedented fluidity and Friedrich's remained monastically chilly and precise, both artists pursued a common goal, the destruction of the material, palpable qualities of landscape in a sensuous continuity of light, atmosphere and color that could evoke an omnipotent force behind the diverse facades of nature. Indeed, the implicitly divine character of these engulfing sublimities often became explicit in Friedrich's

views of Gothic cathedrals and cemeteries, much as they did in the work of such British artists in the orbit of Turner as Francis Danby and John Martin, who illustrated apocalyptic visions from the Bible (nos. 153, 161) in terms of immense spectacles of nature that dwarf man to pitiful insignificance.

Turner's own search for the uncommonly dramatic in nature was constantly stimulated by his intensive and adventurous travels throughout the continent, during which he recorded, as John Robert Cozens and Philip James de Loutherbourg had done before him (nos. 59, 82), views of rugged mountain passes, shimmering lakes, fantastic architectural silhouettes (nos. 118, 121, 122). These pictorial souvenirs of a tourist's experience abroad became common coin in the work of other British artist-travellers of the early nineteenth century, not to mention the work of foreign artists in London, like the Norwegian Thomas Fearnley, who painted scenes that ranged from the fjords of Norway to the shores of Sorrento. Such travelogues, already prophesied in the eighteenth century by works like William Hodges' views of the South Pacific (no. 74), added more and more exotic spices to the romantic diet, and often, as was to be the case with John Frederick Lewis and Edward Lear, demanded that the artist leave the confines of Europe to seek inspiration. So geographically dispersed and so internationalized did these scenes of sublime scenery or picturesque genre become that it is difficult to measure the degree of interaction between the style of the British artist-traveller and that of the local pictorial tradition in the country he visited and recorded; yet such interchanges must have been common and need clarification. We know that Sir David Wilkie, visiting Spain during his continental travels of 1825-28, revealed a precocious admiration for the old masters of Spanish painting, but did Goya and his Spanish contemporaries affect him too? Were there contacts between a British artist like Danby, who lived in Geneva from 1832 to 1836, and such Swiss landscape painters as

Alexandre Calame and François Diday? What was Samuel Prout's relation to those French artists who, like him, exploited a popular market for ramshackle views of northern Gothic cities? Did Joseph Anton Koch's or Ferdinand Waldmüller's views of Alpine scenery leave their mark on such British surveyors of the same icy sublimities as John Brett? Only an international view of British art can begin to answer these questions.

Thanks to recent research, one is beginning to learn considerably more about the continental connections of the best-known movement in mid-nineteenth-century British painting, the Pre-Raphaelite Brotherhood and its satellites. Looked at from a European vantage point, this fervent fraternity of very young artists who banded together in that revolutionary year 1848, in order to achieve nothing less than a complete reformation of art, can be considered the logical continuation of earlier nineteenth-century brotherhoods of youthful artistic rebellion, whether "Les Primitifs" in the studio of David around 1800 or the German Nazarenes, who congregated in Rome shortly after. The latter group, in particular, provided a close prototype for the loves and hates of the later British artists, for their passionate contempt for the prevailing styles of the academics was only surpassed by their attraction to what they felt was the purity, piety, and honesty of art before Raphael, be it Northern or Italian, Van Eyck or Bellini. This archaizing taste for pictorial styles which could stop the last ailing breath of baroque virtuosity and illusionism, as still taught in the academies, was, indeed, an international phenomenon; and a search for incisively sharp outlines, intensely brilliant local color, and painstakingly described surface textures can be found throughout European art of the early nineteenth century, whether one considers Overbeck, Ingres, or William Dyce, the Scottish artist who, through direct contacts with the Nazarenes in Rome in 1827, established the firmest link between their ambitions and those of the much later generation of British Pre-Raphaelites. Although British artists often joined this style of obsessive realism to high-minded religious or literary subjects, as may be seen in Dyce's *Jacob and Rachel* (no. 190) or Holman Hunt's *Rienzi* (no. 215), by the 1850s, contemporary subjects and even pure landscape were also among their repertory, with results that may involve the rewriting of the history of French realism and early impressionism.

A notable case in point is the evolution of Ford Madox Brown, who in the 1830s and 1840s was educated on the continent, under Gustaf Wappers at the Antwerp Academy, and who was also familiar with the works of Delacroix, among others, in Paris. His early paintings, such as the *Body of Harold Brought before William the Conqueror* (no. 210), rephrase these rhetorical styles of history painting learned in Belgium and France; but suddenly, back in England in the 1850s, his works begin to seek out an intensive truth to optical fact that resulted in landscapes painted entirely out-of-doors and often under trying conditions, such as *The Pretty Baa-Lambs* (no. 212) and *Carrying Corn* (no. 213). For those of us conditioned to thinking of Monet's work of the 1860s as the first landmarks of *plein-air* painting, Brown's pictures of the 1850s will come as a jolting revelation in their sunlit glare, which can still make us blink, and their fidelity even to such later, impressionist perceptions as the bluish purples of reflected light.

No less disconcerting in its harsh luminosity and microscopic truth to detail is Holman Hunt's *Strayed Sheep* of 1852 (no. 216), whose fanatical realism was soon to be seen in Paris, at the *Exposition Universelle* of 1855. There it was included in a large survey of nineteenth-century British art that ranged from landscapes by Danby, historical costume pieces by C. R. Leslie and Maclise, animal dramas by Landseer, and harem interiors by J. F. Lewis to a fine selection of the most recent Pre-Raphaelite paintings, of which Millais' *Ophelia* could later inspire no less a poet than Rimbaud. The impact of these British pictures on French artists needs basic

investigation, but at least we have as a preliminary guide the articulate account of Théophile Gautier, whose descriptive powers as an art critic can rival those of Ruskin. His comments on Holman Hunt's *Strayed Sheep* are especially telling and pinpoint the visual paradoxes of its hyper-realism as well as its proto-impressionist discoveries about the color of light:

"Look at it a long time, it's worth the effort. Soon, under the strange green of the grass, bathed in blue shadows and colored russet by the sun, you will follow the tiniest folds of the ground, you will discover plants crumpled by the passing of the herd, and places where a hidden trickle of water filters through—a labor that would drive a Chinese crazy. But since the artist, determined to sacrifice nothing, cannot, for all his skill, reduce mathematically within a canvas one foot square some three miles of horizon, the result is that the details take on the exaggerated importance that a microscope bestows upon objects, and that a blade of grass attracts the eye as much as a tree. Curious phenomenon! In the whole Salon there is perhaps no painting which disturbs one's vision as much as the *Strayed Sheep.* The painting which seems the most false is, in fact, most true."
(Les Beaux Arts en Europe, 1855,
Paris, 1857, p. 42)

If Gautier could respond so intensely and so accurately to this fresh Pre-Raphaelite vision of nature, how, one wonders, did the younger French realists of the 1850s see these works?

The subject matter of many British paintings of the 1850s again raises intriguing questions about possible rapports with the contemporary French pursuit of themes culled from the anonymity of modern life; and indeed, viewed internationally, Britain must once more be given a role of major importance in the introduction of these motifs into mid-nineteenth-century painting. The programmatic realism of Courbet, as represented in works of the early 1850s like

The Stonebreakers and an immense unfinished canvas of firemen rushing through the streets of Paris, is followed, only a few years later, by such works as Henry Wallis' *Stonebreaker* of 1857 (no. 232) and John Everett Millais' *Rescue* of 1855 (no. 227), although the moralizing tenor and underscored pathos of these Victorian paintings may distinguish them from the Frenchman's work. And confronted with other British paintings of the 1850s, like William Powell Frith's *Derby Day* (no. 209), one may well ask whether Baudelaire might not have found this work, or other crowd scenes by Frith of suburban leisure or urban bustle, as quietly revolutionary as the analogous records of nineteenth-century society by another "peintre de la vie moderne," Constantin Guys.

The wealth of narrative incident and the conventional pictorial techniques of *Derby Day* may prevent us from realizing that the locales of Frith's most important paintings—the seaside, the racetrack, the railroad station—announce those of Manet, Degas, and Monet. However, in another British painting of this decade, Augustus Egg's *Outward Bound* (no. 201), the parallels with impressionism of the 1870s are instantly apparent, in pictorial as well as in thematic terms. For here, it is not only a question of the motif of Sunday-afternoon leisure—a couple enjoying an excursion in a boat—but also the flattening intensity of the light and daring precocity of the composition, which matches, as it will later do in Manet's boating scenes, the casualness of the subject. Toying with a telescope that points to unseen distances behind the spectator, this Victorian lady, like the flat expanse of sail above her, is startlingly segmented by the framing edge, whereas her companion, legs crossed and idly puffing on a cigarette, is viewed from an oblique angle whose candor is no less surprising. Probably dating from the late 1850s, Egg's tiny but unforgettably modern canvas should make us realize, yet again, that we still have much to learn about British art, not only for itself, but for its reverberations across the Channel.

Romanticism in Britain, 1760-1860

Frederick Cummings

To build the first cast-iron bridges and to conceive of skyscrapers, to find a cure for smallpox, or to discover the networks and responses of the nerves are romantic endeavors in spirit and in historical origin. To dig up the monuments of antiquity, and with the discovered fragments to recreate a vision of Greece, Rome, or medieval Europe, is romantic. To travel to Tahiti, to attempt to capture Mysore, to discover the people of the South Seas, or to conquer the North American continent is romantic. To be infatuated with and to possess an unslakeable appetite for the new, the unusual and the unknown, is romantic. To covet the exotic, to take delight in grottoes, volcanoes, glaciers, folk-tales, Icelandic sagas, Greek myths, unexplored historical periods and literatures is romantic. To examine emotional responses, to catalogue them, to describe, analyze, recreate, and enter into psychological experiences of every variety is romantic. To explore the entire range of human experience as it has been handed down in poetry, fables, folk-tales, and other literary forms and to read already known works more critically than ever before for new information and new points of view is romantic. To take delight in the world and in all facets of experience with every sense alert and every faculty vibrating is the essence of the romantic point of view.

Romanticism is often said to be a reaction against established social orders and traditional values. However, this places a negative interpretation on the period which is misleading.

In fact, romanticism is characterized by an euphoric commitment to experience. Such a commitment had been important in the visual arts since the Renaissance, but a prevailing artistic style had always absorbed it.

By the 1760s empirical techniques in the sciences, which had already been fruitful in extending human experience, were multiplied and developed within the fields of psychology, history, and literature. More than before, this empirical interest was now taken up and propagated by the artists themselves, who developed new techniques effective for probing history, the emotions, and nature even more intensively.

It is owing to the prevailing evaluation of experience that one of the leading characteristics of the romantic period is its diversity. Indeed, it is this many-faceted point of view which has been a source of confusion and even bewilderment to succeeding generations. However, it can be shown that common assumptions underly this apparent multiplicity, giving the period coherence and unity.

The very diversity of this era has prevented most writers from giving it one name. Thus, many terms have been fabricated[1]—Romantic Classicism, Neoclassicism, Neo-Baroque, and Historicism—which, although they may capture individual characteristics of the age, are inadequate to suggest the variety necessary to its definition.

In the seventeenth century the adjective "romantic" was applied to tales of late medieval romance, the world of the bards and the troubadors. By the eighteenth century, these semi-historical settings gave rise to an intense nostalgia which provided a sought-after stimulus to the imagination. This suggestion of historical inspiration, coupled with the interest in novel experiences and the emphasis on the emotions and the imagination—all make the term romanticism fit perfectly the attitudes of this period. Only the

concept of romanticism, whose original, literary sense has been thoroughly extended in the intervening centuries, is really broad enough to encompass the wealth of invention and the diversity of concepts which emerge and find expression in the visual arts at this time.[2]

William Hazlitt, the critic who links the early and late parts of the romantic era, summed up its leading point of view when he eulogized the infinite complexity and minuteness of nature.[3] The overwhelming, though gradual, realization of this period was that the actual world stretches infinitely beyond the limits of man's senses or his comprehension. Hazlitt recommended that the artist reflect this myriad variety of nature in his art and that, although beyond the total grasp of the human mind, its implications should still be part of his point of view. This realization was accompanied by an attitude of delight in the world, and the process of elaboration and refinement of this delight is the central and unifying motif of romantic art.

Compared with our experiences, the intellectual and emotional contexts of a country squire or a London scholar in 1760 were limited. Today, we easily accept numerous concurrent levels of sensation. Mass communications and streamlined travel have caused the interweaving of many formerly isolated worlds, each with its own character and rationale. The cultural experience of the eighteenth century man was restricted to literature, to the music and works of art available in his country house or in the London exhibitions or theatres, and to rare travel on the continent. Paintings, drawings, and prints were to become the particular visual arts which made it possible for the eighteenth-century individual to enter vicariously into new worlds of information and emotion. Much of the information gathered was either visual or immediately translated into visual form. As a result, the artists were among the first to grasp the popular implication of a series of new areas of experience which then found their first and most complete expression and their widest distribution through the visual arts.

By the middle of the eighteenth century, there was a demand throughout Western Europe for even the smallest fragment of visual evidence about new areas of experience, the South Seas, the Americas and Mexico, the remotest corners of Great Britain, the Alps, and Greece, and there was a general response to this need. For example, in the natural sciences, enlarged numbers of richly illustrated books on insects and animals of every variety were published. The British Admiralty sent Captain Cook to the South Seas with his own artist, William Hodges, particularly to record the novel and the picturesque. Published engravings of his drawings were purchased by a public who appreciated them not only for their exotic qualities but also for their documentary interest. The artists and connoisseurs also promoted the archaeological finds in Italy and Greece which were to provide a visual supplement of information and motifs to the historical and literary texts which had formed part of their common classical education. The visual world of antiquity, in contrast to the discoveries in the South Seas, gave new meaning to a well-established cultural experience.

It is not surprising that this new movement had its beginnings in Great Britain, where John Locke and the empirical philosophers had thoroughly prepared the intellectual climate and where Isaac Newton and other scientists had developed the techniques for the new exploration of phenomena that were to inspire the romantic imagination. At the same time, Great Britain was expansionist in its international interests, carrying on wars in the Americas against the French, and in the East, fortifying its foothold in India. The landed aristocracy was wealthier than ever before, and the economy was greatly stimulated by technological advances like those in weaving, mining, and iron fabrication. The Grand Tour, a requisite for every educated person, and now enjoyed by more individuals than ever before, developed in the upper classes an

awareness and knowledge of the fine arts which led them to patronize artists during and after their travels on the continent.

Before 1760, when George III came to the throne, the largest number of British artists were still portraitists, even though William Hogarth had given legitimacy to a new range of subjects and media, establishing new markets for the younger men. Nevertheless, John Zoffany's success in the 1760s still derived from his portraits of the Royal Family and reflected the enthusiastic patronage of George III and Queen Charlotte who had a penchant for German-speaking artists. The Royal Family also gave commissions to the historical painter Benjamin West, who became the King's Painter, and to George Stubbs, Thomas Gainsborough, and Sir Thomas Lawrence. In addition to extended royal and aristocratic patronage, a new group of patrons of the middle class appeared. The actor David Garrick used portraits of himself by Zoffany, Reynolds, Gainsborough, Mortimer, and numerous others almost as a form of publicity. Early in the nineteenth century it became fashionable to collect works by contemporary British artists, and a group of such collectors including Lord de Tabley, Lord Egremont, and Robert Vernon built important collections.

To increase their incomes, the artists themselves held private exhibitions with admission fees; these were often popular and in the case of John Singleton Copley rivalled those of the Royal Academy. The innovation of public exhibitions which began in 1760 coincides with the establishment of professional societies for artists and the vogue of drawing academies. The Society of Artists of Great Britain held its first annual exhibition in 1760, and it was followed a year later by the Free Society of Artists. The Royal Academy was founded in 1768 and held its first exhibition in 1769. Each of these groups organized annual public exhibitions which became fashionable for bringing artists' works to the attention of the public. Artists who lived in Bath

or Derby could now develop a reputation in London, while relying on a well-established patronage in the provinces.

Although the art of this period is marked by diversity and continuous change, its new and germinal ideas can be reduced to five prevailing concentrations, each with its own new techniques. First is an unprecedented interest in the scientific investigation of nature and its application to works of art. The second is the thorough investigation of the past, not only through the use of literary descriptions but also by using the technique of archaeological verification. Third is the more critical reading of literary texts in search of heightened emotional experience with the accompanying discovery and exploitation of a wide variety of new literary sources. Fourth is an unprecedented and almost bewildering fascination with the present, leading artists not only to greater involvement in portraiture, topography, and current events, but even to criticism and caricature of their own society. Fifth is an intensified concentration on psychological responses, the emotions and the emotional. This development of new interpretations of emotional response required the relinquishing of standardized illustrations and replacing them with that which is felt and observed. This interest included an emphasis on the imagination and extended to the scientific study of the nervous system.

No single or predominant group of visual forms was flexible enough to give expression to each of these concentrations. Each required its own techniques and visual vocabulary. Even within a given category, such as history, archaeological techniques provided a wide array of new visual forms. This kind of enrichment occurred within each of the other areas of concentration, multiplying to a hitherto unexpected degree not only the types of experience available to the general public but also the artistic means for their representation.

The first area of romantic concentration is best illustrated by George Stubbs who undertook, in the 1760s, a group of highly original subjects of a type that had not appeared before in British art. These were his anatomical drawings of the horse, begun in 1757, and his first exhibited lion and horse in combat of 1763. One might refer to his new interests as those of an *animalier,* but few animal painters before him had consistently attempted to paint zebras, tigers, lions, panthers, and the rhinoceros behaving naturally and in their own environment. The emotional intensity and artistic power of such themes as *A Lion Attacking a Horse* (no. 14) reveal Stubbs's insistence that these subjects were to operate at the highest aesthetic levels.

In his wish to surpass ancient art through his studies of nature, Stubbs broke with the prevailing academic theory that gave precedence to antique sculpture. He also made more convincing representations of his subjects through disciplined observations combined with anatomical dissections. His *Lion Attacking a Horse,* inspired by an ancient marble group now in the Palazzo dei Conservatori in Rome, shows two animals struggling in the mortal conflict of primeval instincts amidst the vast panorama of nature. The ferocity and terror of the animals were so heightened that the result was a more monumental and more deeply moving drama seen almost in human terms which was indeed aesthetically and technically superior to his antique model.

Stubbs was then joined by a host of other artists who compulsively studied the figure with an informed awareness of its surface details and its underlying structure. They now represented nature more objectively and with more penetration, achieving a dramatic response as if they had examined the subject through a microscope or had isolated and intensified some segment by means of a magnifying glass. In *The Old Man and Death* (no. 29), Wright of Derby represented a skeleton imbued with lifelike qualities and in

doing so made the presence of death more palpable and intensified the emotional conflict. He is known for representing scientific experiments and for studying different kinds of reflected light, such as that from a glowing ingot in *An Iron Forge* (no. 28). A minute investigation of nature was made by Thomas Bewick, who carried out extensive research through watercolor drawings (no. 84). He dispensed with stuffed animals, often incorrectly mounted, and drew from life in the woodlands or from fresh-killed birds. This resulted in brilliant and diminutive watercolor drawings recording jewel-like feathers and dead specimens. Like numerous other artists, Lord Leighton made detailed nature studies such as the head of *A Thistle* (no. 230) and, like Dürer, William Henry Hunt dramatized a fragment of nature in such works as the *Hawthorne and Bird's Nest* (no. 156). Edwin Landseer drew dissections[4] and painted a host of animals including *Ptarmigan* (no. 173) and *A Boar* (no. 172). Belonging to the same tradition are Bonington's *Two Parrots* (no. 166) and Edward Lear's *Grey Cockatoo* (no. 196). This manner of isolating a segment of nature toward the end of closer inspection, was nurtured through the study of early European art as found in the carefully wrought figures of Raphael, the studies of natural detail by Dürer and the incisively drawn portraits of Holbein.

A similar minuteness of focus was applied to the treatment of light. The critic John Ruskin realized that in Hunt's *Strayed Sheep* (no. 216) the pigments selected made the same light impressions upon the mind as those caused by the light itself, thus recreating by artistic means the same effect as the visual impression itself.[5] A similar observation could be made about Ford Madox Brown's *Summer's Heat* (no. 212) where the artist has recreated his perceptions of the momentary conditions of sunlight falling on the human form. Some twenty years later, Monet and Pissarro were to make similar observations by painting human figures in open sunlight, achieving similar coloristic effects through the same perceptual techniques.

The romantics also turned to literary sources with techniques which resemble those systematically used to probe the secrets of nature. As a result, there was an unprecedented series of discoveries, often by the artists, of an entire range of literature that had not been a part of the emotional life of Western Europeans before. Their new sources included Homer, Ossian, Dante, a broad spectrum of the Elizabethan playwrights, and an unprecedented mining of Shakespeare.

Because literature was a vital source of information about the world, especially about the human emotions, a dramatic synthesis of literature and art emerged during this period which had been impossible before and has not occurred since. Dante's *Divine Comedy* was among the discoveries of the romantic artists. Milton's bold heroes and his tendency toward psychological characterization led to an increased attention and representation of his works by Blake (no. 98), James Barry (no. 62), and William Dyce (no. 189). Medieval songs with a similar epic style, such as the *Chanson de Roland* (no. 70) and the primitive themes of folktales which presuppose an emotional participation by the reader not provided in the simplified literary style, now became the inspiration of major works of art (no. 29). The literary characters of Homeric antiquity, larger, simpler, and more noble than modern men, who seemed to perform on a stage of simpler choices, grander designs, and purer motives than contemporary Europeans, now appear in force in European art. The plays of Shakespeare had prepared British artists for an appreciation of the dramas of Aeschylus (no. 41) and Euripides (no. 33), which were now revived. These took their place alongside the works of other traditional antique authors like Ovid (no. 52), Tacitus (no. 49), and Cicero (no. 42). The heroes of the Old Testament and the visionary book of *Revelation,* neglected since the middle ages, were now given value by Blake (nos. 95 and 96) and Francis Danby (no. 161) for their grandiose images, their suggestion of encompassing designs, and their portrayal of the imaginatively stimulating activities of spiritual beings.

While the artists were discovering new literary sources from the past, writers were producing works in a similar vein which were then illustrated by the artists. A writer like Blake created quite new epic beings resembling those known from *Revelation,* Milton, and Dante, in his *Jerusalem* (no. 99). He also illustrated (no. 94) the poem by his predecessor Thomas Gray entitled *The Bard* (1757) in which the visionary powers of the poet enabled him to subdue an oppressive monarch. The virtuous existence of the Byzantine general Belisarius, as reinterpreted by the French dramatist Marmontel, was a source of inspiration for Benjamin West (no. 50) and, before him, for John H. Mortimer. Francis Wheatley reinterpreted one of the most passionate moments in Rousseau's novel *La Nouvelle Héloïse* (1761) in which a lover dwells with his beloved in an idyllic country place where their relationship is fostered by her patriarchal husband (no. 76). The death of the innocent younger brother of Cola da Rienzi and his own dark passion as leader of a popular revolutionary movement are the subjects drawn by Holman Hunt (no. 215) from Bulwer-Lytton's *Rienzi* (1835).

As the period progressed, the utilization of ancient and contemporary sources became more informed and even more sophisticated. The repetition of the exact subject done by another artist was considered taboo, and there was an unending search for new themes, new approaches to old sources, and new interpretations of traditional subjects.

The scholar, writer, and well-informed guide to antiquities Johann Joachim Winckelmann (1717-1768) was the first major romantic thinker and writer, and he introduces the third romantic concentration, that of history. His passionate eulogy of Greek art in the essay, *Thoughts Concerning the Imitation of Greek Works in Painting and Sculpture* (1755)[6] is the first statement of a new kind of involvement with the materials

of antiquity, and it leads us easily into one of the most important romantic concentrations, the study and use of the past. Winckelmann followed his early essay with a *History of Ancient Art* (1764)[7], in which he used observation, measurement of antique sculpture, and drawings of a wide selection of ancient monuments toward the specific end of revealing the beauty known to the Greeks. Winckelmann insisted that Greek sculpture is closer to an original purity of form that characterized Greek society and which reflected a pure vision of beauty engendered by their pristine culture. His vision of an ideal existence characterizes the nostalgic gleaning of history for numerous decades to follow. Indeed, the techniques he developed of observation, measurement, analysis of literary sources, firsthand observation, and the application of principles drawn from the art of an historical culture to the society of his own time were to be continuing and fruitful romantic techniques.

Employing the techniques refined by Johann Winckelmann, the romantic artists learned to use archaeological evidence to verify literary descriptions in order to obtain a fuller and more accurate view of the past. The great potential of archaeological discoveries as a source for the visual arts may be seen in the influence of the important archaeological finds of the mid-eighteenth century near Naples. In 1711 and 1733 excavations were begun at the base of Mt. Vesuvius in the ancient Roman cities of Herculaneum and Pompeii, unique in being miraculously preserved by the volcanic eruption of 79 A.D. The sites were carefully guarded, and the research was carried on under the enlightened enthusiasm of Charles III, king of the Two Sicilies. The discoveries were engraved and published by the Accademia Ercolanese from 1755 to 1792[8], and the finds were preserved in the museum at Portici which became an essential stop of the Grand Tour. These artifacts provided a slice of life from antiquity with abundant examples of interiors, everyday utensils, and even safety pins, instantaneously preserved and

since undisturbed. Because the context of ancient life was thus revealed intact, the characters known from ancient literature were suddenly brought to life. For the mid-eighteenth century, this created an impact on the imagination like a photograph of the face of the moon in the mid-twentieth century. Everything Greek and Roman was now thoroughly examined in order to establish the individuality of the antique world. For the first time in human experience a remote age, formerly viewed indistinctly, became real and tangible. As an age, it came completely into focus. This striking new dimension of human experience created an intellectual climate in which people began to realize the variety of which history is composed.

The ancient literary texts which described the individuals and the life of antiquity were now sought out, revived, and widely read. Agrippina (no. 49), Achilles, and Hector (no. 11) became individuals capable of arousing the most intense emotions. The evidence brought forth in the excavations was largely visual, and it is natural that the artists were first to grasp its implications. Painters like Gavin Hamilton placed Priam, Hector, and Achilles in interiors which used ancient furniture, utensils, and poses drawn from antique sculpture (no. 11). Benjamin West (no. 49) and, in France, Jacques-Louis David (1748-1825) took up the idea, and it was extended in the archaeological reconstructions of nineteenth-century French artists like J. A. D. Ingres (1780-1867).

So popular was this preoccupation with the visual re-creation of antiquity that such contemporary personalities as Lady Sarah Bunbury (no. 6) wished to be portrayed as an antique vestal; William Hamilton of Bangour (no. 10) wished to be seen as an antique poet; and Viscountess Bulkeley (no. 31) wished to be presented as Hebe, cupbearer to the gods. Like the epic beings Blake admired in Milton and like those he created in his own poetry, the heroes of antiquity were admired as grander, nobler, and physically more perfect than the moderns. The enthusiasm for a society at once larger than life and less complex resulted in an almost irresistible urge to return to a society by definition unsullied and more perfect than any since.

Greece and Rome received a great deal of emphasis in the new evaluation of history, especially in the first half of the romantic period. However, a corresponding point of view led to the concurrent exploration of subjects from early British history.

Although the first work reflecting this interest to be included here is Alexander Runciman's *The Landing of St. Margaret* of 1772 (no. 40), Samuel Wale began exhibiting medieval subjects from the life of Edward IV in 1760, and he was followed in 1762 by Edward Penny with a scene from the life of Jane Shore. John H. Mortimer also exhibited medieval subjects in 1763 and 1764. The same artists who had painted themes from Greek and Roman history also represented medieval subjects. Gavin Hamilton painted an *Abdication of Mary Queen of Scots* commissioned by James Boswell, and Benjamin West's first exhibited medieval subject was in 1773.

The plays of Shakespeare, particularly *Macbeth* (no. 69), *Henry VIII* (nos. 97 and 164), *King Henry VI* (no. 77), and *King Lear* (nos. 51 and 211), were important stimuli to the developing interest in early British history. Josiah Boydell's commissions to numerous artists to illustrate passages in Shakespeare's plays, and the engravings which he published after them, served to popularize these subjects. This interest in medieval and late medieval British history was climaxed by the cartoon competitions for the decoration of the Houses of Parliament of 1843-44 when national subjects were selected.

From the beginning, scenes from medieval history required some suggestion of medieval setting to lend authenticity, and this idea led eventually to accurately reconstituted and costumed pieces.

The interest in medieval subjects in painting coincides with the first significant appearance of historical costume on the London stage in 1762-63. In the same year, Horace Walpole tells of visiting a private theatrical about Jane Shore at Holland House, with Lady Sarah Bunbury in the leading role, in which the actors were dressed in costumes of the period.[9]

David Wilkie's desire for historical accuracy was so acute that he attempted, when possible, to obtain the actual costumes of his figures, as in *Sir David Baird Discovering the Body of Tippoo Sahib* where his models were Indian soldiers then in London (no. 142). Bonington made careful studies for his period subjects (no. 168), and for a portrait, Haydon paid Wellington's valet to obtain the top hat, trousers, and cravat of his master (no. 146). The most extreme examples of researched historical representation occur among the Pre-Raphaelites; a good example is Holman Hunt's *Rienzi* (no. 215), in which every detail was carefully investigated to obtain authenticity.

Although history and literature were stimulating sources of experience for the romantic artist, the present was of even greater fascination. By far the predominant interest of romantic artists was the life and activities of their contemporaries. It is not only the variety of ideas and themes but, in particular, this self-conscious interest in the present, the immediate experience, and the momentary which distinguishes romantic art and particularly that of Great Britain. While earlier artists were relatively restricted in their range of contemporary subjects, British artists now selected from the entire spectrum of contemporary experience. Military exploits with their color, fanfare, and heated emotion were particularly popular. Military heroes became glamorous figures. Benjamin West's *General Kosciusko* (no. 53), David Wilkie's *Sir David Baird* (no. 142), Benjamin R. Haydon's *Duke of Wellington on the Field of Waterloo* (no. 146), and Copley's *Lord Heathfield* (no. 45) engaged the imagination because their contemporaries could see in these heroes

believable reflections of the over-scaled personages of antiquity or of the medieval period.

This self-conscious interest in the present, as practiced by the romantics, brought forth a number of themes which had either been dormant or were completely new. Among these subjects were the race, with the racecourse, horses (no. 12), and jockeys in their vividly colored costumes, matched only by the dash and sleekness of their elegantly dressed owners (no. 209). There were also hunting scenes, such as John Zoffany's *Duke of Richmond* returning after bagging game (no. 38). Fashionable outings in the park, showing elegant men and women conversing together, were painted by Gainsborough (no. 21). Themes of social interest and commentary like George Romney's *John Howard Visiting a Prison* (no. 36), G. F. Watts's *The Irish Famine* (no. 204), and Henry Wallis's *The Stone Breaker* (no. 232) also make their appearance. The self-examination of this period extends even to caricatures of contemporary life like those of James Gillray (no. 89). Technological experiments like Wright's *An Iron Forge* (no. 28), symptomatic of the profound changes wrought by the industrial revolution, contrast sharply with such exotic or orientalizing subjects as Wilkie's *Captain Leigh and his Dragoman* (no. 144) or J. F. Lewis's *Life in the Harem* (no. 179). Portraits of every kind from isolated individuals to situation portraits such as *Queen Victoria and the Duke of Wellington Reviewing the Life Guard* (no. 174) became more popular than ever before. Landscape and animal scenes also belong to this category of contemporary subjects. If one adds the numerous self portraits (nos. 37, 42, 64, 65, 85, 150, and 184), it becomes apparent that the romantic, with all his delight in the past, was most passionately devoted to the present.

The fifth and last of the leading romantic interests to be considered is the fascination with psychological responses, the emotions and the emotional. It becomes increasingly apparent in the scenes taken from everyday life that the key to the subject and composition of a given painting

13 detail

is its emotional orientation. For example, in Copley's *Watson and the Shark* (no. 44), the theme is not so much the anticipated melodrama of a man about to be bitten by a beast as it is the summation of emotional responses among the rescuers of the terrified Watson, since the shark has already devoured his leg. In George Stubbs's *Labourers* (no. 13), which is one of the earliest of these intimate psychological dramas, the subject is quite consciously an emotional interplay among the rustic individuals who are replacing the tailgate of a brick-cart. At the end of this development, William Powell Frith's *Derby Day* (no. 209) is a panoramic catalogue of the individual concern or disinterest of different characters and social classes to a particularly pathetic incident and, as such, is a descendant of Stubbs's *Labourers.* Copley, Wright, and Wilkie, among others, were masters of the psychological study. This became a separate vehicle for imaginative invention, allowing the artist to display his originality and genius. Wilkie's early genre subjects (no. 137) are organized as intimate dramas in much the same way as his imposing historical paintings (no. 143). An artist like Fuseli was especially attracted to extreme emotional situations, and his original dramatic interpretations were considered an important part of his genius. *The Nightmare* (no. 68) is the best example of a situation so extreme that it can be called sensational. Fuseli also attempted compositional devices, recommended by the art theorist Edmund Burke, that give the observer an almost physical sensation of the emotional implications of his drama. In *Macbeth and the Witches* (no. 69), the manipulation of the narrative to include a suggestion of Macbeth's visage from the climax of the play allows a vicarious participation in an almost hallucinatory vision. This supernatural context was designed to elicit an emotional response of almost neurotic intensity. Needless to say, a great deal of inventiveness was applied to the selection and arrangement of dramas such as these.

As in our categories of history and literature, it is

particularly important that new techniques were developed to make the depiction of the emotions more complete, more striking, and yet more convincing. Pre-romantic and romantic painters generally began with the writings and engravings of Charles Le Brun (1619-1690), the seventeenth-century writer on expression, but the best of them made fresh observations and introduced new emotional situations not anticipated in the baroque period. The clue to their relinquishing of pattern-book illustrations appears in such fresh and intimate situations as Wilkie's young girl receiving her first earring (no. 141) or in Stubbs's *Labourers* where commonplace dramas, which were not of interest to the generation of Le Brun, are represented.

The concentration on emotional responses is an underlying theme which draws together a large group of romantic works. For example, Gavin Hamilton's *Priam* (no. 11) is a convincing psychological study of the reactions of each participant to the heartrending plea of a father for the body of his son. Hamilton's perceptive analysis gave this drama emotional conviction just as research among antiquities had given it historical conviction. Stubbs's *Labourers* (no. 13), Copley's *Watson and the Shark* (no. 44), and Wright's *The Old Man and Death* (no. 29) are dramatic re-creations of emotionally moving situations requiring substantial imaginative and intellectual activity on the part of the artist. The intellectual creativity required by the reconstitution of emotional situations raised these scenes of everyday life to a new intellectual level. This was quite unforeseen by a theorist like Reynolds, who attributed a limited value to incidents without rich literary or historical associations. It is this intellectual and imaginative element raised to a new aesthetic level, stimulated by firsthand observation, and supplemented by the scientific technique of tracing the functions of the nerves, that makes these psychological dramas among the most provocative themes in romantic art.

It would take a much longer essay to trace all the

implications of the romantic concentration on the emotions and the emotional. The interest in the imagination, intuition, the spiritual, and the new vitality of Catholicism, are related to it. Out of this interest developed the psychological portrait, a less "tasteful" portrait type, but one which stressed emotional penetration like that which appears in the *Self Portrait* (no. 64) by James Barry. The self-consciousness reflected in this preoccupation with the emotions ultimately made acceptable an emotional self-involvement—even introversion—which would only find its fullest visual realization in the period after 1860.

The spectrum of forms used by romantic artists is almost as varied as the range of their ideas and subjects. No single formal vocabulary can be said to characterize the period as a whole or even one of its parts. Indeed, concurrent diversity in formal matters is as much a distinguishing characteristic of this period as is the choice of subject matter. This very wealth of visual forms in romantic art has been even more confusing to the public and to specialists than has the variety of ideas. The range of treatment extends from the tendency to generalization and breadth in paintings by Sir Joshua Reynolds to the precision and refinement of George Stubbs's anatomical drawings. It continues until the end of the period, when Turner and Wilkie increase their inclination to generalize while Ford Madox Brown and John Brett continue the artistic tradition begun by Stubbs.

The increasingly informed rendition of natural and historical forms made even more complex the already complicated interweaving of artistic manners and techniques. The art forms of a given historical period were often frankly copied. Just as often, the artistic principles of an historical period served the artist and were transformed by him into new formal vocabularies. Gothic sculpture lies behind William Blake's simplified female figures, as the principles of design of medieval manuscripts serve for his compositions and illuminated books. Michelangelo, Mannerist

painting, and antique sculpture all support Fuseli's art. Greek vase painting is the source of Flaxman's schematized and highly abstract illustrations of the *Iliad* and the *Odyssey,* just as Greek and Roman bas-reliefs lie behind the designs for portraits by George Romney. The seventeenth-century Flemish masters, Van Dyck and Rubens, prepare for numerous designs by John Copley, James Ward, and David Wilkie. Italian primitive and early Northern paintings were collected by Prince Albert in the 1840s, and their purity of form and vivid colors were influential in William Dyce's paintings and in his frescoes for the Houses of Parliament. In addition, Dutch seventeenth-century painting was a stimulus for the genre scenes of George Stubbs and David Wilkie. Indeed, the shimmering visual qualities of Dutch painting, and especially the play of light in such works as Jan Vermeer's *View of Delft,* are the ultimate source, confirmed by observation, for the shimmering light in Ford Madox Brown's *Summer Heat* (no. 212).

The interest in a wide variety of historical forms, often quite different from those of the Renaissance with its reference to illusionistic space, finally disrupted the centuries-old Renaissance tradition and established the groundwork for impressionism, the Art Nouveau, and Postimpressionism. This continuing process involved two things: first, an increasing emphasis on empirical values and especially on the minute detail of isolated parts. The refusal to subordinate their interest in minutiae to other considerations led to a disruption of the Renaissance tradition, whereby figures are differentiated in space and related to a space continuing that of the observer by an artificially constructed perspective system. Secondly, the concentration on historical forms for their own sake led to a valuation of the form itself rather than to its historical context. This led to a valuation of historical form for the sake of form or that which has been called in other contexts, art for art's sake.

An emphasis on line and "naïve" spatial arrangements is the first clue to the development of non-illusionistic devices derived from historical

forms other than those of the Renaissance. George Romney's arabesques and two-dimensional patterns drawn in intensely contrasting strokes of black ink on white paper, like sunlight and shade on the Roman bas-reliefs from which these motifs are ultimately drawn, are the first designs suggesting the establishment of quite new formal values. William Blake followed this lead by using medieval manuscripts as a source for his own highly original compositions made up of elongated arabesques. Like the designs of Blake, Flaxman's Homeric illustrations show two-dimensional patterns based on Greek vase painting rather than the illusionistic perspective system of Renaissance art. Samuel Palmer's use of naïve space and his simplification of forms in the Shoreham drawings represents a similar point of view. The interest in linear pattern, simplified design, and primary colors received stimulus from Nazarene painters in Germany, who had developed their style in Rome early in the nineteenth century. Artists like William Dyce were particularly sensitive to the linear purity of the works of Johann Friedrich Overbeck, Carl Philipp Fohr, and Joseph Führich, which was, in turn, learned from fifteenth-century Italian and North European art. In Great Britain, William Dyce followed their example and reinterpreted their sources with a sensitivity to linear considerations that even surpassed his German colleagues. The presence of Prince Albert, his collecting of Italian primitive and early North European art was a stimulus to Dyce, Daniel Maclise (no. 193), and the Pre-Raphaelites to imitate the elongated figures and patterned arrangements of late medieval art. In a work such as Ford Madox Brown's *Summer Heat,* the female figure is like a jamb sculpture of the late Gothic or early Renaissance period, made intensely visual by concentration on light and color. These elongated figures, infused with grace, are the climax of the formal innovations of George Romney, Blake, and Flaxman.

The romantic period is unique within the history of art, because it saw the dissolution of the long-established Renaissance tradition and the beginnings of modern art. It is, therefore, in itself a period in flux and one of rapid, recurrent changes. By 1860 the interest in precise detail, primary colors, and the study of historical forms had become so important that the fertile tradition of psychological dramas and the tendency to emphasize empirical values was subordinated to a new concentration on form for its own sake. With the death of Prince Albert in 1861, and after the Pre-Raphaelites had completed their principal works, the most fertile interests of the romantic period are no longer the stimulus for new forms and ideas. In the works of an artist like Sir Edward Burne-Jones whose principal works originated after 1860, matters of pure design, reflecting the transformation of historical forms into a very personal idiom, are dominant. His psychological interests are no longer focused on the outer world and his contemporaries but develop facets of his own personality and his inner emotional life. The overtly manifested self-consciousness which marked the dramas of the romantic period now becomes introversion and self-involvement. In the period following 1860, emotional interplay between individuals gives way to the introspection of Aestheticism, highly personal figure types, and the resplendent, purely visual feasts of Albert Moore and James McNeill Whistler.

It is an incredible fact that the energy of the romantic artist was equal to the materials increasingly made available to him. His alertness led him to follow closely the new discoveries in archaeology, the sciences, technology, and literature, and their visual implications found immediate reflection in his art. At times, it may seem almost that experience, in itself, was his goal, so important is it for his art and his way of thinking about the world. However, this is rarely the case. It is not the experience alone that moved him; it is rather that specific kinds of experiences were a stimulus to his imagination. For him, the discovery of an antique wall painting or of a nervous function through dissection, although each an insignificant phenomenon, was a significant rent in a veil which opened onto a

universe. His delight in the world, in nature, or in the past, was thus primarily a matter of the imagination and of the emotions. In this respect, the traditional meaning of the concept "romantic" which emphasized a heightened emotional response to the world, is accurate. This view reflects an increased state of energy and a dynamic interchange between interior and exterior worlds that makes the romantic period of special interest to our times. The specific photograph of the moon that gives a glimpse into a universe stretching infinitely beyond man and affecting his feelings about the world serves as a contemporary analogue of a central romantic experience and makes this period of special interest to the second half of the twentieth century.

[1]The leading interpretation of the romantic period among contemporary art historians is that, as a whole, it is dichotomous with a neoclassic and a romantic current. This view originated in its modern form in Charles Baudelaire's Salon reviews, particularly in his analysis of the style of Delacroix as romantic and as the antithesis of that of the *Ingristes*. In turn, this view is a continuation of the controversy which opposed antique to modern art and the relative valuation of the style of Rubens as opposed to that of Poussin. It is curious that this ancient argument which had its most complete formulation in the lectures of the French Academicians should form the basis of discussion by contemporary historians of an historical era. And yet, this is the case. This dichotomous view of the period is the basis for the discussion of Walter Friedlaender, *David to Delacroix*, Cambridge, Massachusetts, 1952, and more recently that of Michel Florisoone, "The Romantic and Neoclassical Conflict," *The Romantic Movement*, The Arts Council of Great Britain, London, 1959, pp. 21-26, to name only two. The same point of view has precipitated into textbooks and characterizes the treatment of H. W. Janson, "Neoclassicism and Romanticism," *History of Art, A Survey of the Major Visual Arts from the Dawn of History to the Present Day*, New York, 1962, pp. 453-88.
[2]The view that the neoclassic and romantic styles are manifestations of deeper, more unified, and interlocking concepts, has been suggested by a number of writers including Mario Praz in his introduction to *The Romantic Agony*, Cleveland/New York, 1951, p. 11 (1st edition published 1933), and more recently by Sir Kenneth Clark in his introduction to *The Romantic Movement*, The Arts Council of Great Britain, London, 1959, pp. 17-20. Robert Rosenblum *(Transformations in Late Eighteenth Century Art*, Princeton, 1957), while

retaining the name of neoclassicism, has stretched its meaning to include a group of underlying themes which characterize this period as a whole, thus drawing close to the intention of Mario Praz. For a discussion of the term "romantic" see Logan Pearsall Smith, "Four Romantic Words," *Words and Idioms, Studies in the English Language,* London, 1925.
[3]William Hazlitt, "On Imitation," *The Complete Works,* ed. P. P. Howe, London/Toronto, 1930, IV, 74.
[4]These anatomical drawings from the collection of D. C. Mansel Lewis were shown in the exhibition, *Sir Edwin Landseer,* Royal Academy of Arts, London, 1961, nos. 146-51.
[5]See the quote from Ruskin to this effect (no. 216).
[6]First published as Johann J. Winckelmann, *Gedancken über die Nachahmung der Griechischen Wercke in der Mahlerey und Bildhauer-Kunst,* Friedrichstadt, 1755, translated by John Henry Fuseli as *Reflections on the Painting and Sculpture of the Greeks,* London, 1765.
[7]First published as Johann J. Winckelmann, *Geschichte der Kunst des Alterthums,* 2 vols., Dresden, 1764.
[8]Regale Accademia Ercolanese d'Archeologia, *Delle antichità di Ercolano,* Naples, 1755-1831, 10 vols.
[9]Countess of Ilchester and Lord Stavordale, eds., *The Life and Letters of Lady Sarah Lennox,* London, 1901, pp. 135-37.

British Landscape Painting, 1760-1860

by Allen Staley

John Brett spent the summer of 1858 in Italy painting his *Val d'Aosta* (no. 234), which appeared at the Royal Academy in 1859. Just over a century before, Richard Wilson returned to England from an extended stay in Italy. His return inaugurated a phase in English landscape painting, of which Brett's picture may be said to represent the culmination, if not indeed the conclusion, and the span of time between these two events provides the approximate limits of this exhibition.

The term "romantic" has many meanings, so many that it has become for some students virtually meaningless. However, it is a word entrenched in the vocabulary of the history of art, and for Turner, or Friedrich, or Delacroix it still comes to mind as the one most immediately appropriate adjective. It suggests a variety of things: discontent with the here and now and with order and discipline, a tendency to exploration, to the exotic and to excess, and appeal to emotion rather than reason. All of these elements are represented in the period of this exhibition, and although they are mixed with other and even contradictory urges, they give the century its dominant flavor and justify the use of the term romantic in a period sense, just as historians use Renaissance for the quattrocento, or baroque for the seventeenth century. There is also a geographic quality to romanticism (as there is about the Renaissance, which, wherever it may have spread, started in Italy). It is primarily a northern phenomenon, and the period under consideration is one in which the arts in Germany as well as in England glowed relatively brightly, unlike so much of history when the visual arts were dominated by the Mediterranean countries.

Conversely, one of the most strongly felt urges during this period, both in Germany and in England, was the lure of Italy, the land of sun and of classical culture. In terms of English landscape painting, interest in Italy did not start with Wilson; John Wootton was there in the 1720s and Alexander Cozens in the 1740s, but Wilson was the first English artist to build a career on exploiting Italy as a place. Once back in England he painted picture after picture showing views of the Roman Campagna and the neighboring hills. His art was based on that of Claude Lorrain, another northerner who worked in Italy a century earlier, but whereas Claude's pictures rarely show recognizable places, Wilson in a painting such as *Tivoli: Temple of the Sibyl and the Campagna* (no. 3) depicts the most famous of ruins and most picturesque of views. Wilson was followed to Italy by numerous other landscape painters, including several watercolorists who accompanied travelling gentlemen and recorded the places of interest visited. To an extent this was prosaic employment, the artists functioning as little more than the modern tourist's camera, but the emotions aroused by Italy in the eighteenth-century mind often found surprisingly rich expression in their works. The most interesting was John Robert Cozens, who visited Italy twice, from 1776 to 1779 with Richard Payne Knight, and again in 1782 with William Beckford, both of whom were or became knowledgeable connoisseurs. Cozens's Italian views were mostly worked up in England from the sketches he had made on the spot and thus, as in the case of Wilson, his responses had been through the emotional alembic of recollection. The appeal in both artists' work lies in their evocation of the mood of a place different from their native land. They do not delineate Italy so much as wrap a few motifs from the Campagna and the Alban Hills in suggestive vapors or bathe them in pale light, evocative of Virgil and Cicero, and of a golden age and a golden place.

Cozens and Wilson belong to the high civilization of the late eighteenth century which was shattered by the French Revolution. The Napoleonic wars put a stop to almost all continental travel until 1815, and the generation of artists who travelled to Italy after the world had been put right did not work for the same classically educated patrons, but for a larger middle-class public. For them Rome no longer was a unique place, whose surroundings were held in pious awe because of classical associations, but simply one of many picturesque cities, which lost its primacy to the more colorful enticements of Venice. When Turner visited Italy in 1819, he made incredibly beautiful drawings of Rome (as well as of Venice), but the pictures which he later painted of the city seem to reflect an emotional and intellectual muddle which he could not straighten out, and (as opposed to those of Venice) they are among his least successful works. For the travelling artists of the nineteenth century remnants of the middle ages had more romantic allure than the afterglow of antiquity. Rouen, Verona, Toledo became their meccas. The works of these artists—Bonington, Prout, Lewis, Lear, and numerous others—were frequently reproduced as engravings or lithographs in volumes which purported to give geographical and historical information. The question of whether Wilson's and Cozens's views of Tivoli or Castel Gandolfo are topographically accurate seems hardly relevant, and in an artist like Bonington, who is notably lax about detail, we still feel the excitement of the artist before the age and picturesque charm of his subject. But later artists generally seem to have wanted to, and to have had to, satisfy their public's curiosity about remote subjects via impersonally literal presentation. The excitement of their art came from the information it gave about remote places, and the more remote the place the more the artist seems to have felt compelled to depict it accurately. The urge to be factually informative culminates in Brett's *Val d'Aosta,* which Ruskin claimed that seeing is as good as visiting the place itself except that we cannot see behind us; in fact, in some ways it is better because the viewer is spared the heat and discomfort of travel.[1]

Brett's picture shows an Italian subject, but that it is Italian is less important than that it is of the Alps, which places it in a special class of romantic views. The first English artist who travelled to Switzerland purposely to see the mountains seems to have been Turner, who did so during the brief interlude in the Napoleonic wars in 1802, but he was preceded by others who travelled through the mountains on their way to Italy. The work of these artists, notably of Francis Towne and John Robert Cozens, shows a fascination with Alpine scenery, both its desolation and its beauty, which achieves in the art of Cozens an almost visionary lyricism. Their response parallels the growth of serious mountaineering in the 1770s. Turner was probably inspired to visit Switzerland partly by Cozens's drawings, partly by the poetry of Thomson, and partly by Philip James de Loutherbourg, whose *Falls of the Rhine at Schaffhausen* (no. 59) anticipates Turner's painting of 1806 (Boston), and whose *Avalanche in the Alps* (Tate Gallery), although not exhibited until after 1802, precedes Turner's *Cottage Destroyed by an Avalanche* (no. 116). But beautiful and influential as Loutherbourg's Alpine scenes are, they are eighteenth-century confections of the decoratively sublime, and they do not suggest an awe of the mountains for themselves. In Turner's art, mountains appear and reappear, and when he was sixty-five he began making annual journeys to the Alps. Like the sea, they held for him some obsessive lure as the quintessence of nature, and they embody a whole range of meanings, from absolute destructive force, as in the *Cottage Destroyed by an Avalanche,* to rhapsodical scenes of transfigured calm, as in the late watercolor of *Fluelen, Lake of Lucerne* (no. 121). The former is, strictly speaking, not a view but an imaginative composition based on memories of the mountains and a passage in Thomson's *Seasons,* but Turner did paint a vast number of actual Alpine views which, as Ruskin labored to prove, are often remarkably accurate.

For Ruskin, Turner's Alpine paintings and watercolors were his central achievement, and Ruskin, himself a good bit crazy on the subject, devoted the long fourth volume of *Modern Painters* to an analysis of *Mountain Beauty* in which he proclaimed mountains "the beginning and end of all natural scenery." In the 1850s Ruskin pushed his protégés Inchbold and Brett into painting the Alps. Like his writings, their paintings are based on precise analytical observation, and they reveal little trace of those feelings of awe and reverence of earlier travellers to the mountains. Brett's *Glacier of Rosenlaui* (no. 233) and *Val d'Aosta* show the most romantic scenery made into the object of fanatically selfless delineation, but the sheer amount of labor put into these pictures makes us as aware of Brett the artist as we are of his more emotion-prone predecessors. The information he gives can be better given by the camera, and the rise of photography made Brett's paintings essentially a dead end (significantly, his mentor Ruskin took the first photographs of the Alps); nonetheless, Brett, in stretching the descriptive possibilities of painting beyond anything previously attempted, represents the extreme fulfillment of the once important function of the artist as bearer of visual information, and he painted the last significant pictures whose purpose was to bring the English public information about foreign places.

The goal of showing places that are interesting of themselves also motivated much painting within England both before and during the period of this exhibition. A tradition of engraved views of England flourished during the late eighteenth and early nineteenth centuries, supporting a substantial printing industry. Turner alone was responsible for some nine hundred prints, of which a large portion consisted of views in England for such publications as Cooke's *Picturesque Views of the Southern Coast of England* or Whitaker's *History of Richmondshire.* These prints were generally based on watercolors, and the eighteenth century saw the growth of a large

school of topographical watercolorists, of whom the best known is Paul Sandby. Both Turner and Girtin were trained under draftsmen who specialized in architectural views, and the tradition of depiction of English buildings and scenery provided the background for the travelling artists of the nineteenth century. However, much of this topographical activity—making commissioned views of country houses or drawings for antiquarian publications—was frankly modest and was looked down upon by artists of pretension. When Gainsborough was asked to paint a view he declined, saying that he had never seen any place in England "that affords a subject equal to the poorest imitations of Gaspar or Claude,"[2] and in 1805 Fuseli, as Professor of Painting at the Royal Academy, told his students that among the least interesting kinds of painting was "that kind of landscape which is entirely occupied with the tame delineation of a given spot; an enumeration of hill and dale, clumps of trees, shrubs, water, meadows, cottages and houses, what is commonly called Views."[3] For Fuseli this was map-work and had been spurned by the great landscape painters of the past, to whom, instead, had been revealed nature's bosom.

The development of romantic landscape painting was in accordance with Fuseli's remarks, away from straightforward topography to the depiction either of views which could evoke moods by associative or exotic appeal, or of nature rather than of places. These two categories are artificial, of course, and they became increasingly mixed up. Turner's *Fonthill Abbey* (no. 115) and Girtin's *Kirkstall Abbey* (no. 114) are views of places, the former commissioned by the structure's owner, but both show their ostensible subjects as relatively small features in the sweep of the landscape. Views were also commissioned to illustrate poetry, Turner's drawing of *Berne* (no. 119), for example, and were expected themselves to be poetic. Edward Lear's *Civitella di Subiaco* (no. 198) is a later example of a topographical view in which the view *per se* has almost disappeared. On the other hand, pictures of rustic scenes, which Gainsborough in the eighteenth century generally composed out of imagination, were in the nineteenth century, as painted by Constable, based on actual places. Between the two, lies the cult of picturesque sketching. Gainsborough may not have known any places in England worthy of comparison with the visions of Gaspar or Claude, but a younger generation of artists and amateurs set out to find them. The word picturesque means like a picture, and theoreticians of the picturesque such as Uvedale Price or the Reverend William Gilpin attempted to isolate precisely those qualities in the English landscape which recalled admired examples of earlier landscape painting. This point of view transformed the sketching tour from visiting places of interest, generally buildings, to looking for scenic beauty of an appropriately pictorial kind. The young Constable praised an effect he saw in the Lake District as "much like the beautiful Gaspar I saw in Margaret St.,"[4] and later an artist such as David Cox was attracted to Wales for similar reasons. Sketching from nature for the sake of nature, rather than for the sake of a view, became an increasingly important practice, which culminated in the Pre-Raphaelites' spending months in the country painting the backgrounds of their figural paintings directly out-of-doors.

Combined with an interest in painting nature as such, in much English landscape painting of the period there is a strong element of sentimental affection for certain aspects of rural life and the countryside, due at least partly to reaction against the growing urbanization of life. The eighteenth-century rural scenes by Gainsborough and Morland belong to the same idyllic world of escape as Marie Antoinette's *Hameau.* For Constable, living in London, his nostalgia for the Stour Valley where he had spent his boyhood was boundless, and the central achievement of his career was the series of six-foot canal scenes which give it visual embodiment. Compared to Gainsborough's or any other

eighteenth-century landscapes, Constable's pictures seem much more naturalistic, the fruit of his constant sketching from nature; but greater naturalism alone was not his goal. Of the paintings by a younger artist, F. R. Lee, he wrote to Leslie, "they pretend to nothing but an imitation of nature—but that is of the coldest and meanest kind . . . *all is utterly heartless.*"[5] Constable proclaimed that for himself painting was "but another word for feeling," and the context of this statement makes clear that he meant feeling for a place rather than for nature as a whole (cf. no. 128). A comparable identification with a certain place can be seen in many other nineteenth-century painters, the Norwich artists with the surroundings of their native city, or Samuel Palmer with Shoreham. Palmer, unlike Constable, was not country-born, and he to a greater extent imposed a preconceived vision upon the world he depicted but, like Constable's, his rural scenes are involved with the whole tissue of life of a specific locality. The romanticization of such vision began to disappear from the work of younger artists, who did not see the same matrix of values in rural life; for Ford Madox Brown landscape was as readily the view out his suburban back window, and admired for the simple delight it offered the eye. Brown's denial of any meaning in his *Pretty Baa-Lambs* (no. 212) might well be interpreted as a denial of the whole outlook of romanticism, but he could, on the other hand, in a picture such as *Carrying Corn* (no. 213), indulge in nostalgia for a pastoral world to which he could walk, but in which he most emphatically did not live.

In addition to the poetry of rural life or of nature, there is another stream, usually called historic landscape, which devoted itself to a more pretentious kind of poetry and which looked to seventeenth-century landscapes with figures by Claude, Nicholas Poussin, and Salvator Rosa for its models. In English painting the archetypal example is Wilson's *Destruction of Niobe's Children,* one version of which (Mellon Collection)

was exhibited at the first exhibition of the Society of Artists in 1760. Reynolds in his *Fourteenth Discourse* criticized Wilson's introduction of supernatural beings into landscapes which were "in reality too near common nature,"[6] but Wilson's attempt to ennoble landscape is comparable to Reynolds's efforts to ennoble portraiture by allegorical embellishments. A continuing ambition to somehow raise the status of landscape parallels the struggles on behalf of the Grand Style by figural painters such as Barry and Haydon. In 1799 Girtin and a group of associates founded a sketching club "for the purpose of establishing by practice a school of Historic Landscape, the subjects being original designs from poetick passages."[7] None of the group ultimately distinguished himself in this area, but in the following few decades historic landscape had an extraordinary flourishing. The most versatile genius of the age made his highest efforts in this realm, and where Turner led others followed. Turner's *Cottage Destroyed by an Avalanche* belongs to this class of painting; it shows an imaginary subject which was apparently inspired by the poetry of Thomson, and Turner composed verse of his own to accompany it. However, it is an atypical example as no human figures are shown and the subject is not drawn from the remote past. More characteristic are such subjects as *The Fifth Plague of Egypt* (Royal Academy 1800, Indianapolis), *Snowstorm: Hannibal and His Army Crossing the Alps* (Royal Academy 1812, Tate Gallery), and so on to *Mercury Sent to Admonish Aeneas* and *Aeneas Relating His Story to Dido* exhibited the year before his death (both Tate Gallery). Turner's chief imitators in this area were John Martin and Francis Danby, who during the 1820s conducted with great popular success a personal rivalry in outdoing each other in scenes of biblical cataclysm. However, as attitudes became more sober during Victoria's reign the taste for invented landscapes declined, and it is difficult to find other than derisory references to Martin after the middle of the century. Ruskin took Turner's historic landscapes very seriously and devoted inordinately long discussions to explaining or elaborating their meanings, but he otherwise dismissed this type of painting as nonsense. In the 1850s he redefined "historical landscape" to mean pictures which give "trustworthy knowledge" about places actually existing, that is, records of the present rather than reconstructions of the past.[8] Thus, Ruskin called Brett's *Val d'Aosta* historical, and he encouraged artists to record the look of places that were likely to be changed or destroyed by the modern world. By his redefinition, pictures such as Constable's *Opening of Waterloo Bridge* (cf. no. 129) and Turner's *Burning of the Houses of Parliament* (no. 120) are historic landscapes and, for us, they, and even more so such paintings as Frith's *Derby Day* (no. 209) or George Samuel's view of *London from Greenwich Park* (no. 102), have genuine interest as historic documents, but the historical fantasies of Danby and Martin, unreal and theatrical as they may be, also have a value, unseen by Ruskin, as documents of some of the more extraordinary reaches of the romantic imagination.

Both Danby and Martin used scale—tiny figures lost in vast spaces and overwhelmed by cosmic violence—as their chief weapon, and their inventions have little direct dependence upon nature. In Turner's pictures the relation between imagination and reality is more complex. *Snowstorm: Hannibal and His Army Crossing the Alps* is based on a storm seen on the Yorkshire moors, and after his trip to Italy of 1819, he often set classical or historical figures into actual landscapes, as in *The Bay of Baiae, with Apollo and the Sibyl* (Royal Academy 1823, Tate Gallery) or *Juliet and Her Nurse* improbably overlooking the Piazza in Venice (Royal Academy 1836, collection Mrs. Flora Whitney Miller). Although Turner attempted in his *Liber Studiorum* to divide his art into neat categories, his worlds of imagination, of literature and history, and of nature became ever more hopelessly intertwined. A similar confusion can be seen in the work of many of his contemporaries,

reflecting a breakdown of the purposes and limitations of landscape painting as they had been generally accepted since the seventeenth century. The enrichment brought to topography, on the one hand, by its allowing itself to become poetic, and to poetry, on the other, by becoming grounded in fact, made a major contribution to the flourishing of landscape painting in England during the late years of the eighteenth and first part of the nineteenth centuries. However, this new freedom, by undermining the traditionally accepted functions of landscape, also contributed to the aimlessness and decline of landscape painting as a significant form of art in later Victorian England. Much of *Modern Painters* consists of an attempt to redefine a role for landscape painting, but Ruskin's efforts had only limited success, and although his protégés, the Pre-Raphaelites, devoted themselves to the most ambitious examination of the natural world, this more often took place in the context of figural painting than in pure landscape.

The stylistic variety of English landscape painting during the period is to a considerable extent accounted for by the variety of kinds of landscape painted. An art whose prime concern was topographical reporting, of necessity, showed its subject with accuracy and with sufficient detail to be informative. On the other hand breadth was supposed to be poetic. The freedom of Gainsborough and Constable belongs to a tradition descending from seventeenth-century landscape painting, and it goes hand in hand with a tendency away from specificity toward generalization, which can be seen from the beginning of the period in Alexander Cozens to the end in David Cox. Constable's art presents a fascinating dialogue between inherited ideals and specific observation, and the progress of his pictures, from sketches to exhibited work, demonstrates how he labored to transmute what he saw into acceptable pictorial form. Even in his sketching there is wide variance in handling depending on what he wished to record and the conditions under which he worked. His cloud

209 detail

studies had to be painted rapidly because they showed transient effects, but he also made careful studies of trees in the most painstaking detail. In Turner the same holds true to a greater extent because of the greater variety of his art. The *Cottage Destroyed by an Avalanche,* which is poetic, is much more broadly handled than his *Bonneville, Savoy,* a painting exhibited at the Royal Academy two years later (Johnson Collection, Philadelphia), which gives topographical information, and in his watercolors the contrast between the microscopic precision of *Berne* and the freedom of *Storm Over St. Peter's* (no. 118) is even more pronounced.

There is, however, a clear movement within the period to more and more literal attention to natural detail. On the theoretical level this can be seen in the contrast between Reynolds's *Discourses,* which urge generalization, and Ruskin's *Modern Painters,* in which nothing is valued more than precise fact. At the beginning of the nineteenth century, John Varley's chief lesson to his students Mulready, Linnell, and William Hunt was "go to nature for everything"; this they reinterpreted into a reverence for natural detail seen at its most extreme in the fruit and flower still lifes of William Hunt. In the 1820s Linnell urged Samuel Palmer to study Dürer and Lucas Van Leyden, and to make niggling studies directly from nature. The extraordinary results produced in Palmer's *Oak Trees in Lullingstone Park* (no. 180) or *Pear Tree in a Walled Garden* (no. 181) are the most memorable manifestations of a whole generation's inclination to find revelations of God in leaves, branches, and blossoms. Although Ruskin's drawings do not have the hallucinatory ferment of Palmer's, he also had profoundly moving experiences before the small things of nature, and his writings convey a mixture of religious mysticism and scientific curiosity. In Ruskin's eyes breadth was a tired-out convention, and Constable represented "the blotting and blundering of Modernism."[9] For the Pre-Raphaelites, as for Palmer earlier, literal copying of natural detail and respect for the art

of the fifteenth century went hand in hand as means of escaping what they considered a decadent tradition.

Science, or pseudoscience, also contributed to the trend to precise handling. A number of works in this exhibition, George Stubbs's anatomical illustrations (nos. 15 and 16) or Edward Lear's bird drawings (no. 196), were intended as scientific illustrations rather than as works of art *per se;* Ruskin's drawing for *The Stones of Venice* (no. 207) likewise served a didactic purpose for which its own aesthetic qualities were more or less irrelevant. These works, even more than topographical illustrations, had to be precisely accurate to be of any value at all. But a scientific attitude motivated much else during the period. Both Stubbs and Joseph Wright of Derby, moving in scientifically and technologically oriented circles, were deeply concerned with contemporary explorations of the natural world, and many of their paintings are essentially naturalists' careful records of things observed. In the nineteenth century Ruskin proselytized for a kind of detailed painting which would provide scientifically factual information, and there are frequent references in histories of Victorian art to eminent botanists' and geologists' lectures based on Pre-Raphaelite pictures. Scientifically oriented observation, however, did not necessarily lead to minuteness, as demonstrated by Constable's cloud studies, which reflect kindred curiosity about the natural world. And in some cases, science justified art that had little or nothing to do with the observation of nature, notably John Martin's imaginative scenes of biblical catastrophes (see no. 153), which were supposed to accord with the most up-to-date theories of the earth's history, based on the discovery of fossils of extinct creatures.

Because it most directly affected the nature of painting itself, the most significant aspect of the exploration of the external world was concerned with light and color. The two are not always synonymous and, in fact, during the eighteenth

century, interest in one tended to exclude the other. Symptomatic of their separation is the eighteenth-century watercolor technique of making a monochrome drawing and then adding color as a finishing touch. Many of the most brilliant effects of light, such as those of Alexander Cozens, are in monochrome. On the other hand, when there is rich color in eighteenth-century painting, as in Gainsborough or Wilson, it stems as much from a kind of rococo artifice as from observation. Wilson's Italian views painted *in situ* are somberly colored; the farther away he got, the more imaginatively tinted became his memory. We do see an attempt to record the prismatic colors of an observed effect in Joseph Wright of Derby's cavern interiors (see no. 30), but the colors are subordinate to the contrast of light and dark of the *contre-jour* effect.

A little before 1800 almost all color departed, and much of the painting of the early nineteenth century is virtually monochromatic. This is in part the result of the development of new materials, specifically of bitumen, which allowed artists to obtain warm moist darks, and which, because it never dries completely, has been so destructive of pictures of this period. However, pigments and mediums are tools, and bitumen was popular because it satisfied a need stemming from the desire to emulate the example of tonal contrast set by seventeenth-century paintings, particularly those of Claude. These paintings are masterpieces of modulation between light and dark anyway, and covered by coats of yellowing varnish they provided models of a rich warm effect with little actual color. Sir George Beaumont, who was England's most influential connoisseur and patron—and the owner of several fine Claudes—proclaimed that the prevailing tone of a picture should be that of a Cremona violin. To this dictum Constable is supposed to have replied by taking a violin outside and laying it on the green lawn. Despite this implied rejection, Constable's pictures are still primarily composed in terms of light and dark rather than color, as is proven by the effectiveness of the mezzotint engravings after them. He stated that his paintings "should have chiaroscuro, if they had nothing else," and the broken colors which so impressed Delacroix belong to details within a tonal context.

At the middle of the century Holman Hunt was still fulminating against the conventions of brown foliage and dark corners.[10] But by then the Pre-Raphaelites could have found numerous examples of vivid coloring, and the typical Royal Academy exhibition was considerably brighter than it would have been forty or fifty years before. The transformation is exemplified by Turner. His early works are generally dark and have surprisingly little color. Stimulated by his trip to Italy in 1819, however, he began to treat light and color as identical. Dark shadows are reduced to smaller and smaller accents, replaced by contrasts of colors, and his late works show an iridescent world dissolved in light. Turner's obsession with color was part of a widespread development. In 1835 George Field published *Chromatography: A Treatise on Colours and Pigments and their Powers in Painting,* and five years later Eastlake translated Goethe's *Theory of Colours* into English. Mulready in the 1820s began to switch from a palette of browns to colors luminously heightened by being painted over a white ground, and his friend William Hunt went even further in his watercolor still lifes by developing an elaborate method of broken brushwork to allow him to follow all variations in reflected colors. These two artists are the main progenitors of the dazzling colors of the Pre-Raphaelites, but it is worth noting Rossetti's claim that Blake's "most original and prismatic system of colour,—in which tints laid on side by side, each in its utmost force, are made by masterly treatment to produce a startling and novel effect of truth,—must be viewed as being, more decidedly than the system of any other painter, the forerunner of a style of execution now characterizing a whole new section of the English School."[11]

The Pre-Raphaelites' interest in color was thus not in itself a new departure, and the artists were in part motivated to make their pictures brighter and brighter so that they would stand out in the Royal Academy exhibitions. The outdoor brightness of Holman Hunt is paralleled by the fanciful but equally bright color of Rossetti's watercolors, which comes from imagination and the example of Flemish painting. However, Hunt, Madox Brown, and many of their colleagues were sufficiently concerned with recording the exact look of things to paint even the subordinate parts of historical subject pictures out-of-doors. Their naturalism had many facets, including relentless geological and botanical detail, but the most significant result of the hours spent painting the details of their pictures in the sunlight was that they saw colors with excruciating freshness, and they painted what they saw. Holman Hunt's *Strayed Sheep* (no. 216) and Ford Madox Brown's *Pretty Baa-Lambs* (no. 212) are unprecedented analytical studies of outdoor light and color, and the essential concern embodied in these pictures, although they are worlds apart in subject, handling, and attitude toward natural detail, is the same as that of impressionism.

However, impressionism is a French phenomenon, not an English one. The naturalistic impulse in English painting stopped short with the pictures of Brown and Hunt and Pre-Raphaelite followers such as John Brett. Just as Brett's *Val d'Aosta* represents the last major record of a view as a view, so it is also the last monumental effort of English naturalism. It is virtually impossible to find anything after 1860 of comparable ambition which is worth taking seriously. What did matter in later Victorian painting was Aestheticism, and Whistler, the one significant painter of landscapes, found nature undiluted a bit sickening and insisted on turning it into decorative abstractions. The growth of this outlook helped end the Pre-Raphaelite impulse towards naturalism, but there are numerous other reasons as well: Ruskin's abandonment of the field, for one; and the

discomfort involved in painting these detailed pictures directly out-of-doors, for another. The basic fact in English painting around 1860, however, was that the Pre-Raphaelites, by choosing to rely entirely on a primitively direct confrontation with nature without the aid of any precedents, had turned their backs on the entire English tradition of landscape painting. They represent the culmination of a century of fruitful dialogue between artist and nature, but by trying to make nature all, and the artist nothing, they undermined the relationship and created no pictorial framework on which they could build; they left themselves no place to go. Further exploration of the natural world, which was to lead to a fundamentally new way of giving structure to experience via abstract means, would require a tradition of artistic discipline which the English had effectively destroyed.

[1]Ruskin, XIV, 234
[2]Mary Woodall, ed., *The Letters of Thomas Gainsborough,* London, 1963, p. 87
[3]Eudo C. Mason, ed., *The Mind of Henry Fuseli,* London, 1951, p. 285
[4]Graham Reynolds, *Catalogue of the Constable Collection in the Victoria and Albert Museum,* London, 1960, p. 58, no. 80
[5]R. B. Beckett, ed., *John Constable's Correspondence: III: The Correspondence with C. R. Leslie, R. A.,* Suffolk Records Society, VIII, 1965, p. 91
[6]Sir Joshua Reynolds, *Discourses on Art,* ed. Robert R. Wark, San Marino, Calif., 1959, pp. 255-56
[7]Dr. Guillemard, "Girtin's Sketching Club," *Connoisseur,* LXIII, 1922, p. 190
[8][John Pollard Seddon], *Memoir and Letters of the Late Thomas Seddon, Artist. By His Brother,* London, 1858, p. 171
[9]Ruskin, V, 423
[10]W. Holman Hunt, *Pre-Raphaelitism and the Pre-Raphaelite Brotherhood,* London, 1905, I, 91
[11]Dante Gabriel Rossetti, *Works,* ed. W. M. Rossetti, London, 1911, p. 588

Explanatory Note

Artists are listed in order of year of birth, and the works of each artist in approximate chronological order. An alphabetical index is on p. 332. In general, the earlier part of the catalogue has been compiled by Frederick Cummings and the latter by Allen Staley, but there is some overlap in the middle. The initials of the author follow the discussion in each entry.

All the works in the exhibition are illustrated. Dimensions are given in inches, height preceding width.

Under *Provenance,* we have listed wherever possible the date when an owner acquired the work, followed by the date and manner in which it left that collection. In the lists of *Exhibitions,* we have generally excluded minor exhibitions for which no catalogue was published. Under *Reproductions,* we have included engravings after the work and, occasionally, early published photographs.

We have attempted to make the *References* more useful to the student by including sources that are generally relevant to the picture or drawing, rather than simply listing all mentions and reproductions. All sources cited in the discussions are included in the *References.*

The following abbreviations have been used throughout the catalogue:

Farington, ed. Greig	*The Farington Diary,* by Joseph Farington, R.A., edited by James Greig, 8 vols., London, 1923-28
Ruskin	*The Works of John Ruskin,* edited by E. T. Cook and Alexander Wedderburn (Library Edition), 39 vols., London, 1903-12
Burlington	*The Burlington Magazine*
JWCI	*Journal of the Warburg and Courtauld Institutes*
OWCSC	*The Old Water Colour Society's Club: Annual Volume*
Walpole Society	*The Walpole Society: Annual Volume*

Otherwise where abbreviated or short titles are used for monographs or articles in the *References* for individual pictures, the full titles may be found in the brief *Bibliography* following the biography of each artist.

Richard Wilson

1713?-1782

Wilson's father was a clergyman with a large family who lived at Penegoes in Montgomeryshire, Wales. Thomas Wright, a minor portrait painter, became his first master when he was sent to London in 1729. His early works were thus portraits which include *Prince George and Prince Edward* (c. 1748-49 National Portrait Gallery, London), sons of Frederick, Prince of Wales. A minor part of his output during these early years was landscapes such as the view of Westminster Bridge of 1745 in the Philadelphia Museum of Art.

He began a tour of the continent in 1750, stopping first at Venice where he obtained a commission from Joseph Smith, the British Consul and patron of Canaletto. His view of Venetian art brought him immediately under its influence as revealed in his figure drawings of this period. Late in 1751 or early in 1752 he travelled to Rome at the time Vernet was there, and W. G. Constable believes that it was he who influenced Wilson to take up landscape painting. His first landscapes for Ralph Howard included scenes of murder and executions with *banditti,* under the influence of Marco Ricci. Probably, Thomas Jenkins secured his first important landscape commission in 1754 from the Earl of Dartmouth for a large group of drawings of Italian views. These highly finished sheets are among Wilson's most complete and most beautiful works. His Italian subjects for which he is best known today include a standard repertoire of views dear to those who took the grand tour. These were painted in the vicinity of Rome and Naples and include views of the Ponte Molle, the Temple of

Minerva Medica, Tivoli, Albano, Lake Nemi, and the Bay of Baiae. His Italian subjects were topographical, but liberties were constantly taken with the figures and landscape elements, and the views were freely interpreted with reference to the paintings of Claude and Gaspard Poussin, who were the most revered masters in landscapes at the time.

About 1757 to 1758 he returned to London and there used the numerous drawings done in Italy as the basis for paintings. Wilson had made excellent contacts before and during his Roman sojourn and, after his return to London, he established an elaborate household near Covent Garden where Thomas Jones, among other pupils, came in 1763. From 1760 to 1768 he exhibited at the Society of Artists, beginning with the *Destruction of Niobe's Children,* a version of which is now in the Mellon Collection. His reputation was such that at the founding of the Royal Academy in 1768, he was asked to be one of the original members.

In addition to Italian subjects, he also painted views of English country houses which include *Woburn Abbey* (collection Duke of Bedford), five large views of *Wilton* for the Earl of Pembroke (collection Earl of Pembroke, Wilton House), and also scenes in Wales such as a view of *Cader Idris* in The National Gallery, London. It is likely that these topographical views for specific patrons formed the basis of his income at this time rather than his landscapes with historical subjects or his Italian views.

Although Wilson's early works are in the taste of Claude, those of his London period show experimentation and an independent development which fuses the landscape forms of Claude with the treatment of light and foliage found in Dutch 17th-century art, particularly in that of Aelbert Cuyp. The best example of this synthesis is the view of *Snowdon from Llyn Nantlle* (Walker Art Gallery, Liverpool), which is a striking composition of pure arabesques, with landscape forms enhanced by almost flat, alternating patterns of light.

Especially in his later years, Wilson was a neglected artist. His chief competitor, apart from the portrait painters, was Zuccarelli, whose decorative and less solid style was popular in England. Adding this to the fact that he lost royal commissions through a breach with the King, his income declined, especially during the years 1770 to 1775. He was given the post of Librarian of the Royal Academy in 1776 to ease his straitened circumstances at a time when he had almost ceased to paint.
F.C.

Bibliography
[William Hodges], "An Account of Richard Wilson Esq. Landscape Painter, F. R. A.," *European Magazine and London Review,* XVII, June 1790, p. 403
Thomas Wright, *Some Account of the Life of Richard Wilson, Esq., R. A.,* London, 1824
Thomas Hastings, *Etchings from the Works of Richard Wilson, with some Memoirs of his Life,* London, 1825
Brinsley Ford, *The Drawings of Richard Wilson,* London, 1951
W. G. Constable, *Richard Wilson,* London, 1953 (with bibliography)

1

Thomas Jenkins, the Roman Cicerone and Dealer Seated to the Left
The Pierpont Morgan Library
Black chalk, heightened with white on gray-green paper; 10¾ x 7¹³⁄₁₆ in.
Inscribed in ink on verso: *Jenkings;* in pencil on verso: *Wilson—Lock sale 1821-387-6.*
c. 1751-53

Edward Edwards in his *Anecdotes of Painters,* 1808, relates that Thomas Jenkins (1722-98) travelled to Rome with Richard Wilson. A letter in the Albani correspondence mentions that they arrived in 1752, Wilson presenting himself to Cardinal Albani in March with a letter of

1

introduction from Sir Horace Mann. His friend Jenkins waited until August 1753 to meet the Cardinal, who received him with enthusiasm. In the same year, the names of Wilson and Jenkins appear in the parish registers of S. Lorenzo in Lucina. Their residence at that time was at the north end of the Piazza di Spagna between the Via delle Croce and the Via delle Carrozze.

Although the only evidence for identifying the sitter as Jenkins is the inscription on the back, the drawing was owned by William Locke of Norbury, who travelled with Wilson from Venice to Rome, knew them both well while in Rome, and later owned the drawing himself. The inscription is not

in Wilson's hand, and Locke must be responsible either for introducing it or for leaving it there.

Thomas Jenkins, truly a man of many parts, was born in Rome in 1722, but he actually studied painting in London under the portraitist Thomas Hudson (1701-79). At the beginning of his career, he painted portraits and historical subjects including a *Hagar and Ishmael* of which a copy by Mosman exists in The British Museum. He apparently achieved some distinction as a painter in Rome since he was created *accademico di merito* of the Academy of St. Luke. However, Jenkins did not restrict his activities to painting. In the period in which he was known to Wilson, at a time when he was in his early thirties, he was something of a contract man, a dealer who could provide fine books, as he did for William Locke, a draftsman for views of Rome, as he did for Lord Dartmouth, and a person who could obtain good antique sculpture for a travelling English nobleman. Already in the 1770s Winckelmann recommended his services to Baron Stosch for the disposal of his collection of gems. His taste was considered good, and his enthusiasm equal to his taste; he was also knowledgeable enough to assist Cavaceppi and Piranesi in their active production of forged antiquities, particularly inscriptions. Later, he was to work with Gavin Hamilton in excavations for antiquities which were then sold to collectors like Charles Townley and to the Vatican. He was fortunate to obtain some very important collections, those brought together by Sixtus V, still at the Villa Montalto-Negroni, those in the Villa d'Este, and works from the Caraffa-Columbrano palace in Naples. By the 1770s he had become a banker, and was apparently involved in an important way in the financial affairs of Clement XIV. Also by this time, he had amassed a collection of works of art important enough to be visited by the Emperor Paul of Russia and Gustavus III of Sweden. His collection was housed in the Casa Celli on the Via del Corso near the church of S. Giacomo, and he also had a villa at Castel Gandolfo, where Goethe visited him. So important did his position in Roman society become, that he

acted almost as British Ambassador, receiving royal visitors and attending at audiences with the Pope. He also acted as a British agent in Rome. In 1797 Jenkins was forced to flee for England as a result of the wars with France, and all of his Roman property was confiscated by the French. Jenkins was ruined. He died soon after his return to England.

Before travelling to Rome, Wilson spent about one year in Venice where he arrived in the autumn of 1750. There is a good possibility that Jenkins and Wilson were in Venice together before they arrived in Rome in 1752. This drawing should be connected as closely as possible with Wilson's Venetian experience. In technique, execution, and refinement, it is intimately related to Venetian draftsmanship, particularly that of Giovanni Battista Tiepolo (1696-1770). The sinuous, undulating outline of the forms, the staccato black spot or slash with the chalk, the blurring of focus at the legs and minor elements, the swiftness, ease and grace of the conception, all reflect Tiepolo's manner.

A date within Wilson's Venetian sojourn would be most acceptable, but we do not know for certain that Jenkins was actually in Venice with Wilson, only that they travelled at least part of the way to Rome together. Thus a dating for this drawing which would include their first months in Rome must be considered a possibility.
F.C.

Provenance
William Locke, Norbury, Derbyshire (died 1810) (sale, Sotheby's, London, 1821, no. 387. Six drawings were in this lot catalogued as *Varia Costumi Italia Fine*)
Rev. J. Burleigh James, Knowbury Park, Shropshire (sale, Sotheby's, London, March, April, May 1877)
Charles Fairfax Murray, London, until 1910
J. Pierpont Morgan, New York (died 1913)
The Pierpont Morgan Library, New York, 1913

References
Charles Fairfax Murray, *Drawings by the Old Masters,*

Collection of J. Pierpont Morgan, London, 1905-12, III, no. 42
Thomas Ashby, "Thomas Jenkins in Rome," *Papers of the British School at Rome*, VI, no. 8, 1913, pp. 487-511
Friedrich Noack, "Des Kardinals Albani Beziehungen zu Künstlern," *Der Cicerone*, 1924, XVI, 412
William T. Whitley, *Artists and Their Friends in England 1700-99*, London, 1928, I, 387
Brinsley Ford, "The Dartmouth Collection of Drawings by Richard Wilson," *Burlington*, XC, 1948, p. 337
Brinsley Ford, *The Drawings of Richard Wilson*, pp. 28, 54, no. 20

2

2
House of Pompey at Albano
The Metropolitan Museum of Art, Rogers Fund, 1906
Black chalk touched with white on gray paper;
8⅝ x 15 in.
Inscribed: *House of Pompey at Albano*
c. 1753-56

The present-day city of Albano is situated in the Alban Hills twelve miles southeast of Rome, between the lakes of Nemi and Albano. In the 18th century it was thought that the ancient baths of Albano were the ruins of part of the palace of Pompeius Magnus (106-48 B.C.). The Romans destroyed Alba, the seat of the Alban kings, about 600 B.C., and during the Empire they built villas in these beautiful hills. Domitian in particular is famous for his villa there, and it became the nucleus of the modern town. Piranesi's view and its accompanying description of this ruin, which he refers to as the house of Pompey, make clear the exact identification.

This drawing was probably made on the spot when Wilson visited Albano in the mid-1750s. It has none

of the artificial devices which were later introduced in drawings regularly produced in the studio. It also has a freshness of observation and an architectonic clarity which help to explain the architectural views of his student Thomas Jones. Wilson did a series of drawings of views in the environs of Rome for William Legge, second Earl of Dartmouth, in 1754, and the Alban hills were included. It could have been done at this time or on another sketching tour during Wilson's years in Rome.
F.C.

References
Giovanni Battista Piranesi, *Antichità d'Albano e di Castel Gandolfo,* Paris, 1836, p. 4, pl. VII

3
Tivoli: Temple of the Sibyl and the Campagna
Brooks Memorial Art Gallery, Gift of
Mr. and Mrs. Morrie A. Moss
Oil on canvas; 37 x 49½ in.
c. 1763-67

Painted soon after he settled in London, this view of Tivoli was probably based on drawings made by Wilson in Italy. The spot was one of the most popular for travellers in the 18th century and, in the mind of the public, it had associations with the antique and with sublime scenery. Wilson shows an artist sketching in the foreground, while a peasant leans over to peer at his work. Far in the distance is the plain of the Campagna which leads ultimately to Rome. Across the gorge can be seen the Temple of Vesta, the Temple of the Tiburtine Sibyl, and the modern city.

The composition of no. 3, with its single tree arched in a graphic pattern against a luminous afternoon sky, shows Wilson departing in a striking way from devices used in his Italian views of the 1750s. His landscape of *Rome with St. Peter's and the Vatican from the Janiculum* (collection Earl of Dartmouth) of about 1753-54 is constructed in the manner of Claude, with solid masses of trees and distinct planes of light marking a progression into deepest space. The graphic silhouette and intricate design of this tree, which makes electric the luminosity and clarity of the light, reveals a study of Dutch 17th-century art. The bizarre chasm between the foreground hillock and the architecture in the middle ground, before the measured recession to the horizon, reveal him experimenting with startling juxtapositions to multiply the implications of spatial recession. In all of these things, Wilson continues in the tradition well established by his 17th-century predecessors, attempting, through experimentation with landscape forms, to refine and to extend their ideas.

At least two versions of the composition are known, one in the collection of Mrs. Frederick W. Hinkle, Cincinnati, and a second which was in the H. A.

3

Baker collection in 1953. Six other versions, listed as attributed or copied, are given by Constable. Variants of the composition are in the collection of E. F. Collingwood and Mrs. Montagu, Ince Blundell Hall. That in the collection of Mrs. Montagu, of which there is a version in the Philadelphia Museum of Art, was commissioned by Henry Blundell for Ince Hall and painted between 1763 and 1767. F.C.

Provenance
Henry de Vere Vane, ninth Baron Barnard, Raby Castle, Darlington, Durham (died 1918)
Scott and Fowles, New York
Mrs. J. Henry Lancashire, New York
Lock Galleries, New York
Mr. and Mrs. Morrie A. Moss, Memphis, Tennessee
Brooks Memorial Art Gallery, 1959

Exhibitions
Anglo-Japanese Exhibition, London, 1910, no. 5
(lent by Lord Barnard)
International Fine Arts Exhibition, Souvenir of the British Section, Rome, 1911, 179, 601, 602, reproduced
Old Masters, Royal Academy, 1912, no. 126
(lent by Lord Barnard)
Paintings from the Collection of Mr. and Mrs. Morrie A. Moss, Memphis, Brooks Memorial Art Gallery, Memphis, Tennessee, 1955, no. 17

References
W. G. Constable, *Richard Wilson,* London, 1953, pp. 89, 223, 268, 292, pl. 116b
Michael Milkovich, *The Moss Collection Paintings,* Memphis, Tennessee, 1964, p. 38 and cover

Alexander Cozens

1717-1786

Alexander was the son of Richard Cozens, one of Peter the Great's principal shipbuilders. His early years were spent in Russia, and by 1746 he was in Rome, a date given on several Roman sketches signed and dated by him. In the same year he travelled from Italy to England. We know nothing for certain of his work before that time, but the dated sheets show that he had already developed into a competent landscape draftsman. In 1749 he was appointed drawing master in landscape at Christ's Hospital, where he continued teaching until 1753. During this period, he was closely associated with the printmaker John Pine (1690-1756), whose daughter, sister of Robert Edge Pine (1742-88), he married. Their son John Robert was born in 1752. In 1760 he sent two paintings to the first exhibition of the Society of Artists, and in the following year he was represented by *An Historical Landscape Representing the Retirement of Timoleon,* a subject from Roman history. From 1765 to 1771 he exhibited with the Society of Artists and from 1772 to 1781 he transferred to the Royal Academy, of which he hoped to become a member. Although he painted in oil, especially when he was interested in becoming an R.A., he was much more prolific as a draftsman. It is almost alone through these drawings and his writings that he is known today.

Cozens' interest in reducing his ideas and impressions to categories and more easily teachable systems mark him as a contemporary of Kant and an 18th-century thinker. His art reflects this inherent tendency to systematize and to reduce his impressions to the essential. In his visual productions, he was attracted to flat patterns of light and shadow and to simplified forms. These result in powerful and often monumental images which have particular appeal for modern taste but often lack a certain refinement which one usually connects with 18th-century art. Like his contemporary Reynolds, Cozens' landscapes suggest that they are infused with ideas, which is often the case. The qualities most important to his monochrome brush-drawings are their implications of atmospheric effects, their subtle and poetic nuances of tone, their peculiarly electric vision of limbs and mountains against the sky, and their rugged, often idiosyncratic selection of views. F.C.

Bibliography
A. P. Oppé, "Fresh Light on Alexander Cozens," *Print Collector's Quarterly,* April 1921, pp. 61-90
A. P. Oppé, "A Roman Sketch-book by Alexander Cozens," *Walpole Society,* XVI, 1928, pp. 81-93
Martin Hardie, "Early Artists of the British Water-Colour School: Alexander Cozens," *The Collector,* XI, 1930, pp. 133-39, 181-87
A. P. Oppé, *Alexander and John Robert Cozens,* London, 1952
A. H. Mayor, "Modern Artist of the eighteenth century," *Metropolitan Museum Bulletin,* n.s. XII, December 1953, pp. 100-04
A. P. Oppé, "Landscape in Oil by Alexander Cozens: Sunset," *Burlington,* XCII, 1954, pp. 20-22
Francis W. Hawcroft, "Water-colour drawing by Alexander Cozens," *Burlington,* CII, 1960, p. 486
H. Zerner, "Alexandre Cozens et sa méthode pour l'invention des paysages," *L'Oeil,* no. 137, May 1966, pp. 28-33

4

4
A Clump of Trees with a Mountain Peak in the Distance
Trustees of The British Museum
Brush, sepia and wash; 9 x 12⅛ in.
c. 1770-80

Cozens' ability to present the unusual is well illustrated by this view. The observer's vantage point is at the level of the ground, below the roots of a tree which rises out of a small hillock. This ancient beech is so massive that its luxuriant growth vibrates across the entire sheet, forming an almost opaque screen of foliage. Its winding branches, compressed into springlike masses of vegetation, press the sky into tiny horizontal cracks and points of light. A mountain, far in the distance, seen through a tiny opening, is the focal point of the composition. Cozens' interest in reducing his vocabulary of forms to a limited number of kinds of brush strokes is well illustrated by the nervously repeated patterns which alternately produce an impression of leaves, grasses, and filtered light. F.C.

Provenance
Presented to The British Museum by the National Art-Collections Fund, 1941

5

The Cloud
Mr. D. L. T. Oppé
Grey and black washes on thin India paper;
8½ x 12½ in.
c. 1775-85

This sheet originally belonged to a sketchbook in the possession of Cozens' pupil Serjeant W. Mackworth Praed. There were in the album eighty-three drawings and four small oil sketches on paper, and numerous of these were studies of clouds. No. 5 is related to his *New Method,* which emphasizes the representation of landscape effects through simplified means by distinguishing carefully among the different classes of landscape forms. The reduction to simple means and effects has, in this case, resulted in a monumental vision of a cloud at sunset.

Cozens was the first to make the representation of clouds a special category of his study and teaching of landscape. His series of aquatints showing their various possible formations was carefully copied and elaborated upon by Constable (no. 126), and Bonington also made such cloud studies (no. 171). The idea of recording atmospheric phenomena for the purpose of representing them in paintings lies behind the study of atmospheric effects in the art of Turner. The same approach and method characterizes the point of view of the impressionists who followed Turner, by emphasizing the important role of color in the study of atmospheric effects. Although Cozens restricts himself to a sombre

5

palette, in his idea of isolating daylight and its atmospheric qualities seen through clouds at different times of the day lies one seed which will find its full maturity in impressionism.
F.C.

Provenance
John Robert Cozens (sale, Greenwood's, London, 9-10 July 1794)
Dr. Curry (sale, Sotheby's, London, March-April 1820, bt. Praed)
Serjeant William Mackworth Praed
Purchased from the descendants of W. M. Praed by A. P. Oppé, London, 1926 (died 1957)

Exhibitions
The Horne Collection, Burlington Fine Arts Club, 1916 (not in catalogue)
Fitzwilliam Museum, Cambridge University, 1920, no. 4
British Art, Royal Academy, London, 1934, no. 1198
Twee Eeuwen Engelsche Kunst, Stedelijk Museum, Amsterdam, 1936, no. 207
Peinture Anglaise, Louvre, Paris, 1938, no. 189
Drawings and Paintings by Alexander Cozens, Graves Art Gallery, Sheffield, The Tate Gallery, London, 1946-47, no. 60 (introduction to catalogue by A. P. Oppé)
The Paul Oppé Collection, Graves Art Gallery, Sheffield, 1952, no. 9
Old Master Drawings, Royal Academy, London, 1953, no. 438

L'Aquarelle Anglaise, Geneva/Zürich (British Council), 1955-56, no. 39
The Paul Oppé Collection, Royal Academy, London, 1958, no. 49
The Romantic Movement, The Tate Gallery, London, (Arts Council), 1959, no. 397
The Paul Oppé Collection, National Gallery of Canada, Ottawa, 1961, no. 26
De Engelse Aquarel uit de 18 de Eeuw, Rijksmuseum, Amsterdam, 1965, no. 13

References
Laurence Binyon, *Landscape in English Art and Poetry,* London, 1931, p. 81
Vasari Society, Series II, Part XIV, 1933, no. I
John Piper, *British Romantic Artists,* London, 1942, p. 12
Iolo A. Williams, *Early English Watercolours,* London, 1952, p. 38, fig. 59
Oppé, *Alexander and John Robert Cozens,* p. 99, pl. 21

Sir Joshua Reynolds

1723-1792

Joshua Reynolds was born in Plympton, Devonshire, the son of the Reverend Samuel Reynolds, Master of the Plympton Grammar School. Having shown an outstanding aptitude for painting and drawing, his father apprenticed him for four years to Thomas Hudson (1701-79), also from Devonshire. He moved to London in October 1740, but did not remain with Hudson the full four years, leaving in the early summer of 1743 for Devonshire to paint portraits. Late in 1744 he returned to London and worked there independently. A second Devonshire period, beginning in 1746, was concluded in 1749 when Augustus Keppel invited him to sail to Algiers and Minorca. Viewing it as an opportunity to reach Italy, he accepted, arriving at Leghorn in January 1750 and travelling on to Rome. He remained there two years studying the art of the old masters, and in May 1752 he journeyed northward to Florence, Parma, Bologna, and Venice, where he stayed three weeks sketching the works of Titian, Tintoretto, and Veronese. After stopping in Paris, he settled in London in 1753, where he was to remain for the rest of his life.

In London, he immediately painted the famous full-length portrait of his friend and benefactor Keppel (National Maritime Museum, Greenwich), a portrait modelled on Ramsay, but revealing powers equalling the best of Reynolds' later productions. With works of this power, he established himself as the most eminent painter in England in the following decade.

His busiest and most productive years were from 1757 to 1761 when he had more than 150 sitters in one year. In the 1760s his most impressive public or heroic portraits were produced. These began with *Keppel* and continued through the *Duchess of Hamilton* (Lady Lever Art Gallery, Port Sunlight) to the allegorical portrait of *Garrick Between Tragedy and Comedy* (collection Lord Rothschild, Rushbrooke), and are climaxed by such works as *Frederick, 5th Earl of Carlisle* (Castle Howard) of 1769.

At this time, the first of numerous portraits of children, *Lady Charlotte Fitzwilliam* (collection T. W. Fitzwilliam, Milten Park), was painted, and its engraving made Reynolds famous in this genre. These intimate portraits are part of a less official side of Reynolds' art which involves such powerful works as the study of *Dr. Samuel Johnson* of 1770 (National Gallery, London).

Although he had not received the patronage of the King, Reynolds was considered the outstanding painter of the period, and his commissions derived from a broad spectrum of British society. His social, artistic, and intellectual talents made him eminently acceptable for election as President of the newly formed Royal Academy in 1768. This marked the beginning of a period in which he painted highly official portraits, often drawing on famous compositions by old masters. Such allegorical portraits as *Lady Blake as Juno,* exhibited at the Royal Academy in 1769, where portraiture was wedded to an elevated conceptual tradition, were intended to give the British painter a more prominent intellectual and social status. *Three Ladies Adorning a Term of Hymen* (National Gallery, London) of 1774 is his most ambitious work of this type.

In 1781 Reynolds travelled through the Lowlands, and on his return replaced his grand manner with new ease, directness, and naturalism which were foreign to his earlier, more pretentious style. In 1782 he had a paralytic stroke but continued to paint. As late as 1788 he completed such masterpieces as *Maria Gideon and her brother William Eardley* (collection Viscount Cowdray, London), one of his most beautiful portraits. However, in 1789 he lost the sight of one eye and gave up painting.

Yearly, in December, it was Reynolds' custom to deliver a lecture at the Royal Academy. Later published as the *Discourses,* these constitute the basic statement of art theory of this period and had a decisive influence even in the early 19th century. Every art student heard or read these classical summaries of 17th- and 18th-century art theory, and they established the way of thinking about art at the time. Even reactions to Reynolds such as those of Blake and Hazlitt were merely departures from him, rather than a totally new theoretical position. Through his writings and compositions, Reynolds had a more extensive influence than any other British artist of his time. He was not as quick, witty, facile, alert, or attractive as Gainsborough, the contemporary with whom he most closely compares. He was not so inventive as John H. Mortimer, nor so penetrating as George Stubbs. But he towers over them as a colorist, in resonance of power as a composer, and in intellect, which at times was almost a burden of his art. Reynolds' is one of the most impressive minds and most formidable talents of the period.

F.C.

Bibliography
The Works of Sir Joshua Reynolds, Knt., 2 vols., London, 1797
James Northcote, *Memoirs of Sir Joshua Reynolds,* 2 vols., London, 1813-15
C. R. Leslie and Tom Taylor, *Life and Times of Sir Joshua Reynolds,* 2 vols., London, 1865
Engravings from the Works of Sir Joshua Reynolds, P. R. A., 3 vols., London, Henry Graves & Co., 1865
The Works of Sir Joshua Reynolds, P. R. A., Grosvenor Gallery, London, 1883-84 (notes by F. G. Stephens)
A. Graves and W. V. Cronin, *A History of the Works of Sir Joshua Reynolds,* 4 vols., London, 1899-1901
F. W. Hilles, *Letters of Sir Joshua Reynolds,* Cambridge, 1929

F. W. Hilles, *The Literary Career of Sir Joshua Reynolds,*
Cambridge, 1936
Sir Joshua Reynolds Loan Exhibition at 45 Park Lane,
London, 1937 (notes by E. K. Waterhouse)
Ellis K. Waterhouse, ''A Review of Reynolds,'' *Burlington,*
LXX, 1937, pp. 105-11
Edgar Wind, '' 'Borrowed Attitudes' in Reynolds and
Hogarth,'' *JWCI, II,* 1938, pp. 182-85
Ellis K. Waterhouse, *Reynolds,* London, 1941
Sir Joshua Reynolds, *Discourses on Art,* edited by Robert
R. Wark, San Marino, 1959
Exhibition of Works by Sir Joshua Reynolds, City of
Birmingham Museum and Art Gallery, Birmingham, 1961

6

6

Lady Sarah Bunbury Sacrificing to the Graces
The Art Institute of Chicago,
Mr. and Mrs. W. W. Kimball Collection
Oil on canvas; 94 x 60 in.
1765

Lady Sarah Lennox Bunbury (1745-1826) is
portrayed here at age twenty, three years after her
marriage to Sir Thomas Charles Bunbury
(1740-1821, Sixth Baronet) of Barton and Mildenhall,
Suffolk, brother of the artist Henry William
Bunbury (1750-1811). Soon after his succession,
George III showed particular attention to the
beautiful Sarah Lennox and perhaps contemplated
marriage. She was the daughter of the second
Duke of Richmond and the granddaughter of the
first Earl Cadogan through her mother. Her cousin
was Charles James Fox, the orator and politician
who became Secretary of State for Foreign Affairs
shortly before his death. Her marriage to Sir
Charles ended in divorce in 1776, and in 1781 she
married Colonel George Napier, son of Baron
Napier, who fought in the American war. Her
sons were the generals Sir Charles and Sir
William Napier.

Although it has been said that Lady Sarah is here sacrificing to the Three Graces at the altar of Apollo (!), she is actually making sacrifice to a symbolic representation of *Amicitia* or friendship. The Three Graces shown nude at the upper left on an antique pedestal are drawn from a Hellenistic sculpture already known to artists like Raphael in the Renaissance. That the Three Graces signify perfect friendship is an idea handed down from the ancient writers. The central figure proffers a wreath of myrtle, which is always green, signifying that friendship propagates itself. Roses climbing the pedestal and the prominent flower at the feet of the brazier are signs of the pleasantness and charm which should always exist between friends contributing to a continued union of good will. Two of the Graces are shown with arms intertwined and the other looks away, suggesting that duplication is a source of benefit to the friend. Ripa in his *Iconologia* stated that the Three Graces should stand for friendship because it has three benefits and stages: the first, the giving of gifts; the second, the receiving of gifts from others; and the third, the continuous exchange of like for like. The intertwining of the arms of the Graces symbolizes this interchange. Their nudity signifies that friendship implies a free spirit which is without deceit. At first it may seem surprising to use Ripa's 16th-century emblem book to interpret Reynolds. However, both it and Alciati's *Emblemata* were published in England in the 18th century and were popular source books for artists in this period. Artists like Blake used such source books, as has been shown especially by P. Nanavutty in an article in the *Warburg Journal* in 1952, and they were used by Reynolds to increase the intellectual content of his portraits. The reference to Cicero's *De Amicitia,* which would have been known to Reynolds, is implied by such a painting as this.

It is known that Lady Sarah was the lifetime friend of Lady Susan Fox-Strangways (1743-1827), later Lady Susan O'Brien. Lady Susan, niece of Sarah Bunbury's brother-in-law Henry Fox, was two years older than her friend, but her features were less classical and more piquant. Two portraits, one by

Francis Cotes (1726-70) and another by Miss Catherine Read (1723-78), both published by Ilchester, show a striking resemblance to the kneeling figure in no. 6. The resemblance between the portraits and the girl pouring the sacrificial libation behind Lady Sarah are evidence enough, coupled with the subject of the painting, to indicate that not only an allegory of friendship is shown here, but that the two friends themselves are portrayed. Moreover, the kind of interchange of like for like suggested by the nude Graces is actually performed by Lady Susan who kneels to pour the libation which Lady Sarah dashes into the sacrificial flames. Thus, although we do not know the circumstances of the commission for this portrait, it must be thought of as a monument to Lady Sarah's devotion to her intimate friend.

The pose of the principal figure, which derives from Guido Reni, and the sitter's costume are in keeping with the slightly esoteric program of the portrait. One needs only to recall Reynolds' portrait of Lady Elizabeth Keppel (collection Duke of Bedford, Woburn Abbey) of 1761-62 or French dress of this period to realize that Lady Sarah's gown is not typical of fashionable costumes of the 1760s. She is shown in antique draperies pinned at the shoulder and tied up at the waist with a band. The brazier, furniture, and Lady Susan's urn are all in the antique taste, harmonizing with the classical architecture and the antique sculptural group. It is the most "neoclassical" of Reynolds' portraits up to this time and is a fitting counterpart in portraiture to Gavin Hamilton's history paintings. The intellectual content is substantial, and its references operate on numerous different levels. It is exactly this kind of portrait, bordering on history painting owing to its intellectual content, that Reynolds pursued in order to raise the status of the portrait painter in Britain from that of a "face painter" to that of a man of learning.
F.C.

Provenance
Sir Thomas Charles Bunbury (died 1821)
Sir Henry Edward Bunbury (died 1860) and descendants, Barton Hall and Mildenhall, Suffolk (the picture was at Barton Hall in 1901)
Charles J. Wertheimer
Mr. and Mrs. W. W. Kimball
The Art Institute of Chicago, 1922

Exhibitions
The Incorporated Society of Artists of Great Britain, London, 1765, no. 104
Great Portraits by Famous Painters, Minneapolis Institute of Arts, 1952, no. 22

References
Leslie and Taylor, I, 247, 248, 252
Sir Walter Armstrong, *Sir Joshua Reynolds,* 1900, ill. opp. p. 20, pp. 167, 196
Countess of Ilchester and Lord Stavordale, eds., *The Life and Letters of Lady Sarah Lennox,* London, 1901, II, ill. opp. p. 12, pp. 104, 136
The Art Institute of Chicago, *Bulletin,* XIV, no. 5, May 1920, pp. 75, 77
J. F. Molloy, *Sir Joshua and His Circle,* London, 1906, I, 179
Waterhouse, *Reynolds,* pp. 12, 56, pl. 101
Nikolaus Pevsner, "Heritage of Compromise," *Architectural Review,* XCI, no. 542, February 1942, p. 37
Minneapolis Institute of Arts, *Bulletin,* XLI, no. 28, 1952, p. 152
Ellis K. Waterhouse, *Painting in Britain, 1530-1790,* London, 1953, pp. 168, 187, pl. 131
The Art Institute of Chicago, *Paintings . . . A Catalogue of the Picture Collection,* Chicago, 1961, p. 399
Ann Hope, "Caesare Ripa's Iconology and the Neoclassical Movement," *Apollo,* LXXXVI, Oct. 1967, supp. (Notes on British Art), pp. 1-4

Reproductions
Engraved by Edward Fisher (1730-c. 1785), 1766

7

7

Comedy
The Visitors of the Ashmolean Museum, Oxford
Pen and brown ink over black chalk; 9 x 7¼ in.
Inscribed on verso: *Sir Joshua Reynolds presents his Compliments/and is sorry he is engaged to-morrow at two*
c. 1772-82

Known drawings by Reynolds are not generally preparatory studies for specific poses or compositions in his paintings. His drawings and sketches were often a means of studying the old masters, of studying a special expression, or for recording a sitter out-of-doors, as in the *Bust of a Young Girl* (no. 9) in the Boston Museum of Fine Arts.

Since his drawings seldom prepare for specific compositions in painting, it is not surprising that this one has been difficult to relate conclusively to a finished picture. A similar pose to that in this drawing is found in the portrait of *Mary, Daughter of Jeremiah Meyer, as Hebe* (collection Anthony de Rothschild, London), exhibited in 1772. However, the young Hebe's draperies are blown behind rather than before her, and are neither so complex nor so fluent in arrangement as those in this drawing, which seems more mature and is probably later in date. There are also striking parallels between this and the half-length portrait of *Giovanna Bacelli as Comedy* (collection Lord Sackville, Knole) of 1782-83, although the features of the sitter are different. In addition we know that Reynolds did a sketch, now lost, of Lady Hamilton as *Comedy* for John Angerstein, which was recorded by Graves and Cronin. This drawing is closely related to a chalk study in The British Museum, showing a figure of similar features and pose, with a mask held before the face, but reversed and seated. As stated in Ripa's *Iconologia*, comedy usually holds a horn and a mask; the horn standing for harmony and the mask symbolizing mimicry. The conception of the figure derives from the extraordinarily graceful water-carrier in Raphael's *Fire in the Borgo* in the *Stanza dell'Incendio* in the Vatican.   F.C.

Provenance
Sir Charles Greville (died 1832)
By descent to his nephew, George Guy Greville, 4th
Earl of Warwick, Warwick Castle (died 1893)
By descent to his son, Francis Greville, 5th Earl of
Warwick (died 1924)
By descent to his son, Leopold Greville, 6th Earl of
Warwick (died 1928)
By descent to his son, Charles Greville, 7th Earl of
Warwick
T. H. Cobb
Karl T. Parker
Presented to the Ashmolean Museum, Oxford, 1944

Exhibitions
Three Centuries of British Drawings, Arts Council,
London, 1951, no. 140
Drawings by Old Masters, Royal Academy (Diploma
Gallery), London, 1953, no. 452

References
K. T. Parker, "Sir Joshua Reynolds . . . Comedy," *Old
Master Drawings,* V, March 1931, pp. 75-78, pl. 57, fig. 20
Report of the Visitors of the Ashmolean Museum, 1944,
pp. 18-19

8

Portrait of Baretti
The Viscountess Galway
Oil on canvas; 30 x 26 in.
1773-74

Giuseppe Marc'Antonio Baretti (1719-89), the
Italian critic and lexicographer, was born at Turin
and lived in his early years at Venice and Milan.
He spent his youth writing literary criticism, and as
a result of a literary quarrel was forced to travel
to England in 1751. There, he became a teacher,
translator, and promulgator of the Italian language
and its literature. His first major work after arriving
in England was a *Dissertation upon the Italian
Poetry,* published in 1753, in which he emphasized

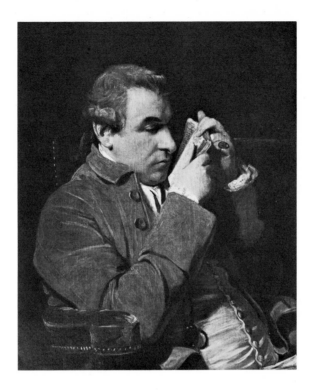

8

the commanding importance of Dante. In his
Italian Library (1757) he mentioned Luigi Pulci and
other Italian writers who were almost completely
unknown at that time in England. In this work, he
translated some of the more striking lines in Dante's
Inferno, including the description of Ugolino in the
Tower of Famine. While in London he compiled an
Anglo-Italian dictionary, published in 1760, for
which a dedication was written by Dr. Johnson, to
whom Baretti was introduced by Mrs. Lennox,
whom he had assisted in preparing her *Shakespear
Illustrated* of 1753. For six years, from 1760 to 1766,
he returned to Italy and published in 1770 his
Lettere famigliari, and he was an intimate of the
intellectual circle which included Garrick, Johnson,
and Reynolds. Johnson among others gave

evidence at his trial for murder in 1769 when Baretti
fatally stabbed with his fruit knife a man who had
assaulted him in the street. His friends supported
him at the trial, and he was acquitted. Through his
contacts with these men, he became secretary to
the Royal Academy. In 1776 he also translated
Reynolds' first six *Discourses* into Italian. He also
wrote essays on Shakespeare and Voltaire which
were brought together in his collected works,
published in Milan in 1838.

Baretti lived with the Thrale family, the friends of
Dr. Johnson and Fanny Burney, from 1773 to 1776,
teaching Italian to their eldest daughter Hester
Maria, afterwards Viscountess Keith. This picture,
for which Baretti sat to Reynolds in 1774, was
painted for Mrs. Thrale's library at Streatham. The
painting was praised by Leslie as one of Reynolds'
finest portraits. It is one of his most impressive
inventions of an intimate and non-intellectual type
and a particularly apt characterization of the sitter.
In this respect, the painting is in striking contrast
with the intellectual involvements of Reynolds'
allegorical portraits.

There are at least two other versions, one bought
by the Herron Museum of Art, Indianapolis, in
1941 (30¼ by 24⅞ in.) and the other, formerly in
the collection of Harold Boyd-Rochfort (29 by 24 in.),
sold at Sotheby's, July 2, 1958, which may be the
painting formerly in the Marquess of Lansdowne's
collection (sale, Christie's, March 7, 1930, no. 67).
Presumably, each of these is different from the copy
by Giuseppe Marchi, painted sometime before his
death in 1808, which appeared at the William
Davies sale, Christie's, June 9, 1821.
F.C.

Provenance
Hester Lynch Thrale Piozzi, Streatham, Surrey (sold in
1816 with other pictures in the Streatham Gallery,
bt. Stewart)
George Watson Taylor (sale, Christie's, London, 13 June
1823, no. 47, bt. in by Major Thwaits; probably sale
Rainy's, London, 16 April 1834)
Lord Hertford

Henry Richard Vassall Fox, Baron Holland (died 1840)
Henry Edward Fox-Strangways, Earl of Ilchester
(died 1905)
The Viscountess Galway

Exhibitions
Royal Academy, 1774, no. 223

References
Leslie and Taylor, I, 334-35; II, 55, 76, 141, 168
Lord Stavordale, *Catalogue of Pictures Belonging to
the Earl of Ilchester at Holland House,* London, 1904,
pp. 140-41, no. 181
Roderick Marshall, *Italy in English Literature 1755-1815,*
New York, 1934, pp. 22-31
Waterhouse, *Reynolds,* p. 64, pl. 158
Anton Scherrer, "A Portrait by Reynolds," *The Bulletin
of the Art Association of Indianapolis,* XXIX, no. 1,
March 1942, p. 7

Reproductions
Engraved by J. Watts, 1780; J. Hardy, 1794; line
engraving by W. Bromly and S. W. Reynolds

9

Bust of a Young Girl
Museum of Fine Arts, Boston, Seth K. Sweetser
Fund
Pen and sepia wash with touches of blue and pink;
10¾ x 8¾ in.
c. 1786

At present, the corpus of Reynolds' drawings is
small and problematical because he was almost
exclusively a painter rather than a draftsman.
But enough drawings by Reynolds are known
to attribute *Bust of a Young Girl* to him securely.

The sitter, whose identity is not known, is of a
characteristic type in Reynolds' art, especially in

his "fancy" pictures or imaginative genre scenes.
A young girl looking directly at the observer, with
head inclined slightly downward so that the eyes
must look up and out, is a typical Reynolds pose.
This shy gesture gives naïveté and innocence,
an effect heightened by wide and shining but
shaded eyes. The attitude appears to have
delighted his patrons and occurs in the portrait
of *Miss Emilia Vansittart* (collection Mrs. Dwight
Morrow, New York), which is almost identical in
pose to the figure in this drawing. The idea of
shading the eyes is also one of which Reynolds was
very fond, and his *Self Portrait* (National Portrait
Gallery, London) shows a lighting of the face with a
diagonal shadow across the nose which is identical.
The drawing style with pen and wash can be found
in Reynolds' portrait of *Oliver Goldsmith* in The
British Museum which is securely related to
Reynolds' painted portrait of the same sitter
(collection Duke of Bedford, Woburn Abbey).

Reynolds portrayed a young woman known to us
only as Robinetta, who may be the sitter drawn
here. Although the final composition, a version
of which is in The Tate Gallery, is different, the
sitter has a very similar nose, mouth, and
almond-shaped eyes. She also parts her hair in
the middle, uses ribbons to divide her coiffure,
with wisps of hair playing around the face, and
has a tendency to keep one hand close to her
mouth. *Robinetta* was painted in 1786 and
engraved by John Jones (1745-97) in 1787.
F.C.

Provenance
Paul Prouté, Paris *(Dessins originaux anciens et
modernes,* Paris, 1964, p. 17, no. 44)
Museum of Fine Arts, Boston, 1964

References
Andrew Ritchie, *English Drawings,* London, 1935, pl. 17

9

1723-1798

Gavin Hamilton was the second son of Alexander Hamilton of Murdieston House, Lanarkshire. He was educated at Glasgow, and about 1748 he travelled to Rome with Ignace Hugford, important as an enthusiast of early Italian art. There, for a time, he became a pupil of Agostino Masucci. From Rome, he travelled on to Naples where he would have seen the finds from Herculaneum and Pompeii in the museum at Portici. He made this tour with James Stuart and Nicolas Revett, with whom he was living in the Palazzo Tomati in Via Sistina, Rome, in 1750. It seems likely that at that time plans were made to travel to Greece, a trip which ultimately culminated in Stuart's and Revett's *Antiquities of Athens* (1764-1816), but which did not finally involve Hamilton himself. In 1752 he returned to London for a time, where he painted portraits, among them the *Gunning Sisters,* and then returned to a permanent residence in Italy.

Hamilton's most important series of paintings was the group of illustrations to Homer, begun about 1761 when the first, *Andromache Bewailing the Death of Hector,* was completed. This group of six Homeric scenes relates in a general way to the great cycle of Primaticcio in the Ulysses Gallery at Fontainebleau, perhaps the most important representations from Homer completed in the Renaissance or later, a series followed by Rubens and Coypel. Hamilton followed the suggestion of the Comte de Caylus, whose *Tableaux tirés de l'Iliade, de l'Odysée . . . et de l'Enéide* was published in 1757, concentrating on the drama of ancient life as it was shown by Homer and Virgil. He

regarded this series, which was to be engraved and circulated widely, as the outstanding conception of his life. He was correct in ascribing to it such importance, since these prints were studied by numerous artists of the later 18th century including Jacques-Louis David (1748-1825). A second series of Homeric subjects was designed by Hamilton which included eight large compositions illustrating the story of Paris and Helen, painted between 1782 and 1784 for the Villa Borghese in Rome.

Apart from his two series of Homeric subjects, he painted the *Discovery of Palmyra by Wood and Dawkins* (1758, on loan to the University of Glasgow) and *The Oath of Brutus* (1763-64, Theater Royal, Drury Lane, London). It was followed in 1771 by *Agrippina with the Ashes of Germanicus* for Lord Spencer (Althorp House). In 1787 he offered for sale to Lord Shelburne a painting of *Apollo Washing his Hair in the Castalian Fount,* and the last work he exhibited at the Royal Academy in 1788 was a representation of *Hygeia.*

While painting such classical subjects as these, Hamilton undertook scenes from English history, such as *Mary Queen of Scots Resigning her Crown,* commissioned by James Boswell in 1765 and painted in Italy. This subject recalls those by Agostino Masucci from English history, such as the *Marriage of James Francis Edward Stuart,* which is known from an engraving after Masucci and is a suggestive source in Rome itself for a similar kind of history painting in period costume.

Late in 1779 Hamilton was introduced to Antonio Canova, the young sculptor who was to become one of the most forceful exponents of the neoclassical style and who admired Hamilton greatly. Canova saw Hamilton's *Death of Lucretia* and numerous other sketches in his studio on a visit of January 5, 1780, and Hamilton, in turn, saw and approved Canova's gesso *Daedalus and Icarus* in June when it was exhibited to a select group of connoisseurs.

He was also an archaeologist of sorts who excavated ancient monuments in order to find sculpture and art objects, and these later entered the great British collections of Townley, Shelburne, and Lansdowne. He discovered such works as the *Wounded Amazon* in 1771, now in the Metropolitan Museum at Tor Colombaro and, in Hadrian's Villa at Tivoli in 1769, the *Hermes,* a Roman copy after a Lysippian original, now in the Ludington Collection, Santa Barbara. The Townley Venus was discovered at Ostia in 1776.

These are some of the most important discoveries of antique sculpture in the period and illustrate completely the neoclassical taste in sculpture which guided collectors until the Elgin Marbles were exhibited in London in 1807. Hamilton was the most important artist in Great Britain working in the taste of Anton Rafael Mengs. He assisted in passing on this taste to the outstanding British collectors of antique sculpture, Thomas Hope, Lord Lansdowne, Charles Townley, and Richard Payne Knight.
F.C.

Bibliography
A. H. Smith, "Gavin Hamilton's Letters to Charles Townley," *Journal of Hellenic Studies,* XXI, 1901, pp. 306-21
Ellis Waterhouse, "The British Contribution to the Neo-Classical Style," *Proceedings of the British Academy,* XL, 1954, pp. 57-74
Brinsley Ford, "A Portrait Group by Gavin Hamilton with some Notes on Portraits of Englishmen in Rome," *Burlington,* XCVII, 1955, pp. 372-78
Robert Rosenblum, "Gavin Hamilton's 'Brutus' and its Aftermath," *Burlington,* CIII, 1961, pp. 8-16, 146
David Irwin, "Gavin Hamilton: Archaeologist, Painter, and Dealer," *Art Bulletin,* LCIV, 1962, pp. 87-102

10

10
William Hamilton of Bangour
Scottish National Portrait Gallery
Oil on canvas; 35 x 27½ in.
Inscribed: *MONIMIA*
c. 1748

William Hamilton (1706-54), the Scottish poet
and author of the *Braes of Yarrow,* was born at
Bangour in Linlithgowshire, Scotland. Between
1724 and 1727 he contributed lyrics for the poet
Allan Ramsay's *Tea-Table Miscellany,* which was a
collection of Scottish and old English songs with
poems by him and some of his contemporaries.
In the Scottish uprisings of 1746, Hamilton took
the side of the Stuarts. He celebrated the

Jacobite victory at Prestonpans in his "Ode to the
Battle of Gladsmuir," and after the defeat of
Prince Charles at Culloden in 1746, he remained in
hiding in the Scottish Highlands. His despair
at the time is reflected in his poem "A Soliloquy
Wrote in June 1746." Afterwards he escaped to
France. However, through the intercession of
friends, and because he did not enter into politics
abroad, he was able to return to Scotland in 1749.
In 1750 he succeeded to the family estates, but his
health was already rapidly failing. Forced to travel
to a milder climate because of his delicate
constitution, he died at Lyons on March 24, 1754.

Hamilton made the earliest Homeric translations
into English blank verse. He also "imitated" Horace,
translated Pindar, and wrote poetry inspired by
the subjects and style of the antique authors.
At the same time, he used Shakespearian
characters as the basis for poems, such as
"King Lear's Speech to Edgar."

The portrait shows William Hamilton as an antique
poet with a simple fillet binding his hair and clad
in classical draperies in imitation of an antique
coin or medallion. The use of classical draperies
for a portrait was not entirely original, having been
done before by Carlo Maratti (1625-1713),
Giovanni Pozzi (1670-1762) in sculpture from 1717
on, and by Edme Bouchardon (1698-1762) in 1727,
but seldom so severely as in this work. The
roundel is adorned with laurel, which appears
as one of the symbols of poetry. Below is a relief
with human figures in tones of gray imitating a
sculptured bas-relief. It illustrates the last part of
Hamilton's poem of 1739, *Contemplation: or the
Triumph of Love.* On the right is shown a tomb
inscribed with the name "Monimia." Before it,
William Hamilton himself sits on the ground with a
sheaf of his writings held in his hand. A cupid with
a laurel crown holds a lyre and an arrow pointed
away from Hamilton toward two women, one
of whom turns while the other contemplates the
poet. The message of the poem is that love cannot
be locked out or be dispelled—even by melancholy;
only death can release one from love.

In the painting, the poet contemplates this prospect
while Cupid holds a lyre, and the poet holds his
sheaf of papers, signifying his devotion to the arts.
Two women, who stand for distraction and pleasure,
are the objects of the arrow of Cupid. The poet,
on the ground, in a melancholy pose, contemplates
his devotion to his art, his love for Monimia who
is in the tomb, and the inevitable and painful
prospect of further, amorous involvements.
A stoic theme is represented, the emulation
of and dedication to the arts, while laying
aside the temporal and more immediate
attractions of the flesh.

Two portraits of William Hamilton of Bangour were
engraved by Sir Robert Strange. The first, after a
drawing by Gavin Hamilton, with the sitter facing
left for the central roundel of this painting, was
prefixed to the 1749 edition of William Hamilton's
works. Another version of this engraving, facing
right, was first published in the 1760 edition of
Hamilton's works. David Laing, (cf. Paterson) who is
generally reliable, wrote that the original picture
was painted at Rome about the year 1748 and
presented by the poet to his friend Sir Stuart
Thriepland. He also quoted the twelve lines of
poetry inscribed on the back of the portrait that
were added at Rouen in 1749, and he says that the
original portrait is now in the possession of Sir
Peter Murray Thriepland of Eingask Castle. There
are certain complications with this tradition since
we do not know for certain that William Hamilton
was in Rome in the late 1740s and no inscription
was recorded on the back of the Edinburgh painting
at the relining of 1909. A copy of this painting,
probably by W. Miller (1740-1810), is in the
collection of the Earl of Stair, Oxenfoord Castle,
Ford, Midlothian.

It is highly interesting to note that Gavin Hamilton
met and talked with William Hamilton of Bangour,
famous for his enthusiasm for Homer, Pindar,
and antique literature generally, as well as old
English and Scottish songs. Although it is not
necessary to posit an origin here for Gavin
Hamilton's general enthusiasm for Greek and

Roman antiquity, it is surely possible to posit a specific origin for his interest in Homer. William Hamilton translated and published the *Parting of Hector and Andromache* from the Sixth Book of the *Iliad,* a subject later painted by Gavin Hamilton (collection Duke of Hamilton, Holyrood House).
F.C.

Provenance
W. F. Watson, Edinburgh
Bequeathed to the Scottish National Portrait Gallery, 1884

Exhibitions
Scottish Art, Royal Academy, 1939, no. 40

References
Charles LeBlanc, *Catalogue de l'oeuvre de Robert Strange,* Leipzig, 1848, p. 58
James Paterson, ed., *The Poems and Songs of William Hamilton of Bangour,* Edinburgh, 1850, frontispiece, pp. xi, xvii, xxxv
Nelson Bushnell, *William Hamilton of Bangour,* Aberdeen, 1957, frontispiece, pp. 89-91
Irwin, *Art Bulletin,* XLIV, 1962, p. 98, fig. 17

Reproductions
Engraved by Sir Robert Strange (1721-92) for the 1749 Glasgow edition of Hamilton's *Poems on Several Occasions*

11
Priam Pleading with Achilles for the Body of Hector
The Trustees of The Tate Gallery, London
Oil on canvas; 25 x 39 in.
c. 1761-65

As related in the *Iliad,* in the war fought to recapture Helen, Troy was besieged by the Greeks. Hector was the champion and mainstay of the city, a good son of King Priam, the loving husband of Andromache, and a favorite of the deity Apollo. With his assistance, the Trojans held out against the Greeks for more than ten years, but at last the Trojans were subdued and Hector was killed along with Patroclus, the favorite of the Greek general Achilles. To dissipate his wrath and to cast infamy on the dead Hector, Achilles dragged his body behind his chariot and left it in the open without the rites of burial. At night Priam went to Achilles' tent and begged for the body of his son in order that it might be honorably buried. Achilles was touched by this entreaty and gave the body to the Trojans.

Gavin Hamilton followed rather closely the description in the Comte de Caylus's *Tableaux* which related that Priam found the Greek general Achilles in his tent surrounded by his friends and served by two warriors. There, the old man fell on his knees, to the astonishment of those present, pleading for the body of his son. Caylus mentioned that exaggeration is in order in representing this scene to show completely the significance of the action, and in Hamilton's painting the warrior covering his face with his cloak, presumably an expression of the deepest emotion, recalls this recommendation.

Dora Wiebenson points out that the composition derives from ancient representations such as the relief on a silver cup from Hoby in the Copenhagen Museum or the relief sculpture in the Villa Borghese (see Winckelmann, *Monumenti antichi inediti,* II, ii, pl. 134) which also shows Priam kneeling and kissing Achilles' hand. Hamilton's version is perhaps closer to the Villa Borghese

relief since it includes the body of Hector on the ground, still tied to the chariot, and Priam kneeling, kissing Achilles' hand. Despite the inclusion of the body, the festive banquet and the nocturnal character of this scene relate Hamilton's *Priam* to an engraved illustration in John Ogilby's *Homer: His Iliads Translated* (London, 1660), which included a series of engraved illustrations largely directed by Abraham Diepenbeck (1596-1675). The rarity of this subject and the striking reminiscences of the earlier illustration lead to the conclusion that it must have served as Hamilton's source along with the antique relief in the Borghese.

Priam Pleading for the Body of Hector is one of a series of Homeric subjects undertaken by Gavin Hamilton in the early 1760s. These were to be among the most important expressions of the revived taste for classical antiquity which we may now appropriately regard as the beginnings of romanticism in Rome. In a letter in the Public Records Office, London, of August 2, 1765 to Viscount Palmerston, Hamilton outlined his plan to undertake a set of six prints illustrating subjects from Homer, including "A Night Piece When Priam Comes to Demand the Dead Body of Hector." The first of these, *Andromache Bewailing the Death of Hector,* was completed in 1761 and engraved by Cunego in 1764. Two others in the series, *Achilles Lamenting the Death of Patroclus* and *The Death of Patroclus,* were completed in 1763 and 1764. *Achilles Dragging Hector's Body Around the Walls of Troy* was engraved in 1769. *Priam and Achilles* was not engraved until ten years later in 1778.

The commissions for each painting in the series were given by different individuals, and the extant examples are of different sizes, as required by the ultimate destination in the patron's house. To obtain these commissions, Hamilton's practice was to prepare an oil sketch which would then be shown to a potential patron, and from it a larger picture would be commissioned at £50 per figure. Canova noted a number of such sketches in

Hamilton's studio in his notebook entry of
January 5 and of June 11, 1780 when he speaks of
"Una cleopatra e altri di incominciati ma di
bellissima invenzione." The engravings, which
Hamilton considered a most important part of the
project, were then made from the finished painting.

In the case of *Priam and Achilles,* no commission
is known, and we know of no large finished work
based on this sketch. The relation of the engraving
to the sketch suggests that no commission was
ever received in this case. The sketch and the
engraving are remarkably close, following each
other in the greatest detail and suggesting that the
engraving was made from the sketch itself rather
than from a larger, finished version. The lack of a
commission would also account for the late
date of the engraving. In a letter of March 13, 1777,
the year before this composition was engraved,
Hamilton refers to the scheme of a Homeric series
of engravings after his own paintings as, "My great
plan in life." To complete his plan, it was essential
to have this scene in the series engraved, which
he finally undertook after many years of waiting.

This hypothesis would suggest a dating in the 1760s
for the sketch itself. Indeed, a date before
August 2, 1765, when Hamilton wrote to Viscount
Palmerston detailing the entire series as later
completed and including this subject as a
night scene, should be accepted as a
terminus for this sketch.
F.C.

11

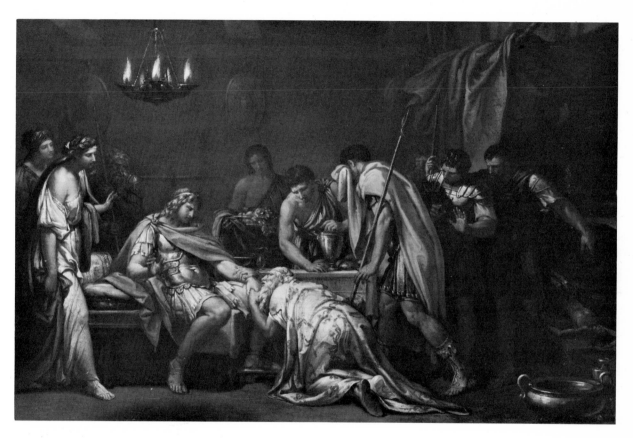

Elena Bassi, Venice, 1959, pp. 59, 137
Irwin, *Art Bulletin,* LXIV, 1962, pp. 93-95
Dora Wiebenson, "Subjects from Homer's Iliad in
Neoclassical Art," *Art Bulletin,* XLVI, 1964, pp. 29-30,
figs. 28, 30, 32
W. McAllister Johnson, "Pictures from the School of
Fontainebleau in Seventeenth Century Guise," *Art
Quarterly,* XXVIII, no. 4, 1965, pp. 293-95, fig. 9

Reproductions
Engraved by Domenico Cunego, 1778

Provenance
Anonymous sale, Christie's, London, 25 March 1966,
no. 143, bt. in
The Tate Gallery, London, 1966

References
Anne Claude Philippe, Comte de Caylus, *Tableaux tirés
de l'Iliade, de l'Odysée d'Homère et de l'Enéide de
Vergile, avec des observations générales sur le costume,*
Paris, 1757, pp. 134-35
Johann Joachim Winckelmann, *Monumenti antichi
inediti,* Rome, 1767, II, ii, pl. 134
Antonio Canova, *I Quaderni di Viaggio (1779-1780),* ed.

George Stubbs

1724-1806

The son of a tanner, and his father's assistant until he was fifteen, George Stubbs studied painting with Hamlet Winstanley (1698-1756), but only for a few weeks. He lived with his mother in Liverpool until he was almost twenty and then for a time in Wigan and Leeds, where he painted portraits for a living. From Leeds, he found commissions in York and moved there around 1744. Although Stubbs had been interested in anatomy from his early years, it is said from the age of eight, he began his first regular study in York, dissecting and drawing human and animal subjects. His knowledge of anatomy created enough interest to secure an appointment to teach the medical pupils of St. Leonard's Hospital, founded in Saxon times. He also studied French and practiced fencing. His talent and knowledge brought him a commission to illustrate a book by Dr. John Burton, *An Essay Towards a Complete New System of Midwifry,* 1751. Obtaining a specimen for the purpose, he prepared drawings and learned the process of etching to make the prints. This prepared him for his greatest publication, the *Anatomy of the Horse,* produced in 1766. Around 1758 he began working in an isolated farmhouse at Horkstow in northern Lincolnshire where he stayed for eighteen months dissecting horses, drawing all the parts and members of numerous specimens. In this work he was accompanied only by his mistress Mary Spencer and his natural son George Townley Stubbs (1756-1815). The idea of preparing a complete study of the anatomy of one species probably developed in his work with the medical students at York, and he expected their help in the

undertaking. But their assistance was not finally forthcoming. About 1759 he came to London where he continued to work on his preliminary drawings (later in Edwin Landseer's collection and now in the Royal Academy, London) and to engrave the plates for *Anatomy of the Horse.*

This unusual training for a British artist was complemented by a trip to Italy in 1754-55, where Stubbs studied the famous collections but remained profoundly skeptical of the technique and knowledge of the Renaissance and antique artists whose works, notably, he did not copy.

His professional artistic life began only after he settled in London in 1760. His first patron was Sir Joshua Reynolds, for whom he painted a *War Horse.* He also worked for the Duke of Richmond and, at Eaton Hall, Cheshire, he painted the *Grosvenor Hunt* in 1762, with portraits of the family and servants. At the same time, he began working for the Marquis of Rockingham at Wentworth Woodhouse, for whom he painted *Lion Attacking a Horse* and *Lion Attacking a Stag* (both now in the Mellon Collection) in 1762. These were followed by a long series of other pictures for the same patron until 1776.

Stubbs was to become the most admired sporting artist of his day with subjects which include portraits of blood horses, dogs, conversation pieces, and hunting and racing scenes. In 1790 a sequence of famous racehorses was commissioned from him for the *Turf Review,* a series of paintings which was exhibited and later engraved. He painted exotic animals such as the *Rhinoceros* (Royal College of Surgeons, London), exhibited in 1772 at Pidcock's Menagerie in Spring Gardens, and many other works for John Hunter (1728-93), who wished to form a collection illustrating the anatomy of the entire animal kingdom.

In his early career he exhibited at the Free Society of Artists, of which he was the Treasurer in 1772 and Director the following year. He was elected an Associate of the Royal Academy in 1780 and an

R.A. in 1781, but he did not deposit a diploma picture and thus did not proceed to full membership. However, he exhibited annually at Somerset House, and the Royal Academicians subscribed to his last publication, begun in 1795, *A Comparative Anatomical Exposition of the Structure of the Human Body with that of a Tiger and Common Fowls,* which was never published although all the drawings were completed and are extant (see nos. 15, 16).

George Stubbs is one of the most remarkable artists of this period. His independence from the art of the past and his complete reliance on experience are fundamental to the new romantic point of view. This contribution is as important as Gavin Hamilton's critical interpretations of classical texts in the area of costume or the penetrating analysis of emotional responses in Wright of Derby's *The Old Man and Death* (no. 29). Stubbs was a brilliant and stylish designer whose compositions have great flash and vitality. He was also extraordinarily skilled in the handling of paint in a way that only the greatest artists achieve.
F.C.

Bibliography
Manuscript memoir of Stubbs by Ozias Humphry in the Picton Library, Liverpool
T. N., "Memoirs of George Stubbs, Esq.," *The Sporting Magazine,* XXXII, May 1808, pp. 55-57; July 1808, pp. 155-57
Joseph Mayer, *Memoirs of Thomas Dodd, William Upcott, and George Stubbs,* Liverpool, 1879
Sir Walter Gilbey, *Life of George Stubbs,* London, 1898
E. Rimbault Dibdin, "Liverpool Art and Artists in the Eighteenth Century," *Walpole Society,* VI, 1917-18, pp. 62-65
Walter Shaw Sparrow, *George Stubbs and Ben Marshall,* London/New York, 1929
Geoffrey Grigson, "George Stubbs, 1724-1806," *Signature,* XIII, January 1940, pp. 15-32
H. F. Constantine, "Lord Rockingham and Stubbs; Some New Documents," *Burlington,* XCV, 1953, pp. 236-38
Denys Sutton, "George Stubbs, Many-Sided Genius," *Country Life,* CXX, 5 December 1957, pp. 1204-10

12

12
Rufus
Art Association of Indianapolis, Herron Museum
of Art
Oil on canvas; 23½ x 30½ in.
c. 1762

Like the famous *Mares and Foals* (collection Earl
Fitzwilliam, Milton, Peterborough), this stallion is
portrayed against an unfigured background. Only a
suggestion of space results from the tiny shadows
slanting from the legs. Such works by Stubbs were
probably designed in a series for a particular
architectural setting. Thus, a frieze of horses
forming a particular owner's stud would complete
the ornamentation of a room. Their nervous
silhouettes, carefully planned to have the greatest
effect against a light background, are extremely
decorative and would have formed an attractive
ensemble. Thus, this composition must be thought
of as having a pendant or being a part of a series.

The commission for this work is unrecorded, but it
was almost certainly painted early in Stubbs's
career. At this time, he was engraving the *Anatomy
of the Horse*. In fact, he was so engrossed with
animals, and he appears to have been so
disappointed with his own attempts at landscape,
that he either subordinated it, used plain
backgrounds, or let other artists paint in the
landscape. This picture is intimately connected
with the *Mares and Foals* of about 1762 in the Earl
Fitzwilliam's collection. But the placement of the
figure in space is so tentative and the Fitzwilliam
painting so much more sure in this respect, that
this should possibly be dated even before the
Fitzwilliam painting.
F.C.

Provenance
Eli Lilly

Exhibitions
Sport and the Horse, Virginia Museum of Fine Arts,
Richmond, 1960, no. 25

13

George Stubbs and Amos Green
Labourers: The Brick Cart
Philadelphia Museum of Art, John H. McFadden
Collection
Oil on canvas; 24¼ x 42¼ in.
Inscribed: *Geo Stubbs pin. 17—*
? 1767

This is one of a pair of pictures, both known
through engravings, which were together in the
Huth sale as late as 1905 and before that in the
Gratwicke sale of 1868; however, the present
whereabouts of the companion piece *Gamekeepers*
is unknown (letter of Basil Taylor, 13 April 1967).
The engraving of *Gamekeepers* was dedicated to
Lord Torrington with an inscription which ascribes
the landscape to Amos Green. Having another artist
complete the landscape is also in keeping with
Stubbs's technique of this period (see no. 14). The
landscape was no doubt carefully introduced
around the figures after they and the dog were
completed. A minor preparatory drawing of the
head of the horse in this painting is in the Picton
Library, Liverpool. The landscapes in both pictures
are by Amos Green, and they compare well with
other known landscapes, one showing fishermen,
in the Hales Owen Grammar School, Hales Owen,
Worcestershire, and another known only through
a photograph in the Witt Library.

Both *Gamekeepers* and *Labourers* were probably
painted for Lord Torrington in 1767, just two years
after his marriage. The story related by Ozias
Humphry (Mayer, p. 29) is probably correct, that
Lord Torrington himself conceived the subject of
this painting. Torrington had often watched his
men at work and thought the subject would make a
good picture in the Flemish style. Stubbs is
supposed to have observed the workmen and,
when they began to quarrel over the manner of
fixing the tailpiece on one of the carts with the
added assistance of a local gossip and adviser, he
selected this moment for representing the group.
The painting was not exhibited in the 1760s and
probably went directly to the person who
commissioned it, Lord Torrington at Southill,
Bedfordshire. A recent technical examination by
the Philadelphia Museum has revealed that the last
two digits of the inscribed date are no longer
legible. However, Gilbey (1898) recorded that these
companion paintings were both dated 1767.

In 1779 another version of *Labourers* was shown at
the Royal Academy (no. 322) which may be that
now at Upton House (panel, 36 by 54 in.; formerly
collection Sir Walter Gilbey), showing a park
landscape with the same group of laborers at the
left and the dog on the right, with an added
entrance lodge to an estate and a fence in the
background. This version is dated 1779 and has a
landscape which would appear, in the photograph,
to be by Stubbs himself. A version of *Labourers,*
referred to as the large version, was in the
possession of Stubbs's daughter in 1809. A third
version, described by Humphry, represented Mr.
Thomson West on horseback, watching the
dispute—a picture purchased from Stubbs by
Mr. West. Still another version was painted for
Erasmus Darwin in enamel on earthenware, and
an oval version in enamel, 38 by 28 in., was bought

very literal ? romantic

by Josiah Wedgwood. A recent x-ray of the Philadelphia painting has revealed a gate lodge and fence identical to those in the Upton House picture.

The subject is original and the objective manner of rendering it is unusual in British art of this period although Stubbs had done something similar in the *Grosvenor Hunt* where the servants were portrayed in a precise and objective manner along with their master. However, *Labourers* shows only servants, that is, the life of the lower classes without moral overtones or caricature or emphasis on their picturesque existence.

These are not anonymous peasants but recognizable portraits of Lord Torrington's workmen, with specific characterizations of the visiting gossip, the sturdy draft horse, and a local fido. Although without an impassioned subject, this painting illustrates that side of romanticism which concentrates on the everyday, holding a magnifying glass up to nature to scrutinize its parts without partiality and leaving with a passionate wonder at its variety.

Stubbs's source for such a picture is to be found in Dutch 17th-century painting. This scene of men loading a brick-cart is particularly reminiscent of the peasants of Jan Victors at his very best, or certain works of Cuyp, but with the addition of direct human contact and psychological self-consciousness, such as one finds only in rare Dutch masters like Frans Hals.
F.C.

13

Exhibitions
Royal Academy, London, 1875, no. 15 (lent by Huth, *Landscape and Figures*)
The Brighton Loan Exhibition, Brighton, 1884
Loan Collection of Pictures by George Stubbs, Vokins's Gallery, London, 1885, no. 4 (lent by Huth)
Loan Exhibition, Manchester, 1909, no. 4
George Stubbs, 1724-1806, Walker Art Gallery, Liverpool, 1951, no. 1
The Romantic Era, Art Association of Indianapolis, Herron Museum of Art, 1965, no. 18

References
Mayer, pp. 29-30, 35
Gilbey, pp. 155, 175, 206, 207
W. Roberts, *Catalogue of the Collection of Pictures formed by J. H. McFadden,* London, 1917, p. 81
Sparrow, p. 19, ill. opp. p. 31
Second Viscount Bearsted, ed., *Catalogue of Pictures and Porcelains at Upton House, Danbury,* London, 1950, pp. 3, 22, no. 85

The National Trust, Upton House, *The Bearsted Collection: Pictures,* 1964, no. 85

Reproductions
Engraved by Henry Birche ([?] Richard Earlom 1742/43-1822) in mezzotint and published by Benjamin B. Evans in 1790, reproduced, Sparrow, opp. p. 31; mezzotint engraving of the figures and horse cart by Stubbs, 1789 (Stubbs, sale, Coxe's, 26 May 1807, no. 11)

Provenance
Probably George Byng, fourth Viscount Torrington, Southhill, Bedfordshire (died 1812)
W. Kinleside Gratwicke, Ham Place, Sussex (sale, Christie's, London, 23 March 1868, no. 54, bt. Whitehead, *A Landscape with Figures; the Brick Cart)*
Louis Huth, London and Possingworth Manor, Waldron, Sussex (sale, Christie's, London, 20 May 1905, no. 135, bt. Agnew)
John H. McFadden, Philadelphia (died 1921)
Philadelphia Museum of Art, 1928

14

Lion Attacking a Horse
Yale University Art Gallery, Gift of the Associates
in Fine Arts
Oil on canvas; 40⅛ x 50¼ in.
Inscribed: *Geo. Stubbs pinxit 1770*

Although the Yale painting is unique in
composition, numerous other versions of this
subject were painted by Stubbs. The earliest was
owned by Charles Wentworth, second Marquis
of Rockingham (1730-82), one of his most
important early patrons. This first version (96 by 131
in., now in the Paul Mellon Collection) may have
been painted as early as 1762 since a receipt of
Stubbs to Lord Rockingham dated December 1762
in the Wentworth Muniments, Sheffield City
Libraries, refers to a painting of a lion. This picture
may also be the one that appeared in the spring
exhibition of the Incorporated Society of Artists
(no. 119) in 1763 under the title *A Horse and a Lion.*
A small painted version (oil on canvas, 8 by 12 in.)
in the Odo Cross collection is suggested by Basil
Taylor as a study for this picture. A similar painting
was exhibited in 1764 at the Society of Artists
(no. 113) entitled *A Lion Seizing a Horse.* Another
Lion Killing a Horse was exhibited in London,
according to James Barry in an undated letter of
about 1764 to Dr. Joseph Fenn Sleigh. Barry was
most enthusiastic about a number of Stubbs's
paintings with exotic animals, calling at least one
of the lions "inimitable." Barry's enthusiasm for
the subject is reflected in the background of his
Orpheus Instructing a Savage People in the Society
of Arts, where a lion attacking a horse, on the order
of the antique group in the Palazzo dei
Conservatori, Rome, is included. A small version
of the same subject, in enamel on copper
(10⅛ by 11⅝ in.), now at the Royal College of
Surgeons in London, is dated 1769. Taylor believes
this is based on the small undated oil (10⅛ by 11⅝
in.) in the Mellon Collection which he places
about 1768-69. Another version in oil on canvas
(27½ by 40½ in.) of about 1790-95 is in the Weld
Blundell collection. Finally, an engraving of the
subject was published by Stubbs in mezzotint in

1788. All of these works except the last precede
the 1770 version at Yale.

His contemporaries explained Stubbs's unusual
selection of subject by reference to a story
published two years after his death. It is said that
he had been to North Africa and had actually seen
the attack of a white horse by a lion. There is no
evidence that Stubbs was ever in North Africa, and
the romantic story of his sitting on the palisades
of the fortress of Ceuta by moonlight, watching a
panorama in which a white horse is attacked by a
lion, is much more a creation of the decade of
Napoleon's sojourns in Egypt than a reality of some
fifty years earlier. Indeed, the story misinterprets
Stubbs's own mentality, which was much more
susceptible to stimulation by a specific lion than
such a visionary scene.

The second theory of the origin of the subject, first
published by Basil Taylor, is much more probable.
When Stubbs was in Rome about 1754, he could
have seen the sculptural group in the courtyard of
the Palazzo dei Conservatori in which a lion has
attacked a horse from the rear and pulled it down,
sinking claws and fangs into its abdomen.

Known versions of this subject before Stubbs
ultimately derive from the Conservatori sculpture,
including an engraving by Ghisi; the small bronze
group from a model of Giovanni da Bologna by
Susini, of which an example exists in The Detroit
Institute of Arts; the 18th-century marble copy
formerly in the Blundell Collection and now in the
Walker Art Gallery, Liverpool; the representation of
the group by Panini in a Roman *capriccio,* now
in the Yale University Art Gallery; the group in the
background of Barry's *Orpheus;* and even the much
more free interpretations of the subject by Rubens.
In fact, this tradition of representation appears to
have great antiquity, relying ultimately on
Italo-Corinthian vase painting.

Although Stubbs did draw upon the specific antique
sculpture, he did so in order to correct and to
improve upon it. While fascinated with the subject,

he realized that the treatment did not succeed in
representing the nobility and power or the
emotional response of the horse, and he must have
suspected that the same was true of the lion. The
dispirited efforts of the horse in the antique
sculpture, his failure to defend himself, and the
lack of anatomical accuracy were not calculated to
impress Stubbs. His version of the *Lion Attacking
a Horse* must be thought of as an improvement on
the sculpture through the carefully observed and
incisive study of nature. This is in keeping with
Ozias Humphry's statement in his memoir of Stubbs
which relates that his motive for going to Rome to
study the finest works of art was to convince
himself that nature is superior even to the
venerable art of antiquity.

The idea of the sculpture must have remained with
Stubbs, and when he had the opportunity to study
a lion at Lord Shelburne's villa at Hounslow Heath
around 1762, he at last found himself in a position
to paint this subject from his own immediate
observations. The result is the highly individual
representation of the lion in the Mellon picture of
1762, showing the startled terror of the horse,
stopped midway in its flight, whipping around to
protect himself with his teeth. This is a convincing
representation of terror and flight, with the nobility
of the horse and the ferocity of the lion emphasized,
and with only a reminiscence of schematic
representations of the passions, such as those of
Le Brun, behind it.

Stubbs's *Lion Attacking a Horse* is striking in its
grasp of the ferocity of the subject, aggressive in
its life-size statement of its own correctness, and
somewhat clinical in its emphasis on accuracy of
parts. But this early version of about 1762 was not
his final solution. The landscape of this early
version was almost peremptory and had little
connection with the figures. That in the National
Gallery of Victoria, Melbourne, which must be a
second stage, emphasizes the swiftness of the
horse and increases the drama by extending the
straining neck and head and by placing the front
leg at a deeper angle. The Melbourne picture is

unsuccessful in relating lion and horse to the landscape, both because it is not the natural habitat, and because there is an awkward juncture between landscape and figure.

No. 14 should be thought of as the ultimate solution to Stubbs's treatment since it is successful in establishing the group in a setting naturalistically appropriate, one which embodies the emotional overtones of the subject, and one which is also visually satisfying. Although this landscape is almost certainly not by Stubbs himself, he must be thought of as determining its general character and its parts. Landscapes in paintings by Stubbs are a thorny problem which can only be resolved by further study. He appears to have avoided or subordinated them whenever possible, especially in his early pictures. In this instance, there is some evidence that the landscape is by George Barret (see Baron, *Life of Edward Tenner,* I, 34).

While more accurate in its representation of the natural habitat of the lion, this composition also reflects the developing taste for sublime landscape. Although Stubbs probably did not think of this subject in theoretical terms in the beginning, concentrating rather on the specific and individual, he must soon have come to realize its aesthetic implications. The Yale composition, with its wild rocks and ominous cloudscape, embodies a highly sophisticated use of landscape to reflect the sublime drama between noble and ferocious beasts and to re-echo that drama by extending its emotional implications to the landscape. Correspondingly, the analytic and specific emphasis in his earlier paintings is subordinated to the overall drama now played on a universal stage. First, it is Stubbs's use of empirical knowledge to correct and to intensify his visual image and, secondly, his final subordination of the creation thus achieved to the demands of the sublime, the highest aesthetic level open to him at the time, that makes this work particularly original and important for the period. In this, Stubbs implies that the elemental drama of life and death of two noble and powerful animals can operate on

the most elevated aesthetic levels, heretofore reserved only for human drama.
F.C.

Provenance
Sir Walter Gilbey (sale, Christie's, London, 12 March 1910, no. 148, bt. Guilles)
Percy Moore Turner (died 1950)
Yale University Art Gallery, New Haven, Connecticut, 1955

Exhibitions
Loan Collection of Pictures by George Stubbs, J. & W. Vokins, London, 1885, no. 30 (lent by Gilbey)
George Stubbs, 1724-1806, Walker Art Gallery, Liverpool, 1951, no. 8

References
T. N., "Memoirs of George Stubbs," *The Sporting Magazine,* XXXII, 55-57; 155-57
James Barry, *Works,* London, 1809, I, 23
George Hamilton, *The English School,* London, 1831-32, III, 134
Gilbey, pp. 156-57, no. 19; p. 212, no. 30
H. Stuart Jones, *A Catalogue of the Ancient Sculptures Preserved in the Municipal Collections of Rome,* Oxford, 1912-26, II, pl. 96
Constantine, *Burlington,* XLV, 1953, p. 237
Robert R. Wark, "A Horse and Lion Painting by George Stubbs," *Bulletin of the Associates in Fine Arts at Yale University,* XXII no. 1, November 1955, pp. 1-7
The Romantic Movement, The Tate Gallery, London, (Arts Council), 1959, p. 216, no. 336
Painting in England 1700-1850: Collection of Mr. and Mrs. Paul Mellon, Virginia Museum of Fine Arts, Richmond, 1963, I, 175
Basil Taylor, "George Stubbs: 'The Lion and Horse' Theme," *Burlington,* CVII, 1965, pp. 81-86

15
Ecorché of a Standing Male Figure
Worcester Public Library, Worcester, Massachusetts
Pencil, red chalk and indigo wash on cartridge paper; 21$\frac{5}{16}$ x 16 in.
c. 1795-1803

George Stubbs began working in 1795 on a project which equalled his ambitious early publication, the *Anatomy of the Horse.* Entitled *A Comparative Anatomical Exposition of a Human Body with that of a Tiger and a Common Fowl,* this work was never completed, although most of the drawings appear to have been. They are now preserved in the Worcester Public Library, Worcester, Massachusetts. The Royal Academy in London agreed to subscribe to the work in 1802, and in 1804 they received the first ten double tables, which included the various views of the human body.

The haunting image of the human form in no. 15, so poignantly related in posture and design to its animal cousin the fowl, illustrates the view that man is a link in the great chain of being. In the comparative representation of human and animal forms, Stubbs was following an analogue which pervaded the thinking about man and his relationship with the animal kingdom as described, for example, by the writer and politician Soame Jenyns: "The farther we inquire into the works of our great Creator, the more evident marks we shall discover of his infinite wisdom and power, and perhaps none more remarkable, than in that wonderful chain of beings, with which this terrestrial globe is furnished; rising above each other from the senseless clod, to the brightest genius of human kind, in which, though the chain itself is sufficiently visible, the links, which compose it, are so minute, and so finely wrought, that they are quite imperceptible to our eyes. . . . Animal life rises from this low beginning in the shell-fish, through innumerable species of insects, fishes, birds, and beasts, to the confines of reason, where, in the dog, the monkey, and chimpanzee, it unites so closely with the lowest degree of that quality

15

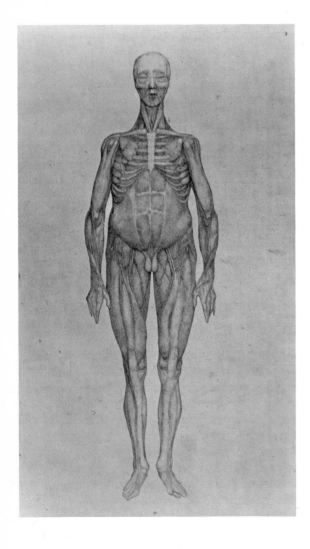

in man, that they cannot easily be distinguished from each other." Stubbs was interested in illustrating the close connection among animal structures by showing similarities in muscles, skeleton, and posture in great detail. The technique of anatomical comparison was very fruitful in making scientific discoveries about human and animal anatomy and especially in pinpointing the special functions of the human form.
F.C.

Provenance
Mary Spencer, London (sale, Phillips, London, 1817)
Probably Thomas Bell, F. R. S.
Dr. John Green, Worcester, Mass.
Worcester Public Library, Worcester, Mass., 1863

Exhibitions
George Stubbs: Rediscovered Anatomical Drawings from the Free Public Library, Worcester, Massachusetts, Arts Council, London, 1958, no. 21

References
Soame Jenyns, "On the Chain of Universal Being," *Works,* London, 1790, pp. 179-185

16
The Owl
Worcester Public Library, Worcester, Massachusetts
Black chalk on thin paper; 15⅜ x 10⅜ in.
c. 1795-1803

See discussion under no. 15.

Provenance
Mary Spencer, London (sale, Phillips, London, 1817)
Probably Thomas Bell, F. R. S., London
Dr. John Green, Worcester, Mass.
Worcester Public Library, Worcester, Mass., 1863

16

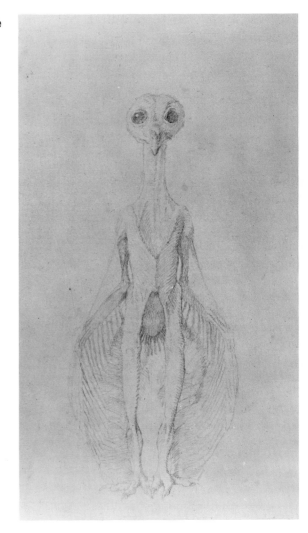

Exhibitions
George Stubbs: Rediscovered Anatomical Drawings from the Free Public Library, Worcester, Massachusetts, Arts Council, London, 1958, no. 54

1725-1809

Born in Nottingham, Paul and his elder brother Thomas left for London probably in 1742. Thomas was appointed private secretary and draftsman to the Duke of Cumberland a year later and accompanied him on his European and Scottish campaigns. After the suppression of the Scots, Paul was appointed draftsman in 1746 to the survey of the Scottish Highlands, begun at that time. To illustrate his mastery in drawing, he submitted copies of prints after Abraham Bloemart and two views, one of Edinburgh Castle, which are now in The British Museum. After his appointment, he sketched topography in the area of Edinburgh, as well as its streets and inhabitants, and he published his first engraved views.

Meanwhile, his brother Thomas Sandby had been appointed Deputy Ranger of Windsor Great Park by the Duke of Cumberland. Paul, leaving the military drawing department in 1751, joined him at Windsor. There, he participated in laying out the grounds and designing architectural elements, as well as sketching a comprehensive series of views of Windsor, its Park, and its inhabitants.

Paul married in 1757 and he spent part of each year in London, finally purchasing a residence there in 1772. He had been a founding member of the Society of Artists in 1754. He sent works to its first exhibition in 1760 and became its Director in 1765. He became a founding member of the Royal Academy and exhibited there regularly from 1768 to 1809. In 1768 he was appointed chief drawing master at the Royal Military College, Woolwich,

and he also had private pupils, among whom may have been Queen Charlotte and her children.

Sandby is thought of primarily as a painter of topography. But it is seldom realized how extensive was his range of subjects or how important for later artists. He made numerous sketching tours through all parts of the British Isles, selecting views important for later artists like Cotman, Girtin, and Turner. He was among the first to make drawing and sketching tours of Wales, and his first Welsh views were exhibited in 1773. He also published numerous prints which drew the interest of artists to little-known parts of Great Britain. He drew the characters of the locale where he travelled, and his watercolor sketches of figures, such as the early *Cries of London* of 1760, are some of his most attractive works.

Sandby's training as a highly disciplined topographical draftsman and his somewhat protected early experience are unusual among artists of this period. He was not engrossed with theories about his art, and he responded to his experiences of landscape with keen, fresh eyes and a brilliant technique. His most important contribution is the wide range of his subject matter in views taken from all parts of Great Britain. He had a fertile and inventive mind which also led him to make numerous technical innovations. It is said that his friend Charles Greville purchased the secret of aquatint engraving in France from Jean Baptiste LePrince (1734-81) and communicated it to Sandby, who was one of the first to make and to improve on the technique of aquatint engraving. He painted in gouache and in watercolor, popularizing the latter medium through his technically brilliant adaptations of the white paper for the rendering of light and air. His treatment of space relies on the paintings of Canaletto and is frequently remarkable for its openness, freshness of observation, and lack of artificial devices.
F.C.

Bibliography
William Sandby, *Thomas and Paul Sandby,* London, 1892
Paul Oppé, "The Memoir of Paul Sandby by his Son," *Burlington,* LXXXVIII, pp. 143-47
(originally published in the *Monthly Magazine,* 1 June 1811)
A. P. Oppé, *The Drawings of Paul and Thomas Sandby . . . at Windsor Castle,* London, 1947
Iolo Williams, *Early English Watercolours,* London, 1952, pp. 29-35
Paul Sandby, 1725-1809, Guildhall Art Gallery, London, 1960

17
The Duke of Cumberland with a Gentleman, His Groom on Horseback, and Dogs
Lent by gracious permission of
Her Majesty Queen Elizabeth II
Pencil, fine brush and watercolor over rough pencil;
6¼ x 16¼ in.
Inscribed in pencil: *Wootton;* and *Duke of Cumberland*
c. 1760

William Augustus, Duke of Cumberland (1721-65), was the son of George II and Queen Caroline. Intended for the Admiralty, he was uninterested in the navy and began a military career. He was a brave officer and was wounded at the Battle of Dettingen in 1742. At Tournai in 1745 he was the head of the British, Hanoverian, Austrian, and Dutch troops, conducting the campaign admirably in the engagement with Marshal Saxe. In 1746 he fought against the Scottish Highlanders, using severe measures which gained him an unfavorable reputation. His resulting unpopularity made it impossible for him to gain the Regency when the Prince of Wales died in 1751. During the Seven

Years' War, he was defeated in the defense of Hanover; thereafter he retired to Windsor.
In his last years, he regained popularity and was influential in displacing the Bute ministry and that of Grenville.

The Duke of Cumberland was particularly important because he was the first to employ artists to paint his stud, initiating a genre which was to become important for artists of the period. The Duke was extremely successful in the breeding of fine racehorses and in 1764 bred Eclipse, one of the most celebrated racers in the history of the English turf. By 1924, ninety-five Derby winners had descended from Eclipse, winning a fortune in prize money. The Duke of Cumberland improved racing at Ascot, and he was also prominent in founding the Jockey Club. He not only employed Paul and Thomas Sandby, he also gave rooms in the Great Lodge at Windsor to Sawrey Gilpin (1733-1807) and commissioned him to paint some of his most famous horses.

No. 17 shows the Duke dressed in a green coat, wearing the Star of the Garter. His companion is in blue. Oppé suggests that this is an alternative idea for the *Great Bridge Over the Virginia River,* where the Duke is shown from a similar point of view, although with different surroundings and attendants. Oppé also points out that this drawing is closer in composition to the view of *The North Face of the Great Lodge with Barnard Smith Lunging a Colt* (Windsor Castle) and its preparatory drawings where the Duke is shown on foot pointing to the exercise. Its relation to the latter work appears the most acceptable suggestion. Small watercolor studies of the spaniels are also at Windsor.
F.C.

Provenance
H. M. Calmann, London
Royal Collections, 1946

Exhibitions
Animal Painting, The Queen's Gallery, Buckingham Palace, London, 1966-67, no. 41

17

References
A. P. Oppé, *The Drawings of Paul and Thomas Sandby,* no. 120, no. 102, fig. 144, no. 386, fig. 143, no. 385, fig. 142, no. 413
A. P. Oppé, *English Drawings . . . at Windsor Castle,* London, 1950, no. S. 422, fig. 66

18
View of Windsor Castle from the Eton Shore
The Duke of Buccleuch and Queensberry, K.T., G.C.V.O.
Watercolor mounted on canvas; 17 x 33¼ in.
Probably 1760-70

Rising on a chalk cliff overlooking the Thames, Windsor Castle was established as the seat of English sovereigns by William the Conqueror. This view from the northwest, looking over the Thames to the buildings on Thames Side and Datchet Lane, shows the panorama of the north walls and terrace on the left and the bell tower at the right end. St. George's Chapel, begun by Edward IV and completed by Henry VIII, appears above the walls. The Round Tower in the middle ward is the central building, with Winchester Tower standing before it on the walls. The state apartments are seen beyond, with the north terrace curving before them, encircling the fine mass of architecture. In the foreground, barges and small boats are seen on the river, and fishermen and a woman frolicking with children are shown in the left foreground.

In the period 1760 to 1771 when Paul Sandby drew frequently in the vicinity of Windsor Castle, the King had not yet taken up residence there, as he was to do in 1778, nor had he begun the repairs which he was to undertake later. At the time Sandby's patron was the Duke of Montagu, who was the Governor of the Castle. A group of seven drawings of Windsor Castle, in the collection of the Duke of Buccleuch, were given by the Duke of Montagu to his daughter, who became Duchess of Buccleuch in 1767.
F.C.

*Clearly known, yet washes are ? fresh /
say detailed = tinted drawing*

Provenance
George Brudenell, Duke of Montagu (died 1790)
Bequeathed to Elizabeth Montagu, Duchess of
Buccleuch (died 1827)
By family descent to Sir Walter Montagu-Douglas-Scott,
eighth Duke of Buccleuch and tenth Duke of
Queensberry, Drumlanrig, Dumfriesshire

References
A. P. Oppé, *The Drawings of Paul and Thomas Sandby*, p. 8

Born at Sudbury in Suffolk, Thomas Gainsborough
was the son of a rather prosperous manufacturer
of woollen fabrics. Having shown talent in
landscape painting, he was sent to London and
became an assistant of the French artist
Hubert Gravelot (1699-1773), who was a drawing
teacher at the St. Martin's Lane Academy. In 1746
he married Margaret Burr, who possessed a
small annuity. His father died at Sudbury in 1748,
and sometime before 1750 Gainsborough returned
to his family home, settling in Ipswich, the beloved
Suffolk country to which he was deeply attached.

His early interest was in painting landscapes,
a taste nurtured by his experience of the
countryside around Ipswich. First he worked in
the style of Jan Wynants and later followed that of
Jacob Ruisdael. However, in Ipswich he found it
essential to paint portraits to make a living.
He was most accomplished at this period in the
small full-length in a landscape setting in the
manner of Hayman, the most splendid example of
which is the portrait of *Mr. and Mrs. Robert
Andrews* (National Gallery, London).

In 1758 he travelled through the Midlands painting
portraits and a year later sold his house in Ipswich
and moved to Bath, where he was received well
and almost immediately given numerous
commissions. From 1761 he sent a series of
full-length portraits to the Society of Artists,
including one of Garrick in 1766 (destroyed,
formerly Stratford-on-Avon Town Hall). From the
rather stiff portraits of Ipswich, his achievement in

this period was to develop an extremely elegant presentation of his sitters in striking and original poses attuned to their own personalities. The best example is *Jonathan Buttall, "The Blue Boy,"* of 1770 (Henry E. Huntington Library and Art Gallery, San Marino).

He only began to show landscapes in London in 1763, and these tend to be subjects of an intimate and highly personal character. These compositions are variations on a limited number of themes like intimate musical exercises using paint, forms and light in an increasingly free and fluid manner as in the *Harvest Wagon* (Barber Institute, Birmingham), probably painted about 1767. These works are released from ponderous ideas, topography, and assiduous attention to visual actuality. They participate in a world of the picturesque, a realm formed wholly of plays of light among landscape forms which ultimately led, by way of Constable and Turner, to impressionism.

Gainsborough's fame in the capital was nurtured on his portraits sent to the London exhibitions, and even though he lived in Bath in the West of England, he was asked to become a founding member of the Royal Academy in 1768. Six years later, he moved to London at a time when he was having dissension with the Academy and refused to exhibit. He received his first commission from the Royal Family in 1777, which firmly established him as a portrait painter, and he again sent to the exhibition—this time a portrait of *The Duke and Duchess of Cumberland.* His achievement in these portraits of his London period was to develop a highly original conception of his sitters, retaining the almost eccentric poses of his Bath period and dwelling on a mood which envelops and gives energy to the sitter's personality. Releasing himself from the demands of actuality almost to the point of denying likeness, he fused his human figures with landscape forms, as in *Mrs. Sheridan* (1774-85, National Gallery of Art, Washington). This harmonious meshing of human and natural forms is realized through a heretofore unequalled fluency with the brush by which paint, hair, and leaves

have similar qualities.

His most diverse subjects were painted in the period of the 1780s when Gainsborough was in his fifties. He continued to produce landscapes, emphasizing more and more the mood and emotional content, and constantly increasing the complexity and intricacy of his forms. He insisted on selecting the subjects himself, and his devices, derived directly from Dutch landscape, now give way to a world completely of Gainsborough's own creation as in no. 22. At this same time, he introduced "fancy" pictures (no. 25), which are the true genre scenes of British art. The name given to the special category for these imaginative presentations of peasant children suggests that they were to be pictures completely devoid of conceptualizations, showing creatures of art and the imagination which appeal wholly to the eye.

As a result of recent researches, Gainsborough's drawings have become much better known. John Hayes insists with certain of Gainsborough's contemporaries that his true greatness is as a draftsman. However, faced with such painted landscapes as no. 22, this is difficult to defend. In both painted and drawn landscapes, Gainsborough established the groundwork which finds consummation in the art of the impressionists. He leaves off literary subjects, dispenses with moral implications, relinquishes associations with the antique and with Italy, and insists upon a world attuned wholly to the eye as the most immediate avenue to the imagination.

One of the greatest painters of this period, Gainsborough's rivals in the history of art are the Venetians and Renoir at his finest.
F.C.

Bibliography
Philip Thicknesse, *A Sketch of the Life and Paintings of Thomas Gainsborough, Esq.,* London, 1788
George W. Fulcher, *Life of Thomas Gainsborough, R. A.,* London, 1856

Lord Ronald S. Gower, *Thomas Gainsborough,* London, 1903
Sir Walter Armstrong, *Gainsborough and his Place in English Art,* London, 1898; (2nd ed., rev., 1904)
William T. Whitley, *Thomas Gainsborough,* London, 1915
M. H. Spielmann, "A Note on Gainsborough and Gainsborough Dupont," *Walpole Society,* V, 1915-17, pp. 91-108
Mary Woodall, *Gainsborough's Landscape Drawings,* London, 1939
Ellis K. Waterhouse, "Gainsborough's Fancy Pictures," *Burlington,* LXXXVIII, 1946, pp. 134-41
Thomas Gainsborough 1727-1788, Arts Council, London, 1953 (catalogue compiled by Ellis K. Waterhouse)
Ellis K. Waterhouse, *Gainsborough,* London, 1958 (with bibliography)
Gainsborough Drawings, Arts Council, London, 1960 (catalogue compiled by John Hayes)
John Hayes, "Gainsborough and Rubens," *Apollo,* LXXVIII, August 1963, pp. 89-97
John Hayes, "Gainsborough's Later Landscapes," *Apollo,* LXXX, July 1964, pp. 20-26
John Hayes, "The Holker Gainsborough," *Apollo,* LXXX, July 1964, supp. (Notes on British Art), pp. 2-3

19
Johann Christian Bach
Bologna, Conservatorio di Musica "G. B. Martini"
Oil on canvas; 29½ x 24⅜ in.
1776

Johann Christian Bach (1735-82), the eleventh son of Johann Sebastian Bach, was born at Leipzig. When his father died of apoplexy in 1750, he became the pupil of his brother Emanuel. Around 1756 he travelled to Italy, studying for a time at Bologna under Giovanni Battista Martini, scholar, teacher, and author of a three-volume *Storia della musica.* They remained good friends, and Bach's letters to Martini are preserved in the Liceo Musicale in Bologna. Subsequently, Bach was

19

received into the Roman Church and became the organist at Milan Cathedral in 1760 for two years, also writing music for the services there. At the same time, he became known as a composer of opera and was invited to London where he took the place at court left vacant at Handel's death in 1759.

Arriving in 1762, he remained for the rest of his life. His works were performed at the King's Theatre, Haymarket, in the building designed by Vanbrugh, and he was appointed music master to Queen Charlotte. His first opera in London, in 1763, was *Orion or Diana Reveng'd* which established him and led him to become the most popular musician in England of his day. He is buried in St. Pancras Churchyard.

Gainsborough, with Bach and his inseparable companion Karl Frederick Abel, who played the viola da gamba, were friends at least from the mid-1770s. They probably met at Domenico Angelo's in Carlisle Street where Zoffany, Bartolozzi, and Cipriani could also be found in lively conversations in the evenings.

Gainsborough assisted in decorating Bach's concert room, which opened in February 1775. A statue of Apollo was placed behind the orchestra, and ten paintings by Cipriani, West, and others, notably a comic muse by Gainsborough, were included as decoration with painted bas-reliefs in the piers of the domed ceiling. In June 1775 Bach was robbed by highwaymen, while Gainsborough in the carriage immediately behind was in the same party. The painter was not robbed. Bach and Abel were connoisseurs and collectors of paintings and prints, and Abel gave Gainsborough one of his coveted instruments in return for two landscapes and some drawings. He also composed a simple work for Gainsborough to play on the harpsichord, and Bach listened until he could no longer bear the amateur's playing and brushed him from the keyboard to take up the work with brilliant innovations of his own.

This portrait, which belongs to the City of Bologna, has not been shown outside Italy. It is known in two versions, of which this is the first. The painting was requested by Padre Martini for a gallery of famous musicians that he was forming in Bologna. In a letter (Bologna, Biblioteca del Conservatorio di Musica "G. B. Martini") of May 22, 1776, Johann Christian Bach wrote to Padre Martini saying how deeply he was impressed by the request for his portrait to add to the gallery of famous men. He mentioned that the portrait was already finished and that he only awaited the right opportunity to forward it. On May 27, 1778 he wrote to Padre Martini that the portrait was being consigned to Sig. Roncaglio, adding that it was an excellent likeness and that it was made by one of the best painters in London. He did not mention Gainsborough's name. The portrait is also

mentioned in a letter of Charles Burney to Padre Martini dated June 22, 1778. It was finally forwarded just before Bach's departure for Paris in July 1778. Gainsborough made a copy for Bach himself that is now in the possession of Lord Hillingdon. F.C.

Provenance
Requested from the sitter by Giovanni Battista Martini for the Liceo Musicale, Bologna, where it arrived in 1778

References
Armstrong, 1898, pp. 101, 102, 191
Whitley, pp. 98, 114, 117, 119, 120, 388
Charles Sanford Terry, *John Christian Bach*, London, 1929, frontispiece, pp. 151, 160
Waterhouse, *Gainsborough*, p. 52, no. 31, pl. 168

20

Lady Anna Horatia Waldegrave (Lady Horatia Seymour) (The "Fireplace" Portrait)
The Detroit Institute of Arts, Gift of Mrs. Edsel B. Ford
Oil on canvas; originally oval canvas with cropped left and right edges in a square frame, the corners of the rectangle now painted in; originally 28 x 24 in. diameter, now enlarged to 30 x 25 in.
1783

Lady Horatia Waldegrave's mother was Maria Walpole, the second illegitimate daughter of Sir Edward Walpole, Chief Secretary of Ireland, and the granddaughter of Sir Robert Walpole, Prime Minister of George I and George II. Her father died when she was one year old, and her mother was married a second time, to the Duke of Gloucester: thus, she became the half-sister of the Princess Sophia Matilda of Gloucester and of His Royal Highness William-Frederick, Duke of Gloucester. Horace Walpole of Strawberry Hill was her uncle. The names Horace, Horatio, and Horatia occur numerous times within the family. She was twenty-one at the time this portrait was painted,

Thomas Gainsborough

20

and here she bears a strong resemblance to her father in his portrait by Reynolds (collection Earl Waldegrave).

Lady Horatia married Lord Hugh Seymour (1759-1801) who served in his youth as a Vice-Admiral and was on the *Latona* under Admiral Howe at the Battle of Gibraltar. In 1782 he settled in London and became an intimate of the circle of the Prince of Wales, and in April 1785 he married Lady Horatia Waldegrave. They were to have seven children, four daughters and three sons.

The whereabouts of this portrait was unknown to scholars after it passed from the Seymour family, and its appearance here brings it back, once again, into the literature on the art of this period. Whitley knew and published the portrait in his monograph

on Gainsborough in 1915. In Mrs. Edsel B. Ford's collection after 1928, its whereabouts was unknown to Waterhouse when he catalogued the portrait in 1958. Soon after it was given to The Detroit Institute in 1967, it was cleaned, removing repaint, especially in the hair and in the corners around the oval. A neutral tone has now been introduced into the corner areas. The shape, which is an oval with cropped edges on left and right, is very rare in Gainsborough's art. Usually his works are rectangular in format even when an oval shape is introduced within to contain the portrait. Ellis Waterhouse in a letter of June 2, 1967 suggests that the unusual shape is probably original and used by the artist because the painting was designed for a particular place.

Because this painting was not in the Royal Academy catalogue of 1783, and because it was placed before the board of the fireplace in the Academy exhibition, it created a great deal of interest at the time and later. Gainsborough was furious at the placement, and this and other objections led him to withdraw completely from the Academy in 1784. However, the placement was probably the fault of Gainsborough himself since he was notorious for sending in his paintings late. The pictures were hung as the catalogue was numbered, and since this picture was not received in time to be included in the catalogue, it would have had to be hung in an anteroom or, alternatively, in a reserve space such as before the fireplace board.

Sir Joshua Reynolds also portrayed Lady Horatia in his portrait of *The Ladies Waldegrave* (collection Mrs. Yerburgh, London), exhibited at the Royal Academy in 1781, no. 187.
F.C.

Provenance
Lady Anna Horatia Waldegrave (Lady Seymour from 1786), Ragley Hall, Alcester, Warwick (died 1801)
By family descent to Hugh F. Seymour, Potterells, Hatfield, Hertfordshire (died 1930)
Duveen Bros., Inc., New York, by 1928
Mr. and Mrs. Edsel B. Ford, Detroit, 1928
Given to The Detroit Institute of Arts, 1967

Exhibitions
Royal Academy, 1783 (uncatalogued)

References
Whitley, pp. 205-07, pl. opp. p. 205
William T. Whitley, *Artists and Their Friends in England 1700-1799,* London/Boston, 1928, I, 319-20
Waterhouse, *Gainsborough,* no. 608

21
A Lady Walking in the Mall
Trustees of The British Museum
Black chalk and stump, heightened with white, on buff paper; 19½ x 12⅜ in.

Inscribed on a label on the back of the mount: *This drawing was given by Gainsborough to Mr. Pearce, Chief Clerk of the Admiralty, and by him to me. He had left it to me in his will, but in the year 1834 chose rather to give it to me and accompanied it with the following written account of the drawing: 'Gainsbro once told me that King George III having expressed the wish to have a picture representing the part of St. James's Park which is overlooked by the garden of the Palace—the assemblage being there, for five or six seasons, as high (?) dressed and fashionable as Ranelagh,—employed him to paint it. 'His Majesty', said Gainsbro, 'very sensibly remarked that he did not desire the high finish of Watteau but a sketchy picture.' While sketching one evening in the park for this picture he was much struck with what he called the fascinating leer of the Lady who is the subject of this drawing. He never knew her name but she was that evening in company with Lady D.—Field, and observing that he was sketching walked to and fro two or three times evidently to allow him to make a likeness. Sir Thomas Lawrence, when he lodged in Jermyn Street, came to my house in Pall Mall, for several successive days, when Lord Derby employed him to paint Miss Farren, to study this drawing.'—William Pearce, 11th Feb. 1834
T. W. Croker, 1842.*
c. 1783

21

The inscription on the back suggests that no. 21 is related to the painting *The Mall* of 1783, now in the Frick Collection, New York. The costume of the lady is almost identical, in the black hat and coiffure, to Reynolds' 1783-84 portrait of *Lavinia, Countess Spencer* (Henry E. Huntington Library and Art Gallery, San Marino). Similar broad-brimmed black hats and tumbling masses of ringlets are worn by the ladies in the Frick picture, who also hold flowers at their bosoms. The inscription on the back suggests that a painting of a fashionable outing in St. James's Park was commissioned by George III; however, the Frick painting was not in the Royal Collections and no painting by Gainsborough fitting Pearce's description is in the Royal Collections today. It is possible that the King was not pleased with the picture or that the inscription is in error. In any case, the pose and glance as well as the costume and technique relate this drawing to *The Mall,* his unique scene of fashionable individuals having an outing in a park.
F.C.

Provenance
William Pearce, London (died 1888)
T. W. Croker
Frederic, Lord Leighton, P. R. A., London (sale, Christie's, London, 11 July 1896, no. 256)
George Salting, London (died 1909)
Bequeathed to The British Museum, 1910

References
Armstrong, 1898, p. 164
Woodall, p. 111, no. 87

22
The Harvest Wagon
Art Gallery of Ontario, Gift of
Mr. and Mrs. Frank P. Wood, 1941
Oil on canvas; 48 x 59 in.
Inscribed: *T.G.*
1784-85

In the winter of 1784-85 Gainsborough painted this landscape showing a group of peasants at evening in the country, climbing into their wagon drawn by three dray-horses and preparing to return, with bundles of sticks, to their cottage or camp. In 1786 the Prince of Wales, then twenty-four years old and an active patron of the arts, bought the painting as a companion to a landscape by Gainsborough already owned by him. Both remained in Gainsborough's possession until his death in 1788 and, with the permission of the Prince of Wales, they were exhibited at the sale of his effects at Schomberg House in 1789. The companion picture, entitled *Upland Valley with Shepherd, Sheep and Cattle,* was in the collection of W. S. Constable Curtis at Mayfield House in 1958.

The composition of this painting relates closely to *The Harvest Wagon* in The Barber Institute, Birmingham, perhaps painted about 1767. Essentially the same components appear in both pictures, and the one in Toronto is a rare example of Gainsborough successfully redoing a composition completed some years before. Waterhouse has pointed out that the motif of the figures in a pyramidal arrangement, reaching up and leaning downward, is based on 17th-century prototypes, and he refers especially to Rubens' *Deposition,* a copy of which was made by Gainsborough.

The Toronto painting illustrates Gainsborough's developing interest in theories of the picturesque. It is at once much less direct, less spirited, more intricate and complex in purely visual ways than the one at Birmingham. The long and variable line of horses and cart, a brilliant invention even in the earlier picture, do not move into the landscape

22

along a strong diagonal but twine over a hillock and into a small dale. The trees are no longer of one variety and simply a pattern of generalized leaves against the sky; they are instead clumps and sprigs of different varieties with a gnarled and broken, aged tree faltering in its growth on the far left. Outcroppings of broken rock and a variety of grasses and plants can now be found. The road itself winds through an almost infinite space and a variety of clouds pick up the movement. Numerous woolly sheep and a furry dog, formerly absent, can now be found. Where the peasants were rather elegantly dressed, they now look like gypsies in rags, and they carry broken jugs and prominently displayed twigs for fires. The energetic horses have now become quaint and rickety drays. In The Barber Institute picture, the drama of two focal points within the group of figures and horses made a taut and exciting composition infused with the energy of Rubens. In the Toronto painting, the eye is stimulated wherever it moves by the continuous alteration of species, textures, spatial planes, light, and clouds. Now, the association with a rustic life and simplicity totally foreign to those who would own the picture predominates. The individuals have been transformed from the world of the fashionable outing to that of the gypsy.

Gainsborough's early interest in the picturesque may have been stimulated by his contacts with Uvedale Tomkyns Price (died, 1764) whose portrait (Alte Pinakothek, Munich) he painted around 1760. More important, we know that Sir Uvedale Price (1747-1829), son of the above, whose *Essay on the Picturesque* was published in 1794, was a friend who had numerous walks and conversations with Gainsborough. The comparison of this landscape with that in The Barber Institute suggests that Gainsborough's ideas were making rapid strides at a time when the younger Price must also have been formulating his views in preparation for his forthcoming publication.

The alterations made between these two compositions reflect in detail the myriad variety which promotes the "natural intricacy" of the picturesque. The wildly overhung and broken banks, the furze-bushes and tussocks, the tufts of grass and broad burdock leaves, even the broken tracks of the cart, the large knots and protuberances of the aging tree, the mosses on its bark, and the blackness of decayed wood are all mentioned by Uvedale Price. According to the suggestions made in Price's writings, which must owe a great deal to Gainsborough, the wandering tribes of gypsies and beggars among men, and the worn-out cart horse among animals are the most picturesque.

F.C.

Provenance
Purchased by George IV when Prince of Wales, 1786
Given to Mrs. Fitzherbert, 1810 (died 1837)
Hon. Mrs. Dawson Damer, 1837 (sale, Christie's, London, 27 March 1841, no. 141, bt. in)
John Gibbons, Birmingham (died 1851)
Thomas Gibbons, Regent's Park, London
The Rev. Benjamin Gibbons, Regent's Park, London (sale, 26 May 1894, no. 24, bt. in)
P. & D. Colnaghi, 1898
Sir Lionel Phillips, Tylney Hall, Winchfield, 1898 (sale, Christie's, 25 April 1913, no. 45, bt. Agnew for Judge Gary)
Judge Elbert H. Gary, New York (died 1927) (sale, American Art Association, 20 April 1928, no. 30, bt. Duveen)
Baron Joseph Duveen
Mr. and Mrs. Frank P. Wood, Toronto

Exhibitions
The Pictures and Drawings of the Late Mr. Gainsborough, Schomberg House, 1789, no. 74 (this catalogue is published in *Burlington,* LXXXIV, 1944, pp. 107-10 and LXXXVI, 1945, pp. 76-78)
British Institution, 1841, no. 127 (lent by H. G. Dawson Damer)
Old Master Exhibition, Royal Academy, London, 1870, no. 82 (lent by Mrs. Gibbons)
Old Master Exhibition, Royal Academy, London, 1890, no. 163 (lent by Rev. B. Gibbons)
Artist's Benevolent Exhibition, Thos. Agnew & Sons, London, 1895, no. 5
Winter Exhibition, New Gallery, London, 1899-1900, no. 181 (lent by Lionell Phillips)
An Exhibition of a Loan Collection of Paintings, Art Gallery of Toronto, 1929, no. 5
Masterpieces of Art, New York World's Fair, 1939, no. 131

Allied Art for Allied Aid, Knoedler & Co., New York, June 1940, no. 7
Loan Exhibition of Masterpieces of Painting, Montreal Museum of Fine Arts, 1942, no. 88
Loan Exhibition of Great Paintings in Aid of Allied Seamen, Art Gallery of Toronto, 1944, no. 21
Old and New England, Rhode Island Museum of Art, Providence, 1945, no. 71
A Thousand Years of Landscape East and West, Museum of Fine Arts, Boston, 1945, unnumbered
40 Masterpieces from American Museums, City Art Museum of St. Louis, 1947, no. 16
Two Cities Collect, Toledo Museum of Art, 1948, no. 12
The Eighteenth Century Art of France and England, Montreal Museum of Fine Arts, 1950, no. 4
Paintings by European Masters from Public and Private Collections in Toronto, National Gallery of Canada, Ottawa, and Montreal Museum of Fine Arts, 1954, no. 34

References
Armstrong, 1898, pl. x opp. p. 40; p. 207
Armstrong, 1904, pp. 156-57, 283
Whitley, pp. 235, 258-59, 322
The Art Collection of the Late Elbert H. Gary, American Art Association, New York, 1928, no. 30
William T. Whitley, *Artists and Their Friends in England,* London/New York, 1949, p. 92 n.
Mary Woodall, *Thomas Gainsborough, His Life and Work,* London/New York, 1949, p. 92 n.
S. N. Behrman, *Duveen,* New York, 1952, p. 144
Robert H. Hubbard, *European Paintings in Canadian Collections: Earlier Schools,* Toronto, 1956, p. 116, pl. LV
Waterhouse, *Gainsborough,* pp. 34, 114 no. 907, 121 nos. 992-93, 125 no. 1027, pls. 99, 270

23

23
Wooded Landscape with a Herdsman and Cow
Richard Cavendish
Black chalk and stump slightly heightened with
white; 11 x 15 in.
c. 1785

There are five Gainsborough drawings of unusually
fine quality at Holker Hall, all dating from the
mid-1780s. John Hayes has suggested that they
were presented by Gainsborough to the Duchess
of Devonshire who sat to Gainsborough twice in
the mid-1780s.
F.C.

Provenance
Probably given by Gainsborough to Georgiana, Duchess
of Devonshire
Probably brought to Holker Hall after its rebuilding
during the 1870s by the seventh Duke of Devonshire
By family descent to Richard Cavendish, Holker Hall,
Lancashire

References
Hayes, *Apollo*, LXXX, 1964, pp. 2-3

24
The Woodman
Mr. and Mrs. K. R. Thomson
Black chalk and stump heightened with white;
20½ x 12½ in.
c. 1787

This is a preparatory drawing from the same model
used by Gainsborough for his famous painting
The Woodman (formerly collection Earl of
Gainsborough), now destroyed. The picture is
known today from the engraving by Jean Pierre
Simon (before 1750- c. 1810). Gainsborough was
working on the painting in June 1787. The model
was an elderly retired smith, really an itinerant
beggar, who lived on incidental charity.
Gainsborough had taken him in and used him as a
model for drawings, for a small sculptured bust, and
for his painting. In the final work, he is shown
standing under a tree looking up at the sky with a
similar pile of faggots on the ground; he is
accompanied by his dog who starts at a clap of
thunder. In a drawing in the collection of Mrs. Cecil
Keith, the same model is seated on the pile of
faggots, and he wears a hat. In no. 24 he is
carrying the pile of faggots on his back. The same
walking stick, stuck through the bundle and placed
upon his shoulder supporting the faggots, appears
in the painting. John Hayes has stressed the rustic
and picturesque character of this model and of the
late drawings of Gainsborough as a whole. He has
suggested that such an individual anticipates
characters of rustic simplicity in the writings
of Wordsworth.
F.C.

Provenance
William Willes, Bournemouth, England (died 1924)
Marshall Spink
Mr. and Mrs. K. R. Thomson, London, 1959

References
Whitley, pp. 285, 296, 322, 323, 329, 331, 332, 371
Paintings and Drawings by Thomas Gainsborough, R. A.,
Cincinnati Art Museum, 1931, no. 74, pl. 74
Gainsborough Drawings, 1960

24

25

Haymaker and Sleeping Girl (The Mushroom Girl)
Museum of Fine Arts, Boston, Maria T. B. Hopkins
and Seth K. Sweetser Residuary Funds
Oil on canvas; not quite completed; 89 x 58½ in.
c. 1788

Although described by Fulcher in the mid-19th
century as a possible reminiscence of the story of
Cymon and Iphigenia in Boccaccio's *Decameron,* a
story which reappears in Dryden's *Fables,* it seems
improbable that a specific literary reference is
implied here. In fact, this mid-19th-century
interpretation embodies a misconception of
Gainsborough's intentions which is almost as
serious as that of Hazlitt, who held Gainsborough
responsible for giving the air of an Adonis to the
driver of a haycart and of modelling his milkmaids
on antique sculpture.

The painting shows the edge of a field at evening
where a young peasant boy has come upon a
sleeping girl, her basket filled with mushrooms,
and a small dog resting beside her. The boy has
stopped, enchanted by her form, to gaze in
abstracted wonder and delight. There are numerous
visual sources which do lie behind this painting
and which are more pertinent than Boccaccio. The
idea for the subject and for the composition comes
from Venetian and Emilian art where creatures of
the woodlands, nymphs, or Venuses are discovered
nude, sleeping in animal skins or on the grass, by
Priapus or by roving satyrs or fauns.

Not only the richness of interwoven strokes of
color, but also the sensuous ripeness, the
innocence and freshness, and the abandonment to
a natural state are drawn from Bellini, Titian, and
Correggio. In this sleeping girl and peasant are
embodied all of that nostalgic yearning to give
oneself totally to a condition of grace and
innocence so important to Venetian art and in the
romantic period reincarnated in works like
Hawthorne's *Marble Faun.*

Already in the 18th century, such paintings of
Gainsborough's were called "fancy" pictures by
Sir Joshua Reynolds in his fourteenth *Discourse.*
The term, as later used by Coleridge, refers to a
particular quality of imagination. Hazlitt describes
these paintings as works on which Gainsborough's
fame chiefly rests, giving some idea of how much
they were appreciated in his own day. With
Reynolds, who did imaginative paintings of
peasants in the 1770s such as *A Beggar Boy and
His Sister* (collection Lord Faringdon),
Gainsborough was an originator of this genre. At
the Royal Academy (no. 176) in 1781, he exhibited
the first of this type, *A Shepherd,* and one of his
most famous "fancy" pictures, *A Girl with Pigs,* was
purchased by Reynolds.

These rustic individuals are often almost the same
characters who inhabited Gainsborough's earlier
paintings of the seventies such as the *Landscape
with Gypsies* in The Tate Gallery, dated in the late
1770s by Waterhouse. However, by subordinating
the picturesque landscape and enlarging the
human figures, he makes a new statement about
their relationship to nature. His first ventures into
this genre are the immediate descendants of
Murillo's peasant children, unintellectual beings
even if occasionally spiritually inspired. Works like
the *Cottage Girl with Dog and Pitcher* of 1785
(collection Sir Alfred Beit, Bart.) reflect Uvedale
Price's view that the wandering tribes of gypsies
and beggars, stricken from their original brightness
by some shadow of warring passion, are the most
picturesque. These are the shadowy children of
nature who are, to a degree, non-human because
they have no more intellectual existence than the
sticks, the craggy trees, and the woods which
they inhabit.

The *Haymaker and Sleeping Girl* is a new venture
within this genre, showing new sources of
inspiration from North Italian art and a departure
from his works of the early and mid-1780s. The boy
and sleeping peasant girl have abandoned
themselves to nature. This nostalgic vision of
unselfconscious abandon is something new in
Gainsborough's art at the very end of his career.

25

It is a departure from the strictly visual and
picturesque qualities of the *Woodgatherers,*
showing his agile mind drawing deeply on new
sources of inspiration.
F.C.

Provenance
Gainsborough Dupont (given to him by Gainsborough in
1788) (Dupont sale, Christie's, London, 11 April 1797,
no. 103, bt. in, in the name of Crofts)
Richard Dupont (G. Dupont's brother)
Richard Gainsborough Dupont (R. Dupont's son) (sale,
Christie's, London, 8 June 1872, no. 67, *Haymaker and*

Joseph Wright
(Wright of Derby)

1734-1797

Sleeping Girl, known as *Mushroom Girl,* bt. White)
W. E. Alexander
William Houldsworth, Halifax, Yorkshire (sale, Christie's, London, 23 May 1891, no. 60, bt. Agnew)
Lord James Joicey, Chester-Le-Street, Co. Durham
sold, c. 1907, to E. M. Hodgkins, Paris
Samuel G. Archibald, Paris and Montreal (sale, Parke-Bernet, New York, 30-31 March 1951, no. 249, bt.
C. G. Doward)
Vose Galleries, Boston
Museum of Fine Arts, Boston, 1953

Exhibitions
9th Annual Exhibition on Behalf of the Artists' General Benevolent Institution, Thos. Agnew & Sons, London, 1903, no. 21

References
Fulcher, 2nd ed., pp. 133-34
Armstrong, 1898, pp. 152-53
James Greig, *Gainsborough,* London, 1909, p. 145
Whitley, p. 349
Spielmann, *Walpole Society, V, 1915-17,*
pp. 95, 96, 98, 108
Waterhouse, *Burlington,* LXXXVIII, 1946, p. 140, no. 18
R. B. K. McL[anathan], "The Mushroom Girl," *Bulletin of the Museum of Fine Arts Boston,* LII, no. 288, June 1954, pp. 39-40
Waterhouse, *Gainsborough,* pp. 37, 105, no. 815, pl. 277

The son of an attorney and brother of a physician, Joseph Wright was born at Derby and spent most his life in that city with only brief periods in London, Bath, and Italy. As a child, he showed an unusual talent for mechanics, making models of machines, clocks, and guns and inventing a pair of proportional compasses for making accurate enlargements of drawings. He was interested in music, and he became accomplished in playing the flute, for which he also wrote scores. At the same time, he showed talent as an artist, and after prudent inquiries his father sent him to London to become a pupil of Joseph Hudson. He remained there only two years, returning to Derby at the age of nineteen, where he took up portrait painting. In 1756 he was in London briefly, once again to study with Hudson.

Wright first exhibited two paintings at the Society of Artists in London in 1765, one of which was *Three Persons Viewing the Gladiator by Candle-Light* (collection Viscountess Mersey). In the following year he sent another subject using artificial light, *A Philosopher giving that lecture on the Orrery, in which a lamp is put in the place of the Sun* (Derby Museum and Art Gallery). Two small candlelight pictures followed in 1767, two in 1768, and an *Academy by Candle-light* in 1769, which Nicolson and Buckley associate with the picture recently at Downe House and now in the Mellon Collection. Wright's specialization in scenes with artificial light is unusual in British art up to this time. His interest in light phenomena was made both bizarre and attractive through his highly original selections of

subject matter, some of which were taken from the developing industrial scene of Derby itself and others from his reading, his travels, and from his knowledge of the art of the past. Often, his early subjects were drawn directly from his own experiences in the area of Derby, and he went everywhere artificial light was employed, painting a *Blacksmith's Shop* (Royal College of Surgeons), *An Iron Forge* (no. 28), and scientific subjects such as *An Experiment on a Bird in the Air Pump* (Tate Gallery). From these he broadened his studies of light phenomena to include moonlight, artificial light seen through a bladder, morning and afternoon landscapes framed by the dim interior of a grotto, light from an erupting volcano at night, the light of fireworks, and light from a stick of charcoal blown white-hot by a young girl.

By 1772 when he painted *Miravan Opening the Tomb of his Ancestors* (Derby Museum and Art Gallery), he had transferred his study of light from his own experiences to literary subjects in which similar effects of artificial light were employed. In order to develop his skill in representing these scenes, he studied the art of the Dutch 17th-century masters such as Honthorst and van Schalcken, who specialized in artificial light effects.

Wright sent his first landscape to the Society of Artists in 1772, beginning a series of works which were to establish him in a new field. His Italian tour from 1773 to 1775 gave this new interest incentive and greatly extended his repertoire of subjects which were already highly inventive. The caverns in the area of Naples, the eruptions of Vesuvius at night, the ancient ruins at Tivoli, Rome, and near Naples, and the tomb of Hadrian with St. Peter's illuminated by fireworks, provided new experiences which he recorded in drawings and later used in his painted landscapes.

In 1775 Wright moved to Bath after the departure of Gainsborough, but he was unsuccessful there and returned to Derby two years later. From 1778 he exhibited at the Royal Academy and was made A.R.A. in 1781. However, he quarrelled with the

Academy, at least in part because of the placement of his pictures in the exhibition, and did not exhibit from 1782 to 1788. He refused the Academy diploma offered in 1784, and in 1785 he held his own exhibition in Covent Garden, sending mostly historical subjects, a few landscapes, and one portrait.

Wright is among the most original and attractive of British artists up to his time. Compared with Reynolds, his portraits are stiff and slightly provincial, the most striking being that of *Sir Brooke Boothby,* 1781 (Tate Gallery). But these are a minor part of his exhibited work. Unlike Reynolds, he was anything but academic. He had none of the ponderous intellectualism of Reynolds but almost nervously discovered the unusual in subject matter and in pictorial sources. In this way, he made contributions which greatly enriched the artistic scene of his period.
F.C.

Bibliography
John Leigh Philips, "Memoirs of the Life and principal works of the late Joseph Wright, Esq. of Derby," *Monthly Magazine,* October, 1797
William Bemrose, *The Life and Works of Joseph Wright, A. R. A.,* London, 1885
S. C. Kaines Smith and H. Cheney Bemrose, *Wright of Derby,* London, 1922
Wright of Derby, The Corporation Art Gallery, Derby, 1934 (catalogue compiled by F. Williamson)
Charles E. Buckley, "Joseph Wright of Derby," *Magazine of Art,* XLV, 1952, pp. 160-67
Benedict Nicolson, "Joseph Wright's early Subject Pictures," *Burlington,* XCVI, 1954, pp. 72-80
Joseph Wright of Derby 1734-1797, The Tate Gallery, London, Walker Art Gallery, Liverpool (Arts Council), 1958 (catalogue compiled by Benedict Nicolson)

26

26
Mrs. Sarah Clayton of Liverpool
Fitchburg Art Museum, Gift of Miss Louise I. Doyle
Oil on canvas; 49½ x 39½ in.
c. 1770

Sarah Clayton (1712-70) is distinctive in her period for achieving success in the enlarged economic realm of technology and manufacturing. Her reputation as an industrialist was achieved in the coal market centered in Liverpool during the "monopoly" period of about 1757 to 1773. By inheritance she came into possession of Parr Hall in 1745 which had on its property a coal mine near St. Helens, eleven miles from Liverpool. Within twelve years she had opened two new pits. With the opening of the Sankey Canal between St. Helens

and Liverpool and its extension to Parr in 1757, she was able greatly to increase distribution. With her two nephews, the Case brothers, she appears to have held a leading position in the Liverpool coal market from this time until her bankruptcy in 1778.

Apart from her activities as an industrialist, she took a lively interest in architecture and painting. Indeed, she wished to be remembered in this way for she is shown holding an architectural plan. As early as 1749, she had recommended John Wood as architect for the Town Hall in Liverpool. She also had an important part in planning Clayton Square in the 1750s and a plan of it falls over the table while she points to the site of her own house, the largest in the square, on the south corner. She took up residence there in 1767 just before Joseph Wright came to Liverpool. Her health was broken by her bankruptcy in 1778. A pastel portrait of Mrs. Clayton, painted when she was a younger woman by her friend Katherine Thornhill, is in the Walker Art Gallery, Liverpool. No. 26 would have been painted by Wright of Derby sometime between his departure for Liverpool late in 1768 and his return to London in the autumn of 1771. F.C.

Provenance
T. A. Tatton (sale, Christie's, London, 28 February 1947, no. 102)
Anonymous sale, Christie's, London, 18 April 1947, no. 74
Anonymous sale, Christie's, London, 25 June 1948, no. 135, bt. Koetser
John Nicholson Gallery, New York, 1952
Charles Childes, Boston, bt. 1953
Miss Louise I. Doyle, by 1953
Given to the Fitchburg Art Museum, Fitchburg, Mass.

Exhibitions
Joseph Wright of Derby, Smith College Museum of Art, Northampton, Mass., 1955, no. 5
Joseph Wright of Derby, 1734-1797, Durlacher Bros., New York, 1960, no. 7

References
Buckley, *Magazine of Art,* XLV, 1952, p. 160
S. A. Harris, "Sarah Clayton's Letter and John Wood of Bath," *Transactions of the Historical Society of Lancashire and Cheshire,* c., 1948, pp. 55-57
Manuscript entry in Benedict Nicolson's catalogue of the works of Wright of Derby, in preparation

27

28
An Iron Forge
Admiral of the Fleet, the Earl Mountbatten of Burma,
K.G., P.C., G.C.B., O.M., G.C.S.I., G.C.I.E.,
G.C.V.O., D.S.O., F.R.S.
Oil on canvas; 47½ x 51 in.
Inscribed: *Jo. Wright Pinxt 1772*

Benedict Nicolson has already written a particularly
sensitive and thorough study of this picture. A
preparatory drawing of the architecture done on
the spot in an actual iron forge is in the Derby
Museum, and the architecture in the finished
painting, heightened in dramatic power by the
lighting, carefully follows the original study. There
are at least two closely related compositions: *The
Blacksmith's Shop* of 1771 (Royal College of
Surgeons, London, in 1958), of which two other
versions existed and are listed by Nicolson in the
Arts Council exhibition catalogue of 1958, no. 8;
and *An Iron Forge Viewed from Without,* signed
and dated 1773, sold to the Empress of Russia
(Society of Artists, 1773, no. 371), and now in the
Hermitage, Leningrad.

Wright was famous for scenes with artificial light
and is often praised in the poetry of the period for
this special interest. Nicolson has described the
procedures used in his studio for staging works
with artificial light, mentioning the influence of
Dutch painters such as Godfried Schalcken and
the Utrecht Caravaggesques like Honthorst as
sources for such figures as that in the foreground
vividly silhouetted against a middle ground light.
If certain of the devices are drawn from the Dutch,
the subject matter is new. The *Forge of Vulcan* as
done by Velasquez and the LeNain brothers was
no doubt known to Wright. But the subject here is
specifically the dramatic forging of a large piece
of iron. Such people as John Wilkinson, iron
manufacturer and developer of an iron boat and the
cast iron bridge, believed that everything
constructed could be made of iron. The possibilities
of the medium and the process of its manufacture
were an important stimulus to the imagination of
the public at that moment. Representing it at night

with artificial light heightened the dramatic effect
and visual impact of the scene. The blunt power
of the tools, the vivid light emitted from the body of
the white-hot metal, the power of the young man
behind, arms crossed, who controls its shape and
destiny, the magnitude of the instruments used to
shape it, and the primitive architecture by which
it is surrounded emphasize the mystery and
excitement aroused by the metal. Apart from the
man actually working with the metal, people of all
ages stand around to watch. The old man, seated,
gazes and dreams and the mother turns away while
the light of the glowing bar catches the faces of
her children. A family portrayed within an iron
forge is an unusual and original idea; surely the
element of allegory was not far from Wright's mind
when he showed the various responses of a human
family to the molding of this metal which would
greatly affect their lives.
F.C.

Provenance
Purchased from the artist in 1772 by Henry Temple,
second Viscount Palmerston, Broadlands, Hampshire
(died 1802)
By descent to his son, Henry John Temple, third
Viscount Palmerston (died 1865)
By descent to his stepson, Hon. William Francis Cowper-
Temple, Baron Mount Temple of Sligo (died 1888)
By descent to his son, Hon. Evelyn Ashley, Broadlands,
Hampshire (died 1908)
By descent to his son, Wilfred William Ashley, Baron
Mount Temple of Lee (died 1939)
By descent to his daughter, Edwina, Countess
Mountbatten (died 1960)

Exhibitions
Society of Artists, 1772, no. 373
British Institution, 1817, no. 97
British Institution, 1845, no. 142
International Exhibition, Victoria and Albert Museum,
London, 1862, no. 124
Royal Academy, London, 1871, no. 245 (lent by Rt. Hon.
W. Cowper Temple)
The Universal and International Exhibition, Brussels,
1935, no. 1138
European Masters of the Eighteenth Century, Royal
Academy, London, 1954-55, no. 420

27
Man in a Turban
J. B. Speed Art Museum, Louisville, Kentucky
Pastel on paper; 16½ x 11½ in.
c. 1770

The identity of the sitter and exact circumstances
of the commission are unknown.
F.C.

28

Joseph Wright of Derby, Arts Council, London, 1958,
no. 13
Englische Malerei der Grossen Zeit, Cologne, etc.
(British Council), 1966-67, no. 12

References
William Bemrose, pp. 14, 122
Francis D. Klingender, *Art and the Industrial Revolution,*
London, 1947, p. 51
Buckley, *Magazine of Art,* XLV, 1952, pp. 163-64
Nicolson, *Burlington,* XLVI, 1954, pp. 75-76

Reproductions
Engraved in mezzotint by Richard Earlom, Jan. 1, 1773
for Josiah Boydell (repr. Klingender, fig. 10)

29
The Old Man and Death
Wadsworth Atheneum, Hartford, Connecticut, The
Ella Gallup Sumner and Mary Catlin Sumner
Collection
Oil on canvas; 40 x 50$\frac{1}{16}$ in.
c. 1773

Charles Buckley first pointed out that this subject
is taken from one of Aesop's fables. The story tells
of an old man, wearied by carrying a bundle of
sticks gathered in a neighboring wood, who has
sunk down exhausted and calls upon death to
release him from his labors. Hearing his invocation,
Death appears immediately at his elbow, terrifying
the trembling old man who insists that he wishes
merely to have his burden restored to his shoulders.

Wright shows the old man, who has seated himself
on a bank, pulling back in horror and reaching for
a stick with which to defend himself from the
ominous vision. Rosenblum has interpreted the
arrow as thrust through the thorax of the skeleton.
But the apparition holds the arrow, the instrument
of death, in his right hand, resting on the shoulder,

29

and pointing away from the man to indicate that death in this case is a matter of choice and is not being inflicted. Part of the rationale of this picture, of Wright's art, and of the beginnings of romantic art is that the painter has thought carefully and freshly about the text and has interpreted it literally and more faithfully than illustrators who have preceded him. Wright has shown the scene in broad daylight as the text suggests, presenting the incident with palpable clarity and attention to naturalistic detail. It is in his careful rethinking of the text and its literal interpretation that Wright achieves the necessary degree of emotional intensity. Fantasy is introduced in the setting by means of Gothic ruins overgrown with vines and the moss-laden trunks of half-dead trees which derive from such works as Jacob Ruisdael's *Jewish Cemetery* (The Detroit Institute of Arts). Rosenblum has pointed out that the crispness of this vision looks forward to Pre-Raphaelite landscape; equally pertinent are its forerunners, such as William Dyce. It should also be said that this same objectivity appears equally in the works of George Stubbs in the 1760s with a similar source of inspiration in 17th-century Dutch painting, although Wright's subjects are frequently even more original and inventive than those of Stubbs. This painting also looks forward to another theme of apparition, *The Nightmare* (no. 68), by Henry Fuseli, an artist who considered himself a master of invention. Wright's *The Old Man and Death* is more sensational than the work of Fuseli, who dwelled on sensationalism, and it is artistically more accomplished and powerful than Fuseli's painting. Another version of the central group is in the Walker Art Gallery, Liverpool. Nicolson finds that work a repetition of the central group rather than a reduced version.

This picture was finished before Wright left for Italy in November 1773. In a letter of April 13, 1774 from Rome to Nancy Wright in London, he mentions his concern about the hanging of the picture at the exhibition. He was particularly anxious to sell it for eighty guineas or even seventy. But it appears that it was not sold until after his death.   F.C.

Provenance
The artist (sale, Christie's, London, 6 May 1801, no. 58, bt. in, sale, Shaw, Derby, 11 October 1810, no. 5, bt.
Sir R. Wilmot, Chaddesden)
Sir Robert Wilmot, Bart., Chaddesden Hall, Derby (died 1842)
Sir Henry Sacheverel Wilmot (died 1872)
Sir Henry Wilmot (died 1901)
Sir Ralph Henry Sacheverel Wilmot (died 1918)
Sir Arthur Ralph Wilmot (died 1942)
Lady Wilmot Mugdrum, Neubruch, Fifeshire, Scotland
H. J. Spiller, London
Wadsworth Atheneum, Hartford, Connecticut, 1953

Exhibitions
The Society of Artists of Great Britain, London, Spring Gardens, 1774, no. 321
Derby, 1883, no. 30 (lent by Sir Henry S. Wilmot)
Derby, 1884, no. 6 (lent by Sir Henry Wilmot)
Joseph Wright of Derby, 1734-1797, Smith College Museum of Art, Northampton, Mass., 1955, no. 12
Romantic Art (Euphorian or Aspects of Romanticism in Art and Literature at Home and Abroad), Trinity College, Hartford, Conn., 1955, no. 5
Joseph Wright of Derby, 1734-1797, Durlacher Bros., New York, 1960, no. 11
Sublimity and Sensibility, Fogg Art Museum, Harvard University, Cambridge, Mass., 1965, no. 39

References
Bemrose, pp. 14, 32, 110, 122
Sacheverell Sitwell, *Narrative Pictures,* New York/London, 1938, fig. 50
C. E. B.[uckley], "An Eighteenth Century English Painting," *Wadsworth Atheneum Bulletin,* series 2, no. 40, April 1953, p. 2
Nicolson, *Burlington,* XLVI, 1954, p. 79
Robert Rosenblum, "Wright of Derby: Gothick Realist," *Art News,* LIX, no. 1, March 1960, p. 27
Robert Rosenblum, "Sources of Two Paintings by Joseph Wright of Derby," *JWCI,* XXV, nos. 1-2, 1962, pp. 135-36

30
A Cavern: Morning
Mr. and Mrs. R. Kirk Askew, Jr.
Oil on canvas; 40 x 50 in.
Inscribed: *J. Wright 1774*

First published in March 1960 in Robert Rosenblum's review of the Durlacher exhibition, this early morning scene is a companion to *A Cavern, Evening* in the Smith College Museum of Art, Northampton, Massachusetts. In Wright's list (no. 2), these two pictures are entitled *Two Grottos by the Sea Side in the Gulf of Salerno.* Both are dated 1774, when Wright was in Italy. Grottoes and caves by the seashore were usually thought of in connection with the area of Naples in the 18th century, and this cave which is on the sea was found by Wright when he was there in the autumn of 1774. In a letter to his brother dated November 11 from Rome, he mentions his recent Neapolitan tour and calls the region "One of the most wonderful parts of the world." Soon after returning, he painted an eruption of Vesuvius, and he described his experiences at Herculaneum and Pompeii, giving some idea, with these cavern scenes, of his conception of the "wonderful," by which he meant something verging on the miraculous. The unique emotional experience provided by a grotto, especially the visual delight in views over water from the craggy apertures of grottoes, had been amply illustrated in British landscape gardening at Stourhead in Wiltshire. Wright places the observer within the cave and heightens the sensation of the bizarre with a minute portrayal of sand and pebbles, unusual plants, and the arched and broken rock, which approaches a Gothic silhouette here formed as a shape of nature. In a later version, this scene will be made even more striking to a literary imagination, through the addition of bandits with captives, in the painting *A Grotto in the Kingdom of Naples, with Banditti, at Sunset* (collection Godfrey Meynell). Variants of the Northampton composition are given by Nicolson who associates these cavern scenes with the art of Pietro Fabris (active 1768-78), who exhibited at the Royal Academy in London, painting such works as *Fishing by*

Torchlight in a Cavern in 1777. **30**

Wright uses overlapping arabesques, with
extended febrile silhouettes which are given
spatial implications through unusually clear light;
and these find an analogy in works like Richard
Wilson's *Snowdon* (Walker Art Gallery, Liverpool).
In both the Wilson and Wright, the special limpid
quality of the light is said to derive from
17th-century Dutch art, particularly the works of
Aelbert Cuyp.
F.C.

Provenance
Thomas Law Hodges, M. P., Hempsted Park
H. Haskett Smith, Trowswell, Goudhurst, Hants (sale,
Christie's, London, 9 May 1896, no. 113, as *Morning)*
Durlacher Bros., New York, 1952
R. Kirk Askew, Jr., New York, 1955

Exhibitions
Joseph Wright of Derby, 1734-1797, Durlacher Bros.,
New York, 1960, no. 12
Alumni Treasures, Addison Gallery of American Art,
Phillips Academy, Andover, Mass., 1967, no. 222

References
Bemrose, pp. 34, 121
Charles E. Buckley, "An English Landscape by Joseph
Wright of Derby," *The Art Quarterly,* Autumn 1955,
XVIII, no. 3, p. 271, n. 3
British Painting in the Eighteenth Century, The Montreal
Museum of Fine Arts, etc. (in collaboration with the
British Council), 1957-58, p. 67 (catalogue compiled by
Dennis Farr)
Oliver Warner, "Sir William Hamilton and Fabris of
Naples," *Apollo,* LXV, no. 385, March 1957, pp. 104-07
Joseph Wright of Derby (Arts Council), 1958, pp. 23-24
Robert Rosenblum, "Wright of Derby: Gothick Realist,"
Art News, LIX, March 1960, p. 54

George Romney

1734-1802

George Romney's father was a joiner, cabinetmaker, and agricultural innovator from the area of Furness in Lancashire. He was apprenticed from 1755 to 1757 to an itinerant portrait painter named Christopher Steele who had travelled on the continent and is said to have studied under Carle Van Loo in France (1705-65). In 1762 he came to London, winning an award from the Society of Arts with the *Death of General Wolfe* two years later. In the same year he travelled briefly to Paris where he met Claude-Joseph Vernet (1714-89), who took him to various exhibitions and to see the Orléans Gallery. Returning to England, he exhibited the *Death of King Edmund* in 1765, for which he again won an award.

In the spring of 1773 Romney travelled with Ozias Humphry, the miniaturist, to Rome where he copied works by Raphael and Michelangelo in the Vatican and also, according to Flaxman, studied the paintings of Giotto and Cimabue. There, he met Wright of Derby and Henry Fuseli, among others. Fuseli whetted his nervous imagination with an interest in esoteric subjects from early European and antique literature, and they both illustrated the *Descent of Odin* by Gray. Leaving Rome, he travelled through northern Italy visiting Bologna, studying the works of Titian in Venice and, in Parma, those of Correggio, whom he greatly admired.

On his return in 1775 a number of literary individuals assisted greatly in establishing Romney as one of the chief personalities in the London art world. Richard Cumberland, the poet and playwright, dedicated an *Ode to the Sun* to Romney in 1776. In 1777 Payne Knight, whom he had met in Rome, sent to Romney a long and detailed letter, published by Hayley, on emotional expression and the sublime in painting, one of the most interesting answers to Burke. In 1778 Hayley published his *Epistle on Painting,* addressing it to him and devoting a significant part to Romney's artistic talent. Romney's introspective, nervous, and highly impressionable temperament was particularly attractive to these literary individuals, who found in him a person combining the talents of the painter with an ingenious faculty for rapidly transforming the most dramatic subjects into graphic form, especially in the drawings and sketches which he would do on the spot.

Romney's introduction to William Hayley, who first sat for him in the autumn of 1777, was one of the most important events in his life. Through him, Romney came into intimate contact with a world of literature and a highly sophisticated theory of art that was to act as a catalyst in altering his view of his own art completely. Hayley urged Romney to select sublime subject matters from English and antique literature and to choose subjects that would affect the observer at the highest aesthetic levels. Romney also sought the advice of Dr. Robert Potter, the translator of classical drama, and William J. Mickle, who translated the *Lusiads* of the Portuguese poet Camoen, about noble and sublime subjects. Through Hayley, Romney met the poets Anna Seward, William Cowper, Charlotte Smith, and Eliza Heron, and he joined in the reading of Milton with Cowper and Hayley.

During the late 1770s he undertook the series of subjects drawn from Aeschylus, probably as a result of Potter's translation which appeared in 1777. After Potter's *Euripides* appeared in 1781-83, his plays became a source of subjects for Romney's art. He also drew numerous biblical themes and illustrated passages from Virgil, Horace, Apuleius, Boccaccio, Shakespeare, Milton, Gray, Hayley, and even did contemporary subjects from the life of John Howard. The fullest elaboration of these themes is to be found in his drawings, with only a residue of his literary interests appearing in the painted works known today. However, it is in the area of the painted figural pieces that discoveries in Romney's work are certain to be made in the future. His output was prodigious, and the catalogue of Ward and Roberts, devoted primarily to portraits, gives an unbalanced view of Romney's production.

Waterhouse's estimate of his portraits as neutral, fashionable, and without sensibility or character reflects Fuseli's summary of Romney's art in Pilkington's *Dictionary of Painters,* and it is not entirely accurate. It is true that the portraits are highly repetitious, and lack the command, individuality, and proficiency of those of Reynolds and Gainsborough. Each may be said to be like a well-made cabinet, which was Romney's own view.

Waterhouse only mentions the "shadowy" side of Romney's art. But his less official side is the most interesting and the most aesthetically satisfying. The various characterizations of Lady Hamilton, his illustrations for literature, and particularly his drawings, best embody his sense of grace and abandon, his facility and free rhythmic play, and the fertility of his mind. This side of Romney's art is little known and even less well understood today. It is only recently that a serious investigation has been undertaken, and yet a balanced view of Romney must include the multitude of drawings, the painted sketches, and figural compositions, with a careful selection from the portraits.

Early in 1782 Romney met Emma Hart, who was to become Lady Hamilton in 1791. She embodied for him the ideal of feminine grace and beauty and inspired many of his finest paintings. After 1788 he became increasingly ill. Although some of his most striking compositional drawings are from the early 1790s when he was particularly interested in Milton, he had numerous strokes in the mid-1790s, leaving him less and less able to paint. In 1799 he gave up his brushes completely and moved to

Kendal, there purchasing Whitestock Hall, Ulverston, where his wife cared for him until his death.
F.C.

Bibliography
Richard Cumberland, *Memoirs . . . written by Himself,* 2 parts, London, 1806-07
William Hayley, *The Life of George Romney, Esq.,* London, 1809
Rev. John Romney, *Memoirs of the Life and Works of George Romney,* London, 1830
Humphry Ward and W. Roberts, *Romney,* 2 vols., London, 1904
Anne Crookshank, "The Drawings of George Romney," *Burlington,* XCIX, 1957, pp. 43-48
George Romney: Paintings and Drawings, The Iveagh Bequest, Kenwood, London, 1961
The Drawings of George Romney, Smith College Museum of Art, Northampton, Mass., 1962 (catalogue compiled by Patricia Milne-Henderson)

31

Study for the Viscountess Bulkeley as Hebe
Lent Anonymously
Pen and brown ink with washes of brown and white; 15⅜ x 7⅞ in.
Inscribed in pencil: 27; collector's mark:
A. A. de Pass, (Lugt 108a)
1776
This is a preparatory design for the full-length portrait of Elizabeth Warren (1759-1826), who married Thomas James, seventh Viscount Bulkeley, in 1777. The finished painting, reproduced by Saxl and Wittkower, is in the collection of Sir Richard Williams-Bulkeley, Bart. Miss Warren first sat for Romney on Friday, May 10, 1776. She is shown

31

holding a jug in her right hand, which identifies her in the allegorical disguise of the daughter of Hera and Zeus and the goddess of youth who filled the cups of the gods.

There are numerous related drawings. John Romney presented one to the Fitzwilliam Museum, Cambridge, that shows the eagle at the top clearly, with Hebe holding the jug in her right hand, and with a stream on the left side. A drawing in the National Gallery of Scotland (D4649) shows the same composition, with her right hand swinging free at the side. A variant of this scheme in The Art Institute of Chicago shows the left hand, probably holding a pitcher at her left hip. A slightly different version of the same composition is in the City Art Museum of St. Louis. There are also related drawings in the sketchbook in the Victoria and Albert Museum, London.

In this drawing, Romney was experimenting with the placement of the hands, the turn of the body, and the arrangement of the draperies. In the final painting, the himation she wears is raised behind the head and more of it appears on her right side. The left hand is raised to the neckline, more of the right leg is showing, the repeated folds across the body now fall between the legs, and the right hand points at the pitcher, which is now placed on the ground. The design of the final painting is more perfect than any of the preparatory drawings. But all of the sketches possess the infinite grace that is one of the most striking features of this design.
F.C.

Provenance
Alfred A. de Pass
By gift to the Royal Institution of Cornwall, County Museum, Truro (sale, Christie's, 22 February 1966, no. 36, bt. Sabin)
Sabin Galleries, Ltd., London
Private collection, 1967

References
Romney, p. 258
Ward and Roberts, I, 82; II, 167
Fritz Saxl and R. Wittkower, *British Art and the Mediterranean,* London, 1948, section 63, no. 4
The Drawings of George Romney, Smith College Museum of Art, Northampton, Mass., no. 5, pl. xxx

32
A Sibyl
Philadelphia Museum of Art, Purchased:
Marie Kimball Fund
Pen and ink over black chalk; verso: black chalk
study of two figures; 19 x 11¼ in.
c. 1775-80

Identification of the subject of this drawing is still problematical. It is related to a series of standing female figures all of which probably prepare for a full-length allegorical portrait of a woman as a sibyl. The figure holds a scroll and stands at the mouth of her cave where her message, traditionally written on a leaf but here on a scroll, will be dropped for the suppliant who must take it before the wind carries it away. This interpretation is supported by two drawings, one of which, recently in the possession of Mrs. Robert Frank, London, shows a more complete view of the rocky background and also shows the sibyl dropping her scroll. Within the Bolognese tradition, sibyls normally have their hair bound with a turban or veil, which in the middle ages symbolized that the message of Christianity was veiled. Although the turban is not absolutely clear in the Philadelphia drawing, it is apparent in that belonging to Mrs. Frank. It is even more clearly shown in a drawing at Yale (62.57.8) catalogued as *Captive or Dejected Woman, Possibly Andromeda,* showing a figure resembling this but writing her prophecy on a scroll.

John Romney lists the subject, "Two designs of the Cumaean Sibyl, foretelling to Aeneas his future

32

destiny," now in the Fitzwilliam Museum, Cambridge. The attractive possibility that no. 32 was an alternate idea for the Fitzwilliam composition is almost certainly incorrect, since the compositions are entirely different.

The format and placement of the figure strongly suggest that this is a study for a portrait and not for a historical composition. The character of no. 32 strongly suggests that Romney is searching for an appropriate pose for a single female figure in a full-length portrait. If this hypothesis is correct, the costume of the lady still does not give a basis for dating the drawing since she is shown in classical dress much like *Viscountess Bulkeley* (no. 31). On the basis of Romney's drawing style, a date in the late 1770s is most acceptable.
F.C.

Provenance
Mrs. Margaret H. Drey, London
Paul Drey Gallery, New York
Philadelphia Museum of Art, 1966

References
Romney, p. 258
The Drawings of George Romney, Smith College Museum of Art, Northampton, Mass., no. 9, pl. xxv

33
Medea Slaying a Child
Mr. and Mrs. A. M. Jaffé
Pen with brown ink and brown wash over pencil;
13⅝ x 12½ in.
Inscribed: oval Haas mark in dull brown; verso:
circular Haas stamp in blue-black; numbered
within in blue ink: 275
1781-83

The drawing shows Medea, a priestess of Hecate and a sorceress of the island of Colchis, as she is described in Euripides' drama. Medea murdered her two children by Jason, leader of the Argonauts, when he attempted to make a beneficial marriage with Glauce, daughter of Creon, king of Corinth.

After successfully plotting the murder of Jason's bride and her father, Medea further revenged herself on her lover by killing their two sons. Here, she is shown preparing to carry their bodies "to a green sepulchre on a hillside where Hera guards the holy precinct." She is shown stepping into the chariot pulled by winged dragons, a gift of Helios. One of the bodies is in the chariot, and she draws the other away over her shoulder to prevent Jason even from embracing for the last time his slaughtered child. It is one of the fiercest subjects undertaken by Romney.

The subject of Medea had interested Romney as early as his trip to Rome. In the Fitzwilliam Museum, Cambridge, there are three compositions of that period showing Medea and her two sons, with Jason hurrying in to save them. He also did a cartoon (Walker Art Gallery, Liverpool) showing Medea distraught over the prospect of murdering her children. A painted sketch of Medea's head, with her hair floating in the air, as she contemplates the murder, is now in the collection of Norton Simon and on view in the Museum of Fine Arts, Boston. Five composition drawings for Medea contemplating the murder of her children are in the Fitzwilliam Museum. Three of these appear in John Romney's list as nos. 10, 11, and 12. These were done in Romney's Roman period and are quite different in composition and subject from no. 33. A study for the head of Medea is also in the Fitzwilliam Museum.

This particular drawing may stem from Romney's association with Robert Potter, famous for his translations of Greek tragedies, who, along with other learned literary friends, suggested subjects of an elevated sort for Romney's art. In a letter of December 26, 1780, Potter wrote to Romney that his translation into English of Euripides' dramas was in press at that moment. We also know that Romney's name was on the subscribers' list for this publication. Romney, who could not read Latin or Greek, awaited the translation anxiously. This illustration of the *Medea* was probably done soon after the publication of Potter's first volume of

33

Euripides, which appeared in 1781.

Although Euripides served as a source of inspiration for Racine and as the basis for Charpentier's opera of 1693, he was not considered a sound dramatist in Great Britain. Playwrights like Dryden found that he did not hold to the classical unities of time and place. Nevertheless, Euripides' plots do appear among the English 18th-century playwrights. Richard West's *Hecuba* appeared in 1726, William Whitehead's *Creusa Queen of Athens* in 1754, James Thomson's version of *Alcestis* called *Edward and Eleanor* in 1739, and even a *Medea* in 1763, by Richard Glover. Johann Lessing also used *Medea* as the original for his heroine in *Miss Sara Sampson* of 1755. The translations of Potter of 1781-83 and that of Michael Wodhull (1740-1816), *The Nineteen Tragedies and*

Fragments of Euripides, published in four volumes in 1782, were the first modern English translations and, no doubt, the principal sources for the artists of the immediate period.

The subject of Medea murdering her two children was known from antiquity in a wall painting at Pompeii. Carle Van Loo did a drawing of this subject which was in the collection of Paignon-Dijon early in the 19th century, and sometime before his death in 1785, Cipriani drew the subject afterwards etched by Bartolozzi. The more fantastic theme of Medea on a dragon or with a team of dragons was painted in Germany by Johann Langenhöffel in 1786, and Albert Christoph Dies etched this subject in 1784.
F.C.

Provenance
Presumably John Romney
Elizabeth Romney (sale, Christie's, London, 24-25 May 1894)
Xavier Haas, Paris (died 1937), and his heirs (Haas Collection, no. 275)
Mr. and Mrs. J. Richardson Dilworth, Jr., 1959
Given to Patricia Milne-Henderson (Mrs. A. M. Jaffé), London, 1962

Exhibitions
The Drawings of George Romney, Smith College Museum of Art, Northampton, Mass., 1962, no. 44, pl. XXVI

References
Romney, pp. 160-61, 258

34

34
Sidonian Recollections
Mr. and Mrs. Thomas J. McCormick
Oil on canvas; 26½ x 23¼ in.
Inscribed: *Sidonian Recollections*
c. 1785-90

Sarah Siddons (1755-1831) was the sister of the actor J. P. Kemble and the eldest member of the acting family of Roger Kemble. Although she played on the stage as a child, she first appeared in London in Thomas Otway's *Venice Preserved*. Her success in this role attracted the interest of David Garrick who brought her to the Drury Lane Theater, but she was not successful there and retired from London to work in the provinces. In 1778 she began a series of engagements in Bath which continued for five years. She appeared once again in London in 1782, this time triumphantly, in Garrick's version of the *Fatal Marriage* by Thomas Southerne. But she found her true stage personality only in 1785 when she appeared for the first time as Lady Macbeth, establishing herself as a tragedienne of great power. She followed this with other tragic heroines, Desdemona, Rosalind, Ophelia, and Queen Katherine, a role which was almost as famous as her Lady Macbeth. Judging from her portraits, Mrs. Siddons was not beautiful, but she had a tall and commanding figure of great majesty. She had large, brown eyes and highly expressive, perfectly symmetrical features and a longish face.

Almost certainly, Romney portrays Mrs. Siddons here in the role of Lady Macbeth, for whose character each of the expressions is appropriate. If this is true, a date after 1785 is in order. Scholars have formerly dated the painting about 1783, but Mrs. Siddons' first roles from 1783 to 1785 were all of tender and melting characters.

These studies of expression are not tragic masks done on the basis of antique masks as has usually been said. Rather, these are studies of expression within the tradition of Le Brun. Normally such studies of terror, fear, and death were translated into oil only in connection with a subject painting. Thus, they are rarely seen except in engravings or drawings, and these are usually by students. In this case, the power of the actress in the highest order of drama forms the basis for a study of the leading emotions of Lady Macbeth. It is a study that penetrates to the focal point of her character and so rises to the level of a subject painting. No doubt it also reflects the intense degree of expression considered desirable in the acting of this period.
F.C.

Provenance
Anonymous sales, Christie's, London, 28 March 1924, no. 12; 27 April 1925, no. 86; 22 March 1929, no. 130

Exhibitions
The Drawings of George Romney, Smith College Museum of Art, Northampton, Mass., 1962, no. 109
Neo-Classicism: Style and Motif, The Cleveland Museum of Art, 1964, no. 80 (catalogue compiled by Henry Hawley)

References
Fritz Saxl and Rudolf Wittkower, *British Art and the Mediterranean,* London, 1948, p. 82, no. 3

35
Portrait of Lady Hamilton as Miranda
Philadelphia Museum of Art, John H. McFadden Collection
Oil on canvas; 14 x 15½ in.
c. 1786

This sketch of the head of Lady Hamilton (1765-1815) prepares for Romney's most ambitious figural composition *The Tempest,* formerly in the Mere Hall Museum, Bolton, and now destroyed. The picture was prepared for the gallery of paintings commissioned by Josiah Boydell, probably in 1786, to illustrate an edition of the works of Shakespeare. There is some confusion about the date when the Shakespeare Gallery originated. The project was conceived in Romney's own house in Cavendish Square, according to Hayley (pp. 106-09), and elaborated upon at a dinner party of November 4 in Josiah Boydell's house where West, Romney, and Hayley were guests. John Romney places the dinner in 1787, and William Hayley in 1786. The 1786 date is supported by James Northcote in a letter of October 3, 1821, in which he says that his picture of Wat Tyler, painted for Boydell and exhibited at the Royal Academy in April 1787, was undertaken in 1786. Hayley is probably quite accurate in this respect, as we would expect him to be, and as we shall see, the actual circumstances of the painting in question support the earlier dating. Commissioning the Shakespeare Gallery was the most important instance of the patronage of history painting in England in the late 18th century, and it culminated in the exhibition of thirty-four paintings in a building in Pall Mall in 1789. At its dispersal in 1805 one hundred and seventy works were included. The paintings were commissioned from prominent artists of the period, subsequently engraved, and the engravings then sold to reimburse the original outlay of funds.

Romney is often given credit for suggesting the idea of the Shakespeare Gallery, and it is possible that he had already made designs and studies for *The Tempest* before the commission was given. The picture was begun in the studio loaned to Romney at Eartham near Felpham, Sussex, on the English Channel, the country residence of William Hayley. Here Romney was invited every autumn, and from late August to early September each year he was able to meet writers such as William Cowper, who came in 1792 to work at the translation of Dante with Hayley, to relax, swim, discuss literature and painting, and to read.

The pose of Miranda in the Philadelphia sketch is in profile to the right while her pose in the final composition was frontal. This is explained by the fact that there were at least two different schemes for the composition. The first, which was more characteristic of Romney's other productions, involved primarily three figures, Prospero, Miranda, and Caliban, watching the rising storm from a rocky promontory, with the sea and only a suggestion of the shipwreck on the left. Of the seven sketches for this subject in the Fitzwilliam Museum, Cambridge, three are composition drawings for Romney's first conception. The lines represented are spoken by Miranda, "If by your art, my dearest father, you have put the wild waters in this roar, allay them."

There are painted sketches of the head of Miranda facing both left and right and at least one with a flash of lightning cutting across the background (Ward and Roberts, cat. no. 18c). Another was in the Kerrigan Collection sale, Parke-Bernet, New York, January 8-10, 1942, no. 276. Still another, reminiscent of the heads of Greuze, was engraved and reproduced in Hayley's *Life of George Romney*

opposite p. 141. At least one other painted sketch of the Philadelphia composition is known (Ward and Roberts, cat. no. 18d), and this or a similar one is reproduced in Maxwell's monograph on Romney.

The first composition was criticized. As John Romney relates, "Some officious individual suggested to Mr. Romney that this picture would not be regarded by the critics as an historical composition, as it consisted of only three figures not sufficiently combined." No doubt the officious individual was William Hayley, who would have been able to persuade Romney to alter his ideas, who would have been referred to by John Romney as officious, and who would also have suggested the more pretentious, literary, and essentially academic alterations which occur in the second composition.

The scheme of the second version is known from the unpublished composition drawing now in The National Gallery of Canada, Ottawa, where Ferdinand leaps overboard from the sinking ship, and his father Alfonso, King of Naples, is restrained from pursuit by three companions. This vastly more ambitious picture, one unlike any before undertaken by Romney, involved numerous figures and allowed him to design a major historical composition with a large variety of emotional responses and actions.

No. 35 relates to the earlier conception of Romney's composition. Traditionally, the sitter is identified as Lady Hamilton. Emma Hart was to become Lady Hamilton in 1791 upon her marriage to the British Ambassador to Naples. Emma's more than generous pile of auburn hair, her enormous eyes, oval face and perfect features combined with an extreme personal grace had entranced Romney since Charles Greville, her protector and Romney's friend, had first brought her to his studio in 1781. She came to embody for Romney the ideal of feminine beauty, and he used her as a model from 1782 until her departure for Italy with Gavin Hamilton as her escort on March 14, 1786. Although Romney's female figures tend to repeat the type of Emma Hart rather than serve as portraits, her

35

features are probably reflected here. It seems likely that this sketch was done either shortly before or shortly after her departure.

The sketch shows Miranda facing upward to the right, her mouth and eyes open in anxious apprehension about the storm. The rising winds have already picked up her flowing auburn hair and now swirl it about her head in a mesh of wisps and broken strokes of paint. This auburn mass relieves her pale flesh in an almost sculptural manner, an impression enhanced by the angular strokes which carve the planes of her face in a bas-relief on the canvas. It is remarkable that Romney, who is best known for his long and elegant rhythms which ultimately derive from late antique bas-reliefs, was also fascinated by the sculptural qualities which could be acheived by intense contrasts of light. This is often what he searched for and achieved in those intensely graphic drawings made up of great brushstrokes of ink reflecting his experience, under the Italian sun, of bas-reliefs bleached with light or obscured by shadow.
F.C.

36

John Howard Visiting a Prison
Yale University Art Gallery, Gift of
Mr. and Mrs. J. Richardson Dilworth, B.A., 1938
Pen with black ink, and watercolor wash in black and shades of gray over pencil; 14¼ x 20⅞ in.
Inscribed: oval Haas mark in pale red, circular Haas mark in blue-black
c. 1792

John Howard (1726-90) had his first experience with prisons early in his career when a ship bound for Portugal about 1755 was captured by a French privateer; the crew and passengers were confined and treated severely. Howard successfully negotiated his own release and that of his fellow captives, settling thereafter at Cardington near Bedford where he pursued philanthropic projects. In 1773 he accepted the office of High Sheriff of Bedford and visited the jail where the prisoners were kept. He found the most horrifying conditions among the guilty and the innocent who could not pay the fees of delivery by which the jailers earned their living. In surveying other British prisons to find a precedent for the county government's paying the wages of the prison staff, he discovered the worst abuses and the same system of jailers' fees prevailing. Devoting all of his energies to righting this inequity, he was able in 1774 to have the House of Commons pass a prison reform bill abolishing jailers' fees and stipulating proper care, treatment, and clean cells for prisoners. After having the new law publicized at his own expense, he began a tour of prisons which was to take him throughout Europe. This resulted in his publishing *The State of Prisons in England and Wales* in 1777, an English translation of a French pamphlet on the Bastille, and *An Account of the Principal Lazarettoes in Europe* in 1789. This remarkable humanitarian died during a tour of Russia after a visit to the hospitals of Kherson on the Dnieper River in South Russia where he attended a young lady suffering from camp fever.

Romney first did a drawing of Howard visiting a prison which was engraved by Bartolozzi and used

36

to preface William Hayley's poem, an *Ode to Howard,* published in 1781. This engraving shows Howard viewing a dejected and weakened prisoner in chains while a stern jailer looks on. The present drawing does not relate to Hayley's poem but relies directly on the writings of John Howard and very possibly on verbal instructions from him. Hayley relates that Romney wished to paint not only Howard's portrait but also a series of pictures that would "display the variety of relief that his signal benevolence afforded to the sufferings of the wretched." Hayley also says that Howard, who knew of Romney's wish to paint a series of scenes on this subject, described in a conversation of 1787 with a friend of Romney, probably Hayley himself, several experiences in foreign prisons which most suited Romney's ability.

The specific scene illustrated is not described in Howard's writings, which are startling because of the cool air of horror which emerges from the crisp and factual paragraphs enumerating savage practices of confinement, torture, and execution. This drawing comes most close to such passages as: "Coventry City and County Gaol . . . To their *dungeons* there is a descent of 12 steps to a passage only 4 feet wide: the four dungeons are

1734/35-1810

about 9 feet by 6: at the upper corner of each, a little window, 11 inches by 7. All are very damp, dirty and offensive; we went down with torches," *(The State of the Prisons in England and Wales,* Warrington, 1784, p. 310). He was particularly offended by the practice of confining men and women together, of allowing women to give birth in the dungeons, of confining the insane with criminals, and of binding prisoners, especially women, in chains. He also objected to the practice of confining the prisoners in dark, underground, airless cells with no provision for sanitation.

Elements of all of these practices can be found in Romney's drawing. An insane man approaches menacingly from behind while light from a manhole or a torch starkly illuminates the figures on the left. The cramped quarters are shown by Howard's own bent head and the crowding of the prisoners, who recline on the wet stone floor without straw. Women are shown together with men, one with a child at her breast. A young woman, either ill or weak from hunger, lies in the foreground. Behind, a death-like figure looms over the group, "delaying to strike, though oft invoked," as in Milton's description of death in the Lazar House in *Paradise Lost.*

While embodying the potent emotions of the horrific sublime, this drawing is important as a social commentary. In *The Disasters of War,* Goya, at this same time and with some of the same devices, made a similar kind of social commentary, and such commentary was to become increasingly important in the visual arts of the 19th century. Before Romney, Wheatley painted the subject *Mr. Howard Offering Relief to Prisoners* (collection Earl of Harrowby), keeping it much more within the vein of the traditional iconography of the Seven Acts of Mercy, which included the act of freeing prisoners, a popular subject in the late Gothic period. The great interest in Howard is further indicated by the sculptural version of the subject by John Bacon (1793, Shrewsbury Prison).

Heemskerck represented a prison interior in a

remarkable drawing in Brussels which was later engraved, and Michael Sweerts (photo Netherl. Art Inst. no. 2694) and Cornelius de Wael (Palazzo Bianco, Genoa) painted this subject in scenes which look forward to Wheatley. Piranesi's etchings of prison interiors were done with the picturesque rather than moral aim of stimulating the eye and the imagination. Romney, in a composite image of Howard's activity, recreates the horror of the events and the stark drama of man's inhumanity to man.

Hayley's poem "Eulogies of Howard, a Vision" was written in 1790. The British Museum sketchbook which contains at least one Howard drawing has an erased date of "June 1790" replaced by the date "July 1792." We know that in the early 1790s, Romney was interested in subjects from Milton, with which this drawing must be connected.
F.C.

Provenance
Xavier Haas, Paris (died 1937), and his heirs (Haas Collection, no. 153)
Mr. and Mrs. J. Richardson Dilworth, Jr., 1959
Yale University Art Gallery, New Haven, 1962

Exhibitions
The Drawings of George Romney, Smith College Museum of Art, Northampton, Mass., 1962, no. 80, pl. XXXVI

References
Hayley, pp. 87-89
Romney, p. 266
Allan Cunningham, *The Lives of the Most Eminent British Painters . . . ,* London, 1832, V, 100
London, 1832, V, 100
Crookshank, *Burlington,* XCIX, 1957, pp. 47-48
George Romney: Paintings and Drawings, no. 62
Ellen Sharp, "Drawings by George Romney at Yale," *Antiques,* XXXVI, November 1964, pp. 602-03

The date of birth of Zoffany is not absolutely certain but a document in the Public Record Office, London, referred to by Manners and Williamson, gives his date of birth as 1735. Zoffany himself told Farington that he was born March 13, 1734 (diary entry for December 18, 1795). The family came from Bohemia, and Zoffany's father was later the architect to the Prince of Thurn and Taxis in Frankfurt. While his father worked in Regensberg in the mid-1750s, Johann studied with Martin Spee (1702?-65), a pupil of Francesco Solimena (1657-1747), and also at this time, he made what must have been a brief journey to Rome. In 1760 he was working with Januarius Zick (1730-97) in the decoration of the Royal Palace in Trier, and he moved to London with his wife in 1761.

The beginnings of Zoffany's life in London were extremely difficult, and his wife returned to Germany within a short time, perhaps because of marital and financial difficulties. He began by working as a painter of clock dials for Stephen Rimbault. Subsequently, he painted draperies for Benjamin Wilson (1721-88) who was preparing for David Garrick a picture of the actor and Mrs. Bellamy in *Romeo and Juliet.* Garrick, who was interested in numerous artists and used their work to extend his own fame, was impressed by Zoffany's talent. He commissioned a portrait of himself and subsequently a series of "conversation pieces" from theatrical sources using portraits of contemporary actors. Among these were *David Garrick and Susannah Cibber in "Venice Preserved"* of about 1763, from *The Plot Discovered* by Thomas Otway (Shakespeare Memorial National Theatre Committee), and *David Garrick as Sir John Brute in "The Provok'd Wife"* (collection Marquess of Normanby, Sandsend) by Sir John Vanbrugh, of about 1765. A source of inspiration for this entire series may actually be the painting by Reynolds of David Garrick in theatrical costume between the muses of tragedy and comedy, exhibited at the Society of Artists in 1762. This in turn derives from Hogarth's *Garrick as Richard III* (Walker Art Gallery, Liverpool). However, Zoffany himself was to popularize this special theatrical genre which includes his most original and interesting productions. These early theatrical conversations were engraved and were the source of Zoffany's rapidly developed fame in England. These also made him a member of the theatrical circles of the day, and there he became a close friend of John Hamilton Mortimer and, through him, of Richard Wilson who painted backgrounds in some of Zoffany's pictures.

In 1765 he received his first Royal commission for portraits of the *Prince of Wales and Prince Frederick as Cupids* (Royal Collections), exhibited in 1766. Other commissions were rapidly forthcoming from the German-speaking court. At the Royal Academy in 1770, he exhibited a group portrait of George III and the Royal Family, now at Windsor, and in 1772 the group portrait of the Royal Academicians the *Life School in the Royal Academy* (Royal Collections), which was immediately purchased by George III. Through his contact with Lord Sandwich, it was suggested that he accompany Captain Cook to the South Seas as artist to the expedition, but this did not finally materialize. Soon after, he received a commission from Queen Charlotte to paint a view of the *Tribuna of the Uffizi* (Royal Collections), and he left for Italy in 1772. After completing his picture, he travelled to Rome the following year and subsequently went on to Vienna, there painting members of the Royal Family. Zoffany was made Baron in 1776.

After returning to England, Zoffany found that the

kind of painting which had made him popular was no longer in vogue. The intimate conversation portraits of the Royal Family which he formerly painted had become almost a cult, partially because of their illustration of a happy family life at court after the trying period of George II. After Zoffany's return from Italy in 1779, the conversation piece was already old-fashioned. He found it difficult to obtain the commissions he had received earlier, and travelled to India, working there from 1783 until 1789 painting numerous, frequently elaborate group portraits. These large complex groupings, based on those he had painted in the sixties were popular in India, even though no longer fashionable in London, and he achieved considerable success.

Zoffany's last picture of this type, and his most important after his return from India, was that of *Charles Townley in his Gallery of Sculptures* (1790, Art Gallery and Museum, Burnley). This painting which portrays Charles Greville, Sir Thomas Astle, Pierre-François-Hugues d'Hancarville, and Townley himself, ultimately derives from the *Tribuna of the Uffizi* and is a group portrait very much within the same vein. This, like his other portraits, has the particular importance of revealing an especially interesting group of personalities, manners, and events of his time, presented with all of the charm and with some of the stiffness which they must have possessed.

F.C.

Bibliography
Lady Victoria Manners and Dr. G. C. Williamson, *John Zoffany, R. A.,* London, 1920
William Foster, "British Artists in India, 1760-1820," *Walpole Society,* XIX, 1931, pp. 80-87
H. Vollmer, "Zoffany, Johann," in Thieme-Becker, *Künstler Lexikon,* XXXVI, 1947, pp. 544-46
Raymond Mander and Joe Mitchener, *The Artist and the Theatre,* London, 1955, pp. 2-73
Johann Zoffany, Arts Council, London, 1960-61

37

37
Self Portrait
National Portrait Gallery, London
Oil on canvas; 20¾ x 16¼ in.
Inscribed: *Zoffany Pinx./1761*

A preparatory pen drawing for this portrait, at one time in the collection of John Lane, is signed and dated 1761, as is the painting. The drawing also shows the curling hair, unusually long in the back and short in front, that Zoffany wore at the time. The pose of the figure, leaning to the left, the position of the hand, and the group of books derive from a work which Zoffany could have known in David Garrick's collection. This was a portrait of Garrick himself painted by Jean-Baptiste Van Loo

(1684-1745) around 1740-42 when Garrick first appeared on the London stage. Garrick is shown leaning on his right elbow on a pile of books and papers, holding a pen in his delicately positioned right hand. Although Garrick, in the Van Loo portrait, faces the observer full face, Zoffany shows a highly sympathetic, reflective view in three-quarter profile. The relationship between these two paintings suggests that Zoffany already knew Garrick in 1761, even though he did not actually undertake commissions for him until the following year.

Perhaps the most famous of Zoffany's self portraits, of which there are many, is that in the Uffizi, Florence, inscribed *Ars longa vita brevis.* A self-portrait drawing is in The British Museum, and another of the same period is in the collection of Miss Beachcroft. A fascinating self portrait with palette, brushes, maulstick, and an elaborate, feathered hat, is in the Accademia Etrusca, Cortona; an early self portrait is in the Mainfränkisches Museum, Würzburg; and there is a late self-portrait miniature formerly in the collection of Ellen Beachcroft, apart from the numerous portraits of Zoffany included in family groups or official commissions like that in the *Tribuna of the Uffizi,* now in the Royal Collections.
F.C.

38

Provenance
J. Scotcher, Ealing
William Bean
National Portrait Gallery, London, 1875

Exhibitions
Johann Zoffany, Arts Council, London, 1960-61, p. 5, no. 6
British Self-Portraits, Arts Council, London, 1962, no. 34

References
G. Scharf, *Catalogue of the . . . National Portrait Gallery,* London, 1881, p. 374
Manners and Williamson, frontispiece, ill. opp. p. 4, pp. 116, 128
Mander and Mitchener, p. 192

38
The Third Duke of Richmond out Shooting with His Servant
Leggatt Trustees
Oil on canvas; 44½ x 53 in.
c. 1765

Charles Lennox, third Duke of Richmond and Lennox (1735-1806), was the third son of the second Duke of Richmond. His younger sister was Lady Sarah Lennox Bunbury who was portrayed by Sir Joshua Reynolds (no. 6). Lennox was educated at Westminster School in London and later graduated from the University of Leiden and travelled on the continent. Subsequently, he entered the army where he became major general in 1761. On August 8, 1750 he succeeded his father as the Duke of Richmond, and he took his seat in the House of Lords in 1756. For a brief time, he was lord of the bedchamber to George II, with whom he very soon quarrelled. Afterwards, he was to remain a member of the opposition party. In 1763 he became Lord Lieutenant of Sussex. In 1765, under the Marquis of Rockingham's ministry, he was appointed ambassador and minister plenipotentiary at Paris, a post which he filled with prudence. Although he was disliked by the King, he became Secretary of State for the southern department but retired after the Earl of Chatham came to power. In his *Memoirs of the Reign of George III,* Walpole wrote of him, "To the Duke of Richmond the king was not tolerably civil, and in truth I believe the seals which I had obtained for his grace were a mighty ingredient towards the fall of that administration." Richmond had an outright quarrel with Chatham whom he called "An insolent minister." Thereafter, according to Walpole, Chatham did not appear in the House of Lords again. He consistently supported the cause of the American colonists, and it was during the debate on Richmond's motion for withdrawal from the colonies that Chatham was stricken while attempting to reply to Richmond's second speech. Richmond continued to play an important role in government, urging Parliamentary reform in 1780, among numerous other bills.

In 1757 he married Lady Mary Bruce, daughter of the Earl of Elgin and granddaughter of the Duke of Argyll. Walpole wrote of the marriage: "The perfectest match in the world—youth, beauty, riches, alliances, and all the blood of the kings from Bruce to Charles II. They are the prettiest couple in England, except the father-in-law and mother." They were to have no children, but the Duke left four illegitimate daughters. He was succeeded by his nephew.

Reynolds portrayed Richmond at least twice, once in 1758 and a second time in 1760. Both portraits are in the collection of the Duke of Richmond and Gordon, Goodwood. Pompeo Batoni painted his portrait while he was in Rome; he was also painted by Romney, and his portrait by Gainsborough is still in the possession of the family. The third Duke of Richmond was sufficiently interested in becoming a patron of the arts to establish at Whitehall in 1758 a gallery of painting and sculpture, including casts of antique sculpture, for the use of students. Giovanni-Battista Cipriani (1727-85), the painter and draftsman, and Joseph Wilton (1722-1803), the sculptor, were appointed directors and teachers.
F.C.

Provenance
Presumably Charles Lennox, third Duke of Richmond, Goodwood, Sussex (died 1806)
The painting was purchased at a sale at St. Martin's Hall, Chichester, 5 March 1963, lot 329, bt. Leggatt. The Richmond family seat at Goodwood is only 4½ miles from Chichester, suggesting that the painting remained in the area since the 18th century

Exhibitions
English Painting circa 1750-1850, Leggatt Brothers, London, 1963, no. 23

References
Sydney Pavière, *A Dictionary of British Sporting Painters,* Leigh-on-Sea, 1965, pl. 48

39
John Cuff with an Assistant
Lent by gracious permission of Her Majesty Queen Elizabeth II
Oil on canvas; there is an early addition of 1¾ in. at the bottom; 35¼ x 27¼ in.
Inscribed: *Zoffany pinx/1772*

John Cuff was Master of the Spectacle Makers Company in 1748. Perfecting and improving the microscope, he produced an instrument made of brass and mounted on a fixed pillar in 1744. He also made microscopes for George III and Queen Charlotte.

The identity of the sitter was confused by Redgrave, in his manuscript inventory of the Royal Collections made for Queen Victoria (V. R. inv., October 6, 1859), who described this painting as *The Lapidaries* and wrote a note in pencil on the stretcher, "Dollard [sic] the Optician in the Strand London." Since that time, the sitter has been identified as Peter Dollond, who was optician to the King and the Duke of York and who perfected the achromatic telescope. The early inventories do not confirm this identification; moreover, Peter Dollond was born in 1731, and the man shown in this portrait is much more than forty-one years old. In fact, a rough draft of the George III inventory of pictures at Kew lists this painting as "Mr. Cuff—optician—Zoffany." It was so identified at the British Institution in 1814.

Although this painting was criticized by Walpole for being too natural, it exhibits a number of characteristics which are dynamic components of the new, romantic point of view. The interest in scientists, scientific undertakings, and instruments is one of the exciting facets of an analytical and empirical interest then operating as a stimulus to artists and thinkers. Equally important is the harsh daylight flooding this interior, allowing for the equal revelation of each object. The source for this is Dutch art, especially the lighted interiors of Vermeer, and De Hooch, but here it is used much less selectively than in Dutch works. Indeed, the

objectivity and open-air quality of this light is a connecting link between French 19th-century art and the Dutch 17th century.
F.C.

Provenance
Presumably purchased by or painted for George III or Queen Charlotte
It is recorded in Princess Augusta's bedroom at Kew c. 1800-05. On August 20, 1828, it was taken to the New Gallery at Windsor and was later, for a short period, at Buckingham Palace

Exhibitions
Royal Academy, 1772, no. 291 *(An Optician with his Attendant)*
British Institution, London, 1814, no. 79 (the sitter called *Mr. Cuffs*)
British Institution, London, 1827, no. 171 *(Two old Men)*
The King's Pictures, Royal Academy, London, 1946, no. 504
British Portraits, Royal Academy, London, 1956-57, no. 353

References
Manners and Williamson, pp. 34-35, 210
C. H. Collins Baker, *Catalogue of the Principal Pictures in the Royal Collection at Windsor Castle,* London, 1935, p. 335
Oliver Millar, *The Later Georgian Pictures in the Collection of Her Majesty the Queen,* in preparation

39

Alexander Runciman

1736-1785

Born in Edinburgh, Runciman was the son of a builder who apprenticed him at the age of fourteen to Robert Norie, a landscape painter connected with a firm of interior decorators. Later he studied at the Falis Academy, Glasgow. After an early period devoted to landscapes, he took up history painting. In 1766 he travelled to Rome with his brother, the painter John Runciman (1744-68). Sir James Clerk of Penicuik appears to have supported him, at least in part, in this venture, and Fuseli suggests that *Ulysses Surprising Nausicaa with her Maids* was done for Clerk. He was in Italy at almost the exact period as James Barry, only five years younger, who arrived in Rome late in 1766. Runciman is the connecting link between Barry and Fuseli, who was seven years younger than Runciman, and who arrived in Rome in February 1770, only a year before Runciman was to leave. They met, and Fuseli described him in a letter of April 27, 1771, as, "In my opinion, the best *Painter of us* in Rome." Runciman was a well-developed artist by this time, and he influenced Fuseli, whose drawings later show many of his mannerisms. Fuseli mentions that Jacob More, a landscapist and figure painter of great interest, was Runciman's pupil and that John Brown was his friend.

After a brief stop in London on his return home, Runciman travelled on to Edinburgh where he was made Master of the Trustees Academy in 1771. Under his influence, it was transformed from a drawing school to an academy modelled after London's, with an emphasis on history painting rather than on the decorative arts which had prevailed under the former French direction. At the same time, he received the commission for his most elaborate and original series of paintings, the decoration of various ceilings at Penicuik House (no. 40). Their unfortunate destruction by fire in 1899 has left us without knowledge of his most important works, drastically reducing the number of his paintings. While at Penicuik he also painted the *Ascension* over the high altar and four single figures for the Church at Cowgate, later St. Patrick's Catholic Chapel. These have been whitewashed. During these years in Edinburgh, he painted an *Agrippina* (Royal Academy 1781) and *The Parting of Lord William Russell and his Wife* (Royal Academy 1781), for which there is a preparatory drawing in the National Gallery of Scotland. The paintings have been lost. He died at a comparatively early age in the street before his house in Edinburgh.

Of Runciman's life perhaps less is known by modern scholars than of the lives of any other artist in this exhibition. Apart from no. 42, two of his known paintings are the *Origin of Painting,* now at Penicuik House, which is believed by Waterhouse to have been done in Rome, and the *Triumph of David,* also at Penicuik House, which is a copy after the same composition by Rubens, now in the Kemble Foundation, Fort Worth, Texas. Apart from these, is the large collection of his drawings in the National Gallery of Scotland, which are especially important since they include the Ossian illustrations, some of which were shown in *The Romantic Movement* exhibition of 1959 in London.
F.C.

Bibliography
[Walter Ross], *A Description of the Paintings in the Hall of Ossian at Pennycuik near Edinburgh,* Edinburgh, 1773
F.[useli], "Alexander Runciman," in Pilkington, *A Dictionary of Painters,* London, 1810, p. 467
Allan Cunningham, *The Lives of the Most Eminent British Painters . . . ,* London, 1832, V, 145-61
John M. Gray, *Notes on the Art Treasures at Penicuik House, Midlothian,* Edinburgh, 1889
L[ionel] C[ust], "Alexander Runciman," *The Dictionary of National Biography,* London, 1917, XVII, 401-02
Ellis Waterhouse, *Painting in Britain, 1530-1790,* London, 1953, pp. 212-13

40
The Landing of St. Margaret
National Gallery of Scotland
Pen, brown ink and wash; 10⅛ x 7½ in.
Inscribed: *A Runciman;* in monogram *AR;* collector's marks: in pen, *David Laing;* Royal Scottish Academy (Lugt 2189); National Gallery of Scotland (Lugt 1969f)
1772

St. Margaret, who died in 1093, was Queen of Scotland and the wife of King Malcolm III Canmore who defeated Macbeth. She was the daughter of Edward the Confessor and granddaughter of Edmund Ironside, and therefore, of the ancient English royal blood. She is said to have been born in Hungary. At the invasion of the Normans, she fled to Scotland to seek the protection of the Scottish King. Soon after, in 1068, she was married to King Malcolm as his second wife. She was canonized in 1251.

The subject is part of a series painted for the cupola of the staircase hall of Penicuik House, built in 1772 and destroyed by fire in 1899. This preliminary sketch is for the splendid figure of St. Margaret, with her retinue, debarking from a ship to be received by the King and approaching the church where white-robed monks await their arrival. It is the first of four scenes from the life of St. Margaret commissioned by Sir James Clerk in 1772. The only visual evidence for the completed composition is the etching of this same group prepared by Runciman with additions in ink showing ships behind and the Gothic architecture of the North in the left background (National Gallery of Scotland, D. 312). The other subjects from the life of St. Margaret were the Royal Wedding, St. Margaret breaking bread and feeding the poor, and the Ascension of St. Margaret. These three scenes were signed in September and October 1772.

These illustrations of the life of St. Margaret preceded the frescoes for the Hall of Ossian, in the same house, which were also designed by Runciman and represented twelve scenes from

40

Michelangelo, and the Carracci. He conceived the entire series as a monument dedicated to the great religious and historical events of his own national past, very much in the spirit of James Barry who later undertook a similar series in the Society of Arts in London (no. 61).

The composition of this drawing, especially the full-blown and winding draperies of St. Margaret, ultimately derives from the windblown figures in Raphael's *Fire in the Borgo* in the Vatican and from Parmigianino's figures. But its style, particularly the manner of handling the pen, reminds one of certain sheets by James Barry, whom Runciman must have influenced. The textured braided hair looks forward to the much more refined drawings of John Brown, and the intensity of chiaroscuro, as well as certain mannerisms of face and limbs, anticipate Fuseli's drawings.
F.C.

41

Provenance
Thomas Sivright
David Laing, Edinburgh (died 1878)
Bequeathed to the Royal Scottish Academy
Transferred to the National Gallery of Scotland, 1910

References
Cunningham, V, 152-57
Gray, pp. 58-59
National Gallery of Scotland, *Catalogue of Scottish Drawings* by Keith Andrews and J. R. Brotchie, Edinburgh, 1960, pp. 199-200, no. D311
David Irwin, "English Neo-Classicism and Some Patrons," *Apollo,* LXXVIII, November 1963, pp. 365-66

41
Orestes Pursued by the Furies
National Gallery of Scotland
Pen, black ink and wash; 17 x 20¼ in.
Inscribed with monogram: *AR;* collector's marks: Royal Scottish Academy (Lugt 2188); National Gallery of Scotland (Lugt 1969f)
c. 1772-75

Orestes was the son of Agamemnon and Clytemnestra. When Agamemnon left his wife Clytemnestra to command the Greek force against Troy, she became the lover of Aegisthus. Upon their return, Agamemnon and his men were treacherously killed by Clytemnestra. To avenge his father's death, Orestes killed both his mother and her lover Aegisthus.

Rather than the straightforward account of the deed as told by Homer in the *Odyssey,* Runciman's version is drawn from the story as reinterpreted by the Greek tragedians. In Aeschylus' *Choephoroe,* Orestes returns from exile at the strict command of Apollo and obtains access to the palace as a stranger bringing news of his own death. First, he

James Macpherson's writings, published from 1761-65. The four large Scottish rivers were portrayed as allegorical figures in the spandrels of the ceiling of this room, forming a physical and historical representation of Scotland.

In a letter to Sir James Clerk written from Rome in 1770, Runciman suggested the subject of the *Marriage of Peleus and Thetis* for the ceiling of the dining room at Penicuik. This suggests that Runciman had a hand in initiating the entire scheme of decoration which was completed by 1773. Like Barry, Runciman had in mind the great cycles of Renaissance frescoes in Rome by Raphael, kills Aegisthus and then forces himself to kill his mother Clytemnestra. At once he is visited by the Erinyes:

All dusky-vested, and their locks entwined
With knotted snakes.

Here we see him after fleeing the palace with the terrible apparitions in close pursuit. In the background is seen the palace itself and two women standing, while the Erinyes appear to Orestes in the air.

The development of Alexander Runciman as a draftsman is still very little known. The drawing style of his Roman period is quite uncertain, and it is impossible to relate this sheet to a known work of those years. It exhibits many of the same mannerisms as the works of his Edinburgh period and is similar to the drawings in the Ossian series, such as the *Death of Oscar* (National Gallery of Scotland.) However, there are certain differences, in particular, the lack of the fine pen work which appears in the Ossian drawings. Still, on the basis of our present knowledge of the preparatory drawings for Penicuik House, the early 1770s must be posited as the period for this drawing.
F.C.

Provenance
David Laing, Edinburgh (died 1878)
Bequeathed to the Royal Scottish Academy, Edinburgh
Transferred to the National Gallery of Scotland, 1910

References
Aeschylus, *Choephoroe*, II. 1046-60
National Gallery of Scotland, *Catalogue of Scottish Drawings* by Keith Andrews and J. R. Brotchie, Edinburgh, 1960, p. 201, no. D297

42
Double Portrait of Brown and Runciman
National Museum of Antiquities of Scotland
Oil on canvas; 24 x 29 in.
Inscribed: *Tempest;* verso: *Alexr Runcimanus et Johannes Bruno, Pictores eximii et mihi amicissimi de Poeta Avoniense disputantes. As. MDCCLXXXIV etc.,* together with a quotation from Cicero's *De Amicitia*
1784

The painter John Brown and his Scottish colleague Alexander Runciman are shown seated together, Brown in an evening coat. The Latin inscription written on the back by the Earl of Buchan describes them as distinguished painters and his friends, discussing the works of Shakespeare. Runciman, on the left, holds a paintbox and brushes, while Brown holds and comments upon the text being illustrated. Portraying these two artists in this way suggests perfectly the kinds of discussions of literary texts which must have occurred frequently among artists of this period. The painting also gives us the information that Brown and Runciman continued to be friends in Edinburgh, a relationship already suggested by resemblances between their works while in Rome.

The Bee for May 8, 1816, comments about this portrait: "His portrait with Runciman disputing about a passage in Shakespeare's Tempest is in the gallery at Dryburgh abbey. It was their joint work the year before Runciman died, 1784." A letter of August 1784 from John Brown to the Earl of Buchan, in the Laing Manuscripts in the Edinburgh University Library, makes clear that the painting is entirely the work of Runciman: "I was yesterday with Runciman and sat for my portrait which he has done a first sitting of on the same canvas on which he has already done his own. The piece is for your Lordship and I think will be an admirable one. He has represented himself sitting at his work, his pallet and pencils in one hand and a portecrayon in the other. I, behind, am seeming to point at and find fault with some part of his work, at which, as being rather irascible and impatient

42

of reproof, he is making a damnable face, as he himself expresses it. I flatter myself your Lordship will be much satisfied with it." F.C.

Provenance
David Stewart, eleventh Earl of Buchan, Dryburgh Abbey, Berwickshire, Scotland (died 1829)
Henry David Erskine, twelfth Earl of Buchan (died 1857)
David Stuart, thirteenth Earl of Buuhan (sale, Nisbet's, Edinburgh, 10 December 1859, no. 344)
David Laing, Edinburgh (died 1878)
Bequeathed to the Society of Antiquaries of Scotland, Edinburgh, 1878
Deposited with the Scottish National Portrait Gallery

Exhibitions
Scottish Art, Royal Academy, London, 1939, no. 22
Eighteenth Century Costume, Scottish National Portrait Gallery, Edinburgh, 1952, no. 60
Scottish Groups and Conversation Pieces, Scottish National Portrait Gallery, Edinburgh, 1956, no. 13
British Portraits, Royal Academy, London, 1956-57, no. 338
Scottish Painting, Glasgow Art Gallery, Glasgow, 1961, no. 41

References
The Bee, Edinburgh, 8 May 1793, p. 31

John Singleton Copley

1738-1815

The son of Irish emigrants, John Copley grew up in Boston. His stepfather Peter Pelham, an engraver and teacher from London, first undertook the training of the young artist. Copley was to become the outstanding American painter of the 18th century before he left Boston for a tour of the continent in 1774 at the age of thirty-nine.

It is a characteristic of Copley's mind that he continuously sought new information and new sources of stimulation for his work. Even before he travelled to England, he had written to West and Reynolds seeking advice about his art, and he was known to the London art world as early as 1766 when he sent the *Boy with a Squirrel* (1765, private collection) to the exhibition of the Incorporated Society of Artists.

On August 26, 1774 he left London for Rome, travelling through southern France to Genoa, Pisa, and Florence. The rooms frescoed by Raphael and Michelangelo in the Vatican were, for him, a revelation which proved a turning point in his career. In Parma he copied Correggio's *Holy Family with St. Jerome;* he returned to London by way of Venice, Mannheim, Cologne, and probably the Lowlands. In October 1775 Copley arrived in London to take up residence at 12 Leicester Square, across the park from the house of Sir Joshua Reynolds. Almost immediately, in 1776, he was made A.R.A. and began a series of paintings that were to be the most significant early expressions of British romantic art.

The first of these is *Watson and the Shark* (no. 44), painted in 1778, which is probably Copley's most original, if not his finest, work. He followed *Watson,* which is unique in his career, with a series of paintings taken from the current scene of British political and military history in the settings in which they were enacted and including actual portraits of the participants. In a letter to Lord Charlemont on March 22, 1783, Copley explained that modern subjects of this type were the most suitable for the artist and of more interest to the people who would view them than the currently fashionable subjects taken from Greek and Roman history. His enormous success in this field proved him to have a better grasp of the artistic taste of the public of London than certain of his less successful contemporaries like James Barry. The subjects which he chose include *The Death of the Earl of Chatham* (1779-81, Tate Gallery), *The Death of Major Peirson* (Tate Gallery) begun in 1782, after which he was elected to full membership in the Royal Academy in 1783, and *The Siege of Gibraltar* (1783-91, nos. 45 and 46). These works were immediately popular, and the engravings, which were widely circulated, were highly profitable. It was the success of Benjamin West in exactly the same area, with the *Death of General Wolfe* (Royal Collections), exhibited in 1771, which served as Copley's inspiration for this undertaking. Significantly, these works are the English prototypes of French endeavors in the same field, like Jacques-Louis David's *Oath of the Tennis Court,* the *Death of Marat,* and the *Death of Le Peletier.*

Apart from these contemporary subjects and during the same period, Copley painted historical and religious compositions. These include a *Nativity,* exhibited in 1777, greatly under the inspiration of his recent Italian tour, and *Samuel and Eli* (Wadsworth Atheneum, Hartford), in 1780. He also painted subjects from earlier English history such as *Charles I in the House of Commons Demanding the Five Impeached Members* (1782-95, Boston Public Library). At the same time, he continued to paint portraits equalling those of his English colleagues, such as *Mrs. Seymour Fort* (?) of about 1778 (Wadsworth Atheneum).

Although Copley is often thought of as an American artist, his outstanding contribution to the history of art as a whole occurred in London. He must be considered one of the brilliant talents of the period, an internationalist who achieved, at moments, the greatness of his French contemporary Jacques-Louis David.
F.C.

Bibliography
Augustus Thorndike Perkins, *A Sketch of the Life and a List of the Works of John Singleton Copley,* Boston, 1873
Martha Babcock Amory, *The Domestic and Artistic Life of John Singleton Copley, R. A.,* Boston, 1882
"Letters & Papers of John Singleton Copley and Henry Pelham, 1739-1776," *Massachusetts Historical Society . . . Collections,* LXXI, Boston, 1914
Frank W. Bayley, *The Life and Works of John Singleton Copley,* Boston, 1915
Martha C. Codman, *The Journal of Mrs. John Amory, 1775-1777,* Boston, 1923
James Thomas Flexner, *John Singleton Copley,* Boston, 1948
John Singleton Copley, 1738-1815, National Gallery of Art, Washington, etc., 1955-65 (catalogue compiled by Jules Prown)
Jules Prown, *John Singleton Copley, 1774-1815,* 2 vols., Washington/Cambridge, 1966 (with bibliography)

43

43
Study for Sir William Pepperell and His Family
Victoria and Albert Museum, London
Black chalk heightened with white on buff paper;
17⅝ x 10⅞ in.; verso: Study for the *Ascension*
1777-78

When he was painting *Watson and the Shark* soon after arriving in London, Copley undertook the group portrait showing Sir William Pepperell (1746-1816), a posthumous portrait of his wife Elizabeth Royall, and his children. This unusually tight and complete drapery study, squared for transfer, is for the figure of Sir William, who, standing with crossed legs and leaning on his wife's chair, smiles at his children in the final painting.

William Pepperell, created baronet in 1774, was an American Loyalist who fled to England at the opening of the Revolution. He was the descendant of Sir William Pepperell (1696-1756), who was commander-in-chief of the New England force against the French in 1745 and was created the first baronet for his services. William, his grandson, was the second son of Sir William's only daughter Elizabeth Pepperell Sparhawk. His name, William Pepperell Sparhawk, was changed at the wish of his grandfather to William Pepperell, and he inherited a large portion of the family lands and property when he came of age in 1767. He graduated from Cambridge in 1766 and married Elizabeth, daughter of Isaac Royall. Although chosen a member of the governor's council, he remained a Loyalist and was proscribed by the people of his county (York) in November 1774. As a result, he sailed for England in 1775. His wife contracted smallpox en route, died, and was buried in Nova Scotia. In 1778 he was banished from Maine, and his vast estates were confiscated. The British government gave him £500 a year, on which he lived along with the proceeds from a small plantation in Dutch Guiana. He was a founder of the British and Foreign Bible Society, and he died in Portman Square, London, in December 1816. Pepperell had one son and three daughters who are seen in the finished portrait now in the North Carolina Museum of Art, Raleigh. The son, however, died young, and the title became extinct.

The drawing was done soon after Copley's return from Italy and illustrates the striking alteration in his method of work at this turning point in his career. In Italy he had seen the large multi-figured productions of the Italian artists. He also learned the technique for preparing these elaborate works through the use of composition sketches, experimental studies of individual compositional elements, and form studies of particular parts to determine the pattern of light and shadow.

This drawing shows an early example of Copley's use of the technique in a particularly tight and detailed form study. It was drawn in the very last stages of preparing the composition, giving the final pose of Pepperell, after a number of alterations in the earlier drawings. Not only the pose (which ultimately derives from antique sculpture), but also the manner of drawing, remind one of the refined form studies, also often squared in this way, by Pompeo Batoni (1708-87). The pose of Pepperell with crossed legs, leaning on his left elbow, is reminiscent of Batoni's portraits of fashionable noblemen travelling on the continent, for example the *Unknown Man* of 1778, now in the Prado. Such works as Reynolds' portrait of *James, Second Earl Waldegrave* of 1759 (collection Earl Waldegrave) could also have served.   F.C.

Provenance
John Singleton Copley, Jr., Baron Lyndhurst (died 1863) (sale, Christie's, London, 26 February 1864, probably no. 672, bt. Clark)
Sale, Christie's, London, 12 May 1869, no. 45, bt. Hogarth
F. Rathbone
Victoria and Albert Museum, London, 1898

Exhibitions
John Singleton Copley, National Gallery of Art, Washington, etc., 1955-66, pp. 90, 93, 139, no. 67

References
Cecil H. C. Howard, "The Pepperell Portraits," *Essex Institute Historical Collections,* XXXI, 1894-95, p. 61
Prown, II, 266, 396, 429, fig. 361

44

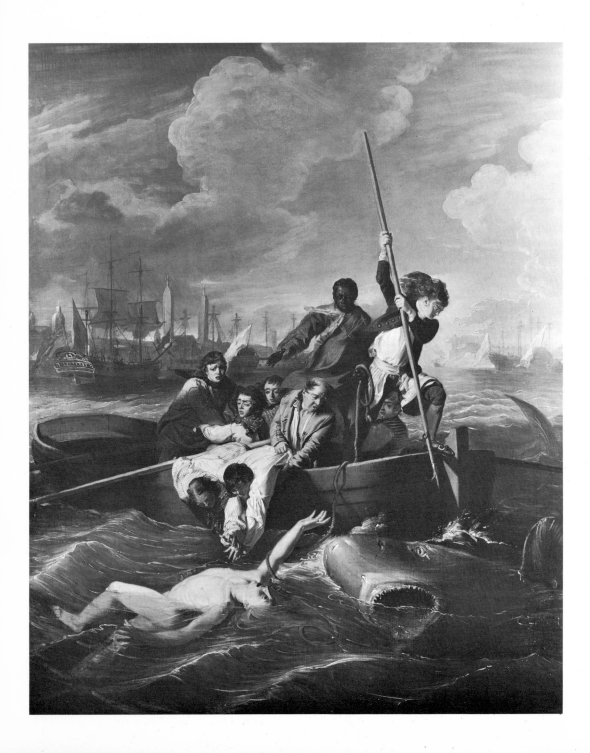

44
Watson and the Shark
The Detroit Institute of Arts, Dexter M. Ferry, Jr.
Fund
Oil on canvas; 36 x 30½ in.
Inscribed: *Painted by J.S. Copley, R.A.,*
London 1782

The three known autograph versions of this
painting have been carefully discussed and
catalogued by Prown and by Gardner and Feld.
The original, commissioned by Brook Watson,
exhibited at the Royal Academy in 1778 (no. 65),
and engraved by Valentine Green in mezzotint the
next year, is in the National Gallery of Art,
Washington. The second, from the collection of
Lord Lyndhurst, Copley's son, has long been at the
Museum of Fine Arts, Boston. No. 44 is the third
version, a vertical, signed and dated 1782. A replica
or copy of the Detroit picture is in the Bayou Bend
Collection, Museum of Fine Arts, Houston, Texas.
Other versions of the composition are cited
by Prown.

Sir Brook Watson, Bart. (1735-1807, see his obituary
in *The Gentleman's Magazine,* October 1807,
pp. 987-88), was elected Member of Parliament for
the City of London in 1784, Lord Mayor of London
for the year 1796, and he was made baronet in 1803.
Orphaned in 1741, Watson was sent to sea at
fourteen. On this voyage he sailed to the West
Indies, where he lost his leg to a shark in Havana
harbor. An army officer, he served in Canada as
commissary under Colonel Robert Monckton at the
battle of Beauséjour and under Wolfe at Louisbourg
in 1758. Returning to London in 1759, he became a
successful merchant, but he did not give up his
military commission or his connections with the
New World. He was in America again in 1775 as
commissary-general to the British Army, and in
1782 he was in Canada assisting in the evacuation
of loyal British from the United States. Watson and
Copley's brother-in-law Jonathan Clarke sailed
from Canada on the *Canadian* in the spring of
1776, and there is an unconfirmed tradition in the
Copley family that he was with Copley on the boat

that took him to England in 1774. Dunlap states that Watson was in Montreal when it was attacked by Colonel Ethan Allen in October 1775 and that Watson took Allen in irons back to London.

The sketch of Watson's life, from one-legged orphan to M.P. and Lord Mayor of London, Deputy Governor of the Bank of England and finally baronet, bespeaks a boldly colorful individual. It was also a part of his success that he was able to make his loss of limb an advantage, lending an aura of glamour to an officer and hero wounded in foreign engagements. His wooden leg was famous in London, as we know from the poem by John Wilkes entitled "Brook Watson and his Wooden Leg" in which he is congratulated for keeping his head even though he lost his limb. Surely the commission for Watson and the Shark is an important part of this capitalization on his romantic career and vivid personality.

The inspiration for treating this subject in a major composition must owe a great deal to the personality of Brook Watson and especially to his ability to tell a good story, since he alone could recreate the drama and terror of the original situation. But in selecting the subject, Copley must have been impressed by numerous elements that would strike the imagination of the London public at the Royal Academy exhibition, establish his name as a painter of historical subjects and, finally, serve as a source of income beyond the immediate commission in a print with a wide distribution. All these matters were at stake with this, his first historical composition in his second appearance at the Royal Academy after his arrival in London.

Copley's tour on the continent had been a revelation, showing him that Raphael and Michelangelo's works were not almost divine effusions, but made by actual men. This gave him courage to attempt complex compositions involving many figures in emotional situations. At least one motif is drawn from the most famous work of men in a boat, The Miraculous Draught of Fishes by Raphael, a tapestry cartoon which he could have

known at Hampton Court Palace or at Buckingham House, St. James's Park (after 1777). The pose of the two sailors leaning out of the boat grappling for the thrashing Watson derives from that of the two figures leaning to pull in nets in Raphael's cartoon. The standing Negro throws out his hands in a gesture reminiscent of a disciple in the same painting. In Rome, only two years before, Copley had studied especially the works and method of Raphael. The grouping of the other figures in a series of interconnected rhythms which interlock to point up the salient features of the drama, shows that Copley had also studied Raphael's compositional devices.

The first composition of Watson and the Shark was a horizontal, with the figures occupying almost the whole of the picture, and the shark placed close to the observer in a physically menacing way, as McCoubrey points out. Indeed, in the horizontal composition, the shark is frighteningly close to the observer, subordinating the other figures and drawing attention to itself rather than to the drama as a whole. McCoubrey argues that the vertical composition is more pat and conventional; however, it shows a number of changes which the artist thought of as improvements on his original idea. In the vertical format, the figures take up less of the total surface, allowing a compact grouping in an interlocked pyramid. More of the sky is shown, and its turbulent clouds participate as emotional echoes of the frenzied action in the central group. In fact, in the final version all parts including the landscape are welded into a compact psychological and physical harmony. A 20th-century viewer would perhaps be impressed by the horizontal composition just because the action is right in the foreground and seems to menace the observer. McCoubrey is correct in stating that the vertical composition is more in keeping with the artistic intentions of the romantic period and is more successful in terms of its point of view.

In the Detroit composition, the figures are all pulled in close together. They are bound by a pyramidal construction which unites and explains each

element and brings into an intimate psychological interplay every other part of the composition. In the horizontal version, the eye wanders over the composition, stopping at individual incidents within the struggle, and thereby losing the emotional impact of the plunging boat hook and the two men grappling for Watson in the water; an intellectual effort is essential to connect them. The psychological drama is the true subject of this painting, and it is more unified and more graspable in one moment of time in the vertical composition. Particularly pertinent is the fact that the moment selected by Copley is that after the shark had bitten off Watson's leg. We know that the man will not be struck again and that he will be drawn into the boat and saved. Copley selected this moment, when each person could be studied for his own psychological response, rather than the more sensational moment of the most intense physical danger.

This is not an example of "newspaper" reporting of a contemporary event. It has seemed to be so primarily because it is a scene describing an event which actually took place. As such, it derives from the psychological drama of George Stubbs's Labourers (no. 13), but it is transformed into heroic terms. Thus, the subject is sublime and owes much to Burke who argued that aesthetic response of a very high order is derived from subjects which demand response to death, physical suffering, horror, and terror.

For the London public of 1778, the interest of the subject was increased greatly by the fact that it involved the unusual and the exotic. The setting is the West Indies, and the Negro and the shark are introduced to compound the unusual. In a London greatly interested in the American continent, an interest already whetted pictorially by West's and Barry's Death of Wolfe, these would have been significant factors in the emotional interest of the subjects. Copley was astute and carefully addressed his picture to his public.
F.C.

Provenance
Noel Joseph Desenfans (sale, Christie's, London,
8 April 1786, no. 396; see Graves, *Art Sales,* I,
149: "1786 April 8 Com. at Christie's Noel Desenfans.
396. Well-known subject of Shark. 44 x 37 out. Fr.")
W. Goddard (sale, Christie's, 5 February 1791, no. 73,
The Shark, bt. Green)
G. P. Anderson, London
W. P. Hunter, London (acquired from Anderson around
1850; sold in London c. 1946 by the heirs of
W. P. Hunter)
M. Knoedler & Co., New York
The Detroit Institute of Arts, 1946

Exhibitions
*The Coast and the Sea, A Survey of American Marine
Painting,* Brooklyn Museum, 1948-49, no. 33
Likeness of America, 1680-1820, Colorado Springs Fine
Arts Center, 1949, no. 19 (catalogue compiled by
Louisa Dresser)

References
William Dunlap, *History of the . . . Arts of Design in the
United States,* New York, 1834, I, 116-18, 120
Augustus Perkins, *A Sketch of the Life . . . of John
Singleton Copley,* Boston, 1873, pp. 21, 118-19
Amory, pp. 70-75
Dr. J. C. Webster, *Sir Brook Watson, Friend of the
Loyalists, First Agent of New Brunswick in London,* St.
John, New Brunswick, 1924
Charles C. Cunningham, *John Singleton Copley,* Boston,
Museum of Fine Arts, 1938, p. 12
New Brunswick Museum, *Webster Canadiana Collection,*
St. John, New Brunswick, 1939-49, I, 323-25
Margaret Jeffery, "A Painting of Copley's English
Period," *Metropolitan Museum of Art Bulletin,* n.s., I,
1942, pp. 148-50
Edgar P. Richardson, *"Watson and the Shark* by John
Singleton Copley," *The Art Quarterly,* X, 1947, pp. 213-18
John S. Newberry, Jr., "Four Drawings by Copley,"
The Detroit Institute of Arts Bulletin, XXVIII no. 2, 1949,
pp. 32-34
John W. McCoubrey, *American Tradition in Painting,*
New York, 1963, pp. 19-20
Albert T. Gardner and Stuart P. Feld, *American
Paintings,* New York, Metropolitan Museum of Art, 1965,
pp. 49-51
Prown, II, 250, 267-74, 459-61, figs. 368-81

45

45

Lord Heathfield
National Portrait Gallery, London
Oil on canvas; 26½ x 23 in.
1787

The son of Sir George Eliott, Bart., Lord Heathfield (1717-90) was created Baron Heathfield of Gibraltar in 1787, three years before his death. He fought with the Prussian army in 1735-36 and in the War of Austrian Succession. In 1748 he married an heiress of the Drake family and a descendant of Sir Francis Drake. Wounded at Dettingen, he was later made lieutenant colonel in 1754. Eleven years later, he was made lieutenant general and selected as Governor of Gibraltar in 1775. As such, he was in charge of its defense when it was attacked four years later (see no. 46).

This sketch was made from Heathfield himself in preparation for the large painting of the *Siege of Gibraltar* (Guildhall Art Gallery, London) commissioned from Copley by the City of London. Copley received the commission in 1783, but his first sketches (no. 46) for the composition were not acceptable to the Court of Common Council because too much emphasis was given to the battle itself and not enough to the officers who guided it. Thus, in January 1787 it was decided to alter the composition to include the officers and men who had defeated the Spanish and their French allies. In July of the same year Copley proposed the changes, and they were approved by the Court of Common Council. The intention was to honor Heathfield and Admiral Howe, the naval commander whose fleet had come to the rescue of the land forces. It was finally necessary to include a portrait group of officers with Lord Heathfield on horseback on the right and the naval conflagration on the left. A second painting, by Dominic Serres, was finally subjoined as a long, narrow predella showing the arrival of Admiral Howe's fleet.

To complete this scheme, Copley had to obtain portraits of the participants, including the Hanoverian officers, for which he was forced to travel to Germany in August. Individual canvases were prepared, the pose and placement of the heads were drawn in with heavy brush lines, and the portraits added later with the dark lines remaining. Fortunately, the portrait of Heathfield did not require this preparation. The result was this brilliant sketch of the alert, hawklike profile of Heathfield directing the battle from his horse, with the yellow flames and smoke rising behind. Sir Joshua Reynolds also portrayed Lord Heathfield in a stalwart and moving portrait in The National Gallery, London.
F.C.

Provenance
John Singleton Copley, Jr., Baron Lyndhurst (died 1863) (sale, Christie's, London, 5 March 1864, no. 57, bt. Scharf)
National Portrait Gallery, London, 1864

Exhibitions
National Portrait Exhibition, Victoria and Albert Museum, London, 1867, no. 486

References
George Scharf, *Historical and Descriptive Catalogue of . . . The National Portrait Gallery,* London, 1881, p. 159
Bayley, pp. 34, 36, 140
Prown, II, 327, 419, fig. 495

46

Study for the Siege of Gibraltar (Figures Clinging to the Mast of a Sinking Longboat)
Victoria and Albert Museum, London
Black and white chalk on green-gray paper squared for enlargement and scaled; 14 x 20⅞ in.
1788-89

The series of studies of Spanish seamen struggling for rescue during the bombardment of the Spanish force that was attempting to capture the English fortress at Gibraltar in 1779 are the most powerful and intense of Copley's drawings. This composition of approximately fifty men groping in the water, clinging to the mast of a sinking boat, and struggling in longboats, in the rigging, and on the

46

decks of ships, in a night battle illuminated by burning and exploding ships, is the most complicated mass of humanity that Copley ever attempted. Indeed, it is perhaps the most ambitious of such paintings in English art. In the number of figures, it is more ambitious than the elaborate series of paintings undertaken by James Barry in the Society of Arts and more so than most of the elaborate figural compositions that Copley would have seen in Italy. Michelangelo's *Last Judgment* is one of the few comparable masses of struggling and terrified humanity that Copley could have known, and he must have been well aware that Michelangelo's was one of the few to which his work could be compared. It is significant that his first idea was to concentrate only on this group of drowning seamen, emphasizing the terror and sublimity of the scene.

Prown has carefully described the circumstances of the commission and the subject itself, and one should read his discussion for a complete record of the painting. In July 1779 the Spanish attempted to capture the British fort on Gibraltar by attacking with a fleet of ten specially built floating batteries, or battering ships. There followed a heavy artillery exchange in which the British used incendiary shot to kindle the Spanish boats. The battle continued during the day and throughout the night, and at about 1:00 a.m. one of the battering ships burst into flames. At 3:00, Sir Roger Curtis set out to capture and rescue the deserting and drowning Spanish officers and men. This scene of conflagration, heroism, and despair was chosen by Copley for the left half of his painting.

This drawing shows two Spanish seamen entwined about and grappling for the mast of the sinking boat which had rescued them only a few moments before, with one of the men supporting a third man, who is wounded. A fourth figure, a British soldier seen from the back and in shadow, is reaching for the oar, extended from Curtis's approaching longboat. The intense shadows and the vivid highlights which play over the flesh are thrown by light from one of the boats, aflame from stem to stern, lighting up the whole scene. The complexity and grace of this grouping of four figures illustrate the mastery of Copley at the height of his career and show how thoroughly he learned the lessons of Italian painting. The prevailing characteristic of Italian art from the Renaissance through the 18th century is an extraordinary grace based on the rhythmic intertwining of forms in space and light. As an English artist, Copley is unusual in grasping this in all its complexity, and in reinterpreting it on an ambitious scale in his own art. A motif drawn from Italian art appears in this drawing and frequently occurs in other works by Copley. This motif is made up of a central form, the mast in this case, which emerges as the dynamic core of a group of forms entwined around it which recreate and expand its basic rhythm. The motif can be seen in the central group of the *Death of Major Peirson* (Tate Gallery), and in the central group *Sir William Pepperell and His Family* (see no. 43), to cite only two examples. The idea is embodied fully in the art of Raphael and Michelangelo and much more intricately in works by Rubens.

The straining of the figures in water, whose speckled foam and current are marked in strokes of white, illustrates a degree of physical and emotional intensity rarely encountered in English art.

Particularly significant is the fact that this is achieved through the gesture and strain of nude male forms and through light rather than facial expression. This shows a departure from Copley's earlier *Watson and the Shark* and West's *Wolfe,* where the emotional representations are based largely on schematic types. Copley has learned from Rubens this new lesson of the use of the entire body in a complete physical gesture to express emotion, and here Copley transforms his source completely to his own uses. The treatment of the nude male figure is much more sophisticated than in *Watson and the Shark* and, once again, a study of Rubens is operative. Finally, the intensity of this group in its physical energy and in its pitch of emotion as well as in its desperate, aqueous situation anticipates, in a striking way, Géricault's *Raft of the Medusa.*
F.C.

Provenance
John Singleton Copley, Jr., Baron Lyndhurst (died 1863) (sale, Christie's, London, 26 February 1864, no. 660 or 662)
Victoria and Albert Museum, London, 1864

References
Richard Redgrave, *A Catalogue of the British Fine Art Collections at South Kensington. Being for the most part the Gifts of John Sheepshanks, Esq. and Mrs. Ellison,* London, 1864, p. 91, no. 618
Prown, II, 322-26, 396, 454, fig. 557

47
Thomas Lane and His Sister Harriot
Museum of Fine Arts, Boston, Emily L. Ainsley Fund
Oil on canvas; 47 x 59 in.
c. 1792

Although dated by Prown about 1783-88, new information about the sitters giving their birth and details of their lives suggests a revised dating. Thomas Lane (born 1768) and Harriot (1776-1860) were the grandchildren of Thomas Lane (died, 1784) director of the banking firm of Lane, Son & Fraser. Their parents were John and Eleanor Everitt Lane. The family and the firm had close ties with New England, and young Thomas, a victim of tuberculosis, lived in Boston from 1786 to 1789 and then travelled to Madeira for his health. Returning to England, he became a business partner of a Mr. Taylor and in 1792 departed with him for Antigua. After settling in Boston in 1801, he married Elizabeth (1768-1802), daughter of Nathaniel Appleton of Boston. His wife died the following year and the subsequent details of Thomas's life are little known. He was in London in 1818, and in 1829 he was again in the Caribbean, this time a resident of Jamaica. The time and place of his death are unknown. Even less is known of his sister Harriot. However, she was still a spinster in 1829, the approximate date of her father's death.

In his will, now in Somerset House, London, John Lane bequeathed to his son Thomas his own portrait painted by Copley which establishes a connection between the Lane and Copley families. Copley was well known to the American colony in London of this period, and they could have met through the New England Club. On the basis of the age of the sitters, the most likely moment for this painting is the period from 1790 to 1792 when Thomas returned from Madeira, and before he left for Antigua. Thomas would have been twenty-four and Harriot sixteen.

This portrait by Copley is of interest because it is based on the somewhat original tradition of the highly civilized and learned man at home in the

47

open landscape and drawing his intellectual and emotional sustenance from it in a Rousseau-like spirit. The idea of painting a man in elegant dress, reclining on the ground and fingering a book in an open landscape, derives from Joseph Wright's striking portrait of *Sir Brooke Boothby* (Tate Gallery), in a lush, green forest interior, lying full length by a tiny brook, amidst succulent grasses and plants, and holding a book of Rousseau's writings. Boothby's portrait dates from 1781 and relates to a tradition which includes Johann Heinrich Wilhelm Tischbein's *Goethe in the Campagna* (1786-87, Städelsches Kunstinstitut, Frankfurt am Main) and Romney's portrait sometimes called *William Pitt as a Boy* (collection Earl of Crawford and Balcarres in 1934). The reclining or semi-recumbent portrait in the late 18th century is fascinating to follow since it includes such works as Benjamin West's *General Kosciusko* (no. 53) and culminates in David's *Mme Récamier* and Canova's *Pauline Borghese*.
F.C.

Provenance
Harriot Eleanor Lane, Camberwell, Surrey, by 1857
By descent to her cousin, John Hawkins, Camberwell, 1860
By descent to his son, George Frederick Hawkins, London (died 1922)
By descent to his wife, Mrs. Frances Alice Hawkins, Hartley Wintney, Hampshire (died 1951)
Leger Galleries, London, 1953
Hirschl & Adler, New York, 1953
Museum of Fine Arts, Boston, 1954

Exhibitions
British Painting in the Eighteenth Century, Montreal Museum of Fine Arts, 1957-58, no. 3 and p. 137

References
Prown, II, 320 and fig. 484
Catalogue of American Paintings, Museum of Fine Arts, Boston, no. 322, fig. 78, in preparation

48

48
A Hussar Officer on Horseback (Study for "George IV as Prince of Wales")
The Cleveland Museum of Art, Norman O. Stone and Ella A. Stone Memorial Fund
Black and white chalk on light blue paper;
10¹³⁄₁₆ x 8¹¹⁄₁₆ in.
1805-08

Prown suggests that this drawing is an early study for Copley's canvas *The Battle of the Pyrenees* of 1813-15 (Museum of Fine Arts, Boston) showing the Duke of Wellington at the battle of Vittoria of June 21, 1813. However, in his caption to the reproduction of this drawing, he suggests that it could also be a study for the equestrian portrait of

George IV as Prince of Wales (Museum of Fine Arts, Boston) of 1804-10. The latter is probably the correct suggestion.

The young man is a Hussar officer raising his sword in a salute. The Hussars did fight in the Peninsular War alongside Wellington, but they were especially connected with the Prince of Wales, and they dominate this equestrian portrait to such a degree that their presence must be considered pertinent. The Prince of Wales, who was to become Prince Regent in 1811, had given his own regiment much rich detailing of costume, and in 1805 his Light Dragoons were permitted to call themselves Hussars (although only in brackets after their names in the Army Lists). Because their costumes were already elaborate, the principal change was the addition of the tall, cylindrical fur hat, or busby, with encircling cords. These hats were attached by a cord from the crest to the body of the man so that the headpiece could not be lost. The pouch harnessed to the waist is the busby bag. The officer's hat was distinguished by a tall feather fixed in the front. This brilliant costume and the men, who wore moustaches in the very first years of its creation, no doubt made a sensation. Since the Prince of Wales was especially linked with their creation, Copley planned his portrait, or was requested to plan his revised composition of 1805, with a pageant of Hussar cavalry behind and prominent Hussar officers in attendance.

Copley's studies of Hussars on horseback include one in The Metropolitan Museum of Art and a study for the two officers to the left of Lord Heathfield in the collection of Vincent Price, which were made in preparation for the equestrian portrait of the Prince of Wales.

Alterations in Copley's plans for the portrait were made in 1805, the year in which the new Hussar costumes were introduced and the year Copley first hoped to exhibit the painting at the Academy. Several officers, a corps of cavalry, and an encampment were placed in the background at this time. For these figures, Copley made careful

studies in his studio, researching the intricacies of the new and dashing costumes. The excitement in the letters of Mrs. Copley about these changes reveals very special occurrences in the studio, and the presence of these fashionable young officers and their colorful appearance in the picture must be the source of her enthusiasm. By July 2, 1808 we learn that he was finishing the large canvas that was not ready for exhibition until the spring of 1810. The Cleveland study must have been drawn in the early phases of preparation since it was finally rejected. The salute with the curved Hussar sword was used later for the composition of Copley's portrait of the *Prince of Orange* of about 1812-13, now in the Royal Collections.
F.C.

Provenance
John Singleton Copley, Jr., Baron Lyndhurst (died 1863) (sale, Christie's, London, 26 February 1864, no. 670, bt. Jupp)
Edward Basil Jupp, London (died 1877)
Martha Babcock Amory, Boston (died 1880)
Linzee Amory, Boston (died 1911)
Harry Shaw Newman Gallery, New York, 1947
Charles D. Childs, Boston, 1950
The Cleveland Museum of Art, 1950

References
Amory, pp. 270-71
Helen Comstock, "Drawings by John Singleton Copley," *Panorama,* Harry Shaw Newman Gallery, II, May 1947, p. 108
Prown, II, 381, 436, figs. 674-76

Benjamin West

1738-1820

Born near Springfield, Pennsylvania, West was the youngest of ten children of Quaker parents; his father was an innkeeper and tradesman. The American artist William Williams, whom he met on a journey to Philadelphia in 1756, assisted him in his early years to obtain information and materials to pursue his interest in painting. He was advised to apply himself to historical subjects and produced a stiff *Death of Socrates* (collection H. A. Stites, Nazareth, Pennsylvania) at this time. In 1760 he had the opportunity to travel to Italy, which he accepted with very limited funds but with good letters of introduction. While there he met Anton Raphael Mengs (1728-79) and Cardinal Albani, Winckelmann's patron. He also travelled to North Italy and was made a member of the academies in Parma, Florence, and Bologna.

West returned to England in 1763, marrying soon after the daughter of a Philadelphia merchant whom he had known before his journey abroad. His first patrons were churchmen, James Johnson, Bishop of Worcester; Thomas Newton, Bishop of Bristol; and Robert Drummond, Archbishop of York. For the latter he painted *The Landing of Agrippina at Brundisium with the Ashes of Germanicus* (no. 49). Drummond introduced him to George III who was delighted with the *Agrippina* and commissioned the *Departure of Regulus* (Royal Collections, Kensington Palace) which was shown at the first Royal Academy exhibition in 1769. In 1772 after his success with the *Death of Wolfe,* he was appointed historical painter to George III, for whom he undertook numerous subject pieces and portraits until 1811 when his annual stipend and his title were rescinded. His many works for Windsor Castle included scenes from early British history like the *Battle of Crécy* (1788), now in the Royal Collections.

In his first London period West used predominantly antique subjects, following Mengs and Gavin Hamilton but with canvases on a scale less than life-size. He climaxed his endeavor by achieving royal patronage. Interest in the discoveries at Herculaneum and Pompeii rustled across Europe at this time, stirring the imagination of the informed and the general public. But the great general interest in new experiences of every kind which marks the 1760s had also impressed West, and now he very wisely altered his tack. In 1771 he exhibited his most original work and the picture which presents his most inventive contribution, *The Death of Wolfe* (versions in The National Gallery of Canada, Ottawa, and Kensington Palace, London). It records the death of General Wolfe, the climactic turning point of the Battle of Quebec in 1759. Without reliance on allegory or other intellectual or literary allusions, and emphasizing the details of military costume, he presented a contemporary hero at the apex of self-sacrifice. The picture makes its presentation with all the traditional devices of the highest order of drama. The novelty of the idea, which had been thoroughly prepared for in the realism of West's antique subjects, struck the imagination of the public. The interest at the time in the potential of the New World, the excitement of national military exploits, the traditional animosity against the French, and the glamour of a military hero all aided in its highly successful reception. The engraving after it was enormously popular and spread West's fame throughout Western Europe. His success in this venture, which he was not to repeat, illustrated to artists like Copley and John Trumbull (1756-1843) the great potential of contemporary military subjects.

West was that kind of artist who rapidly grasps the enthusiasms of other artists and quickly assimilates their interests and style, making them his own. This phenomenon occurred in his Roman period under the influence of Mengs and Hamilton. And it happened to him again in the 1770s when he rapidly assimilated the drawing style of John H. Mortimer, as well as certain of his unusual subjects. After Mortimer's death in 1779, West undertook *Death on the Pale Horse* (sketches of about 1783 and 1802, Philadelphia Museum of Art; final version, 1817, Pennsylvania Academy of The Fine Arts, Philadelphia), an illustration to *Revelation,* a subject which Mortimer had already published in a print. This kind of assimilation was a pattern throughout West's career. In a similar way Fuseli's presence was unhappily influential on West's art after he settled in London in 1780.

The less than life-size scale of his early works was criticized by artists like Haydon, and it was very possibly this criticism that led West late in life to paint a group of enormous canvases. *Death on a Pale Horse,* the composition sketch of 1783, was enlarged to a grandiose size in 1817, and he also completed in 1814 the enormous and complex *Christ Rejected by the Jews* (Pennsylvania Academy of The Fine Arts, Philadelphia). However, West is at his best in his small pictures with unpretentious subjects, particularly when they immediately struck his imagination. His large paintings and portraits, with important exceptions such as that of *Mr. and Mrs. John Custance* (Nelson Gallery—Atkins Museum, Kansas City) which is greatly under the influence of Reynolds, tend to be wooden and stiff, having a limited interest in both their compositions and in their paint qualities.

Although West was frequently at the right place at the right moment, he was essentially an enthusiastic assimilator of the ideas of others. No artist of the period was more secure or more certain of income than he. No other artist was allowed so consistently to pursue his own interests and to paint the most revered historical subjects. And yet, West's technique, his ability to compose, and his handling of paint are seldom entirely satisfying.   F.C.

Bibliography
John Galt, *The Life, Studies, and Works of Benjamin West,* 2 vols., London, 1820
Alfred Neumeyer, "The Early Historical Paintings of Benjamin West," *Burlington,* LXXIII, 1938, pp. 162-65
Charles Mitchell, "Benjamin West's *Death of General Wolfe* and the Popular History Piece," *JWCI,* VII, 1944, pp. 20-33
Edgar Wind, "Penny, West, and 'The Death of General Wolfe'," *JWCI,* X, 1947, pp. 159-62
James T. Flexner, "Benjamin West's American Neo-Classicism," *The New York Historical Society Quarterly,* XXXVI, no. 1, January 1952, pp. 4-41
Grose Evans, *Benjamin West and the Taste of his Times,* Carbondale, 1959
Robert Rosenblum, "Grose Evans, *Benjamin West and the Taste of his Times,*" (review), *Art Bulletin,* XLII, 1960, pp. 76-79

49

The Landing of Agrippina at Brundisium with the Ashes of Germanicus

Philadelphia Museum of Art, Given by
Robert L. McNeil, Jr. Trusts
Oil on paper, mounted on canvas; 13⅜ x 18⅞ in.
Inscribed: *B.West/1766*

Soon after he settled in England in 1763, following a period of three years in Italy, West received one of his most propitious commissions from Dr. Robert Drummond, Archbishop of York, for a subject from Roman history, *Agrippina with the Ashes of Germanicus*. It was to be a fortunate commission since the delighted Archbishop showed it to George III, and West immediately received his order for another Roman subject, *The Departure of Regulus,* which was to be the first in an important series of royal commissions.

West had already painted *The Prodigal Son* for Drummond's colleague, the Bishop of Worcester, and a classical subject, *The Parting of Hector and Andromache,* for another churchman, Dr. Newton. This suggests that the patronage of men of the

49

cloth is a neglected side of the revival of interest in classical subject matters and the introduction of the neoclassical style into England. These men were steeped in Latin and often in Greek literature, and the resonantly stoic themes of the new style particularly attracted them. Drummond commented upon the subject of Agrippina at length when Tacitus was read aloud after a dinner with West, and he made suggestions for its composition. West was so stimulated that he returned home and almost immediately produced a first sketch, presumably this one, to the Archbishop's delight.

The subject is taken from the *Annals* (III, 1-2) of the Roman writer Tacitus (c. 35-c. 117). Agrippina, daughter of Agrippa and Julia, was the wife of Germanicus, the nephew and adopted son of the Emperor Tiberius. Seeing in Germanicus a potential rival to his throne, Tiberius recalled him from successful campaigns in Germany and sent him to the Near East where he became fatally ill and died at Epidaphne in Syria in A.D. 19. Agrippina and her friends, fearing that her husband was poisoned, insisted upon an inquiry. To dramatize her cause, she returned to Rome carrying the ashes of her dead husband. In this painting we see her landing at Brundisium on the east coast of Italy,

surrounded by her children Agrippina the Younger and Caligula. The inquiry into Germanicus' untimely death was undertaken, but the cause of his death was never established.

Robert Rosenblum lists other British representations of the subject by Gavin Hamilton and Alexander Runciman and the only French version, exhibited at an 18th-century Salon by Renou in 1779. Others which might be mentioned are a relief by Étienne d'Antoine (1737-1809) in the Avignon Museum, an etching by Augustin de Saint-Aubin (1736-1807) after Gravelot (1699-1793) a drawing by Simon Julien (1735-1800) in the Budapest Museum, a painting of 1774 by Christian Bernhard Rode (1725-97) in Britz, Germany, and drawing for it in the Budapest Museum. West's composition was engraved by Valentine Green (1739-1813) and Richard Earlom (1742/43-1822). West himself did another version of the subject, exhibited at the Royal Academy in 1773, no. 303, *Agrippina Surrounded by her Children, Weeping over the Ashes of Germanicus* (The John and Mable Ringling Museum of Art, Sarasota, Florida). Two paintings entitled *Agrippina* were exhibited at the Society of Artists in 1768, nos. 120 and 175. A finished version by West is in the Yale University Art Gallery, and another version is at Burghley House.

In this sketch for the final painting, Agrippina, her children, and her attendants have just debarked onto the wharf of the Italian seaport in solemn procession. For this group West may have had in mind the procession of aristocratic Romans on the *Ara Pacis Augustae* now in Rome, fragments of which could have been seen in the collections of the Uffizi in West's day. The architecture in the background recalls the harbor facade of Diocletian's palace at Split as it was published in Robert Adam's book *The Ruins of the Palace of the Emperor Diocletian, at Spalatro,* London, 1764. Both of these monuments were historically pertinent since the *Ara Pacis* was completed some six years before the event depicted occurred, and since the palace of Diocletian overlooked a harbor on the Adriatic like that at Brundisium.

Not only is there Roman architecture, but the clothing of the women is the aristocratic costume of the figures on the *Ara Pacis,* and the Roman officers wear costumes appropriate to their era and rank. In other words West was attempting, and succeeded to an important degree, in recreating a panorama of the antique world so that his contemporaries could enter not only the stage which he had projected but also the drama and emotional life of its inhabitants. His concern was to recreate not only the air of antiquity but its actuality. He achieved this through the techniques of research and archaeological investigation and applied the knowledge gained to the re-creation in his art of the apparatus of antiquity.

In his *Agrippina* West applies this historicizing point of view to a subject from classical literature. But West's extensive research allowed him to surpass the attempts, for example, of a Poussin in a similar venture, and it is essentially this same technique that was employed by Stubbs, whose extensive research allowed him to surpass the antique in the precision of his descriptions of nature. Both Stubbs and West were adamant, not that they follow a style or improve on certain compositional principles from the past, but that through knowledge gained perceptually they recreate a dramatic situation, accurate in the greatest detail, which would, by its very palpability, grip the imagination and transport one into the world created. Stubbs's more immediate and direct technique is related to the emotionally oriented theories of Burke. West's, equally intense in its realism, relies directly on theories of association as later formulated, for example, by Archibald Alison. F.C.

References
Galt, II, 232
Flexner, pp. 32-33
Allen Staley, *"The Landing of Agrippina at Brundisium with the Ashes of Germanicus,"* Bulletin, Philadelphia Museum of Art, LXI, nos. 287-88, 1965-1966, pp. 10-19
Robert Rosenblum, *Transformations in Late Eighteenth Century Art,* Princeton, 1967, pp. 42-43, n. 131

50
The Blind Belisarius
Philadelphia Museum of Art, Purchased: Marie Kimball Fund
Pen and brown ink; 16¼ x 18¾ in.
Inscribed: *B West 1784;* verso: *Doct.— Chepmell/with Mrs—West's/and Mrs. Meugary's kind regards/July 1850*
1784

Belisarius (c. 505-65) was, for a time, the most famous and powerful general of Justinian for whom he repulsed the Ostrogoths from Italy and undertook numerous highly successful campaigns. The story of his blindness and penury derives from a verbal tradition which arose about his personality and was repeated in the *Chiliades* or *Book of Histories* by John Tzetzes, the Byzantine poet and grammarian who lived at Constantinople during the 12th century. Tzetzes portrayed Belisarius as a man who was treated ungratefully and who had to beg for sustenance. It was he who first repeated the words which Belisarius is supposed to have spoken, "He who gives a coin to Belisarius, who emulated virtue, has suppressed jealousy and envy."

Belisarius as a beggar first became a popular subject in painting in the 17th century, and there are two main sources for late 18th-century versions of the subject. The first arises from Salvator Rosa whose painting figured centrally in the Belisarius Chamber of Lord Townshend at Raynham Hall, Norfolk, and was celebrated by

Walpole. Rosa shows Belisarius old and infirm staring at the ground, but not blind and without the child who will later accompany him.

Although a play, *Bélisaire,* was written by Jean de Rotrou in 1643, late 18th- and 19th-century representations of the subject derive from Jean François Marmontel whose novelette *Bélisaire* was published in 1767. Marmontel's version is that followed by the numerous artists who represented the subject in the two generations to follow. François-André Vincent (1746-1816) painted a version in 1776 (Musée Fabre, Montpellier), and David exhibited his famous painting of *Belisarius* in 1781. West's representation still shows the pathetic hero, who has some resemblances to King Lear, now begging and blind, led through the streets of Constantinople. The presence of the child Tiberius, who is Belisarius' guide, companion, and philosophical disputant, reveals that West is following the tradition of Marmontel and David. Indeed, in the Royal Academy catalogue of 1805 (no. 145), *Belisarius and the Boy* by West is followed by *"Vide Marmontel."* The image still carries the

Provenance
Anonymous sale, London, Christie's, 19 July 1963, no. 121, bt. Jones
Philadelphia Museum of Art, 1965

moral overtone that whoever gives to Belisarius, a man without envy and jealousy, will be raised to virtue. The Detroit version of the subject (Royal Academy 1802, no. 139, *"Date Obollum Bellisario"*) is, in fact, a literal representation of this epigram.

Belisarius appears in at least four paintings by West listed in the catalogue of his works by John Galt. He painted two versions of *Belisarius with his Family:* the subject of *Belisarius and the Boy* was prepared for Sir Francis Baring, and a second, and different, smaller version is now in The Detroit Institute of Arts. The composition for which this drawing prepares is likely to be that painted for Sir Francis Baring.

The style of West's draftsmanship at this moment was greatly under the influence of the drawings of John Mortimer, who died only five years before, and it is not surprising that drawings of this type occasionally are found under the name of Mortimer. However, West will soon come firmly under the influence of Fuseli's style, and his drawings will lose the grace and care exhibited by this sheet. F.C.

51

Provenance
Descendants of the artist
David David, Philadelphia
Philadelphia Museum of Art, 1966

References
Marmontel, "Belisaire," *Oeuvres,* Paris, 1819, pp. 209-300
Galt, II, 224, 227
F. Sauerhing, "Belisar in Sage und Kunst,"
Repertorium für Kunstwissenschaft, XVI, 1893, pp. 289-95
Evans, pp. 91, 124 n., pl. 68

51
King Lear
Museum of Art, Rhode Island School of Design
Oil on panel; 17½ x 25½ in.
1789

In the third act of Shakespeare's play, Lear is watching the storm and inviting it to do its worst in a scene which heightens his individual heroism and at the same time emphasizes his pathetic situation. He is accompanied by a cast of fantastic creatures, each of whom in his own way aggravates Lear's desperate situation, starkly delineating the special lines of his tortured character. The Fool sits before a hovel which is approached by the entire group. Edgar, disguised as a madman, has been discovered in the shed and has emerged to add distraction. Gloucester, at first a mysterious presence, emerges from the gloom with a torch, astonishing them all. Lear and Kent both stare at the flame, thus illustrating the line of the Fool, "Look here comes a walking fire." This moment of total fantasy is that selected by West.

This sketch is no doubt that exhibited at the Royal Academy in 1789. It was West's habit to exhibit such sketches, and the high finish of no. 51 would indicate that it was used for this purpose. It was probably also used to submit as a *modello* to Boydell who commissioned the series and paid West £1,000 for his *Lear*. The finished painting was described in the Boydell catalogue as an "astonishing production, matchless in composition and drawing."

No. 51 also served as the basis of the engraving by Sharpe published in 1793. The lighting and the details are identical with those of this sketch, whereas the large painting, now in the Museum of Fine Arts, Boston, is different in many details, especially in the lighting.

The heightened dramatic effect and the element of physical fear brought on by the storm are elements which Burke would have found sublime. The style of the figures, the composition, and the light derive

from Fuseli, who arrived in England only eight years before and very quickly had an impact on West's art.
F.C.

Provenance
Rhode Island School of Design, 1956

Exhibitions
Royal Academy, 1789, no. 88 *(finished sketch for Gallery of Shakespear)*

References
The Pictures in the Shakespeare Gallery Pall-Mall, London, 1810, pp. 56-59, no. xxx
Galt, II, 229
T. S. R. Boase, "Illustrations of Shakespeare's Plays in the Seventeenth and Eighteenth Centuries," *JWCI,* 1947, p. 102
Helmut von Erffa, "King Lear by Benjamin West," *Bulletin of the Rhode Island School of Design,* XLIII no. 2, December 1956, pp. 6-8
Evans, p. 76, pl. 57

Reproductions
Engraved by W. Sharp (1749-1824) and published 25 March 1793

52
Cadmus Slaying the Dragon
Whitworth Art Gallery, University of Manchester
Pen and sepia ink, pencil and wash; 21⅞ x 17⅛ in.
c. 1790

This is a rather literal illustration of the opening lines of Book III of Ovid's *Metamorphoses*. Cadmus was the son of Agenor, king of Phoenicia, and the brother of Europa, who was carried off by Zeus in the guise of a white bull. To avenge her abduction, Agenor sent his eldest son Cadmus in a fruitless search. Apollo directed him to a strange country where he was to found the city of Thebes. Arriving in Bœotia, he halted and directed his men to obtain water from a spring for a libation to Zeus. The men

were killed by a golden-crested dragon, and Cadmus attacked the creature, first with a great rock and then with his spear, finally killing it. The beast is shown here just before Cadmus will pin it to the tree with his spear. Later, its teeth were sown in the ground in accordance with instructions from Athena, and from them grew the warriors who were finally to build the Cadmeia or citadel of Thebes.

This rare subject is not mentioned in Galt's list although it could have been confused with Jason killing the dragon, in the manner of Salvator Rosa. The same subject by West appears in another

53

drawing in pen and pencil, heightened in white on gray paper, in The British Museum (1858. 2.13.92), entitled a *Naked Figure Holding a Javelin.*
F.C.

Provenance
H. H. Margary, through inheritance from a descendant of the artist
Anonymous sale, Sotheby's, London, 22 January 1964, no. 5

53
General Kosciusko
Allen Memorial Art Museum, Oberlin College, Oberlin, Ohio
Oil on panel; 12⅝₁₆ x 17⅜ in.
Inscribed: *B. West/1797; Gen' Co. . . . osko, Lo. do.*

On June 8, 1797 Benjamin West, then President of the Royal Academy, was able to visit the Sablonière Hotel in Leicester Square, London, to meet the Polish patriot and general Thaddeus Kosciusko (1746-1817). Kosciusko had stopped in London for approximately two weeks from about May 30, 1797, en route for America, accompanied by other Polish officers. His plan was to return to the New World where he had fought in the American Revolution in 1776. West was received in the general's rooms where he found him reclining on a sofa surrounded by drawing materials, paper, and his crutch. Kosciusko's wounds, which he suffered as a leader of the Polish armies in the struggle for freedom from Russia in 1794, had not yet healed. After the defeat of the Polish armies at Maciejowice in 1794, Kosciusko was imprisoned for two years until the death of Catherine II. He had suffered extensively,

and his wounds were badly treated. He had been slashed in the head with a sabre, and the wound was bandaged in black. His right leg was injured by a cannon shot, and he was unable to walk without the aid of his crutch. For longer distances, he had to be carried.

Joseph Farington, chronicler of the artistic events of the early 19th century, describes West's visit to the lodgings of the Polish hero in detail: "June 8/1797/. West saw General Kosciuszko yesterday. He went with Dr. Bancroft and Trumbull. —The genl was laid on a Couch—had a black silk band round his head—& was drawing landscapes, which is his principal amusement.—He speaks English & appears to be abt. 45 years of age; and about 5 feet 8 inches high. One side of him is paralytic—the effects of a Cannon Shot passing over him—He had 2 stabbs in his back—one cut in his head.—He asked abt. the meeting at the Nore —is agitated by the thoughts of revolutions and wishes to proceed to America where He expects to find peace. He proposes going to Bristol and from thence to America (Philadelphia). The Emperor of Russia behaved kindly to him—gave him an estate & then allowed him to sell it which He did for abt. 10,000.—He lodges at the Hotel in Leicester fields formerly the house of Hogarth—West shewed me a small picture which He yesterday began to paint from memory of Kosciusko on a Couch." The painting mentioned by Farington is no doubt the Oberlin picture. It is possible that West undertook the portrait from memory because Kosciusko was too modest or too self-conscious to allow himself to be sketched. We know that Kosciusko refused to have his portrait taken by a Swedish artist, and one report states that Cosway, who did a portrait of him, worked through a keyhole.

Such a retreating, glamorous, and at the same time wounded hero must have created a stir in the fashionable London world of that moment, and a portrait of the man would have been of the greatest interest. This was no doubt part of West's motivation in painting this uncommissioned work, and he probably also foresaw possibilities in the

sales of an engraving. His personal interest in the subject and his vivid response to the actual presence of the man must account for the unusually high standard of quality, rich variety of textures, resonant color, and fluidity and delicacy of brushwork.

West has represented the hero surrounded by albums and paper which he used to draw landscapes. West has emphasized this by showing a low window behind the couch with an attractive view of St. Paul's and the Thames in the background. The weapon on the table in the foreground is a sword of honor, presented to him by the Whig Club of England sometime in the first week of his stay in London.

Kosciusko is shown with an abstracted gaze, touching his wounded head. The gaze and gesture are reflective, suggesting his remembrance of the battle fought for his people and the long years of imprisonment which followed. The sentiment of reverie and his suggestion of reflection on the human condition are key elements of the romantic figural piece. Here, it is shown in a guise which relates to a tradition in England of horizontal portraits of famous men. The most sensational of these is the *Death of Chatterton* (Tate Gallery) by Henry Wallis (1830-1916). For others, see no. 47.
F.C.

Provenance
The artist and his heirs (sale, Robins, London, 25 May 1829, no. 138, bt. Bone)
H. P. Bone (died 1855) (the miniature painter was in close contact with the Neeld Family, owners of a large collection of pictures by West)
L. W. Neeld, Grittleton House near Chippenham, Wiltshire (sale, Christie's, London, 13 July 1945, no. 175, *General Kosciussko as a Refugee in London,* bt. Spink)
Spink & Co., London
M. Knoedler & Co., New York, 1945
Allen Memorial Art Museum, Oberlin, Ohio, 1946

1739/40?-1816

Exhibitions
Royal Academy, 1798, no. 618
*Pictures and Drawings by the Late Benjamin West, Esq.,
President of the Royal Academy,* London, 1823, no. 63
The Arts in America in the Eighteenth Century, Allen
Memorial Art Museum, Oberlin, 1946, no. 18
From Colony to Nation, The Art Institute of Chicago,
1949, no. 130
They Gave Us Freedom, Colonial Williamsburg and
the College of William and Mary, Williamsburg, Virginia,
1951, no. 48
The French in America, The Detroit Institute of Arts,
1951, no. 244
Paintings and Drawings from Five Centuries (Allen
Memorial Art Museum), Knoedler Galleries, New York,
1954, no. 54
The Century of Mozart, Nelson Gallery—Atkins Museum,
Kansas City, 1956, no. 106
Masterworks from American University Museums,
Malmo, etc., (College Art Association of America),
1956-57, number varies
Art Across America, Munson-Williams-Proctor Institute,
Utica, New York, 1960, no. 109
Style, Truth and the Portrait, The Cleveland Museum
of Art, 1963, no. 47
Treasures from the Allen Memorial Art Museum,
Minneapolis Institute of Arts, 1966

References
Joel Barlow, *The Columbiad,* Philadelphia, 1809, II, 186
The Port Folio, VI, no. 6, December 1811, p. 552
Farington, ed. Greig, I, 209-10
Rudolf Wittkower, "An Exhibition of American Art in
Chicago," *Burlington,* XCI, 1949, p. 254
Virgil Barker, *American Painting: History and
Interpretation,* New York, 1950, pp. 204-17
Chloe Hamilton, "A Portrait of General Kosciusko by
Benjamin West," *Allen Memorial Art Museum Bulletin,*
IX no. 5, Spring 1952, pp. 81-91 (reprinted in Polish:
"Portret Kósciuszki pędzla Benjamina Westa," *Biuletyn
Historii Sztuki,* XXV, 1963, pp. 77ff)
Wolfgang Stechow, *Catalogue of European and
American Paintings and Sculpture in the Allen Memorial
Art Museum,* Oberlin, 1967, pp. 161-63

The exact birthplace of Towne, who was a landscapist in oil and watercolor, is unknown although it may have been Exeter. He may have studied at Shipley's School located in Castle Court, Strand, London, along with the view painter William Pars (1742-82), Richard Cosway, and Ozias Humphry (1742-1810). In any case he was a close friend of these members of Shipley's School in the mid-1750s. His early works were exhibited at the Society of Artists from 1762 to 1763 and the Free Society from 1763 to 1766, but he only began to exhibit at the Royal Academy in 1775. Until his departure for Rome in 1780, he worked primarily in the area of Exeter, drawing views of country houses and teaching the children of their owners, and he was to become an important member of the cultured society which centered on this capital of Devonshire.

In 1777 he made a tour of Wales that was a turning point in his career, especially for his use of watercolor, the medium in which he was to excel. He visited London from time to time, generally sending his works to the exhibitions through the agency of a friend and not listing his place of habitation. These seclusive habits characterized his activities for the rest of his life. In 1780 he visited Rome, a trip which was the climactic event of his career, there creating the series of splendid watercolors which were later bequeathed to The British Museum. Remaining in Italy only a year, he returned with John "Warwick" Smith (1749-1831) by way of Switzerland where he drew the stark views of Alpine rocks and glaciers whose primitive austerity strike a new note in the art of English landscape. After his return he spent more of each year in London, though remaining in close contact with his Devonshire friends and receiving the patronage of Devonshire people. In 1786 he travelled to the Lake Country with his former pupil James White and a friend, John Merivale. He married Jeannette Hillisberg, a ballet dancer, and in 1807 finally moved his household from Exeter to London; unfortunately, his wife died soon after in April 1808 at the age of twenty-seven.

Towne was a candidate for A.R.A. in 1776, 1797, 1798, and 1803, but he never succeeded in being elected. The lack of appreciation and the appelation of a provincial drawing master applied by the Academicians was a blow which left him embittered. In his later years he continued to exhibit regularly at the Academy or the British Institution, generally sending oils rather than watercolors, which suggests that he still retained ambitions to become an Academician. When he died in London on July 7, 1816, he bequeathed his Roman drawings to The British Museum and left his other sketchbooks and possessions to the Merivale family and to James White. These works tended to remain in seclusion with their descendants until A. P. Oppé published them in the 20th century.

His art was not greatly appreciated in his own day, perhaps because he did not cultivate the fashionable devices of the picturesque. In fact he often deliberately opposed picturesque techniques to achieve more stark and bold effects. In thus simplifying his visual impressions, he tended to concentrate on individual shapes fluently outlined with the pen and unusual spatial juxtapositions which jar one into surprise when compared with those of his contemporaries. It is this very concentration on pattern and bold effects which led to a reawakening of interest in Towne in the 20th century.
F.C.

Bibliography
Winslow Jones, "Francis Towne, Landscape Painter,"
Notes and Gleanings, III no. 26, February 15, 1890,
pp. 17-18
A. P. Oppé, "Francis Towne, Landscape Painter,"
Walpole Society, VIII, 1919-20, pp. 95-126
Adrian Bury, *Francis Towne, Lone Star of Water-colour
Painting,* London, 1962

54

54
Hyde Park, Study of a Tree on the Ground
(In Hyde Park)

The Toledo Museum of Art, Toledo, Ohio, Museum
Purchase 1954
Watercolor on paper; 17¾ x 14½ in.
Inscribed: *F. Towne Delt. 1797;* verso: *This Drawing
taken in Hyde Park June 19th, 1797 on the spot by
Francis Towne, No. 114 New Bond Street, London;*
on mount: collector's mark of G. Davis (Lugt 757a)

Iolo Williams wrote that there are three peaks in
Towne's career, his trip to Wales in 1777, to Italy
and Switzerland in 1780-81, and to the Lake Country
in 1786. Although his Italian and Swiss views are
the climax of his artistic production, his trip to
Wales resulted in a new and bold vision of the stark
grandeur of rocks, water, and cliffs. Even before
this journey Towne was highly accomplished as a
watercolorist, keenly perceptive about the value
of a fluent pen, and aware of the effectiveness of
large areas of flat-colored wash. However, an
almost geometrical boldness comes into his works
in the late 1770s, and this is simplified into even
bolder and grander compositions through his view
of the Swiss Alps on his return from Italy.

Towne's later works, after his return to London,
have received less attention than his Roman and
Swiss drawings, but this watercolor shows the high
standard that he maintained. It has been called the
most beautiful of Towne's studies of trees. That
Towne himself valued it as one of his finest
drawings is suggested by the fact that it is one of

the two London views included in his exhibition
of 1805.

The trees are massed in a highly original manner
so that a series of trunks support a complex and
somewhat undefined plethora of branches. The
twisted limbs and trunks, which become veins in
an organism of living verdure, suggest drawings of
early 19th-century German artists where the
rampant and insuppressible growth of living plants
is symbolic of primeval energies and anticipates
the symbolic attributes of plant growth in
19th-century art theory. This writhing mass of limbs
and leaves is pushed into the middle ground by a
fallen trunk at the front, showing the taut, gnarled
remains of an ancient tree now dead and rotting.

Although Towne uses here a fallen trunk and
shaggy trees, objects favored in picturesque
landscapes, the boldness of this design would not
have pleased advocates of the picturesque. One is
not allowed to wind into the composition on a
gentle, serpentine path. On the contrary, the path
is blocked by an aggressive log lying across the
entire foreground. The flat planes of green and
blue tint, outlined economically with a stroke of the
pen, and the few touches of yellow would not have
possessed enough variety for a picturesque taste.
This bold disparagement of fashionable formulas is
particularly attractive in Towne's intellect and art
today, even though it was not understood well by
his colleagues and contemporaries.
F.C.

Provenance
Gilbert Davis, London

Exhibitions
Francis Towne, Gallery in Lower Brook Street, Grosvenor
Square, London, 1805, no. 17 *(Hyde Park, Study
of a Tree on the Ground)*
*British Water-colours and Drawings from the Gilbert
Davis Collection,* Arts Council, London, 1949, p. 5,
no. 10 *(The Study of Hyde Park)*

References
Oppé, *Walpole Society,* VII, 119-20, p. 98 n.
W. T. Whitley, *Art in England, 1800-1820,* Cambridge,
England/New York, 1928, p. 93
Bury, pp. 95, 103, 118, repr. opp. p. 103, pl. XLII

1740-1779

The son of a miller and customs collector and the nephew of a painter, Mortimer showed early aptitude as an artist and was sent to study under Thomas Hudson in London where he was a fellow pupil of Joseph Wright of Derby. Following the pattern established for art students of the 1750s, he worked with Thomas Hudson (1701-79), then moved to the Duke of Richmond's sculpture gallery where he studied under Giovanni-Battista Cipriani (1727-85) and Joseph Wilton (1722-1803) and was then accepted as a member of the Academy in St. Martin's Lane.

In 1763 he won a first prize at the Society of Artists for a drawing, and the next year, in competition with Romney, he received a first prize for the best historical painting, *St. Paul Converting the Britons,* later presented to the Church of High Wycombe, Buckinghamshire. He became a member of the Incorporated Society of Artists in 1763 and vice president ten years later. During this period he knew Zoffany and was intimately connected with the theater. His riotous life gained him a notorious reputation. Strong, attractive, and frankly vain, he laid the foundation for a reputation of artistic genius, and Cunningham, continuing the posthumous tendency to romanticize Mortimer's personality, referred to him as a fascinating and dangerous companion.

At Brocket Hall in 1771 Thomas Jones, Francis Wheatley, and James Durno (c. 1745-95) assisted him in painting one of the ceilings for Lord Melbourne. He married Jane Hurrell, daughter of a farmer, in 1775 and moved to Aylesbury, Buckinghamshire, settling down and painting works in a moralizing vein such as the *Progress of Virtue* (Tate Gallery) and a companion series, the *Progress of Vice.*

Returning to London, he exhibited for the first time at the Royal Academy in 1778, and was created an A.R.A. in 1779, three months before his death. Greatly admired during his life and after his death, Mortimer was described as a latter-day Salvator Rosa, whose works he imitated. He was considered the embodiment of the brilliant and attractive artistic genius marred by indulgence, an image which appealed to his contemporaries. His imagination was described in the *Universal Magazine* of May 1791 (p. 323) as marked by visions of sublimity which could penetrate with a gloomy enthusiasm the darkest recesses of horror. He was disliked intensely by Fuseli whose genius was of a less graceful and more sensational variety.

Mortimer was one of the highly imaginative and facile artists of his day, approaching Blake in inventiveness but less subjective and mystical. He was interested in unusual subjects apparently because they were esoteric or exotic in their own right. Nebuchadnezzar in the desert with his talons and raven locks was drawn and engraved by him and later by Blake. He also took subjects from the art of the past, portraying Salvator Rosa as a warrior seated in a landscape and studying a book of his own etchings. A series of illustrations to Chaucer and subjects from Cervantes, along with a series of sea monsters, gives some idea of the variety of his intellectual fare. Subjects relating to early English history, such as the *Death of Sir Phillip Sidney,* the *Discovery of Prince Arthur's Tomb,* and esoteric subjects from ancient literature such as *Sextus Pompeius Consulting Erichtho before the Battle of Pharsalia* were also painted and engraved by him.

Frequently Mortimer's works have moral overtones which relate them to the tradition of Hogarth, yet make them as modern as the works of Greuze.

Caricaturing prints by Mortimer and also his figural drawings influenced Gillray and Rowlandson, among numerous others. His vivid conceptions, infused with infinite grace, his unusual choice of subject matter, and his facility as a draftsman, reveal him as one of the distinctive and highly attractive figural artists of the period.
F.C.

Bibliography

A Series of Twelve Heads Illustrative of the Characters in Shakespear's Plays. Designed and Etched by John Hamilton Mortimer, London, Thomas Palser, 1812
Mortimer's Works, A Collection of Fifty Historical Designs, London, Thomas Palser, c. 1816
Geoffrey Grigson, ''Painters of the Abyss,'' *Architectural Review,* CVIII, October 1950, pp. 215-20
Gilbert Benthall, *John Hamilton Mortimer, A. R. A., His Pictures, Drawings and Engraved Works,* typewritten manuscript, 1959, Victoria and Albert Museum, London
Gilbert Benthall, *A Selection from the Catalogue of Pictures, Drawings, and Etchings by John Hamilton Mortimer, A. R. A.,* typewritten manuscript, 1959, Victoria and Albert Museum, London
Gilbert Benthall, *Draft Introduction to an Exhibition of Paintings, Drawings and Etchings by John Hamilton Mortimer, A. R. A.,* typewritten manuscript, 1959, Victoria and Albert Museum, London

55
Fishermen Being Robbed of Their Catch by Bandit
Walter A. Brandt
Pen and brown ink; 11¼ x 15½ in.
1772

In 1772 Mortimer exhibited at the Society of Artist a drawing in pen and ink entitled *Banditti Robbing Fishermen.* The drawing was listed as a companio to another horizontal composition by Mortimer entitled *At Dinner.* The latter was engraved by Samuel Ireland (who owned it in 1784) and retitled *Banditti Regaling.* Benthall was the first to identify tentatively the Ireland engraving with the exhibite drawing of 1772. The compositions of these two works would have served nicely as pendants sinc

they are essentially similar, although reversed arrangements. A slightly later drawing, entitled *Fishermen* (private collection, Detroit), was exhibited at the Society of Artists in 1774 (no. 174). But this drawing, later in the collection of Payne Knight when it was engraved by R. Blyth, shows only fishermen bringing in their catch. Ireland also engraved *A Captain of Banditti and his Family,* showing the seashore and a large catch of fish, a subject related to those above. Indeed, numerous imaginative subjects using similar bucolic characters of a vaguely military type were drawn, painted, and engraved by Mortimer. Probably they should be thought of as important background for Gainsborough's and Reynolds' "fancy" pictures. Later Mortimer gives them moralizing subjects, and they then enter a different intellectual world. These scenes of the activities of bandits refer to the life or presumed life of peasants and outlaws in the Italian Abruzzi and in the area of Naples. The costumes of the soldiers frequently derive from the etchings of Salvator Rosa, and the picturesque individuals are the bandits who appear in a very few pictures actually by Rosa. These are later found in pictures attributed to him, in works by Marco Ricci and in Richard Wilson's early landscapes.

The legend that Salvator Rosa spent time in his youth in company with bandits, a legend that must have influenced artists like George Morland to live with gypsies, is reflected in Lady Morgan's *Life of Salvator Rosa:* "The event which most singularly marked the fearless enterprises of Salvator in the Abruzzi, was his captivity by the banditti, who alone inhabited them, and his temporary (and it is said voluntary) association with those fearful men. That he did for some time live among the picturesque outlaws, whose portraits he has multiplied without end there is no doubt . . ."
F.C.

Provenance
Anonymous sale, Christie's, London, 8 December 1964, no. 128
Walter A. Brandt, London, 1964

References
Lady Morgan, *The Life and Times of Salvator Rosa,* London, 1824, I, 108
Benthall, *John Hamilton Mortimer, A. R. A., His Pictures, Drawings, and Engraved Works,* p. 118

56
Head of Beatrice
Lent Anonymously
Pen in black ink; 13 x 10⅝ in. diam.
1775

The subject is taken from Shakespeare's farce *Much Ado About Nothing.* Beatrice is a creature of mirth and a tease constantly engaged with Benedick in a warfare of words. After a complicated set of intrigues in which the marriage of the lovers Claudio and Hero is allowed to take place, Beatrice and Benedick are persuaded to marry.

Mortimer's Shakespearian heads represent a spectrum of human types drawn from the Elizabethan playwright's works. As such they are unusual in the history of Shakespeare illustrations. More than any other commentary they illustrate the maxim which was to become familiar in this period that Shakespeare is like life, therefore an excellent source for artists. They were extremely popular in the engravings and were frequently copied by amateur draftsmen. The characters selected were the following: Cassandra, Shylock, Caliban, Bardolph, Falstaff, York, Edgar, Ophelia, Richard III, Lear, Beatrice, and the Poet from *Midsummer Night's Dream.* Richard III stood for royalty, Ophelia is the pathetic heroine, Cassandra the tragic heroine, Edgar the hero, Lear the pathetic hero, Shylock the scoundrel, etc. Beatrice is the embodiment of comedy and has all the fanciful characteristics of such a creature but lacks

intellectual qualities. Her seemingly fanciful costume is not so imaginative when compared with the dress of the period. Turbans, feathers, jewels, pieces of satin, and ropes of pearls were all a part of the fashionable coiffure of the 1770s. *Beatrice* is very much *en vogue.* Even the neckline is right, and the lace frill is conceivable for the period.

At present four of Mortimer's original drawings for the Shakespearian series are known. Three of these, *Shylock* (Dyce 629) and *Edgar* (Dyce 630), from the Dyce Bequest, and *Richard III,* from the Benthall Bequest, are in the Victoria and Albert Museum. A related drawing, a study in black chalk of the head of *Bardolph,* recently purchased by the Huntington Art Gallery, San Marino, may be an early study for the engraving of the same subject in this series. Another drawing, of *Richard III,* in red and black chalk (13 by 10 in.), in the

collection of Nicolas Powell, was exhibited in 1964 in the exhibition *Shakespeare in Art* (no. 28), organized by the Arts Council of Great Britain. With the exception of *Richard III* in the Victoria and Albert Museum, all of these drawings are reversed in the final engravings.
F.C.

Provenance
The artist (sale, Christie's London, 25 March 1808, no. 22)
Sale, Hodgson's, London, 21 November 1960, no. 561, *100 Drawings, Etchings and Engravings by Mortimer* (bt. Colnaghi)
Private collection, 1961

Exhibitions
The Society of Artists of Great Britain, 1775, no. 179
William Blake and his Circle, Henry E. Huntington Library and Art Gallery, San Marino, California, 1966, no. 44

References
A Series of Twelve Heads, no. 2
Mortimer's Works, no. ?
Benthall, *Selection from the Catalogue,* p. 132, no. 1a

Reproductions
Engraved by John Hamilton Mortimer, 15 March 1776
Etched by Burnet Reading, 1820

57
Bandit Taking Up His Post
The Detroit Institute of Arts, Director's Discretionary Fund
Oil on fine canvas, mounted on panel; 14 x 10⅛ in.
Inscribed with monogram
c. 1778

The painting of a soldier taking up his post is related to the print *Banditti Taking up his Post* dedicated to Sir Joshua Reynolds and engraved in 1778. There are certain differences between the print and the painting; an extra figure is introduced into the painted background, and the setting is somewhat changed. The engraving is not reversed from the painting. Benthall recorded a *Banditti Taking up his Post* (oil on canvas, 15½ by 12 in.), related to the 1778 engraving, in the Pulteney Hotel, Bath. A rough sketch made of that picture, which has now disappeared and may be identical with the Detroit painting, is in the Benthall manuscripts in the Victoria and Albert Museum.

The Detroit *Bandit* is related to a series of paintings and engravings in a small, vertical format which date from the same period. These are the *Banditti at Market,* dated 1778 (collection Brian Reade, London) and *Banditti Gambling* (formerly National Trust, Overbecks Museum, Salcombe, Devonshire, now lost). Although the dimensions do not correspond exactly, these appear to form a series of the type of the *Progress of Virtue* in The Tate Gallery or the horizontal series, which was engraved, of the various activities and death of a bandit. Both bandit series were inspired by the art of Salvator Rosa, especially his fifty-five etchings of soldiers in various military costumes and positions. Based in general on Rosa's types, but without landscapes, these bandits are transformed into a new idiom by Mortimer. The true subject is almost always a moral and psychological one deriving ultimately from such works by Hogarth as *The Rake's Progress.* In Mortimer's *Banditti at Market,* two men are shown leering at a young damsel, who, incidentally, has a basket of eggs for sale. *Banditti Gambling* shows two men rolling dice but holding

57

their hands ready, near their swords.

Although the subject of this painting is not historical but essentially humble, intimate, and moral, with a limited study of psychological interplay, the characters are highly picturesque and based on a colorful tradition. Mortimer's characters are the most colorful and the most theatrical of the period. They also reflect the incongruous combination of the exotic and the moralizing with a psychological twist which appears in certain kinds of theatrical performances of the period. John Cleland's *Tombo-Chiqui: or, the American Savage* of 1758, James Dance's *The Witches, or Harlequin Cherokee,* a pantomime of

1762 written under the pseudonym of James Love, or an anonymous pantomime of 1760, *The Siege of Quebec; or, Harlequin Engineer* even in their titles give some idea of the theatrical background of Mortimer's subjects. These were largely interludes, pantomimes, comedies, farces, or comic operas, and are generally light and unusual in flavor with a slightly moralizing, yet unpenetrating presentation of character. Mortimer's *Bandit* should probably be thought of in similar terms. Dr. Joseph W. Donohue of Princeton University, who has brought my attention to this material, is currently preparing a study of Mortimer which should clarify his relationship to the theater of this period.
F.C.

Provenance
(?) Pulteney Hotel, Bath
Nathan Chaikin, Paris
The Detroit Institute of Arts, 1966

References
Benthall, *Selection from the Catalogue,* no. 20
Benthall, *Mortimer,* p. 129

58
Fish Devouring Mussels (Fish Spewing up Mussels)
Mr. D. L. T. Oppé
Watercolor and pen; 11⅛ x 16¾ in.
c. 1778

No. 58 shows three fish, perhaps dolphins, on the beach. One has greedily stuffed himself and is fast asleep, out of the waters. Two others are eating voraciously from a group of mussels, oysters, starfish, and other sea life. Both feasting fish are overly fat, and continue to partake in gluttonous fashion in a fierce and unpleasant repast. They derive from Alciati's Emblem no. CLVII which represents a dolphin ejected from the sea onto a rocky shore where sprigs and branches of trees

58

bend over the water. The epigram which heads Alciati's entry tells that dolphins on the earth, when they are out of their familiar element, refer to those who judge too ambitiously what they do not know and who match their ignorance by striving beyond their powers. Alciati's discussion is headed by the lines spoken by the dolphin, "Flood tide has forced me, a dolphin all unwilling on the beach, an example of how great are the perils of the faithless sea."

In his commentary on those who are ejected by the sea, Alciati draws an analogy between the ferocity of the sea and the ferocious human passions which, he says, are led by Satan; gluttons and gormandizers who are pampered and dissipated ferociously compound the error of their own gluttony by further dissipation. Yet in their soft flesh is the worm of putridity which is ultimately the source of their own destruction. The subject of the drawing, then, is that the flesh, like the fierce sea, has within it the seeds of self-destruction.

The image and the moral subject are in keeping with Mortimer's other works of his last period which often have bizarre and picturesque characters who dramatize down-to-earth moralizing themes.

Although published in 1942 by A. P. Oppé as by Rowlandson, this is a typical pen and watercolor landscape drawing by John Mortimer. The sheet which compares most closely is the *Landscape with Crows Near a Dead Body on a Seashore* in the album of Mortimer drawings in The British Museum. Exactly the kind of pen lines seen here appear in the drawing of a struggling triton and sea serpent in The British Museum (B.M. no. 189.c.10.no. 28) and in another study for this same group in the collection of Walter Brandt, London. The style of this drawing relates to Mortimer's last period and is intimately connected with the series of etchings of sea monsters which was published in 1778 and dedicated to Sir Joshua Reynolds.

The former attribution of this drawing to Rowlandson is understandable in view of his reliance, especially in his early works, on Mortimer's style. However, the unique subject of this work, as well as the technique, places it in Mortimer's intellectual sphere rather than in Rowlandson's—two entirely different worlds.
F.C.

Provenance
R. Graves
A. P. Oppé (died 1957)

Exhibitions
The Paul Oppé Collection, Royal Academy, London, 1958, no. 242

References
Alciati, *Emblemata,* CLVII
A. P. Oppé, "Rowlandson the Surprising," *Studio,* November 1942, p. 158 (as Rowlandson)

Philip James de Loutherbourg

1740-1812

Born at Strasbourg in Vieux-Marché-aux-Vins Street, Loutherbourg was the son of Philippe-Jacques Lautterburger who belonged to a family of painters from Basle, Switzerland. Philippe-Jacques *fils* entered the Protestant School in Strasbourg in 1749, but little is known of him before that time. He began his studies in Paris with Carle Van Loo (1705-65), the painter of historical subjects. In 1763 Diderot wrote that he had been studying for five or six years with François-Joseph Casanova (1727-1802), the landscape and battle painter who came to Paris about 1757-58. In 1763 he first exhibited a *Cavalry Combat* at the Academy in Paris. This subject is within Casanova's idiom, and it received the praise of Diderot. He continued to send works to the exhibitions and also began to receive important commissions, among them one from the Prince de Condé in 1765. He became a full member of the French Royal Academy in 1767. Between 1765 and 1775, he collaborated in the illustrations of the six-volume *Fables* of La Fontaine edited by Tessard. At the same time, he was praised for his skill by Michel Dandré-Bardon (1700-83), who recommended him for admission to the Academy of Painting and Sculpture at Marseilles in 1768. His marital life was neither happy nor settled. Although he had at least six children, he abandoned his family in 1771 and sailed for England. In London Louis Monnet, *concessionaire* of the Opéra Comique in Paris, introduced him to David Garrick, in a letter of October 21, 1771, as a painter who excelled in marine painting, landscapes in the style of Berchem, and in battle scenes of the sort learned from Casanova.

Garrick was to become Loutherbourg's first patron in London and, in the exhibition of 1774, Loutherbourg exhibited two portraits of the actor, one as *Don Juan* in Beaumont and Fletcher's *The Chances,* and the other as *Richard III.* He was engaged to paint decor for the performances at Drury Lane after Garrick left in 1776, only terminating his association in 1781. In that year he presented a private exhibition of his *Eidophusikon* which was a panorama of figures and landscapes moved by machinery. He was made R.A. in 1780, at one of the most regular and productive periods of his life.

In 1787 Alessandro Cagliostro (1743-95), a former acquaintance of Loutherbourg's, returning from the affair of the diamond necklace in Paris and imprisonment in the Bastille, came to live with him at his home in Hammersmith Terrace. There, Cagliostro gave Loutherbourg lessons in alchemy and healing by means of physical magnetism. Loutherbourg became so intrigued with its possibilities that he took this up as a profession for a time, but the adventure was finally not a financial success, and he returned to his painting in 1789.

Accompanied by James Gillray, he was sent to Flanders in 1793 to record the deeds of the Duke of York who was in command of the British forces. The result was a large picture, *The Grand Attack on Valenciennes* (collection Lady Hesketh, Easton Neston), based in part on Gillray's drawings and shown in the Historic Gallery, Pall Mall, in 1794. He also painted a companion, again based on researches in drawings by Gillray, *The Victory of Lord Howe on June 1, 1794* (National Maritime Museum, Greenwich) which derives from Copley's *Study for the Siege of Gibraltar* (nos. 45 and 46). In 1807 he became history painter to the Duke of Gloucester, but his health was failing as a result of extended attacks of rheumatism. His last picture, *Landscape with Animals,* was sent to the Academy in 1811, the year before he died.
F.C.

Bibliography
J. Guiffrey, "Philippe-Jacques Loutherbourg et sa femme," *Revue de l'art français,* IV, 1888, pp. 202-07
H. Stein, "Quelques particularités de la vie du peintre Philippe-Jacques Lauterbourg," *Bulletin de la Société de l'Histoire de l'Art Français,* 1915-17, pp. 85-96
A. Girodie, "Notes biographiques sur les peintres Louterbourg," *Archives Alsaciennes,* 1935, pp. 249-55
Geneviève Levallet-Haug, "Philippe-Jacques Louterbourg, 1740-1812," *Trois siècles d'art alsacien 1648-1948,* Strasbourg-Paris, 1948, pp. 77-133

59
The Falls of the Rhine at Schaffhausen
Victoria and Albert Museum, London
Oil on canvas; 53 x 78 in.
Inscribed: *P.I. de Louthbourgh*
c. 1775

Schaffhausen is the capital of the Swiss canton of that name in the northernmost part of Switzerland on the right bank of the Rhine. It is about sixty miles west of Basle, where Loutherbourg's father was born. The city is dominated by the fortress of Unnoth whose walls can be seen on the promontory at the upper right of this painting. Loutherbourg could have seen this spot on one of his travels before his departure for London. As in the case of *The Fête of the Tunny Fishers at Marseilles,* in The Metropolitan Museum, done after his arrival in England, he must have prepared drawings that later enabled him to transform a particularly picturesque view into a large-scale painting.

Loutherbourg was easily influenced by the artists with whom he came into contact, and the different periods of his art are readily distinguishable by his relationships with a given artist at any one moment. For example, his *Laborers Resting* of about 1800 (Strasbourg Museum) relies heavily on the art of George Morland. Certain of his battle scenes of the 1790s rely on Copley, and his early *Caravane en Marche* of 1764 (Musée de Marseille) derives from G. B. Castiglione as interpreted by Fragonard and Casanova with whom he had been working at the time. No. 59 still relies on Loutherbourg's style of

Contrast to Turner's same subject

59

painting in France; it recalls the superb landscapes
with cascades by Hubert Robert (1733-1808) and
Claude Joseph Vernet (1714-89) and should be
dated soon after his arrival in England.
F.C.

Provenance
Joshua Dixon
Bequeathed to the Bethnal Green Museum, 1886

References
Levallet-Haug, p. 108

60

A Midsummer's Afternoon, with a Methodist Preacher
The National Gallery of Canada, Ottawa
Oil on canvas; 38 x 49¾ in.
Inscribed: *P. de Loutherbourgh/1777*

Such scenes as this are described in Richard
Graves's interminable novel of 1772 entitled *The
Spiritual Quixote.* The hero Mr. Geoffrey Wildgoos
and his thickset little companion Jeremiah Tugwel
are characterized in a spirit of burlesque
approximating this scene in the open country whe
an itinerant preacher holds forth before a small
group of attentive listeners. The crying and shoutin
children, the attendant animals, horses, and
carriages, the inspired listeners, and the state of
the weather are all included in Graves's descriptic
of the travels and varied experiences of Geoffrey
Wildgoose. Loutherbourg has shown a wizened
beggar, the awkward country squire and his starin
fleshy wife, and the curious and fashionable folk
from the city, with animals prominently
participating. Such itinerant preachers with a
provocative rhetorical manner, which included
moving harangues on human weakness, were
actually to be found holding forth in the country.
The two most important were John Wesley and
George Whitefield, the latter caricatured by Grave

This painting was at one time called *Wesley
Preaching on a Green.* A note in the Burlington
Fine Arts Club exhibition catalogue states that the
preacher was painted over with a *polichinello*
when first purchased, and after cleaning, the figu
was identified as Wesley. But this is an unlikely
identification. Correspondingly, no specific
passage in the Graves novel is illustrated. Since i
was written only five years before the picture was
painted and continued to be widely read, it would
have been uppermost in people's minds, and the
connection with Geoffrey Wildgoose would have
been inescapable. Loutherbourg was drawing on
vocabulary of types probably developed in Franc
but soon after used by Rowlandson and Gillray, a
these can be seen in *The Fête of the Tunny Fisher*

at Marseilles (Metropolitan Museum, New York), to
which no. 60 is closely related. *The Tunny Fishers*
was probably undertaken soon after he came to
England and no doubt helped to establish him as a
painter of panoramic genre scenes of topical
interest, of which his *Eidophusikon* was a much
more complex example. A smaller version of this
composition was in the collection of John J. Egan
of Philadelphia in 1933.
F.C.

60

Provenance
Col. W. P. Tipping, Brasted Place, Kent
H. Avray Tipping, Harefield House, Harefield, Middlesex
(sale, Sotheby's, London, 10 December 1930, no. 83,
bt. Colnaghi)
The National Gallery of Canada, Ottawa, 1932

Exhibitions
Royal Academy, 1777, no. 216
Georgian England, Whitechapel Art Gallery, London,
1906, no. 130 *(John Wesley)*
Winter Exhibition, Burlington Fine Arts Club, London,
1927-28, no. 80
British Art, Royal Academy, London, 1934, no. 251
Loan Exhibition, Toronto Art Gallery, 1935, no. 43
English Masters, University of Western Ontario, London,
Ontario, 1952, unnumbered
Everyday Life, Carnegie Institute, Pittsburgh, 1954, no. 64
European Masters, Toronto Art Gallery, 1954, no. 39

References
William T. Whitley, *Artists and Their Friends in England,
1700-1799,* London, 1928, II, 351, pl. 7
"Pictures at the Burlington Fine Arts Club," *Country
Life,* LXIII, no. 1620, 4 February 1928, pp. 143-45
Sacheverell Sitwell, *Narrative Pictures,* New York/
London, 1937, pp. 53, 109, no. 82
Levallet-Haug, p. 103, pl. 4
R. H. Hubbard, *European Paintings in Canadian
Collections: Older Schools,* Toronto, 1956, pp. 128,
153, pl. lxi

1741-1806

Barry's father was a businessman who dabbled in building, innkeeping, and shipping. His wish that James, who was born in Cork in Ireland, would take over the seafaring aspect of the business failed after a few unhappy voyages. His early tutor was Dr. Joseph Fenn Sleigh, a close friend and schoolmate of Edmund Burke. In 1763 Barry travelled from Cork to exhibit a medieval Irish subject, *The Conversion by St. Patrick of the King of Cashel,* at the Dublin Society. The unusual and highly nationalistic subject secured him an introduction to Edmund Burke, an event which was to have lasting influence on his life since Burke was to become both his mentor and patron. Barry remained in Dublin and studied for a time at the Academy until he was invited by Burke to travel to London. There Burke introduced him to Sir Joshua Reynolds and found him employment with James Stuart (1713-88), then engaged in publishing the *Antiquities of Athens.* Barry was employed to copy the watercolor drawings in oil, giving him complete access to Stuart's drawings of Athenian sites and antiquities.

In October 1765 with the financial support of Edmund Burke, he embarked for Rome by way of Paris arriving in the late autumn of 1766. He became notorious for his bickering about the traffic in dubious antiquities carried on with well-to-do British travellers, seeing in it ultimate harm for the patronage of the fine arts in Britain. He also spent time studying the works of Raphael, Michelangelo, and particularly those of the Carracci in the Palazzo Farnese. After travelling to Naples in 1768 with

John Runciman, he left Rome in April 1770, going to Florence, Modena, Venice, Parma, and Bologna, before arriving in England in 1771. In Bologna he painted *Philoctetes* (Accademia Clementina, Bologna) and presented it to the Academy, whereupon he was made the only Irish Member of the Accademia Clementina before the 20th century.

Soon after his arrival in London, Barry, who was looked upon as one of the most promising young artists of his day, exhibited in 1771 the *Temptation of Adam and Eve* (National Gallery of Ireland, Dublin) which reveals a careful study of the figures of Annibale Carracci. He was elected a Royal Academician in February 1773. In 1775 he wrote the essay *An Inquiry into the Real and Imaginary Obstructions to the Acquisition of the Arts in England* which was sparked by the suppression of the plan to ornament the interior of St. Paul's and the Society of Arts, in the Adelphi, with figural compositions by contemporary artists. This document, highly critical of the state of artistic patronage, is only one intimation of a vociferous reactionary position assumed by Barry, winning the enmity of the mild-mannered Reynolds who appears actually to have hated him. In this essay, Barry insisted that British artists were capable of producing historical pictures of the highest order, and he set out to prove it by offering to ornament the walls of the Society of Arts with subjects of his own choice, single-handedly and without remuneration. The series, as he conceived it, depicted the rise of Greek civilization through the teachings and inspiration of Orpheus, patron of the arts, and illustrated how the arts would lead contemporary Britain to a similar state of flourishing economy and civilization. Grandiose in conception, this series is Barry's climactic artistic achievement. It was largely completed by 1783, and the fame it brought him is suggested by the fact that he was asked in 1782 to come to America to paint the exploits of George Washington, an invitation which he refused. In the same year he became Professor of Painting at the Royal Academy, but he was expelled in 1799 as a result of dissension with his fellow Academicians.

Barry was not a prolific painter. Apart from the works mentioned, some of his important paintings are the *Creation of Pandora* in the City of Manchester Art Galleries (Royal Academy 1791), *The Death of Wolfe* (The New Brunswick Museum St. John), *Lear with the Body of Cordelia* (1774, Tate Gallery), and the *Self Portrait* in the National Gallery of Ireland, Dublin.

Although a personality of great intelligence and enthusiasm, Barry was often more interested in intricate intellectual programs than in the purely visual matter of painting. His elaborate series in the Adelphi, built on the theme of the uses for British commerce which would arise from the cultivation of the arts, tends to be more conceptually intriguing than artistically satisfying. The idea had been important throughout the 18th century in English literature and thus was not completely original with Barry. These works have numerous innuendoes and a haunting ability to slip from one level of reality to another which recalls the Farnese ceiling and the 17th-century interest in allegory more than the concurrent levels of reality which characterize the potent visual epigrams of William Blake. The truly creative ideas lending energy to the art of the romantic period, the fascination with the minutiae of men's lives in the past, and the endless involvement with the ever new information of the senses as it affects visual experience are foreign Barry's Adelphi series.

F.C.

Bibliography
James Barry, *The Works of James Barry . . . Historical Painter,* 2 vols., London, 1809
Ralph N. Wornum, *Lectures on Painting, by . . . Barry, Opie, and Fuseli,* London, 1848
Thomas Bodkin, "James Barry," *Apollo,* pt. I, XXXII December 1940, pp. 144-47; pt. II, XXXIII, January 1941, pp. 1-5, 27
Geoffrey Grigson, "Painters of the Abyss," *Architectural Review,* CVIII, October 1950, pp. 215-20
Robert R. Wark, *James Barry,* unpublished Ph.D. dissertation submitted to Harvard University, Cambridge, Mass., 1952
Robert R. Wark, "The Iconography and Date of

GS proislews of Michelangelo influence

James Barry's Self-Portrait in Dublin,'' *Burlington,* XCVI, 1954, pp. 153-54
Robert R. Wark, ''A Note on James Barry and Edmund Burke,'' *JWCI,* XVII, 1954, pp. 382-84

61
Male Nude
The Royal Society of Arts, London
Ink and white chalk; 21 x 13 in.
Inscribed: *James Barry R.A.*
c. 1778-83

It has been suggested by Wark that this drawing prepares for an *ecce homo* or similar subject never finally undertaken by Barry. However, it seems likely that it is an alternative idea for one of the semi-nude heroes in Barry's *Crowning the Victors at Olympia,* one of the two 42-foot long canvases in the Society of Arts in the Adelphi, London. Behind a group of figures recalling the Panathenaic Procession on the Parthenon frieze, and with a rearing horse and rider drawn directly from that relief, is a view of the Parthenon itself. In the foreground a procession of heroes is crowned and given victors' palms. Barry would have found drawings of the Parthenon frieze and building in the materials with which he worked when employed by ''Athenian'' Stuart.

If such a pose as this had not been of such general use since the Renaissance, one would be tempted to see in the unusually high right shoulder, the deep incline of the head, and the rich invention of the arms crossing before the body, a reminiscence of such a figure as that on slab XII of the west frieze of the Parthenon. Apparently Barry had planned to use this figure in the frieze of victors, standing with a palm already in his hand. This is one of two studies of this model. The other, shown

61

from a slightly different point of view, is now in the Royal Academy, London. However, this figure was rejected from the final composition altogether.

By comparison with other known Barry drawings, this sheet is executed with care and refinement. Although the highly individual use of parallel lines and cross-hatching characterize his drawings throughout his career, the very fine pen is generally associated with his earlier drawing style. The

lighting, which is almost as delicate as candlelight, has echoes of Italy and especially of Guercino, whose works Barry would have studied in Bologna and who was greatly admired at this time. Robert Wark has doubted that the signature is Barry's own inscription.
F.C.

Provenance
Deposited by the artist in the Royal Society of Arts, London

References
Wark, p. 210, no. 23
Dora Wiebenson, ''Subjects from Homer's *Iliad* in Neoclassical Art,'' *Art Bulletin,* XLVI, 1964, pp. 23-37

62
Satan Calling up his Legions
Trustees of The British Museum
Indian ink wash and reed pen; 27 x 19½ in.
Inscribed: *J. Barry, R.A., P.P., invt.;* verso: *Haviland Burke Collection. Christies July 1852*
c. 1790-95

The scene illustrates the first section of Milton's *Paradise Lost* where Satan stands on the fiery lake calling to his numbed brethren to assist him in establishing a new angelic kingdom after their fall from grace.

> . . . On the beach
> Of that enflamed sea he stood, and call'd
> His legions, Angel forms, who lay entranc'd
> Thick as autumnal leaves, that strow the brooks
> In Vallombrosa . . .
> He call'd so loud, that all the hollow deep
> of Hell resounded . . .
> Awake, arise, or be for ever fall'n.
> They heard, and were abash'd, and up
> they sprung . . .

62

Satan is shown at the brink of the fiery lake with his attendants coming together, and they, in turn, are calling forth others with their trumpets. It is very close to Fuseli's treatment of the same subject. In fact, Collins Baker has pointed out that the first edition of Milton's *Paradise Lost* (1688) with engravings by Sir John Baptist Medina (1655/60-1711) established the subjects selected by the later illustrators up to and including those of Blake. His engravings were used again and again in publications of the text until 1784. Medina also used this subject, *Satan Awakens his Legions,* to illustrate the first book. Indeed, the engraving style

of Medina appears to have influenced Barry's, Blake's, and Fuseli's compositions and drawing manner. This drawing in particular reflects the style of certain of Medina's plates, and serves to explain the close connection between Barry's, Fuseli's, and Sir Thomas Lawrence's representations of the subject.
F.C.

Provenance
(?) Thomas Haviland Burke (The drawing is not listed in the catalogue of the sale referred to in the inscription on the verso)
J. H. Anderdon, London
Given to The British Museum, London, 1868

References
Laurence Binyon, *Catalogue of Drawings by British Artists . . . in the British Museum,* London, 1898, I, 77, no. 12
C. H. Collins Baker, "Some Illustrators of Milton's *Paradise Lost* (1688-1850)," *The Library,* fifth series, III, January-September, 1948, pp. 1-21, 101-19
Wark, pp. 64, 196 no. 19a, 204 no. 7
Gert Schiff, "Johann Heinrich Füsslis Milton-Galerie," *Schweizerisches Institut für Kunstwissenschaft Zürich,* Schriften, Zürich/Stuttgart, no. 5, 1963, pp. 46-48

Reproductions
Engraved by James Barry without date or inscription, 29½ x 19¾ in.

63
Jupiter and Juno on Mount Ida
Sheffield City Art Galleries, Presented by the Sheffield Art Collections Fund
Oil on canvas; 40 x 50 in.
Inscribed: *J. Barry Pinx.*
c. 1790-99

Although this subject occurs infrequently in the 18th century, it is significant that Anníbale Carracci represented it early in the 17th century in the Palazzo Farnese in Rome. Annibale's treatment of the nude figure was studied carefully by Barry, and the poses in this composition, as so frequently occurs in his work, recall moments from the Farnese Gallery. Not only poses of figures and

positions of hands but, in particular, the intimacy of the moment selected derive from interpretation of Annibale Carracci.

Barry painted the subject twice. The first version was undertaken in 1773 and engraved in 1777 when it was dedicated to Charles Townley. The second, shown here, was engraved by Barry himself, but was not published until after his death. However, the inscription on the engraving suggests that the painting was done between 1782, when Barry was appointed Professor of Painting at the Royal Academy, and 1799, when he was expelled from that position.

Barry's late style is well represented by this composition. His earlier works, such as the *Temptation of Adam and Eve* (National Gallery of Ireland, Dublin) or the *Philoctetes* (Accademia Clementina, Bologna), were clearly inspired by the narrative compositions of Annibale's Farnese ceiling. In these the figures are complete, the composition clear, the outline unbroken, and the spatial relationship firmly established. But in his later compositions, figures are casually cut and compressed into the format, the spatial orientation is unclear, and a fantasy of intertwining shapes dominates the composition.
F.C.

Provenance
The artist (sale, Christie's, London, 10 April 1807, no. 121, *Jupiter Beguiled by Juno,* bt. Penrose)
Sheffield City Art Galleries, 1937

References
Grigson, p. 219
Wark, pp. 118, 177, no. 23

Reproductions
Engraved by Barry and published posthumously, July 1, 1809

Coln = Terrible, uhellent

64

64
Self Portrait
The Royal Society of Arts, London
Reed pen and brown ink; 11½ x 9½ in.
Inscribed on verso: *This portrait of Barry the painter
I purchased at the sale of his effects which took
place shortly after his death. It was a favorite candle
light study of his, but never intended to be made
public—as it was his intention that no portrait of
him should be seen past the meridian of his life.
He drew this a few years before his death with pen
and ink, and in his usual painting dress. From my
long acquaintance with him I can answer for its
being a strong characteristic likeness of that artist
and most singular man. Chas. Warren.*
c. 1802

This self portrait is of the same period as the
mezzotint engraving, of which a proof exists in the
National Gallery of Ireland, and may be a
preparatory study for it. On the basis of a letter to
the Society of Arts in which Barry speaks of it as
unfinished, the engraving is usually dated 1802. The
inscription on the back showing that the drawing
was undertaken a few years before Barry's death
is the principal support for a date immediately after
1800. This late dating is also supported by the
technique. The rough, broad and loose hatchings
with a coarse reed pen are characteristic of Barry's
drawings of his last years. This technique derives
from his earlier criss-cross hatchings done almost
in the manner of an engraver. The technique is here
exploited to the point that the crossing lines now
intersect in casually jagged patterns, achieving
an expressionistic power rare in British art of
this period.

The numerous fascinating self portraits by Barry
suggest that he was as self-intrigued as his highly
individualistic and temperamental actions might
imply. There is a painted self portrait looking
wistfully over his right shoulder and another with
palette and brushes in The Tate Gallery. There is a
Self Portrait with a Palette in the National Portrait
Gallery, London, a *Self Portrait,* with virtue
trampling the snake of vice, in the National Gallery
of Ireland, Dublin, a self portrait with palette and
brushes in The Royal Society of Arts, London, a
self portrait accompanied by Burke in the character
of Ulysses now in Cork, the haunting *Self Portrait*
in the Victoria and Albert Museum, the *Self Portrait*
drawing in the Ashmolean Museum, and the profile
roundel in pen in The Royal Society of Arts, to
mention the chief examples.
F.C.

Provenance
The artist (sale, Christie's, London, 10-11 April 1807)
Charles Warren (died 1823)
Given to the Royal Society of Arts, London, after 1807

Exhibitions
British Portraits, Royal Academy, London, 1956-57,
no. 655
British Self Portraits, Arts Council, London, 1962,
no. 44a (uncatalogued)

References
Journal of the Royal Society of Arts, LIV, 1906, p. 477;
CV, 1956, p. 61
Wark, pp. 211-12, no. 27
D. Hudson and K. W. Luckhurst, *The Royal Society of
Arts, 1754-1954,* London, 1954, pl. 3

Angelica Kauffmann

1741-1807

Maria Anna Angelica, who retained her family name of Kauffmann although she married twice, was born at Coire in Switzerland. She was the daughter of a mediocre painter and decorator of church interiors who seems to have been a good teacher. Highly precocious, she became an accomplished musician and artist and rapidly learned several languages, no doubt partially because her father was an itinerant artist who took his family to Italy in her very early years. When she was fourteen, they travelled to Milan where she was able to see and copy the old masters. Her unusual ability brought her to the attention of the Duchess of Modena who sat for a portrait, was greatly pleased, and recommended her to numerous friends. In 1763-64 she was in Rome where she met Johann Winckelmann whose portrait (Frankfurt and Zürich) she painted. She also drew a portrait of Benjamin West (National Portrait Gallery, London) and painted Garrick on his Roman sojourn of 1763 and exhibited the portrait in London two years later. Winckelmann wrote of her immediate popularity in Rome, describing her facility in the English and French languages and her numerous sitters from those countries. He also called her beautiful and mentioned her virtuoso ability as a singer.

While she was studying the paintings of the Carracci in Bologna in 1765, she met Lady Wentworth who persuaded her to travel from Venice to London a year later. There she introduced Angelica to numerous people interested in the arts, including the Royal Family whose penchant for talented Germans and also Italians remains almost notorious.

Sir Joshua Reynolds was her friend, and he painted her portrait (collection Earl Spencer) in 1776, a compliment which she returned, exhibiting his portrait (collection Earl of Morley, Saltram Park) in 1778. Reynolds recommended her for inclusion among the founding members of the Royal Academy in the same year. With his consent, if not intervention, she obtained the commission to ornament the ceiling of the lecture room at Somerset House with roundels representing *Genius, Design, Composition,* and *Painting* which were later transferred to the new quarters of the Royal Academy of Arts at Burlington House. Each year, Angelica submitted a number of paintings to the Academy exhibition, continuing this practice while living in Italy from 1782 until 1796. She remained a particularly popular artist in England where she retained numerous patrons, and her works became extremely well known through the color and stipple engravings of her pictures, many of which were made by William Ryland (1732-83).

Even though criticized by artists like Fuseli, Angelica was a successful and popular artist in her day. After arriving in Venice in 1781, she was commissioned to paint the subject of *Leonardo da Vinci Expiring in the Arms of Francis the First* for the Grand Duke Paul of Russia. The painting was highly successful and gave her an immediate vogue. When she moved on to Rome and to Naples, Queen Caroline, wife of Ferdinand II and an artist in her own right, wished to associate Angelica with her court and gave her a commission to paint the Royal Family. She was also patronized by the Austrian and Polish nobility.

Since Rossi mentioned in his biography that Angelica Kauffmann embodied the ideas of Mengs in her art, she has been thought of as a perfect exemplar of one aspect of neoclassicism. The recent esoteric vogue of neoclassicism has once again given her minor attention. The interiors designed by Robert Adam and Angelica's husband Antonio Zucchi frequently provided for the introduction of painted ovals and roundels under the inspiration of antique interiors at Herculaneum and those of Raphael. Angelica's small roundels and ovals and the engravings after them were perfectly suited for decorative ensembles of this type.

Despite recent attention given to Angelica by scholars, she will probably not again achieve the fame she received in her own lifetime. Her figures, compositional types, and poses are repetitive, and her technical facility and handling of paint are disturbingly unvaried. Her interest today, as it must have been in her lifetime, depends on the variety and ingenuity of the subjects she painted, many of which will appear again and again in the works of later artists. Despite the great range of her subject matter, she relied for the most part on English history and a standard group of classical literary sources which were familiar to her educated contemporaries. However, she does not compare with Fuseli in exploring new literary materials or in interpreting those materials with a new point of view. In fact, her selections tend to be charmingly inventive rather than distinctive and original.
F.C.

Bibliography
G. G. de Rossi, *Angelica Kauffmann,* Florence, 1810
E. Barrington Nash, "Angelica Kauffmann and her Engravers Ryland and Burke," *Magazine of Art,* X, 1887, pp. 259-64
Wilhelm Schram, *Die Malerin Angelica Kauffmann,* Brünn, 1890
Frances A. Gerard, *Angelica Kauffmann; A Biography,* New York, 1893
Lady Victoria Manners and Dr. G. C. Williamson, *Angelica Kauffmann, R. A.,* London, 1924

65

65
The Artist in the Character of Design Listening to the Inspiration of Poetry (Poetry Embracing Painting) (Music and Painting)
The Iveagh Bequest, Kenwood, London
Oil on circular canvas; 24 in. diam.
Inscribed: *For George Bowles Esq.*
1782

Numerous references to Mr. Bowles, whose name is inscribed on this painting, are included in Angelica's list of her works. "Mr. Bowles" was George Bowles, a well-to-do collector of enamels, miniatures, and paintings who lived at The Grove, Wanstead. The painting is described as having

been forwarded from Rome on November 6, 1782: "For Mr. Bowles of London circular picture of two English feet consisting of two figures representing Poetry embracing Painting who is listening eagerly to the suggestions of Poetry, given by the artist to the above named, because the figure representing Painting is the portrait of Angelica Kauffmann."

Mr. Bowles was a continuing patron of Angelica Kauffmann from 1782 until at least 1794, and he brought together a collection of more than twenty of her works. These included a wide range of subjects which are highly revealing about her interests and the taste of collectors of contemporary art in the period. The first commission in 1782 was for a painting of Flora instructing a peasant boy to paint flowers and a companion painting of Ganymede playing at dice, and later in the same year *Cephisa Finding Cupid Asleep in the Wood of Sdallia.* In 1783 *Alexander and Apelles* and *Cleopatra Begging for Mercy at the Feet of Augustus* were sent to Mr. Bowles in England. From Rome in 1786 she forwarded a second self portrait, this time portraying herself grieving before the rascal and blackguard Sacripante, from Ariosto's *Orlando Furioso.* In 1789 from Rome she sent an oval of Queen Margaret of Anjou being attacked by robbers, with a companion painting. In 1794 she painted *Phryne Attempting to Seduce the Philosopher Zenocrates,* and *Praxiteles Giving Phryne his Sculpture of Cupid.* All of these were purchased by the patron who always appears as Mr. Bowles, except for this picture of Angelica as the Muse of painting listening to the inspiration of poetry, which was a gift. At least two versions of this composition were made. A version purchased from Agnew's was in the collection of the Earl of Derby, Derby House, London, in 1924. This may be identical with the picture owned by Sir Richard Brooke and exhibited at Wrexham in 1876.
F.C.

Provenance
Given by the artist to George Bowles, The Grove, Wanstead, in 1782
By descent to his sister, Rebecca Rushout, Lady Northwick, Northwick Park, Worcester (died 1859)
By descent to her son, John Rushout, second Earl of Northwick (died 1859)
By descent to Sir Charles Rushout (died 1869)
By descent to his son, Sir Charles F. Rushout (died 1879)
Sir Archibald P. Primrose, Earl of Rosebery, London (sale, Christie's, London, 5 May 1939, no. 70, bt. Gooden and Fox)
E. E. Cook
Bequeathed to National Art-Collections Fund and presented to Kenwood House, 1955

Exhibitions
English Taste in the Eighteenth Century from Baroque to Neo-classic, Royal Academy, London, 1955-56, no. 394

References
Manners and Williamson, pp. 62, 143, 180, 186, pl. opp. p. 80
The Iveagh Bequest, Kenwood . . . Paintings, London, 1960, p. 19, no. 76 (catalogue compiled by Peter Murray with an introduction by Sir Anthony Blunt)
David Irwin, *English Neoclassical Art, Studies in Inspiration and Taste,* Greenwich, Connecticut, 1966, p. 152, pl. 149
Anne Hope, "Cesare Ripa's Iconology and the Neoclassical Movement," *Apollo,* LXXXVII, October 1967, supp. (Notes on British Art), pp. 3, 4; ill. p. 3

Reproductions
Engraved by T. Burke, 1787

[handwritten annotation: > dramatic, never emotional; ch=th, drawings = > carefully planned / etc]

1741-1825

Fuseli was a member of an old Zürich family which had produced artists since the 15th century. The family was distinguished in literature and the sciences, as well as in art, in a period when Zürich was the intellectual and literary capital of Switzerland. His father was Johann Caspar Fuessli (1706-82), painter of portraits and landscapes and also a lexicographer who compiled the lives of the Helvetic painters (1769-79). His uncles were artists, and one of them, Johann Rudolf Fuessli (1709-93), compiled a general lexicon of artists (1763). Fuseli's younger brother Hans Caspar (1743-86), became an entomologist, an interest shared by Fuseli himself.

Henry Fuseli was directed toward the ministry by his father, and to prepare for it, he was placed in the Collegium Carolinum at Zürich where J. J. Bodmer and Johann Jakob Breitinger taught. These men, who were important for the development of romanticism in German literature, were greatly interested in British poetry and drama, in particular, Shakespeare and Milton. Under their instruction, Fuseli developed his first enthusiasm for these writers. There, he learned Greek and Latin, as well as English, French, and Italian. He also wrote prose and poetry and became a close friend of Johann Kaspar Lavater (1741-1801), a writer on phrenology and emotional expression. With Lavater he took holy orders in 1761, and together they exposed a local bailiff for oppression and extortion in a published pamphlet. Afterwards, they were advised to leave the city for a time, and in 1763 Fuseli travelled to Berlin with J. G. Sulzer, who later wrote a treatise on aesthetics entitled *A General*

Theory of the Fine Arts (1771-74). In Berlin Fuseli immediately set to work assisting Bernhard Rode (1725-97) in preparing a set of illustrations to Bodmer's *Noachide.* Through Sulzer, Fuseli met the British Minister to Berlin Sir Andrew Mitchell, who took him to England as part of a plan to develop closer channels of literary communication between Germany and England. He arrived late in the year 1763. There, Fuseli worked first as a translator, publishing in English Winckelmann's *Gedanken über die Nachahmung der Griechischen Werke in der Malerei und Bildhauerkunst* as *Reflections on the Painting and Sculpture of the Greeks* in 1765. He also wrote an essay on Rousseau and acted for a time as a travelling tutor to Viscount Chewton, eldest son of the Earl Waldegrave.

Encouraged by Sir Joshua Reynolds to become a painter, he did his first oil, *Joseph Interpreting Dreams* (collection Henry Dudley Ryder) and left for Italy to study painting, arriving in Rome in February 1770. He remained eight years, sending drawings and paintings to the London exhibitions and preparing the numerous drawings in the sketchbooks now in The British Museum and the Kunsthaus, Zürich. On his return, he travelled through Lombardy to Zürich where he arrived in the autumn of 1778, and in the spring of 1779 he left for London. While in Zürich he painted the *Oath on the Rutli* (Rathaus, Zürich) and began his *Self Portrait in Conversation with Bodmer* (Kunsthaus, Zürich).

Fuseli began exhibiting regularly at the Royal Academy in 1780 with a subject of his own invention, *Bracciaferro Musing over Meduna, Slain by him for Disloyalty during his Absence in the Holy Land.* The title suggests Fuseli's interest in establishing himself as a master of imaginative and inventive subjects. His first exhibited works created a great deal of interest, and with the exhibition of *The Nightmare* (no. 68) in 1782, his fame was firmly established for the following two decades. In 1786 Boydell commissioned nine works from Fuseli for the Shakespeare Gallery, and he painted four others for Woodmason's edition of

Shakespeare in 1793. He was elected A.R.A. in 1788 and R.A. in 1790.

Taking his cue from Boydell, Johnson, who was also a publisher and an earlier friend of Fuseli, proposed in 1790 an edition of Milton's poems edited by Cowper and illustrated by Fuseli. The scheme was not consummated, and Fuseli pursued it on his own with the assistance of a friend, William Roscoe of Liverpool. He opened the Milton Gallery in 1799 with forty paintings and again in 1800 with seven additional works. The undertaking was a financial failure, but it produced some of Fuseli's finest compositions, such as the *Lazar House,* now known from the preparatory drawing in the Kunsthaus, Zürich. In 1799 Fuseli became Professor of Painting at the Royal Academy, succeeding James Barry, and in 1804 he took the place of Wilson as Keeper of the Academy. His first series of lectures was given in 1801. These, his contributions to the enlarged edition of Pilkington's *Lives of the Painters* (1805), and his essays form a lasting contribution to the intellectual and artistic history of this period.

Fuseli's origin in a family of intellectuals and his training for the ministry in one of the best European schools under some of the most stimulating thinkers of his day are unique. No other British artist of this period had such a background, and this training is reflected in Fuseli's intellectual conception of his own art. Burke's view that the most intense aesthetic experiences were based on emotional involvements, a sense of psychological aggression, and even physical danger are reflected in Fuseli's selection of compositional devices to shock the observer into a recognition of the emotional context of his compositions. He achieves this with intense contrasts of light and shadow, unexpected uses of foreshortening, and sharply contrasting sizes of forms. Fuseli concentrated especially on original subjects and inventive interpretations of those subjects, especially in drawings. Indeed, the drawings are the most immediate evidence of the sparkling genius, the tenderness, the intense and highly eccentric individuality that was Fuseli's.   F.C.

Bibliography
John Knowles, *The Life and Writings of Henry Fuseli,*
3 vols., London, 1831
Johann Heinrich Füssli, 1741-1825, Kunsthaus, Zürich,
1926 (catalogue compiled by Wilhelm Wartmann)
Arnold Federmann, *Johann Heinrich Fussili, Dichter
und Maler,* Zürich/Leipzig, 1927
Johann Heinrich Fussli, 1741-1825, Kunsthaus, Zürich,
1941
Marcel Fischer, "Das römische Skizzenbuch von Johann
Heinrich Füssli," *Neujahrsblatt der Zürcher
Kunstgesellschaft,* Zürich, 1942
Paul Ganz, *Die Zeichnungen Hans Heinrich Füsslis,*
Berne, 1947
Paintings and Drawings by Fuseli, Arts Council,
London, 1950
Eudo C. Mason, *The Mind of Henry Fuseli,* London, 1951
Nicolas Powell, *The Drawings of Henry Fuseli,* London,
1951
Frederick Antal, *Fuseli Studies,* London, 1956
H. A. Hammelmann, "Eighteenth-Century English
Illustrators Henry Fuseli, R. A.," *The Book Collector,* VI,
Winter 1957, pp. 350-60
David Irwin, "Fuseli's Milton Gallery: Unpublished
Letters," *Burlington,* VI, 1959, pp. 436-40
Gert Schiff, "Füsli, puritain et satanique," *L'Oeil,* no. 63,
March 1960, pp. 22-29
H. W. Janson, "Fuseli's *Nightmare*," *Arts and Sciences,*
II no. 1, Spring 1963, pp. 23-28
Hugh Macandrew, "Selected Letters from the
Correspondence of Henry Fuseli and William Roscoe of
Liverpool," *Gazette des Beaux-Arts,* s. 6, LXII, 1963,
pp. 205-08
Gert Schiff, "Johann Heinrich Füsslis Milton-Galerie,"
*Schweizerisches Institut für Kunstwissenschaft Zürich,
Schriften,* Zürich/Stuttgart, 1963, no. 5
Gert Schiff, *Fuseli, Oeuvrekatalog* (in preparation)

66
The Madhouse (The Escapee)
Trustees of The British Museum
Pen and sepia on gray-toned paper; 14¾ x 25 1/16 in.
Inscribed: *Füseli. fec:*
c. 1772

This sheet is more accurately entitled by Schiff
Der Ausbrecher, which means literally "the
escapee." The title *The Madhouse* is not quite
correct and misleads one as to Fuseli's actual
intentions. The event reflects an actual experience
of Fuseli in the hospital of S. Spirito in Rome. A
dying man, already mentally deranged, is seen with
his family and priests who prepare to give the rites
of extreme unction. A priest carrying the host, his
attendants, and one of the children of the family are
seen on the left. Other members of the dying man's
family are mourning over his bed in the center
background. The man himself attempts to flee but
is held back either by an attendant or one of his
own family. He is pursued by three priests, one of
whom throws holy water, another brandishes the
cross, and still another has dropped scripture and
crucifix and grapples the robes of the
terror-stricken and deranged patient.

A similar interest on Fuseli's part in the extremes of
psychological response is also found later in *The
Nightmare* (no. 68). The composition was reworked
in Fuseli's visionary reinterpretation of this theme
under the influence of Romney in his vision of the
Lazar House for the Milton Gallery of 1793; a
preparatory drawing for that work is in the
Kunsthaus, Zürich.

Although much more refined, this drawing is very
close in style to the Ossian series of Alexander
Runciman. The patterns of gray and black wash,
together with fine pen work, are also found in
Runciman's drawings of the same period, and his
style appears to have influenced Fuseli, the younger
of the two artists.
F.C.

Provenance
Presented to The British Museum by J. C. Joyce, 1907

References
Powell, p. 41, no. 35
Frederick Antal, "Fuseli Studies," *Burlington,* XCVI,
1954, pp. 260-61
Antal, *Fuseli Studies,* pp. 32-39
Schiff, *Milton-Galerie,* pp. 39, 76 figs. 36-37, 132 n. 204
Schiff, *Oeuvrekatalog,* no. 515

Reproductions
Engraved anonymously in a slightly reduced version for
Johann Kaspar Lavater's *Essai sur la Physiognomie,*
The Hague, 1783, II, 258 (the French edition of Lavater's
Physiognomische Fragmente, 1775-78); engraved in
full by Thomas Holloway for the English edition,
Essays on Physiognomy, London, 1792, II, 288

67
Martha Hess
The Pierpont Morgan Library
Black chalk, stumped, heightened with white on
light brown paper; 20⅜ x 13⅞ in.
1778-79

Martha Hess was a member of an old and venerabl
Zürich family which included Johann-Jacob, Felix
and their uncle Gaspard Hess, pastor at
Neftenbach. These men knew the poet Friedrich
Klopstock, Fuseli, Johann Kaspar Lavater, and the
poet and teacher Heinrich Bodmer. Fuseli had bee
a friend of the family in Zürich and Johann and
Felix Hess accompanied him when he was forced
to leave in 1762 and travelled to Augsburg and
Berlin. Fuseli returned from Italy, some years late
by way of Zürich where he remained from Octobe
1778 to March 1779. There, he was anxious to
reestablish old acquaintances and to see his ol
circle of friends once again, Bodmer in particular.
During this stay, he made a number of portraits of

66

67

friends, including numerous drawings of Martha Hess. One of these was engraved in profile for the illustration of *Gentleness and Benignity* in volume II (p. 284) of Lavater's *Physiognomische Fragmente.* The identification is made on the basis of the inscription on the etching by Joh. H. Lips of 1780 now in the Kunsthaus, Zürich, where the original drawing is also to be found in the sketchbook made from 1773 to 1778, folio 72, no. 254. Since it is in profile, has a deeply shaded background, and is in many ways identical to the published engraving, no. 67 must represent an early stage in preparing for it. It does, in fact, precede the Zürich drawing since it is taken directly from the model. The

Zürich drawing is very possibly made after no. 67, at an intermediary stage, in preparation for the final engraving.
F.C.

Provenance
R. E. A. Wilson, London, 1935
Roland, Browse and Delbanco, London, 1948
A. P. Oppé, London
The Pierpont Morgan Library, New York, 1954

Exhibitions
Paintings and Drawings by Henry Fuseli, R. A.,
R. E. A. Wilson, London, 1935, no. 26
Paintings and Drawings by Henry Fuseli, Roland, Browse, and Delbanco, London, 1948, no. 18
Fuseli, Arts Council, London, 1950, no. 50
A Selection of Early English Drawings and Watercolours from the Collection of Paul Oppé, Graves Art Gallery, Sheffield, 1952, no. 30

References
Johann Heinrich Füssli, Kunsthaus, Zürich, 1926, nos. 124-25
Johann Heinrich Füssli, Kunsthaus, Zürich, 1941, no. 143s
Powell, no. 40, p. 42
The Pierpont Morgan Library, *Fifth Annual Report to the Fellows of the Pierpont Morgan Library,* New York, 1954, pp. 70-72
Schiff, *Oeuvrekatalog,* no. 547

68
The Nightmare
The Detroit Institute of Arts, Gift of
Mr. and Mrs. Bert L. Smokler and
Mr. and Mrs. Lawrence A. Fleischman
Oil on canvas; 40 x 50 in.
Verso: full-length figure of a woman identified by Gert Schiff as possibly a portrait of Anna Landolt 1781

The subject of *The Nightmare* was imitated in the poem by Erasmus Darwin illustrated by Fuseli "The Botanic Garden Containing the Loves of the Plants":

So on his Nightmare, through the evening fog,

68

Flits the squab Fiend o'er fen, and lake, and bog;
Seeks some love-Wilder'd Maid with sleep oppress'd,
Alights, and, grinning, sets upon her breast.
—Such as of late, amid the murky sky,
Was mark'd by Fuseli's poetic eye . . .

A lady's boudoir and sleeping quarters are shown with a dressing table and still life on the left. Tossing in her sleep, the maiden has thrown off her bedclothes and is shown in a nightgown. As if it were a vision, a bog-fiend and his steed of the night have appeared in her quarters, and she has fainted. During her unconsciousness the fiend has remained and sits upon her body while the literal "night-mare" peers through the draperies, his glowing eyes burning through the darkness and his shadow looming behind him on the curtains.

Far from giving a vision of the unconscious, Fuseli has presented a real vision to shock the observer into a dramatic realization of the psychological state of the swooning maiden. The element of physical danger, which is a significant part of

Burke's notion of the "sublime," is more than palpable here. To compound the horror of the scene, the demon stares at the observer himself, ready to attack him next. It is one of the most aggressive of the psychological pantomimes of the period. In fact, this subject is a summary of the interest in the unusual and the new in aesthetic experiences which characterizes this period. It combines the interest in the unusual with Fuseli's specialty, the presentation of themes of extreme emotion. So startling is the presentation that it achieves a sensationalism which is happily lacking in works like Wright of Derby's *The Old Man and Death* (no. 29) which has a similar visionary subject. However, even Fuseli seldom goes so far in his startling effort to jar the observer into a sense of physical and emotional involvement in the drama he is presenting.

The composition was engraved four times. It was copied by George Morland and, among others, Nikolai Abildgaard (1743-1809) made a free copy of it in 1800. The picture was widely popular as the number of engravings attest. For example, there are descriptions in a letter to Johann Heinrich Merck (1741-91), the German author and critic, of the impression made by the engraved version on Duke Karl August who wrote, "It has been a long time since I have seen anything that has intrigued me so much."

H. W. Janson was the first to identify the Detroit version as the one originally exhibited in 1782. Knowles stated that Fuseli painted a number of versions at different periods in his career, each offering variations of the first drawing. Both vertical and horizontal versions are known and are listed by Schiff.
F.C.

Provenance
H. Haskett Smith, Troweswell, Goudhurst (sale, Viscount Eversley and other collections, Christie's, London, 9 May 1896, no. 78)
Roland, Browse and Delbanco, London, November, 1947
Durlacher Bros., New York, from 1950
The Detroit Institute of Arts, 1955

Exhibitions
Royal Academy, 1782, no. 64
Royal Academy, 1879, no. 15 (lent by H. Haskett Smith)
Paintings and Drawings by Henry Fuseli, Roland, Browse and Delbanco, London, 1948, no. 25
Aspects of British Romanticism, Roland, Browse and Delbanco, London, 1949, no. 9
Romanticism in Eighteenth Century England, Durlacher Bros., New York, 1953, no. 8
The Century of Mozart, Nelson Gallery—Atkins Museum, Kansas City, 1956, no. 36
Homage to Mozart, Wadsworth Atheneum, Hartford, Conn., 1956, no. 17
The Romantic Era, Herron Museum of Art, Indianapolis, 1965, no. 22

References
Erasmus Darwin, *The Botanic Garden Containing the Loves of the Plants, a poem with Philosophical Notes,* London, 1789, Canto III, II. 51-56
Knowles, I, 64-65, 413
Wilhelm Michel, *Das Teuflische und Groteske in der Kunst,* Munich, 1911, p. 28
Cornelius Gurlitt, *Die Deutsche Kunst seit 1800,* Berlin, 1924, pp. 32, 39
Johann Heinrich Füssli, 1741-1825, Zürich, 1926, no. 7
Federmann, pp. 51-52, 169, 173
F. D. Klingender, *Hogarth and English Caricature,* London/New York, 1945, p. 16, figs. 26, 37
Ganz, pp. 65-66, no. 38, pl. 38
Perspex, "Current Shows and Comments," *Apollo,* LI, March 1950, pp. 61-62
Mason, pp. 63, 70, 79, 80
Powell, p. 16
Mario Praz, "Painter Ordinary to the Devil," *Art News,* LI, January 1953, pp. 33-34
Edgar P. Richardson, *"The Nightmare* by Henri Fuseli," *Bulletin of the Detroit Institute of Arts,* XXXIV no. 1, 1954-55, pp. 2-3
Helen Comstock, "Fuseli's *Nightmare,"* The Connoisseur, CXXXVI, December 1955, p. 229
Janson, pp. 23-28
Schiff, *Milton-Galerie,* 1963, pp. 9, 84
Schiff, *Oeuvrekatalog,* nos. 757, 841, 1502, 1503, 1568

Reproductions
Engraved by Laurede in 1782, by de Ville Neuve in 1784, by Theodor Falckeisen (1768?-1814), and published in colored aquatint by Thomas Burke (1749-1815) in 1802

69
Macbeth and the Witches
H.M. Treasury and the National Trust (Collection of Lord Egremont, Petworth House)
Oil on canvas; 66 x 53 in.
1793-94

In the first act of Shakespeare's drama *Macbeth,* two of the generals of King Duncan of Scotland, Macbeth and Banquo, are returning from a victorious campaign against rebels. Suddenly, as they march in the night, three weird sisters or witches appear to them on the heath and voice the prophecy that Macbeth will be Thane of Cawdor and later king.

Fuseli, who was an extremely intelligent and well-read person, had thought carefully about the terror which such a visionary night scene might cause. Knowles quotes Fuseli's discussion of the subject in surprising detail: "When Macbeth meets with the witches on the heath, it is terrible, because he did not expect the supernatural visitation; but when he goes to the cave to ascertain his fate, it is no longer a subject of terror: hence I have endeavoured to supply what is deficient in the poetry . . . I have endeavoured to shew a colossal head rising out of the abyss, and that head Macbeth's likeness. What, I would ask, would be a greater object of terror to you, if, some night on going home, you were to find yourself sitting at your own table, either writing, reading or otherwise employed? Would not this make a powerful impression on your mind?"

It seems astounding to have Fuseli say that he is improving on Shakespeare's poetry, and yet this is a perfect description of the romantic artist's point of view in using a given literary text as a source. Fuseli re-thought the text as it actually happened and realized that by recreating the actuality of the circumstances a more striking drama would be the result because it would be more convincing physically and psychologically. The real fury of this scene comes out particularly in the pen drawing of the same subject in the Kunsthaus, Zürich. Fuseli

69

also thought carefully about the physical placemen in order to achieve the necessary degree of emotional impact. He describes his formal arrangement as a triangular composition and mentions the mystical character of the triangle which must have had some effect, in his view, on the power of the visionary scene. In a startling fashion, he situated the observer on a level with th feet of Macbeth so that the General towers above in an almost menacing way. This looming figure is as apparitional to us as the witches who billow magically out of the ground were to Macbeth. The colossal head mentioned by Fuseli can be made out between the flashes of lightning above the witches' heads.

It was pointed out by Federmann that this picture was painted for Woodmason's Shakespeare Gallery. That this is the Woodmason version is ascertained by the engraving and by the fact that the dimensions of this picture are exactly those given by Knowles. They are also the same as the original measurements of the other three painting in this series. Other versions of this subject are listed by Schiff.
F.C.

Provenance
John Knowles (died 1841)
Almost certainly acquired by George O'Brien, third Earl of Egremont (died 1837; in the 1837 inventory of his seat, Petworth House, Sussex)
By descent to George Francis O'Brien, fourth Earl of Egremont (died 1845)
By descent to George Wyndham, first Baron Leconfield (died 1869)
By descent to Henry Wyndham, second Baron Leconfield (died 1901)
By descent to Charles Henry Wyndham, third Baron Leconfield (died 1952)

References
Knowles, I, 189-90
Rev. Thomas Sockett, *Catalogue of Pictures in Petworth House*, 1856, p. 43, no. 402
C. H. Collins Baker, *Catalogue of the Petworth Collection of Pictures in the Possession of Lord Leconfield*, London, 1920, p. 46, no. 402

Federmann, pp. 53, 170, pl. 45
David Irwin, *English Neoclassical Art,* Greenwich,
Conn., 1966, pp. 38, 128-29, pl. 136
Schiff, *Oeuvrekatalog,* no. 880; also 435, 737, 822, 1010,
1207, 1258

Reproductions
Engraved by William Bromley (1769-1842) without a
publication date. No. 3 for Woodmason's Shakespeare
Gallery

70
Roland at Roncesvalles (Fame)
The Detroit Institute of Arts,
Gift of John S. Newberry
Pen and dark brown ink with brown and gray wash
and traces of white; 22⅝ x 27 in.
Inscribed: *dopo la dolorossa rotta, quando;* verso:
stamped in black *Baroness North's Collection of
Drawings by H. Fuseli &c.* (Lugt 1947); on the verso
is a drawing in pencil and black chalk of a male
nude figure, possibly a preliminary study for the
figure of Roland
c. 1800-10

As related in the *Chanson de Roland,* Charlemagne,
attempting to conquer the last of the Spanish
strongholds held by the Saracens, was encamped
before Cordova. Assured by Marsile, the Saracen
King, with false offers of submission, Charlemagne
and his Frankish armies retreated, leaving Roland,
one of his barons and a kinsman, in command of
the rear guard which contained the flower of the
Frankish army. Just as Roland reached the pass in
the Pyrenees, the Saracen army of 400,000 men
was sighted. Roland prepared to withstand them
and fought three waves of the advance losing all
but sixty of his men. Only then did he consent to
sound his bugle and call for the assistance of
Charlemagne and his troops whom we see
advancing on the distant pass in this drawing.
Roland died in this battle before Charlemagne
actually arrived to be by his side.

Johann Karl Musäus, whose *Volksmärchen der*

70

Deutschen (1782-87) was in Fuseli's library, relates
that Roland died from the very effort of blowing the
horn. So great was his effort in achieving a blast
that would reach Charlemagne some eight leagues
away that he burst the golden horn, split open the
veins of his neck, and his heroic spirit was exhaled
in death. The recently discovered Italian inscription
on the drawing suggests that it could also have
been taken from an Italian source.
F.C.

Provenance
Susan North, Countess of Guilford (died 1837)
Susan, Baroness North (died 1884)
Durlacher Bros., New York
John S. Newberry, Jr., Detroit
The Detroit Institute of Arts, 1956

Exhibitions
The Nineteenth Century: 125 Master Drawings, Solomon
R. Guggenheim Museum, New York, and the University
Gallery, University of Minnesota, Minneapolis, 1962,
no. 43
Romanticism, Agnes Etherington Art Centre, Queen's
University, Kingston, Ontario, 1965, no. 8

The John S. Newberry Collection, The Detroit Institute
of Arts, 1965, no. 52

References
Nicholas Snow, "Fame by Fuseli," *Bulletin of The Detroit
Institute of Arts,* XXXVI, no. 1, 1956-57, pp. 10-11
Schiff, *Oeuvrekatalog,* no. 1403

1742-1803

Born in Radnorshire in Wales, Thomas Jones studied at Oxford from 1759-1761 and later worked in London under Henry Pars (1734-1806) at Shipley's School. Later he drew from sculpture and casts in the Duke of Richmond's gallery under Giovanni-Battista Cipriani (1727-85) and Joseph Wilton (1722-1803) and was admitted to make life drawings at the Academy in St. Martin's Lane. From 1763 to 1765 he was apprenticed to Richard Wilson, at the same time as was William Hodges. His training at Shipley's School, where the miniaturists Cosway and Ozias Humphry (1742-1810) were trained, did not prepare him for Wilson's broad manner, and he was dissatisfied there. Nevertheless, this period was decisive in his career since his later works were composed under the influence of Wilson's compositions. However, his treatment is usually much tighter and more detailed, as well as less inspired than that of Wilson. In 1766 he became a member of the Society of Artists and in this period was a close friend of Joseph Farington (1747-1821), Richard Paton (1717-91), John Hamilton Mortimer, and Francis Wheatley, with whom he made excursions, performed amateur theatricals, and became involved in occasionally dangerous street fights. At this time he collaborated with Mortimer, painting the landscape of his *Death of Orpheus* (Paul Mellon Collection) and also the backgrounds of pictures for Paton.

In 1776 he was able to travel to Italy, a project planned for some years, where he remained until 1783, the major part of his artistic life. The interesting diary of this journey is preserved. One of the useful source books for the period, it is also filled with intimate details about his experiences and friends and records macabre scenes of execution and his terrors in climbing to the ball on the cupola of St. Paul's.

While in Italy, he worked primarily in Rome and Naples where he was received by Thomas Jenkins (no. 1) and James Byers (1733?-1817?). He met Sir William Hamilton, British Ambassador to Naples, Angelica Kauffmann and her husband Antonio Zucchi (1726-95). He also acted as guide and sketching companion to Francis Towne, and William Pars (1742-82) joined him in Naples for a time in May 1781, shortly before his death. The intimate and objective studies made while he was living in Naples first brought Jones to the attention of contemporary art historians in 1954 when forty-nine of his works of this type were sold in London.

After his return from Italy, Thomas Jones painted pictures in the manner of Wilson, based on drawings in his Italian sketchbooks, but with a much more precise touch and with a much less fine treatment of light. In 1787 he inherited property from his family in Wales at Pencarrig, Radnorshire, and he returned there in 1789 giving up painting almost completely and exhibiting only once thereafter at the Royal Academy in 1798.
F.C.

Bibliography
A. P. Oppé, ed., "Memoirs of Thomas Jones," *Walpole Society,* XXXII, 1946-48, pp. 1-162
W. G. Constable, *Richard Wilson,* London, 1953, pp. 139-40

71

71
Penkerrig (Pencarrig)
Birmingham City Museum and Art Gallery
Oil on paper; 9 x 12 in.
Inscribed: *Penkerrig 1772*

After a visit to John Mortimer and his assistants working on the ceiling decoration for Lord Melbourne at Brocket Hall in June 1772, Thomas Jones continued on a tour through Hertfordshire, eastward to Oxford, Gloucester, and into Wales. He travelled through Brecon and arrived at Pencarrig in Carmarthen on July 30, having been accompanied from Abergavenny in Monmouth by his brother John. After a brief stop, he travelled on to Llandrindod-Wells where he remained about three weeks. There, numerous studies in oil on paper were painted. Later, he returned by way of Pencarrig to Brecon and back to London, arriving on December 10.

This view is taken in an area of Wales which is rugged and particularly beautiful. It shows one of the escarpments at the summit of Daren Mountain called Pencarrig-calch, a large mass of millstone

grit and limestone, once a part of the South Welsh coal-mining basin. **72**
F.C.

Provenance
Anonymous descendant of the artist (sale "Of a Lady whose husband was a descendant of Thomas Jones," Christie's, London, 2 July 1954, no. 218, bt. Colnaghi) Purchased for the Birmingham City Museum and Art Gallery, 1954

Exhibitions
Pictures from the City Art Gallery, Birmingham, Thos. Agnew & Sons, London, 1957, no. 45

References
Oppé, *Walpole Society,* XXXII, 1946-48, p. 27

72
House with a Verandah
The Visitors of the Ashmolean Museum, Oxford
Oil on paper; 5¾ x 13¾ in.
Inscribed in pencil on verso: *T.J. Naples Aprile 1782.*

Thomas Jones was fond of sketching in oils on paper and mentions this practice frequently in his *Memoirs.* The flat, Neapolitan rooftop of this type with surrounding parapet walls was called a *lastrica.* Jones commanded such an outdoor space for painting and sketching from his own apartment. His first residence in Naples adjoined Mrs. Sherry's Hotel and was on the second floor of a large house where twelve other floors were used as a warehouse. Thomas had the use of the roof in his apartments near the sea. This view was made from his own *lastrica,* and it is typical of this rather shy and occasionally difficult Welsh artist that he should record this homely wall, perhaps opposite his own rooms. His diary is filled with minute personal details recording experiences which he did not wish to forget and which he looked forward to contemplating in the future. On May 15, 1782 he

took up residence in an apartment on the Vicolo del Canale, only a few doors away from the Italian artist Tito Lusieri (active from 1785), famous for his Pompeiian views, and there he spent highly pleasurable hours in sketching the city, the bay, and the mountains. On May 17, 1781 he began a still life view of his kitchen which he says was painted *con amore* and for relaxation and amusement. He relates, "I still keep this picture by me as a pleasant remembrance of Times past." This sketch of a Neapolitan rooftop must stand in the same category as his detailed representations and descriptions of his rooms, his friends, and any unusual event of his daily sojourns.

Perhaps because it was meaningful primarily to the artist, it has none of the schematization of his large paintings which are modelled on Wilson's compositions. On the contrary, the lights and shadows of a particular time of the afternoon and every broken patch of stucco and brick are recorded in an objective way that is rare in 18th-century art before this time. However, such a treatment can be found in works by Italian landscapists like Lusieri. In view of the curvilinear

and picturesque views of Wilson and the curving lines of Hogarth, the rectilinear qualities of this sketch are remarkable. In France, a tradition for this kind of architectural study of daylight and buildings develops in the works of Pierre Henri de Valenciennes (1750-1819) of Toulouse and can be found in David's view of the Luxembourg Gardens from his place of confinement in the Hôtel des Fermes in 1794 and in Ingres' studies seen from his studio in San Gaetano of 1807. The tradition is climaxed by Corot's early views of Rome. F.C.

Provenance
Anonymous descendant of Thomas Jones (sale, Christie's, London, 2 July 1954, no. 213) Ashmolean Museum, Oxford, 1954

References
Oppé, *Walpole Society,* XXXII, 1946-48, p. 103 John Woodward, *A Picture History of British Painting,* London, 1962, p. 85

Richard Cosway

1742-1821

Son of the master of the public school at Tiverton, Devonshire, Cosway showed a talent for painting at an early age and, after a period of study at a school in Okeford near Bampton, he was sent to London. His uncle Oliver Peard, the mayor of Tiverton and his first patron, paid for his apprenticeship to Thomas Hudson, after which he went to Shipley's School. In 1755 he obtained a prize for drawing at the Society of Artists and repeated with four other premiums in the following years. He also worked under Joseph Wilton and Giovanni-Battista Cipriani in the Duke of Richmond's gallery. His talent as a draftsman enabled him to move from student to teacher at Shipley's School, and he began at the same time to paint miniatures for the lids of snuffboxes. In 1766 he was made a member of the Incorporated Society of Artists; in 1769 he was a student at the Royal Academy, a year later A.R.A., and in 1771 a Royal Academician.

Clever and technically skilled, Cosway quickly became prosperous through his art and by supplementing his income as a picture dealer. John Thomas Smith describes him at Christie's, dressed in his sword with a small three-cornered hat on a powdered *toupé* and an embroidered mulberry silk coat. He bought a fashionable house which became the morning lounge and place of conversation of some of the most distinguished members of London society. His handsomely appointed house contained a collection of old master paintings, majolica, prints, drawings, and arms. The carriage of the Prince of Wales was

frequently at his door and, after being appointed his painter, Cosway was frequently seen at Carlton House. He drew a splendid miniature portrait of Mrs. Fitzherbert and also one of the Prince of Wales and continued to sign himself as his official painter.

In 1781 Cosway married Maria Hadfield, an amateur artist and the daughter of an English hotel keeper in Florence. Because of his wife's health, they travelled to Paris and on the continent, where Richard painted portraits of the Duchesse de Polignac and the family of the Duchesse d'Orléans. Cosway's life in the last decade of the 18th and the first decade of the 19th century, and especially the facts of his relationship with his wife, are little known today. Maria met and corresponded with Jacques-Louis David and Pierre-François-Hugues d'Hancarville, and seventeen letters to Maria from Paris written by Hancarville from 1787 to 1791 are preserved in the Biblioteca Communale in Lodi, Italy. In that town, Maria Cosway lived after the death of her husband, establishing there the Collegio delle Grazie, a school for young women. She also established the Fondazione Cosway within the Collegio, where are preserved today more than 500 drawings by Richard Cosway, together with his interesting library, the source for any further investigation of the later part of Richard's life.
F.C.

73

Bibliography
Sale, Stanley's, London, May 17-19, 22-24, 1821
Sale, Stanley's, February 14-22, March 8-16, 1822
John Thomas Smith, *Nollekens and His Times,* London, 1828, pp. 392-407
Allan Cunningham, "Cosway," *Lives of the Most Eminent British Painters, Sculptors, and Architects,* VI, London, 1833, pp. 1-20
Frederick B. Daniell, *A Catalogue raisonné of the Engraved Works of Richard Cosway, R. A.,* London, 1890
George C. Williamson, *Richard Cosway, R. A.,* London, 1905
E. Ferrari, "I disegni di Riccardo Cosway nella biblioteca di Lodi," *Rassegna d'arte,* XIII no. 9, September 1913, pp. 144-47

73
Horace Beckford at the Age of Thirteen
The Pierpont Morgan Library
Watercolor and pencil; 9⅛ x 5⅝ in.
Inscribed on mount: *Rdus Cosway. R.A. Primarius Pictor Serenissimi Walliae Principis Fecit 1790*

William Horace Pitt-Rivers, third Baron Rivers, was born December 2, 1777. He was the only son of Peter Beckford, M.P. for Stepleton, Dorset, and the grandson, through his mother, of George Pitt (1722?-1803), first Baron Rivers. At the death of his father in 1828, he assumed the name Pitt-Rivers, but he himself was drowned a short three years later (1831) in the Serpentine in Hyde Park. In 1808 he married the daughter of Col. Francis Hale Rigby of Mistley Hall, Essex. They lived together at Sudeley Castle, near Winchcombe in Gloucestershire, once the seat of Lord Seymour and the burial place of Catherine Parr. They had two sons, the fourth and sixth Barons. The line became extinct in 1918 at the death of the sixth Baron, when this drawing may have passed from the family collections.

This sheet, which is in pristine condition, shows well the appealing qualities of Cosway both as draftsman and as miniaturist. It was his habit to finish the face in detail and often with color and to leave the surrounding areas loosely blocked in black chalk or pencil. Here the landscape and figure are fairly complete by comparison with other sheets in which the background and even the figure are suggested by the faintest and briefest of strokes, allowing the face to float on the page in the merest suggestion of a context.

The costume is frankly fanciful, although used by many others apart from Cosway. It was fashionable to be portrayed in the elegant costumes of the period of Van Dyck. A resplendent example of this taste is Cosway's portrait drawing, in a pose reminiscent of this one, of the Prince of Wales (collection Hon. William Ashley). Both in selection of costume and in its imitation of "unfinished" drawings by the old masters, this portrait shows a keen admiration of the art of the past. The entire drawing exhibits well the extreme refinement of Cosway's style and reflects the elegant and informed tastes of the artistic circle most intimately connected with the Prince of Wales.
F.C.

Provenance
Anonymous sale, Sotheby's, London, 18 July 1956, no. 43
The Pierpont Morgan Library, New York, 1956

Exhibitions
The Eighteenth Century, One Hundred Drawings by One Hundred Artists, University Gallery, University of Minnesota, Minneapolis, 1961, no. 14

References
Daniell, no. 10, p. 56 *(Master Horace Beckford)*
The Pierpont Morgan Library, *Eighth Annual Report to the Fellows of the Pierpont Morgan Library,* New York, 1958, p. 81

Reproductions
Engraved in stipple by John Condé, 1792 (13¾ by 9¾ in.); repr. in *The Connoisseur,* XI, 1905, p. 233

William Hodges
1744-1797

Born in London the only child of a blacksmith, Hodges was to become an errand-boy and pupil at Shipley's School in the Strand, where he was noticed by Richard Wilson and became his pupil. There, he assisted with the dead coloring and preparation of the pictures, developing great skill in painting in the manner of Wilson. He first exhibited at the Society of Artists in 1766, and in 1772 sent views of Germany and Switzerland, which probably indicates that he had travelled in those countries. Through the intervention of Lord Palmerston, he obtained the post of draftsman on the second expedition of Captain Cook to the South Seas. He was especially instructed by the Admiralty to record any distinctive or unusual phenomena, and his views document such natural wonders as icebergs (Australian Museum, Sydney) and primitive monuments on Easter Island (National Maritime Museum, Greenwich). After his return in 1775, he completed and engraved the drawings and paintings made on this journey.

In 1776 he exhibited at the Royal Academy for the first time with a view of Otaheite, and in the following year with one of New Zealand. He was in India in 1778 under the patronage of Warren Hastings, and he remained there six years painting views of unusual landscape phenomena. His last trip abroad was in 1790 when he travelled to St. Petersburg and painted landscape views in Russia. He became A.R.A. in 1786 and R.A. in 1789.

Apart from his landscapes, Hodges also painted subject pieces. For Boydell's Shakespeare Gallery, he illustrated scenes from *The Merchant of Venice* and *As You Like It.* Two large allegorical pictures undertaken in the early 1790s, *The Effects of Peace and War,* were failures which convinced him to stop painting. Thereafter in 1795 he opened a bank. However, shortly afterward he died at Brixham, Devonshire, of gout, rather than by suicide as Farington records (September 27, 1806).

Hodges was an imitator of Wilson, and their works are frequently confused. However, his pictures in the manner of Wilson are much less interesting than his views of Cape Town and the fine *Oaitepeha Bay* in the National Maritime Museum. Occasionally, these paintings attain great beauty, and their original subject matter makes them of the greatest interest for the study of romantic art as a whole.
F.C.

Bibliography
Sir William Foster, "British Artists in India," *Walpole Society,* XIX, 1930-31, pp. 40-42
Geoffrey Callender, " 'Cape Town' by William Hodges, R. A.," *Burlington,* LXXIX no. 462, September 1941, pp. 93-95
Bernard Smith, "European Vision and the South Pacific," *JWCI,* XIII, 1950, pp. 73-74
W. G. Constable, "Hodges, William," in *Richard Wilson,* London, 1953, p. 139
L.[ionel] C.[ust], "William Hodges," *Dictionary of National Biography,* IX, 955-56

74

74
A Crater in the Pacific
The Art Gallery and Museum, Brighton, England
Oil on canvas; 40 x 50 in.
1772-75

The only mention of a volcano in Captain Cook's log of his second voyage to the South Seas occurs on August 14, 1744. Cook was in the New Hebrides Islands, each of which has been formed by volcanic action, and a number of which have their own volcanoes. He mentioned, in particular, making an expedition inland to get a better view of the volcano on the Island of Tanna. Cook himself did not reach the volcano on this occasion. However, he did not leave the island until August 25, and there would have been ample opportunity for Hodges to make a tour inland to prepare sketches for this view. However, the islands of the South Pacific are so rich in volcanoes that there would have occurred a number of opportunities, and this particular occasion need not be the one during which this scene was recorded.

This "aerial" view of a volcanic cone may have

been taken from the "somma" ring or jagged outer rim of an earlier cone, vestiges of which can be seen rising behind the further rim. This would have allowed Hodges an unusually complete view of the interior of a largely inactive volcano which has only emissions of steam and sulphurous smoke. Men in European costumes are climbing the well-worn path to the rim; one throws up his arms in amazement and wonder, and others climb the conoidal pile to view the steaming vent.
F.C.

Provenance
Willet Collection
Presented to The Art Gallery and Museum, Brighton, England, 1885

Exhibitions
The Romantic Movement, Tate Gallery, London, (Arts Council), 1959, no. 211

References
Christopher Lloyd, ed., *The Voyages of Captain James Cook Round The World,* New York, 1959, pp. 201-03

1747-1801

Although he is remembered today for the series of engravings the *Cries of London,* which can often still be found in hotel rooms, Wheatley was one of the well-known painters of history, genre and portraits of his day. He was the son of a London tailor who placed him under Daniel Fournier (c. 1710-c. 1766), a drawing master and teacher of perspective. He also studied at the drawing school of William Shipley (1714-1803), and he may have had some instruction in landscape from Richard Wilson. He enrolled as a student at the Royal Academy in 1769. Prizes were awarded him at the Society of Arts in 1762 for a figure drawing and in 1763 for a painting.

In 1770 Wheatley became a member of the Society of Artists, of which he was to become director in 1774. There he became acquainted with John H. Mortimer whom he assisted in painting a ceiling at Brocket Hall for Lord Melbourne, beginning in 1771. One of his first landscapes exhibited in 1774, a *Study on the Coast of the Isle of Wight,* included figures by Mortimer, with whom he left the Society of Artists in 1778 and exhibited at the Royal Academy. Probably under Mortimer's influence, Wheatley developed the rustic genre of gypsy encampments, of which an etching dated 1785 is in The British Museum. In style these derive from Mortimer's scenes of bandits robbing fishermen and bandits at market. In this genre Wheatley was rapidly superseded in popularity by George Morland who made it a specialty.

In 1776 Wheatley had become involved in an affair with Mrs. Gresse, wife of the drawing master to the daughters of George III. Having fallen deeply into debt, he had to flee to Dublin and took Mrs. Gresse with him, borrowing money from Benjamin West which he never repaid. He remained in Dublin until 1783 acquiring initial success painting portraits, beginning with *A View of College Green with a Meeting of the Volunteers* (National Gallery of Ireland, Dublin), which established his reputation and procured for him numerous commissions.

Before 1785 Wheatley's subjects had been largely landscapes and portraits, principally of upper middle-class individuals in outdoor settings with rather standard combinations of backdrop. After 1785 Wheatley exhibited drawings and paintings drawn from modern literature which follow in the tradition of Wright of Derby's literary illustrations. These are drawn from Marmontel's *Contes Moraux,* Rousseau's *Nouvelle Héloïse,* Goldsmith's *Deserted Village,* and from Clara Reeve, Laurence Sterne, and James Farrell. He also painted illustrations for *All's Well that Ends Well, Act II* (The Folger Shakespeare Library, Washington) and *Polixenes and Camillo Welcomed by Perdita* from *The Winter's Tale* (Drury Lane Theatre, London) for Boydell's Shakespeare Gallery. The *Cries of London* were exhibited at the Royal Academy from 1792 to 1795. Wheatley's style, which has much of the grace of Mortimer as well as some of his color and paint qualities, is more closely related to the art of Greuze than that of any other British artist of this period. His grayed colors and his compositions are often infused with reminiscences of that French master whose engravings must also have influenced certain of Romney's studies of Lady Hamilton. Because of his fresh paint qualities and the sheer attractiveness of his art, Wheatley is one of the most engaging minor masters of his period.
F.C.

Bibliography
W. Roberts, *Francis Wheatley,* London, 1910
Francis Wheatley, R. A., 1747-1801, Aldeburgh Festival and City Art Gallery, Leeds (Paul Mellon Foundation for British Art) 1965, (catalogue compiled by Mary Webster)

75
The Wilkinson Family
The Detroit Institute of Arts, Gift of the Founders Society, General Membership Fund
Oil on canvas; 40¼ x 50⅜ in.
c. 1776-78

Although the Wilkinsons are traditionally said to be portrayed in front of the family mansion at Roehampton, it seems unlikely that the Ledoux-like architecture is more than a fashionable setting. This same kind of backdrop appears in the Richardson family portrait by Wheatley in Dublin. Sibella Wilkinson, through whom the picture passed to her descendants, is the oldest girl in the painting and the daughter of John Wilkinson (1728-1808), seen on the right. She later married her cousin Thomas Wilkinson of Clapham. Her younger sister, who was named Marion, later married a Mr. Darval. The John Wilkinson portrayed here is apparently not the famous manufacturer and inventor of materials produced in cast iron although the information is not entirely conclusive on this point. According to a letter from one of his descendants, this John Wilkinson died at the age of forty-seven and had ten children, of whom only two survived. His wife was Sibella Bercisse [Beusse, Buette] of French Huguenot extraction. After the death of her husband, she married a second time, to a Captain Davison.

Traditionally attributed to Coates by the heirs of the Wilkinson family, this picture has also been given to Zoffany and to Benjamin Wilson. This matter has been confused in the publication by John Hulton in which he states that the picture is signed by Benjamin Wilson, which is not the case. Mary Webster, in the Wheatley exhibition catalogue of 1965, has confirmed an attribution to Wheatley by comparison with the portrait of Mr. and Mrs. Richardson (Royal Academy, 1778) now in the National Gallery of Ireland, Dublin, with which it also compares favorably in date. John Steegman in a letter of July 13, 1950 has also indicated a connection between these two paintings. A letter from a descendant of the family, in the Detroit museum archives, identifies the oldest girl in the painting as Sibella Wilkinson and tells that she was born in 1761, giving a working date of 1776-78. The costume and the relation of the picture to the Richardson portrait exhibited at the Royal Academy in 1778 also suggest a dating of 1776-78.

Done when he was barely thirty years of age, this painting is an extremely well-preserved example of Wheatley's early style. Wheatley was a friend of John Hamilton Mortimer, whose works he copied as a young man, and this painting relies on his grayed colors and is less than half life-size, as in the conversation pieces of Mortimer and Zoffany. Like earlier French and English painters of the conversation piece, Wheatley here shows the Wilkinson family out-of-doors. Within this well-established type, there are various possibilities of which a view of the country house or a suggestion of it is most often used. In this painting, the variety of trees, beech, oak, and willow, and the prominence of at least two kinds of plants in the foreground including a hollyhock suggest that nature in its multiplicity, rather than nature as a conventional backdrop, has taken over the scene. It is Wheatley's relaxed and more specific statement of the relation between nature and the sitter, confirmed with even more individuality in the portrait of the Browne family in the Mellon Collection, that was to transform the group portrait into an expression of the sitters' communion with and emulation of seemingly casual nature. In this guise the group portrait in which figures are allowed to become smaller while nature becomes larger, more intricate, and more elaborate, prepares for an intimate correlation of man and nature in the works of artists like Francis Danby in the early 19th century.
F.C.

75

Provenance
John Wilkinson of Roehampton
By descent to Sibella Wilkinson, Clapham, Yorkshire
By descent to Sibella Wilkinson de la Chaumette
By descent to Sibella de la Chaumette Crowdy
(Mrs. James Crowdy)

By descent to James Crowdy
By descent to Dame Rachel Crowdy
By descent to James Fuidge Crowdy (until 1924)
Leggatt Brothers, London (sold 5 December 1924
to Aldred)
J. R. Aldred, Long Island, New York (sale, Parke-Bernet,
New York, 15 May 1946, no. 45)
Scott & Fowles, New York
The Detroit Institute of Arts, 1946

Exhibitions
English Conversation Pieces of the Eighteenth Century,
The Detroit Institute of Arts, 1949, pl. 180
*Paintings Notable for the State of Preservation—
Condition: Excellent,* Worcester Art Museum,
Worcester, Mass., 1951, no. 30
The Century of Mozart, Nelson Gallery—Atkins Museum,
Kansas City, 1956, no. 108

References
John Hulton, *The Leeds Art Calendar,* Autumn, 1947
Edgar P. Richardson, "Conversation for the Eye,"
Art News, XLVII, March 1948, pp. 34, 57
Francis Wheatley, R. A., 1747-1801, Aldeburgh and
Leeds, 1965, p. 45 no. 96

76

76
Julie and St. Preux at Meillerie
Trustees of The British Museum
Indian ink, wash, and pen; 20⁹⁄₁₆ x 14¾ in.
Inscribed: *F. Wheatley delt. 1785; Julia*

This scene shows Julie, the modern heroine of
Rousseau's novel *Julie ou la nouvelle Héloïse,* with
her passionate lover of many years, St. Preux.
Julie's elderly and fully cognizant husband, M.
Wolmar, had invited his wife's lover of the time
before her marriage to live with them at his estate
in Switzerland. The young couple had not seen each
other for many years, he having been exiled before
the marriage; nevertheless, they were still deeply
in love. After a few brief weeks of enchanting,

bucolic existence, M. Wolmar was called away, and
the lovers were left alone in the incredibly beautiful
country place, tended and cared for in ideal fashion
by the exemplary household. On this occasion,
they made a fishing excursion onto the lake and
were driven by the wind to take refuge at Meillerie
where St. Preux had been exiled after his separation
from Julie. He took her away from the boating
party to a wild spot formerly his favorite place for
waiting and meditating on his love. There, a
cascade thundered down the mountainside from
the glaciers above. An inaccessible rock towered
above a spot where fir trees grew out of the rocks,
and beyond, the snow-covered peaks of the Jura

dominated the landscape. Here, St. Preux had
carved Julie's name on the rocks a thousand times
and added verses from Petrarch and Tasso. When
they arrived, St. Preux told her of the special
significance of the spot, broke into tears, and made
an impassioned declaration of his love for her.
She was deeply moved but restrained him for
the moment.

Wheatley frequently illustrated French texts, and
he is often close to Jean-Baptiste Greuze
(1725-1805) in his subjects and in the sentiments of
his art. In no. 76, the cascades of Joseph
Vernet, the craggy trees of Salvator Rosa's
etchings, the nostalgia for a more ideal existence,
and the emotionally moving scenery of the Alps
come together in a scene which is almost a
summary of romantic references and forms. A
companion to this drawing, also an illustration to
Julie, is in The British Museum.
F.C.

Provenance
Purchased by The British Museum from Mr. Rodd, 1866

Exhibitions
Francis Wheatley, R. A., 1747-1801, Aldeburgh Festival
and City Art Gallery, Leeds (Paul Mellon Foundation for
British Art), 1965, no. 40

References
Jean-Jacques Rousseau, *Julie ou la nouvelle Héloïse,*
Paris, 1761, Letter CXXXVI
Laurence Binyon, *Catalogue of Drawings by British
Artists . . . in the British Museum,* London, 1907, IV,
324 no. 5

Reproductions
Etched by F. Wheatley, completed in aquatint by
F. Jukes and R. Pollard, published by I. R. Smith,
14 June 1786

1751-1801

Hamilton was born at Chelsea, the son of a Scottish assistant to the architect Robert Adam. It was with Adam's assistance that Hamilton was able to travel to Italy before he was eighteen years old, and there he studied for a time with Antonio Zucchi (1726-95), the husband of Angelica Kauffmann. In 1769 he became a student at the Royal Academy schools in London and concentrated on history painting. In 1771 he temporarily won a gold medal for the best history painting in a competition at the Academy, but he was disqualified because the picture had been retouched by Zucchi. His first work submitted to the Academy exhibition in 1774 was a subject from English history, *King Edgar's First Interview with Elfrida.* However, from 1780 to 1789 he sent mainly portraits, especially of people connected with the theatre, probably not done on commission but as advertisement of his talents. The popular success of his portrait of his friend *Mrs. Siddons as "Isabella"* contributed to his election as A.R.A. in 1784. He became R.A. in 1789, and thereafter he exhibited numerous historical and literary subjects, such as *Ulysses Sparing Phemius* (Royal Academy 1796, British Museum) and *Moses Receiving the Law on Mt. Sinai* (Royal Academy, 1799; formerly Fonthill Abbey).

In 1779, the year of his marriage to Mary Aylward, he began to produce small pictures to be engraved and published as decorative prints or illustrations, and in this field he acheived considerable popularity. His generous output included designs for *A Voyage to New Guinea and the Moluccas* (1779), Humes's *History of England* (with West and Loutherbourg, 1792-1806), Gray's *Poems* (1800), the Bible (1800), and Milton's *Paradise Lost* (with Fuseli, 1802). His most famous productions of this type were the designs for an ambitious edition of Thomson's *Seasons,* engraved by Francesco Bartolozzi (1727-1815) and P. W. Tomkins (1760-1840) in 1797.

Throughout his career he enjoyed great professional respect. In 1773 the Academy chose him as one of a small committee of artists who were to consider decorating St. Paul's, a scheme which came to nothing. In 1792 he is reputed to have been offered the position of Portrait Painter to the Society of Dilettanti, in succession to Reynolds, but he rejected the proposal on the grounds that portraiture was not his forte. Two years later Farington noted in his diary that West considered Hamilton one of only three artists qualified to supervise the work of students in the Academy schools.

Hamilton's work continues in the decorative tradition of Zucchi, Angelica Kauffmann, and Wheatley. He is pleasant and attractive, and only occasionally attains the power and penetration of his more talented contemporaries.
F.C.

77

Bibliography
Johann Dominick Fiorillo, *Geschichte der zeichnenden kunst,* Göttingen, 1798-1808, pp. 683-84
A. T. Spanton, "William Hamilton, R. A.," *The Connoisseur,* XXI, May 1908, pp. 37-43
C. Reginald Grundy, "William Hamilton, R.A.," *The Connoisseur,* LXXII, August 1925, pp. 198-205
Robert E. Graves, "Hamilton, William," *Dictionary of National Biography,* VIII, 1937-38, pp. 1107-08

77
Joan of Arc and the Furies
Vassar College Art Gallery, Purchase, 1966
Oil on canvas; 31 x 21⅞ in.
c. 1791-1800

The subject is drawn from the play *Henry VI,* which is attributed to Shakespeare, was acted about 1592, and first published in 1623. It deals with the wars in France, particularly the relief of Orléans, early in the reign of Henry VI. The French were guided by Joan of Arc (1412-31) who is described as a minister of Hades, a witch, and a latter-day Circe who lied about her humble origins and gave birth illegitimately, claiming noblemen and kings as the fathers of her offspring. The passage occurs in Act V, Scene iii, where Joan calls upon her spirits to give aid in the battle before Angiers. The demons appear, and she queries, threatens, and pleads with them, inquiring what the outcome of the battle will be. But they hang their heads, deny her requests, and depart even though she offers them her body and even her soul in return for a sign.

This fierce Joan, a modern Bellona, is strange to us after our familiarity with her benign character in 19th-century art, but she is quite believable as the descendant of Romney's *Medea,* an equally fierce and ill-fated heroine. Indeed, George Romney was also interested in the subject of Joan of Arc, and this graceful female figure is closely related to such heroic poses as that of Viscountess Bulkeley (no. 31). According to John Romney, his father's painting was undertaken as a study for Boydell's Shakespeare Gallery, with Lady Hamilton as the model. However, William Hayley quotes a letter of Romney written in 1791 which says that the composition was being prepared for the Prince of Wales. The work, which was not finally completed, showed Joan's head with a raised right arm; the head was later engraved by Norman Hirst. William Hayley was so enthusiastic about the work that he wrote a sonnet in praise of Romney's *Joan of Arc* in which her battle against the English armies is vindicated. A preparatory drawing for Romney's composition is in the Fitzwilliam Museum,

Cambridge. There are so many Romney-like elements in Hamilton's painting, including the pose of Joan and her spirits, the treatment of light, shadow, and the landscape elements, that we can safely infer Hamilton's reliance for subject, and to a degree for composition, on Romney's previous treatment. Although in Boydell's possession, this painting does not appear in the Shakespeare Gallery exhibition catalogues of 1789 or 1790.
F.C.

Provenance
Josiah Boydell (sale, Christie's, London, 17 May 1805, no. 29, bt. Dr. Westrop)
Durlacher Bros., New York

References
William Hayley, *The Life of George Romney,* London, 1809, pp. 158-60
John Romney, *Memoirs of the Life and Works of George Romney,* London, 1830, pp. 154, 265
Humphrey Ward and W. Roberts, *Romney,* New York, 1904, II, 183, no. 14

Reproductions
Engraved by Anker Smith

Son of a goldsmith and watchmaker of Edinburgh, John Brown studied under the artist Charles Pavilon (1726-72), who taught from 1768 to 1772 at the School of Art begun in Edinburgh in 1760 by the Board of Manufacturers. He may also have studied under Pavilon's predecessor William Delacour (died 1767), the first master of the school, since Delacour did a portrait drawing of Brown now in the Scottish National Portrait Gallery.

In 1771, at the age of nineteen, Brown left for Rome with a young friend, David Erskine, whose cousin, later a cardinal, occupied an influential post at the Vatican. There, he became fluent enough in Italian to write poetry in the language, but his poems do not survive. He was also extremely interested in music and wrote *Letters upon the Poetry and Music of the Italian Opera,* addressed to James Burnett, Lord Monboddo, who became his patron in Edinburgh and undertook the publication of these letters in 1789. His close relation with Fuseli is pinpointed in Letter II which includes a detailed description of Cardinal Beaufort's death, a subject represented by Fuseli while in Italy. One of his patrons in Rome was Charles Townley, the antiquarian and collector who invited Brown to travel as his draftsman to Sicily. He returned to Edinburgh in 1781, obtained the patronage and friendship of Lord Monboddo, and assisted in the preparation of his treatise *Of the Origin and Progress of Language* (1773-92).

From David, Earl of Buchan, who founded the Society of Antiquaries of Scotland in 1780, Brown obtained his most important commission in 1781 to do a series of pencil portraits in life size of its leading members. At one time, thirty of these were in the possession of the Society of Antiquaries, Edinburgh. Almost that number is on loan at present to the Scottish National Portrait Gallery.

After a period of five years in Edinburgh, Brown left for London to work for Townley, drawing the sculptures in his collection. Some of these drawings were engraved by Bartolozzi. This was an auspicious moment to be in London, and especially to be a member of the Townley circle, for it was a time when Pierre-François-Hugues d'Hancarville was there preparing his *Recherches sur l'origine, l'esprit et les progrès des arts de la Grèce* (1785). Richard Payne Knight, in his relative youth, joined the group in the evenings, forming one of the most brilliantly cultivated circles of the period devoted to the study and collecting of ancient art. At this very moment, Brown's health began to fail. On embarking by sea for Edinburgh to settle his father's affairs, he became ill and died soon after reaching Leith in September 1787.

Brown was almost exclusively a draftsman rather than a painter and thus is omitted from dictionaries like that of Mathew Pilkington. It was his habit to keep his sketchbook with him constantly at social gatherings, in the streets, and no doubt also at the theater, which was one of his great passions. On these occasions, he frequently drew the guests present in those exceedingly delicate and refined drawings which betray his French teachers while connecting him with the Runciman and Fuseli circle in Rome. These sketches show women walking out-of-doors, in the streets, or in gardens, with the wind billowing their skirts; or men lounging or seated in conversation or study; there are others which concentrate on the braided and intertwined hair of a Roman lady. That he was an accomplished miniaturist, producing masterpieces like the tiny portrait of Alexander Runciman in the Scottish National Portrait Gallery, does not come as a surprise. His works are meticulous in refinement and in quality, and one can only regret that so few

are known to us today.

His social affability, which was greatly admired by his contemporaries, allowed him to enter the most interesting societies of his day. Particularly in his Edinburgh period, he was constantly to be seen at the elegant "Grecian suppers" of Lord Monboddo. F.C.

Bibliography
Lord Buchan, "John Brown with a Portrait," *The Bee,* Edinburgh, May 8, 1793, pp. 24, 27-31
J. M. Gray, "John Brown, the Draftsman," *Magazine of Art,* July 1889, pp. 310-15
W. G. Blaikie Murdoch, "John Brown, A Forgotten Artist," *The Scotsman,* 1928
Nicolas Powell, "Brown and the Women of Rome," *Signature,* XIV, 1952, pp. 40-50

78
The Basilica of Constantine and Maxentius, Rome, With a Scene of Murder in the Foreground
National Gallery of Scotland
Pen and brown ink; 14¾ x 22½ in.
Inscribed: *Tempe della Pace, Intorna da Roma, Giovanni Brown delinto;* collector's marks: Royal Scottish Academy (Lugt 2188); National Gallery of Scotland (Lugt 1969f).
c. 1774

Highly finished and complete in detail, this sheet is primarily an architectural rendering. In this connection, one should remember that Brown was retained as a draftsman of views for Charles Townley, and such a rendering may have been drawn for him. The careful representation of the arches of the Basilica of Constantine and Maxentius in Rome is enlivened by a scene of murder in the foreground. One man has been killed on the left. Another, fallen, in the center, defends himself from a kneeling opponent, while two other figures flee away to the right, and a woman rushes forward from the left to aid the fallen man.

Although the drawing was done in his Roman period, its style differs substantially from no. 79, which is finely brushed while this is drawn with a pen. The drawing of *Three Roman Ladies* was a record of his experience of a scene in a Roman street and part of a series in a sketchbook, as the inscribed number which it bears and its relation to other sheets of this type would lead us to believe. The present architectural view is a finished drawing of the sort Brown sent for exhibition to the Royal Academy in London when he first went to Rome. In subject, it could serve as a companion to the lost *View of the Coliseum, Rome,* exhibited at the Royal Academy in 1774, no. 19. The treatment of architecture, and to some extent of landscape, particularly the knotted trees and the precision with which these are detailed, recalls northern graphic art, especially the engravings of Dürer. The drapery is pulled taut around the female figure much in the same way as in Alexander Runciman's drawing of St. Margaret (no. 40), and the figures show mannerisms used both by Fuseli and Runciman which ultimately derive from schematic representations in 16th-century prints by Marc Antonio Raimondi after Raphael.
F.C.

Provenance
David Laing, Edinburgh (died 1878)
Bequeathed to the Royal Scottish Academy
Transferred to the National Gallery of Scotland, 1910

Exhibitions
Paintings and Drawings by Fuseli, Arts Council, London, etc., 1950, no. 135
Il Settecento a Roma, Amici dei Musei di Roma, Rome, 1959, no. 106

References
Nicolas Powell, *The Drawings of Henry Fuseli,* London, 1951, p. 42
National Gallery of Scotland, *Catalogue of Scottish Drawings* by Keith Andrews and J. R. Brotchie, Edinburgh, 1960, p. 57, no. D276

Violence

78

79
Three Roman Ladies, Seen From the Back
Courtauld Institute of Art (Witt Collection)
Indian ink and gray and brown wash, drawn with
the brush over pencil; 10 x 8¾ in.
Inscribed: *34;* on verso: in pen, *J. Brown invt;* in
Indian ink, pen, and wash a drawing of two men in
conversation; collector's mark of Sir Robert Witt
(Lugt 2228B)
c. 1775-80

This drawing is a central document in a study of the
scholarly resurrection of this remarkable artist.
In 1950 it was discovered that it had been engraved
in 1809 by Claussin, making possible the correct
attribution to Brown rather than to Fuseli. Despite

the signature on the back, its attribution had passed
from Brown to Fuseli owing to its connection with
certain of Fuseli's female figures and the drawing
on the verso which was said to relate to Fuseli's
Self Portrait in Conversation with Bodmer in the
Kunsthaus, Zürich. This discovery made possible
the correct attribution of a series of extraordinarily
delicate and refined sheets, done with a fine brush,
to John Brown. Their style is entirely different from
that of his later portrait drawings which were quite
well known, and it is not surprising that, even
though inscribed, the response to the style of this
sheet was ambivalent until discovery of the Claussin
engraving made the attribution conclusive.

Although Brown has dwelled on the elaborate
character of the costumes and has calculated their
rhythmic interconnections to the point of fantasy,
these are probably accurate records of the Roman
costume of the 1770s. Women in dresses of this
type frequently appear in the drawings of Fuseli,
and Antal's reproduction from the *Gallery of
Fashion* of 1797 makes clear that such swishing
costumes and the tendency to obscure the face
were fashionable characteristics rather than
psychological innuendoes. Powell and Antal called
this costume carnival dress, but Wright of Derby's
description makes clear that this is the everyday
street costume of a Roman lady. He mentions
particularly the elaborate coiffure and the "black
gauze" that hangs from the upper back part of the
head to cover the face, the long trains of the gowns,
and the graceful carriage.

The verso bears an unidentified subject showing
two men seated together in conversation. It is
related to the verso of a *Roman Lady Seen in Back
View,* also in the Witt Collection, signed *John
Brown Romae,* establishing firmly that both of these
drawings derive from Brown's Roman period.
Although both are usually related to Fuseli's *Self
Portrait in Conversation with Bodmer,* exhibited in
London in 1781, their only connection is that in
both cases two men are shown talking. The *Self
Portrait with Bodmer* was begun during Fuseli's
stay in Zürich from October 1778 to March 1779.

79

Exhibitions
Burlington Fine Arts Club, 1924-25, no. 201 (as by Brown)
Ashmolean Museum, Oxford, 1932 (as by Fuseli)
Paintings and Drawings by Fuseli, Arts Council, London, etc., 1950, no. 137 (as by Brown)
The Romantic Movement, The Tate Gallery, London (Arts Council), 1959, no. 625
Il Settecento a Roma, Amici dei Musei di Roma, Rome, 1959, no. 105
Scots in Italy in the Eighteenth Century, Scottish National Portrait Gallery, Edinburgh, 1966, unnumbered (catalogue compiled by Basil Skinner)

References
William Bemrose, *Wright of Derby,* London, 1885, p. 32 (as by Fuseli)
Nicolas Powell, *The Drawings of Henry Fuseli,* London, 1951, p. 45, no. 63 pl. (as by Brown)
Powell, *Signature,* XIV, 1952, p. 48
Frederick Antal, *Fuseli Studies,* London, 1956, p. 127 n. 5, pl. 51
Courtauld Institute of Art, *Hand-List of the Drawings in the Witt Collection,* London, 1956, p. 7 no. 644

Reproductions
Engraved by Ignace Joseph de Claussin, 1809

80

This would rule out any connection between no. 79 and Fuseli's *Bodmer;* nevertheless, it leaves open the dating of this sheet, which must illustrate Brown's mature Roman style and which is related in a general way to Fuseli's art. The verso of this drawing actually prepares for that entitled *The Congregation,* reproduced in the article by Powell, to which it is identical in style.
F.C.

Provenance
Sir Thomas Lawrence (died 1830) (sale, Christie's, London, 17 June 1830, no. 104, *Three Roman Ladies Walking, seen in back view,* as Brown, bt. Rogers)
(?) Charles Rogers
Meatyard, London
Sir Robert Witt, London (died 1952) (bt. from Meatyard)
Courtauld Institute of Art, Witt Bequest, London, 1952

80
Unidentified Lady
The Fyvie Trustees
Black chalk; mounted on canvas; 24 x 16 in.
c. 1780-85

Shown in the costume of the early to mid-1780s, this young woman is drawn in the style of Brown's famous portraits of the members of the Society of Antiquaries now in the Scottish National Portrait Gallery. These portraits were commissioned by the Earl of Buchan during the winter of 1780-81. In style, no. 80 is also close to the portrait drawing of Alexander Runciman by Brown (Scottish National Portrait Gallery, Edinburgh). This is one of the most splendid drawings of his Edinburgh period and

illustrates well, in a highly complete example, his drawing manner after his return from Rome.
F.C.

Provenance
Sir Ian Forbes-Leith of Fyvie, Bart., Fyvie Castle
The Fyvie Trustees, 1966

References
National Gallery of Scotland, *Catalogue of Scottish Drawings* by Keith Andrews and J. R. Brotchie, Edinburgh, 1960, pp. 57-58, no. 369

Even though attempts have been made to identify this artist, his name remains unknown. He was a cultivated and highly imaginative amateur who worked in Rome in 1779 after Fuseli had left for Switzerland and England. The stylistic affinities of this artist and the limited bibliography about him are summarized in the entry below.
F.C.

81

81
Scene with Four People and a Spider
Fogg Art Museum, Harvard University,
Gift of Richard L. Feigen
Pen, brush and black ink; 9⁵⁄₁₆ x 11⁷⁄₁₆ in.
Probably 1779

In 1949 a sketchbook was acquired by Messrs. Roland, Browse, and Delbanco, London, and later exhibited in 1952. It was broken up at the time, dispersing numerous of these drawings to collections in Britain and America. This sketchbook, done in Rome in 1779 according to the inscriptions on various sheets, was associated with Prince Hoare who was an acquaintance of Fuseli and who was in Rome in 1779. Antal, in his monograph on

Fuseli, connected the Master of the Giants with Prince Hoare for the first time in a publication. Later, in 1966, Robert Wark included certain of these drawings in the exhibition *William Blake and his Circle,* organized by the Huntington Library and Art Gallery, San Marino. In the catalogue those drawings were listed as "Attributed to Prince Hoare," and they included two of the type in the Fogg Museum and another entitled *Thor Battering the Serpent of Midgard* which is quite different from those in the Roland, Browse, and Delbanco sketchbook.

Evidence has not been forthcoming to support the attribution to Prince Hoare. A sketchbook in the Victoria and Albert Museum, done when Prince Hoare was in Italy, is not intimately connected with the Fogg drawing or with others by the Master of the Giants. Moreover, the highly conventional portraits by Prince Hoare have no suggestion of the intellectual individuality of drawings by the Master of the Giants. Although these drawings are usually referred to as Fuseliesque, they are also closely connected with the drawings of the Scottish circle in Rome, particularly Alexander Runciman and John Brown.

Numerous sheets by this hand are known, and all are remarkable for their uncanny subjects and their mannered technique. This remarkable drawing shows some ethereal, cloudy, or sulphurous region with a cringing woman whose terror arises from the ominous presence of a spider. Although broad in execution, it is remarkable for its unique subject and typifies the interest of this period in intense psychological responses.
F.C.

Provenance
Probably Roland, Browse, and Delbanco, London, 1949
Richard Feigen, Chicago
Fogg Art Museum, Cambridge, Mass., 1964

Exhibitions
Fantasy and Vision, Richard Feigen Gallery, Chicago, 1962, no. 14

References
Frederick Antal, *Fuseli Studies,* London, 1956, pp. 56, 76, n. 9

John Robert Cozens

1752-1797

John Robert Cozens was the son and also the pupil of Alexander Cozens whose sketches he often used for his own purposes and vice versa. Very little is known of his life, even less than of his father's. He was probably born in London. He sent works to the exhibition of the Society of Artists from 1767 to 1771. In 1776 he exhibited at the Royal Academy a painting entitled *Hannibal in his March Over the Alps, Showing to his Army the Fertile Plains of Italy.* The reception of this work encouraged him to become a candidate for the Royal Academy in 1776, but he received no votes.

One of the most important periods of his life began when he left for Italy in the autumn of 1776 as a draftsman for Richard Payne Knight, the collector, connoisseur, and writer on art. They travelled through the Swiss Alps, where Cozens made some of his most remarkable drawings, and continued on to Florence and Rome. Knight left Rome for Sicily in April 1777, but Cozens did not accompany him. According to a letter of Northcote, he was still in Rome in 1778, and in April 1779 he began his return journey to England.

His second trip to Italy was made with William Beckford, the collector and author of the exotic tale, *Vathek.* This time he travelled by way of Cologne, Augsburg, Venice, and on to Naples by way of Rome. At Naples he stayed with Sir William Hamilton at his villa near Portici. But Cozens then left Beckford's party and continued alone to Vietri, Salerno, and Paestum. He returned to Naples, where he played the violoncello briefly with

Hamilton, and moved on to Rome. There he met Sir George Beaumont, the amateur painter and collector, to whom he gave instruction in landscape drawing, and in September 1783 left for England.

After his return to London, very little is heard of Cozens. He made two or three large drawings from sketches by James Stuart, one of which was engraved in the third volume of the *Antiquities of Athens,* published in 1794. He had a complete nervous collapse in 1793 after which he was deranged until his death in December 1797.

John Robert Cozens is perhaps the most sensitive and at the same time the least pretentious British landscapist of the 18th century. In no way flashy or abrupt, his monochrome landscapes are composed of infinitely subtle nuances of tone and poignant and elegant reiterations of luminous rhythms. From his father, he learned to value the unusual points of view and sharp silhouettes. But under Robert's hand, these devices become subtler, are softened, and often transformed into elongated rhythms, winding through infinite recessions in space. Such devices rely on the tradition of Claude. At other times, he presents monumental visions of mountain or storm-gathered clouds over lakes in scenes which anticipate Turner. At still other times, his works possess that complete stillness of globed light, crystalline in its clarity, which is so frequent in Italy and has come to be viewed as a dominating quality of Italian light. In all of these moods there is a certain constantly changing and willowy design inevitably faithful to nuances of the atmosphere. It is this constant attention to the special qualities of the scene and the atmosphere of the moment, deriving from his father's sensitivity to clouds and atmospheric effects, that makes Cozens especially important for the art of Constable and Turner.
F.C.

Bibliography
A Collection of Drawings by John Robert Cozens, Burlington Fine Arts Club, London, 1922
C. F. Bell and Thomas Girtin, "The Drawings and Sketches of John Robert Cozens," *Walpole Society,* XXIII, 1934-35
A. P. Oppé, *Alexander & John Robert Cozens,* London, 1952

82
Schwartze Lütschine and the Mettenberg (Betwee Lauterbrunnen and Grindelwald)
Leeds City Art Galleries
Watercolor; 14¼ x 20½ in.
Inscribed: *John Cozens 1778*

The Schwartze Lütschine is the stream which flow from the valleys of Grindelwald and Lauterbrunne to the lake of Brienz in the Swiss canton of Berne in the Central Alps. In the background is the remarkable mass of the Mettenberg, one of the chief peaks (10,194 feet) of that range. The intere in Alpine scenery, reflected in drawings and paintings since the period of Dürer, had a dramati revival in the late 18th century. It also took on a slightly new character through an emphasis on th dramatic and unusual in such scenes. The precipitous waterfall, the dark cliffs, and the slim pines framing a snow-covered peak have overtone of the wild and sublime rather than the more domestic picturesque or the views of Italy, well known through the work of Claude, Gaspard Poussin, and their imitators.

No. 82 is an enlarged version of a composition formerly in the collection of Richard Payne Knight only this is signed and dated. The first was probab made in September of 1776 when Cozens was travelling through the Alps in the company of Richard Payne Knight. These form part of a series of Swiss views later in Knight's collection. Some these subjects exist in two or even more versions usually enlarged from the first sketchbook page

82

during the period when Cozens was staying in Rome.

These composition sketches are highly direct confrontations with the view which they dramatize through simplification, with a resulting grandeur which is often startling. These sketches, which are among Cozens' most inspired works, were important for the development of a taste for Alpine scenery in British landscape since they were later admired and copied by artists like Turner and Girtin.
F.C.

Provenance
W. E. Lambert (sale, Christie's, London, 24 March 1817, no. 30)
William Esdaile, London (died 1837)
Edward Cohen
Agnes and Norman D. Lupton
Bequeathed to Leeds City Art Galleries, 1953

Exhibitions
Watercolours and Drawings from the City Art Gallery, Leeds, Thos. Agnew & Sons, London, 1960, no. 21

References
Bell and Girtin, p. 30, no. 1911
Leeds Arts Calendar, VIII no. 27, 1954, p. 16

83
On the Strada Nomentana, Rome
The Toledo Museum of Art, Toledo, Ohio, Museum Purchase, 1958
Watercolor; $13^{11}/_{16}$ x 10¾ in.
c. 1782-83

The Via Nomentana was one of the ancient roads used in Roman times and originally called the Via Ficulensis. It led out of Rome through the Porta Nomentana to Nomentum, fourteen miles northeast of the city. Its ruins and ancient trees made it one of the favorite places of 18th-century artists for sketching Italian scenery.

Unless inscribed by the artist, Cozens' drawings are notoriously difficult to date because he frequently repeated and copied his compositions. This sheet is usually dated in the period of his second Roman journey, about 1782-83. Another version of this same ruin is preserved in the Victoria and Albert Museum.
F.C.

Provenance
William Esdaile, London (died 1837)
Henry Harris, until 1933
Sir Thomas Dalmahoy Barlow, London (died 1945)
Gilbert Davis
(A paper label once on the back of the frame indicates that it was once owned or lent by Thos. Agnew & Sons, London, no. 7728)
The Toledo Museum of Art, 1958

Exhibitions
John Robert Cozens, Burlington Fine Arts Club, London, 1922, no. 11 and pl. viii (lent by Harris)
Watercolour Drawings by J. R. Cozens and J. S. Cotman, Whitworth Art Gallery, Manchester, 1937, no. 59 (lent by Barlow)
Three Centuries of British Water-Colours and Drawings, Arts Council, London, 1951, no. 55 (catalogue compiled by Brinsley Ford)

References
Bell and Girtin, no. 354

83

1753-1828

The son of a farmer who owned a colliery, in which the son worked as a child, Bewick was to become one of the most admired printmakers and naturalists of his day. In 1767, at the age of fourteen, he began his apprenticeship with Ralph Beilby (1744-1817), an engraver from Newcastle. There, he etched swordblades, engraved door-knockers, and did the preliminary roughing-out of woodblocks for such works as the *Ladies' Diary.* Soon he was entrusted with most of Beilby's wood engraving, and undertook numerous projects including, in 1771, the *New Lottery-Book of Birds and Beasts.* In 1774 he completed his apprenticeship and in the following year received an award for a block illustrating Gay's *Fables,* exhibited at the Society of Arts. After a walking tour of Scotland, he was in London with Isaac Taylor and Thomas Hodgson, the printer and publisher. Returning to Newcastle in 1776, he set himself up in business with his younger brother John as his apprentice, and brought enough work from London to last for two years from such former Newcastle acquaintances as William Bulmer, who was to become one of the great English printers at the beginning of the 19th century. In 1779 he engraved *Tommy Trip's History of Birds and Beasts,* Gay's *Fables,* and in 1784, the *Select Fables.* In most of these works, Bewick, depending upon earlier iconographical traditions rather than inventing new designs, generally improved and modernized what had been given to him. In 1785 he undertook the first of the long series of publications devoted to British animals which was to make him famous, the *General History of Quadrupeds,* published in Newcastle in 1790 with a

text by Ralph Beilby. One of Bewick's largest and most famous animal engravings, produced in 1789, the *Chillingham Bull,* showed one of the famous wild cattle, a type which appears in romantic literature. The success of the *Quadrupeds* and the possibility of working directly from actual specimens determined his next undertaking, the *History of British Birds,* his most important publication, brought out in two volumes from 1797 to 1804. This is Bewick's finest effort, and he was not to attain the same standard of quality in his later productions. Although the text of the first volume was still by Beilby, it was edited and amended by Bewick himself. In publications after the *Birds,* his students were often entrusted with the cutting of the blocks which were even occasionally designed by them, for example the *Poems of Burns,* designed by John Thurston. His last outstanding work was the *Fables of Aesop,* produced in 1818, in which he was assisted by his son and two other pupils. His production was interrupted by a serious illness in 1812 which left his hands badly swollen with gout and his eyesight failing.

Bewick's pupils are important since they carry on the legacy of illustrative printmaking which was to flourish in mid-19th-century publications, particularly journals. Among them were his brother John Bewick (1760-95), his son Robert E. Bewick (1788-1849), Robert Johnson (1770-96), William Harvey (1796-1866), and John Jackson (1801-48), to name the most outstanding.
F.C.

Bibliography
Thomas Bewick, *History of British Birds,* 2 vols., Newcastle-upon-Tyne, 1797-1804
Thomas Bewick, *Memoir . . . written by Himself,* London, 1862
Thomas Hugo, *The Bewick Collector,* London, 1866
Austin Dobson, *Thomas Bewick and his Pupils,* London, 1884
Julia Boyd, ed., *Bewick Gleanings,* Newcastle-upon-Tyne, 1886
A Collection of Drawings and Woodcuts by Thomas

Bewick, Fine Art Society, London, 1881 (catalogue compiled by F. G. Stephens)
David Croal Thompson, *The Water-Colour Drawings of Thomas Bewick,* London, 1930
S. Roscoe, *Thomas Bewick; a Bibliography raisonné of editions,* London/New York, 1953
Thomas Bewick, 1753-1828, Arts Council, London, 1965

84

The Natural size.

84
A Starling
Courtauld Institute of Art (Witt Collection)
Watercolor; 7⅞ x 10 1/16 in.
Inscribed: *Thomas Bewick; The Natural Size; The eye a little high/. . .& bright the Body a little more plump*
1791-97

The first drawings for Bewick's *History of British Birds* were done when he went to Wycliffe at the invitation of a Mr. Constable in July 1791 to study stuffed birds in the museum. He brought his drawings back to undertake the woodcuts for printing. However, on comparing the drawings of stuffed birds with actual ones, he found that the poses were often uncharacteristic and that the feathers were frequently set incorrectly in their final places by the taxidermist, resulting in an inaccurate representation of the bird. Realizing this, Bewick began to study birds, both on his own travels out-of-doors and also examples which were killed and brought to him. He had made up his mind not to follow works by other illustrators, which he had learned to doubt in publishing his earlier engravings, and he now decided to work entirely from nature, from birds which were shot, and from observations of birds in their natural habitat. This work was begun in 1791, and the first volume of *Land Birds,* in which *A Starling* was included, was ready for the press by 1797.

Bewick's technique was to prepare a study in color of his subject which would then be copied in a

drawing on the block and cut. His earlier practice had been that of Renaissance wood engravers who drew directly on the block and destroyed the entire preparatory drawing in the process of cutting. Bewick's reason for employing this new technique was to achieve the very sparkle and variety in the woodcut itself of his original visual impression of the bird. To achieve as close an approximation as possible in the black and white through texture alone, it was essential to retain the colored drawing for comparison with the finished print, to correct the block, and to prepare the verbal description. In addition to studies like *A Starling,* which were closely followed in the finished engraving, Bewick also made sketches of dead birds in watercolor, later revised in the illustration. One example is the *Snipe,* carefully signed in Bewick's hand, in the Museum of Fine Arts, Boston. He also made complete studies of individual feathers as notes for the later coloring, printing, and the description of an entire bird. Many of these jewel-like studies and other drawings of the type shown here are in the Hancock Museum, Newcastle-upon-Tyne.

Bewick was admired in particular by the Victorian

artists for his methodical care and accuracy, his study of nature to do the craftsmanly work of illustrating and printing, and also for completing the work with a literary description. Like the intimate focusing on individual parts, such as a feather, these verbal descriptions were undertaken with the greatest care and accuracy, detailing the natural appearance, habits and, especially, the color of each part. Such craftsmanship, in particular the task of a master artisan producing an intimate visual and verbal production from beginning to end, was admired and emulated by John Ruskin and William Morris. Ruskin was enthused about Bewick, and Ruskin's own studies of naturalistic detail find a source of inspiration in Bewick's art. F.C.

Provenance
Sir Robert Witt (in his collection before 1934, bought at an anonymous Sotheby's sale, no date)
Courtauld Institute of Art, Witt Bequest, 1952

Exhibitions
British Art, Royal Academy of Arts, London, 1934, no. 1164, cat. no. 683
English Drawings and Engravings from the seventeenth to the twentieth century, Bucharest, Vienna, Prague, 1935-36, no. 22
Some British Drawings from the Collection of Sir Robert Witt, London, 1948, no. 4

References
Iolo Williams, *Early English Watercolours,* London, 1952, pp. 206-07, no. 318
Basil Taylor, *Animal Painting in England from Barlow to Landseer,* Harmondsworth, Middlesex, 1955, p. 55, pl. 39

Reproductions
Engraved in wood by Thomas Bewick in the *History of British Birds,* Newcastle, 1797, I, 88, repr. in reverse

John Flaxman

1755-1826

One of the few sculptors in this exhibition, Flaxman is shown here as a draftsman. He was born in York and taken to London at the age of six months, where his father, who worked for Roubiliac and Scheemakers, made a living by producing and selling plaster models and casts. Flaxman learned his craft by drawing and modelling under the instruction of his father. He was precocious; in 1767 when he was twelve years old, he sent works to the Free Society of Artists, and from 1770 he sent drawings, waxes and bas-reliefs to the Royal Academy exhibitions. In the same year, he became a student at the Royal Academy schools and remained for at least two years. In 1775 he joined his father in working for Josiah Wedgwood, who had a shop in the Strand. There he designed cameos, friezes, and portrait medallions. He also advised Wedgwood about interior decorations and assisted with the mouldings and architectural details of Etruria Hall. It was primarily through this firm that he supported himself in his early years. By 1780 he had exhibited a design for a sepulchral monument to Chatterton for the Church of St. Mary Redcliffe, Bristol, which suggests that he was receiving substantial commissions for sculpture by that time.

George Romney, who became Flaxman's close friend, introduced him to Mrs. Mathew, a highly literate woman greatly interested in artists and musicians. She read the works of Homer to him in Greek, and he undertook the Gothic interior decorations of her house, which also included designs by other artists for painted windows in imitation of stained glass. At her home, he met Thomas Stothard, William Blake, and the translator of Plato's works, Thomas Taylor, who gave a series of twelve lectures on Platonic philosophy in Flaxman's house in 1784. Through Romney he also met William Hayley, and the Flaxmans spent time in the summers at Hayley's residence at Eartham, near the sea. Hayley was a close friend of William Cowper, the poet and translator, and Flaxman no doubt met him at Eartham, as did Romney.

In 1787 Flaxman left for Rome with his wife, Ann Denman, remaining there seven years to study antique, Renaissance, and medieval monuments, and undertaking his most important early commissions. Indeed, he was so successful in this respect that he remained in Rome well beyond the two years originally projected. Edward Knight of Portland Place had been his patron in London as early as 1781, and he continued to know him in Rome. His patrons were such well-known collectors of antique art as Thomas Hope and Frederick Hervey, Earl of Bristol and Bishop of Derry, for whom he chiselled the *Fury of Athamas* (Ickworth House), his most famous sculptural group, in 1790.

He was particularly successful and influential as a draftsman. From Mr. Udney and Mrs. Nare Taylor he received a commission for seventy-three drawings to illustrate the *Iliad* and the *Odyssey*. When they were circulated, these created a minor sensation in artistic circles leading Thomas Hope to commission a similar series from Dante, and Lady Spencer a series from Aeschylus. All were engraved by Tommaso Piroli (1752?-1824), and all but the Aeschylus of 1795 were published in 1793. His last series of drawings of this type were the illustrations to Hesiod of 1817. Although in a quite general way, these designs reflect the emphasis on noble simplicity of Winckelmann and certain of the types of Canova, their most important source is Greek vase painting. Romney called them simple, grand, and pure, as if they had been made in the age of Homer. The engravings were of the greatest importance for diffusing the taste for purity, simplicity, linear pattern, and non-illusionistic representation to the fields of painting, sculpture, and the decorative arts. The great elegance of Flaxman's designs, their extreme reserve, simplicity, and beauty of pure arabesque made them and their outline technique immediately popular. Even Fuseli acknowledged himself outdone as a designer by these works, and Canova and Schlegel, and the German critics generally, were enthused about them.

Flaxman returned to England in 1794 where he was now a well-known artist and successful as a designer and sculptor of commemorative monuments and groups. He became A.R.A. in 1797 and R.A. in 1800. In 1810 he was appointed Professor of Sculpture at the Royal Academy, and there he delivered the lectures outlining the history of ancient art. He also gave evidence which assisted the British government in purchasing the Parthenon sculptures in 1816.

Robert Rosenblum has pinpointed succinctly Flaxman's principal contribution in a paragraph of his recent book *Transformations in Late Eighteenth Century Art* (p. 189). Flaxman's emphasis on linear arabesque and his use of white spaces as an active participant, with linear pattern alternating with form, dispensed with the closed box techniques of pictorial illusionism, the dominating principle of works of art from Alberti through Boucher. In this way Flaxman prepares for Courbet's and Manet's more complete destruction of illusionist space and Renaissance perspective systems in the mid-19th century and provides one of the sources of the Art Nouveau and of contemporary art.

F.C.

Bibliography

John Flaxman, *Lectures on Sculpture,* London, 1829
Sidney Colvin, *Drawings of Flaxman,* London, 1876
W. G. Constable, *John Flaxman,* London, 1927
Edward Croft-Murray, "An Account Book of John Flaxman, R. A.," *Walpole Society,* XXVIII, 1939-40
Rupert Gunnis, "Flaxman, John, R. A.," *Dictionary of British Sculptors 1660-1851,* London, 1953, pp. 147-51

Robert Rosenblum, *The International Style of 1800: A Study in Linear Abstraction,* Ph.D. dissertation, New York University, 1956
John Flaxman, R. A., Sculptor, Hatton Gallery, King's College, University of Durham, 1958
David Irwin, "Flaxman: Italian Journals and Correspondence," *Burlington,* CI, 1959, pp. 212-17
Margaret Whinney, "John Flaxman," in *Sculpture in Britain 1530 to 1830,* Baltimore, 1964, pp. 183-95
G. E. Bentley, Jr., *The Early Engravings of Flaxman's Classical Designs, A Bibliographical Study,* New York, 1964

85
Self Portrait
Hales Owen Grammar School
Pen and brush with brown ink; 15½ x 14 in.
Inscribed: *John Flaxman Junr. by himself*
c. 1779

During the 1770s a number of Flaxman's works at the Royal Academy exhibitions were portrait reliefs, which is no doubt how he wished to become known, and this drawing illustrates how accomplished he was in this genre. A preparatory study for this portrait is in The Art Institute of Chicago. The preparatory drawing in red chalk was made before a mirror while Flaxman held his sketches far in front with his left hand which, in the mirror image, appears as his right. In order to record his features exactly, he reversed this image for the finished pen drawing now in Hales Owen. He then parted the hair in the middle and arranged the locks so that the longest fell to his left. The heavy folds of his outer coat were drawn across the shoulders and chest in such a way that they suggest antique draperies, but are not, as the contemporary collar indicates. The background was then filled in with overlapping parallel lines to suggest the tonal background of a bas-relief. Together, these drawings prepare for the final relief in wax of 1779 in the Victoria and Albert Museum.

For the technique of this drawing, two sources are apparent. The principal one is the art of John H. Mortimer, whose technique is reflected particularly in the manner of drawing the hand and in the use

85

of stippling in the flesh for texture and to create patterns of shadow and light. The other source is the drawing style of James Barry who used similar parallel and crisscrossing lines to create his backgrounds as in the portrait drawing of Mrs. Sharon Turner (Huntington Library and Art Gallery, San Marino). However, Flaxman's technique is more subtle and refined than Barry's, which uses broader crisscross strokes drawn with the point of the brush.
F.C.

Provenance
Edward Knight of Portland Place, London (died 1812)
By descent to Major Erick Knight, Wolverley House, Worcestershire
Purchased by Dr. Johnson Ball for the Hales Owen Technical School, Hales Owen, Worcestershire, 1945

References
David Irwin, *English Neo-Classical Art, Studies in Inspiration and Taste,* Greenwich, Conn., 1966, p. 154, pl. 153

86
A Young Girl
Museum of Fine Arts, Boston, Anonymous Gift and William A. Sargent Fund
Black chalk on pale gray paper; 11 x 6½ in.
Inscribed: *Italien*
c. 1787-92

Drawn on his Italian tour, probably before the *Iliad* and *Odyssey* illustrations, no. 86 shows Flaxman's technique in a subject not frequently associated with his art. Like his illustrations to Dante and Homer, this study possesses a high order of graphic sensibility. The concentration on textural differentiations with purely graphic means looks forward to the drawings of Van Gogh. The solidity of construction and bluntness of forms, the textured shoestrings and the frill of the dress beneath the chin bring to mind the highly sophisticated graphic achievement of late 19th-century French and Dutch art.

Even in this drawing, which studies solid form, Flaxman shows an interest in arabesque, as in the long and tense outline of the white apron pulled taut across the front of the girl's striped dress and the winding mass of curly hair. But it is rare for him to concentrate on the visual implications of mood as he does here. Simplicity and reserve are the hallmarks of Flaxman's art with those important exceptions where expression was specifically required, as in his sculptural group the *Fury of Athamas.* It is exactly the reflective mood and the element of nostalgia which have captivated him in

86

the expression of this child. The apprehensions open to those who are innocent and uncorrupted by modern, civilizing influence was a favorite theme of the late 18th-century writers, and it is given expression in the historical essays of Voltaire. Such an emulation of innocence and freshness must have been in Flaxman's mind when he made this drawing.   F.C.

Provenance
Museum of Fine Arts, Boston, 1953

87
Dante and Virgil in the Suicidal Wood
The Metropolitan Museum of Art,
Gift of Scott & Fowles, 1918
Reed pen and ink over pencil; 7½ x 10⅛ in.
Inscribed: *I'sentia d'ogni parte tragger guai,/E non vedea persona che'l facesse/Inferno/ Canto 13*
1792-93

This is a variant of the final composition for Flaxman's illustration to Canto XIII of Dante's *Inferno*. Although it was not used for the final engraving, certain elements from it were. The forest of the harpies is the setting in both illustrations, each of which has a splendid, gnarled tree in the foreground, forming an arabesque of lines across the foremost space of the page. However, the text selected for the final illustration was changed. The engraving illustrates the moment when Dante tears a branch from the trunk of a tree and hears the shriek from the living creature within, "Why do you mangle me?"

This sheet illustrates a previous moment (ll. 22, 23), "I heard wailings on every side and did not see the person who made them." The wailing comes not only from the harpies who have nests in the trees but also from the living trees themselves. Stalwart Virgil is shown here leading Dante forward, but in the final version, he will be seen far back in space with a similar cape wrapped around the lower part of his face.

As a variant of the final design for the Dante illustrations, no. 87 gives important information about Flaxman's working method. It comes as a surprise that he changed his mind even after creating such a complete design as this. Curiously, the final design is less satisfying, and Flaxman must have altered his conception because he felt the moment selected was not central enough to the story. The use of a broad reed pen which reveals this drawing as a preparatory sheet is exchanged in the final design for a finer point to give treatment of details.

87

The entire series of 111 drawings for the *Divina Commedia* of Dante was commissioned by Thomas Hope in 1792-93, and it is interesting that this design, although not engraved, was also in his possession.

The revival of interest in Dante is a contribution of the romantic period, and the development of this interest has been richly and microscopically detailed by Paget Toynbee. Jonathan Richardson was particularly important in this revival. His interest in Dante was stimulated when an artist brought to him the beautiful relief of *Count Ugolino and his Sons* by Pierino da Vinci (Ashmolean Museum, Oxford), then attributed to Michelangelo. Searching for the literary source, Richardson became enthused about the then obscure Italian poet and transcribed the passage of Ugolino in his *Discourse on the . . . Advantage of the Science of Connoisseur* (1719), at a point where he was discussing the mutual and individual capacities of poetry, painting, and sculpture as art forms. The moving story, fraught with psychological nuances, the beautiful relief by Pierino, with which it was connected; the context of comparative valuations of the arts, which was one of the extensive light and serious topics of discussion in the 18th century;

and the vivid descriptions by Dante were important sources for Reynolds, who painted *Ugolino,* exhibited at the Royal Academy in 1773, at the same time as he was painting a portrait of Giuseppe Baretti, a translator and promulgator of Dante's poetry and Italian literature in general (no. 8). William Hayley admired Dante, and in his *Essay on Epic Poetry* (1782) made numerous references to the *Divina Commedia.* He was also the first to attempt a translation in the meter of the original. Hayley's and Romney's enthusiasm would have been communicated to their young friend Flaxman when he stayed at Eartham.
F.C.

Provenance
Commissioned by Thomas Hope, Deepdene, Dorking, Surrey (died 1831)
By descent to Lord Francis Pelham Clinton Hope (sale, Christie's, London, 26 July 1917, no. 365)
Scott & Fowles, New York
The Metropolitan Museum of Art, New York, 1918

Exhibitions
Original drawings by John Flaxman, Scott & Fowles, New York, 1918, no. 70 (catalogue essay prepared by Martin Birnbaum)
Fourth Anniversary Exhibition, Drawings, Lyman Allyn Museum, New London, Conn., 1936, no. 173

References
Paget Toynbee, "The Earliest English Illustrations of Dante," *Quarterly Review,* CCXI, 1909, pp. 395-417
Paget Toynbee, "Dante in English Art," *Annual Report of the Dante Society,* 1924, p. 5
Paget Toynbee, *Britain's Tribute to Dante in Literature and Art; A Chronological Record of 540 Years,* London, 1921, p. 36
Bentley, pp. 19-20

88
Penelope's Dream
Professor and Mrs. I. R. C. Batchelor
Pen over pencil; 6½ x 9¼ in.
Inscribed: *J. Flaxman*
1792-93

As related in Book IV of Homer's *Odyssey,* Penelope, Queen of Ithaca, has learned from Medon, the herald, that her suitors are planning to kill her son Telemachus so that one will be able to marry her and have complete control of her throne. The suitors have sailed off to assassinate Telemachus on his return from an expedition to Pylos and Lacedaemon in search of news of his father Odysseus. Full of terror at the news, Penelope returns to her room, whereupon Athena, to ease her troubled mind, sends a phantom disguised as a woman to speak with her in her dreams. The phantom stands at the head of her bed and assures Penelope that the gods will protect her son. Penelope then asks about Odysseus, but the phantom refuses to answer and retires.

The drawings for the *Odyssey* were undertaken in a relatively brief period of time late in 1792 and early in 1793. In a letter of December 15, Mrs. Flaxman wrote that her husband was too busy to write letters because of the work he wished to complete before his departure for England. Apart from sculptures, she mentioned a complete set of drawings on which he was working in the evenings. These were for Dante and for Homer's *Iliad* and *Odyssey.* The Homeric series was commissioned by Mr. Udney, who planned to engrave them, and duplicates were made for Mr. Naylor (Bentley, p. 17). The engraved plates for the *Odyssey* were published on February 1, 1793, but were later lost. The first impressions are mentioned soon after in letters by Romney, recording their presence in England.

This sheet is highly complete and finished, and almost identical to the final engraving. It is one of the most refined in quality and possesses a greater variety of line and textures and a greater certainty and purity than most known Flaxman drawings.

The engravings were often copied, and Flaxman occasionally traced his own drawings to make duplicate sets. The high quality of this sheet and the traces of *pentimenti,* as in the phantom's right upper arm, suggest that this is the first complete realization of this design and, judging from the signature, one with which Flaxman was pleased.
F.C.

Provenance
John Manning, London
Professor and Mrs. I. R. C. Batchelor, Broughty Ferry, 1959

Exhibitions
Twelfth Exhibition of Watercolours and Drawings, John Manning, London, 1959, no. 69

References
T. S. R. Boase, *English Art 1800-1870,* Oxford, 1959, p. 136
Whinney, p. 189
Bentley, pp. 17-18

Reproductions
Engraved by Tommaso Piroli (for other reproductions, see Bentley)

88

1756-1815

Born in Chelsea, James Gillray was the son of a Moravian family, and his father was a veteran and a Chelsea pensioner until his marriage in 1757. Quite early James was apprenticed to Harry Ashby (1744-1818), an engraver of metalwork, whom he soon left, along with several other apprentices, apparently to join a company of strolling players. He returned to London about 1775, when we first hear of him as an artist at the publication of two of his caricature prints, and in 1778 he was admitted to the Royal Academy schools where he studied drawing. His early engravings are not signed, and it is difficult to single out his works before about 1780. At this time, he was already employed by William Humphrey, who opened a publishing and print-selling shop in St. Martin's Lane in 1772. Through Humphrey and his widow, with whom he maintained a connection for the greater part of his life, he received commissions, and their shop formed an outlet for the sale of his prints.

Gillray's first identifiable political caricature is *Grace Before Meat* of 1778, which caricatures George III's support of the Catholic Relief Act. It was the beginning of a specialization which was to gain for him by the early 1780s the leading place among political satirists. An indefatigable worker, his output was extraordinary. His work was based on commissions accepted free-lance to lampoon a particular individual, party, bill, or event. Generally, his work does not reflect a well-devised and coherent point of view as is reflected, for example, in the political and social criticism of William Blake. His subjects include *The Morning*

after Marriage—A Scene on the Continent, which ridicules the clandestine marriage of Mrs. Fitzherbert to the Prince of Wales, and a lampoon on the Duc d'Orléans on his trip to London of 1789-90 before he was guillotined, at a time when the Duke was considered a traitor to his class.

In March 1792 Gillray began to sign his plates; thereafter, they reveal greater care in design and execution, suggesting that by this time, when he was approximately thirty-five, he had made a total commitment to satire as opposed to any other genre. More and more, his prints were carefully thought out and prepared through preliminary studies. At the same time, he wrote elaborate explanatory commentaries in which he showed wit and an originality of style which greatly appealed to the public. The designs and commentaries are infused with a high burlesque in which no reserves in the face of status or position constrict the extravagance. They are devastating, frequently more than crude, even verging on the disgusting, and always infused with a deep-seated irony and sense of the bizarre which is beyond humor.

Gillray not only drew political satires, but was also talented as a social commentator and entertainer. He was a complete master of the grotesque and the ridiculous, which were united in his art with biting sarcasm. He lampooned fashionable dress, hairstyles, artistic tastes, and morals without regard for the feelings of specific individuals. His sources for this specialty are Hogarth and Pier Leone Ghezzi (1674-1755), whose drawings were admired and collected by the aristocratic and artistic travellers to Italy.

Throughout his life, Gillray was subject to states of electric mental activity and depression. He appears to have had a preoccupation with damage to his eyesight which became almost an obsession in his late years and may be related to his final insanity. After years of work as an engraver, he began to wear eyeglasses in 1806. Revealing in this respect is the powerful drawing *Pray Pity the Sorrows of a Poor Blind Man* (collection L. G. Duke, London) in which he portrays himself as a blind and toothless beggar.

Gillray is certain to be of more and more interest to students of this period. Not only are his brilliant talent and his social commentary rewarding, his method of arranging visual images is highly distinctive and related to works of William Blake and Flaxman. For those who are interested primarily in the structure of visual images and the contributions of this period to that specialty, Gillray will require, and will no doubt reward, further investigation.
F.C.

Bibliography
James Gillray, *The Caricatures of Gillray,* London, 1824
Thomas McLean, *Illustrative Description of the Genuine Works of Mr. James Gillray,* London, 1830
Thomas Wright and R. H. Evans, *Historical and Descriptive Account of the Caricatures of James Gillray,* London, 1851
Draper Hill, *Mr. Gillray, the Caricaturist,* Greenwich, Conn., 1965

89

89
Study for "Charon's Boat—or—the Ghosts of 'All the Talents' Taking Their Last Voyage"
The Detroit Institute of Arts, Elliott F. Slocum Fund
Pen and ink, brush, wash in brown, red-brown and gray; 11½ x 18½ in.
Inscribed: *The Stygian Lake; Catholic Bill; Charon's Boat Passing the Stygian Lake/or the last of the/ Broad Bottom Members on their last Voyage*
1807

The scene is the river Styx and the cavernous entry into the Underworld. The event is the fall of William Grenville's ministry, the famous "Ministry of All the Talents." Grenville, who was William Pitt's cousin, resigned the Foreign Office in 1807, along with the Pitt ministry. This resulted from the decision of George III not to consent to any measure being introduced for Roman Catholic relief. He believed a measure in support of Roman Catholicism violated his oath of coronation, and he was so adamant on the point that it actually brought on attacks of insanity. A political ally of George Fox, Grenville became head of a coalition government in 1806 which began with a bad start due to an oppressive tax program, and was further weakened by the death of Fox in 1806. In the spring of 1807 the King asked that an assurance be given that no measures for the relief of Roman Catholics be introduced. Grenville led the refusal, was defeated, and resigned.

In Gillray's drawing, the defeated members of Grenville's ministry, called the "Broad Bottomites," crowd Charon's boat, seen crossing the Stygian Lake to the Underworld where Fox, Cromwell, and Robespierre are cheering in welcome. The Catholic Bill is the sail which propels them forward. In the final print, the feathers of the Prince of Wales, successor to the throne, are lashed to the masthead. Lord Moira, an intimate friend of the Prince of Wales, clings to the mast and holds a cross to his lips. The boat is pushed along by Charles Grey, Viscount Howick, and Grenville and his cabinet are seated, with the Earl St. Vincent holding the tiller. The Bishop of Lincoln, who supported Grenville for the Chancellorship of Oxford, is seen before the sail. Barely perceptible in the foreground, clinging to the boat, is Henry Addington, Viscount Sidmouth, who was Prime Minister from 1801 to 1804. Only squiggles in the drawing, but clearly indicated in the finished print, are figures of harpies flying above who will become William Cobbett, the journalist, and Sir Francis Burdett, who had attacked the fallen ministry. In the upper right, the Fates, shown as three witches on broomsticks, represent Lord Hawkesbury, Home Secretary (1807-08), George Canning, Foreign Secretary (1807-09), and Lord Castlereagh, former Secretary of War.

Gillray's drawings have been almost unknown until very recent years. This sheet, done in his full maturity, is one of the most powerful and complete preparatory studies for a published engraving. It illustrates vividly his deftness and rapidity with the pen well before the famous late self portrait in the L. G. Duke collection, drawn after he had gone mad. A similar subject of 1782 in Draper Hill's list of works, *Charon's Boat or Topham's Trip with Hood to Hell,* was a personal invective against the editor of the *World,* Edward Topham, possibly because he did not pay the artist for his work.
F.C.

Provenance
Jeremy Maas, London
The Detroit Institute of Arts, 1966

References
Thomas Wright and R. H. Evans, pp. 305-07, no. 339
F. G. Stephens and Mary D. George, *Catalogue of Political and Personal Satires in the British Museum,* London, 1876-1942, no. 10748
James Gillray 1756-1815, Drawings and Caricatures, Arts Council, London, 1967, no. 88

Reproductions
Aquatint by James Gillray, 9 by 13½ in., July 16, 1807

1756-1823

Born at Stockbridge, near Edinburgh, of a family of well-to-do mill owners, Raeburn received a systematic education. After leaving school at the age of fifteen, he was apprenticed to a goldsmith and began to paint miniatures soon after. Briefly he received some degree of instruction and exposure to patronage from the less facile David Martin (1736-98), a former pupil of Allan Ramsay (1713-84) and the leading Edinburgh portraitist to whose position Raeburn would succeed. By the age of twenty-one, he was an established portrait painter. In 1778 he married the widow of Count Leslie, a somewhat older woman who brought to their union three children and substantial means.

In 1785 Raeburn made the first of perhaps only three trips to London and travelled on, with the encouragement of Reynolds, to Rome, where he met Gavin Hamilton and James Byers (1735?-1817?). Upon his return to Edinburgh in 1787, he settled down to prosperous activity as a painter of portraits. His rapid advance to the position of the most fashionable portraitist of his period in Edinburgh enabled him to live well, enjoying the best society, keeping a large gallery where his paintings were displayed, and indulging in a variety of interests which included architecture and land speculation. Unfortunately he did not keep diaries and accounts and normally did not sign or date his prolific output.

Raeburn's contact with the London art world was limited, his correspondence with Wilkie providing one link. However, perhaps in connection with a

financial disaster in 1808, he again journeyed to London in 1810 to test the possibility of establishing himself there. Although he was well received by the prominent artists, he decided, possibly on their counsel, to return to Edinburgh. He had sent portraits to the Royal Academy exhibitions occasionally, from 1792, and in 1815 he became R.A. Subsequently, a considerable number of honors were conferred upon by him by institutions as distant as Florence and North Carolina. In climax, when George IV visited Edinburgh in 1822, he knighted Raeburn and, in 1823, two months before the painter's death, he was appointed King's Limner for Scotland.

F.C.

Bibliography

Andrew Duncan, *A Tribute of regard to the memory of Sir H. Raeburn,* Edinburgh, 1824
W. Raeburn Andrew, *Life of Sir Henry Raeburn,* London, 1894
Sir Walter Armstrong, *Sir Henry Raeburn,* London/New York, 1901 (with catalogue prepared by Sir James L. Caw)
Edward Pinnington, *Sir Henry Raeburn, R. A.,* New York, 1904
Sir James L. Caw, *Raeburn,* London/New York, 1911
James Greig, *Sir Henry Raeburn, R. A.,* London, 1911
E. Rimbault Dibdin, *Raeburn,* London, 1925
Ramsay, Raeburn and Wilkie, Arts Council, Scottish Committee, Edinburgh, 1951
Raeburn Bicentenary Exhibition, National Gallery of Scotland, Edinburgh, 1956 (catalogue compiled by David Baxandall)

90
Sir John and Lady Clerk of Penicuik
Sir Alfred Beit, Bart.
Oil on canvas; 57 x 80½ in.
c. 1790

Sir John Clerk, fifth Baronet of Penicuik (died 1798), was the grandson of Sir John Clerk, second Baronet, who was moderately distinguished for his interest in science and antiquities, and for his patronage of the painter Allan Ramsay in the arts. His father was Sir John Clerk-Maxwell, noteworthy for his attempts to advance Scotland's commercial interest. He is particularly remembered for his patronage of Alexander Runciman (no. 40), who painted a series of figural subjects for Penicuik House, the Clerk family seat, illustrating the poetry of Ossian and other subjects relating to Scottish history. The fifth Baronet succeeded his father in 1784. He died without issue and was succeeded by his nephew Sir George Clerk. The similarity of family names can be confusing. To give some idea of the possibilities and to clarify his relationships, the fifth Baronet was the nephew of John Clerk of Eldin and the cousin of Sir John Clerk, Lord Eldin, the distinguished lawyer.

Not a great deal is known about the fifth Baronet, who is portrayed here with his wife. He appears to have maintained the family tradition of a lively interest in the arts, judging from his patronage of Raeburn and the description of Anna Seward who spoke of dining at Penicuik House with "a constellation of Scottish talents." His wife was Rosemary, the daughter of Josiah Dacre Appleby of Kirklington, Cumberland.

This is one of the most original of Raeburn's conceptions. The idea of painting a horizontal, three-quarter length, standing portrait was rarely projected in this period. The idea of silhouetting the figure with his highly fashionable broad-brimmed hat and outstretched arm against the evening sky is unusual and distinctive. As a result of this original placement of the figure in half shadow, flecks and splinters of light are etched

90

along the relaxed arm, posed like the Father's in
Michelangelo's *Creation of Adam.* The developme
of forms within a shadowed light resulting from th
arrangement was formerly used by Reynolds and
Hogarth, who learned it from the Dutch 17th-centu
artists, particularly Rembrandt.
F.C.

Provenance
Sir John Clerk (died 1798)
By descent to Sir George Douglas Clerk (died 1911)
Purchased by Sir Otto John Beit in 1911 (died 1930)
By descent to Sir Alfred Beit

Exhibitions
Shakespeare Gallery, London, 1792
Edinburgh, 1850, no. 38
Edinburgh, 1876, no. 211
Winter Exhibition, Royal Academy, London, 1910, no. 154
Twee Eeuwen Engelsche Kunst, Stedelijk Museum,
Amsterdam, 1936, no. 112
La Peinture anglaise, Musée du Louvre, Paris, 1938,
no. 100
Scottish Art, Royal Academy, London, 1939, no. 111
Old Master Paintings from the Beit Collection, National
Gallery of South Africa, Cape Town, 1949, no. 44
Raeburn Bi-Centenary Exhibition, National Gallery of
Scotland, Edinburgh (Arts Council), 1956, no. 8
(catalogue compiled by David Baxandall)
British Painting, 1700-1960, Leningrad, Moscow (British
Council), 1960, no. 40
Scottish Painting, Glasgow Art Gallery, 1961, no. 59

1756-1827

The son of a prosperous textile merchant who almost immediately after his son's birth became bankrupt, Rowlandson had well-to-do relatives who enabled him to travel and sent him to a boarding school, Dr. Barrow's Academy in Soho. After his father's bankruptcy in 1759, he was put into the care of an uncle, who died in 1764, after which he was taken by his aunt. In 1772 he was sent to study at the newly opened Royal Academy schools, and sometime in the mid-1770s he was invited by an aunt to Paris to study art. This same relative remained his patron and left him a small legacy at her death in 1789.

In his years of study at the Academy, Rowlandson was considered an outstanding figural draftsman in the manner of Mortimer, whose style is frequently reflected in Rowlandson's pen drawings. He first exhibited at the Royal Academy in 1775 with a drawing of *Delilah Visiting Samson in Prison,* which suggests that in the beginning he wished to be a history painter or figural draftsman. This is confirmed by his works sent to the exhibition from 1777 to 1781 which were largely portraits with a limited number of landscapes.

In 1781 he drew and engraved the *School of Eloquence* (Royal Library, Windsor) which relies heavily on Mortimer's caricatures. His success in this venture led him to pursue the genre of popular illustrations and satires. Around 1784 he drew the series entitled *A Tour in a Post Chaise* which established him as a candid and shrewd observer of people and manners. He followed this with a

prolific output of scenes from contemporary life which often involve situation comedy or shrewd commentary in a highly relaxed drawing style. These include *The Enrag'd Husband, The Extravagant Wife, The Amputation, The Bookseller and Author,* to name a few. In 1784 he issued his first political caricatures, entering a field where the brilliant Gillray had already assumed predominance.

Rowlandson's first successful collaboration was with Henry Wigstead, with whom he travelled to southern England in 1789 and published a series of prints, from drawings made on the journey, for which Wigstead wrote the text. In 1797 they took another tour, this time of South Wales, and produced another illustrated book of their tour.

However, Wigstead died in 1800 and Rowlandson began collaborating with the publisher Rudolph Ackermann, who opened a print shop in the Strand in 1795. Their relationship was to continue for the remainder of his career. Their first undertaking was the periodical the *Repository of Arts* with color plates by Rowlandson. In 1809 *The Poetical Magazine* was established, with two plates each month by Rowlandson illustrating a schoolmaster's travels which were written in rhyme by William Combe. This was followed by the *Microcosm of London* from 1808 to 1811 in three volumes for which Augustus Charles Pugin (1762-1832) drew the topographical backgrounds and Rowlandson the figures. From 1812 to 1821 Ackermann published three books about the tours of Dr. Syntax, with poetry by William Combe and illustrations by Rowlandson, a republication and expansion of the material first prepared for *The Poetical Magazine.* In 1814 Combe, who was extraordinarily prolific, writing some eighty books in his lifetime, was also commissioned by Ackermann to write the poetry for *The English Dance of Death,* to be illustrated by Rowlandson. He also illustrated Sterne, Smollett, Goldsmith, Peter Pindar, and numerous other contemporary authors. Rowlandson's illustrations derive from Hogarth and from French representations of contemporary life. They record

situations and events which he experienced on his tours through England, and they poke fun at people by means of exaggerated features, clothing, or habits. Rowlandson's illustrations are frequently spirited, but never possess the talent for pictorial invention, the extravagant intelligence and vividness of Gillray's works.

F.C.

Bibliography
Joseph Grego, *Rowlandson the Caricaturist,* 2 vols., London, 1880
Books Illustrated by Thomas Rowlandson, together with a collection of Original Drawings by him, Grolier Club, New York, 1916
A. P. Oppé, *Thomas Rowlandson; his Drawings and Water-colours,* London, 1923
Arthur W. Heintzelman, *The Watercolor Drawings of Thomas Rowlandson from the Albert H. Wiggin Collection in the Boston Public Library,* New York, 1947
Adrian Bury, *Thomas Rowlandson Drawings,* London, 1949
Robert R. Wark, *Rowlandson's Drawings for a Tour in a Post Chaise,* San Marino, California, 1963
Robert R. Wark, *Rowlandson's Drawings for the English Dance of Death,* San Marino, California, 1966

91
Dressing for a Masquerade
The Barber Institute of Fine Arts, Birmingham University
Pen and watercolor over pencil; 12¾ x 17¼ in.
Inscribed: *Rowlandson 1790*

The engraving after this drawing bears the title *Dressing for a Masquerade (Cyprians)* and thus gives us the subject of the drawing. We are viewing the interior of a house of ill repute. The young women are dressing, one in a man's trousers, hat, and shirt, with an open shirt front. Another ties her short Italianate gown in back, and a third mounts a chair to view her flowing headdress and back in a mirror. They are assisted by two elderly women of

the establishment, one of whom holds a mirror. The **91**
second trundles forth with a flask of wine and a
glass. On the right, a male hairdresser is
demonically preparing the coiffure of a young
woman who apparently holds a letter of assignation.
It appears to bear the word *Pantheon.* The scene
of revelry and excitement is one of complete
disarray. A dog runs through barking; dresses,
masks, combs, and a curling iron are on the floor,
and all the women appear to take great glee in the
general state of clutter and excitement. As in
Hogarth, the scenic disarray suggests the moral
disorder of the individuals. The print was prepared
as a companion to an engraving entitled *Dressing
for a Masquerade (Ladies).*

Another, similar version of the subject, which is
signed and dated on the lower right, appeared in an
anonymous sale at Sotheby's, March 27, 1946,
no. 12, and was bought by Sabin. It was exhibited
by F. I. Sabin in 1948 and is illustrated in *A
Catalogue of Water Colour Drawings by Thomas
Rowlandson* by Philip Sabin, 1948, no. 34.
F.C.

Provenance
Mary Ethel, Dowager Viscountess Harcourt; Stanton
Harcourt, Oxon (sale, Sotheby's, London, 14 July 1948,
no. 119, bt. Bodkin for The Barber Institute of Fine Arts)

References
Grego, I, 272; II, 392
*Catalogue of Paintings, Drawings and Miniatures in
the Barber Institute*, Cambridge, 1952, p. 190

Reproductions
Etched, possibly by Rowlandson, and published by
S. W. Fores (active 1785-1825), April 1, 1790

1757-1827

The myth of William Blake has obscured the man. Despite his wish to be heralded as a prophet, his deliberate creation of a personal mythology which allowed him to repeat similar themes in constantly new guises and contexts, Blake was quite human, as the story of his forcibly removing a soldier from his garden at Felpham and the ensuing lawsuit makes clear.

The son of a moderately prosperous hosier, he was the second child of a family of four. In 1767 he began studying at Shipley's School under Pars. He remained four years, an unusually long time at Shipley's, but he was only ten years old when he began, and in 1771 he was apprenticed to the engraver James Basire (1730-1802). From 1773 Blake prepared the drawings for Richard Gough's *Sepulchral Monuments in Great Britain* (1786-96), bringing him into intimate contact with medieval art for the first time. While working from these monuments, he also composed his early poems on British medieval subjects and made watercolors from English history, such as the *Penance of Jane Shore* (Tate Gallery) and *Edward and Eleanor.* His engraver's apprenticeship ended in 1778, but he continued to live with his family. He entered the antique school of the Royal Academy, drawing from casts and earning his living as an engraver for various booksellers.

This was a critical time in his life, for now he met the people who would have a decisive influence later. Through Thomas Stothard, he met Flaxman who, in turn, introduced him to Mrs. Mathew, an intellectual and patron of young musicians and artists. It was she who read Homer in the original to Flaxman and patronized Tom Taylor, the translator of Plato's works. In her house, ornamented with Gothic details by Flaxman and windows in imitation of stained glass, Blake read and sang his poetry to her guests. Mrs. Mathew also assisted, along with Flaxman, in financing his first book of poetry, *Poetical Sketches by W.B.* (1783).

In 1780 Henry Fuseli, on his return from Italy, became a neighbor of Blake at the time Fuseli was painting *The Nightmare,* beginning their long friendship. At the same time, Blake was courting Catherine Boucher, an uneducated, handsome young woman and member of a large family living in Battersea. They were married in August 1782 and took up residence in Leicester Fields not far from the house of Sir Joshua Reynolds.

When at the end of 1788 the *Songs of Innocence* were written, Blake invented a method of publishing his poetry with his own illustrations by drawing the text and design on one surface, etching away the blank spaces, and printing the plate. Afterwards he added other color and gold by hand. His wife learned the technique and assisted him in the publication of an extended series of illuminated books of extraordinary beauty. These included *Visions of the Daughters of Albion; Europe, A Prophecy; The Book of Urizen; The Song of Los,* and *The Book of Ahania,* among others.

About 1800 Flaxman introduced Blake to William Hayley, who invited him to take a house at Felpham on the seacoast, where he first illustrated Hayley's *Little Tom the Sailor* and began the prophetic books *Jerusalem* and *Milton.*

In 1804-05 he illustrated Blair's *Grave.* He worked for more than a decade on the illumination and publication of *Jerusalem* and *Milton.* When they were finally being printed around 1818, George Cumberland, whom Blake had taught to engrave in outline in the mid-1790s, introduced him to John Linnell who was to commission in 1823-24 a duplicate set of the *Job* series, and the illustrations to Dante, Blake's most powerful series of prints and drawings. Linnell introduced him to a sympathetic group of younger artists which included Samuel Palmer, Frederick Tatham, George Richmond, Francis Oliver Finch, John Varley, and Edward Calvert, and through them Blake had an important influence on the younger generation.

Blake's greatest power was as an imagist. He had a remarkable talent for transforming a concept or verbalism into a concise visual image which had all the elements of the literary text, yet went beyond it in conciseness and immediacy of impact. To develop and propagate this talent, he studied emblem books, engravings of oriental and Mannerist art, and medieval illustrated books whose rhythmic design principles were followed in his own compositions.

Although often utilizing the visionary, more frequently Blake's images appear bizarre because of his visual shorthand. Once translated and put into context, his works have highly specific meanings. His approach to a given text was to embellish and elaborate upon it rather than to give a literal interpretation.

There are two major aspects to the art of Blake. On the one hand, he used his designs as commentaries on social or political events of his own time. In this respect he comes close to Gillray, although Blake's allegories are more obscure and, unlike Gillray's, they reflect a coherent and well-formulated point of view. In this way they serve as companions to his poetry. At other times, his designs are penetrating transformations of a literary text into visual terms. In this connection, he resembles Gavin Hamilton and other artists within the tradition of *ut pictura poesis.* His interpretations and his vocabulary of forms are always highly personal, and this in particular attracted the younger generation of artists in the early 19th century. But his images are never commentaries on his own subjective states. On the contrary, his art is of the mainstream of

Ingres-like drawing

romanticism because it explores an enormous range of literary texts and experiences or, alternatively, comments on those of his fellows. His use of imagery to explore these experiences is unusually rich and varied, establishing a new vocabulary of forms to convey the extraordinary range of his ideas. This same task was posed and undertaken by Wright of Derby, George Stubbs, and Gavin Hamilton in quite different areas of experience.
F.C.

Bibliography
Alexander Gilchrist, *The Life of William Blake with Selections from his Poems and other Writings,* 2 vols., 1st ed., London, 1863; republished with William M. Rossetti's revised and enlarged *Annotated Lists of Blake's Paintings, Drawings, and Engravings,* 2 vols., 1880; republished 1907 with Rossetti list almost identical to 1863 edition
Laurence Binyon, *The Drawings and Engravings of William Blake,* London, 1922
S. F. Damon, *William Blake: His Philosophy and Symbols,* Boston/New York, 1924
Darrell Figgis, *The Paintings of William Blake,* New York, 1925
Geoffrey Keynes, *Pencil Drawings by William Blake,* London, 1927, (2nd series, 1956)
William Blake . . . from Collections in the United States, Philadelphia Museum of Art, 1939
Kerrison Preston, ed., *The Blake Collection of W. Graham Robertson,* London, 1952
David V. Erdman, *Blake: Prophet Against Empire,* Princeton, 1954
Martin Butlin, *A Catalogue of the Works of William Blake in the Tate Gallery,* London, 1957
The Art of William Blake, National Gallery of Art, Washington, 1957
Sir Geoffrey Keynes, *William Blake's Illustrations to the Bible,* Clairvaux, France, 1957
C. H. Collins Baker, *William Blake's Drawings and Paintings in the Huntington Library,* San Marino, 1958
Sir Anthony Blunt, *The Art of William Blake,* New York, 1959 (with bibliography)
David V. Erdman, ed., *The Poetry and Prose of William Blake,* New York, 1965

92

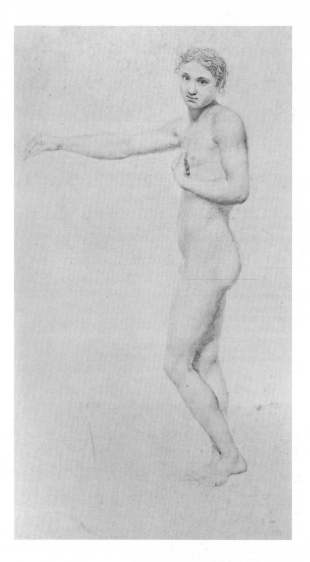

92
Study of a Nude Male Model
Trustees of The British Museum
Black chalk; 18⅞ x 14½ in.
c. 1778

Keynes first published this drawing in 1927. After his visionary works and after Gilchrist's repetition of Blake's strictures on academies and life drawing this study may come as a surprise in Blake's work. Yet, he did careful figural drawings all his life, although they were seldom as precise or as objective as this. Keynes conjectured that such a study was probably done early in Blake's career and possibly is of his favorite brother Robert. It seems more likely that the study was made while Blake was a student at the Royal Academy school. He worked there from 1778, first in the antique school under Georg Michael Moser (1704/07-1783) who had formerly taught at the St. Martin's Lane Academy where drawings from life were made.

The style of this drawing is in perfect accord with the "academies" produced by the R.A. students. Similar drawings of the male figure were made in the Duke of Richmond's academy by Cipriani, and a large group of these is now preserved in the collection of Lord Bruce, at Broomhall, Scotland. The unassuming pose and abstracted gaze of this model, and the refinement which is suggestive of Ingres, must have pleased Blake and led him to preserve this sheet.

The creation of such drawings in the early academies in St. Martin's Lane, in the Duke of Richmond's gallery, and in the Royal Academy itself, has probably not been given sufficient attention. Under the influence of Young's theories of original genius, the British artists were usually all too anxious to begin painting in order to show the brilliance of their conceptions as quickly and as completely as possible. In the 18th century, it is rare for them to value their preparatory, figural drawings greatly. However, just as on the continent there was in England a firmly established, disciplined tradition of draftsmanship. This was to find fruition in the 19th century in the finely wrought drawings of the Pre-Raphaelites. Indeed, such a drawing as this is strikingly close to the sheets of figures by Sir Edward Burne-Jones (1833-98). F.C.

Provenance
John Deffett Francis
Presented to The British Museum, April 1878

References
Gilchrist, 1880, II, 30
Laurence Binyon, *Catalogue of Drawings by British Artists . . . in the British Museum,* London, 1898, I, 128 no. 41
Keynes, *Pencil Drawings,* 1927, no. 3

93

93
A Breach in a City the Morning After a Battle
Charles J. Rosenbloom
Watercolor with pen; 11¾ x 18½ in.
c. 1783-84

The drawing which shows dead warriors, some in armor and with shields and spears, originates from Blake's interest of the late 1770s in medieval subjects. It relates specifically to the series of poems devoted to the horrors of war and the evils of despotism which so engaged his imagination around 1780 and led to such poems as *King Edward the Third, King Edward the Fourth,* and *A War Song to Englishmen.*

Erdman has explained this series of poems as ironical commentaries, in the costume and with the characters of an earlier historical period, on warmongering kings and the destruction they wreak on their subjects. These literary productions are interpreted as a commentary on George III's oppression of the American people, an oppression which involved a civil war. Erdman calls Blake's early poems an outcry against the King's

destruction of vast numbers of his own subjects in a war of despotic oppression and describes them as a propagandistic plea for liberalism. Edward III's wars against the Scots and his bloodthirsty devastation of French towns and legions of French soldiers served as a suitably removed vehicle for Blake's commentaries on the acts of his present monarch. The vivid descriptions in Rapin de Thoyras' *History of England,* translated by Nicholas Tyndal and published from 1723 to 1731, of the Battle of Crécy and the slaughter, during the afternoon and night, of the French army must have impressed Blake's imagination vividly, as they do ours even today.

The analogue of royal despotism from the past and the civil war of 1776 was elaborated upon by Blake in his poem "Gwin, King of Norway," published in 1783 as one of the *Poetical Sketches.* The poem tells of the despotism of the cruel Gwin and his ruthless nobles who were overthrown by the people, led by the giant Gordred, the lightly chained primeval spirit of the land. Blake speaks of the cries of women and babes which fly over the field, the men who die like sheep and groan upon the plain, and he concludes with those who fill the vale of death and are striven for by the eagles. In the drawing appear vestiges of a primeval city,

warriors in medieval armor, and metal shields with zigzag bolts of lightning recalling Nordic emblems. All of these elements are in the poem and probably have essentially the same meaning.

This drawing is probably the version exhibited at the Royal Academy in 1784 as a companion piece to *War Unchained . . . Fire, Pestilence and Famine Following.* Erdman interprets *War Unchained* as a record of the beginning of the American Revolution and a prophecy of the famine and pestilence which are to follow it just as the Black Death followed the wars of Edward. *A Breach in a City,* then, is conceived as a record of the close of the war, showing young and old, and men of both sides murdered by legions on a field where women seek their dead, where only babes and old men remain, and where the land is open to wild beasts and birds of prey.

Robert Rosenblum points out that this composition derives in general from Gavin Hamilton's *Andromache Bewailing the Death of Hector,* engraved by Cunego in 1764. While embodying a theme similar to that used by Hamilton, Blake also removes the action to an earlier historical period. Rosenblum emphasizes that the costumes and warriors here are generalized beyond almost any specific identification. Blake is not representing an event in history, but referring to a specific event in his own day, assuming a propagandistic role by generalizing his characters well beyond contemporary costumes and individuals, and removing his heroes to more simple, heroic times. Gilchrist is correct, then, when he describes this drawing as Blake's commentary on "the supreme despicableness of war in days when war was tyrannously in the ascendant."

Although it lacks the stoicism of David's *Oath of the Horatii* and *Brutus, A Breach in the City* foreshadows their imaginative entry into and commentary upon a prevailing social conflict. If Pierre-Narcisse Guérin's (1774-1833) *Marcus Sextus* of 1799 (Louvre) is to be interpreted as an ironic commentary on the lives lost during the revolution, then Blake's *A Breach in a City* anticipates it without the sophistication of its analogue or its historical accuracy but with greater directness by showing the actual field of dead men scantily disguised in historical costumes.

There are three versions of this subject. The finest is shown here. The care, detail, and emotional conviction of the Rosenbloom drawing suggest it as the first version exhibited at the Royal Academy in 1784. A sheet in the Ackland Memorial Art Center, Chapel Hill, North Carolina, is less detailed, has less conviction, and is a simpler reworking of the Rosenbloom drawing. It also shows certain variations, such as the addition of the babe, the crutch, and the deletion of one fallen soldier. The third version, dated 1805 and entitled *War,* in the Winthrop Bequest, Fogg Art Museum, Cambridge, Mass., also has the babe, adds another crutch, and is further simplified still.
F.C.

Provenance
Probably E. Bicknell (sale, Christie's, London, May 1, 1863, no. 389, bt. Redgrave, *The Plague)*
Samuel Redgrave (died 1876) (sale, Christie's, London, 24 March 1877, no. 178, with another, bt. Noseda)
Rev. Stopford A. Brooke (died 1916)
Marsden J. Perry, Providence, Rhode Island (sale, Anderson Galleries, New York, 11 March 1936, no. 36, reproduced)
Charles J. Rosenbloom, Pittsburgh, 1936

References
Gilchrist, 1880, I, 54; II, Rossetti List 1, p. 207, no. 5
Archibald Russell, *The Engravings of William Blake,* London, 1912, List I
Binyon, p. 23, pl. 2
The Bulletin of the Fogg Art Museum, X no. 2, November 1943, p. 57
Preston, no. 70, pl. 56
Erdman, *Blake: Prophet Against Empire,* pp. 17-18, 71
Blunt, pl. 8b
Robert Rosenblum, *Transformations in Late Eighteenth Century Art,* Princeton, 1967, pp. 154-56, fig. 184

94
The Bard
Philadelphia Museum of Art,
The Louise and Walter Arensberg Collection
Pencil, wash and pen; 25½ x 18½ in.
Inscribed: *Grays Bard;* verso: a second version of the composition; watermark: 1794
c. 1794-1800

The subject is taken from Thomas Gray's Pindaric ode *The Bard* (II, iv), published in 1757. Taken from early British history, the story is based on an incident from the life of Edward I, conqueror of Wales. In order to prevent the Welsh from keeping alive the spirit of popular resistance, Edward condemned all the bards to death. Only one escaped the slaughter, but he sought revenge and later confronted the King and his house, including Queen Eleanor, Mortimer, and Gloucester from an inaccessible rock above the Conway River. The King, like St. Paul in his conversion, has fallen on the shore of the river and gazes upward, terrified. The bard strikes his harp and with the support of his slain companions prophesies the doom of Edward and his line:

> Robed in the sable garb of woe,
> With haggard eyes the Poet stood;
> Loose his beard, and hoary hair
> Stream'd like a meteor to the troubled air.

> Weave the warp, and weave the woof,
> The winding sheet of Edward's race.

A theme related to that illustrated in *A Breach in a City the Morning after a Battle* (no. 93) is intended here. The theme now is the evils of despotism, with the further inference that the artist is also a prophet who will summon patriots to confront and to overwhelm despotic rulers.

Blake treated themes from Gray's *Bard* three times. The first was that exhibited at the Royal Academy in 1785 (no. 607), *The Bard from Gray.* Later, about 1800-01, he did a series of watercolor illustrations to Gray's poems, including *The Bard,* and again in

1809 he signed the tempera painting now in The Tate Gallery, London. (The date itself is now illegible, but a label on the back written by Samu Palmer states that the picture is signed "W. Blake 1809".)

Even though it is closely related to the tempera painting of 1809, the style and composition of the drawing are not compatible with other known sheets by Blake of that date. In his mature works, Blake learned to simplify his compositions, to ma his figures larger, grander, and more powerful, and he tended to use his brush more fluently in th backgrounds and in the actual creation of the design, rather than filling in with black washes around the contours of the figures as he does here. Most likely this drawing is earlier, even though it was used as the basis of Blake's tempera painting. For example, this drawing is not compatible with the style of Blake's series of illustrations to the Bible (nos. 95 and 96) generally dated c. 1799-1810 nor with the style of the illustrations to *Jerusalem* (no. 99) of about 1815-18. The watermark of 1794 gives a *terminus post quem.* Blake was working on the series from Gray around 1800, which is the date given by Grierson for this sheet.

Arthur S. Marks in discussing John Martin's versions of this subject has given further bibliography and has listed other representations of this theme. A representation of *The Bard* by Thomas Jones is in the National Museum of Wales, Cardiff.
F.C.

Provenance
Richard Johnson (sale, Platt's, London, 25 April 1912, no. 702)
Anonymous sale, Sotheby's, London, 20 May 1934, no. 168, bt. Rafael King
Dawson's Bookshop, Los Angeles
Louise and Walter Arensberg Collection, Los Angeles
Philadelphia Museum of Art, 1950

Exhibitions
The Art of William Blake, National Gallery of Art, Washington, 1957, no. 50
Time and the Image, Philadelphia College of Art, 1965, no. 50

References
William Blake, *A Descriptive Catalogue of Pictures, Poetical and Historical Inventions,* London, 1809, p. 35, no. iv
Gilchrist, 1880, I, 56; II, 152; Rossetti List 1, p. 208, no. 6
Sir Herbert J. C. Grierson, *William Blake's Designs for Gray's Poems,* London, 1922, p. 5
National Gallery, Millbank, *Catalogue of the British School,* London, 1929, p. 23, no. 3351
Erdman, *Blake: Prophet Against Empire,* pp. 45-47
Keynes, *Pencil Drawings,* 1956, II, no. 21
Butlin, no. 42, pl. 25
Arthur S. Marks, "The Source of John Martins' 'The Bard'," *Apollo,* LXXXIV, August 1966, supp. (Notes on British Art), pp. 1-2

95

95
And Power was Given Him over all Kindreds and Tongues and Nations (The Seven-Headed Beast of the Apocalypse)
National Gallery of Art, Rosenwald Collection
Watercolor; 15⅝ x 14 in.
Inscribed: *WB inv.*
1799-1810

Blake's power as an imagist is perhaps best revealed by his willingness to undertake a series of illustrations to *Revelation.* The subject of no. 95 is taken from various verses of Chapter XIII in which a fantastic beast with seven heads and ten horns is described as risen out of the sea. A powerful horned dragon, dwelling on the earth, gives him life and is capable of bringing fire from heaven and forcing men to worship this creature, emblematic of blasphemy.

Blake has interpreted the text somewhat freely and subjectively. The dragon is many-headed, multihorned, and peering in all directions at once. His power to destroy those who do not fall before him is conveyed by the flaming sword and mace. Blake has given the creature wings of fantastic size which bear the stars of the firmament and suggest the Devil as he was known to Blake from emblem books. The intricacy and originality of the interwoven design is ultimately based on medieval illuminations, but it is transformed here into a highly original image having the power and conciseness of Dürer's woodcuts.

Blake was drawing subjects from the Bible as early as 1785 when he exhibited three illustrations of the life of Joseph. This was not so rare as it may seem at first since Copley painted a *Nativity* in 1776-77 and illustrations to *Revelation* and other biblical subjects can be found in the art of Benjamin West. In 1793 Blake announced in a *Prospectus to the Public* two large engravings, the first in a series of illustrations to the Bible. But the plan took definite form only in 1799 when Butts gave Blake a commission to paint fifty small pictures from the Bible at one guinea apiece. In a letter to George Cumberland of August 26, 1799, he mentions the project, the idea for which must have come from Blake himself. The illustrations were drawn between 1799 and 1810.

The entire series was intimately connected with Blake's view of the nature and goals of his own art. He believed the Bible the most entertaining and instructive of literary productions and the biblical texts the highest order of literature addressed wholly to the imagination. His illustrations to the *Book of Job,* done in his very last years, form a climax to his artistic achievement. He mentioned the illustrations to *Revelation* in letters to Thomas Butts, describing the perfect union of his ideas with a deep emotional involvement, giving rise to images which seemed direct emanations of his spirit. Because of the high order of the literary texts and the standard of execution, he believed them the most important works of their kind since the productions of Raphael.

F.C.

Provenance
Commissioned by Thomas Butts, London (died 1845)
William A. White
A. S. W. Rosenbach
Lessing J. Rosenwald, Jenkintown, Pa., 1929
Presented to the National Gallery of Art, 1943

Exhibitions
William Blake . . . from Collections in the United States,
Philadelphia Museum of Art, 1939, no. 175
The Art of William Blake, National Gallery of Art,
Washington, 1957, no. 16
William Blake, Andrew Dickson White Museum,
Cornell University, Ithaca, 1965, no. 30
(catalogue compiled by Albert S. Roe)

References
Gilchrist, 1907, Rossetti List 1, no. 176 (deleted in
1880 ed.)
Keynes, *William Blake's Illustrations to the Bible,* no. 166

96

96

The Number of the Beast is 666
The Philip H. and A. S. W. Rosenbach Foundation
Watercolor; 16¼ x 13⅛ in.
Inscribed: *WB inv.*
1799-1810

This biblical illustration follows no. 95 in sequence, in the series of illustrations to *Revelation.* The same two creatures appear, an all-seeing seven-headed beast, emblematic of blasphemy, and his protector, a many-headed dragon. However, the stage has changed so that the illustration now serves for the first two verses of *Revelation,* Chapter XIV, rather than for the closing lines of Chapter XIII as suggested by Keynes. Instead of

over the sea, we aré now on Mount Sinai. A lamb appears at the base of a mountain lifting his hands over the faithful and is worshipped by "An hundred forty and four thousand, having his Father's name written on their foreheads." The second verse opens, "And I heard a voice from heaven, as the voice of many waters, and as the voice of a great thunder." This is the line illustrated.

The subject of the vision, then, is the worship of the Lamb by the Blessed on Mt. Sinai and the resulting consternation of the blasphemous, seven-headed monster. Hearing the divine words, he crouches in fear and is sensibly directed off the scene by his dragon patron.   F.C.

Provenance
Commissioned by Thomas Butts, London (died 1845)
(sale, Sotheby's, London, 26-27 March 1852)
William A. White
Rosenbach Foundation, Philadelphia, 1950

Exhibitions
The Art of William Blake, National Gallery of Art,
Washington, 1957, no. 17

References
Gilchrist, 1880, II, Rossetti List 1, no. 201
Keynes, *William Blake's illustrations to the Bible,* no. 167

97

Queen Katherine's Dream
National Gallery of Art, Rosenwald Collection
Watercolor; 16⅛ x 13½ in.
Inscribed: *W. Blake inv. 1807;* verso: a monogram in red ink, probably that of Mr. Strange

In Shakespeare's play *King Henry VIII,* Act IV, Sc. II, Queen Katherine, deposed as Queen of England and wife of Henry VIII, is nearing death. She tells her companion Griffith that she is meditating on the celestial harmony to which she is going and falls into a deep sleep. A vision appears of six figures with golden visages, clad in white robes, wearing garlands of laurel leaves, and carrying palms in their hands. An extra garland is held over

97

Katherine's head by two figures as they weave around her in a dance, and it is passed to others who repeat the action. Seeing these gestures, she rejoices and lifts her hands to heaven as the dancers vanish.

Shakespeare's meaning was clear to Blake, and he followed the Elizabethan interpretation of the theme rather literally. He shows Katherine on a couch with Gothic motifs, while her companions, Griffith and Patience are at hand, unaware of her dream. The last moments of the vision, with the departing spirits, some of whom have been making music, are shown. Two hold the crown of laurel over Katherine's head, while others fly away with her royal crown.

In his description of the vision, Shakespeare established a pantomime of honor to the departing Queen. The crown of laurel, and the palm, with the gold-colored faces, all signify the honor to be paid to her virtue. Blake follows this program, although he does not include the earthly crown in the same vision, a detail stated in other parts of Shakespeare's text. In this context, it should be remembered that in this period Jane Shore, mistress of Edward IV, embodied the loss of morality. Queen Katherine lifts her arms, rejoicing at the vision which gives her a glimpse of things at hand and promises eternal happiness. Blake's vision portrays Katherine as a paragon of virtue rejoicing in her spiritual rewards.

Blake had engraved this subject after a design of Fuseli for Steeven's edition of Shakespeare in 1805. Three versions of the composition were drawn by Blake himself. All are listed by Rossetti (nos. 86, 87, 88), and all are dated 1807 by him. The first, which had only slight tints of watercolor, was painted for Thomas Butts. The third version was part of a series of illustrations in a volume of Shakespeare belonging to a Mr. Macmillan in 1863. One of these, done in pencil and gray wash, is now in the Fitzwilliam Museum, Cambridge. The second is the Rosenwald sheet which was commissioned by Sir Thomas Lawrence for fifteen guineas. It was praised by Rossetti as one of Blake's most elaborate, beautiful, and imaginative works. Antal has emphasized Blake's close reliance on Fuseli's version of this subject, as engraved by Bartolozzi.

F.C.

Provenance
Commissioned by Sir Thomas Lawrence, London, 1807
Professor Tyler
C. J. Strange by 1863
Sydney Morse, London (sale, Christie's, London, 26 July 1929, no. 16, bt. Colnaghi)
Lessing J. Rosenwald, Jenkintown, Pa., 1930
Presented to the National Gallery of Art, 1943

Exhibitions
The Works of William Blake, Burlington Fine Arts Club, London, 1876, no. 80 (lent by C. J. Strange)
William Blake . . . from Collections in the United States, Philadelphia Museum of Art, 1939, no. 180
The Art of William Blake, National Gallery of Art, Washington, 1957, no. 33

References
Gilchrist, 1880, I, 401; II, Rossetti List 1, 218, nos. 86, 87, 88
Figgis, pl. 88
Frederick Antal, *Fuseli Studies,* London, 1956, p. 85, figs. 31a-b

98
Illustration to Milton's Paradise Lost: The Fall
Harvard College Library,
Gift of John U. and Harold T. White
Watercolor; 19½ x 15⅜ in.
Inscribed: *W. Blake 1808*

This recently "rediscovered" Blake drawing illustrates lines from Book X of Milton's *Paradise Lost* after the fall of man when the guilty Adam and Eve are sought by the Son who calls them forth for judgment. Milton's description of their emotional response at this moment was carefully read by Blake:

> Love was not in their looks, either to God
> Or to each other, but apparent guilt,
> And shame, and perturbation, and despair,
> Anger, and obstinacy, and hate, and guile.

This miracle of description is followed by a discussion between Adam and the Son which further details the emotional situation, and the episode concludes "So judged He man . . ."

While playing on the emotional responses through highly reserved gesture, Blake has transformed the immediate situation into a cosmic image of the implications of the event. The Son and Saviour pronounces judgment while Adam listens, Eve hides her face, and the Serpent leers behind Adam's heel. Sin pours flames from two vials while Death releases its swift and black-tipped shafts.

Three series of illustrations to Milton's *Paradise Lost* were painted by Blake, all of which are discussed by Peckham. The first set, done in 1807, is now in the Huntington Library and Art Gallery, San Marino. It consists of twelve drawings, one for each book of *Paradise Lost* including *Christ Judges Adam and Eve,* of which the Harvard College Library drawing is an enlarged variant.

The second series of illustrations to *Paradise Lost* was painted in 1808 to be added to the large collection of Blake drawings belonging to his

98

friend and patron Thomas Butts. Nine drawings from this series are now in the Museum of Fine Arts, Boston. Peckham was able, cogently, to identify two drawings in Rossetti's third list of works of unascertained method, nos. 17 and 18, with drawings in the Huntington Library and Victoria and Albert Museum. A third, no. 16 in Rossetti's list, given as " 'So judged He man.'—(Paradise Lost) [Butts]," was presumed by Peckham to be the missing illustration in the Butts series, the location of which was then unknown to him. We can now complete the Boston series of illustrations to *Paradise Lost* with the Harvard College Library drawing which is the same size and date as the Huntington, London, and Boston sheets.
F.C.

Provenance
Thomas Butts, London (died 1845)
Fuller (by 1863)
H. A. J. Munro of Novar (sale, Christie's, London, 22-24 April 1868, no. 502, bt. Kibble)
Marsden J. Perry
William A. White, from 1908
Harold T. White
By gift to Harvard College Library, Cambridge, Mass., 1966

Exhibitions
Grolier Club, New York, 1905, no. 91

References
Milton, *Paradise Lost,* X, ll. 103 ff.
Gilchrist, 1907, Rossetti List 3, p. 481, no. 16 (deleted in 1880 edition)
Morse Peckham, "Blake, Milton, and Edward Burney," *Princeton University Library Chronicle,* XI, 1950, pp. 115-16
Baker, p. 12, pl. xi
Gert Schiff, "Johann Heinrich Füsslis Milton-Galerie," *Schweizerisches Institut fur Kunstwissenschaft, Zürich, Schriften,* Zürich/Stuttgart, no. 5, 1963

99

99
**Albion Compelling the Four Zoas to Their
Proper Tasks**
Yale University Art Gallery,
The Frederick Benjamin Kaye Memorial Collection
Pencil; 9⅞ x 12⁵/₁₆ in.
c. 1815-18

Emanating flames and with blazing locks
surrounding his head, this youthful, potent being
wears a quiver on his back and holds an arrow in
his right hand. Although dubbed *Los Kneeling* by
Keynes, it is in fact the resurrected Albion and
illustrates the following text accompanying plate 95
of Blake's *Jerusalem:*

> The Breath Divine went forth over the morning
> hills Albion rose
> In anger: the wrath of God breaking bright
> flaming on all sides around
> His awful limbs: into the Heavens he walked
> clothed in flames
> Loud thundring, with broad flashes of
> flaming lightning & pillars
> Of fire, speaking the Words of Eternity in

> Human Forms, in direful
> Revolutions of Action & Passion, thro the
> Four Elements on all sides
> Surrounding his awful Members. Thou seest
> the Sun in heavy clouds
> Struggling to rise above the Mountains,
> in his burning hand
> He takes his Bow, then chooses out
> his arrows of flaming gold

The passage occurs in Chapter IV of *Jerusalem:
The Emanation of the Giant Albion,* one of Blake's
prophetic works, which relates the fall and
resurrection of Albion, the father of all mankind
and the patriarch and ancestor of England. This
book is divided into four parts each of which poses
a struggle of contraries. In Chapter I, Albion rejects
original perfection, thus accepting chaos and
destruction, and Los opposes such acceptance in
the name of prophecy and creation. With the
opening of Chapter II, the Moral Law is established,
distorting all natural perfections and leading to
crime, jealousy, revenge, war, and finally to the
total despair of Albion. From this repetition of
Albion's history, Los works to create an image of
salvation. In Chapter III, reason triumphs, but it is
the ultimate downfall of Albion, who thus cuts
himself off from the Divine Vision and is ploughed
into the earth with the dead. Chapter IV opposes
error and truth, and out of their confrontation comes
a prophecy of the Last Judgment. The poem
concludes with Albion sacrificing himself for Jesus,
their subsequent union, and the achievement of
immortality in the mystical union of all things.

It is the turning point of Chapter IV which this
drawing illustrates. The voice of a jealous wife, who
signifies the climax of all human error in the
exaltation of chastity, awakens Albion, and he rises
from the dead in wrath, taking his bow and golden
arrows to compel the Four Zoas (body, reason,
emotion, imagination) back to their proper tasks.

This drawing is very much in keeping in format and
conception with the other, massive visionary
designs for *Jerusalem.* The motif of enveloping

flames, which will be heightened to a precious
richness through the use of orange-brown, white,
and actual gold, is a leitmotif of this visionary worl
However, this design was rejected as the final
illustration. The published illustration shows the
resurrection of Albion and his rise in anger with th
wrath of God breaking around him in flames.
Erdman has demonstrated that Blake made
substantial alterations to plate 95 of *Jerusalem.*
Even after it had been etched, he deleted a passag
of twenty-seven lines of text which in turn had
been introduced after another illustration similar
to that on plate 94 had been suppressed. Neither
the discarded illustration nor the rejected text
relate to the Yale drawing which is presumably
a third idea for this plate. This should not come as
surprise since Blake was an extensive reviser and
rearranger of his verses and illustrations.

Blake's reason for discarding the beautiful design
at Yale appears to have been a compositional and
contextual one. The centripetal design of the Yale
drawing was apparently too self-contained to
illustrate effectively a passage leading to the
climactic end of the book. It would appear that
Blake desired a design which would lead on to the
gripping composition, showing the human form
awakening in the bosom of immortality and the
grand centric composition of the triumph of Los
which closes the book.

The golden bow and the arrows of flaming gold,
here held by Albion, are symbols of intellect for
Blake. For example, in his *Milton* (I:9), Blake
himself rhetorically requests a bow of burning gol
which he will use to build the city of Jerusalem.
The flames are emblematic of creative spirit and
energy. Here they are spiritual flames which
consume all accumulated errors, leaving only the
infinite and the holy at the end of the world.

The drawing dates from the last period of Blake's
career. Although the title page of *Jerusalem* bears
the date 1804, the final text of the epic was probabl
not completed before 1815. Erdman suggests that
the etching of the plates for *Jerusalem* was done

1763-1804

from 1815 to 1820, on the basis of the watermark dates of The British Museum copy, which begin in 1818 and run to 1820. The dating is complicated by the fact that certain proofs were made on paper dated 1802, which is too early for the main body of the work. Although the text may have been composed over a long period of time, as Erdman points out, a group of the principal illustrations have a remarkably consistent massiveness of style, a style which is reflected in the Yale drawing.
F.C.

Provenance
Anonymous sale, Sotheby's, 29 July 1925, no. 145, bt. Kaye
Frederick Benjamin Kaye (died 1930)
Bequeathed to Yale University Art Gallery, 1930

Exhibitions
Prints and Drawings from the Yale Collections, Yale University Art Gallery, New Haven, 1957, p. 11, no. D1 *(Male Figure)*

References
Keynes, *Pencil Drawings,* 1956, II, no. 25
David V. Erdman, "The Suppressed and Altered Passages in Blake's *Jerusalem,*" *Studies in Bibliography,* XVII, 1964, pp. 7-9 n. 8, 33-36
Erdman, *Poetry and Prose,* p. 730

George Morland was the son of Henry Robert Morland (1732-97), painter of portraits and genre scenes who may also have been a dealer, with the accompanying necessity of repairing paintings by the old masters, for which he employed his son. From a very early period, George Morland showed an unusual talent for drawing, and his father sent his first works to the Royal Academy exhibition of 1773. From 1777 to 1784 he was bound as an apprentice to his father; during this time, he continued the work of the atelier and copied paintings by Gainsborough and Reynolds and *The Nightmare* (no. 68) by Henry Fuseli.

His career and patronage are unusual in the period. He appears to have ended his professional, and to an important degree his personal, relationships with his father as soon as his apprenticeship was finished. There is some indication that his parents were extremely severe, and he reacted against this in his later life, suffering both economically and professionally from the most unsystematic habits. He refused to be bound by commissions of any sort, and he was especially fearful of being directed by members of the aristocracy by whom he seems to have been awestruck. Generally, he painted subjects of his own choosing for an immediate sale. Since he was inevitably in need of money, this provided an income only for immediate needs. These works would often be given to one of his companions who would in turn sell it to a dealer or buyer. In this way, he was insulated from his immediate public and also was out of touch with the market for his pictures. As a result, he was not

coerced by his patrons; on the other hand, his pictures were quite popular and his dealers appear to have kept him in a state of penury in order to continue to receive paintings. It is significant that Morland was able to support himself through his work, and yet determine almost entirely the form and content of his very personal art.

His subjects of the 1780s, taken from everyday life, show individuals from the upper middle classes in elegant costumes participating in intimate dramas with moral overtones. These included the *Laetitia* series of 1789 which illustrates the fall from virtue of a young woman who eloped against her parents' wishes. Usually these small and unambitious pictures are concerned with themes of middle-class morality, virtue and vice, extravagance and thrift, laziness and industry, discipline and indulgence, the combination of thrift and security bringing happiness, or virtue rewarded by love. Numerous of these were painted and engraved in the 1780s. In general, they are conceived within the tradition of Hogarth, although Morland's works tend to have happy endings rather than the starkly tragic outcomes of Hogarth's more full-blooded productions, which attain the level of high tragedy. Such works are interspersed with studies in the manner of Brouwer of men in taverns. In this early period, he also painted one of his most powerful works, the *Self Portrait* in The British Museum.

Morland's later works like the *Gypsy Encampment* (no. 100) suddenly drop these moralizing themes and show a new interest in the picturesque as envisioned by Gainsborough and the Dutch. His output during the last fourteen years of his life is concerned with Gypsies, the hunt, winter scenes with craggy trees, rustics gathering wood, or itinerant salesmen in country attire bargaining with the wives of farmers. In general, these illustrate Morland's conversion to the cult of the picturesque, a cult involved primarily with visual effects and one which continuously releases itself from moral overtones as a basis of its art.

Morland is a minor master of the period who is

especially attractive in certain of his winter scenes
such as that in the Mellon Collection. He continues
the tradition of Gainsborough in his picturesque
or "fancy" subjects and establishes the pattern to
be followed by Thomas Barker of Bath, and George
Chinnery. Even Thomas Cole's drawings reflect
a study of his style probably as found in Thomas
Barker's lithographs.
F.C.

Bibliography
John Hassell, *Memoirs of the Life of the late George
Morland,* London, 1806
George Dawe, *The Life of George Morland,* London,
c. 1904 (originally published 1807)
Sir Walter Gilbey, *George Morland, his Life and Works,*
London, 1907
George C. Williamson, *George Morland; his Life and
Works,* London, 1907
George Morland, Arts Council, London, 1954

100
Gypsy Encampment with Seated Man Breaking Firewood
The Detroit Institute of Arts, Gift of Henry E. Candler
Oil on canvas; 38 x 50 in.
Inscribed: *G. Morland 1790*

100

Although in modern times this painting has been
entitled *The Fern Gatherers,* it is unlikely that this
is the subject. The picture first appeared under this
title when it was at Agnew's in 1906. In fact, the
composition does not show people gathering ferns;
rather, the artist has painted a Gypsy encampment
with a man breaking kindling for a fire. This may
be the same painting as that exhibited in 1790 at
the Society of Artists (no. 191) entitled *Landscape
with Gypsies* about which Walpole commented,
"G. Morland of Paddington. A young artist of
twenty-five of very great merit." George Dawe,
Morland's biographer and fellow artist, relates
that about 1790 Morland first began to paint
compositions showing Gypsies and rustics in the
forest or in open landscapes. His fascination with
Gypsies, the hunt, and with outdoor life in general
after 1789-90 gives us a clue to a complete change
in his view of what art should be. We are told that

he associated with Gypsies, adopting their way
of life and sleeping in barns with them at night.
Whether or not this story is completely authentic,
it probably contains an element of truth. Such a
point of view on Morland's part would not be unlike
that of Wilkie who wished to obtain the clothing of
the Sultan of Mysore for his painting of *Sir David
Baird* or that of Stubbs who wished to dissect
horses before painting them. Morland's research
was carried on to obtain more information about

the Gypsies, who were to become the principal and
incidentally the most picturesque subject of his
art. The result in his paintings after about 1790 is a
more complete devotion to the cult of the
picturesque in opposition to the moralizing theme
that he had used up to that time.

One of his first productions of this type, and one
which may be identical with no. 100, was a large
picture of Gypsies kindling a fire that was painted

1765-1808

for Colonel Stuart for forty guineas. George Dawe relates an amusing and probably spurious anecdote that Morland painted this work in a particularly slapdash way. Dawe seems to take a certain relish in exposing Morland's unsystematic techniques and criticizes him in particular for his hasty execution. According to the story, the patron saw the picture in the morning when it was begun, and he was promised the finished work on his return the same evening. Dawe insists that Morland altered the composition considerably in order to meet his afternoon appointment.

Knowing Morland's works well, Dawe could have described this picture as large by comparison with Morland's more frequent small canvases, although he also occasionally did even larger compositions like *The Inside of a Stable* of 1791, in The National Gallery, London.

It is unusual for Morland to date a picture on the canvas as in this instance, and it is significant that the majority of his dated works occur in the period from 1790 to 1795 which has been called the meridian of Morland's career. His dating of a significant number of canvases, often of ambitious size, suggests that he was then more systematic and interested in his productions than at any other time in his career. F.C.

Provenance
Probably painted for Colonel Stuart
Charles Romer Williams
Sold to Thos. Agnew & Sons, London, 1906
H. Darell Brown, London (sale, Christie's, London, 23 May 1924, no. 25, bt. Eyre)
Howard Young
Henry Candler
The Detroit Institute of Arts, 1961

Exhibitions
Probably Incorporated Society of Artists, 1790, no. 191
Old Masters, Thos. Agnew & Sons, London, 1906, no. 20
Japan-British Exhibition, London, 1910, no. 34
(lent by H. Darell Brown)

References
Dawe, pp. 50-51, 63, 104
William T. Whitley, *Artists and Their Friends in England 1700-1799,* London/Boston, 1928, II, 370

A painter in watercolor and oil of landscape and architectural views, Freebairn is said to have been a pupil of Richard Wilson. However, Wright (p. 269) challenges this view, suggesting that he may only have been a pupil of Philip Reinagle (1749-1833) to whom he was apprenticed and from whose house he sent his first paintings to the Royal Academy in 1782. Wright may be correct, but it is significant that Reinagle, a pupil and assistant of Allan Ramsay (1713-84), only began painting landscapes as a specialty from about 1794. Before that he had done portraits and animal pieces. Yet Freebairn was already exhibiting landscapes in 1782, and his later subjects were those earlier selected by Wilson: Tivoli, Albano, Nemi, and the Campagna. It seems quite possible that the tradition placing Freebairn, who would have been sixteen when Wilson left London in 1781, in Wilson's studio, may have some basis in fact.

Freebairn exhibited landscapes at the Royal Academy until 1786, the most likely date for his departure to Italy. He was in Rome in 1789 and 1790 when he sent Roman views to the exhibitions. In 1791 he sent two views of the Via Mala in the Grisons, in Switzerland, apparently done on his return journey. He continued to send works to the Royal Academy exhibitions from 1792, when he was back in London, until his death. His patron in Rome was Lord Clive, later Earl Powis, and when he returned to England the patronage of Lord Suffolk and Mr. Penn of Stoke Park were added. He occasionally painted views of Welsh and Lancashire scenery, although his Roman views

were appreciated more in his day. After his death in 1815, a volume called *Outlines of Lancashire Scenery* was published by his son, a printmaker. These views were taken from a sketchbook of Freebairn and were intended for the use of students. From 1806 to 1808 he exhibited at the British Institution and at the Watercolour Society exhibitions. His output was not large. Probably the fifty-four works exhibited at the Royal Academy from 1782 to 1807 represent the main body of his production. Forty of his paintings, engraved by Ziegler, were published as *English and Italian Scenery.* He died at the age of forty-three, leaving a widow and four children. F.C.

Bibliography
The Gentleman's Magazine, LXXVIII, 1808, p. 94
T. Wright, *The Life of Richard Wilson,* London, 1824, pp. 77, 269
L[ionel] C[ust], "Freebairn, Robert," *Dictionary of National Biography,* VII, 678
W. G. Constable, *Richard Wilson,* 1953, p. 142

101
Neptune's Grotto: Tivoli
Dr. and Mrs. Sherman E. Lee
Oil on canvas; 36½ x 48⅜ in.
Inscribed: *Freebairn 1807*

This painting is perhaps the best evidence to support the view that Freebairn was a student of Wilson. The information that he was Wilson's pupil comes from Robert Field's notes, given to Wright, who doubted it, and W. G. Constable found no reason to associate Freebairn with Wilson, placing him in the list of doubtful pupils. Although painted some thirty years after Wilson's death, this painting recalls many elements of his art and supports the authoritative views of Robert Field who was Freebairn's friend.

Although the technique has changed considerably, too many ideas in this painting derive from Wilson not to posit a careful study of his art for its origin. The view of tiny buildings silhouetted against the sky in the upper left, the willowy trunks of trees and their pattern of leaves, and even the manner of painting the foliage are a schematic reminiscence of Wilson's technique. The jagged tree trunk and burdock leaves, the group of willowy figures, the reflections in the water, and the vivid light from the misty cascades in the darkening gloom, are all learned from Wilson.

Grottoes were one of Freebairn's favorite subjects, judging from the titles of his paintings. To select two examples, in 1794 he exhibited the *Subterranean Ruins of Maecenas' Villa at Tivoli* and in 1802 the *Interior of an Ancient Subterranean Ruin in the Vicinity of Otriculum.*

His biographers frequently mention the high finish of his paintings which they called elegant and pleasing but not grand, suggesting that the refinement of this painting exhibits his style well. Its remarkable design, comparable to certain drawings of grottoes by J. R. Cozens, displays the sophisticated and attractive imagination of a minor master heretofore almost completely unknown. F.C.

Provenance
Appleby, London
Dr. and Mrs. Sherman E. Lee, Cleveland, Ohio, 1959

Exhibitions
Royal Academy, 1807, no. 29

References
Wright, p. 269

101

died 1823

102

Samuel's place and date of birth are not known. He received an award from the Society of Arts in 1784, and he exhibited regularly at the Royal Academy and other London exhibitions from 1785 until 1822. All his works sent to the Academy were, with the single exception of *Ellen and Allan Bane* from *The Lady of the Lake,* views of England and Wales, and he apparently never travelled abroad. His most admired picture seems to have been a *View on the Thames from Rotherhithe,* painted during the great frost of 1789. In 1799 Samuel was a member of an organization which called itself "The Brothers" and has since been generally known as Girtin's Sketching Club. This group, of which Thomas Girtin was by far the most distinguished member, met for the purpose of establishing a school of historic landscape by illustrating passages from poetry. However, Samuel in his exhibited work followed no such innovating course. His main occupation seems to have been painting and drawing topographical views, many of which were engraved. His *œuvre* is not marked by great originality or individuality, but demonstrates the high average level attained in English landscape painting of the late 18th and early 19th centuries. Samuel died at work when a brick wall under which he was sketching collapsed and fell upon him.
A.S.

102
London from Greenwich Park
Yale University Art Gallery,
John Hill Morgan, B.A. 1893, Fund
Oil on canvas; 54⅜ x 72⅛ in.
Inscribed: *G. Samuel 1816*

The view is one of the most famous and most
frequently painted in England. In the center of the
picture, under the trees, is the Queen's House at
Greenwich, built by Inigo Jones, and to the right is
Greenwich Hospital. On the horizon is the dome of
St. Paul's, surrounded by the spires of Wren's city
churches. Samuel exhibited a second *London from
Greenwich* at the Royal Academy in 1821.

Colonel Grant, who owned no. 102, called it the
culminating picture of Samuel's career. It is,
nonetheless, a conservative picture when we
remember the innovations of Girtin and Turner of
almost twenty years earlier, and it shows Samuel
carrying the topographical tradition of Sandby and
the 18th century well into the 19th. Its gracious
figures, who have climbed the hill to enjoy the
prospect, seem to breathe the same air as the
characters in Jane Austen's novels, which were
being published at exactly the same time as no. 102
was painted.
A.S.

Provenance
Colonel M. H. Grant

Exhibitions
Royal Academy, 1816, no. 372
British Institution, 1817, no. 136

References
Colonel M. H. Grant, *The Old English Landscape
Painters,* Leigh-on-Sea, 1959, IV, 339-40, pl. 172, no. 346

1767-1849

Son of a member of the bourgeoisie, Agasse began
working at the Ecole de Dessin in Geneva under
Jacques Cassin (1739-1800) and Georges Vanière
(1740-1834), the latter a pupil of Joseph Vien
(1716-1809). His sister Louise-Etiennette was also
a draftsman, and they occasionally did pastel
portraits together. Wishing him to have the best
possible conclusion to his education, Jacques's
father sent him to Paris around 1785 to study under
David, where he remained for almost three years,
returning to Geneva in the summer of 1788. In Paris,
he not only studied the living model and antique
sculpture, but also became interested in the
animaliers and worked at the natural history
museum where he found, among other things, the
skeleton of a rhinoceros. He also practiced
dissection and studied osteology and the rudiments
of veterinary medicine at this time.

Lord Rivers, whose seat was at Stratfield Saye
House, Hants., travelling in Switzerland in 1790, met
Agasse and took him to London where he remained
only a brief time owing to the political and financial
difficulties encountered by his family. His *Farriers
of Lausanne* (Musée d'Art et d'Histoire, Geneva)
was completed in 1796 and shows the results of his
first English sojourn, especially his view of the art
of Morland. Encouraged by Lord Rivers and
distressed by the plight of his family in Switzerland,
he left once again for London in the autumn of
1800. Taking up residence with another artist from
Geneva, A. E. Chalon (1780-1860), he began his
Livre de Verité (Musée d'Art et d'Histoire, Geneva)
which was to record his production for the
next half-century.

During the first decade, Agasse achieved
considerable success with sporting scenes in the
tradition of Stubbs and with representations of
exotic animals. He first exhibited at the Royal
Academy in 1801, but already appeared in J. D.
Fiorillo's *Geschichte der zeichnenden Künste*
(1808) as one of the most celebrated painters of
horses of his day. During this early period, he
painted the two life-size cheetahs now in the
Gallery of Modern Art, New York. He also undertoo
historical subjects, among them *Romulus and
Remus* in 1810, *Androcles and the Lion* in 1811, an
Alexander Subduing Bucephalus in 1812.

In 1813 Lord Heathfield, one of his faithful patrons
died. This appears to mark the beginning of the
slow decline of his reputation in England, even
though the artists, especially Sir Edwin Landseer,
later admired his works.

In June 1819 he was painting an elephant, a lion,
panthers, and other animals in the menagerie of
Edward Cross in Exeter Change, the Strand, and h
had probably worked there as early as 1803, as we
learn from the journal of his relative Louis-André
Gosse who was studying medicine in England. He
continued to remain a friend and painted portraits
of Mr. and Mrs. Cross in 1838. In 1827 he received
royal commissions, probably through Cross for
no. 103, and George IV was delighted with the
result; however, Agasse's overly direct and slight
naïve manner did not endear him to the King, and
the patronage was not continued. In 1828 another
faithful patron, Lord Rivers, died, and Agasse's
position appears to have declined steadily. He
exhibited at the Academy for the last time in 1845
and died four years later.
F.C.

Bibliography

Daniel Baud-Bovy, *Peintres Genèvois 1766-1849,* Geneva, 1904, II, 89-130, 141-48

12 Reproduktionen nach Gemälden von Jacques-Laurent Agasse, Winterthur, 1947

C. F. Hardy, "The Life and Work of Jacques-Laurent Agasse," *The Connoisseur,* pt. I, XLV no. 180, August 1916, pp. 191-98; pt. II, XLVII no. 185, January 1917, pp. 8-17

C. F. Hardy, *Jacques-Laurent Agasse, Peintre Genèvois, 1767-1849,* trans. by D. Plan, Geneva, 1921

103

The Nubian Giraffe

Lent by gracious permission of
Her Majesty Queen Elizabeth II
Oil on canvas; 50⅛ x 40 in.
Inscribed: *JLA*
1827

A giraffe and its two Arab keepers are shown with Edward Cross, an importer of foreign birds and animals for the Royal Menagerie, Exeter Change. Cross had supplied animals for George IV from 1824 onward. During the years 1825 to 1829, his account includes a charge of £100 for supervising the arrival of the giraffe and its journey to Cumberland Lodge and for staying with it for almost six weeks during the period that it remained out-of-doors (Royal Archives, Windsor, Georgian Papers, 25624-5). Two Egyptian cows can be seen in the background.

George IV gave a commission to Agasse "For a picture of the Giraffe & Keepers," for which £200 was to be paid for the painting and £18.17s. for the frame. His receipts are dated January 23, 1829 (Royal Archives, Windsor, Georgian Papers, 26557). His *Livre de Verité* records the picture under October 1827 and lists a reduced copy 21 by 17 in.

The giraffe was captured in 1826, while still a calf, on the plain of Sensar in the Sudan by troups of Mehemet Ali, Pasha and later Viceroy of Egypt. The mother of two calves was shot, and the young,

103

strapped to the backs of camels, were carried to Cairo during a journey lasting forty-five days. Mehemet Ali presented the larger of the two animals to Charles X of France, and the smaller was given to George IV. Sailing on the *Penelope,* the young giraffe travelled from Alexandria to Malta where it remained six months and was then sent on to London arriving August 11, 1827. Two days later, with its Arab keepers, it went on to Windsor and was received with delight by George IV.

Two Egyptian cows, seen in the background of the picture were kept with the young giraffe, possibly as wet-nurses. However, separation from its mother and the ensuing exhausting journey and change of climate had seriously weakened the animal, which lost the use of its legs. One Mr. Bittlestone made

an elaborate pulley to enable it to stand, but it finally died in the summer or autumn of 1829. Subsequently, the skin was stuffed and given to the Zoological Society by William IV and, after the dispersal of the museum, it was acquired by Dr. Crisp, a zoological pathologist.
F.C.

Provenance

Painted for George IV; recorded in the inventory of "Carlton Palace" no. 643; later at Windsor, no. 1111; to the Zoological Gardens, London, in 1924

Exhibitions

The Romantic Movement, The Tate Gallery, London (Arts Council), 1959, no. 8
Animal Painting, Van Dyck to Nolan, The Queen's Gallery, Buckingham Palace, London, 1966-67, no. 26

References

Baud-Bovy, pp. 124, 148

R. Lydekker, "On Old Pictures of Giraffes and Zebras," *Proceedings of . . . the Zoological Society of London,* II, 1904, pp. 339-41

Berthold Laufer, *The Giraffe in History and Art,* Chicago, 1928, p. 89

Basil Taylor, *Animal Painting in England,* 1955, p. 53, pl. 62

L. S. Lambourne, "A Giraffe for George IV," *Country Life,* CXXXVIII, 1965, pp. 1498-1502

Oliver Millar, *The Later Georgian Pictures in the Collection of Her Majesty the Queen,* in preparation

1769-1830

Lawrence was the fourteenth of a family of sixteen children born at Bristol of a Supervisor of Excise and afterwards an innkeeper. By 1779 Fanny Burney described him as a most lovely boy, astonishing for his skill in drawing. Also by 1779 his father had become bankrupt as an innkeeper and moved to Oxford, where Lawrence made portrait drawings and had an engraving published after his likeness of William Hoare. By 1780 they were living in Bath, and Lawrence was drawing profile portraits in pastel. Thomas Barker was working there at the time and gave Lawrence some minor instruction in the use of oils as well as the opportunity of viewing private collections in the area. Lawrence undertook subject drawings and copied Raphael's *Transfiguration* which obtained for him a prize at the Society of Artists in London in 1785. The following year, he painted his first picture, an enormous *Christ Bearing the Cross.*

Probably in the summer of 1787, Lawrence settled in London permanently and studied for three months at the Royal Academy, making sketches in oil. Thereafter, his pastel portraits declined in number. *Lady Cremorne* (collection Lt. Cmdr. C. Windham, R.N.) and his first full-length portrait of *Eliza Farren, Countess of Derby* (Metropolitan Museum of Art), who is portrayed in the open country and shown in a furtive, somewhat shy pose fraught with psychological overtones, give the first indication of the distinctive and psychologically apt portraiture that he was to produce. *Eliza Farren* was shown in the Academy exhibition on the same wall as Reynolds' *Mrs. Billington as S. Cecilia* (New

Brunswick Museum, St. John), and it was Lawrence's psychological interest rather than Reynolds' intellectual involvements that struck the imagination of the public when these two paintings were compared.

As a result of these impressive, early achievements and because of the social connections that he had developed through a sympathetic and attractive personality, Lawrence was made A.R.A. in 1791 and R.A. in 1794. In 1792, when Reynolds died, he became Painter in Ordinary to the King, at the age of twenty-three.

In the period of the 1790s, he produced some of his finest works, including the portrait of *Atherley* (no. 104) and in 1794 the remarkable characterization of the collector and antiquarian *Richard Payne Knight* (collection Major W. M. P. Kincaid-Lennox). His chief rivals in the period were John Hoppner (c. 1758-1810), who was Painter to the Prince of Wales, and Sir William Beechey (1753-1839).

In 1815, the year he painted *Mrs. Jens Wolff* (Art Institute of Chicago), Lawrence travelled to Paris on his first trip abroad to see the works collected by Napoleon. He travelled to Aix-la-Chapelle and Vienna in 1818 to paint portraits of the Emperor of Russia and the King of Prussia. This tour was extended to include Rome, where Lawrence also painted the Pope and Cardinal Consalvi, establishing the nucleus of the series of portraits which were to become the gallery entitled the Waterloo Chamber at Windsor. When they were exhibited in Rome before Lawrence's departure, they created a sensation on account of their rich color and broad technique, and he was called the English Titian. Now considered the outstanding portrait painter of his day, he succeeded Benjamin West as President of the Royal Academy on his return to London in 1820.

During his lifetime, Lawrence achieved a fame with his contemporaries unequalled even by Reynolds. His contacts among the banking families, the

nobility, and with the King, which were climaxed by his official journey to Vienna, gave him a distinction in his period which compares to a degree with that of Rubens.

His sheer skill in the manipulation of paint is dazzling. His presentation of character is frequent highly individual and subtly attuned to the personality of the sitter. In the originality and glamour of his portraits, he looks forward to Mane who must have studied not only his manner of handling broad flat areas of paint but also his colo his juxtaposition of crisp light and dark forms, and his subtle relationships of blacks, grays, and white Lawrence began as a draftsman, and he became one of the most important collectors of old master drawings of his period. His own drawings are exceedingly skilled and beautiful, forming a most attractive and intimate counterpart to his portraits in oil.
F.C.

Bibliography
D. E. Williams, *The Life and Correspondence of Sir Thomas Lawrence, Kt.,* 2 vols., London, 1831
Lord Ronald Sutherland Gower, *Sir Thomas Lawrence,* London, 1900
Oswald G. Knapp, *An Artist's Love Story,* London, 1904
George Soames Layard, *Sir Thomas Lawrence's Letter Bag,* London, 1906
Sir Walter Armstrong, *Lawrence,* London, 1913
Kenneth Garlick, *Sir Thomas Lawrence,* London, 1954 (with bibliography)
Kenneth Garlick, "A Catalogue of the Paintings, Drawings and Pastels of Sir Thomas Lawrence," *Walpole Society,* XXXIX, 1962-64

104

104
Arthur Atherley as an Etonian
(Portrait of an Etonian)
Los Angeles County Museum of Art,
The William Randolph Hearst Collection
Oil on canvas; 49½ x 39½ in.
c. 1790-91

Arthur Atherley (1770-1844) is portrayed here
before a landscape with a distant view of Eton
College, which he attended. Later, he was at Trinity
College, Cambridge, became a Member of
Parliament for Southampton, and was particularly
interested in Parliamentary reform. A study for the
head, with suggestions of a blue rather than red
coat, is in the collection of Col. H. D. M.
Crichton-Maitland, Igtham, Kent.

In this type of portrait, the essential individuality
of the sitter is dramatized by Lawrence through the
personal selection of clothing, cut of hair, carriage,
and pose, elements which were later to be
conceived of as "style" by writers like Baudelaire.
This dramatization of the personality of the sitter
through clothing, pose, and in some cases by mood,
is essential to one kind of romantic portraiture.
Lady Sarah Bunbury (no. 6) by Sir Joshua Reynolds
is a completely different type of portrait. It is an
allegorical portrait infused with intellectual
overtones, a type made popular in England by
Reynolds. Lawrence's *Lady Louisa Manners as
Juno* (Cleveland Museum of Art) derives from this
tradition but is somewhat rare in the art of
Lawrence who was not as attracted to intellectual
conceits of this type. In the portrait of Atherley,
the extraordinary elegance, the broad brushwork,
the large, unbroken areas and simple patterns of
color with vivid passages of darkest shadow look
forward to the art of Manet who must have studied
such portraits with care.
F.C.

Provenance
Mrs. Killett, London
Mrs. Pesne, London
Lord Duveen, 1936
Miss Marion Davies, Los Angeles, California
Hearst Magazines, Inc., Los Angeles
Given to Los Angeles County Museum of Art, 1947

Exhibitions
Royal Academy, 1792, no. 209 *(Portrait of an Etonian)*
Masterworks of Five Centuries, Golden Gate
International Exposition, San Francisco, 1939, no. 131
British Painting in the Eighteenth Century, National
Gallery of Canada, Ottawa, etc., 1957, no. 39
Sir Thomas Lawrence, Regency Painter, Worcester Art
Museum, 1960, no. 4
Masterpieces of Art—Century 21, Seattle World's Fair,
1961, no. 20

References
Williams, I, 128
Gower, p. 107
Armstrong, pp. 111, 162
Garlick, *Sir Thomas Lawrence,* pp. 25, 67, 88, pl. 18
Catalogue of Paintings, Los Angeles County Museum of
Art, Los Angeles, 1954, II, p. 87, pl. 96
William T. Whitley, *Artists and Their Friends in England,
1700-99,* London, 1928, II, 386
Garlick, *Walpole Society,* XXXIX, 1962-64, pp. 24, 268

105

106

105

Satan as a Fallen Angel with Beëlzebub
Colonel Michael Barne
Red and black chalk; 9¾ x 8 in.
c. 1797

Lawrence is probably illustrating the following
lines from Milton's *Paradise Lost,* showing Satan
and his principal companion after his fall and
before his complete revival and the return of
his power:

Thus Satan talking to his neerest Mate
With Head up-lift above the wave, and Eyes
That sparkling blaz'd,—

Probably this study was done around 1797 when
Lawrence was preparing his Diploma picture, one
of the requirements for entrance into the Royal
Academy, with the subject from Milton, *Satan
Calling up his Legions* (Royal Academy, London).
This was the period in England of the most intense
interest in Miltonic subjects. Fuseli was in the
process of preparing his Milton Gallery, and
Romney, Barry, Richard Westall (1765-1836),
Edward Burney (1760-1848), and William Hamilton
were all engaged in making various series of
drawings to illustrate Milton's poems.   F.C.

Provenance
By family descent to Col. Michael E. St. J. Barne,
Sotterly Hall, Beccles

References
Garlick, *Walpole Society,* XXXIX, 1962-64, p. 255, no. 2

106

Miss Sarah Martha (Sally) Siddons
The Pierpont Morgan Library
Black and red chalk on very light brown paper;
9¼ x 7⁹⁄₁₆ in.
Inscribed: *T.L. May 1798*

Sarah Martha (Sally) Siddons (1775-1803) was th
eldest daughter of Mrs. Siddons, the actress and
friend of Sir Thomas Lawrence. She was sent to
boarding school in Calais with her sister in 1790
and remained there about two years. Lawrence w
romantically involved with both Sally and her sist
Maria and was engaged to each of them at differe
times. Unfortunately, the sisters were consumptiv
and both died young—Maria in the autumn of 179

and Sally less than five years later, when she was twenty-eight. Sally Siddons, in particular, was prone to stimulate Lawrence's mercurial affections, and he became engaged and broke his engagement to her more than once. In the spring of 1798, after breaking his engagement to Maria, he gave his affection to Sally who wrote to him in April making clear her attachment while deploring his inconsistency. Sally continued to be in love with him but a shadow was cast over their relationship when, in the autumn of the same year, Maria, on her deathbed, implored her sister never to marry Lawrence. She obtained a solemn pledge to this effect before her mother, a pledge communicated by letter to Lawrence himself.

Two versions of the drawing are known. The first, inscribed: *T.L. Thursday 1797* and *This drawing is Miss Siddons,* was engraved by R. J. Lane in 1830. No. 106, dated May 1798, is the second and repeats the composition of the 1797 drawing.

Lawrence painted two portraits of Sally Siddons in oil. One of these is the picture in the Wallace Collection. A second portrait of Sally, looking to the right, is in the collection of Walter P. Chrysler, Jr. A sketch for the latter was with the Leger Galleries, London, in 1935 and is reproduced in *Apollo* for September 1935, p. 167. There are a number of portrait drawings of Sally Siddons: seated in profile to the left (Courtauld Institute of Art, Witt Collection); seated, head bowed in profile to left (collection Miss Juliet Brodie, Brodie Castle); head only, looking to the right, engraved R. J. Lane; head and bust, facing (Huntington Art Gallery, San Marino); profile to the right, engraved by R. J. Lane. F.C.

Provenance
J. P. Morgan (died 1943)
The Pierpont Morgan Library, New York, 1945

Exhibitions
The First Quarter Century of the Pierpont Morgan Library, The Pierpont Morgan Library, New York, 1949, no. 109

References
Knapp, opp. p. 49
Lady Eliza Priestley, "An Artist's Love Story," *The Nineteenth Century,* no. 338, April 1905, pp. 642-54
Armstrong, pp. 40-46, 188
Garlick, *Walpole Society,* XXXIX, 1962-64, pp. 243, 244, no. 5

107
Benjamin West
Amherst College, Bequest of Herbert L. Pratt
Oil on panel; oval, 28⅞ x 23⅞ in.,
within rectangle 29¼ x 24 in., unfinished
Inscribed: *Benjamin West PRA by Sir Thomas Lawrence PRA; Benjamin West PRA Th. Lawrence PRA:* underneath the jabot is a tiny circle with letters: *MH* (the collector's mark of Matthew Hutchinson)
c. 1811

When this work was shown in the West exhibition in 1950, it was dated c. 1794, that is, shortly after West became President of the Royal Academy. It has also been related by Morgan and Toole to the full-length portrait by Lawrence exhibited at the Royal Academy in 1821, now in the Wadsworth Atheneum, Hartford. However, it is clear that this painting is a study for the portrait of West exhibited at the Royal Academy in 1811. The present whereabouts of the finished portrait is unknown, but it was engraved by H. Meyer in 1813, and a careful comparison with this preparatory sketch illustrates their close relationship. In both, the hair is short and groomed in much the same way, rather than long and more lank as in the Hartford portrait. The hairline is also that of 1811 rather than much further receded as in 1821. The lighting, with the left side of the face in shadow, and the light coming from high on the right, is that of the 1811 portrait. The general firmness of flesh and the keen light of the eyes is that of West in 1811, and the costume, with a high, black collar encircling the neck from

107

the left and slightly covering the cravat, corresponds to the 1811 portrait.

It is possible that no. 107 was left unfinished because the composition, with the left hand supporting the cheek, was unsatisfactory, or because the half-length of the final version was finally more desirable. The rejected canvas remained, along with some two hundred other unfinished portraits, in Lawrence's possession until his death.

The technique used here by Lawrence on panel recalls the sketches of Romney. First, the figure was drawn on the sized canvas with black chalk or charcoal. The underpainting was laid in with a broad, rough brush or sponge. The darker undercoat of the oval was then hastily and thinly introduced with a very wet brush, allowing the paint to run down the canvas. The head and certain of the outlines were added with the brush, and the building up of the focal point of the canvas, the face and the area round it, begun.

Romney's unfinished portraits may result from a lack of immediate inspiration, the absence of a sitter, or a shift in his own mood or interest. More than half of Lawrence's unfinished works were commissions bypassed because of the demands of more impressive or more insistent sitters. Others, like the *West* at Amherst, were the result of altered plans. Numerous portraits must have been undertaken with the view that they would be finished by assistants. We know that it was his practice to have assistants complete his work. This study shows a painting as it might have been turned over to a particularly able student to be finished with Lawrence's supervision and his final touching to improve faulty details.

Such unfinished productions in the work of earlier masters were appreciated in the 18th century by writers like Diderot. And in the 19th and 20th centuries, such informal productions have come to be valued more and more for their informality. The lack of high finish is considered more stimulating to the eye and to the imagination because it displays the artist's technique. Showing the artistic process, it makes the image more dynamic by allowing it to appear in a state of flux, and because it reveals a related series of forms within one format, each of which appears to exist on a different level of experience.
F.C.

Provenance
The artist (sale, Christie's, London, 19 June 1830, no. 419, bt. Hutchinson)
Matthew Hutchinson (sale, Christie's, 22 February 1861, no. 138)
James Hughes Anderdon (died 1879)
Horatio Noble Pym, Foxwold Chase, Brasted, Kent (died 1896) (sale, Christie's, 22 November 1912, no. 70, bt. Renton)
Herbert Lee Pratt, Glen Cove, Long Island (died 1945)
Bequeathed to Amherst College, 1945

Exhibitions
National Portraits, Victoria and Albert Museum, London, 1868, no. 17 (lent by J. H. Anderdon)
Winter Exhibition, Royal Academy, London, 1877, no. 255 (lent by J. H. Anderdon)
Benjamin West: His Times and His Influence, Amherst College, Amherst, Mass., 1950, no. 6
Sir Thomas Lawrence as Painter and Collector, Columbus Gallery of Fine Arts, Columbus, Ohio, 1955, no. 33
Sir Thomas Lawrence, Regency Painter, Worcester Art Museum, Worcester, Mass., 1960, no. 14

References
Horatio N. Pym, *Odds and Ends at Foxwold,* London, 1887, p. 8
Armstrong, p. 169
The Herbert Lee Pratt Collection, Amherst College, Amherst, Mass., 1946, p. 17
Charles H. Morgan and Marget C. Toole, "Benjamin West: His Times and His Influence," *Art in America,* XXXVIII, December 1950, pp. 259-60
Garlick, *Sir Thomas Lawrence,* p. 62, pl. 73
Garlick, *Walpole Society,* XXXIX, 1962-64, pp. 195 no. 1, 322

108
Sir Richard Page Croft, Sixth Baronet
Richard Page Croft
Black and red chalk; 15 x 10¼ in.
1818

Sir Richard Page Croft (1762-1818) had become intimate with the Royal Family as a physician, and he took delight in his role, as his letter to his sister dated October 19, 1817 makes clear. He was *accoucheur* to Princess Charlotte in 1817. Her death led to an outburst of public feeling against him. He became depressed and shot himself on February 13, 1818.

Lawrence was a friend of Elizabeth Croft and her circle which included Mrs. Jens Wolff, and she had left a memoir which describes this drawing. The portrait is of her brother who was portrayed in his coffin but transformed by Lawrence to appear asleep in his armchair. The drawing, which Miss Croft refers to as unfinished, was praised by artists like Wilkie, and Lawrence himself was pleased with it. We are told that he was so delighted with this work that he would send for it to show artists who dined with him.
F.C.

Provenance
Elizabeth Croft and descendants

Exhibitions
Lawrence, Royal Academy, London, 1961, no. 69

References
Elizabeth Croft, "Recollections of Sir Thomas Lawrence," in Layard, pp. 114-15, 244-45
Garlick, *Walpole Society,* XXXIX, 1962-64, p. 223

Thomas Barker
(Barker of Bath)

1769-1847

Barker's father, although prepared for the law, had turned to animal painting, perhaps prompted by a visit to Wright's Gallery in Derby. He reduced himself to uncomfortable circumstances and was employed, possibly as a decorator, at a tinware factory in the area of Pontypool, Monmouthshire, at the time of Thomas's birth. The family subsequently moved to Bath, and there the talents of the precocious boy attracted the attention of Charles Spackman, a wealthy coach-builder. Spackman undertook his education in a grammar school and set him to work copying among his collection of Netherlandish and Italian paintings. The arrangement proved financially successful for Spackman and beneficial to the young painter. In about 1790 Spackman sold Barker's *Woodman,* inspired by William Cowper's poem *The Task,* to Thomas Macklin, the London publisher of the *Poets Gallery,* for 500 guineas, and it was engraved by Francesco Bartolozzi (1727-1815). In 1790 Spackman also organized an exhibition of Barker's work in Bath, drawing minor attention to the painter. And from the same year, or the following, Spackman underwrote a three-year sojourn in Italy for Barker, who continued to supply his patron with pictures. Deprived of this support by Spackman's bankruptcy in 1794, Barker quickly attained considerable success. He concentrated on English, Welsh, and Italian landscapes, such as the *Mountainous Landscape with a Watermill* (Mellon Collection), and genre scenes and fancy pictures, such as *A Boy Extracting a Thorn from his Foot* (1810, Victoria and Albert Museum). However, he occasionally produced portraits, religious subjects

like *Christ in the Garden* (Royal Academy 1829), and history pieces like *The Trial of Queen Caroline* (painted and exhibited at Bath, 1821). He exhibited often at the British Institution from 1807, but only six times at the Royal Academy, from 1791. In 1813 he published *Forty Lithographic Impressions from Drawings . . . of Rustic Figures,* and in the next year *Thirty-two Lithographic Impressions from Pen Drawings of Landscape Scenery.* At the same time, his picturesque, rustic characters were copied extensively on a variety of transfer-printed English ceramics and fabrics. By about 1810 Barker was able to erect his handsome "Doric House" on Sion Hill, Bath, from the designs of his friend Joseph Gandy (1771-1843), the draftsman of the architect Sir John Soane (1753-1837). Here, in 1825, he decorated one wall with a monumental *Massacre at Scio.* However, the expenditures caused by his taste for an urbane life and the decline of Bath as a fashionable watering-place placed his latter years under an economic cloud.

F.C.

Bibliography
Sir Edward Harington, *A Schizzo on the Genius of Man; in which . . . the merit . . . of T. Barker, the celebrated young painter of Bath, is particularly considered,* Bath, 1793
Forty Lithographic Impressions from Drawings by Thomas Barker, Selected from his Studies of Rustic Figures after Nature, Bath, 1813
Thirty-two Lithographic Impressions from Pen Drawings of Landscape Scenery by Thomas Barker, Bath, 1814
Thomas Barker, *A Descriptive Account of the Historical Picture, the Trial of The Queen,* Bath, 1821
R[obert] H[arrison], "Barker, Thomas," *The Dictionary of National Biography,* London, I, 1937-38, pp. 1131-32
Percy Bate, "Thomas Barker of Bath," *The Connoisseur,* X, October 1904, pp. 107-12; XI, February 1905, pp. 76-81
E. Harrison Barker, "Thomas Barker of Bath," *The Connoisseur,* XI, 1905, p. 190

109
Interior of a Mill
Allen Memorial Art Museum, Oberlin College,
Oberlin, Ohio
Oil on canvas; 40½ x 26 in.
Inscribed: *Tho. Barker Pinx. 1807*

The miller in this view of the interior of a country
mill is a descendant of Gainsborough's peasants
and Morland's rustics. However, nothing in
Gainsborough or Morland prepares one for the
shock of the miller's gaze. The man supports
himself with his stick in an awkward stance from
which he must move in a moment. He glances
upwards, arrested in the motion itself, as if a visitor
had suddenly appeared and caught his attention.

This momentary and vivid action is enhanced by
an equally rare psychological intensity. The anxious
face of the miller is splashed with light from a
source low down at the front, leaving pools, crisp
edges, and brims of illumination within. The wide,
round eyes of the haggard face taunt the observer
with a querulous uncertainty. Momentary attitudes
in the works of Frans Hals, for example, are used
to jolt us enthusiastically into the delights of the
senses. This pale miller draws us reflectively into
the lengthening shadows of his existence. In this
rustic peasant, Thomas Barker has created one of
the most gripping moments in the relaxed cult of
the picturesque.

The same model appears in certain of the
lithographs published by Barker in 1813.
F.C.

References
Lawrence Gowing, "Barker," *Kindlers Malerei-Lexikon,*
Zürich, 1964, I, 202-03
Wolfgang Stechow, *Catalogue of European and
American Paintings and Sculpture in the Allen
Memorial Art Museum,* Oberlin, 1967, p. 10

109

James Ward

1769-1859

Son of a warehouse manager for a wholesale frui
and cider merchant in the manufacturing district
of Thames Street, London, James Ward was a
member of a family of five and had almost no form
education. John Raphael Smith (1752-1812), to
whom he was apprenticed around 1782, was his
first teacher. Ward remained only about a year wi
Smith, who was more taskmaster than teacher, an
after that, he attached himself to his brother
William for three years. In 1785 the Wards moved
to Kensal Green, where the painter George Morla
came to live with them and married James's siste
Anne. Working day and night at printmaking for h
brother, James Ward became the outstanding
mezzotint engraver of his period. It took him only
two years, after completing his apprenticeship, to
obtain the appointment in 1794 of Mezzotint
Engraver to the Prince of Wales, despite his humb
birth and contacts. This period of his life was
climaxed by his marriage to Emma Ward
about 1794-95.

Ward's contacts with Morland developed in him
profound interest in painting and he began to pa
under his brother-in-law's instruction, at first
copying Morland's own paintings. Slowly, he
developed his own style, although all of his
productions in the 1790s were done in Morland's
manner and with his subjects. In 1792 he began
exhibiting at the Royal Academy. Realizing that h
could not become a full Royal Academician if he
were too well known as an engraver, he gave up
lucrative commissions. Beginning with portraits

cattle and livestock for local landowners, he became known at first as an *animalier*. This prepared him well for his first truly successful picture, and one of the finest he ever painted, *Fighting Bulls with a View of St. Donat's Castle in the Background* (Victoria and Albert Museum). This was undertaken after seeing Rubens' landscape *View of the Château de Steen, Autumn* (National Gallery, London), purchased by Sir George Beaumont in 1803 and exhibited in the studio of Benjamin West where Ward saw it. It was Ward's plan to submit his picture to the Royal Academy with a painting of a boa serpent attacking a Negro on a white stallion, which he thought would gain him access to the Academy. However, the picture was rejected by the academicians, and he exhibited his paintings in his studio.

After 1805 his range slowly increased to include religious subjects and the lucrative genre portraits of blood horses and their masters, climaxed by the series of twenty-four portraits of famous horses painted from 1823 to 1826. He also painted landscapes, the most famous of which is *Gordale Scar, Yorkshire* of 1811-15 (Tate Gallery). To this he slowly added historical subjects, first with an emphasis on animals such as the *Fall of Phaeton* exhibited in 1808, and later broadening to include female nudes. His most ambitious undertaking in history painting was the gigantic project arising from a competition held by the British Institution in 1815 for the best historical composition to illustrate the triumph of Wellington. Ward's composition sketch, for which he received a prize of £1,000, still exists at Chelsea Hospital. Preparing himself with prayer and meditation, he undertook the enlargement of the format on three different occasions until it became 35 by 21 feet and had to be moved on rollers for painting. Finished in 1821, it was shown at the Egyptian Hall and was thoroughly condemned by the public and the press.

During the difficult period of preparing this picture, Ward's wife and daughter died. Although it was a time when he commanded his largest annual income, it was also the most difficult period of his

life and one which damaged his reputation and his self-confidence considerably.

Although continuing to paint animals, particularly horses, exhibiting in 1828 his striking *L'Amour du cheval* (Tate Gallery), his later period, which is often neglected, included a surprising number of historical compositions. His last years are generally passed over with little attention, and this is the period in his life which one would wish to know more about. In 1830 he exhibited *Diana and Actaeon* (Royal Academy, no. 326), *Duncan's Horses* in 1834 (Royal Academy, no. 34), the *Weird Sisters from Macbeth* in 1838 (Royal Academy, no. 86), and *Charles II at the Battle of Worcester* in 1847 (no. 10).

In 1829 he married Charlotte Fritch and to gain money held a public sale of his own works, which proved a failure, an event repeated in 1841. Having sold no pictures for many years, he applied for assistance from the Academy in 1847 and was awarded an annual stipend. His last work, sent to the exhibition of 1855, was *The Morning Grey with Cattle*. Suffering from poverty, he had become bitter by this time and totally dissatisfied with anything to do with art and exhibitions.

We can say with his biographers of the early 20th century that James Ward must still await a true reevaluation. He was an uneven artist who is thrilling at his best in such works as the *Fighting Bulls* of about 1803. In his study of the many facets of animal painting, especially in his interest in their emotional life and responses, he looks forward to Landseer. His striking watercolor drawings of weasels, ducks, geese, and swans are often beautiful even though he can frequently be crude. His early painted sketches on small panels in the manner of Rubens are frequently brilliant in color and delicious in handling of paint. He is a finer artist than B. R. Haydon whom he resembles in his pretentious ambition to paint historical subjects in the manner of the old masters.
F.C.

Bibliography
James Ward, *Ward's Gallery of Paintings, Drawings, Models and Engravings,* London, 1841
Julia Frankau, *William Ward, A. R. A., James Ward, R. A.,* London, 1904
C. Reginald Grundy, *James Ward, R. A.,* London, 1909
Elliott O'Donnell, ed., *Mrs. E. M. Ward's Reminiscences,* London, 1911
W. Shaw Sparrow, *A Book of Sporting Painters,* London/New York, 1931, pp. 71-82
James Ward, Arts Council, London, 1960 (catalogue compiled by Dennis Farr)

110
Lioness and Heron (Lioness Disturbed)
Ponce Art Museum (The Luis A. Ferré Foundation)
Oil on canvas; 44 x 58 in.
Inscribed: *JWD/1816*

This painting is somewhat unusual in Ward's art as he himself was aware when he wrote on April 11, 1848, "The world knows nothing of what I can do in that way but from Mr. Earle's picture."

Signed and dated 1816, this is almost certainly the *Lioness Disturbed* that was exhibited at the British Institution in 1817. The landscape, which Delacroix must have seen, is remarkable, and the picture has great importance for such artists as Sir Edwin Landseer and Antoine Louis Barye (1796-1875). Although it stands within a tradition well established by Jacques-Laurent Agasse in the first decade of the century, it is unusual for its boldness of design and its breadth of execution. Such a picture goes beyond the fairly objective animal portraits of artists like Agasse (no. 103) in showing a concern to represent animals in situations demanding emotional response. In this case, the lioness, disturbed by some creature or sound, has turned in an almost furious way to bare her fangs, snarl, and to peer intently at the intrusion. Anatomists like Sir Charles Bell and artists like B. R. Haydon were concerned to represent animals with their own instinctual responses rather than with human emotions wedded to animal physiognomies, for which such masters as Rubens were soundly criticized.

110

This new naturalism goes beyond the simple "portraits" of animals by such artists as Stubbs, although his *Lion Attacking a Horse* anticipates such theories. This is a logical continuation of the developing interest in human psychology and its continuous exploration in art and in science through the use of comparative anatomy. Knowledge of the human nervous system was greatly expanded by Sir Charles Bell, who was the first to distinguish between motor and sensory responses and who also wrote a treatise on expression for the use of artists in 1806. He used the technique of comparing the emotional responses of animals and human beings to make clear the unique capacities of each. Bell held lectures on anatomy which numerous of the artists attended, and his ideas were thus infused into the visual arts. Ward's painting is an early example of the impact of his ideas and a perfect illustration of the use of research into the phenomena of experience in order to make works of art conform to our precise knowledge of the exterior world. F.C.

111

Provenance
Mr. Earle
Hugh Robert Hughes, Kinmel Park, Abergele, Wales, 1885 (died 1911)
J. Staats Forbes (died before 1908) (sale, Christie's, London, 2 June 1916, no. 164, bt. Buck)
Anonymous sale, Robinson, Fisher & Harding, London, 8 October 1925, no. 174
Ponce Art Museum, Ponce, Puerto Rico, 1959

Exhibitions
British Institution, 1817, no. 176
Royal Academy, London, 1885, no. 58 (lent by H. R. Hughes)
Guildhall, London, 1894, no. 86 (lent by J. S. Forbes)
Animals in Art, Bristol Art Gallery, 1908, no. 160 (lent by executors of the estate of J. Staats Forbes)

References
Grundy, p. 48, nos. 565, 566, pl. 10
Julius S. Held, *Museo de Arte de Ponce, Fundación Luis A. Ferré, Catalogue I, Paintings of the European and American Schools,* Ponce, 1965, pp. 192-93

111
Marengo, the Barb Charger
His Grace the Duke of Northumberland, K.G., T.D.
Oil on panel; 32 x 43 in.
Inscribed: *J. Ward, R.A. 1824*

This spirited portrait of Napoleon's famous charger
belonged to a series of twenty-four famous horses
by Ward. It is likely that he received the idea from
Stubbs, whose Turf Gallery of sixteen famous
horses was exhibited in 1794. In 1823 Ward was
painting for George IV three of the royal horses
including Nonpareil, Soothsayer, and Monitor
which formed part of this series.

Marengo, named after the small town in North Italy
where Napoleon was victorious over the Austrians
in 1800, was imported from Egypt as a six-year-old
in 1799. Napoleon, who preferred gray or cream
horses, rode him at the Battle of Marengo and was
greatly impressed with his speed, vitality, and
sureness under fire. Thereafter, this horse carried
the Emperor at Austerlitz, Jena, and Wagram and
survived the Russian expedition of 1812. At
Waterloo, Marengo was ridden by Napoleon during
the first part of the battle, but later was captured
by the British and brought to England by Lord Petre.
J. J. Angerstein bought him and kept him at New
Barnes near Ely until 1831 when he died at around
thirty-eight years of age.

The title of the print bears the line "The
Background, Emblematic of his Master's Downfall."
The sunset and red sky are easily interpreted. The
crow, according to Alciati, symbolizes the death
of kings or princes. Normally, it stands for concord
or harmony. Alciati represents four crows balanced
in pairs on either side of a scepter, because
rulership is maintained or falls by the concurrence
and harmony of the people. If this harmony is
suppressed, discord follows, bearing the fate
of kings.

James Ward is generally thought of today as
following in the humble and non-intellectual
tradition of Morland. However, his painting the

*Genius of Wellington on the Car of War, Supported
by Britannia and Attended by the Seven Cardinal
Virtues, Commanding Away the Demons, Anarchy,
Rebellion and Discord with the Horrors of War*
(sketch, Royal Hospital, Chelsea), had an elaborate,
Rubensian program. It illustrated grandiose
intellectual and pictorial pretensions even more
startling than those of Haydon. These are reflected
on a much more intimate and attractive scale
in this painting.
F.C.

Provenance
Purchased from the artist by Hugh Percy, third Duke of
Northumberland
By descent to the present owner

Exhibitions
Royal Academy, 1826, no. 219
The First Hundred Years of the Royal Academy, Royal
Academy, London, 1951-52, no. 126
The Romantic Movement, Tate Gallery, London (Arts
Council), 1959, no. 372
Sport and the Horse, Virginia Museum of Fine Arts,
Richmond, 1960, no. 51

References
Andrea Alciati, *Emblemata,* XXXIIX, III
Somerset House Gazette, 1824, XL, 208
M. Phipps Jackson, "Two famous chargers, Copenhagen
and Marengo," *The Magazine of Art,* 1893, XVI, 306-07
Frankau, pp. 106, 129
Grundy, p. 46 no. 452, p. 57 no. 21, p. 58 no. 29, p. 71
no. 68
Stella A. Walker, *Horses of Renown,* London, 1954,
pp. 72-74

Reproductions
Lithograph by James Ward, 13¼ by 17⅞ in., as one of a
series of celebrated horses published by R. Ackerman
on May 1, 1824 and again on August 1, 1824 (repr.
Walker, *Horses of Renown,* opp. p. 80)

George Chinnery

1774-1852

George Chinnery was the grandson of a celebrate
writing master, and the son of William Chinnery,
a merchant and an amateur painter of Fleet Street
who exhibited at the Free Society of Artists in 176
and 1766. With whom Chinnery studied painting is
unknown, but he first exhibited at the Royal
Academy in 1791 when he was seventeen years ol
In 1794-95 he travelled to Ireland, marrying in the
same year and remaining until 1802, when he
deserted his family. In Dublin, Chinnery was
influenced by the works of the miniaturist John
Comerford (1770-1832), and at the time he painted
numerous miniatures on ivory, some of which wei
included in the Arts Council exhibition of 1957. The
art of miniature painting was not foreign to him
even in his first London period when he had studie
the works of Richard Cosway, whose style is
reflected in numerous of his portrait drawings
both at this time and later.

After leaving his wife and two children in 1802,
Chinnery returned to London and sailed for Madra
where his family had owned the firm of Chase,
Sewell, and Chinnery. Almost at once he receivec
numerous commissions for oil portraits, ivory
miniatures, and portrait drawings, allowing a
degree of financial security which he had not befoi
known. In 1807 he was induced to go to Calcutta
to paint the portrait of Sir Henry Russell who had
recently been appointed Chief Justice of Bengal.
He also painted portraits of the Earl of Moria, Sir
Gilbert Elliott, both Governors General, and other
dignitaries, and he lived like other Europeans in
India at this time on a sumptuous scale with a

household of ten to fifteen servants and a salary estimated at over £500 a month.

In 1817 his wife and daughter joined him in India. Despite his success, he was not able to support his debts, and in 1822 he deserted his family once again, travelling to the Danish settlement of Serampor, possibly to escape arrest for debt. In 1825, with debts of £40,000, he fled India and left his wife, who remained, supported by an allowance from her husband.

In September 1825 he travelled to Macao which was then the principal seaport for foreign trade in China. Chinnery lived there for the rest of his life, filling sketchbooks with innumerable views of every part of the city. When his wife attempted to join him, he removed temporarily to Canton, nearby, where European women were not allowed. From Macao he continued to send numerous works to the Royal Academy exhibitions.

Chinnery is very little understood today partially because numerous of his works remain unknown and others have been destroyed. He was an uneven painter, remarkable at times for his delicacy and originality and at other times dull, repetitive, and merely topographical. However, his landscapes and particularly his landscape watercolors and pen drawings are frequently beautiful.
F.C.

Bibliography
James Orange, "The Life and Work of George Chinnery, R. H. A., in China," *The Studio*, LXXX, 1920, pp. 82-93; XCIV, 1927, pp. 230-39
Sir William Foster, "British Artists in India," *Walpole Society*, XIX, 1930-31, pp. 13-20
George Chinnery, 1774-1852, London, Arts Council, 1957 (catalogue compiled by Allan Carr)
Henry and Sidney Berry-Hill, *George Chinnery 1774-1852, Artist of the China Coast*, Leigh-On-Sea, 1963

112

112
Design for a Title Page
The Pierpont Morgan Library
Pen and gall-nut ink on paper; 7$\frac{1}{16}$ x 8$\frac{15}{16}$ in.
Inscribed in shorthand and dated 1821

This drawing shows two dilapidated dwellings with domestic animals in an Indian village in or near Madras, where Chinnery was living in 1821. It was his habit to draw incessantly, going out in the very early morning with pen and watercolors to record landscapes, buildings, bridges, or peasants in their daily activities. Numerous sketchbooks of these studies, often done with the greatest rapidity and fluency, are preserved. Canaletto has been mentioned as a possible source for Chinnery's drawing style, especially in the works of his Macao period. Something more objective, occasionally suggestive of Canaletto in a most general way, does make its appearance in the Macao drawings, and it may have something to do with the neatness and clean lines of a city which was essentially Portuguese in origin and character. But Chinnery's Indian drawings are highly picturesque, as this sheet suggests, and their source is much closer to

London of the 1790s than to Venice. The style and subject of this remarkable drawing reflect the manner of George Morland and his follower Thomas Barker of Bath. Particularly, Barker's series of picturesque views entitled *Thirty-Two Lithographic Impressions from Pen Drawings of Landscape Scenery* (Bath, 1814) offer striking parallels in technique which must illustrate a common source in Morland for the drawing style in landscape of these two men. Indeed, this source would also assist in explaining the origin and technique of Chinnery's paintings of Chinese peasants. A dilapidated cottage, much closer in style to Morland and offering a transition to the developed treatment of this sheet, is reproduced in the monograph by Berry-Hill.

The rapid inscription in the upper right corner of no. 112, concluding in a date of 1821, and that on the lower right are similar to those found on other studies by Chinnery. These annotations are in a system of shorthand developed by W. B. Gurney, who became Short-Hand Writer to the House of Lords in the 1820s.

The ultimate destination of Chinnery's drawings of this type is uncertain. James Orange mentioned four presumed title pages or frontispieces in his possession, from the early years of Chinnery's residence in Macao in the 1820s, which may be connected with this sheet.
F.C.

Provenance
The Pierpont Morgan Library, 1960

References
The Pierpont Morgan Library, *Tenth Report to the Fellows of the Pierpont Morgan Library*, New York, 1960, pp. 65-66
Orange, *The Studio*, XCIV, 1927, pp. 230-39
Berry-Hill, pl. 29

1775-1802

Born at Great Bandy Leg Walk in Southwark, Girtin grew up in London. Few details are known about his early life. In 1789 he was apprenticed to Edward Dayes, a topographical watercolorist, and he may also have colored prints for the engraver John Raphael Smith, where he is said to have met Turner. From around 1791 to 1795 he worked for an amateur antiquarian and topographer, James Moore, making drawings for him and working up Moore's sketches into finished watercolors that could be engraved. Girtin's first exhibited work at the Royal Academy, in 1794, was a watercolor view of *Ely Cathedral* (Ashmolean Museum), which is based on a sketch by Moore and reflects the influence of Dayes. For a period of three years, probably from late 1794 until the end of 1797, Girtin, along with Turner, was employed by another amateur, Dr. Thomas Monro. Dr. Monro was an alienist under whose care John Robert Cozens was placed when he became insane in 1794. Apparently as a result, Monro gained temporary possession of many sketches by Cozens, and he set Turner and Girtin to making finished drawings based upon them, Girtin drawing the outlines and Turner washing in the effects. The exposure to Cozens was of profound importance for both artists, and his influence was probably the strongest single factor in the development of Girtin's mature style. Girtin also copied older masters, notably Canaletto, who strongly influenced his drawing style, and Piranesi, and he seems to have been interested in the landscapes of Rembrandt and Rubens, although the nature and extent of their influence have been

the subject of some debate. In 1799 he was one of the founders of a sketching club which met for the purpose of illustrating passages from literature.

Beginning in 1796, if not earlier, Girtin travelled extensively and regularly in Scotland and the north of England; he seems to have been especially drawn to Yorkshire scenery, which provided the subjects of several of his best works. In the autumn of 1801 he went to Paris, ostensibly in search of relief from the asthma from which he suffered, and he remained there until May of 1802. He died in the November following his return, at the age of twenty-seven.

Girtin apparently made only one oil painting, which is now lost. Shortly before his death he opened an exhibition of a circular panorama of London, the *Eidometropolis,* which Girtin and Loshak believe was painted in 1797-98, but most other students place after 1800. It was apparently painted in tempera and is known through a bad engraving and several preparatory watercolors in The British Museum. He also etched a series of *Twenty of the Most Picturesque Views in Paris and Its Environs,* which were aquatinted and published posthumously. However, it was as a painter in watercolors that Girtin made his great contribution. It used to be believed that the change from the 18th-century tinted drawing, based on a monochrome underpainting, to the 19th-century watercolor painting, conceived throughout in terms of color, was due to Girtin. This is no longer tenable, but it is true that Girtin and Turner between them in the last years of the 1790s brought a new breadth and richness, both of handling and of content, to the medium, and they had a vast influence on almost all watercolor painting of the ensuing century.
A.S.

Bibliography
Randall Davies, *Thomas Girtin's Water-Colours,* London, 1924
Martin Hardie, "Thomas Girtin: The Technical Aspect of His Work," *OWCSC,* XI, 1934, pp. 1-20
Jonathan Mayne, *Thomas Girtin,* Leigh-on-Sea, 1949
Thomas Girtin and David Loshak, *The Art of Thomas Girtin,* London, 1954 (see review by Paul Oppé, *Burlington,* XCVII, 1955, pp. 392-95, and further correspondence, *ibid.,* XCIX, 1957, pp. 58-60)

113
Lindisfarne Castle, Northumberland (Holy Island Castle)
The Metropolitan Museum of Art,
Rogers Fund, 1906
Watercolor; 15⅟₁₆ x 20⅞₁₆ in.
Inscribed: *Girtin*
1796 or 1797

This drawing is apparently a result of the trip to Scotland and the north of England which Girtin made in 1796. Several other drawings based on Girtin's visit to Lindisfarne exist, most of which Girtin and Loshak suggest were painted in 1797. At the Royal Academy in 1797, Girtin exhibited two views of *St. Cuthbert's Cathedral, Holy Island.*

This watercolor was done at a time when Girtin was probably still engaged with Turner in making copies after John Robert Cozens for Dr. Monro, and it shows Cozens' influence. Girtin and Loshak suggest that its composition is based on a drawing such as Cozens' *Part of Vietri and Raito* (Powell Collection). The looming hill, curving shoreline, foreground figures, and smoke all recall Cozens, as does the romantic grandeur which Girtin has imparted to the scene. The strong vertical accent which gives the drawing much of its impact, is characteristic of Girtin's earlier work and reflects his training and experience as a draftsman of architectural subjects.

The blue color also reflects the influence of Cozens, but its strength shows Girtin attempting to give more force and vigor to his colors than he would have found in any 18th-century precedent. Such strong blues came in for criticism from Girtin's old master Edward Dayes, who upon seeing a drawing by a follower of Girtin exclaimed, "O ye gods! the blue bag—the blue bag!" Girtin's paper is also noteworthy; he was the first artist to use rough cartridge paper and consciously exploit its imperfections for part of the effect of his drawings. According to the Redgraves, he could only get the paper he liked at a stationery shop in Charing Cross and had to buy it folded. When he unfolded it to make a large watercolor, the crease was more absorbent than the other parts of the paper and caused a dark discoloration. This apparently is the source of the stain down the middle of no. 113. The defect was considered proof of the authenticity of the works in which it appeared, and thus it gradually gave them greater value.

A.S.

Provenance
Hopkins
Palser, 1906

References
Richard and Samuel Redgrave, *A Century of Painters of the English School,* London, 1866, I, 393-94, 397
Girtin and Loshak, pp. 62-63, 159, no. 185, fig. 32

113

114

monument, neither it nor the watercolor in the Victoria and Albert Museum show it primarily as an object of topographical or antiquarian interest In the Victoria and Albert drawing the point of view is low, and the tower is silhouetted against a sunset sky. In no. 114, as in several other drawing by Girtin, we have a raised, almost bird's-eye view, looking down on the Abbey nestled in the landscape. Kirkstall Abbey provides the focus, but the subject of no. 114 is the sweep and grandeur of the landscape as a whole. The horizontal vastness of no. 114 provides a contrast to the vertical emphasis of the earlier no. 113. Its greater sobriety of color is also evident, and hand in hand with these changes comes a calmer and mellowe mood, replacing the overt drama of no. 113.

Girtin's obituary in *The Gentleman's Magazine* (reprinted in Mayne, p. 77) states that in the latter part of his life Girtin sedulously studied Rubens. Although the connection has been questioned by Loshak, the sweeping panorama of no. 114 which curiously (and symptomatically) did not receive any discussion by Girtin and Loshak, does sugge a kinship with the landscapes of Rubens. However as Laurence Binyon puts it, it was perhaps more a case of discovered kinship than derivation, and the mood of Girtin's work is quite different. A.S.

114
Kirkstall Abbey
Trustees of The British Museum
Watercolor; 12⅝ x 20⁷⁄₁₆ in.
Inscribed: *Girtin 1800*

This is one of two late views of *Kirkstall Abbey* by Girtin; the other is in the Victoria and Albert Museum and is not dated. Girtin and Loshak imply, without arguing their reasons, that the Victoria and Albert watercolor is the later of the two. Both belong to a group of Yorkshire scenes which represent the peak of Girtin's achievement. Jonathan Mayne and other scholars have noted the similarity of outlook between these views and the poetry of Wordsworth. The opening of *Lines*

Composed a Few Miles Above Tintern Abbey, for example, written and published in 1798, describes just such a panoramic view as Girtin was wont to paint.

Both men seem to conceive of the landscape as almost holy, reflecting the fact that for most people, nature was becoming less and less of an everyday experience. Girtin's views of Yorkshire are not the outgrowth of the habitual experience of the native, but of the brief visit of the city-dweller, which he was, just as Wordsworth's *Tintern Abbey* describes the responses and thoughts of one who had not seen that landscape for five years.

Although no. 114 shows a picturesque and famous

Provenance
Chambers Hall, Southampton (gift to The British Museum, 1855)

References
Laurence Binyon, *Catalogue of Drawings by British Artists in the British Museum,* London, 1900, II, 228, no. 38
Laurence Binyon, *Thomas Girtin, His Life and Works,* London, 1900, pl. V
Hugh Stokes, *Girtin and Bonington,* London, 1922, ill. p. 32
Davies, pl. 40
E. M. O'R. Dickey, *A Picture-Book of British Art,* London, 1931, p. 169, fig. 168
Mayne, pp. 65-66, pl. 40
Girtin and Loshak, p. 187, no. 388

1775-1851

Turner was born in Maiden Lane, Covent Garden, London, the son of a barber, and he grew up in this urban environment. He entered the Royal Academy schools in 1789, and at about the same time he began to study under the topographical draftsman Thoman Malton. He may also have had some connection with John Raphael Smith and with Edward Dayes, Girtin's master, and between 1794 and 1797 Turner and Girtin were employed by Dr. Thomas Monro to make finished watercolors from sketches by John Robert Cozens. Turner exhibited a watercolor at the Royal Academy in 1790, and most of his early activity was as a watercolorist. His first oil painting was exhibited six years later. He was elected an Associate of the Royal Academy in 1799 and a full R.A. in 1802. For the rest of his life he was a loyal Academician, but in 1804 he built his own gallery and for several years he held private exhibitions of his works while continuing to send pictures to the Academy.

In 1802, during the brief Peace of Amiens, Turner made his first visit to the continent, a visit significant because it granted him both an exposure to the old masters in the Louvre and his first look at the Alps, which provided many of his subjects in the following years. Because of the resumption of hostilities between France and England, he did not journey abroad again until 1817, when he travelled up the Rhine. In 1819 he made his first trip to Italy, a visit of considerable importance although some of its results did not appear until some time; he first exhibited

a view of Venice only in 1833. He continued to travel frequently on the continent until 1845.

In the first part of his career, Turner was influenced by several earlier masters, especially Claude Lorrain. The extent of his desire to emulate Claude is indicated by the stipulation in his will that two of his pictures left to The National Gallery should hang next to paintings by the French master. While Turner's earlier pictures tended to be composed primarily in light and dark, after his 1819 trip to Italy his palette began to lighten, and color played an ever-increasing role. His output was enormous, and he tried his hand at virtually every kind of landscape composition. His work in watercolor, a medium he used both for sketching and for finished compositions to sell, was of equal importance to that in oil, and his mastery of watercolor technique certainly influenced his later innovations in oil painting. He was also responsible for a huge number of prints, the most important being his *Liber Studiorum,* published in mezzotint from 1806 until 1819, in imitation of the *Liber Veritatis* of Claude Lorrain.

Turner always had a loyal following, and he managed to accumulate a sizable fortune. However, he was also controversial from the first, and in the 1830s, as his art departed more and more from convention, he began to provoke outraged criticism in the press. This, in turn, inspired the young Ruskin to begin writing *Modern Painters* in Turner's defense, and as a result of this advocacy Turner retained a surprisingly high reputation all through the Victorian era. As a man, Turner seems to have been a miserly but generally respected eccentric who lived as a recluse. He refused to sell several of his finest pictures, and in the latter part of his life he bought back many works. Upon his death the contents of his studio were left to the English Nation, and they are now divided among The Tate Gallery, The National Gallery, and The British Museum.
A.S.

Bibliography
The most extended comment on Turner's art is that of Ruskin which appears not only in the five volumes of *Modern Painters* but scattered throughout the thirty-nine volumes of Ruskin's collected works.
Walter Thornbury, *Life of J. M. W. Turner, R.A.,* 2 vols., London, 1862 (2nd edition, 1 vol., 1877; this book is notoriously inaccurate but is, nonetheless, an indispensable source)
Walter Armstrong, *Turner,* 2 vols., London, 1902
A. J. Finberg, *A Complete Inventory of the Drawings of the Turner Bequest,* 2 vols., London, 1909
A. J. Finberg, *The Life of J. M. W. Turner, R.A.,* Oxford, 1939 (2nd edition, revised by Hilda Finberg, 1961)
Martin Butlin, *Turner Watercolours,* London, 1962
John Rothenstein and Martin Butlin, *Turner,* London, 1964
Lawrence Gowing, *Turner: Imagination and Reality,* New York, 1966 (accompanying an exhibition at the Museum of Modern Art)
Jack Lindsay, *J. M. W. Turner: A Critical Biography,* London, 1966

115
Fonthill Abbey (South View of the Gothic Abbey—Evening—Now Building at Fonthill, the Seat of W. Beckford, Esq.)
The Montreal Museum of Fine Arts, Purchased 1963, Horsley and Annie Townsend Bequest
Watercolor on paper backed on panel;
28½ x 41¾ in.
1799-1800

Fonthill Abbey in Wiltshire was built between 1796 and 1807 by James Wyatt for William Beckford, the author of *Vathek* and heir to a fortune made in West Indian sugar. This structure, the most spectacular example of Gothic-revival sublimity, was sold by Beckford in 1823; the tower collapsed in 1825, and now only one wing remains standing.

On May 27, 1799 Joseph Farington recorded in his diary that Beckford had written from Portugal asking Turner to go to Fonthill, but that Turner did not know what the commission would be. Turner spent three weeks at Fonthill in August and September, and on September 11 Farington noted that he was to make several drawings of the

Abbey. At the Royal Academy in the following May, Turner exhibited five watercolor views of the Abbey. On July 10 Farington recorded that Turner had made seven drawings (possibly an error) for which he was thinking of asking Beckford forty guineas apiece; however, Farington later noted that he had received only thirty-five guineas each.

Turner had apparently paid an earlier visit to Fonthill, as a drawing by him of Fonthill House, the Palladian mansion in which Beckford resided before building the Abbey, was engraved in W. Angus's *Select Views of Seats, etc.,* published in March 1800. When Turner visited Fonthill in 1799, the top of the tower was uncompleted, and he presumably had to finish his watercolors from the architect's designs. There are four sketchbooks containing drawings of Fonthill and an unfinished upright watercolor of the same size as no. 115 in The British Museum. These show the top of the tower unfinished. The five exhibited watercolors are all reproduced in Cundall's book.

Turner's watercolors of Fonthill Abbey are in the tradition of commissioned views of gentleman's seats but, like Girtin, who painted a series of comparably large watercolors of Harewood House at about the same time, Turner stretched the conventional 18th-century topographical view almost out of recognition. The five exhibited watercolors are all landscape compositions first, and delineations of the building second, and no. 115 provides the nearest view of the Abbey of any of them. These large watercolors were clearly intended to compete with oil paintings, both in effect and in sheer size. Unfortunately, unlike many 18th-century views which have been well preserved as a result of being kept in a portfolio, such watercolors were often framed and hung as if they were oil paintings, with the consequence that they have suffered discoloration from excessive exposure to daylight.
A.S.

115

Provenance
William Beckford, Fonthill, commissioned 1799
J. Allnutt, Clapham (sale, Christie's, London, 19 June 1863, no. 319, bt. Cox)
John Heugh, Tunbridge Wells (sale, Christie's, London, 24 April 1874, no. 100)
H. W. F. Bolckow, M.P. (sale, Christie's, London, 18 June 1892, no. 142)
Frederic Nicholls, Toronto
Sir Henry Pellatt, Toronto (died 1939)
Gordon Edwards, Ottawa

Exhibitions
Royal Academy, 1800, no. 566 *(South View of the Gothic Abbey (Evening) now building at Fonthill, the seat of W. Beckford, Esq.)*

Loan Collection of Paintings of the English, Old Dutch, Modern Dutch, French and other European Schools, Art Museum, Toronto, 1909, no. 60
Canada Collects: European Painting, Museum of Fine Arts, Montreal, 1960, no. 109

References
Thornbury, II, 371, 408
Farington, ed. Greig, I, 289, 307
Finberg, *Inventory,* I, 120-24, 176, cf. nos. XLVII, XLVIII, LXX-P
E. G. Cundall, *Fonthill Abbey: A Descriptive Account of Five Water-Colour Drawings by J. M. W. Turner, R.A.,* privately printed for Ralph Brocklebank, Esq., Tarporley, 1915
E. G. Cundall, "Turner Drawings of Fonthill Abbey,"

Burlington, XXIX, 1916, pp. 16-21
Finberg, *Life,* 1961, pp. 60-61, 67-68, 71, 305, 464 no. 65

Reproductions
Engraved by T. Crostick in *The Anniversary,* 1829

116

116

Cottage Destroyed by an Avalanche (The Fall of an Avalanche in the Grisons)

The Trustees of The Tate Gallery, London
Oil on canvas; 35½ x 47½ in.
c. 1810

In the catalogue of his exhibition of 1810, Turner accompanied no. 116 with a poetic composition of his own invention:

> The downward sun a parting sadness gleams,
> Portentous lurid thro' the gathering storm;
> Thick drifting snow, on snow,
> Till the vast weight bursts thro' the
> rocky barrier;
> Down at once, its pine clad forests,
> And towering glaciers fall, the work of ages
> Crashing through all! extinction follows,
> And the toil, the hope of man—o'erwhelms.

Grisons, or Graubünden, is the easternmost canton of Switzerland, which Turner did not visit on his 1802 trip to Switzerland. Nor, although Farington notes that Turner saw very fine thunderstorms among the mountains, is there any record of his having seen an actual avalanche. Turner was strongly impressed by Swiss scenery and painted several views of it after his return, but no. 116 seems to be a product of his imagination. It was probably inspired by Loutherbourg's *An Avalanche in the Alps, in the Valley of Lauterbrunnen,* exhibited in 1804 (Tate Gallery), which also shows a cottage being destroyed, and he may have had

in mind the lines from Thomson's *Winter,* which
are cited by Lindsay:

> In peaceful vales, the happy Grisons dwell,
> Oft, rushing sudden from the loaded cliffs,
> Mountains of snow their gathering terrors roll,
> From steep to steep, loud thundering,
> down they come,
> A wintry waste in dire commotion all;
> And herds, and flocks, and travellers,
> and swains,
> And sometimes whole brigades of
> marching troops,
> Or hamlets sleeping in the dead of night,
> Are deep beneath the smothering
> ruin whelmed.

Presumably it was because of Thomson that Turner
set his avalanche in the Grisons rather than in a
part of the Alps he had seen. Thomson's *Seasons*
provided a primer of images for romantic
landscape painting, and Turner, from 1798 until
he started to use his own verses, constantly
accompanied his pictures in the Royal Academy
catalogues with lines from Thomson.

No. 116 is one of Turner's most concentrated
images of the destructive violence of nature, and
in contrast it makes Loutherbourg's treatment of a
similar subject seem prettily decorative. Turner
painted many later pictures of the hostile forces of
nature, notably of storms at sea, and in *Snow
Storm, Avalanche and Inundation in the Val
d'Aosta* of 1837 (Art Institute of Chicago) he
returned to a subject very much like that of no. 116.
No. 116 has frequently been considered as linked
with *Snow Storm: Hannibal and His Army Crossing
the Alps,* which Turner exhibited in 1812 (Tate
Gallery). Both pictures contain driving storm and
huge boulders, but whereas in the *Hannibal* the
composition consists of a great swirling vortex
which pulls the eye into a deep space, in no. 116
the crossed diagonals of boulder, avalanche, and
storm stay near the surface and there is little
suggestion of space. Turner's bold and even
abstract use of the palette knife is the most

extreme example in his early work of the
innovations in technique which drew constant
attack from conservative connoisseurs.
A.S.

Provenance
Turner Bequest to The National Gallery
The Tate Gallery, 1910

Exhibitions
Turner's Gallery, London, 1810, no. 14 *(The Fall of an
Avalanche in the Grisons,* accompanied by eight
lines of verse)
Turner's Early Oil Paintings, Tate Gallery, London,
1931, no. 56
Turner, Stedelijk Museum, Amsterdam, etc., 1947-48,
no. 16
Turner, Biennale, Venice, and Palazzo Venezia, Rome,
1948, no. 18
*Engelse Landschapschilders van Gainsborough tot
Turner,* Museum Boymans, Rotterdam, 1955, no. 50

References
Farington, ed. Greig, II, 43-44
Ruskin, III, 239; XIII, 122-23, 496
Hilda Finberg, "Turner's Gallery in 1810," *Burlington,*
XCII, 1951, pp. 383-86
Finberg, *Life,* 1961, pp. 82-84, 167, 472 no. 151
Rothenstein and Butlin, p. 31, pl. 48
Lindsay, pp. 91, 106-07

117
The Church of SS. Giovanni and Paolo, Rome
Trustees of The British Museum
Watercolor and gouache; 9 x 14⅝ in.
1819

The church of SS. Giovanni and Paolo, with its
12th-century campanile, stands on the Coelian Hill.
The view is from the Palatine. Beyond the church
on the right are visible the statues on the facade
of San Giovanni in Laterano. A painting of the
same view by Turner's friend Sir Charles Eastlake,
dated 1823, is in the Rhode Island School of Design.

On his Italian trip of 1819, Turner was in Rome
from early October to the middle of December,

interrupted by a brief trip to Naples. He had
previously been in Venice for approximately a
fortnight. While in Rome Turner worked
industriously, making pencil sketches to serve as
memoranda for future paintings, and some fifteen
hundred such black and white drawings are
preserved in The British Museum. However, there
are only about forty watercolors. Turner did not
make drawings in color directly from nature which
as Sir John Soane's son noted in a letter of
November 15, somewhat surprised the fashionabl
visitors to the city: "At Rome a sucking blade of
the brush made the request of going out with pig
Turner to colour—he grunted for an answer that
would take up too much time to colour in the open
air—he could make 15 or 16 pencil sketches to
one coloured, and then grunted his way home."
Thus, Turner presumably made a drawing such
as no. 117 in his lodgings, based on his pencil
notations and memory.

The few watercolors Turner made in Venice in
1819 are amazing documents of his response to
Italian light, and in the most famous of them,
San Giorgio from the Dogana, Sunrise (British
Museum), the city seems to dissolve in the glow.
In a drawing such as no. 117 the lightness remain
but there is also a respect for the monumental
solidity of Rome. The geometric clarity of the
modelling of the complex of buildings recalls the
responses of many other northern artists to the
Eternal City, most conspicuously Corot, whose
first visit to Rome was in 1825.

Ruskin wrote that Turner's powers were at their
height on his first Italian visit, and in Rome he
taxed them to the utmost. Ruskin claimed that the
amount of detail in the distances of these drawing
could only be seen in actuality by a person with
the strongest faculties of eyesight but that there
was no exaggeration: "They are in all respects th
most fine and the most beautiful ever made by
the painter."
A.S.

117

Provenance
Turner Bequest

References
Ruskin, XIII, 299, no. 109, 377-78
Finberg, *Inventory,* I, 563, no. CLXXXIX. 39
Thomas Ashby, *Turner's Visions of Rome,* London and
New York, 1925, p. 27, pl. 20
Finberg, *Life,* 1961, pp. 261-62

118
Storm over St. Peter's
Museum of Fine Arts, Boston, Gift at the request of
the late Ellen T. Bullard
Watercolor; 8⅜ x 11⅛ in.
c. 1820-30

The subject of no. 118 has traditionally been
identified as St. Peter's in Rome but, as suggested
by Miss Barbara Reise, it is equally or more likely
that it represents Venice. The dome could be
either that of San Giorgio Maggiore or Sta. Maria
della Salute, and the empty foreground, with a hint
of reflection, seems to suggest water. However,
whatever the view, Turner's purpose was obviously
not accurate topographical description. The
watercolor was made from memory and
imagination, and he may not have intended to
depict any specific place.

The arched cloud and stormy subject of no. 118
recall several drawings in the Turner Bequest.
There is no definite record of when they were done.
Finberg put them in a group of miscellaneous
drawings "after about 1830," but more recent
students have tended to date them in the 1820s.
Edward Croft-Murray proposes that one of these,
Paestum in a Storm, was intended as a preliminary
idea for the vignette of *Paestum* published in
Samuel Roger's *Italy* in 1830. Similar handling may
be seen in *A Tree in a Storm* which, Martin Butlin
suggests, because of its subdued, almost
monochrome color, also belongs to the 1820s.
When Turner paid his second visit to Venice in
1835, he imposed this stormy vision on the city. A
watercolor in The British Museum, reproduced by
Butlin, is close in subject and mood to no. 118 but
has more color and detail drawn with the point
of the brush, a later mannerism of Turner's which
does not appear in no. 118. Two additional scenes
of storms at Venice dating from the 1835 trip,
both reproduced by Rothenstein and Butlin, are in
the Fitzwilliam Museum and the National
Gallery of Scotland.
A.S.

118

Provenance
Ellen T. Bullard, Boston
Museum of Fine Arts, Boston, 1959

Exhibitions
Joseph Mallord William Turner: Watercolors and Drawings, Otto Gerson Gallery, New York, 1960, no. 39

References
Finberg, *Inventory,* II, 1191, 1213, cf. nos. CCCLXIV-224, CCCLXV-27b
Butlin, pp. 40, 50, cf. nos. 11 and 20
Turner Watercolors from the British Museum, National Gallery of Art, Washington, etc., 1963-64, p. 20, cf. no. 46 (catalogue by Edward Croft-Murray)
Rothenstein and Butlin, cf. pl. 101

119

119
Berne
Vassar College Art Gallery,
Gift of Matthew Vassar, 1864
Watercolor; 8¾ x 10⅞ in.
c. 1830-33

No. 119 was engraved as the frontispiece to the eleventh volume of Murry's *Byron* in 1833. Thus it was not directly connected with any one poem; however, it probably was originally intended to accompany *Manfred,* which is set in the Bernese Alps. Turner had apparently not visited Berne when he made this drawing, but based it on sketches made by another hand. This was his practice for most of the Byron illustrations, many of which show views in Greece and the East. Turner was responsible for various Byron illustrations in the 1820s, but the main project for Murry's seventeen-volume edition was probably only undertaken after 1830, following the great success of his illustrations to Samuel Roger's *Italy.* The vignette style and the extremely tight detail are characteristic of Turner's illustrations for poetry, which were intended for reproduction by steel

engraving. Many such drawings were sold during Turner's lifetime, and they created a very different concept of his work than we generally hold today.

The Byron drawings were exhibited in London in 1834, and a large number of them were acquired by D. T. Griffith, who later acted as Turner's dealer. In the 1850s, no. 119, along with three other Turner drawings, was acquired by Ruskin on the behalf of Elias Magoon, a Baptist clergyman in New York whose collection was to form the nucleus of the Vassar College Art Gallery. Ruskin did not particularly like Turner's drawings for Byron, finding them all "more or less artificial and unequal," and he wrote that they were drawn with such labor that they were more trouble to look at than it was worth. However, he told Magoon that the drawings he had selected for him contained "essence of Turner."
A.S.

Provenance
(?) D. T. Griffith, London, 1834
John Ruskin, London
Dr. Elias Magoon, New York, 1856

Exhibitions
(?) Colnaghi, London, 1834

References
Ruskin, XIII, 445-46
A Catalogue of the Art Collection Presented by Matthew Vassar to the Vassar College, New York, 1869, no. 292
Armstrong, II, 242
W. G. Rawlinson, *The Engraved Work of J. M. W. Turner, R.A.,* London, 1908, 1913, I, p. lvii; II, 247-48, 253 no. 422
Jean Thornton Fotheringham, "Some Ruskin Letters Hitherto Unpublished," *Vassar Journal of Undergraduate Studies,* I, 1926, pp. 232-41
Finberg, *Life,* 1961, pp. 328, 346

Reproductions
Engraved by E. Finden in Murry, *The Life and Works of Byron,* London, 1832-34, frontispiece of vol. XI
(The Bernese Alps)

Joseph Mallord William Turner

120

120

Burning of the Houses of Parliament (The Burning of the Houses of Lords and Commons, 16th of October 1834)
Philadelphia Museum of Art,
John H. McFadden Collection
Oil on canvas; 36¼ x 48½ in.
c. 1835

Early in the evening of October 16, 1834, the Houses of Parliament caught fire. The conflagration attracted such immense crowds that the army had to be called out to help the police keep control and, according to a correspondent of *The Gentleman's Magazine* (quoted by Whitley), when at half-past nine the roof of the House of Lords fell in, "so struck were the bystanders with the grandeur of the sight at this moment that they involuntarily (and from no bad feeling) clapped their hands as though they had been present at the closing scene of some dramatic spectacle." Several artists witnessed the scene, among them J. J. Chalon, who exhibited a picture of the subject at the British Institution the following February, and Constable, who made a rough sketch from Westminster Bridge and gave it to Leslie. Turner filled nine pages of a sketchbook with watercolor sketches of the fire made from the South bank of the Thames (British Museum). This is one of the infrequent occasions that Turner made use of watercolor to record his impressions direct from nature rather than making pencil sketches and coloring them later; as Martin Butlin notes, the particular circumstances ruled out any other medium. The nine sketches were made with such haste that the wet watercolor stained the blank pages opposite. A watercolor sketch in Boston with the same page size may also record the fire, and a smaller sketchbook with pencil sketches is also in The British Museum.

In 1835 Turner exhibited two paintings of the fire: no. 120 at the British Institution in February, and the second, now in The Cleveland Museum, at the Royal Academy in May. A third, smaller painting, recorded by Armstrong, may be a replica or copy of no. 120. In addition a finished watercolor, taken from a closer vantage point than either the Cleveland or Philadelphia pictures or any of the watercolor sketches, is in The British Museum, and Finberg lists another watercolor at Farnley Hall.

We have a detailed account by Edward Villiers Rippingille of Turner's work on no. 120 on the varnishing day before the opening of the exhibition at the British Institution. The picture when it was sent in was "a mere dab of several colours and 'without form, and void' like chaos before the creation." Turner worked incessantly for several hours, to the fascinated amusement of his fellow artists. Rippingille noted that Turner worked almost entirely with his palette knife, and at one point he was observed "rolling and spreading a lump of half-transparent stuff, the size of a finger in length and thickness, over his picture." Unfortunately, nobody had the nerve to ask him what it was. When he was finished Turner closed up his paint box and left, without looking again at his picture or speaking a word to anybody. John Scarlett Davis also mentioned Turner's performance in a letter quoted by Thornbury: "I am told it was good fun to see the great man whacking away with about fifty stupid apes standing round him, and I understand he was cursedly annoyed—the fools kept peeping into his colour box and examining all his brushes and colours."

Whereas the view in the Cleveland picture is from downriver and shows the fire at considerable distance, that in no. 120 is from directly across the Thames, and flames fill the left half of the picture. The size of Westminster Bridge, which reflects the light of the fire, is grossly exaggerated, adding to the compositional drama. The crowds in the foreground correspond to those described in the accounts of the fire, but the figures on the right seem to be looking not at the fire but out at us and resemble the densely packed mobs in several other late works such as *Heidelberg Castle in the Olden Time* or *The Opening of the Walhalla* (both Tate Gallery). In no. 120 they seem to embody human insignificance before the uncontrollable

destructive force of the fire. Lindsay proposes that Turner's two paintings may have had symbolic meaning, the burning of the center of government reflecting the malaise and conflict consuming the country as a result of agitation for the Reform Bill. However, there is no real evidence to substantiate this interpretation, and as the disaster was so obviously suited to Turner's abilities and inclinations, it is certainly not necessary to postulate a symbolic message to explain his painting it.

The burning of the Houses of Parliament seems to have triggered in Turner an interest in nocturnal scenes. In no. 120 he contrasts the warm colors of the flames with the cold blue of the night sky and the pale light of the gas lamps in the foreground. *Keelmen Heaving in Coals by Moonlight* (National Gallery of Art, Washington), also exhibited in 1835, makes play of the contrast between moonlight and the artificial light of flares, and a number of dramatically illuminated night scenes date from his trip to Venice in the same year. Lawrence Gowing even suggests that the fire broke down a barrier between fantasy and reality and that the great imaginative force of Turner's late works was released by his reactions to the event. The destruction of the Houses of Parliament also had vast significance for the evolution of English painting in general, as most of the major new developments of the 1840s were connected with the program of decorating the new building designed by Sir Charles Barry.

A.S.

Provenance
C. Hall, 1835
Charles Birch, Edgbaston, by 1852
Lloyd Bros., London (sale, Foster's, London, 13 June 1855, no. 59, bt. Wallis)
Henry Wallis (sale, Christie's, London, 17 November 1860, no. 209)
Fisher, London
C. J. Palmer, Portland Place, London (sale, Christie's, London, May 1868, bt. Agnew)
J. Graham
Holbrook Gaskell, Woolton, by 1885 (sale Christie's,

London, 24 June 1909, no. 97, bt. Agnew)
John Howard McFadden, Philadelphia
Philadelphia Museum of Art, 1928

Exhibitions
British Institution, London, 1835, no. 58
Royal Birmingham Society of Artists, 1852, no. 114
Works by the Old Masters, Royal Academy, London, 1907, no. 113
Old Masters, Knoedler and Co., New York, 1912

References
E. V. Rippingille, "Personal Recollections of Great Artists," *The Art Journal,* 1860, p. 100
Thornbury, 2nd ed., 452-53
F. G. Stephens, "The Private Collections of England: LXXIX—Allerton, Liverpool," *Athenaeum,* 1884, p. 438
Armstrong, I, 117; II, 236
Finberg, *Inventory,* II, 909-10, cf. nos. CCLXXXIII, CCLXXXIV
W. Roberts, *Catalogue of the Collection of Pictures Formed by John H. McFadden,* privately printed, London, 1917, pp. 85-87
William T. Whitley, *Art in England: 1821-1837,* Cambridge, England, 1930, pp. 292-94
Finberg, *Life,* 1961, pp. 350-52, 354, 499 no. 458
Butlin, pp. 50-51, cf. pl. 16
Rothenstein and Butlin, pp. 52-54
Gowing, pp. 33, 42-43, 45
Lindsay, pp. 178-81

121
Fluelen, Lake of Lucerne
The Cleveland Museum of Art
Watercolor; 11½ x 18¾ in.
c. 1845

Turner visited Switzerland every summer from 1840 through 1844. In the winter of 1841-42, after having made a long stay at Lucerne, Turner approached his dealer D. T. Griffith with a plan to paint finished watercolors from his sketches if Griffith could get commissions for them. This resulted in his making ten finished drawings in 1842; the following year he repeated the offer and made five more; and, after a year's interval, in 1845 he made eight. We know the details of

121

Turner's making these drawings from Ruskin who, in the catalogue of his Turner drawings exhibited in 1878, attempted to give the history of each of the twenty-three finished Swiss watercolors (actually twenty-two showed Swiss subjects; one, now in Cincinnati, was of Coblentz). To Ruskin these watercolors were Turner's greatest and culminating achievement, and much of *Modern Painters* is written about them. Ruskin, himself, was the original purchaser of many of them, and fourteen of the twenty-three were at one time or another in his possession.

No. 121 certainly belongs with this group. It is the same size, is in the same style, and shows the same class of subject as those of the series whose

history can be traced. It has sometimes been identified as the *Fluelen, Lake of Lucerne* which Turner painted for his patron and friend Munro of Novar in 1845 and which was later acquired by Ruskin, but this is wrong; Ruskin made an etching after that drawing which shows a different view, with figures on a shore in the foreground. However, no. 121 may be one of the other drawings made in 1845. When Ruskin was finishing his catalogue, he was beginning to have his first mental breakdown and his listing of the last eight drawings is somewhat confused and incomplete. Although there is no conclusive evidence, the most likely possibility is that no. 121 is the watercolor made for Ruskin which he described as "a faint Lucerne with floating vapours, they and the mountains

passing away." In the last paragraph of his *Catalogue of Turner's Sketches and Drawings Exhibited in Marlborough House,* published in 1857, Ruskin had referred to this "faint Lucerne." Arguing that Turner's great genius lay in painting clouds, Ruskin concluded: "The first words which he ever wrote, as significative of his aim in painting, were Milton's, beginning 'Ye mists and exhalations.' And the last drawing in which there remained a reflection of his expiring power, he made in striving to realise, for me, one of these faint and fair visions of the morning mist, fading from the Lake Lucerne."

Ruskin, in the 1857 passage, did not refer to the drawing as being in his possession, which he usually did, so it may have left him already. Certainly it seems to have been gone well before 1878, and Ruskin's editors in 1904 were unable to trace it or identify it beyond Ruskin's slight descriptions. It is apparently number 10 in the list of Turner drawings belonging to Ruskin included in Thornbury's *Life of Turner,* published in 1862; however, this included other drawings no longer in Ruskin's possession and seems to have been based on a list drawn up by Ruskin sometime earlier. The Cleveland drawing was apparently acquired in the 1850s by a Reverend C. Upham Barry in the Isle of Wight, who does not appear in any of Ruskin's diaries or correspondence, but he may have obtained it for or because of his daughter, a Mrs. Hewitt, who is listed as the watercolor's subsequent owner. She is quite possibly the Mrs. Hewitt to whom Ruskin was writing letters in 1857, beginning "My Dear Ward" (whatever that may mean), and to whom, according to Ruskin's editors, he gave drawing lessons.

John Gage, in the catalogue of the exhibition *Ruskin and His Circle,* has identified the source for no. 121 among the sketches Turner made in Switzerland in 1841, now in the Turner Bequest in The British Museum (T.B. CCCLXIV, 381; CCCXXXII, 28; CCCLXIV, 282, 331). However, no. 121 is not a variant of the drawing made for

Munro, as Gage states. Not only is the view from the opposite direction, but whereas in the Munro drawing Fluelen is looked down upon from above, in no. 121 the vantage point seems to be from a boat on the lake.

As Louis Hawes has pointed out, no. 121 repeats a type of composition frequently used by Turner in which the whole picture is centered on a large, elliptical area of bright light. This composition appears in the early *Snowstorm: Hannibal Crossing the Alps* of 1812 and in many late pictures, most notably *Shade and Darkness—the Evening of the Deluge* of 1843 (both Tate Gallery). The combination of mist and mountain also recalls the *Snow Storm, Avalanche and Inundation in the Val d'Aosta* of 1837 in The Art Institute of Chicago, and it is astonishing how out of the same vocabulary Turner makes images in one of cosmic violence and in the other of divine radiance and calm.
A.S.

Provenance
(?) John Ruskin, Herne Hill, London, 1845
Rev. C. Upham Barry, Ryde, Isle of Wight, c. 1850 (died 1883)
Mrs. P. G. Hewitt, his daughter (sale, Christie's, London, 25 March 1884, no. 139, bt. in?)
Ralph Brocklebank, Sr., Haughton Hall, Tarporley, Cheshire, 1887 (died 1892)
Ralph Brocklebank, Jr., (sale, Christie's, London, 7 July 1922, no. 34, bt. Agnew)
Thos. Agnew & Sons, London
Grace Rainey Rogers, New York (sale, Parke-Bernet, New York, 18 November 1943, no. 41)
Walter F. Wedgwood, New York
Durlacher Bros., New York
The Cleveland Museum of Art, 1954

Exhibitions
Loan Collection of Pictures and Drawings by J. M. W. Turner, R.A., Guildhall, London, 1899, no. 150
Birmingham Art Gallery, 1899
Whitworth Institute, Manchester, 1912
Forty-fifth Annual Exhibition of Selected Water Colour Drawings, Thos. Agnew & Sons, London, 1912, no. 21
Fifty-sixth Annual Exhibition of Water Colour Drawings, Thos. Agnew & Sons, London, 1923, no. 19
Paintings, Drawings, and Prints by J. M. W. Turner,

John Constable, R. P. Bonington, Museum of Fine Arts, Boston, 1946, no. 44
Paintings by J. M. W. Turner, Art Gallery of Toronto, 1951, and National Gallery of Canada, Ottawa, 1952, no. 58
Turner in America, John Herron Art Museum, Indianapolis, 1955, and Dayton Art Institute, 1956, no. 47, pl. 47
Joseph Mallord William Turner: Watercolors and Drawings, Otto Gerson Gallery, New York, 1960, no. 43
Ruskin and His Circle, Arts Council Gallery, London, 1964, no. 104

References
Thornbury, I, 323; II, 395-96
Ruskin, XIII, 316, 459-60, 475-85, 556, 602, cf. pl. XXIV
Armstrong, II, 264
R. Radcliffe Carter, *Pictures and Engravings at Haughton Hall, Tarporley, in the Possession of Ralph Brocklebank,* London, 1904, pp. xi, 87, pl. 77
Henry Sales Francis, "A Water Color by J. M. W. Turner," *Cleveland Museum of Art Bulletin,* no. 9, 1954, pp. 201-03
Louis Hawes, "Turner in New York," *Burlington,* CVIII, 1966, p. 312

122
The Apse of the Church of St. Laurent, Eu
Trustees of The British Museum
Pencil and watercolor; 9 1/16 x 12 13/16 in.
c. 1845

Eu in Picardy, nineteen miles northeast of Dieppe, was the site of Louis-Philippe's summer château. Turner made his last trip to the continent in September 1845, visiting Dieppe and wandering along the coast to Eu and Tréport. At Eu his presence was learned of, and he was summoned to dine with the King. In no. 122 the pitched roofs of the château are discernible beyond the church.

No. 122 was originally part of the *Eu and Tréport Sketchbook,* which was broken up by Ruskin when he was cataloguing and arranging the Turner Bequest in 1857. This was one of the first drawings which Ruskin chose to put on view in a trial exhibition for the Trustees of The National Gallery. Ruskin paid for the frames himself, and he arranged the drawings and the catalogue following an imaginary itinerary in which the artist landed at Tréport, visited Eu, and travelled up the Rhine

122

to Switzerland and Venice. No. 122 was fifth in Ruskin's series; he supposed that after a day of walking the tourist arrived in the town of Eu, seeing the church by moonlight and in the sea fog. Ruskin was puzzled by what appears to be a vineyard or hop-garden in the lower left of the watercolor, but decided that Turner had intended to represent "the good people of Eu going to evening service."

As was his habit throughout his life, Turner probably sketched the view on the spot in pencil and colored it from memory. His use of color is extremely free and not descriptively realistic. The drawings from this trip were apparently the last watercolors made by the artist.
A.S.

Provenance
Turner Bequest

Exhibitions
Turner Watercolors from the British Museum, National Gallery of Art, Washington, etc., 1963-64, no. 78

References
Ruskin, XIII, 192-93, no. 5
Finberg, *Inventory,* II, 1169, no. CCCLIX-16
Finberg, *Life,* 1961, pp. 410-11

John Constable

1776-1837

Constable was born at East Bergholt, Suffolk, the son of a prosperous miller. In 1799 he went to London to study at the Royal Academy schools. For the rest of his life he lived mainly in London, but he retained strong links with the Suffolk countryside of his childhood, and Dedham Vale and the River Stour provide the subjects of a major portion of the works of his maturity. In the earlier part of his career he painted portraits and even an altarpiece, but he soon decided to dedicate himself to landscape painting. Constable never travelled abroad and, except for visits to the Peak District of Derbyshire in 1801 and to the Lake District in 1806, he never went on the customary sketching trips to areas of acknowledged picturesque beauty. Most of his works are based on a few localities for which he felt personal affection: his native Suffolk, the neighborhood of Salisbury, where he was a frequent visitor of his friend Archdeacon John Fisher, and Hampstead, where in 1819 he began to spend the summers and where he eventually bought a house. He set himself the goal of being "a natural painter," a recorder of the English countryside, and to this he restricted himself throughout his life.

Official success came slowly to Constable; he was elected an A.R.A. only in 1819, when he was forty-three years old, and it was another decade before he became a full Academician. This is frequently cited as an example of the obtuseness of official bodies in recognizing creative genius, but it could be argued that Constable's delayed success went hand in hand with his slowness in developing. Although he had been struggling to find his own path since the beginning years of the century, Constable's output before 1814 or 1815 was not particularly distinguished. His first monumental achievement was *The White Horse* of 1819 (Frick Collection), and most of his major works date from after 1820. In 1829 Constable's wife died, and for the rest of his life he suffered from fits of depression which are reflected in the stormy agitation of much of his later painting. In 1830 he began a series of mezzotint engravings, under the title *English Landscape Scenery,* which are marked by a similar tumultuous gloom.

Constable had the usual ambitions for public success, and he regularly prepared carefully finished works to submit to the Academy exhibitions. In recent years it has been the fashion to praise these more pondered works at the expense of his sketches and studies from nature. The latter, however, have an immediacy of observation and a freshness of handling which frequently disappeared in the finishing process. Constable's great virtue was certainly the depth and originality of his feeling for nature, including not only the topography of the landscape, but also the life of the countryside, the weather, and the sky; whether he was able to orchestrate all these elements, so directly and beautifully recorded in the sketches, into the large pictures without a diminution of feeling is open to question.

Among his English contemporaries, Constable had relatively little impact, but his *Hay Wain* (National Gallery, London) had a notable success in the Paris Salon of 1824, and in the following years several other of his works crossed the channel. His influence on Delacroix is well known, and his importance for the Barbizon artists is incalculable. His reputation began to grow at the end of the 19th century, but in America, where his pictures were bought by the Duveen-nurtured generation of millionaires, he has achieved more respectability than respect, and his works have tended to be placed among the more forgettable old masters rather than among those of the innovating figures of modern art, with which they belong. Proper assessment of his work has also been inhibited by the large numbers of forgeries, imitations, and inferior works which wrongly have been ascribed to him.
A.S.

Bibliography
Charles Robert Leslie, *Memoirs of the Life of John Constable, R.A.,* London, 1843 and 1845 (later editions by the Hon. Andrew Shirley, London, 1937; and by Jonathan Mayne, London, 1951)
Sir Charles J. Holmes, *Constable and His Influence on Landscape Painting,* London, 1902
R. B. Beckett, *John Constable and the Fishers: The Record of a Friendship,* London, 1952
Graham Reynolds, *Catalogue of the Constable Collection in the Victoria and Albert Museum,* London, 1960
Graham Reynolds, *Constable the Natural Painter,* London, 1965
John Baskett, *Constable Oil Sketches,* London, 1966

123
View in the Lake District
Philadelphia Museum of Art
Pencil and watercolor; 6½ x 12 in.
1806

In the autumn of 1806 Constable paid a two-month visit to the Lake District. The trip was financed by his uncle David Pike Watts, and Constable stayed at his uncle's house on Lake Windermere. Constable drew constantly on the trip, and over forty drawings are now known, twenty-three in the Victoria and Albert Museum. The earliest date on any of them is September 1, the latest is October 19. From the middle of September to the middle of October he went on a sketching tour of Borrowdale. In the following years, 1807 to 1809, he exhibited several Lake District scenes resulting from this trip.

An old note on the mount of no. 123 signed by G. D. identifies it as no. 192 in the sale of Isabel Constable's estate on June 17, 1892. No. 192 was identified in the sales catalogue as *A Welsh Valley.* However, Constable is not known to have ever visited Wales, and no. 123 seems in subject, style,

123

Provenance
Isabel Constable (the artist's daughter) (sale, Christie's, London, 17 June 1892, no. 192, *A Welsh Valley*)
(?) G. D. (from note on mount)
Boies Penrose, Devon, Pa. (gift to the Philadelphia Museum of Art, 1930)

Exhibitions
A Century of British Art from 1737 to 1837,
Grosvenor Gallery, London, 1889

References
Leslie, ed. Mayne, pp. 18-19
Beryl and Noel Clay, "Constable's Visit to the Lakes,"
Country Life, LXXXIII, 1938, pp. 393-95
Reynolds, *Catalogue,* pp. 56-63
Reynolds, *The Natural Painter,* pp. 31-35

124

and technique to belong with his Lake District watercolors. These romantic views of mountain scenery are in the tradition of John Robert Cozens, and they probably reflect the direct influence of Girtin's watercolors. As Graham Reynolds has pointed out, they are essentially derivative and, attractive as they are, they represent a dead end in Constable's development. Two of the drawings in the Victoria and Albert Museum are inscribed with notes comparing the scenery to landscapes of Gaspard Poussin, which indicate the degree to which Constable was still looking at nature through the eyes of other artists.

Constable seems to have enjoyed the Lake District. His notes are generally enthusiastic, and on one drawing he wrote, "The finest Scenery that ever was." However, he later told his biographer Leslie, "the solitude of mountains oppressed his spirits." After 1806 he never again deliberately travelled to a region of such scenic grandeur but limited himself to more prosaic aspects of the English landscape. As Leslie commented, "His nature was peculiarly social and could not feel satisfied with scenery, however grand in itself, that did not abound in human associations."
A.S.

124
Fir Trees at Hampstead
Victoria and Albert Museum, London
Pencil; 9⅛ x 6¼ in.
Inscribed: *Wedding day. Hampstead Octr. 2. 1820*

This is a detached sketchbook page which has been mounted together with no. 125; the original leaf size, which has been trimmed in no. 124, was 6⅜ x 9¾ inches, and the paper bears a watermark, truncated in no. 124, "Whatman 1818." Reynolds has identified nine separated leaves from this sketchbook which Constable used in 1820 and 1821.

The inscription refers to the anniversary of Constable's wedding, which took place on October 2, 1816. The Constables first took a house at Hampstead in the summer of 1819, and for the rest of his life Hampstead and its Heath provided his most convenient sketching ground. He had a special affection for many of the trees at Hampstead, and in a lecture he gave in 1836 he discussed the distressing fate of a favorite ash tree at the entrance to the village which had been killed by having a sign nailed to it. No. 124 demonstrates the loving attention to the precise form of individual trees which Constable shows in many of his studies. Its careful detail might be compared to that of the oil *Study of the Trunk of an Elm Tree,* which may date from approximately the same time (Holmes dates it c. 1815, but Reynolds *[Catalogue,* no. 235, pp. 141-42] suggests "c. 1821?"). A larger oil painting of *Trees at Hampstead* (Victoria and Albert Museum), not dependent on no. 124, may be the *Study of Trees from Nature* which Constable exhibited at the Royal Academy in 1822.

Blake is said to have seen a drawing of fir trees in one of Constable's sketchbooks (no. 124?) and to have exclaimed, "Why this is not drawing, this is inspiration!" To which Constable replied, "I never knew that before; I meant it for drawing." Despite Constable's study of trees, Ruskin chose this aspect of his art to pillory, and in both the third and fourth volumes of *Modern Painters* he reproduced details of trees by Constable. In the former, under the heading "Good and Bad Tree-Drawing," he contrasted Constable's trees with Turner's, and in the latter, he dismissed an aspen by Constable as "wholly false in ramification, idle, and undefined in every respect."
A.S.

Provenance
Isabel Constable (presented to the Victoria and Albert Museum, 1888)

Exhibitions
Constable, City Art Gallery, Manchester, 1956, no. 113

References
Leslie, ed. Mayne, p. 328
Ruskin, V, 162-64, cf. pl. 5; VI, 101, cf. pl. 27
Martin Hardie, "Constable's Water-Colours," *OWCSC,* XII, 1935, p. 13, pl. VI
Beckett, p. 78
Reynolds, *Catalogue,* p. 129, no. 203, pl. 155

125

125
A Cart and Horses
Victoria and Albert Museum, London
Pencil; 6⅜ x 9⅜ in.
Inscribed: *Augst 21st. 1821*

No. 125 comes from the same sketchbook as no. 124, with which it is mounted. Reynolds suggests it was possibly drawn at Hampstead, as Constable wrote to Fisher from there on August 4 and September 20, 1821, without mentioning any excursions in the meantime.

Constable had great affection for the details of rural life, and there exist numerous studies by him of carts and ploughs, which often show the regional differences of the forms of agricultural equipment in various parts of England. Similar carts and horses appear in many of his pictures.

Nos. 124 and 125 are brilliant examples of the richness Constable could achieve in the black and white medium. Both drawings demonstrate the importance that the study of light and shadow held for the artist; as he said to his friend Leslie, "I was always determined that my pictures should have chiaroscuro, if they had nothing else." Because of this emphasis, the relative interest of Constable's pencil studies, as opposed to his watercolors, is much greater than that of any of his landscape contemporaries, and Constable's paintings are composed much more in terms of light and dark than of color.
A.S.

Provenance
Isabel Constable (presented to the Victoria and Albert Museum, 1888)

References
Leslie, ed. Mayne, p. 207
Reynolds, *Catalogue,* p. 136, no. 220, pl. 165

126
Study of Clouds and Trees
Royal Academy of Arts, London
Oil on paper mounted on board; 9½ x 11¾ in.
Inscribed, verso: *Hampstead,/Sept. 11, 1821./ 10 to 11 Morning under the sun/ Clouds silvery grey on warm ground/ Sultry. Light wind to the S.W. fine all day—but rain in the night following*

On September 20, 1821 Constable wrote from Hampstead to Archdeacon Fisher, mentioning some tree studies and continuing: "I have likewise made many *skies* and effects—for I wish it could be said of me as Fuseli says of Rembrandt, 'he followed nature in her calmest abodes and could pluck a flower on every hedge—yet he was born to cast a steadfast eye on the bolder phenomena of nature.' We have had noble clouds and effects of light & dark & colour—as is always the case in such seasons as the present." Constable's remark about the nobility of the skies during one season is significant, for although there are groups of cloud studies dating from three different years, 1820, 1821, and 1822, in each case, the dated examples almost all belong to the months of

September and October. He painted no. 126 nine days before writing to Fisher.

Constable explained in further detail his reasons for making such studies in a second letter to Fisher, dated October 23, 1821: "I have done a good deal of skying. I am determined to conquer all difficulties, and that most arduous one among the rest. . . . That landscape painter who does not make his skies a very material part of his composition, neglects to avail himself of one of his greatest aids. Sir Joshua Reynolds, speaking of the landscapes of Titian, of Salvator, and of Claude, says, 'Even their *skies* seem to sympathize with their subjects.' I have often been advised to consider my sky as *a white sheet thrown behind the objects.* Certainly, if the sky is obtrusive, as mine are, it is bad; but if it is evaded, as mine are not, it is worse; it must and always shall with me make an effectual part of the composition. It will be difficult to name a class of landscape in which the sky is not the keynote, the standard of scale, and the chief organ of sentiment. You may conceive then, what a 'white sheet' would do for me, impressed as I am with these notions, and they cannot be erroneous. The sky is the source of light in Nature, and governs everything: even our common observations on the weather of the day are altogether suggested by it. The difficulty of skies in painting is very great, both as to composition and execution; because with all their brilliancy, they ought not to come forward, or, indeed, be hardly thought of any more than extreme distances are; but this does not apply to phenomena or accidental effects of sky, because they always attract particularly. I may say all this to you, though *you* do not want to be told that I know very well what I am about, and that my skies have not been neglected, though they have often failed in execution, no doubt, from an over-anxiety about them, which will alone destroy that easy appearance which Nature always has in all her movements."

Graham Reynolds has established that all Constable's sky sketches of 1821 have some foliage in them, as in no. 126, and the earliest dated pure cloud studies are from 1822. Most of the studies have inscriptions on the back noting the exact time they were made, describing the conditions and also mentioning subsequent meteorological developments; for example, although no. 126 was painted on a fine day, rain followed at night. Thus, these notes must have been written from memory, when Constable was able to place his specific observation in a larger pattern of the weather.

On the back of one of the cloud studies of 1822 in the Victoria and Albert Museum, Constable appears to have written "cirrus" (according to Reynolds [*Catalogue,* no. 250], the inscription is nearly illegible). This would confirm that Constable was familiar with the meteorologist Luke Howard's *The Climate of London,* published in 1820, in which appear the names of cloud forms, cumulus, nimbus, cirrus, which are still in use today. Around this connection Kurt Badt wrote his provocative book, discussing not only Constable's cloud studies, but also those of his continental contemporaries Dahl and Blechen, and the relations between 19th-century romanticism and science in general. Constable was, like many artists of his time, interested in science, but Badt's hypothesis that Howard's book spurred Constable to create his cloud pictures is certainly overstated. If that had been the case, Constable surely would have given some hint of it in his letters to Fisher, his closest friend and confidant, and he would have made more use of Howard's nomenclature that the one example that has been tenuously identified. Also, Paul Oppé pointed out that Constable's interest was concentrated on the "mobility, buoyancy and, above all, lighting" of clouds, and that these interests are purely matters of vision and not concerns of the scientific analyzer.

Badt also claims that earlier artists, such as Alexander Cozens, unlike Constable and his generation, studied clouds in order to make an effect with them in landscape compositions, rather than from interest in their forms as such. This statement probably misrepresents the attitudes of both parties. Although Constable did love and study natural phenomena for their own sakes, his letters to Fisher show that a prime concern in making these studies was to improve the effects of the skies in his landscape compositions. Although we may recognize the lyrical beauty and perhaps an element of psychological release in a study such as no. 126, that does not lessen the practical value it had for the artist. Constable's notations about the wind and weather on these studies were certainly made in part to help him categorize them in order that he might correlate the proper sky with the other aspects of the landscape which he wished to show. An indication of how he thought of these sketches is given by the inscription on another Hampstead cloud study (Melbourne), on which he noted the conditions were "very appropriate to the 'coast at Osmington'," which he had visited several years earlier. He was willing to allow his friends to employ these studies, much as he must have done himself, and on March 26, 1836 he sent Leslie "a few skies, such as we thought might suit your picture." The enrichment of the skies in Constable's own pictures after 1821-22 is evident; in his later work clouds are ever more prominent, and the sky generally is "the chief organ of sentiment."
A.S.

Provenance
Isabel Constable (presented to the Royal Academy in 1888)

Exhibitions
Constable, City Art Gallery, Manchester, 1956, no. 48
Treasures of the Royal Academy, Royal Academy, London, 1963, no. 224

References
Kurt Badt, *John Constable's Clouds,* London, 1950
Leslie, ed. Mayne, pp. 83, 85, 93-94, 253, 257, 282, pl. 30
Beckett, pp. 78, 81-82
A. P. Oppé, *Alexander & John Robert Cozens,* Cambridge, Mass., 1954, pp. 48-51
Reynolds, *Catalogue,* pp. 142-43, 149-50
Reynolds, *The Natural Painter,* pp. 84-90

126

127

127
Landscape Study: Figures by a Clump of Trees
Royal Academy of Arts, London
Oil on paper mounted on board; 9⅜ x 11½ in.
c. 1821

Reynolds dates this sketch c. 1823 on the basis of its similarity to a study in the Victoria and Albert Museum (*Catalogue,* no. 258) which is dated October 4, 1823, and he suggests that both were made at Hampstead. However, another closely similar study, with figures like those in no. 127 and also in the Royal Academy, has on its back a copy of an old inscription "4 Afternoon 27 Sept 1821 Wind . . . West very warm and bright . . ." Although the clump of trees and sunset effect in no. 127 are comparable to the Victoria and Albert sketch, the terrain is flat and parklike while that in the Victoria and Albert painting seems rougher. The receding perspective of trees on the left in no. 127 should also be compared to the *View of Salisbury Cathedral* in the National Gallery in Washington, which Reynolds dates between 1820 and 1822.

Constable began to make small oil sketches directly from nature before 1810, and throughout his career he recorded many of his most immediate responses to nature in this fashion. He made a large number of such sketches in the vicinity of Hampstead in the years following 1819, when he first began to spend his summers there (see also no. 124). Constable did not make these sketches to sell, but kept possession of them to refer to when composing his larger pictures. Graham Reynolds has estimated that some four hundred oil paintings, consisting in good part of such sketches, were in Constable's studio at the time of his death. Nos. 126 and 127 are part of a group of fourteen presented to the Royal Academy in 1888 by Constable's daughter Isabel, at the same time that she presented a much larger body of her father's work to the Victoria and Albert Museum. A.S.

Provenance
Isabel Constable (presented to the Royal Academy in 1888)

Exhibitions
Constable, City Art Gallery, Manchester, 1956, no. 57
Treasures of the Royal Academy, Royal Academy, London, 1963, no. 210

References
Reynolds, *The Natural Painter,* pp. 84, 89-90, 141, pl. 32

128
Study for 'A Boat Passing a Lock' (The Lock)
Philadelphia Museum of Art,
John H. McFadden Collection
Oil on canvas; 53¾ x 48 in.
c. 1822-24

The subject shown is the lock at Flatford on the River Stour in Suffolk. Dedham Church is discernible in the distance. There exist numerous versions of this composition, which R. B. Beckett has sorted out. No. 128 is the full-size sketch for the picture which Constable exhibited at the Royal Academy in 1824. Beckett suggests that Constable's first reference to the subject may be in a letter to Fisher of October 31, 1822,

128

in which he mentions that he has an excellent subject for a six-foot canvas without, however, describing it further. On February 21, 1823, he wrote again to Fisher, "I have put a large upright canvas in hand, and I hope to get it ready for the Academy." This presumably refers to *The Lock,* as Constable's other projected large pictures of this time were all horizontal. Illness prevented Constable from having it or any other large picture ready for the 1823 exhibition. On December 16, 1823 he wrote to Leslie that he would probably have *The Lock* done for the next Academy exhibition, and on January 17, 1824 he mentions having it in hand. The finished picture was no. 18 in the Royal Academy Exhibition of 1824 and was bought on the opening day of the exhibition by

James Morrison of Basildon Park, in the possession of whose descendants it still remains.

There exist several other versions of the composition, many of them of obviously dubious authenticity. Constable, however, did make at least one copy, mentioned in a letter of November 26 and a journal entry of November 28, 1825, which Beckett identifies as the picture belonging to Major A. W. Foster. This version was used for the mezzotint begun by Lucas in 1832 and it appeared in the sale of Constable's pictures on May 16, 1838. Constable also reworked the composition into a horizontal picture, of which there exists a version in Melbourne, as well as his diploma picture in the Royal Academy. The latter is signed and dated 1826 and shows the lock-keeper in a different position than in the other pictures here mentioned. Two drawings in the Fitzwilliam Museum and one in The British Museum are related to the later horizontal composition. The drawing in The British Museum is a straightforward view in pencil on paper watermarked 1824 and shows a superstructure with a horizontal beam over the lock, which does not appear in any of the painted versions. However, an X-ray photograph reveals that Constable had originally included the superstructure in no. 128, and that he subsequently painted it out.

Although in fact slightly smaller, Constable's exhibited picture of *The Lock* is one of six so-called "six-foot" canvases of canal scenes which Constable sent to the Royal Academy between 1819 and 1825. The others are *The White Horse* (1819, Frick Collection), *Stratford Mill* (1820, private collection), *The Hay Wain* (1821, National Gallery, London) *View on the Stour* (1822, Huntington Library, San Marino, California), and *The Leaping Horse* (1825, Royal Academy). These were the most ambitious pictures that Constable had yet undertaken, and to establish their compositions he prepared full-sized oil sketches, the best known of which are the two for *The Hay Wain* and *The Leaping Horse* in the Victoria and Albert Museum. No. 128 clearly served the purpose

of a sketch in which Constable with broad free brush work could give shape to his composition and juggle the elements he wished to include, without having to worry about niceties of detail and finish. In the case of no. 128, Constable established the shape of the composition while at work on the sketch by extending the canvas on both top and bottom and cutting it down on the right side. A similar adjusting of the size can be seen in the sketch for *The Leaping Horse,* which has been extended on the top and right-hand sides. Whether Constable actually began these sketches as sketches is not clear. In the first edition of *The Life of Constable* (1843, p. 51), Leslie asserted that Constable had intended a sketch for *The Leaping Horse* to be the picture and afterwards turned it into a sketch, "not an unusual occurrence with him." Although Holmes's suggestion that no. 128 was painted on top of a finished picture is not sustained by technical examination, the handling of certain parts of the landscape indicates that Constable originally painted them with greater precision than now appears. This in turn would suggest that no. 128 may have only become a sketch when Constable realized he was making so many changes that for the finished picture he should start anew on a fresh canvas.

The most important change was presumably that of shape. Without the additions to top and bottom, no. 128 would be approximately forty-three inches high, and no longer an upright composition. We do not know how much picture Constable cut away from the right side; conceivably no. 128 could originally have had proportions comparable to *The White Horse* and the other horizontal canal scenes. Beckett suggests that the "large upright landscape" mentioned by Constable on February 21, 1823, was the Philadelphia version of *The Lock;* if so, he must already by then have made his subtraction and additions to give the picture its present shape. In his mention of January 17, 1824, Constable described the picture as "my upright Lock."

The exhibited picture follows closely the

composition of no. 128, as altered, with the main difference being its greater precision of detail. The chief gain resulting from the finishing process is the articulation of space: the view over the meadows has become clearer and Dedham Church seems much further in the distance. Other details such as the legs of the lock-tender or the man and dog looking over the edge of the lock, which are sketchily vague in no. 128, are clearly defined in the finished version. What appears to be a man on horseback on the extreme left of the sketch has disappeared, although his horse remains, and the fishing pole across the foreground has also been omitted.

No. 128 does not seem to have been preceded by any other directly related studies. However, W. G. Constable has suggested that the seeds of the composition are to be found in a sketch of about 1811 in the Victoria and Albert Museum, *Barges on the Stour, with Dedham Church in the Distance* (Reynolds, *Catalogue,* no. 104). The same or similar locks also appear frequently in many other sketches and pictures by Constable, and a man operating a lock in comparable fashion to the tender in no. 128 appears in the middle distance in the *Dedham Mill* of 1820 (versions in the Victoria and Albert Museum, Tate Gallery and Currier Gallery, Manchester, N.H.). This was the environment of Constable's childhood, and his abiding affection for it was one of the motivating forces of his entire career. In the letter to Fisher of October 23, 1821 in which he described his "skying," Constable wrote: "The sound of water escaping from mill-dams, etc. willows, old rotten planks, slimy posts, and brickwork—I love such things. Shakespeare could make everything poetical; he tells us of poor Tom's haunts among 'sheep cotes and mills.' As long as I do paint, I shall never cease to paint such places. . . . Painting is with me but another word for feeling, and I associate my 'careless boyhood' with all that lies on the bank of the Stour. Those scenes made me a painter, and I am grateful."

Constable seems to have held *The Lock* in special

affection. When he sent the picture to exhibition, he wrote to Fisher on April 15, 1824 that he had never been "more fully bent on any picture." He recounted that all his friends told him it was his best, and Constable agreed: "It is a good subject and an admirable instance of the picturesque." When the picture was at the Academy, Constable wrote again to Fisher to tell of its success: "Indeed it forms a decided feature and its light cannot be put out, because it is the light of Nature— the Mother of all that is valuable in poetry, painting or anything else, where an appeal to the soul is required." In 1825 Constable borrowed back the picture which he had exhibited and sold, so that it might be engraved by Samuel Reynolds, and when he had it in his studio, he wrote once again to Fisher: "It looks most beautifully silvery, windy and delicious. It is all health, and the absence of everything stagnant." These remarks were made about the finished picture rather than no. 128, but those qualities which Constable was especially pleased with are equally present in the sketch, perhaps more so because undiluted by a finishing process which was extraneous to what Constable most deeply valued. Many critics have seen Constable's greatest achievements in the full-size sketches, and although this is not the place to argue the relative merits of sketches vs. finished pictures, the large sketches such as no. 128 are revelations of Constable's ability to carry over that emotional response to nature, so directly felt in his drawings and small first sketches, into the thought-out studio composition. W. G. Constable has even proposed the idea that these are not in fact sketches for the more finished pictures, but that Constable painted them afterwards, "to express his idea of what a painting should be, in contrast to one tailored to suit Royal Academy standards." The evidence of change of size, etc., in no. 128, makes this hypothesis untenable, at least for no. 128, but the proposal seems to be an outgrowth of the dilemma, felt by many admirers of Constable, that his greatest works came as by-products made in the preparation of what are often less effective finished paintings.
A.S.

Provenance
Ernest Gambart, London (sale, Christie's, London, 3-4 May 1861, no. 294, bt. Leatham)
E. A. Leatham, Misarden Park, Gloucestershire (sale, Christie's, London, 18 May 1901, no. 121, bt. Vicars)
Thos. Agnew & Sons, London
John Howard McFadden, Philadelphia
Philadelphia Museum of Art, 1928

Exhibitions
Seventh Annual Exhibition, Thos. Agnew & Sons, London, 1901, no. 8

References
Leslie, ed. Mayne, p. 115 *et passim*
Catalogue of Oil Paintings by the Old Masters in the Possession of E. A. Leatham, Esq., Misarden Park, Gloucestershire, 1898, p. 5
Holmes, p. 247
W. Roberts, *Catalogue of the Collection of Pictures formed by John H. McFadden, Esq., of Philadelphia,* London, 1917, pp. 3-5
Andrew Shirley, "John Constable's 'Lock': the Newly Discovered Study," *Connoisseur,* CXXVII, 1951, pp. 71-75, 132
Frank Simpson, "Constable's 'Lock': a Postscript," *Connoisseur,* CXXIX, 1952, p. 39
R. B. Beckett, "Constable's 'Lock'," *Burlington,* XCIV, 1952, pp. 252-56
Beckett, *Constable and the Fishers,* pp. 82, 120-21 *et passim*
W. G. Constable, " 'The Lock' as a Theme in the Work of John Constable," in Franz Philipp and June Stewart, eds., *In Honour of Daryl Lindsay: Essays and Studies,* Melbourne, 1964, pp. 128-44, pl. 117
Reynolds, *The Natural Painter,* pp. 70-73, 142, pl. 41

129
Waterloo Bridge
Cincinnati Art Museum
Oil on canvas; 21$^{11}/_{16}$ x 30$^{11}/_{16}$ in.
Probably 1823-24

Waterloo Bridge, designed by C. R. Rennie, was opened by the Prince Regent on June 18, 1817, the second anniversary of the Battle of Waterloo. It seems certain, although there is no definite record, that Constable was present to watch the ceremonies. Although the event had little in common with the rural scenes which provided his usual subjects, he decided to paint a picture of it, and for the next seventeen years, until 1834, he struggled with the project.

The history of the various versions of Constable's *Waterloo Bridge* is tortuous, and despite Denys Sutton's admirable article, the subject is still confusing. We do not know where Constable was on June 18, 1817, nor if he made any sketches on that day. His first recorded mention of the composition comes in a letter of two years later, July 17, 1819, in which he tells Fisher that he had "made a sketch of my scene on the Thames." In August of the same year he showed a treatment of the subject to Joseph Farington who criticized it as a "bird's-eye view." There are other references from 1820, 1822, and 1823, which tell us little more about the picture except that the Bishop of Salisbury considered it equal to Canaletto. In the winter of 1823-24 Constable thought that he might have the *Waterloo* and *The Lock* (see no. 128) ready for the 1824 Royal Academy. On January 17, 1824 he wrote to Fisher: "I have just completed my little Waterloo Bridge. It looks very well indeed," and on January 22 he wrote again, "I have done the little 'Waterloo', a small balloon to let off as a forerunner to the large one." However, no *Waterloo* appeared at the 1824 Academy, and when Constable was pressed by Fisher, he replied in July, "I have no inclination to pursue my Waterloo, I am impressed with an idea that it will ruin me." He did, nonetheless, return to the subject in 1825, and a large painting of *Whitehall Stairs*

129

between them, Whitehall Stairs leading down to the river. The view in no. 129 is from a lower vantage point and would seem to have been made from a boat in the river. Also, Sutton suggests that the wall and landing stage shown in no. 129 may not be the same as in the exhibited picture, that is, not the foot of Whitehall Stairs, but are possibly from further down the river toward the bridge.

Stylistically, no. 129 could date anywhere between 1819 and 1825. It, however, is not a bird's-eye view and is, thus, not the version which Constable showed to Farington in August 1819. Sutton suggests that it may be the "little" *Waterloo* which Constable completed and twice referred to in letters of January 1824. Sutton and Reynolds agree that the references imply a finished picture of the type which Constable was likely to exhibit, a condition certainly met by the Cincinnati painting. The question arises, however, that if Constable intended to exhibit a *Waterloo* in 1824 and had no. 129 ready by January, why did it not appear at the Academy in May along with *The Lock*? The answer may be that some unknown incident prevented it, and that this is hinted at in Constable's unexpectedly sour reference of the following July.

Of the many other versions of the subject, two, a pencil drawing once in the Gregory Collection and an oil sketch in the Royal Academy (both reproduced by Sutton), show the view from the same vantage point as in no. 129. These presumably are the studies upon which Constable based the more finished treatment of no. 129, and the former would seem certainly to have been drawn from nature. There are numerous small differences between no. 129 and the pencil drawing, but it differs from the sketch in the Royal Academy only in greater detail and a much vaster sense of space. Control over horizontal recession was one of the chief gains achieved by Constable in painting his finished pictures.

No. 129 recalls many other views over the Thames, notably those of Canaletto, to which the Bishop of Salisbury compared this or another version, and

or *The Opening of Waterloo Bridge* finally appeared at the Royal Academy in 1832. Even then, it was apparently not completed to Constable's satisfaction, and in 1834 he wrote that he was working on it, "and shall make it look like something before I am done with it."

There are two main groups of Waterloo views: those showing the ceremonies, including flags, troops, and state barges, and those, such as no. 129, which depict the river view unencumbered by ceremony. The exhibited picture of 1832 (private collection) shows the ceremony and,

presumably, it and several related sketches come after the simpler views, although Reynolds gives the date 1819 to a sketch showing the ceremony (Victoria and Albert Museum). In the exhibited picture, the distant view of the bridge, with St. Paul's beyond, is approximately the same as in no. 129, but the foreground details are considerably altered. In July 1827 Constable was able to visit the gardens of Pembroke House, overlooking the Thames, and the foreground of the exhibited picture shows what he could see from there, including the bow front of the neighboring house, the wall and garden of Fife House and,

those of Samuel Scott. *Waterloo Bridge* is Constable's only important urban composition, and the difficulties that this departure from his usual practice caused are revealed by the length of time he struggled with it. However, one sees little reflection of Constable's trouble in no. 129. This picture is quite different from the finished version; there the emphasis falls on the panoply of the ceremony with a corresponding air of excitement, but in no. 129 nature's placid mood and the loveliness of the view are depicted with a temper not unlike that which animates many of Constable's earlier rural scenes.
A.S.

Provenance
Helen Johanna Shore Nightingale, London, and family descent (sale, Robinson and Foster's, London, 2 July 1928, no. 106)
Mary Hanna, Cincinnati

Exhibitions
The City by the River and the Sea, Dayton Art Institute, 1951, no. 34
Art and City Life, Columbus Gallery of Fine Arts, 1952
Birth of Impressionism, Wildenstein and Co., New York, 1963, no. 12

References
Farington, ed. Greig, VIII, 225, 268-69
Leslie, ed. Mayne, pp. 119-20 *et passim*
H. Granville Fell, "Constable's 'Waterloo Bridge'," *Connoisseur,* XCVIII, 1936, pp. 186-91
Ella S. Sipple, "Another Version of Constable's Waterloo Bridge," *Burlington,* LXX, 1937, p. 295, fig. B
Denys Sutton, "Constable's 'Whitehall Stairs' or 'The Opening of Waterloo Bridge'," *Connoisseur,* CXXXVI, 1956, pp. 248-55
Beckett, pp. 158, 161, 179 *et passim*
Reynolds, *Catalogue,* pp. 119-21
Louis Hawes, Jr., review of Reynolds, *Catalogue; The Art Bulletin,* XLIII, 1961, pp. 161-62

130

130
View at Hampstead
Victoria and Albert Museum, London
Watercolor; 4½ x 7½ in.
Inscribed, verso: *Hampd December 7, 1833 3 oclock—very stormy afternoon—& High Wind*

This is one of many views by Constable looking towards London from Hampstead with the dome of St. Paul's in the distance. Reynolds cites four such drawings in The British Museum, the last dated November 9, 1831, two years before no. 130. In 1832 Constable exhibited at the Royal Academy *Sir Richard Steele's Cottage, Hampstead,* which is lost but known through prints and sketches (see Baskett, p. 82), and which included a comparable view of St. Paul's. No. 130 was presumably made from the drawing room of Constable's house in Well Walk, Hampstead, which had a commanding view over London.

The drawing shows the dramatic contrasts of light and dark and the somber mood that characterize much of Constable's later work. It should be noted, however, that no. 130 was drawn in the winter and

that Constable indicated on it that it was a stormy afternoon. Girtin and Loshak cite this drawing as a contrast to Girtin's views of London in his *Eidometropolis,* pointing out that, even when painting London, Constable was little interested in the city as such but in the atmosphere and weather hanging over it.
A.S.

Provenance
Isabel Constable (gift to the Victoria and Albert Museum, 1888)

References
Holmes, p. 113 (ill.), p. 251
Martin Hardie, "Constable's Water-Colours," *OWCSC,* XII, 1935, p. 10
Thomas Girtin and David Loshak, *The Art of Thomas Girtin,* London, 1954, p. 105, fig. 94
Reynolds, *Catalogue,* pp. 209-10, no. 358, pl. 259

John Sell Cotman

1782-1842

Cotman was the son of a Norwich hairdresser. In 1798 he went to London where he found a job coloring prints for Rudolph Ackermann. As an artist he had no formal training. In 1799 he was employed to make drawings for Dr. Thomas Monro, for whom Turner and Girtin had previously worked; in 1800 he exhibited six drawings at the Royal Academy; and in that or the following year he became a member of the Sketching Club, in the formation of which Girtin had been the leading light. Cotman remained a member of this group through 1804, making drawings from Ossian and other literary sources. In 1800 and 1802 he made sketching trips to Wales. His watercolors of this time are dependent upon Girtin, but in 1803 he began to develop an individual style marked by a strong sense of pattern and delicate clear washes of color with a minimum of shadow. This reached fruition in the last of three trips to Yorkshire which Cotman made in 1803, 1804, and 1805. In 1806 he returned to his native Norwich and two years later he became a member of the Norwich Society of Artists. In Norwich he began to paint in oils as well as watercolor, and he tried to set himself up as a portrait painter, without much success. For the rest of his life he supported himself and his family as a drawing master. In 1812 he moved to nearby Yarmouth, but returned to Norwich in 1825. In 1834 he was appointed teacher of drawing at King's College in London, and he died in London eight years later. He was elected an Associate of the Old Water Colour Society in 1825, but never became a full member.

In Norwich Cotman was encouraged toward antiquarianism by his patron Dawson Turner. He made a vast number of drawings of the medieval architecture of Norfolk and of Normandy, which he visited three times for the purpose, his only foreign travel. This study resulted in the publication of several volumes of etchings of antiquarian subjects. While living at Yarmouth, he painted and drew numerous seascapes, and after about 1825 much of his work consisted of invented or historical subjects. His later watercolors are painted in strong colors, with a marked preference for bright blue and yellow, and to gain these stronger colors he developed a technique of mixing his pigments with pastes.

Cotman did not basically share the naturalistic orientation of most of his contemporaries, and the distinctive element in most of his work is a somewhat aestheticizing refinement of pattern and shape. However, in his most successful works, the Yorkshire watercolors of 1805, this instinct was brought into harmony with a deeply felt response to the landscape. He seems to have been an extremely sensitive and unstable man who often acted impulsively and foolishly. Most historians agree that his move to Norwich was a mistake, not only because it condemned him to a life of drudgery as a drawing master, but more important because it isolated him from the progressive elements of English painting. Of the Norwich school of artists he is the brightest star, but he developed his style and did his best work while a resident of London, and his later work, although still highly individual, never reached the same levels. Cotman had two sons, Miles Edmund and John Joseph, who became artists, and the work of the former is very similar to that of his father. A.S.

Bibliography
A. P. Oppé, *The Water-Colour Drawings of John Sell Cotman,* London, 1923
Sydney D. Kitson, *The Life of John Sell Cotman,* London, 1937
Paul Oppé, "Cotman and His Public," *Burlington,* LXXXI, 1942, pp. 163-71
Victor Rienaecker, *John Sell Cotman: 1782-1842,* Leigh-on-Sea, 1953

131
Greta Woods from Brignal Banks
Leeds City Art Galleries
Watercolor; 7¾ x 11⅜ in.
Inscribed, verso: *On the Greta, Yorkshire*
c. 1805

Each summer for three years, beginning in 1803, Cotman paid an extended visit to Yorkshire, where he gave drawing lessons to the family of Francis Cholmeley of Brandsby Hall, fifteen miles north of York. On the third visit he went also to Rokeby Park, situated in northern Yorkshire at the junction of the Greta and the Tees Rivers, where he stayed for over a month with its owner John Morritt, a friend of the Cholmeley family.

The scenery along the Greta is among the most famous and beautiful in England, and it inspired Cotman to his highest achievement. Of this scenery he made both studies directly from nature and more formalized watercolors painted in the studio. No. 131 is of the latter class. Kitson has published in the *OWCSC* the pencil drawing upon which it is based (now also in Leeds). The drawing and the watercolor show the identical view, but in the latter Cotman has given more order to the foreground foliage and added the geometrically shaped pattern of cloud and rain to the sky. The emphasis on the play of shapes is characteristic of Cotman, as is the mastery of delicately controlled flat washes of color. However, the extraordinary sense of calm, embodying both intimacy and detachment, is nowhere else so beautifully

131

132
Horses Drinking
Trustees of The British Museum
Sepia wash; 11 x 8³⁄₁₆ in.
c. 1806

One of the drawings which Cotman exhibited at th
Royal Academy in 1806 was entitled *Horses
Drinking.* Kitson suggests that no. 132 may be a
study for this exhibited drawing, and that it may
also be the drawing which Cotman exhibited at
Norwich two years later as *Horses Drinking:
a Sketch for a Large Picture.* From the evidence
of some outline tracings, Kitson writes that the
"large picture" seems to have been based on
Dutch paintings by Nicolas Berchem and Karel
du Jardin. However, there is nothing particularly
Dutch, beyond the genre subject, in a drawing
such as no. 132. In a remarkably witty and fanciful
way it demonstrates Cotman's strong sense
of pattern, which here verges on the abstract.
A.S.

Provenance
James Reeve, Norwich
The British Museum, 1902

Exhibitions
(?) The Norwich Society of Artists, 1808, no. 75 *(Horses
Drinking: a Sketch for a Large Picture)*

References
Kitson, p. 94, pl. 41
Rienaecker, pl. 19, fig. 32

expressed as in these Yorkshire drawings. Cotman
retained his strong sense of design throughout
his life, but he never again responded so
deeply to natural scenery.
A.S.

Provenance
Palser, London
Agnes and Norman Lupton (bequest to Leeds, 1952)

Exhibitions
Twee Eeuwen Engelsche Kunst, Stedelijk Museum,
Amsterdam, 1936, no. 201
Early English Watercolours, Leeds City Art Galleries,
1958, no. 16

Watercolours and Drawings from Leeds, Thos. Agnew &
Sons, London, 1960, no. 82

References
Sydney D. Kitson, "John Sell Cotman (1782-1842),"
OWCSC, VII, 1930, pp. 4-5, 7-8, pl. VI
Kitson, pp. 80-84

Strangely artistic-academic
Outlined planes of light

132

133
A Spanish Arquebusier
Leeds City Art Galleries
Watercolor silhouette on cardboard;
10 x 6½ in. (image)
Inscribed: *J. S. Cotman*
c. 1837

This is a late drawing made when Cotman was employed as a drawing master in King's College, London. His method of teaching was to make drawings for his students to copy, and as his classes increased in size, he worked ever harder to prepare a large number and variety of such models. Shortly before his death, he wrote to Dawson Turner of the "thousand upon thousand" drawings he had made: "Subjects that I only hear my boys whisper or wish to go on with, whether Horses, Dogs, Men in Armour, Classical Figures, Coats of Arms: anything and everything." No. 133 reflects this activity, but it apparently was not actually made to be copied. It seems to be one of several such brightly colored drawings which Cotman made in silhouette on cardboard to decorate the room of Hannah Maw, the daughter of one of his patrons. Three other drawings of soldiers are also in Leeds, and a drawing of a knight on horseback is reproduced by Kitson. In this latter drawing, the knight bears a banner inscribed "Hannah the Fairest." The arquebusier in no. 133 is based on an illustration in Jacques de Gheyne's *Maniement d'Armes,* published in 1608. Another watercolor of the same subject, by an unknown hand, is in the National Maritime Museum, Greenwich.
A.S.

133

Provenance
J. H. Maw, London
E. Derwent Wood, R. A., London, Maw's grandson
(sale, Christie's, London, July 1926)
Sydney D. Kitson (bequest to Leeds, 1938)

Exhibitions
Works by John Sell Cotman, The Tate Gallery, London, 1922, no. 225
Watercolours and Drawings from Leeds, Thos. Agnew & Sons, London, 1960, no. 93

References
Kitson, pp. 348-50, cf. p. 137

Samuel Prout

1783-1852

Bibliography
Ruskin, XII, 303-15; XIV, 367-454
E. G. Halton, *Sketches by Samuel Prout* (Studio Special Number), London, 1915
Jane Quigley, *Prout and Roberts,* London, 1926
C. E. Hughes, "Samuel Prout (1783-1851),"
OWCSC, VI, 1929, pp. 1-30

134

Prout was born in Plymouth, where he was a boyhood friend of Benjamin Robert Haydon, his junior by two years. During the early part of his career he travelled extensively in England making drawings of picturesque places and buildings, many of which were published by the antiquarian John Britton in his *Beauties of England and Wales* and *Architectural Antiquities of Great Britain.* After the end of the Napoleonic wars, Prout made his first trip to the continent in 1818 or 1819, and for the rest of his life he specialized in continental views. Prout was the most popular of a large group of artists who, in the second quarter of the 19th century, provided the English public with a steady flow of decaying monuments and dilapidated European streets picturesquely inhabited by colorfully clad peasants. To create an effect of crumbling stone and weathered wood, Prout developed a style of drawing with a broken line, which became something of a repetitive and easily recognizable mannerism.

The first drawing that Ruskin knew was by Prout, and throughout Ruskin's life he praised Prout's work to a degree that few modern observers would feel it deserved. However, Ruskin admired Prout not only for the quality of his art (which Ruskin made clear that he liked because of its depiction of places that interested him), but also for his essentially middle-class outlook and appeal, and out of a liking for the man himself. Prout was a delicate semi-invalid all his life, yet he travelled constantly for the sake of his art, and he seems to have had an almost saintly personality. A.S.

134
View in Ghent
The Beinecke Rare Book and Manuscript Library, Yale University
Pen and ink, and watercolor; 3¾ x 2⅜ in.
After 1819

No. 134 is mounted in the Denham Album, for which see no. 188. It shows the projecting polygonal northeast corner of the town hall in Ghent, which was built in the flamboyant Gothic style between 1518 and 1535. A watercolor view of the lower portion of the corner from a slightly different angle is in The British Museum and is reproduced by Halton. No. 134 is much smaller, and consequently less highly elaborated than the watercolors of continental views which Prout usually exhibited. It is, however, about the same size as the many engravings and lithographs of his work, which appeared regularly and spread his reputation far beyond the limited circle of purchasers of watercolors.

The busy foreground scene is characteristic of Prout, so characteristic in fact, that in his *Hints on Light and Shadow, Composition, etc. as Applicable to Landscape Painting* and the subsequent *Prout's Microcosm: The Artistic Sketchbook of Groups of Figures, Shipping and Other Picturesque Objects,* he published numerous lithographed examples of such figures and gave amateurs instructions on how to dispose of them effectively in a picturesque composition. Prout also frequently used the motif of a piece of cloth draped out a window or over a balcony to give a highlight, and in his works we can see what appears to be bed linen hanging improbably from a variety of buildings including the Temple of the Sibyl at Tivoli and the Doge's Palace in Venice. A.S.

Provenance
Same as no. 188

References
Halton, cf. pl. I

David Cox

1783-1859

135

Cox was born in a suburb of Birmingham, the son of a blacksmith. He was apprenticed to a local miniature painter and then worked as a scene painter in a Birmingham theater. In 1804 he moved to London. Except for a few lessons from John Varley, he was self-taught. He exhibited at the Royal Academy from 1805 through 1808, and in 1812 he was elected to the Old Water Colour Society. Between 1813 and 1859 he exhibited on the Society's walls no less than 849 watercolors. Like many of his colleagues he supported himself as a drawing master, and he published several books of drawing instructions. In 1814 he moved to Hereford to teach at Miss Croucher's Academy of Drawing, and he lived in Hereford until 1827, when he returned to London. In 1841 he retired from teaching, although not from painting, and he moved back to his native Birmingham.

Cox made only three brief trips abroad, to the Low Countries and France in 1826, 1829, and 1832, but he went on frequent sketching tours of Yorkshire, Derbyshire, and, especially, Wales. At the end of his life he visited Wales every summer, and Bettws-y-Coed, where he stayed, became something of an artists' colony, with Cox its revered patriarch.

Cox was primarily a painter in watercolor. In 1840 he had instruction in oil painting from William James Muller, a younger artist, and for the rest of his life he worked seriously at painting in oils, without, however, giving up watercolor. He made charming figural studies and painted many

architectural subjects, but he most frequently depicted the countryside, making a specialty out of windswept fields and moors under cloudy skies. His late works are broadly handled and stormily dramatic and, surprisingly, they were much admired despite the Victorian trend to ever-greater tightness and precision.
A.S.

Bibliography
N. Neal Solly, *Memoir of the Life of David Cox,* London, 1873
William Hall, *A Biography of David Cox,* London, 1881
F. Gordon Roe, *Cox the Master,* Leigh-on-Sea, 1946
Trenchard Cox, *David Cox,* London, 1947

135
Greenwich Hospital
The Metropolitan Museum of Art, Rogers Fund, 1907
Pencil and watercolor; 7⅝ x 14⁵⁄₁₆ in.
Inscribed: *Greenwich*
c. 1831

Cox exhibited views of the vicinity of Greenwich at the Old Water Colour Society regularly from 1823 through 1831. Most of these seem to have been scenes on the river rather than views of the Hospital itself. However, in 1831 he exhibited a watercolor titled *Part of Greenwich Hospital,* and although no. 135 is probably too unfinished to have been exhibited itself, it seems likely that it is related to the exhibited work.

1785-1841

Following his trip to France in 1829, Cox exhibited several views of Paris and apparently developed a short-lived interest in architectural subjects. Although these works never had the popularity of his pure landscapes, the geometry of architecture brought a welcome discipline to his art, and works such as no. 135 or the well-known *Porch of St. Philip's Church, Birmingham* of 1836 (Birmingham) now seem to have a strength and control generally lacking in Cox's more diffuse landscapes.
A.S.

Exhibitions
Drawings, Lyman Allyn Museum, New London, Conn., 1936, no. 178

References
Solly, p. 67

136

136
On the Sands (Lancaster Sands)
Birmingham City Museum and Art Gallery
Oil on panel; 9 x 13¾ in.
c. 1850

This is one of several late paintings of the seashore by Cox which frequently have been compared to pictures by Boudin. The best known are a painting of *Rhyl Sands* on the coast of Wales, which is in Birmingham and is dated 1854-55, and a related broadly treated oil sketch in Manchester. The date of 1850 is ascribed to no. 136 by Solly, Cox's first biographer, who identifies the subject as *Lancaster Sands.* Cox exhibited a *Lancaster Sands* at the Society of British Artists in 1842.
A.S.

Provenance
David Cox, Jr., Brixton Hill, London
Joseph H. Nettlefold (bequest to Birmingham, 1882)

Exhibitions
Works by David Cox, Museum and Art Gallery, Birmingham, 1890, no. 104

Swansea, 1953, no. 83
Pictures from the City Art Gallery, Birmingham, Thos. Agnew & Sons, London, 1957, no. 44
Victorian Painting, Nottingham University, 1959, no. 14
David Cox Centenary Exhibition, City Museum and Art Gallery, Birmingham, 1959, no. 110

References
Solly, *p. 209*
Catalogue of Paintings, City Museum and Art Gallery, Birmingham, 1960, p. 39

David Wilkie was the son of a minister and the grandson of a miller from Cults, just north of Edinburgh. He first studied at the Trustees Academy in Edinburgh with John Graham and later, travelling through Fife, painted portraits in the manner of Raeburn. In 1805 he moved to London where his small, carefully wrought pictures of Scottish peasant life, such as *The Village Politicians* (Earl of Mansfield), attracted the attention of the most active patrons of British art at the moment, Sir George Beaumont and Lord Mulgrave.

The Scottish peasant scenes were enormously popular and brought him to the attention of the wealthiest and most fashionable patrons, including Julius Angerstein, for whom *The Village Festival* (Tate Gallery) was painted in 1811, and the Prince Regent, for whom he painted *Blind Man's Buff* (1811-12, Royal Collections). These genre scenes were interspersed with portrait drawings and paintings, including the fine study of the *Duchess of Buccleuch* (Dr. Batchelor, Broughty Ferry). Wilkie's early works brought him a reputation which had seldom been attained by a British artist who was not a portraitist. This resulted in numerous official honors which included the A.R.A. in 1809 and R.A. in 1811. In 1823, at the death of Sir Henry Raeburn, he was appointed King's Limner for Scotland. He was considered for President of the Royal Academy but was not elected, perhaps in part because he was too greatly favored by the King. He was Painter in Ordinary to William IV and to Queen Victoria, and he was knighted in 1836.

Travelling to Spain and Italy in 1825 in order to restore his fragile constitution, he saw the paintings of Velasquez, Murillo, the North Italians, and Rubens, a revelation which at the time had as important an effect on his art as had the Dutch formerly. He concluded what he no doubt had already learned from his British masters, that color, richness, depth, and fluency of brushwork were essential, activating elements in painting. Although his pictures had already begun to increase in size and to become broader in technique, this journey abroad was the final incentive toward his late style.

After his continental tour, Wilkie broke through the constricting mold of his painstaking early productions and broached the entire range of romantic subject matters, scenes from contemporary life, literature, history, landscape, and portraiture. At the same time, he maintained the interest in psychological interplay which characterized his early work. The study of emotional responses is at the core and is the true subject matter of his art. This interest is coupled with a vast appetite for the ephemera of a wide range of visual experiences which includes all objects and textures that are light, delicious, crisp, and stimulating to the eye.

Working at a much more rapid pace and exhibiting five and six pictures per year, he produced some of his most powerful and certainly his most original compositions. *The Defence of Saragossa* (Royal Collections), *Peep-O-Day Boy's Cabin* (Tate Gallery), *Josephine and the Fortune Teller* (no. 143), *The Irish Whiskey Still* (National Gallery of Scotland), and *Sir David Baird Discovering the Body of Tippoo Sahib* (Lady Baird, on loan to Edinburgh Castle) are among his finest works and compare well with the achievement of the French romantic painters. These were interspersed with a series of commanding portraits which, in originality of composition, solidity of construction, and brilliance of pictorial fanfare equal those of Reynolds and Lawrence. That of *Viscount Arbuthnot* (Laurencekirk Council, St. Lawrence's

Hall) is among the most haunting and beautiful of these.

Wilkie last travelled abroad in 1840, visiting Constantinople and the Near East to see the places where the biblical events had taken place. He drew incessantly on his voyage, producing some of his most beautiful figure and costume drawings. He died on the return voyage.

Although still little known to the general public, especially in America, Wilkie is a major artist of the romantic period. The range of his subject matter is broad, his technique is solidly grounded and frequently brilliant, and his compositions are infused with a variety and richness of forms and figures that are rare in British painting. One of the finest draftsmen of the British School, his drawings are as attractive and as striking as his paintings. Like the French romantic artists, he frequently drew with watercolor and chalks in combination. These give his drawings rich color combined with precise technique and a sinuous line which is ultimately modelled on the Italian and Flemish masters and like theirs possesses great generosity of form and penetrating apprehensions of grace.
F.C.

Bibliography
Allen Cunningham, *The Life of Sir David Wilkie*, 3 vols., London, 1843
Sir David Wilkie's Sketches in Turkey, Syria and Egypt, 1840 & 1841, London, 1843
Works of Sir David Wilkie, R.A., Christie's, London, 25-30 April 1842
Works of Sir David Wilkie, R.A., Christie's, London, 20-21 June 1860
Lord Ronald Sutherland Gower, *Sir David Wilkie*, London, 1902
Ramsay, Raeburn and Wilkie, Arts Council of Great Britain, Scottish Committee, Edinburgh, 1951
Paintings and Drawings by Sir David Wilkie, National Gallery of Scotland, Edinburgh, Royal Academy, London, 1958 (catalogue compiled by John Woodward)

137
The Blind Fiddler
The Trustees of The Tate Gallery, London
Oil on panel; 22¾ x 31¼ in.
Inscribed: *D. Wilkie, 1806*

This subject was commissioned by Sir George Beaumont in 1806 when John Jackson, the portrait painter, brought his friends and patrons Lord Mulgrave and Sir George Beaumont to Wilkie's studio. Beaumont's letter of June 15 describes Wilkie working on the picture, and another letter of Wilkie to Sir George of August 20, 1806 tells that it is finished. The price paid was fifty guineas.

Wilkie rose to immediate fame on the basis of his first pictures exhibited in London, *The Village Politicians,* in 1806 and *The Blind Fiddler,* of the following year, which shows an itinerant musician playing in the home of a shoemaker. The picture is composed and painted in the manner of the interiors of David Teniers. It is traditional to emphasize in such works the interest in anecdote and humble simplicity which relate paintings of this type to Wordsworth's poetry. However, the painting is romantic not only because of its rustic simplicity but, more important, because of its concentration on highly specific psychological responses which are, in fact, its chief subject. Not only Teniers but Greuze and the writers on expression around 1800 form the intellectual background of such a work. These early paintings by Wilkie establish the vogue for artists such as Frith, C. R. Leslie, and E. M. Ward in the early Victorian period who will portray intimate psychological dramas in everyday settings. The popularity of such subjects in the school of Düsseldorf and their frequent recurrence in American art also derives from the carefully prepared prints after Wilkie's early paintings.
F.C.

Provenance
Commissioned by Sir George Beaumont, 1806
Presented to The National Gallery, London, 1826
Transferred to The Tate Gallery, London, 1919

137

Exhibitions
Royal Academy, 1807, no. 147
Pictures Painted by D. Wilkie, R.A., 87 Pall Mall,
London, 1812, no. 6
British Institution, London, 1825, no. 138
Paintings and Drawings by Sir David Wilkie, National
Gallery of Scotland, Edinburgh and London, 1958, I, no. 4

References
Cunningham, I, 95-96, 118-22, 131-33, 137-46; III, 524
M. R. S. Raimbach, *Memoirs and Recollections of the
Late Abraham Raimbach, Esq.,* London, 1843, p. 156

J. Burnet, *Practical Essays on Various Branches of the
Fine Arts,* London, 1848, p. 105
Farington, ed. Greig, IV, 1924, pp. 41-42, 44, 47-48, 116,
122, 124, 133-34, 140, 149-50; V, 1925, p. 136
W. Whitley, *Art in England 1800-1820,* London, 1928,
pp. 120-21
Benjamin R. Haydon, *The Autobiography and Memoirs,*
London, 1926, I, pp. 38, 46, 398; II, 780-81
W. B. Pope, ed., *The Diary of Benjamin Robert Haydon,*
Cambridge, I, 1960, pp. 143, 145; V, 1963, p. 415

138
Study for the Letter of Introduction
Victoria and Albert Museum, London
Oil on panel; 15 x 11¾ in.
1813

We first hear of Wilkie's painting, the *Letter of
Introduction* (National Gallery of Scotland), in a
letter to his sister on May 17, 1813. Later, in his
journal of October 21, he noted that the final
picture was almost completely painted on that day
Allan Cunningham relates that Wilkie, who looked
quite youthful, had in mind his own introduction
to Caleb Whitefoord (1734-1810), who received him
on his arrival in London with the query, "How old
are you?" which baffled the young man.
Whitefoord, an Edinburgh man, was a wine
merchant, diplomat and friend of Franklin who
collected paintings and purchased works from
living artists.

The finished painting for which this picture
prepares was not a commission. It was sold to
Samuel Dobree just before the Royal Academy
exhibition in which it was included the following
year. Dobree paid £250 for the picture, only 24
inches high, giving some idea of the great
popularity of Wilkie's works at the time.

The library in this sketch differs in almost every
detail from the finished painting. However, the
space is similar and the bookcase is the same. Th
use of a wooden panel covered with a white
ground, a wash of color applied with a sponge, an
the actual forms in oil added on top is a technique
based on the oil sketches of Rubens which were
greatly admired at this time. However, Wilkie's
loving attention to detail and his use primarily of
still life relate this more closely to Dutch interiors
and remind one of Zoffany's portrait of *John Cuff*
(no. 39) which precedes it by half a century.
F.C.

Provenance
Wilkie sale, Christie's, London, 30 April 1842, no 606
(A Library)

John Sheepshanks (died 1863)
Given to the Victoria and Albert Museum, 1857

Exhibitions
Paintings and Drawings by Sir David Wilkie, The
National Gallery of Scotland, Edinburgh, 1958, I, no. 16;
II, pl. 9

References
Cunningham, I, 380, 383-86

139
**Going to the Drawing-Room Holyrood House (Study
for the "Entry of George IV into Holyrood House")**
The National Gallery of Canada, Ottawa
Pen and brown ink; 11⅞ x 17¹³⁄₁₆ in.
Inscribed: *D. Wilkie 1822*

In August of 1822 George IV made an official visit
to Edinburgh, landing at Leith and travelling on to
the capital. It was the first visit of a sovereign to
Scotland since that of Charles II in 1650, and it was
a memorable occasion, especially for Wilkie who
was both a Scot and a painter remembering
Rubens' portrayal of the triumphal entry of Marie
de' Medici into Marseilles. Wilkie had been asked
to paint a further work for the collection of George
IV while he was still Prince of Wales, and he
conceived the subject of the preaching of John
Knox at St. Andrews. However, the King requested
that another subject be selected, and Wilkie, like
Turner, travelled to Edinburgh with the plan of
painting an event from the King's visit to Scotland.
His preparations were made carefully, probably
through his friend Sir Walter Scott, who organized
the reception, and Wilkie was on hand in court
dress and powdered hair at Holyrood House to be
received. In a letter to his sister of August 16, he
described the arrival, the fine day, the spectacle
of the procession, and the King alighting in his
brilliant costume, and the officials on hand to meet
him. Wilkie was introduced to the King, and on
numerous occasions he watched or was present
during the royal ceremonies. The selection of the
final subject was made by George IV himself, the

138

moment being his arrival and receiving of the key to the Palace of Holyrood House, with the nobles of the North surrounding.

Wilkie first showed sketches and discussed the matter with Sir Robert Peel on December 15, 1822, but this drawing was probably made before that date in the autumn months. Wilkie carefully studied the architecture, the locale, the portraits of the individuals, and all the peculiarities of northern costume, including tartans, claymores, and dirks, in preparation for the painting whose subject appealed to him because of its dash, variety of character, feathers, splendor, and pomp. The final painting was not presented to the King until 1830.

This sheet is a preparatory drawing closely connected with the final composition, of which two versions are known, one in Holyrood House and a reduced variant in the Scottish National Portrait Gallery, Edinburgh. No. 139 shows a carefully observed and quickly recorded study of the visit of an official party to the Palace from the same spot where the receiving of the key took place. The procession moving to the left, the horse, and the Highlander with shield, who was later moved before the horse, are all used in the final painting. The lady alighting from her carriage has the same headdress as the woman being kissed by the King in Wilkie's pen drawing *King George IV Holding a Drawing-Room* in the Royal Collection, Windsor. Wilkie described the drawing room which he saw at Holyrood House in a letter to his sister of August 23, 1822. But the Windsor drawing is dated October 10, when Wilkie was staying on the Isle of Wight. It gives us the exact moment of the Ottawa drawing.

Numerous studies for the final composition are known in the Ashmolean Museum, Oxford and in other collections, including one in the possession of Villiers David shown in the Wilkie exhibition, 1958, no. 14. There are two other drawings in the Royal Collection, also of 1822, which are closely connected. Wilkie's pen manner, which reveals a

139

study of Rembrandt's graphic art, is shown here at its finest and most complete.
F.C.

Provenance
Wilkie sale, Christie's London, 25 April 1842, no. 68, bt. Nieuwenhuijs *(Going to the Drawing Room Holyrood House)*
P. & D. Colnaghi & Co., London
The National Gallery of Canada, Ottawa, 1954

Exhibitions
Constable to Bacon, Queen's University, Kingston, Ontario, 1962, no. 65

References
Cunningham, II, 82-91, 95-96, 104-06
A. P. Oppé, *English Drawings . . . at Windsor Castle,* London, 1950, nos. 662, 663
T. S. R. Boase, *English Art 1800-1870,* Oxford, 1959, pp. 157-58, pl. 59a.

140

pensioner and a study for Commodore Trunnion.
As far as we know, he did not carry further its
transformation into the character of Trunnion.
Cunningham's feeling that it rose far above a mere
portrait is understandable because of its stylish
and penetrating presentation of character.
However, it remains a portrait. Freshly and swiftly
drawn on the spot, it looks forward to Manet and
Degas in its breadth, vivid color, and power of
technique. It is the most famous of Wilkie's
drawings and shows him, correctly, as one of the
finest of British draftsmen.
F.C.

Provenance
Edward Hawke Locker, Windsor (died 1849)
National Gallery of Scotland, Edinburgh, 1928

Exhibitions
Royal Academy, 1824, no. 445 *(A Study for Commodore
Trunnion, made in Greenwich Hospital)*
British Art, c. 1000-1860, Royal Academy, 1934, no. 1222
Scottish Art, Royal Academy, 1939, no. 763
Portrait Drawings by Scottish Artists 1750-1850, National
Gallery of Scotland, Edinburgh, 1955, no. 86
Paintings and Drawings by Sir David Wilkie, National
Gallery of Scotland, Edinburgh, 1958, I, no. 41, no. 66
Old Master Drawings, P. & D. Colnaghi & Co., London,
1966, no. 85

References
Cunningham, II, 106-07

Reproductions
Engraved in aquatint by F. C. Lewis (1779-1856), 1826

141

140
A Greenwich Pensioner
National Gallery of Scotland
Black chalk and colored washes; 14⁵⁄₁₆ x 9¹⁵⁄₁₆ in.
Inscribed in brown pen: *D. Wilkie, 1823*

Allan Cunningham relates that Wilkie had long
wished to illustrate the character of Commodore
Trunnion from Tobias Smollett's *Peregrine Pickle.*
Having taken the invigorating boat ride from
London to Greenwich, he came upon one of the
old pensioners and realized that this man would
serve for the character. However, Smollett
described Trunnion as a great, if quixotic, warrior
who had lost an eye and also a heel in service.
Wilkie called his drawing a portrait of a Greenwich

141
Study for "The First Ear Ring"
The Art Museum, Princeton University
Black chalk, pencil and watercolor;
12½ x 10¼ in.
Inscribed: *D. Wilkie—1833*

This is the earliest dated sketch for Wilkie's
painting *The First Ear Ring* (Tate Gallery), which
was included in the Royal Academy exhibition of
1835, no. 88, and a second version in 1836, no. 123.

The subject is a scene from everyday life, but in
this period such scenes frequently have an
intellectual basis and are not allowed to remain
pure genre. The painting is a study of the innocent

expression of a young girl, placing it within the tradition of interests of Johann Kaspar Lavater, Petrus Camper, and Sir Charles Bell. In the Academy catalogue of 1836, the painting was accompanied with the line, *"Il faut souffrir pour être belle."* Wilkie's interest was in the expression of coupled vanity and fear of the young and inexperienced child. This early drawing shows her left hand clinging to a cloth which will later become the arm of her mother who will stand behind. In the final composition, her right arm will cross to join the left in a cascade of interlocking shapes of the sort dear to Rubens and his British followers.

Related studies for *The First Ear Ring* include: an oil sketch on panel signed 1835 in the collection of Major A. W. Foster; a composition drawing in The Tate Gallery dated July 3, 1834; a study for the girl's head in The British Museum; and a study for the attendant, formerly in the possession of Messrs. P. & D. Colnaghi, London.
F.C.

References

Not specifically identifiable in the Wilkie sale, Christie's, London, 28 April 1842
Parsons, London, 1928
Dan Fellows Platt, Englewood, New Jersey
Given to The Art Museum, Princeton University, 1928

References

Paintings and Drawings by Sir David Wilkie, The National Gallery of Scotland, Edinburgh, 1958, I, no. 74

142

142
The Orderly of Sir David Baird and Three Companions
Philadelphia Museum of Art, Given by David Keppel
Crayon or soft pencil heightened with orange and white on tan wove paper; 11¼ x 15⅜ in.
Inscribed on the mount: *This drawing is a study of heads for the painting representing the discovery of the body of Tippoo Saib by Sir David Baird / Sir David Wilkie / 37;* verso: head of a man with a moustache representing the pioneer, or military workman, reversed for the same painting.
c. 1835-36

Sir David Baird (1757-1829) was born at Newbyth, Aberdeenshire and entered the British army in 1773. He served in India, South Africa, and Egypt, and was for a time commander-in-chief in Ireland. The painting *Sir David Baird Discovering the Body of Tippoo Sahib,* for which this drawing is a study, depicts an incident in the last war fought against Tippoo Sahib (1753-1799), who led the Indian troops against the British during the 1780s and '90s. In the first Mysore war, the British troops were cut to pieces, and Sir David Baird was severely

wounded in the thigh. With other captives he was imprisoned from 1780 until March 1784 in the fortress of Seringapatam, capital of Mysore, situated on an island in the Cavuery River. During this internment, the prisoners were treated with oriental barbarity, and many were poisoned or tortured to death. In 1799 Baird returned to India as senior brigade commander. On the storming of Seringapatam on May 4, 1799, which Baird led, Tippoo Sahib, now Sultan of Mysore, was killed. Wilkie's painting depicts Baird discovering the Sultan's body beneath a heap of the slain in the fortress where he himself had been cruelly confined years before. Wilkie's source was Theodore Hook's *Life of Baird:* "About dusk, General Baird, in consequence of information he had received at the palace, came with lights to the gate, accompanied by the late killadar of the fort and others, to search for the body of the Sultaun, and after much labour it was found, and brought from under a heap of slain, to the inside of the gate.

The painting was commissioned for 1500 guineas by Sir David's widow. The enormous canvas (138 by 107 in.), now in the Sir David Baird Collection, Edinburgh Castle, was completed in 1838 and exhibited at the Royal Academy in 1839 no. 45. The painting was commissioned in September 1834, when Wilkie was staying at Fern Tower, the home of Lady Baird. In April 1835 he was working on studies for the principal figure, and in August he had made the drawing in chalk on the canvas, delighted with its generous size.

The Philadelphia drawing represents an advanced stage in Wilkie's planning. This study of heads in various attitudes of terror, awestruck fear, and intense fascination is for a group directly to the left of the figure of Baird. In the final composition three of these heads were removed and only the orderly to the left, fixed by the gripping scene of the dead monarch, remained. The relationship of this drawing to the final painting becomes clearer when it is realized that the chin and ear of the man to the right are covered by a blank area which will become the arm and shoulder of Baird himself

This drawing is a study of form, with special reference to the complicated artificial lighting from a torch thrust downward by a Scottish guardsman on the right and by a lantern held by a kneeling man on the left. A watercolor drawing of Baird and the troops with him, in the Witt Collection (no. 3590), Courtauld Institute, London, shows a later stage in the composition, with the two heads directly behind Baird's shoulder omitted and only a suggestion of the upturned head behind the orderly. In the London drawing, the orderly has lost his moustache, but the lighting of the face in the Philadelphia sheet is that to which Wilkie ultimately returned in the painting.

From the first, he planned for the eyes of Baird to look down upon the body of Tippoo Sahib. But in October 1835 he altered the figure of Baird to show him with left arm raised (ordering the removal of the body to the palace), showing more movement and command than in an early sketch in the Royal Scottish Academy where Baird, both arms lowered, is stunned by the scene before him. This alteration, which improved the composition greatly, necessitated uplifting the eyes of the general and giving a downward gaze to the man beside him.

At this same time, Wilkie mentioned in a letter of October 15, 1835 that he had given more action to those around Baird. This must refer to the agitated figures in the Philadelphia drawing. In the winter of 1835-36 Wilkie worked on six major paintings for the opening of the Royal Academy exhibition in April. As a result, he progressed slowly on the immense picture of Tippoo Sahib, which he thought of as an *opus magnum*, like Rembrandt's *Night Watch.* However, in July 1836 he completed the head of Baird. During this period of work on the principal figure, Wilkie could have made studies of the heads surrounding him, and once again, this is a possible moment for the Philadelphia drawing, although the date of October 1835 is more probable. F.C.

Provenance
Wilkie sale, Christie's, London, 28 April 1842, probably no. 20, in the addenda of original studies for the picture of Sir David Baird which included *A Group of Four Heads, Coloured, very fine*
David Keppel (died 1956)
Philadelphia Museum of Art, 1942

References
Theodore Hook, *The Life of . . . Sir David Baird,* London, 1832, I, 218
John Woodward, *British Painting,* London, 1962, pl. 115

143
Josephine and the Fortune Teller
National Gallery of Scotland
Oil on canvas; 83 x 62 in.
Inscribed: *David Wilkie f. 1837*

The Royal Academy catalogue for 1837 appends to the entry for no. 144 the following lines: "When fortune placed a crown on Josephine's head she told me that the event, extraordinary as it was, had been predicted. It is certain she put faith in fortune-tellers—*Burien.*" This antiseptically phrased passage is typical of the style of Louis-Antoine Fauvelet de Bourrienne (1769-1834) whose *Mémoire . . . sur Napoléon,* in which these lines appear, was first published in 1829 and translated into English in 1830. Fauvelet de Bourrienne's matter-of-fact description was scarcely likely to inspire the imagination of our warm-hearted Scot. A more likely source for Wilkie's picture than this multi-volume life of Napoleon is John Memes's *Memoirs of the Empress Josephine,* published in 1831 and reedited many times thereafter. His vivid account tells the prophecy of Josephine's destiny in the first person: "One day, some time before my first marriage while taking my usual walk, I observed a number of negro girls assembled round an old woman, engaged in telling their fortunes. I drew near to observe their proceedings. The old sibyl, on beholding me, uttered a loud exclamation, and almost by force seized my hand. She appeared to be under the greatest agitation . . . 'what read you concerning me in futurity?'—'What do I see in the future? You will not believe me if I speak.'—'Yes, indeed, I assure you. Come my good mother, what am I to fear and hope?'—'You will be married soon; that union will not be happy; you will become a widow, and then—then you will be *Queen of France!' ''*

The fear and hope described by Memes is carefully portrayed by Wilkie who represented the scene in the street arcade of a tavern. Josephine herself is seen in a languishing pose with an abstracted gaze, recalling Prud'hon's portrait in the Louvre. A number of preparatory drawings for the painting are known. A composition study in the City Museum and Art Gallery, Birmingham, is dated 1836. One of Wilkie's most beautiful drawings for the Negro servant is in the collection of the Duke of Buccleuch. Another study for the fortune teller, formerly in the Leslie Wright Collection, Birmingham, is now in the City Museum and Art Gallery, Birmingham.

Although subdued in color, no. 143 possesses the broad and fluid brushwork of Wilkie's late style. Although without his glowing color, it possesses the fluidity of Lawrence's brilliant brushwork and adds to that extended passages with interlocking forms of great rhythmic subtlety, learned from Copley and Rubens.
F.C.

Provenance
John Abel Smith, Dale Park, Chichester, Sussex (died 1871)
Dudley Robert Smith, London (died 1897)
Bequeathed to his daughter, Ada Margarette, wife of Henry Reynolds, Lord Moreton (died 1944)
Capel Moreton, 5th Earl of Ducie, Tortworth Court, Falfield, Gloucestershire (sale, Christie's, London, 17 June 1949, no. 137a, not in printed catalogue)
National Gallery of Scotland, 1949

Exhibitions
Royal Academy, 1837, no. 144
British Institution, London, 1842, no. 12 (lent by John Abel Smith)
Ramsay, Raeburn and Wilkie, National Gallery of Scotland, Edinburgh, 1951, no. 34

The First Hundred Years of the Royal Academy,
Royal Academy, London, 1951-52, no. 47
Paintings and Drawings by Sir David Wilkie, National
Gallery of Scotland, Edinburgh, 1958, no. 107

References
Louis-Antoine Fauvelet de Bourrienne, *Memoirs of
Napoleon Bonaparte,* ed. R. W. Phipps, New York, 1905,
I; IV, 48
John Memes, *Memoirs of the Empress Josephine,*
New York, 1838, p. 21
Cunningham, III, 222
National Gallery of Scotland, *Catalogue of Paintings
and Sculpture,* Edinburgh, 1958, p. 289

143

144

Captain Leigh and His Dragoman

Victor D. Spark
Chalk, pen, wash, watercolor, heightened with
Chinese white; 16⅚₁₆ x 12⅝ in.
1840

David Wilkie left London August 15, 1840 for a
tour of the Near East, in particular the Holy Land,
to see the places where the events recorded in the
Bible actually took place. He travelled by way of
Rotterdam and the Lowlands up the Rhine to
Cologne, to Munich, where he met George Von
Dillis (1759-1841) and proceeded to Vienna. From
there, he travelled down the Danube by steamer
to Constantinople where he arrived in October. In
January 1841 he sailed for Smyrna, Rhodes, the
Holy Land, and Jerusalem, which he approached
with excitement and awe. In April he began his
journey home by way of Alexandria and Malta, and
died on June 1, after the boat had departed from
Gibraltar. The event is recorded in J. M. W. Turner's
Burial of Sir David Wilkie at Sea (Tate Gallery), one
of the most poignant pictures of this era.

Sir David Wilkie

Benjamin Robert Haydon

1786-1846

144

Delacroix travelled to North Africa in 1832, some ten years before Wilkie, and British artists had been travelling to the South Seas and to India for some generations, returning with drawings and paintings of the unusual dress and customs of the people to satisfy their countrymen's curiosity and taste for the unusual. His drawings published in *Wilkie's Sketches in Turkey, Syria, etc.* (1843) are among the finest by any artist who travelled to the Near East and rival those of Delacroix. Wilkie's tour is particularly important for later British painting because he went specifically to the Holy Land to view and to record the people and places where the ancient religious events had occurred. Holman Hunt was to follow in his footsteps some fourteen years later. Wilkie was preceded by the landscapist David Roberts, who traveled through the Holy Land in 1838, and John Frederick Lewis, whom Wilkie met in Constantinople in 1840.
F.C.

Provenance
Wilkie sale, Christie's, London, 29 April 1842, no. 588, bt. Simpson *(Captain Leigh, with his Dragoman)*
Sir George Campbell, Garscube, Glasgow
Victor D. Spark, New York

Exhibitions
Glasgow, 1901, no. 891 (lent by Lady Campbell)

References
Cunningham, III, 336
Lord Gower, p. 116

It is reasonable to identify this drawing with no. 588 in the Wilkie sale of 1842 which is described as "Captain Leigh with his Dragoman, Fine." It was probably drawn on November 11, 1840. On November 10 Wilkie was accompanied by Captain Leigh from his residence in Pera, which is the European quarter, into the old section of Constantinople. The following day, he held a dinner to which Captain Leigh was invited and of which Wilkie wrote in his diary, "passed with the friends in the house a jolly evening." Captain Leigh is shown here with a resplendent saber, smoking a hookah, with his Turkish servant behind, and he may be relaxing after dinner on this very evening.

Haydon was born in Plymouth, Devonshire, the son of a printer and publisher. He had a good education at the grammar school in Plymouth, where he studied Latin and Greek. Later he was also able to read some Italian, and he had some knowledge of French. He read widely among the books in his father's shop, in particular the *Discourses* of Sir Joshua Reynolds, which had a permanent effect in convincing him to pursue history painting. He went to London in 1804 to study at the Royal Academy schools, working there under Henry Fuseli. Sir David Wilkie was his close friend in this early period, but they were to have a permanent rift in a very few years over money borrowed by Haydon, an incident which was paralleled in Haydon's relationship with John Keats.

His first painting at the Academy was *Joseph and Mary Resting on the Road to Egypt* (1806), which was bought by Thomas Hope. This was followed by his first successful commission from Lord Mulgrave for the *Assassination of Dentatus* (Marquess of Normanby, Sandsend), exhibited in 1809. *Dentatus* was improved through Haydon's study of figures from the Parthenon metopes brought by Lord Elgin from Greece and first exhibited in London in 1807. The painting was hung in the octagon room, an anteroom of the Academy exhibition galleries, and this so disturbed Haydon that it remained a continuing source of irritation between him and the Academy, of which he never became a member. Haydon's antipathy was nurtured by the example of James Barry, whose posthumous cause he espoused. Like Barry, he called for governmental patronage of the arts, suggesting in 1812 the ornamentation of the Houses of Parliament with historical subjects and later urged that churches be embellished with works by contemporary artists. Both ideas were to bear fruit, although not for Haydon.

His first two paintings had been unusually large, but he now began to paint on a grandiose scale equal to the largest works of West and of James Ward. In 1814 he completed the *Judgment of Solomon* (J. B. Gold, Richmond, Surrey) which was 130 by 154 inches. *Christ's Triumphal Entry into Jerusalem* (St. George's Seminary, Cincinnati, Ohio, 192 x 228 in.), exhibited in 1820, was one of his largest works and took him six years to complete. These are self-conscious arrangements of figures rather than compositions welded and fused together like those of Rubens on this scale, and they are only slightly less wooden than those of West in the same vein.

After his disaster with the Academy in 1809, Haydon's tendency was not to send works to the annual exhibitions. Such paintings as *Christ's Entry Into Jerusalem* were exhibited privately with an entrance charge in order to raise money. He accompanied his exhibitions, with which he travelled to provincial towns, with elaborate and detailed descriptions. He also gave lectures on art which were later published.

Haydon's most important contributions were in his writings on art theory, his lectures, and his teaching. For example, he was the first to demonstrate verbally, through drawings, and by comparison with other Greek sculptures that the Elgin Marbles represented a central moment in the development of Greek art. His analysis of their style as the establishment of a harmonious balance between a scientific knowledge of human anatomy and the most sophisticated design principles is an evaluation essentially accepted today.

His analysis of Greek sculpture involved the use of new techniques, such as measurement of the sculptures, comparison of proportions, dissection of human specimens to verify anatomical accuracy, and an evaluation of psychological responses as they relate to pose and arrangement. This contribution to connoisseurship is imposing and was climaxed by his pamphlet of 1816 *On the Judgement of Connoisseurs Being Preferred to that of Professional Men—The Elgin Marbles, etc.* This pamphlet was an attack on Richard Payne Knight, whose taste had been nurtured on the ideals of Winckelmann, Mengs, and Gavin Hamilton, and who was not prepared to grasp completely the dynamic 5th-century sculptures from the Parthenon. Apart from his art criticism, Haydon kept a detailed diary of his daily activities, and the memorable passages culled from these interminable entries by Tom Taylor form one of the most moving biographies of the 19th century.

The six years without income when he was painting *Christ's Entry into Jerusalem* forced Haydon to incur heavy debts, and he endured his first bankruptcy and imprisonment in 1823. This was one of the great shocks of his life, and his art and ideas were never so forceful or so penetrating thereafter. Although Haydon continued to paint, producing a work almost every two years and subsequently exhibiting it, he never again achieved the power of his *Solomon* and *Jerusalem.*

His later works are generally historical and include *Alexander Taming Bucephalus* (1826-27, Petworth House), *The Raising of Lazarus* (1820-23, Tate Gallery), and *Marcus Curtius Leaping into the Gulf* (1836-42, Royal Albert Museum, Exeter). However, his limited excursions into the field of humorous genre were highly successful. In 1827 he painted the *Mock Election* (Royal Collections), and in 1829 *Punch or May Day* (Tate Gallery). These are painted with a liveliness and freshness much more in keeping with his energetic and impressionable temperament, and they reveal his true talent. Despite the fact that there was a great taste for these works in this period, Haydon did not pursue this kind of painting because he did not consider it of the highest order.

Especially after the burning of the Houses of Parliament in October 1834, he recommended th project of decorating the new building with frescoes. Believing firmly that he was almost the only artist in England prepared to paint the huma figure on the scale required and with the kind of subjects desired, he studied fresco technique an was convinced that he would receive an importan part of the commission. He submitted a cartoon to the competition of 1843 with a subject from Milto *Adam and Eve.* Haydon was especially astoundec at the number of young artists who appeared in strength in the cartoon competitions. In the presence of their carefully drawn and vigorous compositions with numerous figures, his own styl and Miltonic subject appeared old-fashioned, and he lost. It was a shattering personal and financial blow since he had hoped to pay his debts with the new income. In June 1846 he committed suicide by attempting to shoot himself and then by cutting his throat.

F.C.

Bibliography
Benjamin Robert Haydon, *Lectures on Painting and Design,* 2 vols., London, 1844-46
Tom Taylor, ed., *The Life of Benjamin Robert Haydon,* 3 vols., London, 1853
Benjamin R. Haydon, *Correspondence and Table-Talk,* ed., Frank W. Haydon, 2 vols., London, 1876
Clarke Olney, *Benjamin Robert Haydon, Historical Painter,* Athens, Georgia, 1952
Willard Bissell Pope, ed., *The Diary of Benjamin Robert Haydon,* 5 vols., Cambridge, Mass., 1960-63
Frederick Cummings, "B. R. Haydon and His School," *JWCI,* XXVI, 1963, pp. 367-80
Frederick Cummings, "Nature and the Antique in B. R. Haydon's *Assassination of Dentatus,*" *JWCI,* XXV, 1962, pp. 145-57
Frederick Cummings, "Phidias in Bloomsbury: B. R. Haydon's Drawings of the Elgin Marbles," *Burlington,* CVI, July 1964, pp. 323-28

145

145
Head of the Horse of Selene
Trustees of The British Museum
Black and white chalk on grey paper;
21⅞ x 29¹⁵⁄₁₆ in.
Inscribed: *1809*

The sculptures from the Parthenon were brought from Athens to England under the auspices of the seventh Earl of Elgin, who was Ambassador to Constantinople from 1799. Greece was still in Turkish possession, and Elgin was able to remove and transfer the sculptures which are now in The British Museum. They were exhibited at Gloucester House in Park Lane from June 1807 until the summer of 1811. Haydon was granted permission to make drawings in May 1808. He was followed by Benjamin West, who worked there in September 1808, and preceded by the architect Charles R. Cockerell, who drew from the sculptures as early as August 1806. The sculptures were purchased from Lord Elgin by the British Government in 1816.

The Parthenon sculptures were the most important group of Greek sculptures brought to Western Europe, but their artistic merit and their central

place in the development of Greek art was first made clear through the writings of Haydon. This is one of the central achievements in the history of connoisseurship and Haydon's outstanding personal contribution within the history of art. His drawings of the sculptures, which have not been exhibited since his death and which have rarely been reproduced, were one of the devices which enabled him to perceive the special qualities of the sculptures. This technique was supplemented through measurement, calculation of proportions, and anatomical dissection.

In no. 145 he concentrates on one of the best preserved fragments in the collection, the *Head of the Horse of Selene,* formerly at the right end of the east pediment of the Parthenon. He was fascinated by the protrusion of the eye from the socket and greatly intrigued by the inclusion of detail, the folds of skin in the eyelid, and the sense of alternating bony and fleshy qualities. Checking this against his observation of a real horse's head, he concluded that the Greeks had made anatomical dissections to obtain their information and to make their works follow the rationale of nature, yet combining their observations with refined compositional principles and an enthusiastic grasp of the animal's energy, alertness, and power. Actually, George Stubbs had come to this realization from quite a different direction, and other artists were in the process of doing the same, but the authority of Greek sculpture gave the discovery enormous importance for the early 19th-century artists who were to follow.
F.C.

Provenance
Benjamin Robert Haydon, London (died 1846)
Frederick Wordsworth Haydon, London
Purchased by The British Museum, London, 1881

References
Laurence Binyon, *Catalogue of Drawings by British Artists . . . in the British Museum,* London, 1900, II, 277
Frederick Cummings, "Phidias in Bloomsbury: B. R. Haydon's Drawings of the Elgin Marbles," *Burlington,* CVI no. 106, p. 325 fig. 17, p. 327

146

146
George IV and the Duke of Wellington on the Field of Waterloo
Board of Commissioners, Royal Hospital, Chelsea
Oil on canvas; 68 x 80 in.
1842-45

Haydon conceived the subject of the Duke of Wellington visiting the field of Waterloo in January 1842. The subject and the composition, to a degree, derive from his earlier painting *Wellington Musing on the Field of Waterloo* (1838-39, St. George's Hall, Liverpool). He was not able to begin work seriously on the composition until January 8, 1844. On November 30 he obtained Wellington's hat from his valet, took it home in a hatbox and painted it in. He also asked for a pair of his boots, an entire suit, and Wellington's cravat in order to give authenticity to his work. These were promised to him by the valet. In November he studied Rubens' treatment of landscape at The National Gallery, probably from the view of the *Château de Steen,* and was impressed particularly with the treatment of weeds, plants, and flesh. The painting was finished by December 4, 1844.

1786-1863

The event represented is imaginary and was conceived by Haydon as having occurred some seven years after the battle of Waterloo. The Duke of Wellington, whom Haydon revered, is seen behind, pointing to the battlefield and describing the placement of troops. George IV, who had died in 1830, accompanies him, wearing the cross of St. George, patron of the Knights of the Garter. Haydon wished to make George IV as dandy-like and as dashing as possible, in keeping with a prevailing view of his character. The rank growth of weeds, prominently placed on the left and even more luxuriant than those in a painting by Rubens, suggest the passage of time and the afterlife of battlefields.
F.C.

References
Clarke Olney, *Benjamin Robert Haydon, Historical Painter,* Athens, Georgia, 1952, pp. 244, 287
Willard Bissell Pope, ed., *The Diary of Benjamin Robert Haydon,* Cambridge, Mass., 1963, V, 124, 340-43, 385, 398-402, 596 no. 121

Mulready was born in Ireland, but his family moved to London when he was five years old. He learned to draw from the sculptor Thomas Banks, and at age fourteen he entered the Royal Academy schools. He was also one of a group of young artists who worked under the watercolorist John Varley. Others of the group included John Linnell and William Henry Hunt. Mulready was apparently the most talented, and the loyalties of the group went to him rather than their teacher; what they held in common was an almost reverent respect for the details of nature, an interest not conspicuously shared by Varley. Before he was eighteen years old Mulready had married Varley's sister. Although they had four sons, the marriage was notoriously unhappy, and they separated a few years later. In later life Mulready lived alone, with apparently few interests other than his art.

Mulready's first exhibited works were landscapes. In 1809 he began to exhibit genre scenes, and these, particularly scenes of children's activities, remained his specialty throughout his life. He was a devotee of boxing, and he frequently depicted boys quarreling or fighting. His early genre pictures were strongly influenced by Wilkie and, like Wilkie's, they were highly popular. In the winter of 1815-16 he was elected both Associate and full Academician. In the 1820s Mulready's style began to change, and his later works are painted in a light palette and with a precision of line that is quite individual. Mulready all his life was active as a drawing master. In his later years he regularly attended the life class of the Royal Academy, and

his academy studies form an important part of his *oeuvre.* In 1843 he published a series of illustrations to *The Vicar of Wakefield,* which provided the basis for several of his own pictures and those of some of his colleagues (cf. no. 227).

Mulready had an important influence on the Pre-Raphaelites, who admired both his brilliant coloring and his draftsmanship. To Holman Hunt he "was most painstaking and student-like to the last, and single-handed had striven to reach an unattainable perfection," although Hunt criticized his taste for "Dresden-china prettiness." The basic account of his life was written by F. G. Stephens, one of the original members of the Brotherhood. In 1855 Mulready was represented by a large group of works in the *Exposition Universelle* in Paris, where he was made a Knight of the Legion of Honor. His admirers considered him England's counterpart to Ingres.
A.S.

Bibliography
James Dafforne, *Pictures by William Mulready, R. A.,* London, n.d.
F. G. Stephens, *Memorials of William Mulready,* London, 1867
William Mulready: 1786-1863, City Art Gallery, Bristol, 1964 (exhibition catalogue, edited with introduction by Arnold Wilson)

147

The Mall, Kensington Gravel Pits
Victoria and Albert Museum, London
Oil on canvas; 14 x 19¼ in.
c. 1811

In 1811 Mulready moved to Robinson's Row,
Kensington Gravel Pits. His neighbor there, the
landscape painter Augustus Callcott, procured for
him a commission to paint this picture and a
companion, *Near the Mall,* which is also in the
Victoria and Albert Museum. The area has since
been entirely rebuilt. According to Stephens,
no. 147 is partly an accurate depiction of the Mall
and partly composed, and it is said to show the
house in which Mulready lived. The patron declined
to accept either picture, apparently because they
were too literal, and Callcott himself refused to
recommend them. This was enough to discourage
Mulready from exhibiting the pictures, and he
only sent them to the Royal Academy over
thirty years later.

The picture's sobriety of coloring and its
composition primarily in terms of masses of light
and dark are characteristic of Mulready's early
work. Although the effect is broad, the picture is
painted with small detail, as can be seen in the
bricks of the wall to the right, and it reflects the
concern for precise fact that Mulready shared with
Linnell and William Hunt. The Dutch
17th-century derivation of Mulready's early
style is obvious, although in his genre paintings
this came largely via Wilkie, and in landscape
possibly from Old Crome, whose works (for
example, the *Blacksmith's Shop near Hingham* in
the Philadelphia Museum of Art, exhibited at the
Royal Academy in 1808) frequently show
comparable combinations of genre figures and
dilapidated buildings and are similarly composed
in light and dark. Comparison between the two
artists demonstrates Mulready's greater discipline
and his crisp precision of handling. The boys in
the foreground are of the type which populates
Mulready's early genre subjects. A preliminary
drawing in pen and sepia ink is in the Victoria and

147

Albert Museum.
A.S.

Provenance
Said to have been commissioned by a Mr. Horley,
who rejected it
Mr. Welbank (Mulready's doctor)
John Sheepshanks (bequest to the Victoria and
Albert Museum, 1857)

Exhibitions
Royal Academy, 1844, no. 330
*Pictures, Drawings and Sketches of William Mulready,
R. A.,* Society of Arts, London, 1848, no. XXV
*Pictures, Drawings, Sketches of the Late William
Mulready, R. A.,* South Kensington Museum, London,
1864, no. 34
*The First Hundred Years of the Royal Academy:
1769-1868,* Royal Academy, London, 1951-52, no. 228
William Mulready, City Art Gallery, Bristol, 1964 no. 6

References
Art Union, 1844, p. 161
Dafforne, pp. 6, 35-36
Stephens, pp. 64, 66-68, 118
Colonel M. H. Grant, *The Old English Landscape
Painters,* Leigh-on-Sea, 1960, VII, 573-75, pl. 305,
ill. no. 616

148

148
The Sonnet
Victoria and Albert Museum, London
Oil on panel; 14 x 12 in.
c. 1839

The boy has written a sonnet and now bends over to see the look in the girl's eyes as she reads it. Mulready prepared a full-size chalk study for no. 148 which is reproduced by Stephens (National Gallery of Ireland). This accords with his later practice, begun in the 1820s, of basing his pictures on careful drawings, rather than painting at once from the object. The resultant refined inventiveness of his compositions is no place more evident than in no. 148. Arnold Wilson has suggested that the

figures are adapted from Michelangelo's *Jeremiah* on the Sistine ceiling. The crossed legs of the man and the hand across the mouth of the girl would both depend upon the prophet's pose.

The bright colors are thinly painted over a white ground so that the luminosity of the ground is allowed to show through. Mulready's technique was to stipple his flesh tones and then to glaze over them to gain smoothness of finish. In many places the paint is so thin that the pencil lines of the underdrawing are visible. The cartoon shows that Mulready had intended to paint foliage before the tree trunks on the right, and its outlines are still visible in the painting itself. The thinness of the background and a similarly careful composition appear in *Open Your Mouth and Shut Your Eyes,* another small painting of approximately the same size which Mulready also exhibited at the Royal Academy in 1839 and which also is now in the Victoria and Albert Museum. John Sheepshanks, who commissioned no. 148, was a wealthy cloth manufacturer from Leeds who retired to London and began to collect contemporary British paintings. He was Mulready's chief patron, and as a result of his bequest, Mulready is exceptionally well represented in the Victoria and Albert Museum. A.S.

Provenance
Painted for John Sheepshanks (bequest to the Victoria and Albert Museum, 1857)

Exhibitions
Royal Academy, 1839, no. 129
Pictures, Drawings and Sketches of William Mulready, R. A., Society of Arts, London, 1848, no. LI
Pictures, Drawings, Sketches of the Late William Mulready, R. A., South Kensington Museum, London, 1864, no. 80
British Art 1000-1860, Royal Academy, London, 1934, no. 559
La Peinture Anglaise, Louvre, Paris, 1938, no. 97
William Mulready, City Art Gallery, Bristol, 1964, no. 6

References
"On the Size of Works of Art," *Art Union,* 1839, p. 81
"Stanzas . . . Suggested by Mulready's Picture

The Sonnet," *Art Union,* 1840, p. 164
"The Sheepshanks Collection," *Art Journal,* 1857, p. 240
Dafforne, pp. 29-30
Stephens, pp. 92, 101, 112, 119, ill. (of cartoon) opp. p. 118
F. Feuillet de Conches, "Mulready: Peintre de Genre, de l'Academy Royale," *L'Artiste,* XVIII (nouvelle periode), 1883, pp. 250-51
Raymond Lister, *Victorian Narrative Paintings,* London, 1966, p. 36, pl. 3

Reproductions
Engraved by J. C. Armytage, *Art Journal,* 1876, opp. p 136

149
Seated Nude with Snake
Victoria and Albert Museum, London
Red and black chalk; 18¾ x 14 in.
After 1840

During the last twenty years or so of his life, Mulready made numerous academy studies of nudes. He regularly attended both the life school at the Royal Academy and a private life academy in Kensington. Most of these drawings are elaborately wrought in a technique of red and black chalks, as seen in no. 149. F. G. Stephens calculated that Mulready worked on a single drawing from the life two hours a night, six nights a week, for two weeks, the normal time a pose was held at the Royal Academy, and that with additional work at home, he probably devoted as much as fifty hours of work to one drawing.

Mulready's interest in the nude led him to make his last two important pictures both scenes of women bathing which, however, were not so much admired as his drawings. During Mulready's lifetime, several of his life studies were purchased by the Department of Science and Art to be used as examples in art schools, and the Redgraves pronounced them among "the greatest works of the kind by the greatest masters," which would lay the foundation for better drawing in the British school.

The serpent in no. 149 seems to be the product of

1787-1849

149

William Etty, seventh child of a miller and baker, was apprenticed to Robert Peck, publisher of the Hull Packet, a weekly newspaper, when he was eleven years old. He remained for the next seven years working as a typesetter. During his apprenticeship, he used his spare time for reading and drawing, and when it was terminated, he moved to London to prepare himself for student membership in the Royal Academy. Fuseli accepted him in 1806 as a probationer, a year later as a full member, and in the same year he became Lawrence's pupil for a brief time and continued to revere him as his master. By 1811 he was exhibiting regularly, beginning with a *Sappho* and a *Telemachus Rescuing Antiope* at the Royal Academy.

The death of Etty's uncle, a banker, in 1809, left him in comfortable circumstances, and his life afterwards was devoted almost exclusively to his art. He was able to travel to Paris in 1815 with a wave of foreign visitors who wished to see the treasures from all parts of Europe brought together by Napoleon. A year later, he went on to Italy going only as far as Florence. Stopping in Paris on his return, he studied for a few weeks in the studio of Jean-Baptiste Regnault (1784-1829). From 1822 to 1824 he travelled on the continent, spending a period of time in Rome and seven months in Venice. He was in Paris in 1830 during the July Revolution, and his last years, which were economically quite comfortable, allowed him to travel frequently. In 1840 he was in Holland and Belgium, investigating schools of art, just after his appointment to the

Council of the Normal School of Design, and in 1841 he travelled to Antwerp, Ghent, and Bruges. He embarked on his last trip to the continent in 1843, going to Orléans in order to prepare a series of three paintings from the life of Joan of Arc.

Etty, a retiring man with an asthmatic and rheumatic frame, and one who was the victim of an unhappy love affair, was devoted to the human figure. In the tradition of the Venetians and Rubens, his pictures are largely studies of the semi-nude or nude. His London rooms were filled with prints after Raphael, Rubens, and Poussin. In fact, he devoted the whole of his career to the continuous, almost obsessive production of studies and large groupings of figures in which the literary element is incidental to the arrangement of human forms. Even after he became a member of the Royal Academy in 1828, he refused to cease his studies at the life school. Only late in his life did he take up seriously the genre of still life and landscape.

It is his concentration on formal, to the exclusion of literary values that makes Etty a surprisingly modern artist and relates him closely to the French School of painters. A work such as *Pluto Carrying Off Proserpine* (collection I. Oscar Herner) is like the large machines of Delacroix, and his *Wood Nymphs Sleeping* and *Satyr Bringing Flowers* (formerly Munro Collection) anticipate Courbet. In these works there is almost no attempt at psychological penetration which might give motivation, but rather an obsessive study and restudy of forms. In this, he looks forward to Cézanne. As William Charles Macready, the actor whose portrait he painted, wrote on April 7, 1846 of his exceptional interest in formal values, "He is *revelling* in colour and in form."

In 1843 Prince Albert gave him a commission for one of the frescoes in the Garden Pavilion on the grounds of Buckingham Palace. The subjects were taken from Milton's *Comus,* and the composition is known to us from his painting *Circe and the Sirens Three* (Art Gallery of Western Australia, Perth). This venture under royal patronage was

a half-hearted attempt to make a straightforward academy study into a picture of Eve. A version or copy of no. 149, also with a snake, is in the Lady Lever Art Gallery in Port Sunlight. Yet another life study of a seated female figure with a snake, dated 8-13 August 1842, is in The Tate Gallery and was included in the Mulready exhibition of 1864 at South Kensington.   A.S.

Provenance
John Sheepshanks (bequest to the Victoria and Albert Museum, 1857)

References
Richard and Samuel Redgrave, *A Century of Painters of the English School,* London, 1866, II, 320-24
Stephens, pp. 120-22

singularly unsuccessful, partially because of Etty's lack of experience in working with fresco; his work was later painted over with a composition by William Dyce. Nevertheless, Etty was an extremely popular artist in his day, amassing a fortune of £17,000 by 1849. His particular patrons were the increasingly wealthy class of merchants and industrialists which included men like Joseph Gillot, the manufacturer of pens.

F.C.

Bibliography
William Etty, Arts Council, London
1849, pp. 13, 37-40
Alexander Gilchrist, *Life of William Etty, R. A.,* 2 vols., London, 1855
William Gaunt and F. Gordon Roe, *Etty and the Nude,* Leigh-on-Sea, 1943
James M. Biggins, *Etty and York,* York, 1949
William Etty, Arts Council, London, 1955 (catalogue compiled by Dennis Farr)
Dennis Farr, *William Etty,* London, 1958

150
Self Portrait
City of Manchester Art Galleries
Oil on panel, painted oval; 16⅞ x 13⅛ in.
1825

According to Gaunt and Roe, no. 150 was painted in 1825 when Etty was 38, immediately after he returned from his trip to France and Italy. The note in the *Art Journal* on the engraving by C. W. Wass tells that the painting was made for his mother. Placing the head in an oval and emphasizing the profile, Etty produced the effect of a carved gem, or an ancient coin or medal. The result is a type like Gavin Hamilton's portrait of *William Hamilton of Bangour* (no. 10). Although the costume does

150

not have antique draperies, the reference to ancient forms is present. New is the richness of color and contrasting light and shadow. The red and blue cravat combine with rich and creamy flesh tones, set off by black hair, which was not Etty's natural coloring, to produce a Venetian sumptuousness of light. This highly individual presentation of the sitter was learned from Gainsborough and Lawrence. It cloaks him in a world of poetic imagination which uses the shadow and color of the Venetians, which Etty considered the triumph of modern art, combined with antique form to create a fusion of ancient and modern that would have pleased critics like Augustus von Schlegel.

A replica, painted for Charles Etty, the artist's

brother, is in the collection of Thomas H. Etty, Leidschendam, Holland, and a free copy is in the collection of J. Lunn, Bradford, Yorkshire. A version in the Fogg Museum, Cambridge, Massachusetts, appears to be a studio copy. Two other self portraits painted about 1843-45 are in the City Art Gallery, York, and in the National Portrait Gallery, London.

F.C.

Provenance
Collection of the artist
Sir Joseph Whitworth, Bt.
Presented to the Manchester Corporation, 1882

Exhibitions
William Etty Retrospective, Society of Arts, London, 1849, no. LXXVII
Royal Jubilee, Manchester, 1887, no. 672
William Etty Retrospective, City Art Gallery, York, 1911, no. 81
British Art, City Art Gallery, Manchester, 1934, no. 658
William Etty Centenary, City Art Gallery, York, 1949, no. 50
William Etty, Arts Council of Great Britain, London, 1955, no. 12
British Self Portraits, Arts Council of Great Britain, London, 1962, no. 73

References
Art Journal, 1849, p. 68
Gaunt and Roe, 1943, p. 113
Dennis Farr, pp. 49, 165, nos. 152a-g

Reproductions
Engraved by C. W. Wass, 1849

151

151
Reclining Male Nude Leaning on a Staff
The Art Museum, Princeton University
Oil on canvas; 25 x 30 in.
c. 1825

Throughout his life, Etty made oil sketches at the Academy from the nude figure. This study is unusually precise and highly finished. Seldom are his colors so restrained and at the same time so delicate and fresh as in this example. The pose recalls that of the *Ilissus* (British Museum) from the west pediment of the Parthenon. Its relationship with this sculpture, its extreme naturalism, and the relatively tight manner of handling the paint all suggest an early date. It is perhaps closest in treatment to Etty's *Prometheus* (Lady Lever Art Gallery, Port Sunlight), for which the same model could have served.
F.C.

Provenance
Hugh Chisholm
Paul Magriel
The Art Museum, Princeton University, 1961

Exhibitions
William Etty-Atkinson Grimshaw, Durlacher Brothers, New York, Rhode Island School of Design, Providence, Rhode Island, 1961, no. 18

152
Venus and Her Satellites (The Toilet of Venus)
(There Beauty's Lovely Goddess Smiles) etc.
Ponce Art Museum, The Luis A. Ferré Foundation
Oil on panel; 30½ x 42½ in.
c. 1835

Venus is shown winding pearls into her hair while she is being dressed by numerous attendants. One ties her sandal, another holds a shield which will act as a mirror, still others, personifying the Three Graces, stand to the right, holding a crown of flowers. Mars, asleep on a couch, is seen from the back. His sword has fallen on the floor and is covered with flowers. Beside him stands a pot of laurel. On the right, a poet plays a cithara, adding the delights of song to the appeals to other senses. The scene occurs before the portico of a Tuscan Doric temple. The columns of the temple surround the figure of the goddess Athena, who is in shadow and thoroughly imprisoned by the forest of columns, a phantom in this world of sensuous delight dominated by the goddess of love. The white garment of Venus and the pot of laurel signify her chastity and purity. The sleeping Mars, whose sword is covered with flowers, indicates that war is lulled into sleep by her powers. Even reason is put in the shade by the triumph of Venus, who is here goddess of all the senses. In January 1835 Etty wrote of the darkness hanging on the cold and heartless London winter. Certain of his pictures seem almost to have been painted to dispel those damp mists. This was one of his favorite pictures, embodying the grace and

abundance of Italian art and the abandonment of Venice to color and delicious warmth, qualities which Etty most admired. It includes a plethora of objects, each of which is a delight in its own right, and adds pink, amethyst, and yellow colors, which embody the sensuous delight and sunshine that Etty sought in the dark London winter.

A smaller version of this composition, a copy, judging from a photograph, is in the City Art Gallery, York. A study for the group of the Three Graces is in The Metropolitan Museum of Art, New York. F.C.

Provenance
Rev. Edward Pryce Owen (purchased from the artist 1835)
Hugh D. Owen
Antony Gibbs (by 1888)
Sir Morville Nathaniel Wraxall (died 1898)
Frost & Reed, Ltd., London, February 1955
Anthony Devas (sale, Christie's, London, 16 July 1965, no. 94)
Ponce Art Museum, 1965

Exhibitions
Royal Academy, 1835, no. 94
National Exhibition, Leeds, 1868, no. 1191 (lent by Hugh D. Owen)
Old Masters, Royal Academy, London, 1878, no. 275 (lent by Hugh D. Owen)
A Century of British Art, 1737-1837, Grosvenor Gallery, London, 1888, no. 247 (lent by Antony Gibbs, as *Disrobing of Venus*)
International Exhibition, Glasgow, 1888, no. 203 (lent by Antony Gibbs)
Guildhall Exhibition, London, 1892, no. 91, reproduced in supplement, facing p. 52 (lent by Antony Gibbs, as *Venus Disrobing*)

References
William Etty, "Autobiography," *Art Journal,* XI, 1849, pp. 13, 40
Alexander Gilchrist, *Life of William Etty, R. A.,* London, 1855, II, 30-32, 337
William Etty, Arts Council of Great Britain, London, 1955, no. 42
Dennis Farr, *William Etty,* London, 1958, pp. 73-74, 156, cat. no. 100, pl. 56
Julius S. Held, *Museo de Arte de Ponce, Fundación Luis A. Ferré, Catalogue I, Paintings of the European and American Schools,* Ponce, 1965, pp. 61-62

1789-1854

Martin came from a peripatetic North-of-England family. He was the youngest of four brothers who achieved among them a remarkable amount of notoriety. His eldest brother William was an indefatigable inventor and pamphleteer who proclaimed himself "Philosophical Conqueror of All Nations" and ended his days wandering the streets of Newcastle, carrying a homemade gong and wearing a tortoiseshell helmet. Another brother, Jonathan, set fire to York Minster, destroying the medieval roof of the choir, and spen the rest of his life in Bethlem Hospital. John Martin, himself, acquired the nickname of "Mad Martin," although he does not seem to have share his brother's actual insanity. He was, however, an inventor as well as a painter. Among his invention were an Elastic Iron Ship, proposals for lighthouse and mine safety, and ambitious projects for London's water supply and sewage disposal. Man of these seem to have been quite sensible; a Metropolitan Sewage Manure Company, initiated by Martin, was chartered in 1846 by Act of Parliament.

As an artist, Martin had some slight training from an Italian painter in Newcastle, Boniface Musso. In 1806 he went to London, and during the next five or six years he supported himself off and on as a glass painter. He first exhibited a picture at the Royal Academy in 1811. In 1814 his *Clytie,* which he sent to the Academy, was ruined when a Academician spilt a pot of varnish over it. As a result Martin became a lifelong foe of the Academ Although he continued to exhibit there occasionally, he was, along with Haydon, one of its bitterest critics in the Parliamentary hearings of 1836.

Martin's specialty was scale: tiny figures in vast landscapes or architectural complexes which are usually being torn apart by cosmic disturbance. The chief sources for these pictures are early Turners such as *The Fifth Plague of Egypt* of 1800 (Indianapolis) or *The Destruction of Sodom* of about 1805 (Tate Gallery). They may also have been influenced by the architectural fantasies of Piranesi and of the Englishman, Joseph Michael Gandy. Martin's first great success was *Joshua Commanding the Sun to Stand Still,* shown at the Royal Academy in 1816, and he followed it in the 1820s with a series of paintings of spectacular catastrophes, which attracted huge popular acclaim but considerably less enthusiasm from artists and critics.

In the 1820s Martin turned his attention to engravings, partly in an attempt to reach a wider public, partly out of a feeling that his paintings were not well displayed at the Royal Academy and other places of exhibition. He published engravings both after his exhibited pictures and of independent compositions, including series of illustrations of *Paradise Lost* and of the Bible. Circulation of these prints brought Martin a much wider reputation than he could have gained by his paintings alone. In France his name became a synonym for the sublime, and he had a strong influence on such diverse artists as Gustave Doré and Thomas Cole.

In the last three years of his life, Martin painted a trilogy of large pictures of *The Last Judgement* (Tate Gallery and collection of Mrs. Robert Frank). After the artist's death, these were engraved and sent on an extended exhibition tour that carried them to America and lasted into the 1870s. By the end of the century, however, Martin's great reputation had just about evaporated. Many of his pictures have disappeared, so that he is better known from his prints, and only since World War II

has there been a serious revival of interest in his work.
A.S.

Bibliography
Ruthven Todd, "The Imagination of John Martin," in his *Tracks in the Snow: Studies in English Science and Art,* London, 1946, pp. 94-122
Thomas Balston, *John Martin, 1789-1854: His Life and Works,* London, 1947
Jean Seznac, *John Martin en France,* London, 1964

153
The Seventh Plague of Egypt
Museum of Fine Arts, Boston. Francis Welch Fund
Oil on canvas; 57 x 84½ in.
Inscribed: *J. Martin 1823*

The picture was shown in 1824 at the opening exhibition of the Society of British Artists, which had been founded as a rival to the Royal Academy. Martin's painting was the center of attraction, although he had not become a member of the new Society.

The subject is described in Exodus 9:23: "And Moses stretched forth his rod toward heaven: and the Lord sent thunder and hail, and the fire ran along upon the ground; and the Lord rained hail upon the land of Egypt." Turner had exhibited a picture of the same subject at the Royal Academy in 1800, mistitling it *The Fifth Plague of Egypt* (Indianapolis).

Scenes of Biblical catastrophes were enormously popular in the early 19th century. Not only did they provide spectacular extravaganzas, as they still do in the movies, they also embodied one of the most central of romantic themes: the smallness and helplessness of man before the forces of the universe. In addition, they corresponded with prevailing scientific thought about the history of the world. The discovery of the fossils of extinct species and the excavation of buried cities of the past were taken as proof that biblical disasters such as the Flood had indeed

taken place. According to the theory, appropriately termed "catastrophism," the earth took form not by gradual evolution but by a series of violent cataclysms corresponding to the biblical disorders. One of the leading proponents of this theory, the eminent French paleontologist Baron Cuvier, was interested enough in Martin's depictions to visit his studio several times, and he complimented Martin on the scientific accuracy of his *Deluge.* Martin was also friendly with another geologist, Gideon Mantell, and under his influence painted a picture of the prehistoric Iguanadon, which was engraved as the frontispiece of Mantell's book, *The Wonders of Geology.*

The elaboration of the architecture is characteristic of Martin and is similar to that of his *Fall of Babylon* of five years before. In *The Seventh Plague* the detail is Egyptian, and there are pyramids in the background, while in *The Fall of Babylon* can be seen the hanging gardens and a ziggurat beyond. Balston has pointed out that Martin repeated the same compositional scheme, with even more grandiose architecture, in *The Fall of Nineveh,* which he exhibited privately in 1828. The architectural emphasis in these pictures may have been inspired by such pictures as Turner's *Decline of the Carthaginian Empire,* exhibited in 1817 (Tate Gallery); however, Turner's most imposing architectural confections came only in the 1830s in such pictures as *Caligula's Palace and Bridge* and *Regulus Leaving Carthage* (Royal Academy 1831 and 1837, both Tate Gallery), and these probably reflect an equal awareness of the inventions of Martin. Martin's long colonnades also suggest the regency architecture of John Nash but, again, Nash's structure most akin to Martin in feeling is Carlton House Terrace which was only begun in 1827. So, if there is any question of influence, it may be that of painter upon architect.
A.S.

Provenance
John George Lambton (later Earl of Durham), Lambton Castle, 1825, and family descent (sold, Lambton Castle, 18 April 1932)

[handwritten annotation: Terrible in color, stage-setting (scenic fallacy) linear patterning, much like Turner of photo, line giving dim picture]

153

P. & D. Colnaghi & Co., London
Museum of Fine Arts, Boston, 1960

Exhibitions
Society of British Artists, London, 1824, no. 22 *(The Seventh Plague in Egypt,* with a quotation from Exodus 9:22-24 and 26)
British Institution, London, 1825, no. 119 (lent by J. G. Lambton)
Art Treasures of the United Kingdom, Manchester, 1857, no. 422 (lent by the Earl of Durham)
North-East Coast Exhibition, Gateshead, 1929

References
Balston, pp. 77-79, 275
D. Dunham, "A Footnote to the History of Egyptology," *American Research Center in Egypt, Inc., Newsletter,* 42, July 1961

Reproductions
Engraved in mezzotint in Martin's *Illustrations of the Bible,* 1835

154
View of Shepherd's Bush and the Grounds of Norlands
Smith College Museum of Art, Gift of Malcolm Stearns, Jr.
Watercolor; 6½ x 9⁹⁄₁₆ in.
Inscribed: *J. Martin, 1836*

Shepherd's Bush is part of Hammersmith, in western London. The area is now built up, but before the middle of the 19th century it still consisted largely of open country. From his home in Allsop Terrace, near Baker Street, Martin would make sketching excursions into the nearby countryside. According to his son, Hanger Hill, which is slightly beyond Shepherd's Bush, was Martin's chief sketching ground.

Martin is unusual among English landscape painters in that his imagination, not natural scenery provided the meat and potatoes of his art. Although he did go on occasional sketching tours, he was essentially a city-dweller whose chief contact with nature came from one-day visits to the suburbs. His fame rested on his grandiose inventions, and

1790-1864

154

his watercolors from nature have received little attention; they are not mentioned at all in most histories of English watercolor painting. Although Martin's tight, almost niggling, technique is far from the breadth and freedom of the most admired English watercolorists, his watercolors are often quite lyrical, and the smokestack in the distance of no. 154 shows a recognition, generally absent from the work of his contemporaries, of the transformations that the industrial revolution was wreaking upon the look of the countryside.
A.S.

Provenance
Charles Scarisbrick, Lancashire
Roland, Browse & Delbanco, London
Malcolm Stearns, Jr., Haddam, Mass.

Exhibitions
One Hundred Years of English Landscape Drawing,
Busch-Reisinger Museum, Cambridge, Mass., 1960,
no. 30
English Landscape Painters, Phoenix Art Museum, 1961
Romanticism, Agnes Etherington Art Center,
Queen's University, Kingston, Ontario, 1965

References
Balston, pp. 171-72
Smith College Museum of Art, *Bulletin,* no. 40, 1960,
p. 51

Hunt was the son of a tin-worker who lived near Covent Garden. He was a cripple from birth, and his uncle reputedly stated, "as he was fit for nothing, they made a artist on him." His father apprenticed him to John Varley, where he was a fellow student with Mulready and Linnell. He subsequently studied at the Royal Academy schools and was employed by Dr. Thomas Monro, for whom he both made copies of earlier English drawings, those of Gainsborough in particular, and painted landscapes. He first exhibited oil paintings at the Royal Academy in 1807; however, he soon gave up painting in oil, and the entirety of his later work is in watercolor. He was elected a member of the Old Water Colour Society in 1826.

Early in his career, Hunt was patronized by the Earl of Essex, who employed him to paint views at Cassiobury, near Bushey in Hertfordshire. Because his infirmities immobilized him, Hunt stopped painting topographical views about 1820, although he continued to make drawings of interiors. In the 1820s a large part of his exhibits consisted of drawings of gamekeepers, gardeners, millers and other rural types, which in the following decade began to degenerate into humorously anecdotal drawings of rustic children. He also painted still lifes throughout his career, and after about 1850 he so limited his work to small drawings of fruit, flowers, and bird's-nests that he is frequently known as "Bird's-nest Hunt." These still lifes became extremely popular, and in 1855 the French were amazed to discover that they commanded higher prices than painting by Ingres or Delacroix.

Hunt began drawing in a linear style, based on Canaletto; as he grew older his work became minutely detailed, and color became more and more important. The coloring of his early drawings is in transparent washes and is subordinate to the outline, while his later still lifes are elaborately worked in opaque body color, or gouache, and line has disappeared.

Hunt was enormously admired by the Pre-Raphaelites and by Ruskin, who in 1879 sponsored an exhibition of his works to show "what real painting is, as such, wholly without inquiry concerning its sentiment or story." In the 1850s Ruskin commissioned Hunt to make drawings to be placed as examples in the provincial schools of art. He especially admired Hunt's painting with broken colors, and Ruskin's amazingly advanced instructions for prismatic coloring in *The Elements of Drawing* are largely based on Hunt's practice. Hunt himself took his coloring seriously, and at the end of his life he wrote to Linnell that he wished people would look at his still lifes of fruit "as bits of colour instead of something nice to eat." However, he seems to have been completely inarticulate about his methods and, when asked for instruction, his advice was simply "to fudge it out."
A.S.

Bibliography
F. G. Stephens, "William Henry Hunt (1790-1864),"
OWCSC, XII, 1935, pp. 17-50 (reprinted with additions
from *Fraser's Magazine,* November, 1865, pp. 525-36)
Ruskin, XIV, 373-84, 440-48
John Lewis Roget, *A History of the 'Old Water-Colour'
Society,* London, 1891, I, 389-93, 467-71; II, 189-202

155

155
Farmer in a Barn
Birmingham City Museum and Art Gallery
Watercolor; 10¾ x 7⅛ in.
c. 1825-1835

In the 1820s and early 1830s Hunt exhibited a large number of rustic genre subjects such as no. 155 at the Old Water Colour Society. Examples are *The Miller* (1824, no. 286), *A Blacksmith's Shop* (1829, nos. 59 and 275), *A Gardener's Store Room* (1830, no. 112), *Interior of a Barn* (1833, no. 130), and numerous drawings of gamekeepers. He subsequently gave up this type of subject, and his later work consists primarily of anecdotal drawings of children and still lifes such as no. 156.

Although Hunt's interest in color is most clearly seen in the later still lifes, it is also evident in his figural drawings. He once remarked, "It is astonishing the number of colours you can work into flesh." No. 155 demonstrates his use of a broken treatment—hatching, stippling, scraping—in order to exploit variations in light and color. The lighting effect, with the farmer's face seen by reflected light, and the view of the figure from the rear are characteristic of Hunt.
A.S.

Provenance
J. Leslie Wright (bequest to Birmingham, 1953)

References
Roget, II, 197

156

156
Hawthorne and Bird's Nest
Fogg Art Museum, Harvard University
Watercolor and gouache; 6⁹⁄₁₆ x 10⅜ in.
Inscribed: *W Hunt*
c. 1850-60

Hunt painted bird's-nests through most of his life, but no. 156 is certainly late. A similar drawing showing two bird's-nests which belonged to Ruskin is reproduced in volume XIV of Ruskin's collected *Works*. William Ward, from whom no. 1⁵ was acquired, was employed by Ruskin to make copies of Turners, and it is possible that no. 156 came to him from Ruskin.

No. 156 demonstrates the reverently close attentio Hunt paid to natural detail. He once remarked, "I feel really frightened when I sit down to paint a flower." Ruskin noted that Hunt's flower pieces were necessarily less finished than the fruit drawings because flowers so readily change thei form, but he praised the straightforward executio of such drawings and compared them favorably to more polished Dutch flower paintings: "When

1792-1882

the thing to be represented is minute, the touches which express it are necessarily minute also—they cannot be bold on the edge of a nutshell, nor free within the sphere of a bird's nest—but they are always frank and clear, to a degree which may seem not only imperfect, but even harsh or offensive, to eyes trained in more tender or more formal schools. This broken execution by detached and sharply-defined touches became indeed, in process of years, a manner in which the painter somewhat too visibly indulged, or prided himself; but it had its origin and authority in the care with which he followed the varieties of colour in the shadow, no less than in the lights, of even the smallest objects. It is easy to obtain smoothness and unity of gradation when working with a single tint; but if all accidents of local colour, and all differences of hue between direct and reflected light, are to be rendered with absolute purity, some breaking of the texture becomes inevitable. In many cases, also, of the most desirable colours, no pigment mixed on the palette, but only interlaced touches of pure tints on the paper, will attain the required effect."
A.S.

Provenance
Purchased from William Ward, 1898

References
F. G. Stephens, "John Linnell," *Portfolio,* III, 1872, p. 46
Ruskin, XIV, 382-83, cf. pl. XXVI

Linnell was born in Bloomsbury, the son of a carver and gilder who made frames and also sold pictures and prints. He did not attend school, and by the time he was ten or twelve years old he was put to work making copies after George Morland, which his father sold. In 1805 he became a student of John Varley, the watercolorist; his companions in Varley's studio were Mulready and William Hunt, and the former, who was six years older, had a greater influence on Linnell than Varley himself. Linnell also studied for several years at the Royal Academy schools, and he and Hunt followed Turner, Girtin, and Cotman in the beneficent employ of Dr. Thomas Monro. Linnell first exhibited at the Royal Academy in 1807, when he was fifteen, and in 1813 he became a member of the Old Water Colour Society, which temporarily, from 1813 until 1820, admitted oil paintings. When the Society reverted to its original purpose, Linnell presented himself as a candidate for election as an Associate of the Royal Academy. He was an unsuccessful candidate every year from 1821 through 1841, when he gave up. In the 1860s, when his reputation was much higher, the Academy solicited Linnell to join, but he refused.

Linnell painted almost every kind of picture, including portraits, landscapes, and biblical subjects. He also painted portrait miniatures and worked as a printmaker. Until 1847 he largely supported himself as a portrait painter, but after that time he occupied himself almost exclusively with landscape. Linnell took no interest in topography but painted "aspects of Nature." He rarely went on sketching tours after his student days; in the latter part of his life all his pictures were based on the surroundings of his home in Surrey and thus are somewhat repetitive.

Linnell holds a secure place in the history of English art because of his friendship with Blake, whom he met in 1818. Linnell's support allowed Blake to engrave his illustrations to the *Book of Job,* and Linnell actually drew the outlines, which Blake colored, of the second set of watercolors. He commissioned the *Divine Comedy* illustrations and was the mainstay of Blake's last years. Linnell also introduced Samuel Palmer to Blake, and he himself had a major influence on Palmer, who in 1838 became his son-in-law. As a person Linnell seems to have been difficult. He is generally accused of having made Palmer's life miserable, and Constable hated him. Linnell felt that Constable's hostility was a main reason that he was never elected to the Royal Academy, but it was probably only one of many. In 1812 he became a Baptist and a religious zealot who based his life on close study of the Bible. He refused to be married in church and insisted on working on Sunday out of principle, and in later life he published several pamphlets on biblical interpretation. He was also notoriously miserly and laid by a huge fortune. He taught his own children, dug his own well, baked his own bread, and brewed his own beer. After living in London and Hampstead until he was sixty, he built a home at Redhill in Surrey, and there for another thirty years he ruled in patriarchal grandeur over his children and grandchildren, reading the Bible and painting landscapes until his death in his ninetieth year.
A.S.

Bibliography
Alfred T. Story, *The Life of John Linnell,* 2 vols., London, 1892

157

157
Southampton from the River near Netley Abbey
Lawrence Gowing
Oil on canvas; 13 x 36¾ in.
Inscribed: *J Linnell/1825*

The following entry is based largely upon information kindly supplied by Mr. Lawrence Gowing. The picture is recorded and illustrated in Linnell's manuscript book of landscapes and described as "1824-25/ Southampton from the River near Netley Abbey/ Painted for Mr. Hall of Southampton 25 Gns./ Canvas 1 ft 6 x 3 ft." A watercolor study belonging to the same owner shows the identical view, omitting the figures, and is inscribed *Southampton 1819.* Gowing notes that this inscription was evidently added later and that the date may not be reliable. However, Linnell did visit Southampton at the end of August 1819, when he stayed with an engraver named D. C. Read who had sought Linnell's help in becoming a painter. While there, Linnell spent ten or twelve days painting a view of Netley Abbey, and he met Chambers Hall, for whom he later painted no. 157 and several other pictures. Linnell exhibited at the British Institution in 1828 an *Itchen Ferry near Southampton,* for which Story records the same measurements as no. 157, and which Gowing suggests may be the same picture. According to Story the *Itchen Ferry* was painted for Chambers Hall, but exchanged for an *Evening—Storm Clearing Off* of 1819. Story lists further the *Netley Abbey* of 1819, a *View of Southampton,* painted in 1819, and a later *View of Southampton (by Moonlight)* of 1836, exhibited at the Royal Academy in 1837.

Linnell also sold to Read, his host, a view of *Southampton Quay* which became a sore point between Linnell and Constable. Linnell secured for Read a job as drawing master in Salisbury, where Read met Constable and complained that Linnell had overcharged him for the picture, a story which Constable seems to have passed about among members of the Royal Academy, thus injuring Linnell's chances of election. Read himself later painted a view of Southampton, which in the description of Constable's friend Archdeacon Fisher sounds like a caricature of no. 157: "Imagine a tint composed of blacking, rust of iron and cabbage water laid on with a scrubbing brush. In the very centre stares the Sun. In the distance Southampton buried in an atmosphere of mud. In the foreground, plashy beach with the Sun reflected."

Chambers Hall, for whom no. 157 was painted, also owned an important collection of watercolors by Girtin (including no. 114), which he gave to The British Museum. Linnell's picture reflects some of the sweeping horizontal breadth of a Girtin, combined with the same precision of observation and handling which at this time he was urging upon Samuel Palmer. His interest in sunset and moonlight effects, as seen in no. 157, was also of obvious significance for the younger Palmer.
A.S.

Provenance
Painted for Chambers Hall, Southampton

Exhibitions
Samuel Palmer and His Circle: The Shoreham Period, Art Council, London, 1957, no. 111 (as *Itchin Ferry: Sunset*)

References
Story, I, 125-27, 133-37; II, 263-64
R. B. Beckett, *John Constable and the Fishers,* London, 1952, pp. 79, 143

158

158
Portrait of Carlyle
Scottish National Portrait Gallery
Oil on canvas; 29½ x 24½ in.
Inscribed: *J. Linnell/ 1844*

No. 158 was painted in 1843 and 1844 and is one of Linnell's last portraits before he gave up portraiture to devote himself to landscape. It was not commissioned but painted on Linnell's own initiative, and it remained in the possession of the artist's family until 1916. Carlyle was reluctant to take the time to pose for Linnell. He originally agreed to only two sittings; then, in the spring of 1844 at Linnell's request he allowed him two more. Despite the landscape setting, the picture was painted in Linnell's studio in Bayswater under a skylight. During the sittings the artist and his subject argued about theology.

All Linnell's portraits tend to be small and to have a look of unpretentious and unadorned honesty as opposed to the grand flattery of the 18th-century tradition. One would expect this to have appealed to Carlyle, but he told William Allingham that no. 158 was "an entire failure as a likeness." However, Carlyle disliked most pictures and most portraits of himself, and he claimed that Watts's portrait of 1868 (Victoria and Albert Museum) made him into "a delirious looking mountebank full of violence, awkwardness, atrocity and stupidity, without recognisable likeness." Nonetheless, as David Piper has noted in his *English Face* in a chapter on portraits of Carlyle (which does not include no. 158), from a sense of duty to history he repeatedly exposed himself to long-suffering as a sitter for artists. Linnell's portrait was made relatively early, before Carlyle had grown the beard which he is seen wearing in Ford Madox Brown's *Work* and the portraits by Watts and Whistler (Glasgow).
A.S.

Provenance
The artist
Presented to the Scottish National Portrait Gallery in 1919 by Mrs. Riches, a descendant of the artist

Exhibitions
Royal Academy, 1844, no. 428
Winter Exhibition, Royal Academy, London, 1883, no. 16 (lent by the Linnell family)

References
Story, I, 249, 300-05; II, 252
Helen Allingham and D. Radford, eds., *William Allingham, A Diary,* London, 1907, p. 267
Isaac Watson Dyer, *A Bibliography of Thomas Carlyle's Writings and Ana,* Portland, Maine, 1928, pp. 545-46
David Piper, *The English Face,* London, 1957, pp. 281-94

159
Summer Evening, Boys Bathing, Harrow in the Distance
Harris Museum & Art Gallery, Preston, England
Oil on canvas; 14½ x 23 in.
Inscribed: *J. Linnell 1849*

This picture was painted in the few years after Linnell gave up portrait painting and before his move to Redhill. Regent's Park would have been an easy walk from Linnell's home in Bayswater; Harrow is on a hill about eight miles to the northwest. The soft touch belongs to Linnell's later landscape style, but after 1860 he rarely indicated in his titles that his pictures showed specific places. The curving line of the shore is a favorite compositional device in English landscape painting, and its frequent appearance traces back to the watercolors of John Robert Cozens. Both it and the effect of reflected sunset light in the water are anticipated in somewhat different form in Linnell's *Southampton from the River* (no. 157), painted a quarter of a century earlier.
A.S.

Provenance
Richard Newsham, Preston (bequest to Preston, 1883)

Exhibitions
British Institution, 1849, no. 313 *(A Summer's Evening)*
Winter Exhibition, Royal Academy, London, 1883, no. 31 *(A Summer Evening: Regent's Park)*
Japan-British Exhibition, London, 1910, no. 71

References
James Hibbert, ed., *Catalogue of the Pictures and Drawings of the Newsham Bequest to the Corporation of Preston, Prepared by the Testator Richard Newsham, Esquire,* Preston, 1884, p. 35, no. 55
Story, II, 269 (listed as *A Summer Evening: Regent's Park*)
Ambassadors of Art, Harris Art Gallery, Preston, 1954, p. 31, ill. p. 30

159

1793-1861

Danby was born in County Wexford, Ireland, and grew up in Dublin, where he studied with the landscape painter James O'Connor. In 1813, with O'Connor and another friend, he paid a visit to London. On their return to Dublin, Danby stopped at Bristol, where he married and where he was to remain for the next eleven years painting views of the local scenery. In 1820 he sent to the British Institution in London a grandiose and gloomy picture, *The Upas Tree* (Victoria and Albert Museum); this was the first of a series of imaginative landscapes exhibited during the 1820s which made Danby's reputation. In 1824, encouraged by Sir Thomas Lawrence, Danby moved to London, and in 1825, following the exhibition of his *Delivery of Israel Out of Egypt* (Preston), he was elected an associate member of the Royal Academy. Danby's great pictures of the 1820s were felt at the time to have been painted in direct emulation of John Martin's scenes of biblical catastrophes, and his rapid official success, the result of the Royal Academy's desire for a rival to Martin, who was an implacable enemy of that body and one of the founders of the competing Society of British Artists (see no. 153). In 1829 Danby was put up for full membership in the Academy, but was defeated by one vote by Constable, who was seventeen years his senior and had been an Associate since 1819. In the same year, Danby left England, apparently because of a marital scandal in which his wife deserted him for the painter Paul Falconer Poole. In 1832 he arrived in Geneva accompanied by a Welsh mistress and ten children, seven from his marriage and three illegitimate. He remained in

Geneva for fours years, painting, building boats, and plagued by debts. Little is known about his other years abroad. In 1840 he returned to England and exhibited a vast painting of *The Deluge* at a rented hall in Piccadilly. Most of Danby's later works are melancholy sunset or nocturnal scenes, formally composed and tightly painted. The best known of them, *The Evening Gun* (Royal Academy 1848, location unknown; a half-size replica belongs to Lord O'Neill), made a sensation at the *Exposition Universelle* of 1855 and was later recalled by Ford Madox Brown as "a most solemn and beautiful work." Although Danby's reputation remained high, especially among younger artists such as Brown, and although he exhibited regularly at the Royal Academy, he was never elected to full membership. He lived for most of his later years in embittered isolation at Exmouth in Devonshire.
A.S.

Bibliography
"British Artists: Their Style and Character. No. III—Francis Danby, ARA," *Art Journal,* 1855, pp. 77-80
Geoffrey Grigson, "Some Notes on Francis Danby, A.R.A.," in *The Harp of Aeolus and other Essays on Art, Literature & Nature,* London, 1947, pp. 66-78 (reprinted with additions from *The Cornhill Magazine,* CLXII, 1946-47, pp. 99-109)
H. W. Haüserman, "Francis Danby at Geneva," *Burlington,* XCI, Aug. 1949, pp. 227-29
Francis Danby, 1793-1861, City Art Gallery, Bristol, etc., 1961 (catalogue of an Arts Council exhibition, edited with introduction by E. W. Adams)

160

delicate mood in these early pictures, as well as their small scale, also suggest central European "Biedermeier" painting of approximately the same time, but there is no evidence of any direct contact or influence. After leaving Bristol in 1824, Danby seems to have completely abandoned this type of painting.
A.S.

Exhibitions
Francis Danby, 1793-1861, City Art Gallery, Bristol, etc. (Arts Council), 1961, no. 8

160
View of the Avon Gorge
City Art Gallery, Bristol
Oil on panel; 13⅝ x 18⅜ in.
Inscribed: *Fr. Danby 1822*

This is one of several views by Danby showing the environs of Bristol. They share none of the striving after grandiose effects which by 1822 characterized the more ambitious works Danby was sending to the Royal Academy and for which he is better known. Rather, the mainspring of these early landscapes seems to have been a loving attention to geological and, especially, botanical detail. The sense of detail is emphasized by the precise shadows cast by the crisp sunlight. Nature is shown as intimate and hospitable, a place in which picnicking city-dwellers stroll and enjoy the scenery. Danby's mildly sentimental affection for landscape scenery, here emphasized by a foreground figure pointing out the view, both belongs to 18th-century tradition and anticipates early Victorian attitudes toward nature, as shown, for example, in the landscapes of Ford Madox Brown. The qualities of light, of detail, and of

161
Subject from the Revelations
Robert Rosenblum
Oil on canvas; 24¼ x 30¼ in.
c. 1829

At the Royal Academy in 1828, Danby exhibited a large painting based on a passage in the Book of Revelation, which he entitled *An Attempt to Illustrate the Opening of the Sixth Seal.* This scene of supernatural cosmic violence was sensationally successful and was purchased for 1,000 guineas by William Beckford. In the following year, Danby exhibited two further pictures of subjects from Revelation: no. 4 in the Academy catalogue, showing the fourth angel of the Apocalypse, and no. 317 in the Academy catalogue (no. 161), which Danby accompanied with the following quotation from Revelation 10:1, 2, 5, 6:

"And I saw another mighty angel come down from heaven, clothed with a cloud: and a rainbow was upon his head, and his face was as it were the sun, and his feet as pillars of fire.

161

readiness that it had applauded the spectacular extravaganza of *The Opening of the Sixth Seal*. The brilliant red sunset is a motif which appears throughout Danby's career in combination with many different subjects. In no. 161 the flaming red provides an appropriately lurid setting for the picture's message of the end of time.
A.S.

Exhibitions
Royal Academy, 1829, no. 317
English Romantic Paintings 1800-1900, Maas Gallery, London, 1965, no. 6

References
Art Journal, 1855, p. 80

162

"And he had in his hand a little book open; and he set his right foot upon the sea, and his left foot on the earth.

"And the angel which I saw stand upon the sea and upon the earth lifted up his hand to heaven.

"And sware by Him that liveth for ever and ever; who created heaven, and the things that therein are; and the earth, and the things that therein are; and the sea, and the things which are therein—that there should be time no longer."

According to the *Art Journal,* the popular reaction to these two paintings was disappointing; although each showed "a grandeur of conception which no other living painter could put forth," they were considered a letdown from Danby's painting of the previous year. The *Art Journal* even suggested that disappointment over the reception of these pictures may have been the reason that Danby left England in the same year. We now know that this was not the reason, but we can also understand why the public might not have responded to this strangely quiet and visionary work with the same

162
Pagan Rites
Smith College Museum of Art, Gift of Miss Frances C. Powers
Watercolor; $7^{11}/_{16}$ x $9^{1}/_{8}$ in.
c. 1849

At the British Institution in 1849, Danby exhibited *A Mountain Chieftain's Funeral in Olden Times* (no. 52). This was described in the *Art Journal* as "a night procession . . . the figures and objects being seen of course by torch-light." The present drawing would seem almost certainly to be related perhaps as a preliminary sketch. A small painting in the Mellon Collection entitled *The Funeral of Alaric* shows a similar torchlit procession. The combination of elegiac subject with a formally symmetrical composition is characteristic of Danby's later works.
A.S.

References
"The British Institution," *Art Journal,* 1849, p. 78

Charles Robert Leslie

1794-1859

Born in London of American parents, Leslie grew up in Philadelphia where he had his first lessons in painting from Thomas Sully. In 1811 a group of Philadelphia merchants took up a subscription to send the young artist to London to study for the next two years. However, once in England, Leslie remained for the rest of his life, returning to America for five months in 1833-34, when he had a brief appointment as drawing master at West Point. Leslie's first associates in London were the expatriate American artists Benjamin West and Washington Allston, to whom he took letters of introduction from Sully. He was also a friend of Washington Irving, and contemporaries considered their styles and outlooks analogous.

Throughout his career Leslie specialized in painting scenes drawn from literary sources. His most popular works were illustrations of *Don Quixote,* but his sources of subjects also included Shakespeare, Molière, and Goldsmith. Unlike earlier illustrations of literature such as those of Fuseli, who projected into his subjects a highly personal vision, Leslie's pictures are straightforward depictions whose success depended on the viewer's recognizing a favorite passage or scene from a work with which he was already well acquainted, either from reading or seeing it performed on the stage. Leslie's art represents perfectly the toning down of romantic emotion into Victorian domestic sentimentality, and it was immensely popular. He was elected an Associate member of the Royal Academy in 1821 and a full member five years later.

Leslie was a close friend of John Constable, and his life of the landscape painter, published in 1845, is a classic artistic biography which remains the prime source for the artist's life. Although Leslie was a conservative and essentially timid artist in comparison to Constable, the latter's influence did lead to a discernible new breadth and luminosity in Leslie's mature works. His lectures to the Royal Academy students, published in 1855 as *A Handbook for Young Painters,* expressed a by then conservative point of view which drew a scornful attack from Ruskin, at the time in full fig as defender of the Pre-Raphaelites.
A.S.

Bibliography
Tom Taylor, ed., *Autobiographical Recollections by the late Charles Robert Leslie, R.A., with a Prefatory Essay on Leslie as an Artist, and Selections from his Correspondence,* 2 vols., London, 1860

163
Woman and Child under a Garden Trellis
Trustees of The British Museum
Watercolor; 10¾ x 8¹⁄₁₆ in.
c. 1840 (?)

No. 163 is undated, but its breadth of handling and outdoor freshness suggest that it may come from the latter part of Leslie's career, when he was somewhat influenced by his friend Constable. In 1840 Leslie painted a picture of his youngest son George Dunlop Leslie playing in a garden, which shows comparable sunlit brightness but much greater detail (Victoria and Albert Museum). Watercolors by Leslie are relatively rare.
A.S.

163

164
Scene from Henry VIII—Act IV, Scene 2
Amherst College
Oil on canvas; 24 x 32 in.
1849-1850

The painting represents the scene from Act IV of Shakespeare's *Henry VIII* when the dying Queen Katherine of Aragon receives Capucius, the ambassador of Henry VIII, at Kimbolton and commends through him her daughter and her women to the King. The two figures in the background are Griffith, the Queen's gentleman-usher, and Patience, her maid. The scene is shown in exact accordance with the stage directions and text of Shakespeare's play. Blake's

164

atypical of Leslie's art, which usually bubbles with playfully high spirits and mild humor. The painting of the ball scene from *Henry VIII,* which Leslie exhibited in 1849 and which he described as containing many figures, would have been more in his usual vein of subject. It may be that Brunel in commissioning the companion piece asked Leslie to emphasize a different aspect of the play. The quietly posed grouping of a few figures in a 16th-century period setting is reminiscent of the costume pieces painted by Bonington in the 1820s and seems to belong to a more introspective kind of romanticism than we normally associate with paintings from the middle of the century.
A.S.

Provenance

Isumbard Kingdom Brunel, London (sale, Christie's, London, 20 April 1860, no. 220, bt. Wallis)
J. Dugdale, Wroxall Abbey, Warwickshire
G. Michelmore & Co., London
Folger Shakespeare Library, Washington, 1928
Amherst College, 1961

Exhibitions

Royal Academy, 1850, no. 136 *(Scene from Henry VIII,* accompanied by a long quotation)
Art Treasures of the United Kingdom, Manchester, 1857, no. 378 (lent by I. K. Brunel)
International Exhibition, London, 1862, no. 343 *(Queen Katherine,* lent by J. Dugdale)
Exhibition of the Works of Old Masters, Royal Academy, London, 1870, no. 168 *(Death of Queen Katherine)*
Royal Jubilee Exhibition, Manchester, 1887, no. 900 *(Death of Queen Katherine)*

References

Taylor, I, liv; II, 296-99, 324

Reproductions

A photograph was published in 1857 at the time of the Manchester exhibition

watercolor of *Queen Katherine's Dream* (no. 97) is based upon a subsequent moment in the same scene.

During his life, Leslie painted five scenes from *Henry VIII.* His diploma picture in the Royal Academy, painted in 1826, shows the opening episode of Act III, scene 1, in which Queen Katherine asks one of her companions to stop working and sing. He repeated this subject in a picture exhibited at the Royal Academy in 1842. In 1849 he painted for the engineer Isumbard Kingdom Brunel, who was forming a room of

Shakespearean pictures, the incident from the ball at York Place in which Cardinal Wolsey recognizes Henry VIII and Anne Boleyn in disguise (Act I, scene 4). This picture was no. 55 in the Royal Academy exhibition of 1849. The Amherst picture, exhibited the following year, was commissioned by Brunel as a companion piece. In a letter of December 27, 1849, Leslie described it as nearly finished. Leslie's fifth picture from the play was a smaller repetition of this picture, painted for John Naylor of Leighton Hall near Welshpool.

The sober, even somber mood of the painting is

James Holland

1800-1870

165

Holland was born at Burslem, Staffordshire, where his father was employed in the pottery works, and his first training was as a painter of decorative flowers on pottery. He came to London in 1819 and set himself up as a flower painter in watercolors. However, around 1830 he turned to topographical landscape views, and he continued to paint scenes comparable to those of Prout and Bonington until his death. He first travelled abroad to France in 1830; in 1835 he visited Venice, in 1837 Portugal, and he made numerous subsequent sketching tours on the continent, although in later life he tended to specialize in views of Venice. Holland was elected an associate of the Old Water Colour Society in 1835, but he resigned in 1842 to become a member of the Society of British Artists. He subsequently left that body and was reelected an associate of the Old Water Colour Society in 1856 and a full member in 1857.

Like those of many of his contemporaries, Holland's views are primarily architectural, and they often show considerable inventiveness in the treatment of perspective. He painted both in oil and watercolor. His experience with the former seems to have influenced his handling of the latter, and his later watercolor views are painted largely in opaque pigments to achieve an effect of sumptuously rich color.   A.S.

Bibliography
Hugh Stokes, "James Holland," *Walker's Quarterly,* XXIII, 1927
Randall Davies, "James Holland: Some Contemporary Notices," *OWCSC,* VII, 1930, pp. 37-54

165
Greenwich Hospital
Fogg Art Museum, Harvard University,
Gift of Harold Broadfield Warren
Watercolor; 17¼ x 12⅛ in.
Inscribed: *J. H 1840*

Holland taught himself as a landscape painter by sketching on the banks of the Thames in the vicinity of Greenwich, and there exist numerous views by him of Greenwich Hospital, dating from all periods of his career. In 1836 he exhibited a large painting of the Hospital at the Royal Academy. The marked perspective and play of sunlight and shadow in no. 165 are similar to a view of the Hospital from the opposite side reproduced by Davies. Both are relatively early works, executed before Holland started to make heavy use of gouache. His later views tend to have more emphasis on color, somewhat at the expense of inventive design.
A.S.

Provenance
Given to the Fogg Art Museum in 1937 by Harold Broadfield Warren

Exhibitions
Watercolors by the Masters: Dürer to Cézanne, Minneapolis Institute of Arts, 1952, no. 38

Richard Parkes Bonington

1802-1828

Bonington was born near Nottingham. When he was fifteen years old, his family left England because of depression in the Nottingham lace industry. They spent two years in Calais, then went on to Paris. In Calais, Bonington learned watercolor painting from Louis Francia, a native of Calais who had spent many years in England and had been a friend of Girtin. In 1820 Bonington entered the atelier of Baron Gros at the École des Beaux Arts, where he remained until 1822. In that year he exhibited two watercolor views at the Salon. He travelled extensively in France and the Low Countries, in part to make drawings which were lithographed in his own *Restes et Fragmens* [sic] *d'Architecture du Moyen Age* and in Baron Taylor's *Voyages Pittoresques et Romantiques dans l'Ancienne France,* and in the summer of 1825 he visited London. Delacroix was in England at the same time; the two met, and after their return to France they shared a studio for several months. Their friendship was of importance for both artists, and for a while their work was very close. Through Delacroix, Bonington met Baron Charles Rivet, and with Rivet he travelled in Italy in the spring of 1826. For Bonington the most significant part of their trip was a stay of three weeks in Venice, scenes of which form a large part of the output of the last two years of his life. He exhibited at the Royal Academy in London for the first time in 1827, and he paid brief visits to London in 1827 and in the spring of 1828. Bonington had begun to suffer from tuberculosis on his Italian trip of 1826. In the summer of 1828 his health declined rapidly. He returned to London to consult a specialist, and he died there on September 23, a month before his twenty-sixth birthday.

Bonington was primarily a painter of landscapes and of picturesque continental cities. He also painted subjects drawn from literature, particularly the novels of Scott, and from French history. The latter are often scenes of intimate moments from the lives of the great, which have a distinct and personal charm. Most of Bonington's works are small. Their spontaneous and natural ease of handling is probably the most essential aspect of his appeal, but it was criticized both by Constable and by Delacroix, although in the latter's case the criticism was joined with frankly envious admiration.

It is a standing question whether Bonington should be considered a French or an English artist. Despite his French training and the fact that he spent his entire working life, except for brief journeys, in France, his success in Paris was certainly in part due to his appeal to the prevailing Anglophilia. Bonington's work was instantly popular in both countries, so popular that it was soon widely imitated, and his reputation still suffers from the many inferior works wrongly ascribed to him.
A.S.

Bibliography
Albert Dubuisson and C. E. Hughes, *Richard Parkes Bonington,* London, 1924
Roger Fry, "Bonington and French Art," *Burlington,* LI, 1927, pp. 268-74
The Hon. Andrew Shirley, *Bonington,* London, 1940 (see the review by A. P. Oppé, *Burlington,* LXXIX, 1941, pp. 99-101)
RP Bonington, 1802-1828, Castle Museum and Art Gallery, Nottingham, 1965 (exhibition catalogue, edited with introduction by Marion Spencer)

166

166
Two Parrots
The National Gallery of Canada, Ottawa
Black, red and white chalk on grey paper;
7⁷⁄₁₆ x 10¼ in.
Inscribed twice with the number 60
c. 1820

A companion drawing, showing three parrots and numbered 61, is in the Oppé collection. Lot 97 in the sale after Bonington's death consisted of four "Sketches of Birds, in Black and White Chalk very Spirited," which may have been related drawings. All of Bonington's chalk drawings seem to come from his student period around 1820, which is presumably the date of no. 166. Parrots appear in several of Bonington's later depictions of historical or exotic themes; see, for example, his painting of *Henry III and the English Ambassador* and the watercolors *A Venetian Scene* and *An Odalisque* (all in the Wallace Collection). However, none of these is particularly close to the studies in no. 166. The freedom of handling reflects the virtuosity that so impressed Bonington's contemporaries. The liveliness of these birds,

gained in part from the suppression of precise detail, might be contrasted with the careful delineations of a professional bird artist such as Edward Lear, whose *Grey Cockatoo* (no. 196) dates from approximately ten years later.
A.S.

Provenance
Anonymous sale, Sotheby's, London, 17 October 1956, lot 46, bt. Colnaghi
The National Gallery of Canada, 1956

Exhibitions
Constable to Bacon: An Exhibition of Nineteenth and Twentieth Century British Art, Agnes Etherington Art Centre, Queen's University, Kingston, Ontario, 1962, no. 66

References
Dubuisson and Hughes, p. 168

167

Marly from the Terrace of St-Germain-en-Laye
Mr. S. Bowes Lyon
Oil on canvas; 11½ x 15½ in.
Inscribed: *R.P.B., Marly, 1823*

The view from the terrace of St-Germain is one of the most famous in France. The Seine is below, the wooded heights of Marly are beyond to the south, and on the horizon is visible the aqueduct built by Louis XIV to carry water from the Seine to the reservoirs of Louveciennes to supply the fountains of Versailles and Marly. The structure in the foreground is the *Pavillon Henri IV,* a remnant of the *château neuf* of St-Germain built during the reigns of Henri II and Henri IV.

This painting has generally been accepted as the only surely signed and dated landscape by Bonington from before 1825, and thus it has been the touchstone for assessing his early art. Dated when he was only twenty-one years old, it demonstrates an extraordinarily rich use of paint and naturally fluent ease of handling. The composition of the vertical mass of the pavilion

167

set off against the vast horizontal landscape is more structured than we normally see in his work. A watercolor by Turner (British Museum), dating from approximately the same time and engraved in *The Rivers of France,* shows the same view. The contrast of the two shows how extraordinarily advanced Bonington's painting is for this date, and how essentially French. The real affinities of no. 167 are with French landscape painters such as Paul Huet and Corot.

A.S.

Provenance
Mrs. H. H. Spender-Clay
The Hon. Lady Bowes Lyon

Exhibitions
R. P. Bonington and His Circle, Burlington Fine Arts Club, London, 1937, no. 9
La Peinture Anglaise, Louvre, Paris, 1938, no. 1
Engelse Landschapschilders van Gainsborough tot Turner, Museum Boymans, Rotterdam, 1955, no. 1
Masters of British Painting: 1800-1950, Museum of Modern Art, New York, etc., 1956-57, no. 13
Pictures, Watercolours and Drawings by R. P. Bonington, Thos. Agnew & Sons, London, 1962, no. 14

References
Shirley, pp. 47, 57, 90, pl. 20

168
Male Costume, 1580
Nottingham Castle Museum
Pencil; 7 x 10 in.
Inscribed: *1580*
c. 1825

Shirley dates no. 168 as 1825, which is the year that Bonington and Delacroix met in London. It is said that the meeting took place when both were sketching in the Meyrick Collection of armor. Although the precise source for no. 168 has not been identified, it is similar to some of the drawings made from the Meyrick Collection and would seem to be the product of comparable study. Bonington made use of the costume of the center

168

figure in his watercolor of *Henry IV and the Spanish Ambassador* (Wallace Collection), where it reappears on the Ambassador. The pose is not repeated so it would seem that Bonington drew no. 168 not as a preparatory sketch but as a study of costume, which he later employed for a detail of the watercolor.

No. 168 reflects the antiquarian interests which Bonington shared with Delacroix and many of their contemporaries, and which go hand in hand with the poems of Byron and the Waverley novels. Bonington's interest in a romantically colorful past is manifested equally in drawings such as no. 168, in his costume pictures, and in his studies of picturesque medieval and Renaissance architecture. No. 168 was apparently intended as no more than a sketch made for reference purpose, but even so it evokes some of the glamorous appeal that armor and costume of the past held for Bonington's generation.

George Cattermole, listed as the drawing's first owner, was himself a popular painter of historical costume scenes in watercolor, who carried on the tradition of Bonington past the middle of the century.

A.S.

Provenance
George Cattermole
(?) M. Gosselin, 1924
Luc Albert Moreau, 1934
Arthur Tooth and Sons, London
Nottingham Castle Museum, 1949

Exhibitions
R. P. Bonington: 1802-1828, Nottingham Castle Museum, and Southampton Art Gallery, 1965, no. 140

References
Dubuisson and Hughes, ill. opp. p. 26
Shirley, p. 100 and pl. 73

169
The Doge's Palace, Venice
The National Gallery of Canada, Ottawa
Oil on canvas; 31½ x 25½ in.
c. 1826

The staircase in no. 169 reappears as the setting o Delacroix's *Execution of Doge Marino Faliero* of 1826 (Wallace Collection). Whether Delacroix's picture depends on no. 169, or vice versa, is not clear. The stairs seem to be based on the *Scala dei Giganti* in the courtyard of the Doge's Palace, but they are so freely reinterpreted in ever detail that their depiction would not have to depen on Bonington's trip to Venice of 1826. Delacroix's painting, based on Byron's play *Marino Faliero, Doge of Venice,* shows an event that took place in the 14th century, while the *Scala dei Giganti* an the surrounding façade date from after the fire of 1483, so in Delacroix's case an accurate representation would have been an anachronism The scale of the figures in no. 169 is smaller than in the Delacroix, and the effect of the architectur consequently is more imposing.

169

René Huyghe has questioned the picture's attribution to Bonington. Although acknowledging that it shows Bonington's influence, he feels that it is by a French hand and suggests the friend of Delacroix and Bonington, Baron Schwiter. Whether this proposed reattribution is tenable is open to question. The outlines of Bonington's *œuvre* are the least clearly defined of any 19th-century artist, and decisions about many aspects of his art probably should wait until Bonington and his associates have received more adequate study than has yet been given them. In any case, no. 169 is a spectacular example of that community of interests shared by Delacroix and Bonington at the point of intersection of their careers. A.S.

Provenance
Carlier René Longa, 1940
The National Gallery of Canada, 1956

Exhibitions
Delacroix: ses maîtres, ses amis, ses élèves, Musée des Beaux-Arts, Bordeaux, 1963, no. 214

References
Shirley, p. 103
Maurice Gobin, *R.P. Bonington 1802-1828,* Paris, 1955, pl. 50
René Huyghe, *Delacroix,* New York, 1963, pp. 166, 522 n. 8, pl. 119 (as school of Bonington)

170
The Castelbarco Tomb, Verona
Nottingham Castle Museum
Watercolor; 7 x 5¼ in.
Inscribed: *[R] PB. 1827*

Count Guglielmo da Castelbarco (died 1319) was a friend and adviser of the Scaligeri and a major benefactor of the church of S. Anastasia, before which stands his tomb. Ruskin called the Castelbarco Tomb "the most perfect Gothic sepulchral monument in the world."

Bonington's one visit to Italy lasted from April 4 until June 20, 1826. He was in Verona between April 18 and 20. He did not make this watercolor, which is dated 1827, at the time, but based it on a pencil drawing now in the collection of the Marquess of Lansdowne. Most of Bonington's Italian views were painted after his trip, and it is possible to identify many of the sketches that served as their basis among those now in the Lansdowne collection. This group of drawings was bought by the third Marquess of Lansdowne at the sale of Bonington's remaining works at Sotheby's, June 29, 1829.

As Bonington painted his watercolor away from the tomb itself, it is not surprising that he took some liberties. Ruskin's earliest drawing of the tomb (Bembridge School, Isle of Wight), done on the spot eight years later, shows a round arch over the portal below the tomb, rather than the post and lintel construction with a rectangular panel above, as shown in no. 170. Ruskin's drawings also show a rectangular opening in the wall to the right of the portal, where Bonington's watercolor is rather blurred, and traces of an arch in the wall beneath. It is characteristic of the difference between the generation of Bonington and that of Ruskin that the former would be less fussy about exactness of detail. If Bonington was loose with his details, his drawing gives the tomb a dramatic monumentality that Ruskin never attempted.

The vertical composition appears frequently in Bonington's Italian views. The richness of coloring reflects the impact upon him of the Venetian painting which he saw during his trip. The genre figures in the foreground, whose small size makes the tomb above them bulk even larger, are also typical of Bonington's later work. A.S.

Provenance
W. A. Coats
Major J. A. Coats (sale, Christie's, London, 12 April 1935, no. 3, bt. P. M. Turner)
Fine Art Society, London, 1935
Nottingham Castle Museum, 1935

Exhibitions
Works of Cotman and Bonington, Paterson Gallery, London, 1913, no. 39
R. P. Bonington and His Circle, Burlington Fine Arts Club, London, 1937, no. 110
Watercolours by British Landscape Painters, Castle Museum, Norwich, 1956, no. 9
British Watercolour Painting During Three Centuries, British China Friendship Association, Peking (British Council exhibition), 1963, no. 60
R. P. Bonington: 1802-1828, Nottingham Castle Museum, and Southampton Art Gallery, 1965, no. 223

References
Ruskin, IX, 175
Dubuisson and Hughes, ill. opp. p. 75
Shirley, pp. 67, 114, pl. 131

170

171
Four Studies of Cloud Effects
Leona E. Prasse, Cleveland, Ohio
Watercolor and some pencil; four drawings:
a. 2¼ x 6³⁄₁₆ in.
b. 2¼ x 4¹³⁄₁₆ in.
c. 2 x 6³⁄₁₆ in.
d. 2¼ x 5¹⁄₁₆ in.
Drawing a. is faintly inscribed: *RPB*
c. 1825-28

These four small drawings of clouds belong to a
sizable group of such drawings, which the artist
presumably made late in his short life. Similar
watercolors of clouds are in the Mellon Collection
and a group of four such drawings, which had
been bought originally by Paul Signac, were lent
to the Bonington exhibition at the Musée
Jacquemart-André in 1966 by Mme Cachin-Signac

Although Constable's are by far the best known,
many other English artists also made beautiful
studies of clouds, among them Alexander Cozens
(cf. no. 5) and Joseph Wright of Derby in the
18th century, and Turner and Bonington in the
nineteenth. Bonington's studies are rapid notation
in which the capture of transient color is his
prime concern, and they are concentrated on more
spectacular effects than those of Constable.
A.S.

Provenance
Herbert N. Bier, London

References
Bonington: Un Romantique anglais à Paris, Musée
Jacquemart-André, Paris, 1966, cf. no. 52

171

1802-1873

Landseer was born in London; his father, two brothers, and two sisters were also artists. He studied at the Royal Academy schools, where Fuseli, the keeper, called him "my little dog boy," and he also worked under Benjamin Robert Haydon and dissected animals with John Frederick Lewis. As a student of animal anatomy, he owned George Stubbs's drawings for *The Anatomy of the Horse,* which were presented to the Royal Academy after Landseer's death, and he himself made accomplished anatomical drawings.

Landseer first exhibited at the Royal Academy at the age of twelve, and he had his first success in 1818 with *Fighting Dogs Getting Wind* (collection of Pierre Jeannerat). In 1821 Géricault on his visit to London saw Landseer's *Rat Catchers* at the Royal Academy and praised it in a letter to Horace Vernet. Landseer was elected A. R. A. when he was twenty-four, the earliest permissible age, and he became a full Academician in 1831. He was knighted in 1850, and in 1865, upon the death of Sir Charles Eastlake, he was offered but declined the presidency of the Royal Academy.

Throughout his life Landseer specialized in pictures of animals. In 1824 he paid his first visit to Scotland, and in subsequent years he returned regularly. He made numerous landscape sketches from nature in Scotland, and many of his later exhibited pictures show stags and other Highland wild life. He also had a knack for making animals express human sentiments, and he exploited this in a series of comical dog pictures, *Jack in Office,*

Alexander and Diogenes, and *Dignity and Impudence,* among others, which became immensely popular, especially through engravings, and now seem abysmally coy. Landseer's early pictures are broadly and richly painted, while his later work tends to be tighter and dryer, and it was acknowledged even by the artist that as his popularity rose in the Victorian period the quality of his painting declined. He is reported to have said that if people knew as much about painting as he did they would never buy his pictures.

Landseer moved in aristocratic circles. He was a favorite of Queen Victoria and a frequent guest of the Royal Family in Scotland. He was also close to the Russell family, especially Georgiana, wife of the sixth Duke of Bedford. In his later years he suffered from alcoholism and mental breakdown.

During the Victorian period Landseer probably achieved wider popularity than any other artist in history. This, however, was mainly the result of the sentimental appeal of his anthropomorphic animals and was followed by the inevitable plummet in reputation. Recently there has been some resurgence of interest in Landseer, based on recognition of the painterly quality of his earlier works and his sketches and on a new ability to see his art within the context of European romanticism. A.S.

Bibliography
Algernon Graves, *Catalogue of the Works of Sir Edwin Landseer, R. A.,* London [1874]
Frederick G. Stephens, *Sir Edwin Landseer,* 3rd ed., London, 1880
James A. Manson, *Sir Edwin Landseer, R. A.,* London, 1902
Sir Edwin Landseer, R. A., Royal Academy, London, 1961 (exhibition catalogue with introduction by John Woodward; essays, "Landseer as a Craftsman" by Derek Hill, and "Landseer in the Highlands" by Humphrey Brooke)

172

**172
A Boar**
Nelson Gallery—Atkins Museum, Gift of Mr. and
Mrs. Milton McGreevy through the Westport Fund
Pencil, watercolor and gouache on tan paper;
8½ x 11 1/16 in.
Inscribed: *E L 1820;* verso, in another hand:
*Portrait of a boar in the possession of Colonel
Hamilton, Priors Ongar, Essex/ Drawn by
Sr. Edwin Landseer in the year 1818 or 1819 when
he was a very young man./ Charlotte Hamilton*

No. 172 may have been made in connection with
Landseer's preparatory studies for *The Seizure of
a Boar,* which he exhibited at the British Institution
in 1821. Executed when Landseer was seventeen
or eighteen years old, no. 172 demonstrates his
extraordinary precocity. His virtuosity in
suggesting the appearance of animals' hair and
skin is also evident in his oil paintings, and he was
later frequently criticized for concentrating upon
surface texture and sheen while neglecting the
underlying structure.
A.S.

Provenance
Colonel Hamilton, Priors Ongar, Essex
Nelson Gallery—Atkins Museum, 1956

Exhibitions
Drawings: Collection of Milton McGreevy, Nelson
Gallery—Atkins Museum, Kansas City, 1965, no. 96

**173
Ptarmigan**
Henry P. McIlhenny
Oil on panel; 19¾ x 26 in.
c. 1833

Landseer painted a series of pictures of game birds
for his patron William Wells of Redleaf. These
included *Dead Pheasant* and *Death of the
Woodcock* of 1823, and *Ptarmigan, Grouse, Black
Cock and Grey Hen, Snipe and Woodcock,
Partridges,* and *Dead Wild Duck,* all painted in
1833. A label on the back of the frame indicates
that no. 173 was shown in the Landseer exhibition
of 1874 as *Blackcock.* However, it may be that at
some time the frames of *Ptarmigan* and *Blackcock*
were exchanged, as both pictures remained in
the Wells collection until 1890. A slightly smaller
picture of *Ptarmigan* was lent to the 1874
exhibition by Unwin Heathcote.

Most of the subjects of the Wells series were
shown either dead or dying. Landseer was
frequently criticized for the cruelty of such
depictions; however, in these works the reason for
showing the moment of death was probably
because game birds just after being shot were
conveniently available as models while still in their
natural habitat. The pictures are halfway between
the traditional still life of dead game, in the manner
of Jan Fyt or Frans Snyders, and scenes of living
wild animals. Landseer painted relatively few
pictures of birds, compared to four-footed animals
such as stags, probably because of the difficulty
of studying them alive. Wells also owned a small
Dead Roe Deer and Ptarmigan, and in 1869
Landseer exhibited *Ptarmigan Hill,* a curious
picture in which the fowl are amicably

173

accompanied by a pair of spaniels.

The background of no. 173 is similar to many of
Landseer's landscape sketches of the Highlands.
Comparable landscapes are *Lake Scene: Effect of
a Storm* (Tate Gallery) and *The Eagle's Nest*
(Victoria and Albert Museum), both painted in the
Cairngorms in 1833.
A.S.

Provenance
William Wells of Redleaf (sale, Christie's, London,
10 May 1890, bt. Agnew)
Mrs. Robert Frank, London

Exhibitions
British Institution, 1833, no. 129
(?) *The Works of the late Sir Edwin Landseer, R. A.,*
Royal Academy, London, 1874, no. 352 *(Blackcock)*
Winter Exhibition, Grosvenor Gallery, London, 1890,
no. 164
Paintings and Drawings by Sir Edwin Landseer, R. A.,
Royal Academy, London, 1961, no. 62

References
Graves, p. 17
John Canaday, *Mainstreams of Modern Art,* New York,
1959, p. 142, fig. 160

174

174

Queen Victoria and the Duke of Wellington Reviewing the Life Guard
Private Collection, London
Oil on canvas; 22 x 34 in.
c. 1839

The subject of no. 174 is a review which took place at Windsor on November 1, 1839. The site is the castle end of the Long Walk in Windsor Park. The troops lining the walk are the 2nd Life Guards. Queen Victoria is on her grey charger Comus. Whether the Duke of Wellington was actually present at this review is questionable. In a long account of the review published the next day in the *Windsor and Eton Express* (cited in *Christie's Bi-Centenary Review*) his name is not included in the list of those attending. Prince Albert of Saxe Coburg, who was to become the Prince Consort three months later, was a guest at Windsor at the time and present at the review, and it has been suggested that Landseer originally portrayed him, in which case the dog in the foreground may be his pet greyhound Eos. But why was the Prince replaced by the Duke of Wellington, with whom Queen Victoria was then so angry over the Tories' attitude towards Albert that she did not want him invited to her wedding? Whatever the reason, no. 174 remained in the artist's possession rather than entering the Royal Collection, and it was not exhibited until after Landseer's death.

No. 174 is the most ambitious composition among several equestrian studies painted by Landseer of Queen Victoria at the beginning of her reign. The idea of this sketch was apparently carried no further, but the artist did paint several versions of the Queen alone on Comus (Royal Collection, and collections of H. M. the Queen Mother and of Lord Fairhaven). In the same year Sir Francis Grant painted an equestrian group portrait of the Queen riding with Lord Melbourne and members of the court which was shown at the Royal Academy in 1840 (Royal Collection), and it was Grant who a few years later painted a large equestrian portrait of *Queen Victoria Reviewing the Troops*

(Christ's Hospital, Horsham). However, in the first years of Queen Victoria's reign, Landseer was clearly the royal favorite, and on one occasion his neighbors in St. John's Wood were amazed to see the Queen waiting at his door while Landseer changed his clothes in order to ride with her. John Woodward, in the introduction to the catalogue of the 1961 Landseer exhibition, asserts that Queen Victoria's taste was for the freely painted sketch, so brilliantly exemplified by no. 174; as a result of Prince Albert's influence, Landseer's later works for his royal patrons became more tightly painted.
A.S.

Provenance
The artist's sale (Christie's, London, 8 May 1874, no. 132, bt. Agnew)
Lord Cheylesmore (sale, Christie's, London, 7 May 1892, no. 57, bt. McLean)
Leggatt Brothers, London, 1958
H. A. J. Silley, C. B. E. (sale, Christie's, London, 22 July 1966, no. 92, bt. Leggatt)

Exhibitions
The Works of the Late Sir Edwin Landseer, R.A., Royal Academy, London, 1874, no. 244 (lent by the Executors of Sir E. Landseer)
Paintings and Drawings by Sir Edwin Landseer, R. A., Royal Academy, London, 1961, no. 23

References
Graves, p. 22
L. E. Buckell, "Landseer and the Life Guards, 1839," *Journal of the Society for Army Historical Research,* no. 156, 1960, p. 143
Christie's Bi-Centenary Review of the Year: October 1965-July 1966, London, 1966, pp. 54-55

175

The Challenge (Coming Events Cast Their Shadows Before)
His Grace the Duke of Northumberland, K.G., T.D
Oil on canvas; 38 x 83 in.
c. 1844

The composition is apparently based on a wash drawing, *Stag at Ardverikie,* in the collection of th Duke of Abercorn. However, in the drawing the mountains across the lake are silhouetted black against the water and sky, while in the painting the are lighter. A cabinet-size version of no. 175 was sold in the Landseer sale in 1874.

Following Landseer's first visit to the Highlands in 1824 stags became his most favored subjects. In 1843 Landseer exhibited *The Sanctuary* (Royal Collection), a painting of similar horizontal proportions showing an exhausted stag that has just swum across a loch to escape its hunters. *The Sanctuary* was the first of his Highland drama and he followed it with no. 175 in 1844, *The Stag at Bay* in 1846, and numerous other comparable inventions. No. 175 is in many ways the most memorable, both because of its subject of impending solitary struggle, and because of the almost unworldly beauty of the barren landscape and starlit sky. Both John Woodward and Derek Hill in the catalogue to the Landseer exhibition o 1961 suggest that no. 175 may be connected with landscapes by Caspar David Friedrich which Landseer could have seen on his one continental trip in 1840. Hill also suggests, quite plausibly, that no. 175 may have inspired Holman Hunt's *Scapegoat* (Port Sunlight), who expires on a simil barren shore, before the flaming violet Mountain of Moab across the Dead Sea in the background.
A.S.

Provenance
Family descent

Exhibitions
Royal Academy, 1844, no. 165 *(Coming Events Cast Their Shadows Before)*

175

1803-1878

The Works of the Late Sir Edwin Landseer, R. A., Royal
Academy, London, 1874, no. 199
Winter Exhibition, Grosvenor Gallery, London, 1890,
no. 128
Paintings and Drawings by Sir Edwin Landseer, R. A.,
Royal Academy, London, 1961, no. 74

References
Graves, pp. 26, 38-39
Stephens, pp. 85, 88
Manson, pp. 128-29

Reproductions
Engraved by John Burnett, 1846; C. G. Lewis, 1852;
Thomas Landseer and Charles Mottram, 1872

Grant was the younger son of a Perthshire laird,
Grant of Kilgraston. He was educated at Harrow
and Edinburgh High School, and as a young man
he began to lead a fashionable life in Edinburgh
and among the fox-hunting circles in
Leicestershire. He maintained his own hunting
establishment at Melton Mowbray, he married a
niece of the Duke of Rutland, and by 1830 he had
run through his inheritance. To prepare himself to
make a living, he first studied law, but failing at
that, he turned to art. Except for some lessons from
the sporting artist John Ferneley, Grant was
self-taught, but he had natural abilities and he was
able to capitalize upon his social position. He first
exhibited at the Royal Academy in 1834 a
conversation group, *Breakfast Scene at Melton*
(collection of Viscount Errington), and during the
1830s his work consisted largely of sporting
pictures and portraits of the rural aristocracy. His
first major success was an equestrian portrait of
Queen Victoria riding at Windsor with Lord
Melbourne and members of the court, which he
exhibited in 1840 (Royal Collection). This led to
other commissions from court circles and for the
rest of his life Grant was England's most
fashionable portrait painter. He was elected an
Associate of the Royal Academy in 1842 and a full
member in 1851. In 1866, following the death of
Eastlake, he was elected President of the Royal
Academy, much to the distaste of Queen Victoria,
who knighted him anyway but wrote disapprovingly
that Grant "boasts of *never* having been in Italy or
studied the Old Masters." After a successful
career, which he never allowed to interfere unduly

176

with his fox-hunting, Grant died and was buried at Melton Mowbray.

Grant was a gifted aristocratic amateur who turned professional. He was in no sense a significant innovator, and in many ways he was a holdover from the 18th century and the Regency, indeed just as were his landed patrons. His earlier sporting pictures often recall Ben Marshall, and his portraiture carries on the tradition of Lawrence, but it often has an easy directness and charm raising it above the level of most of his early Victorian colleagues.
A.S.

Bibliography
John Steegman, "Sir Francis Grant, P. R. A.: The Artist in High Society," *Apollo,* LXXXIX, 1964, pp. 479-85

176
Mary Isabella Grant
Leicester Museum and Art Gallery
Oil on canvas; 50 x 40 in.
c. 1850

Mary Isabella Grant was the daughter of the artist. In 1852 she was married to Sir Francis Geary of Oxon Hoath, near Tonbridge in Kent. She died in 1854. Grant exhibited no. 176 at the Royal Academy in 1850, and in the following year he presented another portrait of his daughter to the Academy as his diploma picture. This latter picture, which is approximately the same size as no. 176, shows Miss Grant seated holding a dog in her lap. Stylistically, no. 176 might also be compared to Grant's *Portrait of Mrs. Livesay* of 1851 (Bristol), which shows similar early Victorian detail and affectionate sentimentality within the context of the 18th-century tradition of large-scale figures in a landscape setting.
A.S.

Provenance
Sir Francis Geary, Oxon Hoath

Thos. Agnew & Sons, London
Leicester Museum and Art Gallery, 1954

Exhibitions
Royal Academy, 1850, no. 126 *(Miss Grant)*
Thos. Agnew & Sons, London, 1954 (as *Lady Geary*)

References
Leicester Museums and Art Gallery, *Catalogue of Local Portraits,* Leicester, 1956, pp. 48-49, no. 55

Reproductions
Engraved by Thomas Faed, 1851

Lewis was a native of London. His father Frederic Christian Lewis was a well-known engraver, and his uncle George Robert Lewis was a painter of portraits and landscapes. Two brothers were also artists. He was trained by his father, served for a time as a studio assistant to Sir Thomas Lawrence and exhibited pictures before he was fifteen years old. He was first active as a painter of animals, and in the 1820s, under the patronage of King George IV, he painted deer and sporting subjects in Windsor Park. However, he withdrew from this field, apparently because he did not wish to compete with Edwin Landseer, who had been a childhood friend. In 1827 Lewis was elected an associate member of the Old Water Colour Society and from then until the late 1850s he painted almost exclusively in watercolor.

From 1832 to 1834 Lewis was in Spain. This visit was inspired by Wilkie's Spanish trip, and Lewis dedicated to Wilkie one of the two volumes of lithographs of Spanish scenes which he subsequently published. His views of picturesque Spain were so popular that he was dubbed "Spanish Lewis." However, the Spanish travels were only a prelude to a more ambitious journey. In 1837 he was in Paris; from there he travelled to Rome, and in 1840 he went on to Corfu, Athens and Constantinople, where his path crossed with Wilkie's. In 1842 he went to Cairo, and he remained there until 1851. Thackeray visited him in 1844 and wrote a description of him living the life of an oriental pasha, but otherwise Lewis seems to have tried to avoid contact with the British Isles. From

1838 to 1850, with one exception in 1841, he did not exhibit in London. In 1848 he was dropped from the membership of the Old Water Colour Society as a result of his inactivity; however, Lewis wrote promising henceforth to abide by the Society's regulations and was reinstated.

In 1850 Lewis sent to the Society's exhibition a large, microscopically elaborate watercolor named *The Hhareem,* which immediately caused a sensation (Victoria and Albert Museum, cf. no. 179). In 1851 he returned to England, and from 1852 through 1857 he exhibited eight additional Eastern watercolors. These drew unstinted praise from Ruskin; about Lewis's *Frank Encampment in the Desert of Mt. Sinai,* exhibited in 1856, he wrote, "I have no hesitation in ranking it among the most *wonderful* pictures in the world," and he declared that since the death of Veronese nothing comparable had been painted. Despite Lewis's bad behavior of a few years earlier, he was elected president of the Old Water Colour Society in 1855. However, in 1858 he resigned from the Society in order to concentrate his energies on oil painting, which he felt would be more lucrative than watercolor. He was elected an A.R.A. in 1859 and a full member of the Academy in 1865. For the rest of his life he industriously produced oil paintings of Eastern subjects which do not differ radically, except in medium, from his watercolors of the 1850s.
A.S.

177

Bibliography
"British Artists: Their Style and Character: No. XXXII—John Frederick Lewis," *Art Journal,* 1858, pp. 41-43
Randall Davies, "John Frederick Lewis, R. A. Some Contemporary Notices with Comments by the Editor," *OWCSC,* III, 1926, pp. 31-50
Hugh Stokes, "John Frederick Lewis," *Walker's Quarterly,* no. 28, London, 1929
Brinsley Ford, "J. F. Lewis and Richard Ford in Seville, 1832-33," *Burlington,* LXXX, 1942, pp. 124-29

177
Study for "The Proclamation of Don Carlos"
The Visitors of the Ashmolean Museum, Oxford
Watercolor and gouache on three joined pieces of
paper; 17⅜ x 23⅛ in., irregular
c. 1833-37

Don Carlos was the younger brother of King
Ferdinand VII of Spain. In the summer of 1833,
Ferdinand voided the law forbidding female
succession to the throne, thus making his daughter
Isabella heir to the monarchy rather than Don
Carlos. Don Carlos refused to renounce his rights,
and after the death of Ferdinand VII on September
29, 1833, he was proclaimed King by the clerical
party. This set off the Carlist wars, which were to
continue on the behalf of Don Carlos and his heirs
through the rest of the 19th century.

Lewis was in Spain from 1832 until 1834, and had
firsthand exposure to the opening events of the
Carlist wars. In the midst of civil war, he continued
to travel extensively, making sketches of
picturesque subjects. He apparently projected two
ambitious treatments of the war, *The Proclamation
of Don Carlos* and *The Christino Spy before
Zumulcarregui*. In the sale of Lewis's works in
1877, after his death, four drawings were listed as
studies for the picture *The Proclamation of Don
Carlos*. However, there is no record of the finished
picture ever having been exhibited or sold, and it
is possible that it never was painted. Another
sketch for the picture, showing a different group
of figures, is now also in the Ashmolean Museum.

Lewis's Spanish work is best known from his two
volumes of lithographs, *Lewis's Sketches and
Drawings of the Alhambra* and *Lewis's Sketches of
Spain and Spanish Character*. These, as their
titles indicate, have primarily topographical and
picturesque interest. No. 177 is more ambitious in
that it depicts contemporary history, but even here
Lewis approaches history in terms of local color,
rather than showing the most dramatic and
significant aspects of events. It is a brilliant
example of Lewis's virtuoso abilities as a draftsman

before his trip to the East, abilities that are often
concealed by the insipid prettiness of many of his
subjects, and there are echoes of the Spanish
work of Wilkie, such as his *Defence of Saragossa,*
which had been exhibited in 1829 (Royal
Collection). Lewis dedicated one of his volumes
of Spanish views to Wilkie.
A.S.

Provenance
(?) The artist's sale (Christie's, London, 5 May 1877,
nos. 298-301)
The Ashmolean Museum, 1941

Exhibitions
30th Annual Exhibition of Early English Water-colours,
Walker's Galleries, London, 1934, no. 62

References
Davies, *OWCSC,* III, 1926, p. 47
Ford, *Burlington,* LXXX, 1942, p. 128, n. 4

178
Two Camels
The Metropolitan Museum of Art, Gift of Mr. and
Mrs. Charles K. Wilkinson, 1961
Watercolor and gouache over black chalk on
brownish paper; 14⅝ x 20⅝ in.
Inscribed: [de] *sert of Mt. Sinai J. F. Lewis*
c. 1843

There exist large numbers of uncompleted sketches
of Eastern subjects by Lewis, almost none of
which are dated. It is probable that he executed
them in the East and that they provided the basis
for the elaborately finished watercolors and
paintings which he continued to paint and exhibit
in London for over twenty years after his return

178

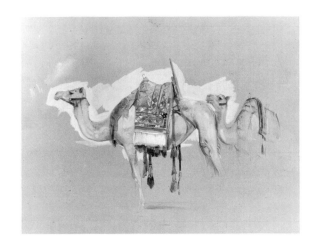

from Cairo. However, it is not known whether he
also made some of these sketches while living in
England. The sale of Lewis's estate after his death
consisted largely of such drawings, which suggest
that he made them only for his own use and
not to sell.

Lewis visited Mt. Sinai in 1843 and possibly in
other years as well. Camels such as those in no. 17
appear in several of his finished Eastern subjects,
for example, *A Frank Encampment in the Desert
of Mt. Sinai,* which Ruskin praised so lavishly in
1856, but he does not seem to have made specific
use of this drawing in any of his known later work.
A.S.

Provenance
(?) The artist's sale (Christie's, London, 4 May 1877,
no. 130, *Studies of Camels, Desert of Mt. Sinai,*
bt. Critchell)

179

179
Life in the Harem
Victoria and Albert Museum, London
Watercolor and gouache; 23⅞ x 18¾ in.
Inscribed: *JFL* (monogram) *1858*

This drawing has occasionally been confused with *The Hhareem,* which Lewis sent to the Old Water Colour Society's exhibition in 1850 and which is now also in the Victoria and Albert Museum. No. 179 is, however, dated 1858. In that year Lewis had resigned from the watercolor group in order to devote himself to painting in oil and make himself eligible for election to the Royal Academy. In 1858, among Lewis's exhibits at the Royal Academy was *An Inmate of the Harem* (no. 122),

but this was an oil painting and not to be identified with no. 179. Scenes of harem life were subjects which Lewis repeated over and over after his trip to the East until his death, and the same motifs and compositions often reappear, making it difficult to distinguish between various versions.

The style of no. 179 is essentially the same as that of Lewis's *The Hhareem* of 1850 and of his other exhibited watercolors of the 1850s. It is primarily in body-color, or gouache, and is painted with the stippled precision of a miniaturist. The brilliant colors look more like those of an oil painting than those we usually associate with watercolor, and it is easy to see how Lewis could so readily change mediums without in the least altering the look of his works. To many historians of English watercolors, Lewis's use of the medium was misuse and a sign of decadence. Because of this and despite his obvious virtuosity and the brilliance of his *œuvre,* Lewis has received little sympathetic attention in this century.

Ruskin associated Lewis's Eastern subjects with his training as an animal painter, suggesting that he had thus prepared himself "to portray the comparative animal life of the southern and eastern families of mankind." A work such as no. 179 seems like a final languid distillation of the romantic interest in the exotic East which attracted so many French and English painters of the 19th century. Lewis's interest in effects of the brilliant sunlight of the East is also noteworthy, and most of his interiors show light filtering through elaborate lattice-work shutters.

No. 179 was painted when Pre-Raphaelitism was in full bloom. Ruskin called Lewis, whom he admired immensely, a Pre-Raphaelite, and he combined his defense of the younger artists with praise of the older. However, there is no likelihood of influence of Lewis's work on the Pre-Raphaelites, or vice versa, as Lewis only returned from the East, with his style established, three years after the Brotherhood was founded. There are obvious similarities, but Ruskin was probably right when,

in 1858, he said that Lewis was the one artist in England painting without reference to Pre-Raphaelite dogmas, neither in imitation nor defiance.
A.S.

Provenance
(?) Mozley, Liverpool (sale, Christie's, London, 27 May 1865, no. 156, *Interior of a Turkish Harem,* 25 x 19 in.)
(?) John Noble (sale, Christie's, London, 4 July 1891, no. 30, *Harem Life,* dated 1858, bt. Vokins)
Purchased by the Victoria and Albert Museum, 1893

References
Ruskin, XII, 363; XIV, 160
William Gaunt, *A Concise History of English Painting,* London, 1964, p. 184, pl. 142 (incorrectly dated 1850)

1805-1881

Palmer started life in the suburbs of London. His father, a bookseller, approved of his becoming an artist, and he began to learn the conventions of drawing from William Wate, a minor and now forgotten landscape artist. In 1819, when he was fourteen years old, he had works accepted at both the British Institution and the Royal Academy. In 1822 he met John Linnell, who immediately began to exercise a strong influence on him. Linnell encouraged Palmer to study engravings by Dürer and Lucas Van Leyden and to draw the human figure, and together they visited the collection of early Flemish and German pictures belonging to Charles Aders. This exposure disillusioned Palmer with the conventional effects of English landscape painting that he had learned so far. In a notebook of 1824, we find him writing to himself, "Look for Van Leydenish qualities in real landscape, and look hard, long and continually."

Linnell introduced Palmer to several of his friends, among them William Mulready, who joined with Linnell in urging upon Palmer a precise, severe attention to detail. And Linnell was responsible for the single most important event in Palmer's life: on Saturday, October 9, 1824 he took him to see William Blake. By then Palmer already seems to have experienced visions on his own, and he and Blake hit it off immediately. Shortly after the visit he wrote: "The scene recurs to me afterwards in a kind of vision; and in this most false, corrupt, and genteely stupid town my spirit sees his dwelling (the chariot of the sun), as it were an island in the midst of the sea—such a place is it for primitive

grandeur, whether in the persons of Mr. and Mrs. Blake, or in the things hanging on the walls." Palmer became one of a group of young artists who gathered around Blake in the last years of his life. Although two of the others, Edward Calvert and George Richmond, produced striking works under the spell of Blake, Palmer alone was able to develop out of Blake's influence, on the basis of his own studies, a sustained creation both deeply personal and highly original.

In 1826 or 1827 Palmer moved to the village of Shoreham in Kent. Blake visited him there at least once before his death in 1827, and Linnell and Palmer's other associates were frequent visitors. But for the most part, this was a period of isolation in which Palmer could identify with nature and with the rustic life of the surrounding valley. At Shoreham he produced his best works, combining visionary exaltation and the close study of nature which Linnell continued to encourage. This lasted until 1833 or 1834, when the impulse waned, and Palmer began to tire of the restricted world of Shoreham. The passage of the Reform Bill of 1832 upset him, and the accompanying rick-burnings and social agitation apparently brought disillusionment with rural life. In 1832 he bought a house in London and took a sketching trip to Devonshire. In 1835 and 1836 he visited North Wales, and in 1836 he left Shoreham for good to live in London. In September 1837 he married Linnell's daughter and set off on a honeymoon trip to Italy which lasted two years. Linnell had an imperious temperament, and he seems to have made his son-in-law's life miserable. Palmer spent the rest of his life unhappily in a series of suburban homes, struggling to make a living by his art. He became a member of the Old Water Colour Society, and he was active as an etcher. Towards the end of his life he made ambitious series of illustrations to Milton and Virgil.

Palmer's son, who was also his pious biographer, destroyed most of the early notebooks and sketchbooks, feeling that the visionary excesses were an embarrassment. A sketchbook of 1824 is

divided between the Victoria and Albert and British Museums, and six varnished sepia drawings, done in 1825 when Palmer was most immediately influenced by Blake, are in the Ashmolean Museum. These unfortunately are too fragile to travel. The earliest works in the present exhibition date from 1828 when Palmer was fully established at Shoreham. Around 1832 the tension of his work began to soften, and by the time of Palmer's Italian trip his style had changed completely. His later works have seemed an anticlimax to most modern observers. They are, however, often both sensitive and accomplished, and they would receive more respect if they did not suffer from comparison with the extraordinary production of Palmer's youth.
A.S.

Bibliography
A. H. Palmer, *The Life and Letters of Samuel Palmer,* London, 1892
Laurence Binyon, *The Followers of William Blake: Edward Calvert, Samuel Palmer, George Richmond and Their Circle,* London, 1925
Geoffrey Grigson, *Samuel Palmer: The Visionary Years,* London, 1947
Martin Butlin, *Samuel Palmer's Sketch-Book, 1824,* Clairvaux, 1962

180
Oak Trees in Lullingstone Park
The National Gallery of Canada, Ottawa
Pen, ink, watercolor and gouache on grey paper;
11⅝ x 18⁵⁄₁₆ in.
Inscribed: *S. Palmer*
c. 1828

Lullingstone Park is a few miles from Shoreham. No. 180 is one of several studies from nature commissioned by John Linnell on a visit to Shoreham in September 1828. Palmer wrote to George Richmond that Linnell had told him that by making such studies he could earn a thousand pounds a year, but "tho' I am making studies for Mr. Linnell, I will, God help me, never be a

180

earlier drawings, although full of visionary oddities, are built out of a vocabulary based on the study of early engravings, and they often verge on the incoherent. After 1828, while the traits of Palmer's personality in no way disappear, his art is enriched by a constant dialogue with the natural world, a world, however, apprehended so closely that it becomes transformed into a part of Palmer's own visionary being.

Geoffrey Grigson notes that William Gilpin, the advocate of the picturesque, in his *Remarks on Forest Scenery* of 1791 instructed artists to study lichens, "the green velvet moss" of oaks, and "little rich knots and fringes." These are the elements of nature which Palmer described as contrary to art, but which so beguiled him that they became central elements of many of his drawings. As a student of landscape, Palmer must have been acquainted with Gilpin's writings, although what he thought of them is not known. A study of gnarled trees, such as no. 180, is in the tradition of picturesque sketches, but the vitality of Palmer's drawing far transcends the normally genteel picturesque view. A.S.

Provenance
John Linnell
Herbert Linnell
Walker's Galleries, London
The National Gallery of Canada, 1937

Exhibitions
Early English Watercolours, Walker's Galleries, London, 1937, no. 88
The Work of Samuel Palmer, Durlacher Bros., New York, 1949, no. 7
Five Centuries of Drawings, Museum of Fine Arts, Montreal, 1953, no. 256
Samuel Palmer and His Circle: The Shoreham Period, Arts Council, London, 1957, no. 17
The World of W. B. Yeats, University of Victoria, Victoria, B. C., 1965, no. 23

References
William Gilpin, *Remarks on Forest Scenery and Other Woodland Views,* London, 1791, I, 10-11
"Early English Water-Colours," *Walker's Monthly,* June, 1937, no. 114, ill. p. 3

naturalist by profession." He was still working on the commission in December, and in a letter of December 21 to Linnell he complained about the difficulty of being the naturalist Linnell wished him to be. Although he admitted nature's "lovely gentleness of mild attraction," he found difficulty in reconciling its charm and multiplicity with "the unwinning severity, the awfulness, the ponderous globosity of Art," and he cited an example: "Milton, by one epithet, draws an oak of the largest girth I ever saw, 'Pine and *monumental* oak'; I have just been trying to draw a large one in Lullingstone; but the poet's tree is huger than any in the park: there, the moss, and rifts, and barky furrows, and the mouldering grey (tho' that adds majesty to the lord of the forests) mostly catch the eye, before

the grasp and grapple of the roots, the muscular belly and shoulders, the twisted sinews."

There exist at least three closely related studies of oak trees (Grigson, nos. 60-62), and Palmer's letter could refer to any of them. As can be seen in no. 180, he did try to show the grasp and grapple, the muscle, and the sinews of the gnarled old trees, but equally attended to are the moss and bark of surface detail. Palmer's studious care is obvious, but he nonetheless manages to endow his trees with emotional drama and patriarchal dignity.

The naturalistic drawings made for Linnell are of great importance in Palmer's development. His

Geoffrey Grigson, "Samuel Palmer at Shoreham," *Signature,* Nov. 1937, pp. 9-11, ill. opp. p. 17
A. P. Oppé, "Drawings at the National Gallery of Canada," *Burlington,* LXXXIX, 1941, pp. 54, 56, pl. E
Grigson, pp. 58-69, 74, 82-83, 89-91, 170, no. 62

181
Pear Tree in a Walled Garden
Mr. and Mrs. Victor O. Jones
Watercolor and gouache; 8¾ x 11⅛ in.
c. 1829

The artist's son suggests that this study was made either in the garden of "Waterhouse," Palmer's home in Shoreham, or in a corner of the garden of a Mr. Groombridge. This latter place was so fertile and rich that Palmer took Linnell and other visitors to see it (note in catalogue of 1926 exhibition).

In May 1829 Palmer wrote to Linnell urging him to visit Shoreham, "tho' living in the country, I really did not think there were those splendours in visible creation which I have lately seen." A passage from the letter to Linnell of the previous December, in which he had discussed the oaks at Lullingstone, also suggests some of the associations, as well as the excitement, which he found in the blossoming of spring: "Terrestrial spring showers blossoms and odours in profusion, which, at some moments, 'Breathe on earth the air of Paradise': indeed sometimes, when the spirits are in Heav'n, earth itself, as in emulation, blooms again into Eden . . .''

The treatment of the richly flowering tree is akin to another drawing, *In a Shoreham Garden* (Victoria and Albert Museum), which is of the identical size, but vertical rather than horizontal. Neither is dated; the date of c. 1829, generally ascribed to them, is due to Grigson, who sees in these drawings the development of a new visionary

frenzy based on Palmer's study of nature. In no. 181 the size and rhythm of the foreground leaves and the insistently superabundant blossoms of the tree have a compulsive extravagance suggestive of the tumultuous state of Palmer's mind.
A.S.

Provenance
Samuel Palmer
A. H. Palmer, Tilford, Surrey, and Vancouver, B.C. (sale, Christie's, London, 4 March 1929, no. 45)
Victor Rienaeker
Mrs. K. T. Parker, Oxford
Mrs. Paul J. Sachs, Cambridge, Mass.

Exhibitions
Drawings, Etchings and Woodcuts by Samuel Palmer and other Disciples of William Blake, Victoria and Albert Museum, London, 1926, no. 56 *(Study of a Wall Fruit Tree in Blossom)*
Two Centuries of English Painting, Stedelijk Museum, Amsterdam, 1936, no. 223
Aquarelles de Turner, Oeuvres de Blake, Bibliothèque Nationale, Paris, 1937, no. 114
La Peinture Anglaise, Louvre, Paris, 1938, no. 216
The Work of Samuel Palmer, Durlacher Bros., New York, 1949, no. 11
Samuel Palmer and His Circle: The Shoreham Period, Arts Council, London, 1957, no. 29

References
A. H. Palmer, pp. 175, 178
Geoffrey Grigson, "Samuel Palmer at Shoreham," *Signature,* Nov., 1937, pp. 11, 14, ill. opp. p. 16
Grigson, pp. 90-92, 174, no. 77, pl. 33

182
Moonlit Landscape
The Art Museum, Princeton University
Pencil and sepia wash; 3¹¹⁄₁₆ x 4½ in.
c. 1829-30

No. 182 is one of numerous moonlit scenes by Palmer. It is similar to *A Kentish Idyl,* a slightly smaller sepia drawing, which Grigson dates c. 1829-30. Palmer repeated the effect of dappled moonlit clouds, which appears with slight variation in *A Kentish Idyl,* also in a number of other drawings.

Palmer's interest in nocturnal effects developed well before his move to Shoreham and continued throughout his life. It was certainly encouraged by his devotion to Milton, whose lines from *Comus,*

> . . . there does a sable cloud
> Turn forth her silver lining on the night,
> And casts a gleam over this tufted grove.

had previously inspired Wright of Derby's moonlit *Lady from Comus* in Liverpool. In 1829 Palmer's nurse gave him an edition of Milton, inside the front cover of which he made a list of all those passages which referred to the moon. There are also numerous moons in Blake, notably in his woodcut illustrations to Dr. R. J. Thornton's *Virgil Eclogues* (1821), which had the most immediate effect of any of Blake's works upon Palmer and his circle; in a note written in 1825, Palmer contrasted their "mystic and dreamy glimmer" to the "gaudy daylight" of this world. Palmer's sketchbook of 1824 is full of moons, and his letters from Shoreham contain descriptions of "perfumed and enchanted twilight" and of the delights of nocturnal walks on midsummer eves. Some of the significance he attached to these scenes is suggested by a passage from his letter of December 21, 1828 to Linnell: "Creation sometimes pours into the spiritual eye the radiance of Heaven: the green mountains that glimmer in a summer gloaming from the dusky yet bloomy east; the moon opening her golden eye, or walking in brightness among innumerable

181

182

islands of light, not only thrill the optic nerve, but shed a mild, a grateful, an unearthly lustre into the inmost spirits, and seem the interchanging twilight of that peaceful country, where there is no sorrow and no night."

This small sepia drawing was unknown to Grigson. It conceivably could be one of two sepia landscapes of approximately the same size which were included in the Palmer exhibition of 1926 (nos. 77 and 79), but which Grigson was unable to locate. However, neither of the brief notices in the 1926 catalogue precisely describes no. 182. In 1829 Palmer submitted to the Royal Academy two "little moonshines," in which he felt that there was more look of light than he had achieved previously and less of his "wonted outrageousness." Both were rejected and it is now impossible to identify them.
A.S.

Provenance
Frank Jewett Mather, Jr., Princeton

Exhibitions
The Work of Samuel Palmer, Durlacher Bros., New York, 1949, no. 46

References
A. H. Palmer, pp. 15-16, 176, 178
Grigson, pp. 85, 92-93, 174-75, cf. no. 79, pl. 35, p. 195

183
The Harvest Moon
City Museum and Art Gallery, Carlisle
Watercolor and gouache; 4⅞ x 5½ in.
c. 1830-31

For Palmer's interest in nocturnal scenes see no. 182. Grigson, who proposes a date of c.1830-31 for no. 183, suggests that it may be a drawing leading up to the *Harvest Moon* which Palmer exhibited at the Royal Academy in 1833. However, the exhibited picture has disappeared and its actual appearance is not known. As Palmer's style began to broaden in the early 1830s, he painted several scenes of bustling harvest activity, for example, another *Harvest Moon* (Tate Gallery) and *A Pastoral Scene* (Ashmolean Museum), both in tempera. Grigson is probably correct in dating no. 183 somewhat earlier than these works. It does show a new mellow richness, characteristic of the end of Palmer's Shoreham period, but the huge dominating moons do not reappear in the later works.
A.S.

Provenance
Dr. and Mrs. Gordon Bottomley (bequest to the City Museum and Art Gallery, Carlisle, 1949)

Exhibitions
Second Annual Exhibition of Watercolours, Cotswold Gallery, London, 1924, no. 32
Samuel Palmer and His Circle: The Shoreham Period, Arts Council, London, 1957, no. 40

183

The Romantic Movement, The Tate Gallery and Arts Council Gallery, London, 1959, no. 803

References
Grigson, pp. 93, 179, no. 93, pl. 46

184
Portrait of the Artist as Christ
Kerrison Preston
Oil on panel; 13½ x 9¼ in.
c. 1833

In the most notable image of Palmer, other than no. 184, the *Self Portrait* drawing of about 1828 (Ashmolean Museum), he appears beardless and with short hair. However, in a letter of May 17, 1829 to Linnell, he wrote, "the artists have at last an opportunity of wearing the beard unmolested I understand from the papers that it is become the height of fashion! I hope they will avail of this . . ." Palmer took his own advice, and as shown in a miniature by George Richmond (National Portrait

184

Gallery) and a related drawing by Richmond, dated February 7, 1830 (private collection), by the following year he had grown long hair and a beard and had taken on a distinctly Christlike appearance. A later drawing by Henry Walter (British Museum), probably done on a trip Palmer and Walter jointly made to Wales in 1835, shows him with the beard and hair trimmed short. The date of c. 1833, proposed for no. 184 by Mr. L. G. Duke, is thus after the Richmond drawing and miniature but before Palmer had trimmed his locks to a somewhat more conventionally acceptable appearance.

The change between the Ashmolean drawing and no. 184 is great. The earlier drawing is an amazing revelation of Palmer's obsessed yet sensitive character, while in no. 184, he takes on the forbidding blankness of a hierarchical Byzantine Christ. It has been suggested in *The Burlington Magazine* that this self portrait is based on Dürer's self portrait of 1500 in the Alte Pinakothek, Munich, in which Dürer is seen with hair falling to his shoulders and staring eyes. Dürer had been one of Palmer's heroes since Linnell had introduced his engravings to Palmer in 1822.

Whether Palmer actually thought of no. 184 as a self portrait is questionable. It is more likely that he intended it as a portrait of Christ, using himself as model. His letters to George Richmond of 1832 and 1834 show that this was a period of religious fanaticism in his life; the rapturous descriptions of nature in his letters of the 1820s have given way to a predominating concern with Christian theology. In 1832 he wrote that he intended to obtain prints of the holy Bishop Fisher and of his fellow-martyr Sir Thomas Moore, "and hang them cheek by jowl in my little chapel, that they may frown vice, levity, and infidelity out of my house and out of my heart." Palmer quite obviously believed in the power of images, and it seems likely that no. 184 was intended to serve a similar function. It would have been natural to use himself as a model: in the relative isolation of his later Shoreham years there were few other models available, and he must

have been aware that his hirsuteness gave him a Christ-like appearance, if only via the suggestion of Richmond's miniature. Despite the visionary freedom of his art, Palmer's religion tended to be violently orthodox, and it seems improbable that he would have thought of himself as worthy of a halo, or that he would have had the temerity to identify himself with his redeemer. The traces of a crown within the halo suggest that he had considered showing Christ as King, a natural inclination for Palmer, who was deeply disturbed by the Church of England's temporal problems resulting from the passage of the Reform Bill. A.S.

Provenance
Hugh Squire
L. G. Duke, London

Exhibitions
English Romantic Paintings: 1800-1900, Maas Gallery, London, 1965, no. 22

References
A. H. Palmer, pp. 178-82
"Notable Works of Art Now on the Market," *Burlington,* CV, Dec. 1963, supplement, pl. XXV
Illustrated London News, Christmas number, 1963, ill.

185
View of Tivoli
Philadelphia Museum of Art, Given in Memory of J. Leonard Sessler by Mr. and Mrs. Arthur Goldsmith and Mabel Zahn
Pencil, watercolor and gouache on tinted paper; 12⅞ x 16⅜ in.
c. 1838 or 1839

Immediately after their marriage in September 1837, Palmer and his wife went off to Italy where they remained for over two years while Palmer worked industriously painting landscape views. On September 16, 1838 he wrote to George Richmond from Corpo di Cava, that they hoped "to grapple with Tivoli" before spending the winter in Rome.

185

In the posthumous exhibition of Palmer's works at the Fine Art Society in 1881, an outdoor study of *Tivoli and the Campagna of Rome* was dated 1839. Palmer continued to paint Italian views after his return to England; another treatment of the same subject was dated 1845 in the 1881 exhibition catalogue, and his exhibits at the Old Water Colour Society from 1843 through 1845 consisted largely of scenes of Italy.

No. 185 is presumably a view drawn on the spot, rather than a later reworking. According to A. H. Palmer, his father's practice was to make elaborate studies out-of-doors, spending several consecutive days on a single drawing. To save time in sketching he used warm middle-tint paper and body-color (or gouache), which is very evident in no. 185. The rapid notation in pencil of foreground detail also differs from the more polished technique of Palmer's finished works.

In contrast to the relatively private nature of Palmer's Shoreham views, no. 185 shows what is probably the all-time favorite subject of landscape painting, the so-called Temple of the Sibyl and the neighboring waterfalls at Tivoli. Although there is nothing left of Palmer's Shoreham mannerisms, he does represent the scene under a transfiguring sunset. As A. H. Palmer noted about most of the studies from his father's honeymoon trip, it presents "a golden and glittering" Italy. Palmer lost his visionary intensity, but he retained throughout his life a Virgilian idealism, and the crumbling temples and shepherds with their flock appear and reappear in his later work.
A.S.

Provenance
Bryan Hook
Alexander Finberg, London
Mrs. Clegg
Mrs. Holden White
Philadelphia Museum of Art, 1956

Exhibitions
Water-Colour Drawings and Etchings by Samuel Palmer, Cotswold Gallery, London, 1927, no. 3 (lent by Bryan Hook)

Nineteenth and Twentieth Century European Drawings,
National Gallery of Art, Washington, etc. (American
Federation of Arts), 1965-66, no. 43

References
A. H. Palmer, pp. 60-61, 76, 194, 206
Ira Moskowitz, ed., *Great Drawings of All Time,* New
York, 1962, IV, no. 990 (text by Theodore Heinrich)

186

186
Study of Barley, Oats and Wheat
The Art Museum, Princeton University
Pencil, watercolor and gouache; 10⅞ x 15¹/₁₆ in.
Inscribed extensively with descriptive notes
c. 1846 or 1847

The date ascribed to no. 186 is due to A. H. Palmer
(note in 1926 exhibition catalogue). In 1846 the
nature of the works Palmer sent to the exhibition
of the Old Water Colour Society changed radically;
from the Italian views exhibited in 1845, he
switched to domestic subjects with titles such as
The Corn Field and *The Listening Gleaner.* He
presumably drew no. 186 to help him with his new
class of subjects.

This is a later example of the close, niggling study
of nature which Palmer's mentor and father-in-law
John Linnell had urged upon him as early as 1822.
He made numerous such studies; a comparable
drawing of a bough loaded with apples, also
inscribed with descriptive notes, is dated 1830,
from the midst of the Shoreham period (Fitzwilliam
Museum). No. 186 shows the absolutely literal and
microscopically close study of nature's forms and
appearances, which in the 1840s, in the first volume
of *Modern Painters,* Ruskin was urging upon the
young artists of England, and it is comparable to
many of Ruskin's own studies of natural detail.
A.S.

Provenance
A. H. Palmer, Tilford, Surrey, and Vancouver, B. C.
(sale, Christie's, London, 4 March 1929, no. 34)
Durlacher Bros., New York
Frank Jewett Mather, Jr., Princeton

Exhibitions
*Drawings, Etchings and Woodcuts by Samuel Palmer
and Other Disciples of William Blake,* Victoria and
Albert Museum, London, 1926, no. 100
Durlacher Bros., New York, 1938
The Work of Samuel Palmer, Durlacher Bros., New York,
1949, no. 28

David Scott

1806-1849

David Scott was a native of Edinburgh and spent most of his life there. He was the son of Robert Scott, an engraver, and brother of William Bell Scott, the poet, painter, and friend of Rossetti. He was trained as an engraver, but by the age of twenty he had decided to become a painter and to devote himself to high art of the most ambitious kind. In 1828 his first exhibited work was *The Hopes of Early Genius Destroyed by Death,* a title indicative of Scott's neurotically morbid outlook and portentously appropriate to his own life. A year later he was elected to the Scottish Academy (later the Royal Scottish Academy). In 1832 he went to Italy and spent over a year in Rome, returning to Edinburgh in 1834. He was an unsuccessful competitor in the cartoon competitions for the Parliament frescoes in 1843. Plagued by ill health, he died at the age of forty-three.

Scott's output is very uneven, and his achievements often fall sadly short of his ambitions. He was, however, aware of his own failings and of the shortcomings of the British art about him and he struggled desperately, if self-consciously, to rise above them. He was one of the few artists of his generation to look seriously at Blake, and he considered his own art an attempt to unite Blake's concern with the infinite to man's historical appearances. He was also aware of progressive European painting. He admired David and his followers, who were anathema to most Englishmen, and he was affected by the German Nazarenes, with whom he came into contact in Rome. The journals of his travels reveal a searching interest

in the past and a surprising attention to such figures as Caravaggio and Canova, as well as more obvious heroes such as Michelangelo.

In his later years Scott became a landmark in the intellectual life of Edinburgh as the gloomy romantic genius of the place. He was visited by Margaret Fuller and by Emerson, whose portrait by Scott is in the Concord Public Library. After his death, William Bell Scott labored in behalf of his memory, writing a memoir of his life and publishing his illustrations to *The Pilgrim's Progress* (he had previously published a series of illustrations to *The Rime of the Ancient Mariner).* Largely due to his brother's pushing, David Scott's reputation stood high with the Pre-Raphaelites. Rossetti and Madox Brown both considered him a British counterpart to Delacroix (see no. 210), and Rossetti included a eulogistic passage about him in Gilchrist's *Life of Blake.*

A.S.

Bibliography
William Bell Scott, *Memoir of David Scott, R. S. A.,* Edinburgh, 1850
John M. Gray, *David Scott, R. S. A., and His Works,* Edinburgh, 1884

187
Philoctetes Left in the Isle of Lemnos by the Greeks in Their Progress Towards Troy
National Gallery of Scotland
Oil on canvas; 39¾ x 47 in.
c. 1839

Philoctetes was a Greek hero in the Trojan War. On the way to Troy he was bitten in the foot by a serpent. This produced so fetid a wound, and Philoctetes's cries of pain were so terrible that his comrades left him on the uninhabited island of Lemnos. Subsequently the Greeks learned that Troy could only be taken by the bow and arrows of Hercules, which Philoctetes had inherited, so Odysseus and Diomedes returned to Lemnos and

brought him to Troy. A play by Sophocles is based upon these later events. No. 187 shows him abandoned on the island, writhing in pain while he bathes his foot, the bow and arrows conspicuous beside him.

Robert Rosenblum has cited several treatments of the subject of Philoctetes by romantic artists. The theme of isolation and suffering must have been one with which Scott, living in Edinburgh and in ill health, would readily have identified. Rosenblum points out, however, that Philoctetes had been cited by Lessing as an example of unrestrained and ignoble anguish which the artist should spurn; his model instead should be the restrained and noble suffering of Laocoön. Ironically, or perhaps intentionally in an effort to prove that Philoctetes could be dignified, Scott based his figure on the *Laocoön* group. He was, of course, familiar with that monument of antiquity from his stay in Rome. At one point in his journal he declared the author of the *Laocoön,* along with Caravaggio and Rembrandt, as one of the three most forceful minds exerted in art. They had all worked toward natural truth, whereas Raphael and Michelangelo were modists in comparison. Scott's main picture painted in Rome was *The Agony of Discord: Or the Household Gods Destroyed,* in which the central figure was also based on the *Laocoön.* He exhibited that picture at the Royal Scottish Academy only in 1840, the same year in which he exhibited no. 187. William Bell Scott quotes him as being pleased with the *Discord's* similarity to the *Laocoön*—"it is drawn as the *Laocoön* is modelled" —however, he repainted it in Edinburgh before exhibiting it, and it was presumably at this time that he painted the *Philoctetes.*

Scott's *Philoctetes* shows the use of a classical vocabulary in both subject and form for the most turgid romanticism. Although Scott disliked Fuseli (he criticized his "leathery, extravagant mode" and felt that, whereas Blake dealt with the infinite Fuseli treated the superstitious), the *Philoctetes* shares something of his morbid violence. Also, in the stormy meeting of classic tradition with

187

romantic emotion there is an analogy with the early Delacroix of *The Barque of Dante,* and, even more, with Géricault, an analogy justifying the Pre-Raphaelites' relating Scott to French romanticism.
A.S.

Provenance
George Cousin, Edinburgh
Presented to the National Gallery of Scotland by
J. W. Cousin, 1890

Exhibitions
Royal Scottish Academy, Edinburgh, 1840, no. 131
Loan Exhibition, Royal Scottish Academy, Edinburgh, 1863, no. 299 (lent by George Cousin)

References
W. B. Scott, pp. 211-12, 238
Gray, p. 38
"David Scott," *Burlington,* XCI, 1949, p. 153, ill. p. 152
Graham Reynolds, *Victorian Painting,* London, 1966, p. 27, pl. 7
Robert Rosenblum, *Transformations in Late Eighteenth Century Art,* Princeton, 1967, pp. 13-14

William Dyce

1806-1864

William Dyce was born in Aberdeen in 1806. He graduated from Marichal College in his native city, and among Victorian artists he was outstanding for his education and for his breadth of interests. In 1829 he won a prize for an essay on electricity and magnetism; he was an important figure in the High Church movement, and he published several essays on theological subjects and on the revival of early church music. He visited Italy four times in his life and probably had a more thorough knowledge of Italian trecento and quattrocento art than any other English artist of his day. On his first trip to Italy in 1825, he interested himself in Titian and Poussin, but on his second visit in 1827, he fell in with the German Nazarenes in Rome. On his return to Scotland he apparently attempted to emulate their example, with little success, and for the next several years his main occupation, first in Aberdeen, then in Edinburgh, was painting portraits conventionally based on Lawrence and Raeburn. In 1837 he was appointed Master of the Trustees Academy in Edinburgh, and in the same year he travelled abroad on the behalf of the newly formed Schools of Design in London to study methods of education in France and Germany. In 1838 he became Superintendent of the Schools of Design, a position he held during a stormy tenure until 1843. By this time the great undertaking of decorating the new Palace of Westminster with frescoes was underway, and Dyce, as an artist already familiar with both early Italian frescoes and their revival in the hands of the German Nazarenes, played a leading role. In 1845 he received the first commission for a fresco in the House of Lords,

and in the following winter he went to Italy to study fresco techniques. Dyce also received in 1847 the much larger commission of frescoing the Queen's Robing Room in the Palace of Westminster. This project occupied him for the rest of his life and was left uncompleted at his death in 1864.

During the 1840s Dyce's position shifted from that of an educator, with somewhat eccentric interests in German and Italian art, to a dominant position among English painters as the leader of an acknowledged revolution. He was elected an Associate of the Royal Academy in 1844 and a full member in 1848. He was clearly the favorite artist of Prince Albert, who was chairman of the commission responsible for the Parliament frescoes, and he received commissions from the Prince for a fresco in the garden pavilion in the grounds of Buckingham Palace (see no. 189), for a large fresco, *Neptune Resigning to Britannia the Empire of the Sea,* in the stair hall at Osborne House, and for pictures of the *Madonna and Child* and of *St. Joseph,* now also at Osborne House.

Dyce's example had an important influence on the formative years of the Pre-Raphaelites, and he was one of the older artists most sympathetic to them; in fact, it was Dyce who first made Ruskin look seriously at a Pre-Raphaelite picture, Millais's *Christ in the House of His Parents.* In 1855 Ruskin criticized Dyce as representing a false branch of Pre-Raphaelitism which imitated early painting rather than studying nature. Perhaps stung by this, Dyce did, in the last few years of his life, follow the lead of the younger artists in his scrupulous attention to natural detail. His best-known works are the microscopically precise landscapes which he painted after 1855 as a diversion during his holidays, while his main energies were concentrated on the frescoes for the Houses of Parliament.
A.S.

Bibliography
James Dafforne, "British Artists: Their Style and Character: No. LI—William Dyce," *Art Journal, 1860,* pp. 293-96
James Stirling Dyce, "The Life, Correspondence, and Writings of William Dyce, R. A. 1806-64: Painter, Musician, and Scholar," unpublished typescript in the Aberdeen Art Gallery
Quentin Bell, *The Schools of Design,* London, 1963
Allen Staley, "William Dyce and Outdoor Naturalism," *Burlington,* CV, 1963, pp. 470-76
Centenary Exhibition of the Work of William Dyce, R. A. (1806-1864), Aberdeen Art Gallery, and Thos. Agnew & Sons, London, 1964 (exhibition catalogue edited with introduction by Charles Carter)

188
Bacchus Nursed by the Nymphs of Nysa
The Beinecke Rare Book and Manuscript Library, Yale University
Watercolor; 4½ x 3¾ in.
c. 1827

Bacchus was the son of Zeus and Semele. To save the infant god from the wrath of Hera, Zeus conveyed him to Mt. Nysa where he was brought up by the nymphs.

Dyce exhibited a picture of this subject at the Royal Academy and the Liverpool Academy in 1827 and at the British Institution in 1828. The exhibited picture is now lost, but a small version is in the Aberdeen Art Gallery, where there is also a pen-and-ink drawing. The compositions of the painting and the drawing in Aberdeen differ in numerous details from one another, and no. 188 differs considerably from both of them, most notably in its vertical rather than horizontal shape. The Yale drawing is broadly handled and seems obviously an early sketch, which Dyce then

188

was put together during the 1830s and 1840s by Mrs. John Charles Denham and her husband, and it contains drawings by a number of leading artists of the early 19th century, including Lawrence, Flaxman, William Hamilton, Cosway, and Wilkie. Denham was an amateur artist and a frequent honorary exhibitor at the Royal Academy. In addition to drawings the album contains several letters to Denham, including one from Dyce dated June 20, 1853 in which he apologizes for being rude and says that fresco painting makes him nervous (p. 21 verso). All the drawings in the album, including the one by Dyce, seem to be earlier than this, and Dyce, in fact, is the youngest artist included.

A.S.

Provenance
Catherine Case Copeman Denham (1812-1861)
Frances Copeman (her niece)
Louisa Jane Copeman (sister of Frances Copeman, died 1921)
James Miles's Book Shop, Leeds, 1924
Sir Harold (later Lord) Mackintosh, Knaresborough, by 1935
Given by Edward J. Beinecke to the Yale University Library, 1953

189

worked up with increasing refinement into a finished picture.

Bacchus Nursed by the Nymphs of Nysa was the most important picture painted by Dyce between his first trip to Italy in 1825 and his second in 1827. It shows that his main source of inspiration at this time was Titian; the painting is little more than a pastiche of Titian's great *Bacchanals*. On his second trip Dyce's orientation changed radically; Raphael replaced Titian as the dominant ideal, and such broadly drawn and richly colored studies disappeared from his *œuvre*.

No. 188 is mounted on page 59 verso of the Denham Album, which also includes no. 134. The album

189

The Attendant Spirit, from Milton's "Comus"
Lent anonymously
Black chalk on cream paper, mounted on canvas; 18¾ x 12½ in.
c. 1844

In 1843 Prince Albert commissioned a group of artists to paint a series of frescoes in the lunettes of the octagonal central room of a garden pavilion in the grounds of Buckingham Palace. This was just before artists were to be selected to paint the frescoes in the new Houses of Parliament, and the garden pavilion was intended as a kind of trial run. The artists originally chosen were Clarkson Stanfield, Thomas Uwins, Sir William Ross, Sir

Charles Eastlake, Leslie, Maclise, Landseer, and Etty, a cross section of the leading reputations of the day. Etty was unable to cope with the medium of fresco, and in 1844, amidst considerable bitterness, his commission was taken away and given to Dyce. Ironically, Dyce had given Etty technical advice about fresco painting to help him with this commission. The frescoes no longer exist, as the garden pavilion fell into disrepair and was pulled down early in this century.

The subjects of the frescoes were to be from Milton's *Masque of Comus,* each artist illustrating a scene of his own choosing. Dyce's showed the concluding scene, when the attendant spirit in the guise of a shepherd returns to their parents the two brothers and their sister, who had been lost in the woods and under the spell of the evil Comus. On a tablet above the fresco were inscribed the opening lines of the song with which the spirit addresses the parents:

Noble Lord and Lady bright
I have brought ye new delight.
Here behold, so goodly grown,
Three fair branches of your own.

No. 189 is a drawing for the fresco, possibly a fragment of a larger cartoon. It shows the kneeling spirit, from the right side of the composition; the figure behind is one of the brothers. The drawing corresponds in all details to the portion of the fresco to which it is related (reproduced in Gruner and Jameson). The Raphaelesque quality of Dyce's draftsmanship is obvious, so obvious indeed, that, before being identified by its present owner, no. 189 was thought to be an Italian drawing of the 16th century.
A.S.

References
L. Gruner and Mrs. Jameson, *The Decoration of the Garden-Pavilion in the Grounds of Buckingham Palace,* London, 1846
Alexander Gilchrist, *Life of William Etty, R. A.,* London, 1855, II, 149-53, 163-71
T. S. R. Boase, "The Decoration of the New Palace of Westminster, 1841-1863," *JWCI,* XVII, 1954, pp. 334-35
Dennis Farr, *William Etty,* London, 1958, pp. 95-97

190

190
The Meeting of Jacob and Rachel
Hamburger Kunsthalle
Oil on canvas; 22⅞ x 22⅞ in.
c. 1853

The subject is from Genesis 29:1-12. Dyce exhibited two pictures of *Jacob and Rachel* at the Royal Academy: in 1850 and in 1853. This is the second of the two. The earlier picture is now lost, but it is reproduced in an engraving in the *Art Journal* (1860, p. 296) and in a photograph published by Colnaghi in 1857. The chief difference between that picture and no. 190 is that in the former the figures are three-quarter length, cut off at the knees by the bottom of the painting. The

earlier Jacob was bearded and there are numerou[s] variations in detail, but the essential poses of the figures are the same. Two other versions of the three-quarter length composition are in the Leicester Art Gallery and in the church of St. Lawrence, Knodishall, Suffolk. These two are close to one another but vary from the original; Jacob is beardless and a vase on the wall behind Rachel has disappeared. In addition, Dyce commissioned Holman Hunt to paint a copy of his picture when it was at the Royal Academy in 185[0]. Hunt's copy was smaller than any of the known pictures, and we would expect it to repeat the details of its model; so it is apparently yet anothe[r] unlocated version. James Dafforne, writing during Dyce's lifetime, said that the artist had repeated the subject four times. The four would be: the lost picture of 1850, the versions at Leicester and Knodishall, and no. 190.

There is also a drawing of the subject in the Aberdeen Art Gallery in which the figures are who[le] length. This has generally been taken as a preparatory study for the Hamburg picture, but in detail it corresponds more closely to the Leicester and Knodishall pictures. Rachel's vase, which reappears on the wall in no. 190, is on the ground[;] Jacob has a wine flask strapped to his hip, as in a[ll] the three-quarter length versions, but not in the Hamburg picture; and there are palm trees in the background, which, again, have disappeared in no. 190. The most logical explanation for this drawing is that it was made when Dyce was painti[ng] the Leicester and Knodishall pictures as an experiment to see how the composition would look in whole length. When Dyce actually painte[d] the whole length version, he had made so many changes and had so altered the composition tha[t] he apparently thought of it as an independent picture rather than a replica, and he exhibited it as such at the Royal Academy.

The most interesting change in the picture of 185[3] is the suppression of the palm trees in the background. Whereas in the earlier versions Dyc[e] placed his figures in what he clearly meant as a biblical landscape, in the Hamburg picture they seem to be standing before a Scottish loch. The background is reminiscent of a broadly sketched view of *Castle Threave, Dumfrieshire* by Dyce in a Scottish private collection. A few years later Dyce carried this much further in a pair of pictures of *The Man of Sorrows* and *David in the Wilderness* (both collection David Stewart) which show the biblical figures placed emphatically, if anachronistically, in the Highlands of Scotland.

Keith Andrews has compared no. 190 to Joseph Führich's 1836 painting of the same subject (Österreichische Galerie, Vienna) without, however, claiming actual influence. Their juxtaposition demonstrates how strongly Nazarene are Dyce's clear outlines, precise drawing, and hard bright colors. Dyce's *Jacob and Rachel* also has an obvious connection with Holman Hunt's *Hireling Shepherd,* which was begun in 1851 and exhibited in 1852 (Manchester), a connection which is hardly fortuitous, as Hunt in 1850 had had the closest of exposures to Dyce's composition. A.S.

Provenance
Possibly Sir C. Lindsay (sale, Christie's, London, 19 May 1866, no. 50, bt. Wallis)
G. C. Schwabe, London, by 1871 (bequest to Hamburg in 1886)

Exhibitions
Royal Academy, 1853, no. 140
Winter Exhibition of Old Masters, Royal Academy, London, 1871, no. 59 (lent by Schwabe)

References
Dafforne, *Art Journal,* 1860, pp. 295-96
Walter Armstrong, "A Pioneer Collection of English Pictures," *Art Journal,* 1886, p. 2
W. Holman Hunt, *Pre-Raphaelitism and the Pre-Raphaelite Brotherhood,* London, 1905, I, 206-07
G. Pauli, *Die Kunst des Klassizismus und der Romantik* (Propyläean-Kunstgeschichte XIV), Berlin, 1925, pl. 487
Leicester Museums and Art Gallery, *Collection of Paintings* [catalogue], Leicester, 1958, pp. 17-18, cf. no. 54
Keith Andrews, *The Nazarenes: A Brotherhood of German Painters in Rome,* Oxford, 1964, pp. 82, 131, pl. 74b
Graham Reynolds, *Victorian Painting,* London, 1966, pp. 37, 59, pl. 31

191
Welsh Landscape with Two Women Knitting
Sir David Scott
Oil on millboard; 13⅞ x 19⅞ in.
1860

The women wear traditional Welsh peasant costume, of which the most distinctive feature is the tall black beaver hat over a frilled white cap, such as is worn by the standing woman on the right. Dyce painted one previous picturesque genre subject, the *Highland Ferryman* (Aberdeen Art Gallery) which, when shown at the Royal Academy in 1859, was noted as a departure from the artist's usual practice. However, Dyce undertook these pictures and his other late landscapes primarily as a diversion from his preoccupation of the 1850s, painting frescoes in the Queen's Robing Room of the Palace of Westminster.

The peak in the distant background is Snowdon. This mountain appears in at least two other views by Dyce, an oil painting in Hamburg and a watercolor in the Ashmolean Museum. We know that Dyce visited Wales for six weeks in 1860, and this painting almost certainly dates from that trip. Upon his return home, Dyce wrote to his brother-in-law Robert Dundas Cay on October 20: "These trips for change of air always pay. I made £400 by my trip to Ramsgate two years ago and £620 by my last year's trip to Arran, and I hope to make an equally good thing out of the Welsh excursion." *Pegwell Bay* (Tate Gallery), Dyce's best-known painting, which he subtitled *A Recollection of October 5th, 1858,* is a product of the earlier trip. From the 1859 holiday come *A Scene in Arran* (Aberdeen Art Gallery) and probably *The Man of Sorrows* and *David in the Wilderness* (both collection David Stewart). The payment for these trips came largely from within Dyce's family as both *Pegwell Bay* and *A Scene in Arran,* as well as several other of his pictures, were bought by his father-in-law James Brand. No. 191, *A Scene in Arran,* the two pictures in the Stewart collection, and pictures of *Christ and the Woman of Samaria* (Birmingham), and *Henry VI During the Battle of*

Towton (Guildhall, London) are all on panels of millboard of the same size, approximately fourteen by twenty inches. Dyce apparently bought these prepared boards in large numbers as they were easy to carry with him on his travels. However, we know that he did not paint directly from nature, but that even his most detailed views were worked up from sketches.

In his letter to Cay, Dyce discussed the geological differences between the Welsh and Scottish landscapes, noting that the granite of Scotland tended to take smooth rounded shapes, while the slate of the Welsh mountains by splitting in flakes left the peaks sharp and angular. He described various Welsh formations in detail, accompanying his description with diagrammatic drawings. Dyce's Welsh and Scottish views show clearly the geological distinctions pointed out in his letter. His interest in scientific observation has, of course, much to do with the preaching of Ruskin, and these pictures are inconceivable without the prior example of the detailed naturalism of the Pre-Raphaelites. However, Dyce's painting always retains a clarity and sober discipline which readily distinguishes it from the sometimes staggering profuseness of the younger artists. A.S.

Provenance
Mrs. Robert Frank, London

Exhibitions
English Romantic Paintings, 1800-1900, Maas Gallery, London, 1965, no. 8

References
J. S. Dyce, ch. XL, *passim*
Staley, *Burlington,* 1963, pp. 474-75

191

Daniel Maclise

1806-1870

There is question about Maclise's birth date. O'Driscoll, his biographer, gives it as January 25, 1811, but Cosmo Monkhouse in the *Dictionary of National Biography* cites a record of his baptism on February 2, 1806. He was born in Cork, Ireland, the son of Alexander McClish, a merchant of Scottish descent. Maclise studied at the Cork Academy and achieved some reputation in his native city as a maker of portrait sketches. In 1827 he went to London to study at the Royal Academy schools, where in the following few years he won all the highest awards, including a travelling fellowship to Rome, which he declined. He exhibited regularly at the Academy from 1829 on, and was elected A.R.A. in 1836 and a full Academician in 1840. From 1830 through 1838, under the name Alfred Croquis, Maclise drew a series of caricatures of eminent literary figures for *Fraser's Magazine,* and his friends consisted primarily of writers rather than artists, his most intimate associates being John Forster and Charles Dickens.

Although Ruskin and the Pre-Raphaelites criticized Maclise's work as artificial and too facile, he was the most widely respected figural artist to come to maturity in the 1830s and 1840s. His oil paintings are primarily of literary subjects, painted with a hard, metallic precision. The best-known is *The Play Scene from Hamlet,* exhibited at the Royal Academy in 1842, which allowed full scope to his tendency to melodramatic theatricality (Tate Gallery). His most important works, however, are in the Houses of Parliament. In the late 1840s he

painted two of the frescoes in the House of Lords, *The Spirit of Chivalry* (see no. 193) and *The Spirit of Justice.* These were followed by the two large scenes of *The Meeting of Wellington and Blucher after the Battle of Waterloo* and *The Death of Nelson,* which Maclise painted between 1859 and 1865 in the Royal Gallery of the Palace of Westminster. These long narrow paintings, each over forty-five feet long, are both vast scenes of carnage, painted in gory detail and with endless invention. Although these were and are the most admired of the Parliament paintings, Maclise's huge reputation plummeted during the latter years of the 19th century, and today it is still near rock-bottom.

A.S.

Bibliography
W. Justin O'Driscoll, *A Memoir of Daniel Maclise, R. A.,* London, 1871
William Bates, ed., *The Maclise Portrait Gallery of 'Illustrious Literary Characters,'* London, 1883

192

192
The Debut of Paganini
Victoria and Albert Museum, London
Pencil; 14⅛ x 10¾ in.
Inscribed: *The Debut of Paganini/Harmonics & Seul Corde/ Sketched at Opera House*
1831

Nicolo Paganini (1784-1840), Italian composer and virtuoso on the violin, made his London debut at the Drury Lane Theatre on June 3, 1831. His English visit followed an extended tour on the continent, and it was preceded by extensive publicity. Paganini was a genius who behaved and looked like one, and by the time he arrived in England his musical abilities were considered as emanations

of diabolical powers. It is said that while he was in London, mobs followed him on the streets and touched him to see if he were actually made of flesh and blood. Paganini was also drawn by Ingres in 1819 (Louvre) and was the subject of a small oil painting by Delacroix (Phillips Collection, Washington). It seems likely that Delacroix's painting was made following Paganini's Paris debut on March 9, 1831 (see Maurice Serullaz, *Mémorial de l'Exposition Eugène Delacroix,* Paris, 1963, p. 107). Thus, it and Maclise's drawing probably date within a few months of one another.

No. 192 came to the Victoria and Albert Museum in the bequest of Maclise's friend John Forster, along with the original drawings for his character sketches in *Fraser's Magazine.* However, it was not reproduced in that periodical. It is larger than the drawings for *Fraser's* and apparently was made as an independent drawing for its own sake. A.S.

Provenance
John Forster, London (bequest to the Victoria and Albert Museum, 1876)

References
Armand Dayot, *La Peinture Anglaise,* Paris, 1908, ill. p. 218
Portrait Drawings, Victoria and Albert Museum, London, 1953, pl. 21

193
The Spirit of Chivalry
Sheffield City Art Galleries
Oil on canvas; 49¼ x 35¼ in.
c. 1845

After the competition of 1844 to choose artists for the new Houses of Parliament (see no. 210), the commissioners announced that six arched compartments in the House of Lords would receive the first fresco decorations. Three of the compartments were to contain personifications or abstract representations of *Religion, Justice,* and *The Spirit of Chivalry;* the other three would show appropriately corresponding scenes from English history. The commissioners also announced that they had asked six artists, Richard Redgrave, W. Cave Thomas, C. W. Cope, J. C. Horsley, Maclise, and Dyce to prepare cartoons, colored sketches, and specimens of fresco; however, they were not binding themselves to employ these artists, and there would be yet another competition in June 1845, in which their works would be shown and other artists could also compete.

193

The subject assigned to Maclise was *The Spirit of Chivalry.* In the catalogue of the 1845 competition his cartoon was number 41, a portion of the subject in the fresco was 42, and his colored sketch was 43. Although, as one of the commissioned artists, Maclise was not eligible to win a prize, it was generally acknowledged that his contribution was the highlight of the exhibition. The *Art Journal* hailed his cartoon as "alone sufficient to make this exhibition remarkable" and suggested that it should immediately have a place in the National Gallery. In 1846 he was commissioned to paint the fresco of *The Spirit of Chivalry* in the House of Lords. It was completed by April 1848, and Maclise immediately followed it with a companion fresco of *The Spirit of Justice,* for which the commission had been taken from Cave Thomas and given to Maclise.

No. 193 may be the colored sketch shown in the competition of 1845, but this is not certain. The commissioners in announcing the competition specified that the sketches need be no larger than eighteen by eighteen inches, and most of those shown were in watercolor. Another study of the subject by Maclise now hangs in the Palace of Westminster. There are numerous small differences between no. 193 and the finished fresco: in the latter, for example, the central figure carries her laurel wreath in her left hand rather than wearing it, and the knight in the right foreground wears his helmet and has his sword at his side. Also, the frescoed space has an arched top which cuts across the two side arches. Otherwise, the fresco follows the general compositional scheme depicted in no. 193.

The arched architectural background seems to have been established beforehand as a unifying factor, and variations of it appear in all six frescoes. Surrounding the object of chivalric attention are personifications of war, religion, and civil government: a warrior king, an archbishop with his hand on the altar, and two statesmen. Around them are a sculptor, a painter, a poet crowned with laurel, a philosopher and an architect. Among the

1810-1844

figures in the foreground are a bard enwreathed with ivy, "exciting youth to deeds of high emprise by his strains," a troubadour at the foot of his lady love, and a palmer from Palestine clad as a pilgrim. On the right, a kneeling knight utters a vow to the service of chivalry. The lady behind him clasps his hand and his sword-belt, which is inscribed "A Dieu et aux Dames," and her companion attaches a glove to the knight's helmet, held by his page.

Maclise's conception and composition ultimately stem from Raphael's *School of Athens,* but at a rather far remove. The crowded, piled-up composition recalls some of the later works of the German Nazarenes, such as Overbeck's *Triumph of Religion in the Arts* of 1840 (Städelsches Kunstinstitut, Frankfurt). The large first sketch of Overbeck's composition came to England about this time and was given by Prince Albert to Queen Victoria for Christmas in 1847. Maclise visited Paris in the summer of 1844, studying "dim old frescoes" in the churches and "the miles of canvas at Versailles"; however, no. 193 shows little French influence, much less than Ford Madox Brown's competition entry of 1844 (no. 210). No. 193 is closer to Brown's *Chaucer at the Court of Edward III* (Sydney, Australia), which was begun in Rome in 1845 after Brown had come into contact with the Nazarenes.

The hard, clear drawing and modelling and the figural types, especially the women, are typical of Maclise. Despite its special function, no. 193 is a good example of his art and of what was most admired in the English painting of the 1840s.
A.S.

Provenance
Purchased from the artist in 1852 by Grundy
John Wardell, Dublin (sale, Christie's, London, 29 May 1880, bt. Permain)
Sir F. T. Mappin, Sheffield (presented to the Mappin Art Gallery, Sheffield, 1887)

Exhibitions
(?) Cartoon competition, Westminster Hall, London, 1845, no. 43
Exhibition of Arts, Industries and Manufactures, and Loan Museum of Works of Art, Dublin, 1872, no. 458 (lent by Wardell)
British Subject in Narrative Pictures: 1800-1848, Arts Council, London, 1955, no. 24
Victorian Painting, Nottingham University, 1959, no. 44

References
The Art Union, 1845, pp. 170, 255, 257
F. K. Hunt, *The Book of Art: Cartoons, Frescoes, Sculpture and Decorative Art as Applied to the New Houses of Parliament: Illustrated by Engravings on Wood,* London, 1846
O'Driscoll, pp. 90-92
Allan Cunningham, *Lives of the Most Eminent British Painters, Sculptors and Architects,* London, 1880, III, 421
T. S. R. Boase, "The Decoration of the New Palace of Westminster, 1841-1863," *JWCI,* XVII, 1954, pp. 332, 338, 353
Keith Andrews, *The Nazarenes,* Oxford, 1964, p. 126, cf. pl. 67

Von Holst was the son of a music teacher from Riga. He was born in London, but he travelled several times in Germany, and there are strong Germanic overtones to his art. From the evidence of inscriptions on his drawings, he seems to have been as at home in German as in English. He entered the Royal Academy schools in the early 1820s and became a pupil of Fuseli, whose influence shaped Von Holst's art. So dependent is Von Holst's style upon that of Fuseli, that until recently a large part of his work has been attributed to the older artist. Among the wrongly attributed works are several erotic drawings which Von Holst made for George IV. He also made numerous illustrations to Goethe's *Faust,* and in many of these can be seen the influence of Delacroix's *Faust* illustrations, published in 1827, as well as that of Fuseli. In 1841 Von Holst won a prize at the British Institution for a huge painting of *The Raising of Jairus's Daughter.* He died three years later at the age of thirty-three.

Von Holst was keenly admired by the Pre-Raphaelites, who even frequented a certain restaurant, Campbell's Scotch Stores, because it contained pictures by him. His influence is important for Rossetti's early drawings, especially his illustrations to *Faust* done in the 1840s. Rossetti later described Von Holst as one of the few connecting links between the generation of Fuseli and Blake and the Pre-Raphaelites. However, Von Holst's life was too short and too irregular to allow any real fulfillment of his talents. His best works are his drawings.
A.S.

Bibliography
Gert Schiff, "Theodore Matthias Von Holst," *Burlington,*
CV, 1963, pp. 23-32

194

194
Les Adieux
The National Gallery of Canada, Ottawa
Watercolor; 14⁹⁄₁₆ x 10⁵⁄₁₆ in.
Inscribed: *Holst 1827 Les Adieux*

Gert Schiff has identified the source of this drawing
as *Ginevra,* a poem by Shelley, written in 1821 and
published in 1824. The girl Ginevra has just married
a rich man, Gherardi, whom she does not love.
Between the ceremony and the wedding feast, her
lover Antonio accosts her. She gives to him, as a
pledge of her faith, the wedding ring which she
has just received and promises to take her own life.
Von Holst returned to this poem several times; in
1842 he exhibited a picture, *Ginevra from the
Nuptial Altar Went,* at the British Institution, and
Schiff has published a picture in a Viennese private
collection showing Gherardi finding Ginevra on
her bridal bed after she has killed herself.

The style of the drawing is dependent upon Fuseli's,
but Von Holst has sweetened and prettified Fuseli's
sinister eroticism and given a curvilinear flow to
the composition, thus bringing the drawing into
line with more conventional romantic taste. Schiff
has pointed out that its bright coloring,
comparative flatness, and straight unbroken lines
foreshadow such early Pre-Raphaelite
representations of Renaissance Italy as Millais's
Lorenzo and Isabella (Liverpool). Von Holst was
seventeen years old when he made this drawing.
A.S.

Provenance
P. & D. Colnaghi & Co., London
The National Gallery of Canada, 1952

References
T. S. R. Boase, *English Art 1800-1870,* Oxford, 1959,
pl. 19b
Schiff, *Burlington,* CV, 1963, p. 31

William Davis

1812-1873

Davis was a native of Dublin, and he began his
professional career there as a portrait painter.
However, insufficient patronage forced him to
migrate to Liverpool where he became a member
of the Liverpool Academy which, during the middle
years of the century, was a thriving provincial
body. Davis's first exhibits in Liverpool were of
figural subjects and still life, but after 1853 his work
was exclusively landscape. The earliest reflect the
influence of another Liverpool painter, Robert
Tonge; however, after Tonge left Liverpool because
of his health in 1853, Davis's work soon began to
show strong Pre-Raphaelite bearings. In 1855 he
sent to the Royal Academy a painting named *Early
Spring Morning—Cheshire,* about which Rossetti
became so enthusiastic that he prevailed upon
Ruskin, who had failed to notice it, to praise it
anyway in his *Academy Notes.* Davis also attracted
the admiration and friendship of Ford Madox
Brown. He participated in the Pre-Raphaelite
group's Russell Place exhibition in 1857, and he
was a member of their exhibiting society, the
Hogarth Club.

Among a small circle, Davis's reputation was
extraordinarily high: William Michael Rossetti, for
example, reviewing the International Exhibition of
1862 described him as approaching nearer to the
true ideal of landscape than any other artist except
Turner. This admiration, however, was not
widespread. Despite Rossetti's urgings, Ruskin,
once he had looked, disliked his work and said so.
Davis's sales were limited to a handful of Liverpool
collectors, and he seems to have been neurotical

bitter about his lack of success and his ill treatment at the hands of the artistic establishment. In 1870 he moved to London in an attempt to improve his fortunes, and he died there three years later leaving an impoverished family, on whose behalf Madox Brown organized an exhibition of Davis's work and even finished some of his uncompleted paintings.

Davis's landscapes have much in common with those of Brown. His subjects are always unpretentious scenes of the English countryside. Occasionally they show a freshness of vision and an inventiveness which seems to prefigure aspects of French impressionism and Postimpressionism, but he achieved no sustained development. None of his pictures is dated, so the chronology of his work is somewhat unclear. There are large groups of paintings by Davis in the museums in Liverpool and Birkenhead.
A.S.

Bibliography
Frederick George Stephens, "William Davis, Landscape Painter, of Liverpool," *Art Journal,* 1884, pp. 325-28
H. C. Marillier, *The Liverpool School of Painters,* London, 1904, pp. 99-113

195
Old Mill and Pool at Ditton, Lancashire
Walker Art Gallery, Liverpool
Oil on canvas; 20⅞ x 14⅛ in.
Inscribed: *W. Davis;* verso: *Old Mill at Ditton Lancashire W. Davis.*
c. 1856-60

The painting is not dated. Although it may have been exhibited in 1864, stylistically it is similar to two paintings recently acquired by the Walker Art Gallery, *Near Leixlip on the Liffey* and *Junction of the Liffey and Rye,* both of which bear old inscriptions dated 1857. In 1856 Davis exhibited a picture of a similar subject at the Royal Academy, *Wallasey Mill, Cheshire* (no. 378), which Madox

Brown described in his diary as showing some leafless trees and some ducks and praised as "far too good to be understood."

Ruskin in the fourth volume of *Modern Painters,* published in 1856, made an attack upon the Pre-Raphaelites' inclination to "duck-pond delineation," which seems to refer to pictures such as this by Davis. In his *Academy Notes* of 1855, after seeing Davis's picture at the Academy which Rossetti had called to his attention, Ruskin added a supplementary note expressing disappointment: he found no evidence of inventive power and little tact in choice of subject. In 1857 he wrote a letter to Davis, which apparently had been solicited by Rossetti and in which he again criticized Davis's subjects. No. 195 is an example of the kind of picture that provoked this dislike. On the one hand, it has no pretensions of detailed scientific observation; and on the other, it lacks the usual spaciousness and breadth of English landscape painting. The subject is restricted and has little interest other than its purely visual appeal. There is no space; mill, plants, and pool all seem to exist on one vertical plane, forming a brightly colored two-dimensional pattern. This emphasis on the picture surface to the exclusion of more traditional concerns, while it alienated Ruskin and was too sophisticated for popular success, was certainly the aspect of Davis's art which so strongly attracted Brown and Rossetti.
A.S.

Provenance
John Bate (bequest to the Walker Art Gallery, 1885)

Exhibitions
Possibly Liverpool Academy, 1864, no. 101
(Old Mill at Ditton)

References
Ruskin, VI, 30; XIV, 30, 32-33
Ford M. Hueffer, *Ford Madox Brown,* London, 1896, p. 125
Marillier, p. 113

195

Edward Lear

1812-1888

Lear was born in the suburbs of London, the youngest of twenty-one children of a Danish-born stockbroker. When he was thirteen, the family broke up as a result of his father's bankruptcy and thereafter he lived with an older sister. He was homely and immensely self-conscious about it, weak-eyed, asthmatic, bronchial, and, most devastating of all, epileptic. Because of all this he never married, and although he was widely liked he spent much of his life alone.

From the age of fifteen Lear supported himself by drawing. In June 1830 he obtained permission to draw in the Zoological Gardens, and in November 1830 he began to publish his *Illustrations of the Family of Psittacidae, or Parrots,* a remarkably ambitious undertaking for a boy of eighteen. In the following years he worked extensively on the bird publications of John Gould. From 1832 to 1836 he drew in the private menagerie of Lord Derby at Knowsley Hall. While there, he made for Lord Derby's grandchildren his first *Book of Nonsense,* which was first published in 1846, and for which, with its sequels, Lear is best remembered today.

Because the detailed work of zoological illustration was too hard on his eyes, Lear decided to become a landscape artist instead. In 1837 he went to Rome, where he lived on and off for the next decade, and in 1841 he published his first book of landscape illustrations, *Views in Rome and its Environs.* This was followed by six further volumes recording Lear's travels throughout the Eastern Mediterranean. He made a point of visiting

relatively inaccessible and unknown places, such as the interior of Albania, and most of his books contain lively texts describing the places he visited as well as reproductions of his drawings. In 1846 Queen Victoria saw one of Lear's publications and summoned him to give her a series of drawing lessons. Soon after, Lear himself became a student. He first exhibited a picture at the Royal Academy in 1850 and apparently felt it was not up to snuff. In 1852 he entered the Royal Academy schools in order to improve his figure-drawing. In the same year he became a student of Holman Hunt (see nos. 197 and 216), and for the rest of his life he considered himself a confirmed Pre-Raphaelite.

During the latter 1850s and early 1860s, Lear lived much in Corfu. His activity as a travelling artist culminated in 1873-75 with a tour of India and Ceylon, and a continuing project of his later years was a series of landscape illustrations to Tennyson's poems, which did not reach publication during his lifetime. From 1871 until his death he lived at San Remo on the Italian Riviera.

Lear was an immensely industrious artist; at his death one friend alone inherited over ten thousand drawings. Naturally, from such a large output there is wide variation in quality, but Lear's calligraphic style of drawing is generally easily recognizable.
A.S.

Bibliography
Lady Strachey, ed., *Letters of Edward Lear,* London, 1907
Lady Strachey, *Later Letters of Edward Lear,* London, 1911
William B. Osgood Field, *Edward Lear on my Shelves,* privately published, Munich, 1933
Angus Davidson, *Edward Lear: Landscape Painter and Nonsense Poet,* London, 1938
Edward Lear: 1812-1888, Aldeburgh Festival, etc. (Arts Council), 1958 (exhibition catalogue, edited with introduction by Brian Reade)

196
Grey Cockatoo
Harvard College Library, Gift of W. B. Osgood Fiel
Pencil, pen and watercolor; 17¼ x 11¼ in., irregular
Inscribed: *58* (and extensive color notes)
1830

In the Field collection in the Harvard College Library there is an extensive series of drawings b Lear of parrots which bear dates from June to September 1830. These were all apparently intended for his *Illustrations of the Family of Psittacidae, or Parrots,* a series of large lithograph which Lear began to publish on November 1, 1830. No. 196 belongs to this group, although it is not dated, nor was it reproduced in the *Family of the Psittacidae.* The undertaking was Lear's first bird book, and considering his age and inexperience it represents an extraordinary achievement. In the following years Lear made many other bird drawings, notably for John Gould's *A Century of Birds from the Himalaya Mountains,* published in 1832, and Gould's *Birds of Europe,* issued betwee 1832 and 1837. The accuracy of Lear's illustrations is noteworthy, and these publications long remained standard works of reference.

The most considerable study of Lear's bird art has been made by Brian Reade, who claims Lear was responsible for a distinct advance in the scientific comprehension of bird forms, to whom not only wa Gould indebted, but whose best works in the *Family of the Psittacidae* are superior to anything in Audubon. Although for several years Lear was a hard-working professional, he abandoned zoological illustration when only in his mid-twentie because of the strain of the detailed work upon his eyes. However, as Reade points out, many of the human figures in Lear's later nonsense drawings take on bird-like forms. The color notations and watercolor tests are characteristic of Lear's bird drawings, and he continued to make such notations on his later landscape drawings. Or the verso of no. 196 is a pencil drawing of a woma
A.S.

196

Provenance
William B. Osgood Field (presented to Harvard, 1942)

References
Field, p. 245, no. 58
Brian Reade, "The Birds of Edward Lear," *Signature,*
n.s., no. 4, 1947, pp. 3-15

197
The Quarries of Syracuse
Walker Art Gallery, Liverpool
Pen and sepia ink and watercolor; 13⅞ x 19⅞ in.
Inscribed in ink, lower right: *Siracusa/12 June
1847/(Jackdaw Gardens)/(138);* also in pencil,
bottom center, and with numerous color notes

Lear visited Sicily in May and June 1847 with John
Proby (later Lord Proby). In a letter of October 16,
1847 to Chichester Fortescue, he wrote, "Siracuse
only wanted your presence to make our stay more
pleasant. . . . We abode in a quarry *per lo più,* and
left the place sorryly." No. 197 is a good example
of Lear's drawing style in the 1840s. His method
was to make a pencil drawing with some color on
the spot, and then later, in the evenings, to pen out
the lines in ink. The two inscriptions, in pencil
bottom center and in ink bottom right, testify to
these two periods of work. The color notes all over
the drawing are also typical of Lear. He obviously
intended such drawings as working sketches upon
which he could later base finished pictures.

Lear's later use of this drawing is of particular
interest. In the summer of 1852 he asked Holman
Hunt's advice about how to turn his sketches into
pictures. Hunt advised him against trying to paint
pictures in the studio from such skeleton outlines,
but he looked through Lear's drawings, and picking
out a view of *The Quarries of Syracuse,*
presumably no. 197, he suggested that all the
elements of the picture, limestone rocks, fig trees,
and the rest, could be found in England. As a result,
when Hunt went to Fairlight, near Hastings, a few
weeks later to paint his *Strayed Sheep* (no. 216),
Lear accompanied him and painted *The Quarries
of Syracuse* under Hunt's direction. The two shared
a house, and in return for Hunt's tutelage, Lear
gave him lessons in Italian. He became a loyal
devotee of Pre-Raphaelitism, and for the rest of his
life he addressed Hunt, who was fifteen years his
junior, as "Pa" or "Daddy." Hunt returned to
London early in December; Lear went up to town
before him, but returned in the new year to work
further on his picture. On January 23, 1853, he

197

wrote to Fortescue from Hastings: "I am now doing
a huge picture of Syracuse quarries; ½ starved
Athenians judiciously introduced here and there.
Since August I have been, as I told you, painting
on an oly different principle, and so far with
great success." He finished the painting in time
to send it to the Royal Academy in April. There it
was won as an Art Union prize by Earl Beauchamp,
and it is now in the collection of the present Earl
Beauchamp. The view of the distant city over the
quarries is the same in the painting as in the
drawing, but the foreground is much more detailed,
with the jackdaws, noted on the drawing, forming
a conspicuous feature. In Lear's list of paintings
he included a second *Quarries of Syracuse* of the
same date as the property of Lord Tennyson.   A.S.

Provenance
Purchased by the Walker Art Gallery, 1943

Exhibitions
British Watercolours, 1850-1914, Australia and New
Zealand, 1952-53, no. 59
*Victorian Watercolours and Drawings in the Walker Art
Gallery,* Walker Art Gallery, Liverpool, 1966, no. 64

References
W. Holman Hunt, *Pre-Raphaelitism and the
Pre-Raphaelite Brotherhood,* London, 1905, I, 328-36
Lady Strachey, ed., *Letters,* pp. 4, 27, 314
Davidson, pp. 76-82

198

198
Civitella di Subiaco, Sunrise
Worcester Art Museum, Charlotte
E. W. Buffington Fund
Oil on canvas; 36⅞ x 59 in.
c. 1855

This painting was until recently attributed to Francis Danby. It is, however, definitely by Lear, and its composition is closely repeated in two drawings Lear prepared for his projected series of landscape illustrations to Tennyson's poetry (Houghton Library and Worcester Museum). These drawings illustrate the line, "Morn broadened on the borders of the dark," from Tennyson's poem *A Dream of Fair Women.*

Lear visited Subiaco in May 1840, and two drawings from there, dated May 12 and May 15, 1840, neither directly related to this painting, are in the Houghton Library. In his volume of lithographs, *Views in Rome and its Environs,* published in 1841, number five is a view of *Civitella di Subiaco.* Its depiction of the town on the distant hill is close to no. 198, but it is seen in full daylight, and the foreground is entirely different. In the list of his works prepared by Lear in 1877, five pictures of *Civitella di Subiaco* are listed, dating from 1840 to 1855. The last of these, no. 117 on the list, is entitled *Civitella di Subiaco, Sunrise,* and is presumably no. 198. It was purchased by William Nevill, an old friend of Lear's who also owned one other picture listed as from 1855. Lear was

notoriously inaccurate about dates, but the pictures were certainly in Nevill's possession by September 1858, when Lear visited him and described his home as "beadornamented by my own paws." Another view of *Subiaco,* signed and dated 1843, and presumably no. 30 on Lear's list, was recently advertised on the London art market.

By 1855 Lear had already been a student of Holman Hunt. His treatment of the clouds in the upper left corner is especially reminiscent of Hunt. The tree in the foreground is characteristic of Lear; but the picture's prior attribution to Danby is understandable, as Danby in his later years specialized in scenes of flaming sunrises and sunsets. Although Lear also often revelled in brilliant colors along the horizon, his pictures are rarely as murky as this, and it is quite likely that he had Danby's works in mind when painting it. The drawings in the Houghton Library and at Worcester are closer to Lear's conception in this painting than any of the known earlier views of *Civitella di Subiaco,* but they are certainly after the picture rather than studies for it. Both belong to related series of drawings for the Tennyson illustrations, a project conceived in 1852 but only put into effect in 1871. The group in the Houghton Library dates from around 1885.
A.S.

Provenance
William Nevill, London (before 1858; died 1873)
Major Clowes (sale, Christie's, London, 28 Oct. 1960, no. 36)
Mrs. Robert Frank, London
Durlacher Bros., New York
Worcester Art Museum, 1961

References
Lady Strachey, ed., *Letters,* pp. 114, 314
Burlington, CII, Feb. 1960, cf. p. xxv (adv.)

199
Corfu from near the Village of Virò
Museum of Art, Rhode Island School of Design
Oil on paper mounted on canvas; 14¾ x 9⅜ in.
Inscribed: *Corfu/ E Lear/ 1858,* and on the
stretcher: *Corfu from near the Village of Virò*

Lear was in Corfu at the beginning of the year in
1858 and, after a trip to Palestine, again during the
summer. The island was then administered by the
English, and it was Lear's home for much of the
time from 1855 until 1864, when England ceded
Corfu to Greece.

The bright colors and precision of detail reflect the
continuing influence upon Lear of Holman Hunt.
It is characteristic of Lear to put the main object
of interest, the Citadel of Corfu, in the far distance.
The peephole view, forming a kind of vignette, is
comparable to many early Victorian engravings
of landscape views. Alden Murray has pointed out
that it also recalls the lacy frame of a Victorian
valentine and the romantic stage decorations
of the 1840s.
A.S.

Provenance
Mrs. Robert Frank, London

References
Alden Murray, *"Corfu* by Edward Lear," *Bulletin of
Rhode Island School of Design,* XLIII, Dec. 1956, pp. 9-11

199

1816-1863

A native of London, Egg studied at Sass's Academy
of Art and at the Royal Academy schools, where
along with Frith, Dadd, and others, he was one of
"The Clique." A consistent exhibitor at the Royal
Academy from 1838, he was elected an Associate
member in 1848 and a full Academician in 1860.
Egg was a close friend of Dickens, Wilkie Collins,
and the group of writers for *Punch,* and he
appeared regularly in Dickens's amateur
theatricals. Because of ill health, he spent much
of the latter part of his life in the Mediterranean;
he died of an attack of asthma in Algiers at the
age of forty-seven.

Egg began his career as an artist by painting
costume pictures in the manner of Leslie, with
perhaps less narrative subtlety and charm, but a
richer handling of paint. He was one of the first
established artists to support the Pre-Raphaelites,
and he commissioned Holman Hunt's *Claudio and
Isabella* (Tate Gallery). His work of the late 1840s
probably had some influence on the
Pre-Raphaelites (compare his *Launce's Substitute
for Proteus's Dog* [Leicester] with Millais's *Lorenzo
and Isabella* [Liverpool]), and in the 1850s he
seems in turn to have been affected by the younger
men, especially in his paintings of subjects drawn
from modern life. His most ambitious works were
gloomily didactic subjects painted in series. During
his lifetime the most famous were the pair of
pictures showing *The Life and Death of
Buckingham,* which the purchaser found so painful
he had to separate them. Today Egg is best known
for the three-picture drama of modern life, *Past*

and Present (Tate Gallery), which shows the horrible consequences of marital infidelity.
A.S.

Bibliography
"Notes on the Life of Augustus L. Egg," *The Reader, A Review of Literature, Science and Art,* 1863, pp. 462, 486-87, 557-58; new vol., pp. 42-43, 91, 516-17
Peter Ferriday, "Augustus Egg," *The Architectural Review,* CXXXIV, 1963, pp. 420-22

200
The Opera Mantle (Anticipation)
Harris Museum & Art Gallery, Preston, England
Oil on canvas; 13½ x 11½ in.
1851

The picture was commissioned as a companion to a *Girl Making a Bouquet of Flowers* by Egg (now also in Preston), which is signed and dated 1849. The girl is reading the opera bill for Meyerbeer's *Le Prophète,* which had its English premiere at the Royal Italian Opera House, Covent Garden, on July 24, 1849.

Rossetti, seeing the picture exhibited in 1851, described the girl's features as slightly out of drawing, but he praised the color as the most gorgeous of any work in the exhibition. Egg in this respect, especially in his use of white, is close to Millais, and it seems probable that he had an influence on the younger artist. The type of painting of a single girl in elegant costume was made extremely popular in early Victorian England by the publication of volumes of poetry with engraved illustrations known as *Keepsakes* or *Books of Beauty.* The Pre-Raphaelites professed to scorn the triviality of *Keepsake* art, but many of Millais's most successful early works are small single figures of women, closely comparable to this painting by Egg.　　　　　　A.S.

Provenance
Commissioned by Richard Newsham, Preston, 1851 (bequest to Preston, 1883)

200

Exhibitions
Exhibition of Sketches and Drawings, Old Society of Painters in Water Colours, London, 1851, no. 35 *(Anticipation)*
Ten Decades of British Taste, 1851-1951, R. B. A. Galleries, London (Institute of Contemporary Arts) 1951
Some Pre-Raphaelite Paintings and Drawings, Aberystwyth and Swansea (Arts Council), 1955, no. 25
Victorian Painting, 1837-1887, Thos. Agnew & Sons, London, 1961, no. 35
Victorian Paintings, Aldeburgh Festival, etc. (Arts Council), 1962, no. 16

References
Dante Gabriel Rossetti, *Works,* London, 1911, p. 582 (reprinted from *The Spectator,* 1851, p. 860)
James Hibbert, ed., *Catalogue of the Pictures & Drawings of the Newsham Bequest to the Corporation of Preston, Prepared by the Testator, Richard Newsham, Esquire,* Preston, 1884, p. 21, no. 20, ill.

Reproductions
Engraved by S. W. Reynolds, Jr.

201
Outward Bound
The Visitors of the Ashmolean Museum, Oxford
Oil on board; 6¾ x 9 in.
Late 1850s

This small sketch is undated, but it surely dates from Egg's later years. Unlike his *Travelling Companions* in Birmingham, which shows the Mediterranean coast near Menton, the background of *Outward Bound* seems to be northern. The picture reflects the vogue for scenes of seaside holidays which followed on the great popular success of Frith's *Life at the Seaside* (Royal Collection), but it lacks the anecdotic narrative of Frith. Its boldness of composition and effect of outdoor light are closer to the more adventurous art of the Pre-Raphaelites. The foreshortened position of the man is reminiscent of that of the drunken guard in the foreground of Holman Hunt's *Flight of Madeleine and Porphyro* (R. A. 1848; Guildhall, London).
A.S.

Provenance
Robert Braithwaite Martineau, London (died 1869)
Miss Helen Martineau
Ashmolean Museum, 1941

Exhibitions
Victorian Pictures, Leicester Galleries, London, 1941, no. 47
Victorian Painting, Nottingham University, 1959, no. 19

Richard Dadd

1817-1886

Richard Dadd had one of the most extraordinary careers of any artist. Born in Chatham and brought up in Rochester, in the 1830s he became a student at the Royal Academy schools, where he was a member of "The Clique," along with Frith, Egg, and others. He seems to have been the most talented of the group, which disbanded when Dadd received a commission to paint over one hundred pictures for Lord Foley's town house. At this time his ambition was said to have been to paint works of imagination, and his early exhibits tended to be drawn from the more fanciful reaches of English literature, several being based on *A Midsummer Night's Dream.*

In 1842, at the suggestion of David Roberts, Dadd was invited to accompany Sir Thomas Phillips on a trip to the Near East. On this trip, which carried them to Damascus, Baalbek, and up the Nile to Thebes, Dadd started to show signs of mental imbalance. He wrote to Frith, "at times the excitement of these scenes has been enough to turn the brain of an ordinary weak-minded person like myself, and often I have lain down at night with my imagination so full of wild vagaries that I have really and truly doubted my own sanity." It has been suggested that a sunstroke suffered on this trip caused Dadd's later troubles, but this does not correspond with modern medical belief.

Upon his return to England in 1843, Dadd submitted to the cartoon competition for the Houses of Parliament a design of *St. George and the Dragon* in which the dragon had so inordinately long a tail

that his friends tried to persuade him not to enter it. In the following few months, schizophrenia seems to have taken over. In September, Dadd's father took his son to the country for a rest. Their trip ended violently at Cobham in Surrey when Dadd stabbed and killed his father, then immediately fled to France. He was arrested near Fontainebleau, his arrest supposedly interrupting further homicidal plans, including the murder of Emperor Ferdinand of Austria. Dadd was returned to England and incarcerated in mental hospitals for the rest of his life. He was first at Bethlem Hospital (Bedlam) in London; then, in 1864 he was moved to the newly built Broadmoor, outside the city, where he died in 1886, over forty years after he was first arrested.

Dadd was allowed to paint during all this time. He apparently was under sympathetic care, and it may even be that Dr. Hood, the resident physician at Bethlem, suggested some of his subjects. According to the memoirs of Frith's daughter, of whom Dadd's sister was the governess (another sister was the wife of John Phillip, R.A.), Dadd's works were sold to pay the expenses of keeping him. Some were destroyed in an attempt to wipe out any record of his tragedy, but surprisingly many are known today.

Almost all of Dadd's works are scrupulously signed and dated, and they frequently bear long, carefully printed inscriptions describing their subjects. In the 1850s he made an extensive series of drawings, subtitled "Sketches to Illustrate the Passions," of which at least twenty-five have been recorded. His best-known work is *The Fairy-Feller's Master Stroke* (Tate Gallery) dated "quasi 1855-64," which carries his prior interest in imaginative, fanciful subjects to an obsessive degree of microscopic elaboration unmatched by the most detailed work of the Pre-Raphaelites. He also painted landscape, genre, and historical subjects. Many of these are ostensibly straightforward treatments of traditional themes, but almost all show clear evidence of the artist's mania, especially noticeable in his emphasis on his figures' vacant staring eyes and

the extreme precision of his often very strange
ancillary detail.
A.S.

Bibliography
"The Late Richard Dadd," *The Art Union,* October,
1843, pp. 267-71
Sacheverell Sitwell, *Narrative Pictures,* London, 1937,
pp. 69-74
John Rickett, "Rd. Dadd, Bethlem and Broadmoor: An
Attempt at a Biography," in *Ivory Hammer 2: The
Year at Sotheby's, Two Hundred and Twentieth Season,
1963-1964,* London, 1964, pp. 22-25 (ills.) and
7 unnumbered pages of text.

202

202
The Ballad Monger
Trustees of The British Museum
Watercolor; 10¹/₁₆ x 14¹/₁₆ in.
Inscribed: *The Ballad Monger. A Reminiscence/
Sketch by Richard Dadd 1853. Bethlem Hospital*

Dadd's inscription suggests that no. 202 recalls a
street scene observed by the artist before he
was hospitalized in 1843. However, this
extraordinary drawing seems obviously to have
some pathological significance, and, whatever
Dadd's intentions in making it, it has an element of
latent violence far removed from *The Cries of
London* or from the relative insipidity of most early
Victorian genre scenes. Among the titles of the
ballads displayed are *Me and My Lad* and
The Assassin.
A.S.

203

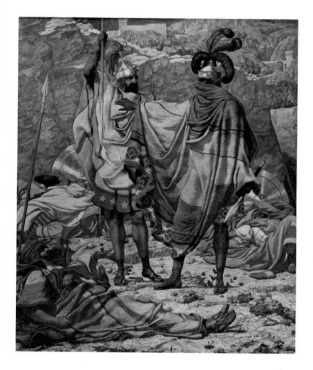

203
Mercy. David Spareth Saul's Life
Charles Handley-Read
Oil on canvas; 23¾ x 19 in.
Inscribed, verso: *Mercy. David spareth Saul's life.*
1st Samuel. Chapt. 26. . . . by Richard Dadd. 1854
(this inscription has been covered in relining)

Part of the inscription on the back of the picture
has been obliterated; this may have been a
reference to Bethlem Hospital, reminders of which
friends of the artist's family wished to destroy.

The setting is the Wilderness of Ziph. Saul,
pursuing David, has encamped with his army at
Hachilah, before Jeshimon. David and a
companion, Abishal, stealing into their camp by
night, find Saul asleep, his spear stuck in the
ground at his head, and all his followers asleep
around him. The painting shows Abishal, his spear
raised to smite the sleeping Saul, stopped by David,
who refuses to harm his King. The subject is rare
in painting but not unknown. At the Society of
British Artists in 1835, John Martin exhibited a
David Spareth Saul at Hachilah, and he included an
engraving of the subject in his *Illustrations of the
Bible* published between 1831 and 1835.

In 1854 Dadd was in the midst of his series of
watercolors of "Sketches to Illustrate the
Passions." These include such subjects as *Love*
and *Jealousy* (both illustrated by scenes from
Shakespeare, *Romeo and Juliet* and *Othello*
respectively, and both now in the American
Shakespeare Festival Theatre, Stratford, Conn.),
and at least one Old Testament subject, *Cain
Murders Abel,* dated October 24, 1854, which is still
at Bethlem Hospital. There is no evidence that
Dadd intended no. 203 as one of the series, which
are otherwise all in watercolor, but it is obviously
related. Rickett has suggested that the series of
Passion drawings, which during 1854 are dated to
the day and appear at weekly intervals, form part of
a curriculum suggested to Dadd by Dr. Hood, his
physician at Bethlem. As Dadd was in Bethlem as a
result of his uncontrolled homicidal passions, the
subject of the present painting may also have been
chosen because of its therapeutic relevance to
his own condition.

The strange foreshortening and distortions of the
sleeping figures are characteristic of Dadd. The
background is presumably based upon memories
of his travels in the East twelve years before.
A.S.

Provenance
Clifton, London
K. J. Hewett, 1961
Mrs. Robert Frank, London

Exhibitions
Victorian Painting: 1837-1887, Thos. Agnew & Sons,
London, 1961, no. 43

References
Rickett, *The Ivory Hammer,* 1964

George Frederic Watts

1817-1904

Watts was born in London; as a child he suffered from ill health and did not go to school. He frequented the studio of the sculptor William Behnes and attended the Royal Academy schools for a short time, but he was largely self-taught as an artist. In 1837 he first exhibited at the Royal Academy, and in 1843 he won a first prize in the initial cartoon competition for the Houses of Parliament. With his prize money he set off for Italy, where he became the guest of Lord Holland, the British Minister to the Court of Tuscany. He remained in Florence until 1847, returning to England in that year to win another prize in the Parliament competitions. During the following few years, he painted his first major allegorical picture, *Of Time and Oblivion* (collection of the Hon. Mrs. Hervey-Bathurst), as well as four large realistic pictures (see no. 204). In 1851 he met Mrs. Thoby Prinsep, and for the next quarter of a century he was the Prinseps' permanent guest at Little Holland House in Kensington. The Prinseps kept a semi-bohemian salon with Watts the genius in residence; Julia Margaret Cameron was Mrs. Prinsep's sister, and among their regular guests were Tennyson, Thackeray, and Gladstone.

In 1852 Watts offered to decorate Euston Station with frescoes, without pay, but he was turned down; he did, however, between 1853 and 1859 paint a large fresco of *Justice* in the New Hall of Lincoln's Inn. For the rest of his life he occupied himself with painting portraits and large allegorical pictures. Watts was the leading portraitist of the Victorian era and his pictures of the eminent of the day

provide a record which is often frightening in its penetration. The allegories have stood the test of time less well, and their "timeless" messages now generally seem banally pretentious. Watts was like Tennyson in wanting to express great truths at a time when science had undermined inherited beliefs. If what they found to say is no longer compelling, it was nonetheless said in richly lyrical language. Watts's earlier works after his Italian trip were strongly influenced by Titian; his later ones have a subtle delicacy of color, which by the end of his life became quite abstract. After 1870 he was also active as a sculptor.

During the 1850s Watts remained outside of the Royal Academy, but in 1867 he was elected A.R.A. and R.A. in the same year. In 1864 he married Ellen Terry, then aged sixteen, but they separated the year after. In the 1880s and 1890s his reputation was enormous; he had a one-man exhibition at the Metropolitan Museum of Art in 1884-85, and he twice declined a baronetcy. After 1875, when Little Holland House was demolished, Watts lived at various places, eventually settling with his second wife at Limnerslease, Compton, Surrey, which became a museum after his death.
A.S.

Bibliography
G. K. Chesterton, *G. F. Watts,* London, 1904
Mrs. Russell Barrington, *G. F. Watts: Reminiscences,* London, 1905
M. S. Watts, *George Frederic Watts: The Annals of an Artist's Life,* 3 vols., London, 1912
Ronald Chapman, *The Laurel and the Thorn: A Study of G. F. Watts,* London, 1945
George Frederic Watts, 1817-1904, The Tate Gallery, London, 1954 (catalogue of an Arts Council exhibition, compiled with introduction by David Loshak)

204
The Irish Famine (The Irish Eviction)
The Trustees of the Watts Gallery
Oil on canvas; 71 x 78 in.
1849-50

The subject is based on the Irish potato famine of 1848. Watts had never been to Ireland when he painted no. 204, but he did go there shortly after to visit the poet Aubrey de Vere. When urging Watts to come, de Vere wrote that in painting no. 204 he must have had "a second-sight vision" of what he would actually see in Ireland.

The period between Watts's return from Italy in 1847 and his move to Little Holland House in 1851 seems to have been one of dislocation and depression, and during this time he painted four gloomily realistic subjects dramatizing the sufferings of the poor, *Found Drowned, Under a Dry Arch, The Seamstress,* and no. 204 (all in the Watts Gallery). These comprise an isolated group of works in Watts's *œuvre;* he retained his social consciousness to the end of his life, but, as David Loshak has pointed out, its expression later took "the form of abstract hostility to the rich rather than concrete sympathy with the poor." The hostility is most explicitly shown in Watts's *Mammon* of 1884-85 (Tate Gallery).

In 1849 Watts was still under the influence of Italy, and his monumental triangle of figures suggests that he was attempting to paint a modern counterpart to a Renaissance *Holy Family* or *Rest on the Flight into Egypt.* In several ways, no. 204 anticipates the realistic orientation of several adherents of Pre-Raphaelitism a few years later. Ford Madox Brown's *Last of England* (Birmingham) shows a similar modern version of the Holy Family and both Brown, in *Work* (Manchester) and Walter Deverell, in his *Irish Vagrants* (Johannesburg) depict displaced Irishmen akin to those of Watts. No. 204 also reflects the international impulse towards realism that grew up around 1848, and its monumental gloominess provides the closest English parallel to the paintings of Courbet. A.S.

204

Provenance
The artist

Exhibitions
Watts, Grosvenor Gallery, London, 1881-82

References
M. S. Watts, I, 108-09, 126
Chapman, 42
Watts (exhibition catalogue, Arts Council), 1954,
pp. 8, 30
Wilfrid Blunt, *Watts, (The Masters, 37),* London, 1966,
pp. 4, 7, pl. VI

205
Portrait of Emily, Lady Tennyson
Fogg Art Museum, Harvard University, Gift of
Anonymous Donor and Mr. and Mrs.
Henry A. Rudkin
Pencil; 13⅞ x 10 in.
Inscribed: *Signor/Little Holland House/July 21,
1858/1858* (Watts was called "Signor" by
his friends)

Lady Tennyson (née Emily Sellwood) was the wife
of the Poet Laureate. Her role in her husband's life
is best indicated by Max Beerbohm's cartoon in
which Woolner, carving a bust of Tennyson, is
asked by Mrs. Tennyson, *"when* do you begin
modelling his halo?" Watts painted at least seven
portraits of Tennyson, the first in 1857.

When Watts was living in Florence as the guest of
Lord and Lady Holland, he made a large number
of pencil portraits of their guests and
acquaintances; a group of thirty-three of these still
survives in the possession of the descendants of
Lord Holland. Numerous other pencil drawings
exist of Watts's Little Holland House circle of

205

Provenance
Mrs. Lillian Chapman
H. C. Green
J. S. Maas & Co., London

Exhibitions
Watts, Manchester, 1905
*Works by the Late George Frederic Watts and the
Late Frederick Sandys,* Winter Exhibition, Royal
Academy, London, 1905, no. 118
Pre-Raphaelites—Art Nouveau, Maas Gallery, London,
1964, no. 145

References
Charles Tennyson, *Alfred Tennyson,* London, 1950,
cf. ill. opp. p. 81

1819-1900

Ruskin was the child of prosperous middle-class
parents of Scottish ancestry. He grew up at Herne
Hill in South London, and in 1837 he entered
Oxford. In 1835 the family went on a tour of France,
Switzerland, and Italy, and in 1840-41, because of
John's health, they spent the winter in Italy.
Henceforth Ruskin travelled abroad regularly, most
frequently to Switzerland. In 1836 an attack upon
Turner in *Blackwood's Magazine* provoked him to
write a defense. Although not published, it led to
Ruskin's first great book *Modern Painters,* which
was published in five volumes from 1843 through
1859. In 1849 he published *The Seven Lamps of
Architecture,* and in 1851 and 1853, *The Stones of
Venice.* In 1851 he came to the defense of the
Pre-Raphaelites and he proselytized vigorously on
their behalf through the rest of the decade,
publishing annually from 1855 through 1859 a
forthrightly one-sided review of each year's
exhibitions. After 1859 much of his energy was
taken up by political, social, and scientific
concerns, and his writing about art became more
sporadic. In 1869 he was appointed Slade Professor
of Art at Oxford.

All his life Ruskin drew regularly. His first drawing
master was a Charles Runciman, and he also had
lessons from Copley Fielding in 1835, and later
from James Duffield Harding, but the chief
influence on Ruskin's early drawing style was
Samuel Prout, whose mannerisms he imitated with
considerable success. In 1842, however, he
reversed himself entirely. The reason was his
exposure to Turner's recent Alpine sketches (see

friends. While the Italian portrait drawings are
primarily impressive for their display of Watts's
virtuosity as a draftsman, the later drawings such
as no. 205 also reveal his increasing sensitivity as a
recorder of personality. As in his later portraits
in oil, the emphasis of no. 205 is upon the inner
person, which in Watts's depiction assumes tragic
dimensions. A pencil sketch on the verso carries
these revelatory qualities to the point of caricature.
There is also a slighter pencil sketch of a
recumbent male nude on the verso. An oil portrait
of Lady Tennyson by Watts is reproduced in
Charles Tennyson's *Alfred Tennyson.*
A.S.

no. 121), which amazed Ruskin by their lack of artifice. This revelation led to two almost mystical experiences, first at Norwood near his home in May, and later in the summer at Fontainebleau, when he realized that he had never been taught to draw "what was really there" and that nature composed itself "by finer laws than any known of men." His new attitude of absolute reverence to nature animates the first volume of *Modern Painters,* and almost all of Ruskin's subsequent drawings are marked by a fanatical concern with precise, factual observation.

Ruskin was not a professional artist, and his drawings are generally studies rather than finished compositions. However, he was more than amateur; he illustrated his books with his own drawings, he occasionally exhibited his works, and he also sold them. In the 1850s he taught drawing at the Working Men's College along with Rossetti, and he wrote two books on how to draw, *The Elements of Drawing* and *The Elements of Perspective.* He was an "artistic" member of the Pre-Raphaelites' exhibiting organization, the Hogarth Club, and in 1861 George Price Boyce recorded in his diary that Ruskin was planning to give up writing to devote himself to painting. His output was enormous; the catalogue in his collected *Works* lists 2,145 drawings, and it is very far from complete.

Ruskin's unhappy marital and emotional life has been the subject of several recent books. In the 1870s and 1880s his mental stability began to give way entirely, and he ended his life living as a recluse at Brantwood on Lake Coniston.
A.S.

Bibliography
Everything published by Ruskin in his lifetime and much that was not, including material from his letters and diaries and from writings about Ruskin, is included in the thirty-nine volumes of the Library Edition of his *Works,* admirably edited by E. T. Cook and Alexander Wedderburn and published from 1903 to 1912. Volume XXXVIII contains a bibliography and a catalogue of his drawings

Derrick Leon, *Ruskin: The Great Victorian,* London, 1949
The Diaries of John Ruskin, edited by Joan Evans and John Howard Whitehouse, 3 vols., Oxford, 1956-59
Ruskin and His Circle, Arts Council Gallery, London, 1964 (exhibition catalogue, edited by Elizabeth Davison, James S. Dearden and John Gage; introduction by Sir Kenneth Clark)
Ruskin a Verona, Museo di Castelvecchio, Verona, 1966 (exhibition catalogue, edited with introduction by Terence Mullaly)

206
Landscape
The Art Institute of Chicago
Pencil, pen and ink, and watercolor; 12⅝ x 17⅞ in.
c. 1845

No. 206 is one of many drawings of tree forms made by Ruskin in the 1840s. It might be compared with his *Stone Pine at Sestri,* drawn in April 1845, and the *Sketch of Tree Growth,* drawn at Macugnaga in the Italian Alps later in the same year, both of which are now at Oxford. Ruskin spent a month at Macugnaga, and no. 206 might well have been drawn during this visit. Its unfinished condition is characteristic; Ruskin relentlessly pursued the details that interested him without giving attention to the composition as a whole. His major redirection as an artist was due to discovering the beauty in patterns of branches. This was in 1842, and through the rest of the decade many of his drawings, such as no. 206, demonstrate the continuing fascination and excitement which this aspect of nature held for him.
A.S.

Provenance
Charles Deering, Chicago

References
Ruskin, IV, cf. pl. 12 opp. p. 346; XXI, cf. pl. LXVII

207
Loggia of the Ducal Palace, Venice
The Metropolitan Museum of Art, Rogers Fund, 1908
Watercolor over pencil; 18½ x 11½ in.
c. 1849-1850

Ruskin was in Venice from November 1849 until March 1850 working on *The Stones of Venice,* and this drawing presumably dates from that visit. The first volume of *The Stones of Venice* was published in March 1851; to accompany it Ruskin prepared folio illustrations, *Examples of the Architecture of Venice,* which were published in three parts. No. 207 was reproduced as plate 15, the last illustration in the third part, published on November 1, 1851.

In his preface to the *Examples* Ruskin stated that "the power of drawing, with useful accuracy, objects which will remain quiet to be drawn, is within every one's reach who will pay the price of care, time, and exertion," and for the present drawings he claimed no higher artistic merit than that of faithful studies. The advertisement for the *Examples* which appeared at the end of the first volume of the *Stones* gave similar warning that the chief value of the plates would be "their almost servile veracity," but it also admitted that many of the subjects would be found to possess much picturesque value. In his preface Ruskin noted that he had used the daguerreotype without scruple in completing many of the subjects in the series and expressed regret that artists in general did not make more use of the camera. However, he stated that its strong contrasts of light and shadow were most effective in subjects presenting little variation in distance, so he apparently did not have the help of the camera in preparing no. 207. Many of the *Examples* are details of flat wall surfaces, or of capitals and ornament, and no. 207, with its perspective depth and view of Saint Mark's through the arcade, is one of the most elaborate views of the series.

In his note on the lithograph after no. 207, Ruskin warned that the reader might like the capitals here shown, but he, in fact, included the plate to show the decline of Venetian architecture in the Renaissance, and he compared these capitals, carved in the 15th century, unfavorably to the earlier Gothic capitals. He also pointed out that the two nearest columns and the intervening balustrade were of red marble, rather than the Istrian stone of the others; this was because the head of Doge Marino Faliero was shown to the public from between these columns after his execution. Ruskin did not like lithography, and he tried to have as many plates as possible in the *Examples* printed in mezzotint; however, where color was important, as here, he had his drawings reproduced in tinted lithographs.
A.S.

Provenance
Sir James Knowles, London (sale, Christie's, London, 28 May 1908, no. 357)

References
Ruskin, IX, pp. xxiv-xxvi, 1, 8-9; X, 429-32; XI, pp. xxiv-xxv, 311-14, 348, pl. 15; XXXVIII, 295, no. 1879 (as *Renaissance Capitals of the Loggia*)

207

R. E. F. [Roger Fry], "Recent Acquisitions of Drawings," *Metropolitan Museum of Art Bulletin,* IV, no. 2, 1909, p. 25

Reproductions
Ruskin, *Examples of the Architecture of Venice,* London, 1851, III, no. 15 (tinted lithograph)

208
St. Nicholas, Lake Lucerne
The Beinecke Rare Book and Manuscript Library, Yale University
Pencil and watercolor; facing sketchbook pages, each 5¼ x 8¼ in.
Inscribed: *St. Nicholas. Lake Lucerne. White Cloud Clasping Pilate*
c. 1861

None of the drawings in this sketchbook are dated, however it would seem to have been used during the late autumn of 1861 when Ruskin stayed in Lucerne from October 16 until December 27. In 1854 Ruskin began to plan an illustrated history of Switzerland and started to make drawings for it. He visited Switzerland eight out of the ten following years, both for the sake of this project and to study the sites of Turner's Swiss views. In the fourth volume of *Modern Painters,* subtitled *Of Mountain Beauty* and published in 1856, Ruskin discussed Turner's treatment of the mountains, and in the fifth volume, published in 1860, he devoted a long section to cloud effects. As a result of preparing these volumes, the nature of Ruskin's own drawing changed; whereas in his earlier drawings he had concentrated on solid things, botanical, geological or architectural, now much of his sketching began to record clouds and atmosphere, and in a drawing such as no. 208 we see him making a rapid notation of the kind of effect that appears in Turner's late watercolors. Ruskin later placed a number of such sketches on view at Oxford, two of which, one inscribed *Pilate, 25th Nov. 1861,* are reproduced in volume xxi of his *Works.*

From a letter of October 23, 1861, we know Ruskin's daily routine at Lucerne: "Morning I get up a little before seven—breakfast at eight, reading Livy; write my letters; read on at Livy till I've had enough, go out and draw till about one or two, taking care not to tire myself—then row, quietly, with little pauses and landings and sketches till five; dress for dinner at six, read Xenophon in evening—the papers at tea, at eight." His activity in the morning was probably concentrated on drawing ambitious

208

1819-1909

views of Lucerne for his history of Switzerland, of which several exist, while no. 208 appears to be a product of the more leisurely afternoons. Ruskin's diary is full of references to his rowing and sketching on the lake, for instance, the entry of Saturday, November 2: "Wet day but lovely sunset. Sketching in twilight on lake." No. 208, which appears to have been made from a boat, could have been made on any such outing. A second double-page sketch of *St. Nicholas* in the same book, inscribed "evening" and showing the mountains in violet, was probably made on the same day. Ruskin's diary and his letters are full of ecstatic descriptions of the sunsets, and after his return to London he wrote Charles Eliot Norton on January 6, 1862: "I've seen a good deal—but nothing ever to come near it. The long, low light,— the floating frost cloud—the divine calm and melancholy—and the mountains all opal below and pearl above. There's no talking about it, nor giving you any idea of it."

As Norton owned this sketchbook, it may be that Ruskin presented it to him to make up for the inadequacy of words. However, Norton prepared

an exhibition of Ruskin's works in Boston in 1879, and it is also possible that the sketchbook was among the large number of drawings which Ruskin sent him then. If so, the inscription may be from this later date.
A.S.

Provenance
Charles Eliot Norton, Cambridge, Mass.
Miss Elizabeth Norton
Yale University, 1944

References
Ruskin, XVII, pp. xliii-xlv; XXI, cf. pl. LXIII; XXXVI, 385-405 *passim.*
Diaries, II, 554-59

Frith had no youthful ambition to be an artist; he would have preferred to have become an auctioneer. However, his father, the landlord of the Dragon Hotel in Harrogate, persuaded him to study art and placed him, at age sixteen, in Sass's School of Art in London. From Sass's, Frith proceeded to the Royal Academy schools, where he became part of a group of young artists known as "The Clique." These artists, Frith, Augustus Egg, Henry O'Neil, Richard Dadd, and John Phillip, met once a week; their purpose seems primarily to have been the selection of subjects to illustrate. Frith first exhibited at the British Institution in 1838 and at the Royal Academy two years later. His early works were primarily illustrations of scenes from Shakespeare, Cervantes, and Molière. However, as a member of The Clique, his interests were said to be in pictures of ordinary life. He approached this goal in the 1840s with a series of pictures of *Dolly Varden,* based on Dicken's *Barnaby Rudge,* but his first major venture in painting scenes of modern life was his *Life at the Seaside (Ramsgate Sands),* which he conceived while on holiday at Ramsgate in 1851. This picture, when exhibited at the Royal Academy in 1854, had an instant and enormous success, and was bought by Queen Victoria. Frith followed it by the large paintings *Derby Day* (no. 209), exhibited at the Royal Academy in 1858, and *The Railway Station,* exhibited privately in 1862, and he continued to paint scenes of modern life for the rest of his long life.

Frith's outlook was one of hearty philistinism, and

the three volumes of his *Autobiography* exude an air of smug self-satisfaction. He scorned most progressive movements in art, a scorn reflected in the article "Crazes in Art, Pre-Raphaelitism and Impressionism" which he published in *The Magazine of Art* in 1888. The Pre-Raphaelites equally detested Frith, and their view of him has generally prevailed, but such unlikely critics as Whistler and Sickert were his professed admirers. It is also noteworthy that Frith's concern with ordinary life and his choice of subject for his three great pictures, the seaside, the race track, and the railroad station, prefigure important elements of the iconography of French impressionism.
A.S.

Bibliography
W. P. Frith, R. A., *My Autobiography and Reminiscences*, 3 vols., 3rd ed., London, 1887
An Exhibition of Paintings by William Powell Frith, R. A., 1819-1909, Corporation Art Gallery, Harrogate, and Whitechapel Art Gallery, London, 1951 (exhibition catalogue edited with introduction by Jonathan Mayne; foreword by James Laver)

209

209
Derby Day
The Trustees of The Tate Gallery, London
Oil on canvas; 40 x 88 in.
1856-58

After the popular success of his *Life at the Seaside* at the Royal Academy in 1854, Frith sought for another subject "capable of affording me the opportunity of showing an appreciation of the infinite variety of everyday life." He saw his first horse race in 1854; two years later he visited Epsom for the first time, and this visit provided the basis for *Derby Day.* The race itself held no interest for Frith except as providing an opportunity of studying life and character, and in his picture horses and

jockeys form decidedly insignificant parts of the composition. What Frith wanted to show, and did show, was a "principal incident": the hungry child acrobat distracted by the unpacking of a picnic hamper; this he surrounded with an astonishing accumulation of the fashionable and unfashionable, gamblers, gypsies, policemen, fancy women, and beggars, all depicted in loving anecdotal detail.

According to Frith's *Autobiography,* which provides an account of his progress on the picture, his time at the Derby was too short for sketching, so he made mental notes. He also made use of photographs, although he neglected to mention this in his *Autobiography.* He employed a photographer, a Mr. Howlett, to stand on the roof of a cab and photograph "as many queer groups of people as he could." One such photograph, showing the distant grandstand, is now known. After the race, on May 21, 1856, Frith began a rough drawing of the composition, which he finished on May 24. Incorporating so many figures

and incidents into a composition apparently presented no problems. For Frith, this seems to have been a natural talent: "I cannot say I have ever found a difficulty in composing great number of figures into a more or less harmonious whole." Considering the painter's professed lack of interes in this essential aspect of his art, it is amazing how well the composition of *Derby Day* does work, and Frith's inventiveness in the variety of groupings amounts to sheer genius.

Following the rough charcoal drawing, Frith made numbers of studies from models for all the prominent figures. Then, on his usual seaside holiday to Folkestone, he prepared a careful oil sketch incorporating color and effect. This was followed by a large sketch which took many week and a second to try a different grouping of the central figures (Bethnal Green Museum; the variou known sketches and versions are discussed by Martin Davies). Frith began sketching the figures in charcoal onto the picture itself on January 20,

1857, and on February 9 he spent his first day in painting. Frith's *Autobiography* contains numerous anecdotes about his models, several of whom were of the professions depicted in the picture. For the horses, Frith had the assistance of the animal painter, John Frederick Herring, Senior, who made a highly finished watercolor from which Frith copied the two horses in the right background (British Museum). On Herring's drawing there is a slight sketch by Landseer of the anatomical construction of a horse, which presumably was also intended as an aid for Frith.

After "fifteen months' incessant labour," Frith exhibited the picture at the Royal Academy in 1858, where it was phenomenally successful, so successful that it had to be protected first by a policeman and then by a guardrail from the pressure of the crowds. This latter distinction pleased Frith enormously, as a rail had been used only once before, for Wilkie's *Chelsea Pensioners* in 1822. After the exhibition he retouched the picture, making some changes which had been advised by Prince Albert. He had long since sold it, on the basis of his first oil sketch, to Jacob Bell, a wealthy druggist and onetime schoolmate of Frith's at Sass's. Bell paid Frith £1500, the artist retaining the copyright and the right to borrow the picture back for engraving. Frith subsequently sold the copyright for engraving for another £1500 to the French dealer Ernest Gambart, who also paid an additional £750 for exhibition rights. This constituted, at the time, one of the highest amounts ever paid to a living artist for a single work, but Frith soon surpassed it with the £5,250, including engraving and exhibiting rights, he received for *The Railway Station*. Bell died in 1859, bequeathing *Derby Day* to The National Gallery, but it went first to Paris to be engraved, and then was sent on an exhibition tour around the world, entering The National Gallery only in 1865. As recently as 1922, it was described as attracting more visitors to that august institution than all the Gallery's other pictures combined.

The instant popular appeal of *Derby Day* was

not accompanied by equal critical acclaim. Ruskin quite aptly described it as "a kind of cross between John Leech and Wilkie, and a dash of daguerreotype here and there and some pretty seasoning with Dickens's sentiment." He wrote that he had never seen an abler example of "the entirely popular manner" of painting, but this manner was necessarily "because popular, stooping and restricted." The Pre-Raphaelite group was keenly conscious that Frith did not share its ideals; and in their attitude toward Frith we can feel the dislike of the self-conscious avant-garde for an artist who, they felt, pandered to popular taste. William Michael Rossetti called *Derby Day* commonplace and lacking in beauty, grandeur, dramatic intensity, or "that depth of humour which has passion at the bottom of it." Even the *Art Journal,* no friend of the Pre-Raphaelites, called the picture vulgar. On the other hand, Whistler, of all people, later praised the *Derby Day* and compared its background favorably to Manet. In recent years there has been some recognition that Frith's breezy freshness has more in common with modern attitudes than the pondered seriousness of his high-minded contemporaries.

It is occasionally said that Frith's great paintings of modern life from the 1850s owe a debt to the example of Pre-Raphaelitism. Actually, however, he began his *Ramsgate Sands* before the Pre-Raphaelites undertook any comparable ventures. Millais's *The Woodman's Daughter,* exhibited in 1851 (see no. 224), is usually cited as the first Pre-Raphaelite depiction of modern life, but it is, like Frith's *Dolly Varden,* based on a literary source; the first major Pre-Raphaelite attempt in this direction was made by Ford Madox Brown in the summer of 1852, when he began *Work, The Last of England,* and *An English Autumn Afternoon.* In their modern subjects, both Frith and the Pre-Raphaelites belong to an English tradition whose founder and most distinguished practitioner was Hogarth.
A.S.

Provenance
Jacob Bell (commissioned the picture in 1856; bequest to the National Gallery, 1859; however the picture did not enter the Gallery until 1865)
The National Gallery, London, 1865
The Tate Gallery, 1951

Exhibitions
Royal Academy, 1858, no. 218
Marylebone Literary Institution, London, 1859
Between 1859 and 1865, under the auspices of Ernest Gambart, the picture was sent on a worldwide exhibition tour, which included Europe, Australia and America
Franco-British Exhibition, London, 1908, no. 385
The First Hundred Years of the Royal Academy, 1769-1868, Royal Academy, London, 1951, no. 359

References
Ruskin, XIV, 161-62
Thomas Sutton, "On Some Uses and Abuses of Photography," *The Photographic News,* VII, 1863, p. 67
William Michael Rossetti, *Fine Art, Chiefly Contemporary: Notices Re-printed, with Revisions,* London, 1867, pp. 263-65
Frith, I, 268-69
E. R. and J. Pennell, *The Whistler Journal,* Philadelphia, 1921, p. 78
Walter Sickert, "The 'Derby Day'," *Burlington,* XLI, 1922, pp. 276-78 (reprinted in Osbert Sitwell, ed., *A Free House,* London, 1947, pp. 202-04)
Captain Reginald White, letter to *The Sunday Times* (London), 8 Aug. 1926
"The Most Famous Derby Picture and the Photograph Used for Details," *The Illustrated London News,* 9 June 1934, p. 924
A. M. Hind, "A Sheet of Studies for Frith's 'Derby Day'," *The British Museum Quarterly,* X, 1935, pp. 18-19
Martin Davies, *National Gallery Catalogues: The British School,* London, 1946, pp. 53-54
Helmut Gernsheim, *Masterpieces of Victorian Photography,* London, 1951, p. 12
Graham Reynolds, *Painters of the Victorian Scene,* London, 1953, pp. 11, 13, 59-60
Graham Reynolds, *Victorian Painting,* London, 1966, pp. 33, 57, pl. 24

Reproductions
Engraved by A.-T.-M. Blanchard

1821-1893

Brown was born in Calais, the son of a retired ship's purser, who, although English, lived on the continent. In 1833 the family moved to Belgium so that their son could study art, which he did under a series of masters culminating in Gustaf Wappers in Antwerp. From 1840 until the summer of 1844 he lived in Paris. In the latter year he submitted works to the cartoon competition in Westminster Hall to choose artists to decorate the Houses of Parliament (no. 210), and he settled in London. He spent the winter of 1845-46 in Rome.

Brown's early works reflect the variety of styles to which he was exposed: his Belgian academic training, French romanticism, and the archaism of the German Nazarenes whose works he saw in Rome. His most ambitious works of the later 1840s, *Chaucer at the Court of Edward III* (Sydney, Australia), *Our Lady of Good Children* (Tate Gallery), and *Wickliffe Reading His Translation of the Bible to John of Gaunt* (Bradford), show strong Nazarene influence and were of great importance for the young members of the Pre-Raphaelite Brotherhood. Brown stated about a smaller work of this period that his goal was "to substitute simple imitation for scenic effectiveness, and purity of natural colour for scholastic depth of tone," and in order to do so he attempted to paint "a Holbein of the 19th century." In 1848 Dante Gabriel Rossetti introduced himself to Brown and was for a short time his pupil; they remained lifelong friends. Brown was not a member of the Pre-Raphaelite Brotherhood, but he was very close to it, and the intensified naturalism of his paintings in the 1850s stemmed from interests he held in common with Holman Hunt and Millais. In 1851 Brown painted his first picture entirely in the open air (no. 212). In the following year he began his two great paintings of modern life, *The Last of England* (Birmingham) and *Work* (Manchester). The former was completed in 1855, the latter only in 1865. In that year Brown had a retrospective exhibition of his work for which he wrote long explanations of all his pictures, thus insuring that henceforth *Work* and *The Last of England* would be looked upon as sociological tracts. They are, however, also monuments of the realism of the 1850s. Brown wrote of *The Last of England,* "absolutely without regard to the art of any period or country, I have tried to render this scene as it would appear," and this attitude characterizes most of his work of the 1850s.

Around 1860 Brown's art changed radically. Along with Rossetti, Burne-Jones, and William Morris, he was a founding member of the decorating firm of Morris, Marshall, Faulkner and Company (later Morris and Company). As a result of designing for the firm, a concern with decorative values replaced the rigorous naturalism which had characterized his art during the preceding decade. Brown's most important later works are his murals in the Town Hall in Manchester, which occupied him from 1878 until his death in 1893.

Brown was a blunt, knotty individual whose personality is well reflected in his art. He was an implacable hater of the official artistic establishment; after 1853 he stopped exhibiting at the Royal Academy, and he was the chief promoter among the Pre-Raphaelite circle of their various attempts to exhibit independently, notably of the exhibition held in Russell Place in 1857 and of the Hogarth Club, a private exhibiting society founded the following year. During the 1850s he lived mainly in and around Hampstead and, because of financial difficulties, in relative isolation. In 1865 he moved to Fitzroy Square in Bloomsbury, where his home became an intellectual and artistic gathering place. He was the grandfather of the writer Ford Madox Ford.   A.S.

Bibliography
"Work" and Other Paintings by Ford Madox Brown, 191 Piccadilly, London, 1865 (exhibition catalogue with notes by the artist)
Ford M. Hueffer, *Ford Madox Brown: A Record of His Life and Work,* London, 1896
Ford Madox Brown, 1821-1893, Walker Art Gallery, Liverpool, etc., 1964-65 (exhibition catalogue, edited with introduction by Mary Bennett)

210
The Body of Harold Brought Before William the Conquerer (Wilhelmus Conquistador)
City of Manchester Art Galleries
Oil on canvas; 41½ x 48¼ in.
Inscribed: *F MADOX BROWN 1844-61*

On October 16, 1834 the British Houses of Parliament were destroyed by fire. A new building to replace them, the present Houses of Parliament designed by Sir Charles Barry, was begun the following year. By 1841 construction was far enough along that a commission, headed by Prince Albert, was appointed to supervise the decoration of the new building. The commissioners decided that the interiors should be decorated with monumental frescoes, an undertaking without precedent in Britain, and to this effect they sponsored a series of competitions to select the artists. The first competition, in which the artists were asked to submit cartoons for frescoes illustrative of English history or literature, took place in 1843, and there were additional competitions in 1844 and 1845. Ford Madox Brown then living in Paris, did not participate in the first competition, but in 1844 he submitted two cartoons which he had executed in France, *Adam and Eve* (no. 84 in the competition catalogue; illustrating *Paradise Lost)* and *The Body of Harold Brought Before William the Conquerer* (no. 7 in the competition catalogue). This large cartoon (13 by 15 feet) is now in the South London Art Gallery, Camberwell, where there are also some related drawings. No. 210. was shown alongside the cartoo

210

in 1844, apparently as a sketch for color. After the competition, in which Brown had no official success, this smaller version remained on the artist's hands until 1861, when T. E. Plint, the Leeds stockbroker for whom Brown was painting *Work,* commissioned him to rework it into a finished picture. Plint died before this was completed, and the commission was taken up by James Leathart of Newcastle, who owned a large group of Brown's works (cf. no. 212). In his 1865 catalogue, Brown stated that he had entirely repainted the picture in 1861, but, in fact, it corresponds exactly in every major compositional feature to the original cartoon of 1844.

Brown's entry in the catalogue for the 1844 competition was accompanied by two quotations explaining the subject: "After the battle, the body of Harold was found and brought to William the Conqueror"—(Hume); and "William, on the day of battle, wore round his neck the principal relics of the tubful which he had guilefully caused to be placed beneath the table at which he had forced Harold to swear to aid him in obtaining the crown of England"—(Auguste Thierry). In 1865 Brown wrote that he had studied the Bayeux tapestry, but did not follow it, preferring to be deliberately anachronistic: "twenty years ago, extreme exactness in matters external and archaeological was less in vogue than it is now; properly speaking the medieval feeling in art did not as yet exist— men *thought Renaissance* and *called* it *Gothic.* With me in those days, the dramatic interest in a subject outweighed every other consideration, such was the example set by Delacroix in France, and by David Scott, the British Delacroix here—set, though not followed."

The reference to Delacroix is significant. Although the figures carrying Harold are ultimately derived from Raphael's *Entombment* in the Villa Borghese, the main inspiration for Brown's picture seems to have come from Delacroix's great machine for the Gallery of Battles at Versailles, *The Crusaders Entering Constantinople* (now in the Louvre), which Brown would have seen exhibited at the Salon in

1841. Brown's concern with the "dramatic interest of a subject" led to a personal expressionism which was to crop up again in his later years, and which is apparent here in the grimacing faces and grotesque details such as the two figures in the lower left corner.
A.S.

211

211
Lear Curses Goneril's Infidelity
Whitworth Art Gallery, University of Manchester
Pen and sepia ink over faint pencil; 7⅜ x 10⅞ in.
Inscribed: *Ford M. Brown, Paris/44*

Brown, in Paris in 1844, executed a series of sixteen outline drawings illustrating *King Lear.* These are all now in the Whitworth Art Gallery. Several preliminary sketches are in Birmingham.

The incident shown in no. 211 is drawn from Act I, Scene 4. Lear has been rudely received in the palace of the Duke of Albany and has been told by Goneril that he must get rid of part of his entourage. In response Lear has called for his horses, which appear in the background of the drawing. Also present are Albany, rather puzzled by the conflict, the Fool, and Kent. In this scene, Lear actually curses Goneril twice, first asking nature to make her sterile, and then calling down blasts and fogs upon her.

In 1843 Delacroix published a series of thirteen lithographs of scenes from *Hamlet.* These

certainly provided inspiration for Madox Brown's illustrations to *Lear.* As we have seen from Brown's explanation of no. 210, Delacroix was an important influence upon him at this time. However, Lear's emphatically expressive gesture projected across the picture plane has more in common with French neoclassicism than with Delacroix's *Hamlet* illustrations. The roughness of Brown's drawings corresponds to the emotional violence of Shakespeare's play, and Hueffer has suggested that Brown deliberately avoided attractiveness in order to retain a feeling of primitive barbarism.

Brown later etched one of his *Lear* illustrations as a frontispiece for *The Germ,* and he worked up three of the compositions into pictures, although no. 211 was not among them. In the 1890s Sir Henry Irving owned the series of drawings, and he used them as a basis for his production of *King Lear* at the Lyceum Theatre in November 1892. Irving also employed Brown to design three scenes in the first and second acts.
A.S.

212

The Pretty Baa-Lambs (Summer Heat)
Birmingham City Museum and Art Gallery
Oil on panel; 24 x 30 in.
Inscribed: *F. MADOX BROWN 1851-59*

Brown began *The Pretty Baa-Lambs* in the summer of 1851 while living in Stockwell. According to a diary entry written in 1854, it was painted almost entirely in the sunlight, "which twice gave me a fever while painting." Brown painted the picture from his painting-room, which was on a level with the garden. His wife and his daughter were the models for the lady and child. The sheep were brought every morning in a truck from Clapham Common, and the background was painted on the Common. Brown had essentially completed the picture in five months' work between May and October 1851, but he altered the head of the woman in the spring of 1852 before exhibiting the picture at the Royal Academy; he worked on no. 212 further in the autumn of 1852 and the spring of 1853 before sending it to an exhibition in Glasgow. In 1852 he made a small copy, which he sold in 1854 for five pounds (Ashmolean Museum). His work of 1852 and 1853 may have consisted of repainting parts of the draperies over a wet white ground, a technique yielding greater brilliance which Hunt and Millais had developed and which Millais revealed to Brown in the summer of 1851. Brown had previously admired the brilliance of Hunt's and Millais's pictures and had advised his friend Lowes Dickinson to adopt a pure white ground at once. The medium he originally used in no. 212 was "Roberson's undrying copal (flake white)." As soon as he learned the secret of the wet white ground (for the technique of which, see Hunt, I, 277), Brown put it to use in *Christ Washing Peter's Feet* (Tate Gallery), which he began in the autumn of 1851.

The picture remained unsold until 1859 when Brown worked further on it before it was finally purchased by James Leathart. This later work resulted in the addition of the panoramic background. According to Holman Hunt, and from the evidence of the 1852 copy, the picture originally had a lower horizon, stopping at the hedgerow and cottage at the edge of the grazing land. The further background was apparently added to lessen the stark contrast of the vertical figures against the horizontal landscape. It may have been based on a lost landscape of *Southend,* showing the estuary of The Thames with the Nore lightship and the Isle of Sheppy in the distance, which Brown began in 1846, but completed only in 1858 and exhibited in 1859.

When *The Pretty Baa-Lambs* appeared at the Royal Academy in 1852, William Michael Rossetti described it in *The Spectator* as "a pretty touch of home sentiment," painted in 18th-century costume and set in "the long summer hours before the gloaming." To other critics it was incomprehensible, and the *Art Journal* concluded that it was "a facetious experiment upon the public intelligence." Brown, in his catalogue of 1865, acknowledged the confusion and wrote an explanation which tried to set things straight: "This picture was painted in 1851, and exhibited the following year, at a time when discussion was very rife on certain ideas and principles in art, very much in harmony with my own views, but more sedulously promulgated by friends of mine. Hung in a false light, and viewed through the medium of extraneous ideas, the painting was, I think, much misunderstood. I was told that it was impossible to make out what *meaning* I had in the picture. At the present moment, few people I trust will seek for any meaning beyond the obvious one, that is— a lady, a baby, two lambs, a servant maid, and some grass. In all cases pictures must be judged first as pictures—a deep philosophical intention will not make a fine picture, such being rather given in excess of the bargain; and though all epic works of art have this excess, yet I should be much inclined to doubt the genuineness of that artist's ideas, who never painted from mere love of the look of things, whose mind was always on the stretch for a moral. This picture was painted out in the sunlight; the only intention being to render that effect as well as my powers in a first attempt of this kind would allow."

Despite Brown's disclaimers of complexity of meaning, his *œuvre* contains several other pictures of mother and child or nurse and child, *Our Ladye of Good Children* (Tate Gallery), *Out of Town* (Manchester), *An English Fireside of 1854-55* (private collection), *The Last of England* (Birmingham), and *Take Your Son, Sir* (Tate Gallery); in all of them, as in no. 212, the *Madonna* image is more or less present. Also, for pious Victorians the religious symbolism of sheep could not be dismissed lightly. Those in no. 212 are not unlike the sheep in Holman Hunt's *Hireling Shepherd,* which was painted at exactly the same time, and upon which Hunt happily concurred in imposing a weighty load of symbolical meaning (see also no. 216). Nonetheless, Brown's insistence on the purely visual appeal of his picture is a significant relief from much Victorian cant. The remark about the promulgation of certain ideas refers to Holman Hunt and Millais; the ideas were of outdoor painting. Hunt and Millais in the summer and fall of 1851 spent long hours out-of-doors, painting the backgrounds of *The Hireling Shepherd, Ophelia,* and *The Huguenot* (no. 225) directly from nature. But they painted their figures in the studio, while Brown went a step further and painted the whole picture in the sunlight. In fact, *The Pretty Baa-Lambs* seems to have been the first sizable figural picture intended for exhibition that was painted entirely out-of-doors. As such it is an important forerunner of such pictures as Monet's *Women in the Garden* (Louvre), painted in the following decade, and of impressionist *plein-air* painting in general. As the critic R. A. M. Stevenson exclaimed to Ford Madox Hueffer, "By God! the whole history of modern art begins with that picture. Corot, Manet, the Marises, all the Fontainebleau School, all the Impressionists, never did anything but imitate that picture."

As Brown noted, *The Pretty Baa-Lambs* represents his first attempt at painting in the sunlight, and it shows a notable advance over his earlier paintings. Cast shadows are intense blue (note, for example, those against the baby's white gown), and areas of diffused light, such as the baby's face, are purple

212

and violet from reflected light. Brown continued to paint out-of-doors in his other major paintings of the 1850s, *Work* and *The Last of England,* but, in terms of naturalistic observation, *The Pretty Baa-Lambs* is his most revolutionary undertaking. A.S.

Provenance
James Leathart, Newcastle, July 1859 (until 1896)
Henry Yates Thompson
Mrs. Edith M. Yates Thompson (sale, Sotheby's, London, 27 June 1956, no. 81, bt. Colnaghi)
Birmingham City Art Gallery, 1956

Exhibitions
Royal Academy, 1852, no. 1291
Works of Modern Artists, Glasgow, 1854-55, no. 241
Liverpool Academy, 1859, no. 39
"Work" and Other Paintings by Ford Madox Brown, 191 Piccadilly, London, 1865, no. 11
A Pre-Raphaelite Collection (Leathart Collection), Goupil Gallery, London, 1896, no. 20
The First Hundred Years of the Royal Academy: 1769-1868, Royal Academy, London, 1951-52, no. 278
Pictures from the City Art Gallery, Birmingham, Thos. Agnew & Sons, London, 1957, no. 51
The Liverpool Academy 1810-1867, Walker Art Gallery, Liverpool, 1960, no. 71
Ford Madox Brown, 1821-1893, Walker Art Gallery, Liverpool, etc., 1964-65, no. 21

References
Art Journal, 1852, p. 175
The Spectator, 1852, p. 472
"Work" and Other Paintings, pp. 6-7, no. 11
Hueffer, pp. 84-85, 160, 162-63, 413, 436-37
W. M. Rossetti, ed., *Praeraphaelite Diaries and Letters,* London, 1900, pp. 108-14, 193
W. Holman Hunt, *Pre-Raphaelitism and the Pre-Raphaelite Brotherhood,* London, 1905, I, 277; II, 96
Ford Madox Hueffer, *Ancient Lights and Certain New Reflections,* London, 1911, p. 207
Robin Ironside and John Gere, *Pre-Raphaelite Painters,* London, 1948, p. 23 and pl. 12
Catalogue of Paintings, City Museum and Art Gallery, Birmingham, 1960, pp. 16-17

213

213
Carrying Corn
The Trustees of The Tate Gallery, London
Oil on panel; 7¾ x 10⅞ in.
Inscribed: *F. Madox Brown Finchley/54*

Painted from nature in September and October 1854 while Brown was living at Hampstead, the picture shows a harvest scene just before sunset. Concurrently, while he was working on this picture in the evenings, in the mornings Brown was painting another small landscape, *The Brent at Hendon,* which is now also in The Tate Gallery. A third small landscape, *The Hayfield,* painted the following year, is in an English private collection.

During this period Brown kept a diary which provides day-to-day documentation of his progress. The first mention describes the site: "About three out to a field, to begin the outline of a small landscape. Found it of surpassing loveliness. Cornshocks in long perspective form, hayricks, and steeple seen between them—foreground of turnips —blue sky and afternoon sun. By the time I had drawn in the outline they had carted half my wheat;

by today all I had drawn in was gone." His subsequent entries record continuing difficulties. October 3, 1854: "To work at the cornfield from quarter past three till quarter to six: did next to nothing. It would seem that very small trees in the distance are very difficult objects to paint, or else I am not suited to this sort of work; for I can make nothing of this small screen of trees, though I have pottered over [them] sufficient time to have painted a large landscape, the men of English schools would say. . . ." October 11: "The field again.— Sunshine when I did not want it, cold and wind when it went. Worked at the trees and improved them—found the turnips too difficult to do anything with of a serious kind. I don't know if it would be possible to paint them well; they change from day to day." October 12: "Saw my turnips were all false in colour: ruminated over this disgrace, and tried to retrieve it. . . ."

And so on. At the time Brown was desperately poor, and visits to the field were interspersed with visits to the pawnbroker. He intended his landscapes as potboilers, "little subjects that will paint off at once." However, Brown invariably bogged down in difficulties; he spent long amounts of time upon the pictures, and then sold them for ridiculous prices; for *Carrying Corn* he received twelve pounds. His project of making money out of these pictures was impractical to say the least; he did not have the training, nor the experience, to paint landscapes with ease. However, because of this, he approached landscape with a remarkably fresh eye. He seems to have been oblivious of anything to be learned from previous landscape painting which could help him slide over his problems. Freed from traditional English interests in atmospheric effects and from most conventional devices to create space, such as repoussoir trees and contrasts of warm and cool colors, Brown's landscapes diverge considerably from the mainstreams of 19th-century naturalism, leading from Constable to Monet. Despite, or because of, Brown's working directly out-of-doors and his scrupulously conscientious labor, his landscapes seem highly stylized, more like Samuel Palmer

1822-1907

than Constable. Brown was almost certainly unacquainted with Palmer's Shoreham works, but his subject is essentially the same: a twilight world of pastoral harmony. His work is not deliberately visionary, as is Palmer's, but its immediacy and obsessive clarity make it verge on the hallucinatory. Brown described himself in his diary at the time as "intensely miserable, very hard up, and a little mad," and these idyllic scenes seem to have become for the artist vehicles of release into which he unknowingly projected an emotional load transcending his original mundane moneymaking goals.
A.S.

Provenance
Sold to D. T. White (dealer), 27 June 1855
B. G. Windus, Tottenham (sale, Christie's, London, 19 July 1862, no. 37, bt. in; Christie's, 15 Feb. 1868, no. 299, bt. Tebbs)
Henry Virtue Tebbs, London (sale, Christie's, London, 10 March 1900, no. 39, bt. Radley)
Frederick Anthony White, London (sale, Christie's, London, 20 April 1934, no. 46, bt. Martin)
The Tate Gallery, 1934

Exhibitions
Pre-Raphaelite Exhibition, Russell Place, London, 1857, no. 11
"Work" and Other Paintings by Ford Madox Brown, 191 Piccadilly, London, 1865, no. 16
Works of Ford Madox Brown, Grafton Galleries, London, 1897, no. 26
La Peinture Anglaise, Louvre, Paris, 1938, no. 11
Ford Madox Brown, 1821-1893, Walker Art Gallery, Liverpool, etc., 1964-65, no. 32

References
"Work" and Other Paintings, p. 9, no. 16
Hueffer, pp. 101-02, 439
W. M. Rossetti, ed., *Praeraphaelite Diaries and Letters,* London, 1900, pp. 125-43 *passim,* 149, 165, 175, 185
Robin Ironside and John Gere, *Pre-Raphaelite Painters,* London, 1948, p. 24, pl. 17
John Rothenstein, *The Tate Gallery,* London, 1958, pp. 82-83

Windus was the son of wealthy Liverpool parents. He studied for a short time under William Daniels, a Liverpool portrait painter, and then at the Liverpool Academy. He became a member of that body in 1848. Before 1850 Windus followed the prevailing taste for pictures of literary or historical subjects, but with a tendency towards the illustration of themes of extraordinary obscurity. Stylistically, his early works seem most strongly influenced by Etty, although Windus was one of the few prominent artists of his generation who was not directly exposed to Etty's influence in the life class of the Royal Academy. His subject pictures of the later 1840s are morbidly dramatic with strong contrasts of light and dark.

In 1850 Windus visited the Royal Academy Exhibition in London, and in front of Millais's *Christ in the House of his Parents* he apparently underwent instantaneous conversion. He persuaded his fellow members of the Liverpool Academy to invite the members of the Pre-Raphaelite Brotherhood and their friends to show at their annual exhibitions, and during the next decade, due largely to Windus's pushing, Pre-Raphaelites regularly won the Academy's annual prize. Windus, a slow and hesitant worker, produced only two pictures under Pre-Raphaelite influence in the 1850s, but these are his best-known works: *Burd Helen,* which he exhibited at the Royal Academy in 1856 (Liverpool) and *Too Late,* shown in 1859 (Tate Gallery). Ruskin praised *Burd Helen* lavishly, but the gloomy subject of *Too Late* provoked an incredible outburst, the gist of which

was that Windus should get some fresh air and exercise. This, combined with other personal calamities, seems to have so depressed the artist, that it brought his painting career almost to an end and during the rest of his life Windus produced only a handful of small pictures and sketches, done for his own pleasure.

As a man Windus seems to have been neurotically melancholy and ultra-sensitive, so much so that he became paralyzed as an artist. However, when he could channel his sensitivity, he was a painter of remarkable individuality. In his Pre-Raphaelite phase, he was the one Liverpool artist to achieve reputation outside of his native city. It is unfortunate, however, that interest in his two Pre-Raphaelite pictures has not been accompanied by attention to his earlier work, which is in many ways equally accomplished and interesting.
A.S.

Bibliography
E. Rimbault Dibdin, "William Lindsay Windus," *The Magazine of Art,* XXIII, 1900, pp. 49-56
H. C. Marillier, *The Liverpool School of Painters,* London, 1904, pp. 241-54
Mary Bennett, "William Windus and the Pre-Raphaelite Brotherhood in Liverpool," *Liverpool Bulletin,* VII, 1958-59, pp. 18-31

214

The Interview of the Apostate Shaxton, Bishop of Salisbury, with Anne Askew in Prison
Walker Art Gallery, Liverpool
Oil on canvas; 34 x 43¾ in.
c. 1849

The painting shows the Protestant martyr Anne Askew, who was executed for heresy in 1546. Shortly before her execution, Shaxton, the ex-Bishop of Salisbury who had been arraigned with her but saved his life by recanting, visited her in an attempt to persuade her to do likewise, an attempt which she dismissed with scorn.

Windus exhibited a painting of a parallel subject, *Cranmer Endeavoring to Obtain a Confession of Guilt from Catherine Howard* (Walker Art Gallery) at the British Institution in 1849, the same year no. 214 was shown at the Liverpool Academy. The competitions to select artists to decorate the Houses of Parliament had inspired a flurry of interest in subjects from British history during the 1840s, but they do not explain why Windus was attracted to these relatively obscure confrontations. He may have thought of the pictures as a pair, exemplifying in no. 214 female virtue, and in the case of Catherine Howard, from whom Cranmer drew a confession of adultery, its opposite.

The two pictures are the most impressive examples of Windus's art before he fell under the sway of Pre-Raphaelitism. The modelling of the figure of Anne Askew is reminiscent of Etty, but the Caravaggesque lighting is not. It may owe something to the example of Windus's first mentor William Daniels, but Windus uses light and shadow in a sophisticated and personal way to underline the sinister mood of the meeting. With his introduction to Pre-Raphaelitism in the following year, Windus underwent a radical change, replacing the brownish murk of this picture with the overall brightness of *Burd Helen.* It is an indication of the appeal of Pre-Raphaelitism that Windus completely abandoned the style in which he had been working so effectively as soon as he had contact with the

214

new movement.
A.S.

Provenance
Presented by Alderman John Lea, J. P., to the Walker Art Gallery in 1913

Exhibitions
Liverpool Academy, 1849, no. 96
Liverpool School of Painters, Harrogate, 1924, no. 38

References
Bennett, *Liverpool Bulletin,* VII, 1958-59, pp. 23, 29
Graham Reynolds, *Victorian Painting,* London, 1966, pp. 66, 90, pl. 44

William Holman Hunt

1827-1910

Hunt was the son of a London City merchant. At an early age he became a clerk to an estate agent. Having shown some talent in drawing, he entered the Royal Academy schools in 1844, and he struggled through them during the next several years. At the Academy schools he met John Everett Millais and Dante Gabriel Rossetti, and the three, along with four rather inconsequential friends, in November 1848 formed the Pre-Raphaelite Brotherhood. Hunt was primarily responsible for the Brotherhood's slim theoretical underpinnings, which in essence were little more than a desire to be high-minded and a concern with literal, detailed realism. These interests in turn stemmed largely from Hunt's reading of *Modern Painters.*

Hunt was, along with Millais, a chief target of the hostile criticism which the Brotherhood attracted, and for several years he had an extremely difficult time of it. However, his *Light of the World* (Keble College, Oxford), which he began in 1851 and exhibited in 1854, struck the appropriate chord of Victorian religiosity and became one of the best-known and most popular of 19th-century paintings. In 1853 he set off for the Holy Land in order to paint the life of Christ in its natural setting. The two chief products of Hunt's first trip to the East were *The Scapegoat* (Port Sunlight) and *The Finding of Christ in the Temple* (Birmingham), upon which Hunt labored from 1854 until 1860, and which he then sold for 5500 guineas, at the time a record price for a picture. Hunt made several later trips to the East in order to paint further religious subjects. These now seem like some of the most

extraordinary aberrations of Victorian taste, but their success was phenomenal, and Hunt was piously enshrined among the Great Victorians.

It is usually said that Hunt alone of the Pre-Raphaelites stayed true to their principles throughout his life. However, his later works are far inferior to his best Pre-Raphaelite pictures of the early 1850s. His two-volume *Pre-Raphaelitism and the Pre-Raphaelite Brotherhood,* published in 1905, presents a detailed record of the movement and of his own career, but the account is probably somewhat marred by Hunt's refusal to allow any credit to Rossetti and Madox Brown, and by his tendency to color his youth with the pietism of his old age. One result of this has been that Hunt's early works are often regarded in the light of his later ones as symbolic religious tracts, while, as in the case of Madox Brown's, the fact that they are major monuments of the realism of the 1850s is often overlooked. Hunt's painstaking study of natural appearances and his insistence upon painting directly out-of-doors led to works of vigorous originality which still look like nothing else.
A.S.

Bibliography
[Frederick George Stephens], *William Holman Hunt and His Works: A Memoir of the Artist's Life, with Descriptions of His Pictures,* London, 1860
William Holman Hunt, *Pre-Raphaelitism and the Pre-Raphaelite Brotherhood,* 2 vols., London, 1905
Otto von Schleinitz, *William Holman Hunt,* Leipzig, 1907

215
Rienzi Vowing to Obtain Justice for the Death of His Younger Brother Slain in a Skirmish between the Colonna and Orsini Factions
Mrs. E. M. Clarke
Oil on canvas; 32½ x 47½ in.
Inscribed: *William Holman Hunt PRB 1849*

In the Royal Academy catalogue, no. 215 was accompanied by the following quotation: "But for that event, the future liberator of Rome might have been but a dreamer, a scholar, a poet—the peaceful rival of Petrarch—a man of thoughts, not deeds. But from that time, all his faculties, energies, fancies, genius, became concentrated to a single point; and patriotism, before a vision, leaped into the life and vigour of a passion."

The picture is based on *Rienzi: The Last of the Roman Tribunes,* the historical novel published in 1835 by Bulwer-Lytton, which describes the life of the 14th-century Roman republican. The event shown is from the first chapter. Cola di Rienzi and his young brother have been walking on a summer evening along the banks of the Tiber. While Rienzi has gone to fetch a manuscript from a nearby convent, his brother is accidentally caught up and killed in a skirmish between adherents of the warring Orsini and Colonna families. The Colonna who sympathize with Rienzi's loss, are ready to revenge the death as long as they believe it was done by an Orsini, but they discover it was done by one of their own men. At this point, Rienzi tries to feel his brother's heart, finds his hand covered with blood, raises it on high, and cries out, "Justice! Justice." The dead brother still holds a garland of flowers he had been making for their sister. The two soldiers on the right have been left behind to help with the corpse. The figure on the left is Adrian di Castello, a young member of the Colonna family who later becomes an important figure in the novel and now sympathetically offers friendship to Rienzi. Rienzi, however, is busy thinking dark, revolutionary thoughts. Their fulfillment forms the substance of the novel, which describes his leadership of a popular revolution and the overthrow of the Roman nobility.

Hunt began his *Rienzi* in the summer of 1848 and exhibited it at the Royal Academy in 1849. It was his first picture as a member of the Pre-Raphaelite Brotherhood and the only one to bear the initials PRB. One of the professed purposes of the Brotherhood was to choose serious subjects, and no. 215 was serious in a timely way. Hunt later wrote: "Like most young men, I was stirred by the spirit of freedom of the passing revolutionary time. The appeal to Heaven against the tyranny exercised over the poor and helpless seemed well fitted for pictorial treatment." In the same year Hunt began his picture, a new edition of *Rienzi* was published to which Bulwer contributed a preface suggesting that the book had had an influence on Italian youth and thereby upon the recent revolutionary events in Europe. He described the novel as an account of "the exertions of a Roman, in advance of his time, for the freedom of his country." Hunt was directly acquainted with the fortunes of Italy via Rossetti, with whom in 1848 he shared a studio; his memoirs describe the impression made upon him by the political exiles, Rossetti's father among them, who frequented the Rossetti household.

The other prime concern of Pre-Raphaelitism was the direct study of nature. If we can trust Hunt's account, the genesis of the movement was a conversation between Hunt and Millais of late 1847 or early 1848 in which the two agreed that closer adherence to nature should be their goal. Fortified by his reading of Ruskin, Hunt resolved, although his current painting *The Eve of St. Agnes* (R. A. 1848, Guildhall, London) was an interior night scene, that he would paint his next out-of-doors "direct on the canvas itself, with every detail I can see, and with the sunlight brightness of the day itself." *Rienzi* was the next picture, and Hunt put his ideas into practice. In the summer of 1848 he took his canvas to the garden of F. G. Stephens' father to paint a fig tree in full sunlight. He also painted there the foreground grass and dandelions,

215

and he painted the hill and trees of the background at Hampstead. This was done not for the charm of minute finish, "but as a means of studying more deeply Nature's principles of design." For the shields and spears, Hunt took his canvas to the Tower of London. The tower in the background of the picture corresponds to the fortified mansions of the Roman barons described by Bulwer in the opening page of the novel.

After Hunt had painted his landscape details out-of-doors during the summer, he drew the figures from the nude in the studio, and during the following winter he painted them into the picture. He painted the head of Rienzi from Rossetti in order to show the proper racial character. Millais posed for Adrian; a sketch is reproduced in *Pre-Raphaelitism and the Pre-Raphaelite Brotherhood.* Both Hunt and Millais in his picture of the same year, *Lorenzo and Isabella* (Liverpool), employed elaborate and inventive figural compositions. Hunt could not paint with the fluency of Millais, but the organization of his composition is worked out with an intellectual clarity which Professor Waterhouse has claimed worthy of comparison with Poussin.

The picture was well received when exhibited at the Royal Academy in 1849. Hunt's bright colors and precise drawing led the reviewer for the *Art Journal* to call it "an imitation of the works of the early Italian schools," but the same reviewer also declared it assuredly the work of a man of genius. After the exhibition the picture remained unsold until Augustus Egg induced the collector John Gibbons to buy it. This apparently was purely an act of generous support to a young artist, as the owner kept the picture in a closet rather than hanging it. In 1886 Hunt discovered the painting had been damaged by an improper varnish. He repaired it himself, and in so doing he repainted much of the sky and parts of the background, but apparently the figures were not affected.

The subject might be compared with a neoclassical tradition of fervent patriotic oaths, of which

Jacques Louis David's *Oath of the Horatii* is the most famous example. Bulwer-Lytton's novel also inspired Richard Wagner's first successful opera, which had its premiere six years before Hunt began his painting.

A.S.

Provenance
John Gibbons, 1849 (sold 1860s)
Frederick William Cosens, c. 1868 (sale, Christie's, London, 17 May 1890, no. 107, bt. Clarke)
Thomas Clarke, Woolton (sale, Christie's, London, 29 Jan. 1926, no. 41, bt. C. S. Clarke)

Exhibitions
Royal Academy, 1849, no. 324 (accompanied by a quotation from Bulwer-Lytton's *Rienzi)*
Liverpool Academy, 1858, no. 300
Holman Hunt, Fine Art Society, London, 1886
The Art of William Holman Hunt, Walker Art Gallery, Liverpool, 1907, no. 23
The First Hundred Years of the Royal Academy 1769-1868, Royal Academy, London, 1951-52, no. 296

References
Hunt, I, pp. 91, 107, 111-15, 134, 142, 172, 181-83, ill. opp. p. 166
von Schleinitz, p. 20, pl. 14
E. K. Waterhouse, "The Exhibition 'The First Hundred Years of the Royal Academy'," *Burlington,* XCIV, 1952, p. 52, pl. 21

216
Strayed Sheep (Our English Coasts)
The Trustees of The Tate Gallery, London
Oil on canvas; 17 x 23 in.
Inscribed: *W H Hunt 1852 Fairlt.*

When Holman Hunt exhibited his *Hireling Shepherd* (Manchester) at the Royal Academy in 1852, an admirer, Mr. Charles Maude, commissioned him to paint a repetition of the group of sheep in the background. Hunt agreed to do so, but he later sought and received permission to paint an independent picture of sheep. He spent the summer and autumn of 1852 at Fairlight, near Hastings, painting this picture. Because he had spent more time on it than he had intended, Hunt decided that he must ask more than the £70 originally agreed upon. Through the winter of 1852-53 he delayed delivering the picture to Maude, and he considered painting yet another sheep picture to satisfy the commission. His correspondence of this time is full of unhappy references to the painting. However, Maude agreed to pay him £120 for the picture, which Hunt gratefully accepted. It was shown at the Royal Academy in 1853 where it was well received, and in the following year it won the £60 prize of the Birmingham Academy.

Although usually known as *Strayed Sheep,* the picture was shown at the Royal Academy with the title *Our English Coasts, 1852.* F. G. Stephens suggested that this might have been intended as a satire of England's defenselessness against foreign invasion. Stephens also stated that the picture was "of men, and not of sheep," and in this picture, as in *The Hireling Shepherd,* there probably is allegorical reference to the pastoral flock. However this is not belabored, and Hunt never proposed any symbolic explanation for the painting.

While Hunt was at Fairlight, he had the company of Edward Lear, who was taking instruction from Hunt in landscape painting (see no. 197). Thus Hunt was codifying and clarifying his theories of how to paint nature at the time he was putting them

216

as the example of the Pre-Raphaelites' research into the effects of sunlight and suggested that it was one of "the earliest manifestations of the open-air school," i.e., of impressionism. Ruskin mentioned the picture in his 1859 *Academy Notes,* along with two Turners, as an example of magnificent effect of sunshine color "of a kind necessarily unintelligible to the ordinary observer," and in 1883 in his Oxford lectures, *The Art of England,* Ruskin returned to the picture, declaring that it was the first and most complete example of the new attentive landscape which had arisen: "It showed to us, for the first time in the history of art, the absolutely faithful balance of colour and shade by which actual sunshine might be transported into a key in which the harmonies possible with material pigments should yet produce the same impressions upon the mind which were caused by the light itself. . . . the pure natural green and tufted gold of the herbage in the hollow of that little sea-cliff must be recognized for true merely by a minute's pause of attention. Standing long before the picture, you were soothed by it, and raised into such peace as you are intended to find in the glory and the stillness of summer, possessing all things."
A.S.

Provenance
Commissioned by Charles Maude, Bath, 1852
Anonymous sale, Sotheby's, 10 June 1882, no. 463, bt.
Fine Art Society
George Lillie Craik, by 1886
Bought from Mrs. Craik by the National Art-Collections Fund and presented to The Tate Gallery, 1946

Exhibitions
Royal Academy, 1853, no. 534 *(Our English Coasts, 1852)*
Birmingham Academy, 1854
Exposition Universelle, Paris, 1855, no. 840
Art Treasures of the United Kingdom, Manchester, 1857, no. 488 (Modern Masters)
National Exhibition, Leeds, 1868, no. 1310
Whitechapel Art Gallery, London, 1883, no. 136
Holman Hunt, Fine Art Society, London, 1886, no. 17
Royal Jubilee Exhibition, Manchester, 1887, no. 36
Special Loan Collection of Modern Pictures, City Art Gallery, Birmingham, 1891, no. 171

into practice in no. 216. It is in a lighter and brighter palette than any of his previous pictures, and, indeed, than almost any previous picture. The real subject of the picture is sunlight, not sunlight as a general visual effect, but seen in terms of specific observation: shining through a sheep's ear, transforming the colors of the foreground plants and turning the sea into prismatic greens and violets. Stephens made special mention of the haze over the horizon of sea near the cliff, which originated from the exhalations arising from the

cliff. At the same time Hunt painted a smaller picture, which he titled *Fairlight Downs: Sunlight on the Sea.*

In 1855 no. 216 was exhibited in Paris at the *Exposition Universelle,* where it received considerable attention. Delacroix admired it, and Maxime du Camp described its colors as false, fantastic, and discordant, as if seen through a prism. At the end of the century another French critic, Robert de la Sizeranne, used *Strayed Sheep*

Loan Collection of Pictures, Guildhall, London, 1894, no. 127
International Exhibition, Glasgow, 1901, no. 394
Ruskin, City Art Gallery, Manchester, 1904, no. 334
The Collected Works of W. Holman Hunt, City Art Gallery, Manchester, 1906, no. 10
The Collected Works of W. Holman Hunt, Leicester Galleries, London, 1906, no. 30
The Art of William Holman Hunt, Walker Art Gallery, Liverpool, 1907, no. 68
The Pre-Raphaelite Brotherhood, City Art Gallery, Birmingham, 1947, no. 38
The Pre-Raphaelites, Whitechapel Art Gallery, London, 1948, no. 37
The Pre-Raphaelite Brotherhood, The Tate Gallery, London, 1948, no. 12

References
Eugène Delacroix, *Journal* (trans. Lucy Norton), London, 1951, p. 286
Maxime du Camp, *Les Beaux Arts à l'Exposition Universelle de 1855,* Paris, 1855, p. 313 (quoted in *Art Journal,* 1856, p. 79)
[Stephens], p. 23
William Michael Rossetti, *Fine Art, Chiefly Contemporary: Notices Re-printed with Revisions,* London, 1867, pp. 237-38
Ruskin, XIV, 225-26; XXXIII, 222
Robert de la Sizeranne, *La Peinture anglaise contemporaine, 1844-1894,* Paris, 1895, pp. 76-78 (English translation by H. M. Poynter, *English Contemporary Art,* London, 1898, pp. 75-77)
Hunt, I, 321, 327-38, ill. opp. p. 412
von Schleinitz, p. 33, pl. 25
Ford Madox Hueffer, *Ancient Lights and Certain New Reflections,* London, 1911, p. 219
Janet Camp Troxell, ed., *Three Rossettis: Unpublished Letters to and from Dante Gabriel, Christina, William,* Cambridge, Mass., 1937, p. 37

Reproductions
Engraved by C. Cousen, *Art Journal,* Nov. 1877, opp. p. 292 (as *On the Hill Side*)

217

217
Cairo—Sunset on the Gebel Mokattum
Whitworth Art Gallery, University of Manchester
Watercolor; 6¾ x 14 in.
Inscribed: *WHH* (monogram) *Cairo 1854*

On his first trip to the East, Hunt visited Egypt in the spring of 1854 before proceeding on to Jerusalem. He was not happy there; he could not find suitable models, he did not wish to be a *paysagiste,* and he was disappointed, anyway, with the scenery: "The country offers nothing with more than antiquarian interest as landscape; the Pyramids themselves are extremely ugly blocks, as one always knew, and arranged with most unpicturesque taste. . . . one might as well sketch in Hackney Marsh." He did, however, find the desert beautiful. Its brilliant colors, which must have been startling to this young Englishman, form the main interest of no. 217 and of Hunt's other Eastern watercolors. Hunt had given unprecedented brilliance of color to his *Strayed Sheep* (no. 216) of 1852, but in his Eastern works the palette is at an even higher pitch. In no. 217, differences of color, rather than darkening, correspond to the different lights. The foreground shadows are blue and purple, the illuminated buildings of the middle distance are orange, and the hills are a vivid pink in the sunset.

Hunt had no experience in painting extensive landscapes before his trip to the East, and as a

1828-1882

result he relied heavily on a few compositional schemes. The foreground figures and the wall running across the picture are repeated with only slight variation in another Eastern watercolor, *Jerusalem During Ramazan,* now also in the Whitworth Art Gallery.

A.S.

Provenance
Ernest Gambart, London
Thomas Plint, Leeds (sale, Christie's, London,
7 March 1862, no. 196, bt. Agnew)
Jesse Haworth, Manchester (died 1920)
Mrs. Haworth (died 1937)
Whitworth Art Gallery, 1937

Exhibitions
Pre-Raphaelite Exhibition, Russell Place, London, 1857,
no. 41 *(Sketch from a House in New Ca. . Looking
towards Gebel Mokattum)*
Art Treasures, Royal Institution, Manchester, 1878,
no. 184
Royal Jubilee Exhibition, Manchester, 1887, no. 1229
The Collected Works of W. Holman Hunt, City Art
Gallery, Manchester, 1906, no. 52
The Art of William Holman Hunt, Walker Art Gallery,
Liverpool, 1907, no. 25
*Works by Pre-Raphaelite Painters from Collections in
Lancashire,* The Tate Gallery, London, 1913, no. 43
The Pre-Raphaelites, their Friends and Followers,
Lady Lever Art Gallery, Port Sunlight, 1948, no. 114
Winter Exhibition, Royal Society of British Artists,
London, 1948, no. 332
*Pre-Raphaelite Paintings, Drawings and Book
Illustrations,* Whitworth Art Gallery, Manchester, 1961,
no. 20

References
Hunt, I, ill. p. 377
von Schleinitz, p. 44, pl. 35

Rossetti was born in London, but he was of Italian descent on both sides; his father was a political refugee from Naples and a Professor of Italian at King's College, London. He studied at Sass's School and from 1846 to 1848 at the Royal Academy schools. In March 1848, he introduced himself to Ford Madox Brown and became Brown's pupil. He soon found the work which Brown prescribed irksome and left, but the two remained close friends throughout their lives. Rossetti then shared a studio with Holman Hunt, and in November of the same year he, Hunt, Millais, and four associates founded the Pre-Raphaelite Brotherhood. Rossetti's first painting *The Girlhood of Mary Virgin* was begun under Hunt's supervision in the autumn of 1848 and exhibited the next spring (Tate Gallery). He followed it with a painting of the *Annunciation* which he exhibited in 1850 (Tate Gallery), but then, in the face of mounting hostility to Pre-Raphaelitism, he ceased exhibiting his work publicly, and for a decade he largely gave up painting in oil. The one significant exception is *Found* (Wilmington), which Rossetti never completed, a modern urban drama of a fallen woman, à la Holman Hunt's *Awakening Conscience.* For the rest, during the 1850s he devoted his energies to drawings and watercolors. Most of his watercolors are of literary subjects. He identified strongly with the Dante of the *Vita Nuova,* which he had translated in 1847-48 and which frequently provided his subjects during the earlier part of the decade. In the later 1850s the Arthurian legends became his prime source of pictorial inspiration. Rossetti also made large numbers of sensitive portrait drawings, especially of Elizabeth Siddal, whom he met in 1850 and married in 1860. She died in 1862 of an overdose of laudanum, an event which drastically altered Rossetti's life. After 1862 he tended to live in rather morbid seclusion, and his later art, consisting almost entirely of single figures of women, shows a marked decline from that of the 1850s.

There has been endless debate over the roles of Rossetti and Holman Hunt in the formation of the Pre-Raphaelite Brotherhood. Rossetti had the most conspicuous personality of the group, and his qualities of imagination undoubtedly were responsible for much of the Brotherhood's vitality in its formative years. However, he had little sympathy with the naturalistic leanings which dominated the movement during the 1850s and for which Hunt was the chief proponent. As Rossetti stopped exhibiting as soon as Pre-Raphaelitism became a public issue, during its most vital period his work was relatively little known. He did, however, attract the friendship of Ruskin who, after his split with Millais, became Rossetti's patron and champion. He also attracted as disciples two Oxford students, William Morris and Edward Burne-Jones, and in 1857 he led them and some friends in a project of decorating the newly built Oxford Union with Arthurian frescoes. In 1861 he was among the founding members of the decorative arts firm eventually known as Morris and Company. Rossetti's influence on both Morris and Burne-Jones, and thus on later Victorian aestheticism, was enormous, but this had little to do with Pre-Raphaelitism as it was understood by the original members of the Brotherhood.

Rossetti's training as an artist was totally inadequate, and signs of his struggle to overcome technical limitations by weight of imaginative personality are generally evident; even his best works, in which the personality shows through most clearly, are frequently marred by glaring faults. Rossetti was a poet as well as a painter and was the brother of Christina Rossetti. Another sister, Maria, also wrote and eventually entered a convent.

His brother, William Michael Rossetti, was one of the original seven members of the Pre-Raphaelite Brotherhood, although only an amateur as an artist, and he later was active as a critic and the movement's historian.
A.S.

Bibliography

The Rossetti literature is vast; for an extensive bibliography see William E. Fredeman, *Pre-Raphaelitism: A Bibliocritical Study,* Cambridge, Mass., 1965, pp. 90-132
William Michael Rossetti, *Dante Gabriel Rossetti as Designer and Writer,* London, 1889
Henry Currie Marillier, *Dante Gabriel Rossetti: An Illustrated Memorial of His Art and Life,* London, 1899
Oswald Doughty, *A Victorian Romantic: Dante Gabriel Rossetti,* 2nd ed., London, 1960
Oswald Doughty and John Robert Wahl, eds., *Letters of Dante Gabriel Rossetti,* vols. I and II, Oxford, 1965

218
Woman in a Bonnet
The Art Institute of Chicago
Pencil, pen and ink, touched with brown wash; 7⅞ x 5½ in.
Inscribed: *C G D R* (monogram) *Sept. / 46*

This drawing was made when Rossetti was eighteen years old. The monogram appears on a number of other early drawings; the initials C G D R stand for the artist's full given name Charles Gabriel Dante Rossetti, which he later rearranged, dropping the Charles.

The chief stylistic influence on no. 218 is the French illustrator Gavarni, who was one of Rossetti's youthful heroes. In letters written to his brother from a visit to Boulogne in 1844 he wrote delightedly of purchasing "sublime" Gavarni prints, and he was still buying them on a trip to Paris with Holman Hunt in 1849. Randall Davies owned and published a Rossetti drawing of two streetwalkers accosting a timid citizen, which is pure imitation of Gavarni, and in which the drawing style and the costumes are virtually identical with no. 218. Rossetti's liking

218

for Gavarni was largely because of subject, and when he actually saw the Parisiennes in 1849 he was sorely disillusioned: "My dear sir, we have not seen six pretty faces since we have been at Paris, and those such as would not be in the least remarkable in London. . . . As for Gavarni, he is a liar and the father of it."
A.S.

Provenance
Charles Deering, Chicago
The Art Institute of Chicago, 1927

Exhibitions
Dante Gabriel Rossetti and His Circle, The University of Kansas Museum of Art, 1958

References
Marillier, pp. 215-16
Randall Davies, "Rossetti's Earliest Drawings," *Burlington,* LXXVI, 1940, p. 22
Doughty and Wahl, eds., *Letters,* I, 23-29, 65, 72

219
The Sleeper
Trustees of The British Museum
Pen and ink; 8⅞ x 4¾ in.
Inscribed: *E. A. Poe/ D. G. Rossetti;* and on a separate attached piece of paper: *The Sleeper*
c. 1848

No. 219 illustrates a poem of the same name by Edgar Allan Poe. The time is midnight, in the month of June:

> All beauty sleeps! and lo! where lies
> (Her casement open to the skies)
> Irene, with her destinies!
> Oh, lady bright! can it be right—
> This window open to the night?
> • • •
> I pray to God that she may lie
> Forever with unopened eye,
> While the dim sheeted ghosts go by!

According to William Michael Rossetti, Poe "prove singularly fascinating" to Rossetti in his youth. Poe was included in the list of immortals which Rossetti and Holman Hunt drew up in August 1848 and Rossetti later described Theodore Von Holst, who had an important influence on him in the 1840s as "in some sort, the Edgar Poe of painting." Illustrations to Poe's "Ulalume" and "The Raven" are in Birmingham. These have traditionally been dated c. 1848 on the basis of another Poe illustratio once in the possession of Dr. H. A. Munro, which Marillier lists as "dated 'June, 1848' (?)."

219

No. 219 belongs with this group. The careful cross-hatching, reminiscent of etching, appears in several other drawings by Rossetti from the same year. The almost timid handling, with its thin lines and stiff angularity replacing the more vigorous style of no. 218, is characteristic not only of Rossetti but of much Pre-Raphaelite drawing in the period immediately around and following the formation of the Brotherhood. Rossetti retained and cultivated the air of naïve charm of no. 219 in much of his work of the 1850s.
A.S.

Provenance
Purchased by The British Museum from Watford Wilson and Co., through the H. L. Florence Fund, 1936

References
W. M. Rossetti, *Rossetti as Designer and Writer,* p. 243 n.
Marillier, pp. 23-24, 234, cf. nos. 6, 7
Dante Gabriel Rossetti, *Works,* ed. W. M. Rossetti, London, 1911, p. 592
Catalogue of Drawings, Museum and Art Gallery, Birmingham, 1939, p. 311

220
Elizabeth Siddal
Trustees of The British Museum
Pencil; 7¼ x 4⅝ in.
c. 1852-60

Elizabeth Eleanor Siddal, called by Rossetti "Guggums" and by Ruskin "Ida," was discovered in 1849 by Walter Deverell in a bonnet shop, and she served as model for several Pre-Raphaelite pictures between 1850 and 1852, notably for Sylvia in Holman Hunt's *Two Gentlemen of Verona* (Birmingham) and for Millais's *Ophelia* (Tate Gallery). After 1852 she was Rossetti's exclusive model; they were married in 1860. Her health was bad long before their marriage, and after her

220

delivery of a stillborn daughter in 1861 it declined rapidly. She died an apparent suicide from an overdose of laudanum in February 1862.

Rossetti made countless drawings of her. After calling on Rossetti on October 6, 1854, Ford Madox Brown wrote in his diary, "Saw Miss Siddal, looking thinner and more deathlike and more beautiful and more ragged than ever; . . . Gabriel as usual diffuse and inconsequent in his work.

Drawing wonderful and lovely Guggums one after another, each one a fresh charm, each one stamped with immortality, and his picture never advancing." Again, on August 6, 1855, Brown wrote: "He showed me a drawer full of 'Guggums'; God knows how many, but not bad work I should say for the six years he has known her; it is like a monomania with him. Many of them are matchless in beauty, however, and one day will be worth large sums."

These drawings reveal Rossetti at his most tender and sensitive, and in their accumulated effect they are probably his most impressive achievement. Many of them show Miss Siddal either asleep or, as no. 220, reclining wearily in a manner that seems to reflect her declining health and spirits. Ruskin looked through a volume of such sketches in September 1860 and wrote to Rossetti the next day: "I think Ida should be very happy to see how much more beautifully, perfectly, and tenderly you draw when you are drawing her than when you draw anybody else. She cures you of all your worst faults when you only look at her."
A.S.

Provenance
Colonel Gillum, Tottenham (bequests to The British Museum, 1910)

Exhibitions
Drawings and Sketches by Old Masters and by Artists of the English School, British Museum, London, 1912, no. 418 (dated c. 1854)

References
William Michael Rossetti, ed., *Ruskin: Rossetti: Preraphaelitism: Papers 1854 to 1862,* London, 1899, pp. 19, 40
Ruskin, XXXVI, 341
William Michael Rossetti, "Dante Gabriel Rossetti and Elizabeth Siddal," *Burlington,* I, 1903, pp. 273-95

221

221
Passover in the Holy Family
The Trustees of The Tate Gallery, London
Watercolor; 16 x 17 in., unfinished
1854-56

In 1870 Rossetti published a sonnet based on no. 221. To it he appended a note explaining the subject: the scene takes place on the house porch where the Holy Family is preparing for the Passover. Christ holds a bowl of blood from which Zacharias sprinkles the posts and lintels. The shoes, which John fastens, and the bitter herbs being gathered by Mary are also part of the ritual. On the left Joseph has brought the sacrificial lamb, and Elizabeth is lighting the pyre, but as the

drawing is unfinished, these two figures are only faintly suggested. Although the subject is invented Rossetti was concerned with explaining the facts correctly, and in a letter of September 15, 1869 he asked William Michael Rossetti to thank their sister Maria for her most complete information. The sonnet is as follows:

> Here meet together the prefiguring day
>   And day prefigured. "Eating, thou
>   shalt stand,
>   Feet shod, loins girt, thy road-staff in
>   thine hand,
> With blood-stained door and lintel,"—
>   did God say
> By Moses' mouth in ages passed away.
>   And now, where this poor household
>   doth comprise
>   At Paschal-Feast two kindred families,—
> Lo! the slain lamb confronts the Lamb to slay
>
> The pyre is piled. What agony's crown attained
>   What shadow of Death the Boy's fair
>   brow subdues
> Who holds that blood wherewith the porch
>   is stained
>   By Zachary the priest? John binds the shoe
>   He deemed himself not worthy to unloose;
> And Mary culls the bitter herbs ordained.

William Michael Rossetti gives 1849 as the date of Rossetti's original designs. A pair of pencil drawings, one showing the same subject as no. 221 but with a slightly different composition, the other of *The Eating of the Passover,* are reproduced by Marillier. Ruskin saw these two drawings in 1854 or 1855, declared himself very much struck by them, and commissioned no. 221. Both pencil drawings passed into the possession of Ruskin's friend Henry Acland. Ford Madox Brown recorded in his diary on September 5, 1854 that Rossetti wanted "costumes to paint a watercolour of the Passover"; however, it is not clear whether Rossetti had actually begun no. 221 at this time or was only considering it. On the first of July 1855, Rossetti wrote to his mother that he was painting for Ruskin a watercolor, begun some time ago, of the *Preparation for the Passover in the Holy Family.* There are frequent additional references to the watercolor in both Ruskin's and Rossetti's correspondence. In October Ruskin borrowed the uncompleted drawing to show it to the Archdeacon of Salop. Rossetti, in a letter to Browning dated February 6, 1856, described the *Passover* drawing as not quite done, due to other work intervening. However, the drawing never was finished. Sometime in the spring of 1856, Ruskin visited Rossetti's studio when the artist was away. He was so displeased with the reworking Rossetti had given another watercolor he had commissioned, *Beatrice at the Marriage Feast,* that he walked off with no. 221. In a subsequent letter he wrote, "I have had serious thoughts of refusing to *give up* the picture now returned, lest you should spoil the Zacharias; but it would be a pity not to finish it." Although this letter implies the picture had been returned again to Rossetti, it never was finished and presumably remains in the state in which Ruskin abducted it. Rossetti obviously had trouble with the head of Christ, which is on a separate piece of paper stuck to the original sheet; Ruskin later pointed this out to Selwyn Image and told him, "he put it in and scraped it out so many times, that I feared he would end by scraping the whole thing clear away—so I carried it off."

Ruskin's interference and his attempts to tell Rossetti how to paint are usually criticized as the meddling of a busybody. Rossetti, however, did frequently get in trouble from overworking his drawings; so there is justification for Ruskin's desire to protect no. 221. In later years no. 221 was one of Ruskin's favorite drawings. He placed it on exhibition at Oxford, and he referred to it several times in his Oxford lectures. Of all the works by Rossetti which Ruskin commissioned or owned, no. 221 was the only one to remain in his possession to the end of his life.

Although there is no documentary evidence, the date 1849 which William Michael gave for the first designs for no. 221 seems appropriate. Stylistically, the drawing retains the angular stiffness of

Rossetti's earlier compositions. The thatch-covered porch recalls the shed in Holman Hunt's *Early Britons Sheltering a Missionary from the Druids* (Ashmolean Museum), which was also begun in 1849. The interest in the domestic life of the Holy Family can also be seen in Rossetti's *Girlhood of Mary Virgin,* exhibited in 1849 and, especially, in Millais's *Christ in the House of His Parents,* which was begun in 1849 and exhibited in 1850 (both Tate Gallery).

Coventry Patmore saw *The Passover* drawing at Ruskin's, probably in 1855, and wrote to Rossetti that the symbolism was too remote and unobvious to be effective. To this Ruskin replied in a letter to Rossetti asking what the mischief Patmore meant by symbolism: "I call that Passover plain prosy Fact. No Symbolism at all." Rossetti, on the other hand, replied in a letter to Patmore conscientiously justifying what he had attempted to show: "Its chief claim to interest . . . would be as a subject which must have actually occurred during every year of the life led by the Holy Family, and which think must bear its meaning broadly and instantly —not as you say 'remotely'—on the very face of it,—in the one sacrifice really typical of the other. In this respect—its actuality as an incident no less than as a *scriptural* type—I think you will acknowledge it differs entirely from Herbert's [*Our Saviour, Subject to His Parents at Nazareth,* Royal Academy 1847; Guildhall Art Gallery, London] some years back, Millais's [*Christ in the House of His Parents*] more recently, or any other of the very many both ancient and modern which resemble it in so far as they are illustrations of Christ's life 'subject to His parents,' but not one of which that I can remember is anything more than an entire and often trifling fancy of the painter, in which symbolism is not really inherent in the fact, but merely suggested or suggestible, and having had the fact made to fit it." Religious pictures do not form a major part of Rossetti's *œuvre,* and he did not again attempt a work of such overt biblical symbolism. Holman Hunt's *Shadow of the Cross* (Manchester) is a later Pre-Raphaelite return to the theme of premonitions of the Crucifixion which

lays itself open to Rossetti's criticism of being an entire fancy of the painter. However, it should be pointed out that there is no biblical source for Rossetti's subject either, and there is an element of hairsplitting in the distinction which he draws between his work and Millais's.

According to William Michael, Rossetti had originally planned the design as part of a triptych. The other two subjects were to be *The Virgin Planting a Lily and a Rose* and *Mary in the House of John.* The former was never painted; watercolors of the latter are in The Tate Gallery and the Wilmington Society of the Fine Arts. The design of no. 221 served as model for the memorial window executed by Frederick Shields in the church at Birchington-on-Sea, where Rossetti died and is buried.   A.S.

Provenance
Commissioned by Ruskin, 1854 or 1855 (died 1900)
Arthur Severn, Brantwood
Presented to The Tate Gallery by the National Art-Collections Fund, 1916

Exhibitions
Ruskin lent the drawing to Miss Bell's school at Winnington in the 1860s, and later placed it on loan at Oxford
Old Masters, Royal Academy, London, 1883, no. 364
Pictures Ancient and Modern Including a Special Selection from the Works of Dante Gabriel Rossetti, New Gallery, London, 1897-98, no. 44
The Pre-Raphaelite Brotherhood, City Art Gallery, Birmingham, 1947, no. 100
Ruskin and His Circle, Arts Council Gallery, London, 1964, no. 244

References
Dante Gabriel Rossetti, *Works,* ed. W. M. Rossetti, London, 1911, pp. 210, 668
W. M. Rossetti, *Rossetti as Designer and Writer,* pp. 24, 26, 27, 48, 67, 149, 273, no. 271
Marillier, pp. 53, 67-68, 206, 238, no. 53, cf. ill. opp. p. 68
W. M. Rossetti, ed., *Ruskin: Rossetti: Pre-Raphaelitism,* London, 1899, pp. 18, 27-31, 92-94, 104, 107-08, 115-17, 123, 139-40
Selwyn Image, "Some Personal Recollections of John Ruskin," *Saint George,* VI, 1903, p. 299
Ruskin, XIX, 206 n.; XXXIII, 288, pl. 34; XXXIV, 168; XXXVI, 199, 206, 221-22, 225, 227, 232, 234, 237, 588
Doughty and Wahl, eds., *Letters,* I, 260, 275-76, 287, 290; II, 740, 743

222

222
The Tune of Seven Towers
The Trustees of The Tate Gallery, London
Watercolor on three joined pieces of paper;
12⅜ x 14⅜ in.
Inscribed: *DGR* (monogram) *1857*

This is one of a group of watercolors made by
Rossetti in the years 1856 to 1858 showing medieval
themes. In several of them the subjects come from
the Arthurian legends; although no precise source
has been identified for no. 222, it stems from the
same background. Rossetti's first treatment of an
Arthurian subject was a watercolor of 1855, *King
Arthur's Tomb,* which is vaguely based on
Tennyson's *Morte d'Arthur,* but shows an incident
that is described neither in Tennyson nor in Malory.
In 1855 Rossetti also received a commission from
the publisher Edward Moxon to make designs for
an illustrated edition of Tennyson. He chose
several Arthurian themes, explaining to a friend
that he wanted subjects "where one can allegorize
on one's own hook," without being too closely tied
down by any distinct idea of the poet's. The freely
invented subjects of Rossetti's medieval

watercolors of the following years represent a
further step in this direction.

Rossetti apparently designed no. 222 late in 1856
or early in 1857. In an undated letter to William
Morris he described it as not done yet, but
suggested it might still be ready for the Russell
Place exhibition, which took place in June 1857.
However, the drawing did not make it to the
exhibition. In the letter, Rossetti wrote, "I've got
rid of its *black* stage I hope," which suggests he was
having his usual technical difficulties, the results
of which are still evident in, for example, the figure
on the right. A drawing for this figure is at
Birmingham. At some point Rossetti apparently
decided to expand his original composition, as
the paper has been added to on both right
and left sides.

In 1857 Rossetti was close to William Morris and
Edward Burne-Jones, and their admiration
probably encouraged him in inventing these
quaintly medieval scenes. In the autumn of 1857
they all went to Oxford to decorate the newly built
Oxford Union with frescoes of the Arthurian
legends. William Morris, who was independently
wealthy, bought several of Rossetti's medieval
watercolors, including no. 222, and these works
are of importance for both his development and
that of Burne-Jones. The titles *The Tune of Seven
Towers* and *The Blue Closet,* another of the group
bought by Morris, inspired poems in Morris's
Defence of Guenevere, published in 1858. These,
however, have relatively little to do with Rossetti;
when a later owner included quotations from them
in a catalogue, Rossetti objected that the poems,
although beautiful "don't at all tally to any
purpose" with the pictures. On the other hand,
Rossetti's vision of an overdecorated Middle Ages
was the point of departure for the firm of Morris
and Company, and the combined chair and zither in
no. 212 is like a prototype piece of Arts-and-Crafts
furniture. Thematically and stylistically these
soulful people, whiling away their hours with music,
are the ancestors of all the sad-eyed knights and
maidens of Burne-Jones.

Music-making is an important element in several
of Rossetti's watercolors of this period, notably
The Blue Closet and *The Wedding of St. George*
(both Tate Gallery) and *A Christmas Carol* (Fogg
Art Museum), as well as no. 222. F. G. Stephens, a
fellow PRB, described *The Blue Closet* as "an
exercise intended to symbolize the association of
colour with music." Stephens did not mention
no. 222, but the remark was probably meant to hold
true of the whole group. Rossetti's fascination
with music and with musical values was an
important legacy for later Victorian aestheticism,
as can be seen in the works of Burne-Jones,
Albert Moore and, especially, Whistler.

Rossetti's watercolors of 1857 have generally been
looked on as a high point in his art, although not
always for the same reasons. Ford Madox Hueffer
wrote that they have "the abstract, inconsequent
charm of the fairy-tale told in earnest," Hueffer,
however, felt that they pushed charm, naïveté, and
decorative elaboration too far, thus driving out
weightier values. The opposite view appears in an
essay by Roger Fry, written at the time the
watercolors were acquired by the Tate Gallery:
"Rossetti's form became clear, definite and truly
expressive almost exactly in proportion as he was
concerned with the accessories of his drama . . .
when he was most occupied with the central core
of his theme, with the passion, his form fell to
pieces, he became a mere illustrator and not a
very good one." Fry considered no. 222 as one of
the most successful of the group, full of "delightful
inventions of design, the boldest and most
surprising motives." He specifically praised the
repeated diagonals of the bell rope and the staff of
the banner, which Hueffer found distracting and
unnecessary, and admired the play with the shapes
of the belfries, but he felt the figures, although
beautifully placed, were marred by overemphasis
on psychological expression. Fry was England's
leading apologist for the Postimpressionists and
for Matisse, and his attention to Rossetti, a
surprising exception to his usual dislike of
Victorian art, draws attention to the extraordinarily
abstract qualities of surface design in these works,

1829-1896

qualities too often hidden by the literary and biographical haze that accompanies most approaches to Rossetti's work.
A.S.

Provenance
William Morris, London, 1857
George Rae, Birkenhead, 1864
The Tate Gallery, 1916

Exhibitions
Dante Gabriel Rossetti, Burlington Fine Arts Club, London, 1883, no. 18
The Pre-Raphaelite Brotherhood, City Art Gallery, Birmingham, 1947, no. 104
The Pre-Raphaelites, Whitechapel Art Gallery, London, 1948, no. 69

References
Catalogue of Mr. George Rae's Pictures, Redcourt, Birkenhead, privately printed, n.d.
W. M. Rossetti, *Rossetti as Designer and Writer,* pp. 43, 44, 78, 275, no. 105
F. G. Stephens, *Dante Gabriel Rossetti,* London, 1894, p. 41
Ford Madox Hueffer, *Rossetti: A Critical Essay on His Art,* London, 1896, pp. 86-106
Marillier, pp. 80-81, 239, no. 65, ill. opp. p. 80
Val C. Prinsep, R. A., "A Chapter from a Painter's Reminiscence: The Oxford Circle: Rossetti, Burne-Jones, and William Morris," *Magazine of Art,* n.s., vol. 2, 1904, pp. 170, 172
Roger Fry, "Rossetti's Water Colours of 1857," *Burlington,* XXIX, 1916, pp. 100-09 (see also D. S. MacColl, "Monthly Chronicle," *ibid.,* pp. 80-81)
T. Martin Wood, "The True Rossetti," *Studio,* LXIX, 1917, pp. 3-15, ill. p. 9
Doughty and Wahl, eds., *Letters,* I, 238-39, 324-25
William Gaunt, *Rossetti (The Masters,* no. 89) London, 1967, p. 7, pl. VI

Millais came from a Jersey family which settled in London when he was ten years old. He was a child prodigy who entered the Royal Academy schools at age eleven and during the next six years won all the awards the Academy had to offer. In 1844 he met Holman Hunt, and in 1848 Dante Gabriel Rossetti, and he was, with them, one of the founding members of the Pre-Raphaelite Brotherhood. Although Millais's artistic ideals came largely from Hunt, and he was less important in formulating the outlook of the movement than either Hunt or Rossetti, he became the central figure in the critical storms which the Brotherhood provoked. In 1851 it was Millais who requested Coventry Patmore to ask Ruskin to come to the Brotherhood's aid, which Ruskin did. Ruskin immediately took a patronizing interest in the young artist, and in the summer of 1853 Millais accompanied the Ruskins on a vacation trip to Scotland. During the trip Millais painted Ruskin's portrait and developed an attachment with Mrs. Ruskin, which led to her gaining an annulment of her marriage to Ruskin and her marriage to Millais in 1855. As a consequence of his marriage and of being elected an Associate of the Royal Academy in the autumn of 1853, Millais gradually dropped out of Pre-Raphaelite circles, in which Ruskin during the latter 1850s was playing an ever more important role. In 1863 Millais was elected a full Royal Academician. He had a large family, a large house in Palace Gate, shooting lodges in Scotland, and he produced a steady stream of highly popular pictures to pay for it all, making himself one of the most prosperous artists in history. In 1885 he was

created a baronet, and in February 1896, he succeeded Lord Leighton as President of the Royal Academy; however, Millais's health was by then failing, and he died in August of the same year.

Millais's abilities were prodigious. His first Pre-Raphaelite painting *Lorenzo and Isabella* (Liverpool), begun when he was nineteen years old, shows freshness of invention and qualities of draftsmanship that make the entire further course of the movement seem in some ways an anticlimax. In the early 1850s he shared Holman Hunt's concern with minutely literal treatment of natural detail (see no. 225), and it was this side of Millais's art which Ruskin tried to encourage. After 1853 his art began to broaden, reaching a new lyricism and emotive richness in his *Blind Girl* (Birmingham) and *Autumn Leaves* (Manchester), both exhibited in 1856. Unfortunately, in the following years the broadening process degenerated into slovenliness. Although Millais's abilities remained great, he conspicuously misused them in order to achieve a large output and a large income. He was not a profound thinker; during his Pre-Raphaelite days, the companionship of Hunt and Rossetti seems to have stimulated an intellectual rigor which evaporated as soon as Millais lost his closeness with them. His later works reveal a banality of mind, which accounts for their widespread popularity but makes the contrast with Millais's early masterpieces extremely depressing.
A.S.

Bibliography
M. H. Spielmann, *Millais and His Works,* Edinburgh and London, 1898
John Guille Millais, *The Life and Letters of Sir John Everett Millais,* two vols., London, 1899
Werner Weisbach, "John Everett Millais," *Zeitschrift für Bildende Kunst,* X, 1899, pp. 179-83, 214-19, 246-54
Mary Lutyens, *Millais and the Ruskins,* London, 1967
Millais: PRB: PRA, Royal Academy, London, and Walker Art Gallery, Liverpool, 1967 (exhibition catalogue, compiled, with introduction, by Mary Bennett)

223

The Disentombment of Queen Matilda
The Trustees of The Tate Gallery, London
Pen and ink; 9 x 16⅞ in.
Inscribed: *JE Millais 1849 PRB* (initials in
monograms)

The subject is based on an incident described in
Agnes Strickland's *Queens of England,* published
between 1840 and 1848. In 1562 the Calvinist troops
under Chastillon sacked the church of the Holy
Trinity in Caen. The tomb of Queen Matilda, the
wife of William the Conqueror, was broken open,
and one of the Calvinists, taking a ring from the
corpse's finger, presented it to the abbess.

Millais was at work on no. 223 in May 1849, and it is
mentioned in "The P.R.B. Journal" which William
Michael Rossetti began to keep on May 15, 1849.
On May 17, William Michael noted that Millais "had
put in some fat men, finding his general tendency
to be towards thin ones," and on May 23, that he
had drawn in most of the populace.

This highly finished and elaborate drawing is the
most extreme example of Millais's drawing style
in the first years of the Pre-Raphaelite
Brotherhood. Some of the same tendencies to
linear stylization can be seen in his *Lorenzo and
Isabella,* which he exhibited in 1849 (Walker Art
Gallery, Liverpool), but not carried so far. Mary
Bennett has suggested that Millais's drawings of
this time owe something to the Lasinio engravings
of the frescoes in the Campo Santo at Pisa, which
the Pre-Raphaelite Brothers had been studying the
night they formed their group, and also something
to Rossetti. Several of Millais's mannerisms in
no. 223, such as the hand clasped to the mouth to
express timid fear, are close to gestures frequently
employed by Rossetti in his drawings of the same
time, and the horizontal format, crowded with
figures, is reminiscent of that of Rossetti's *Hist!
Said Kate the Queen,* also begun in 1849. Millais,
however, was close to Rossetti only in the first flush
of Pre-Raphaelite enthusiasm; as that waned their
vastly different temperaments came between them.

223

Millais's drawing style also soon began to change,
and his drawings after 1850 are more
naturalistically oriented.
A.S.

References
J. G. Millais, I, ill. p. 63; II, 490
William Michael Rossetti, ed., *Praeraphaelite Diaries
and Letters,* London, 1900, pp. 209-10, 212

Provenance
William Brocklebank
Mrs. Brocklebank
Purchased by the National Gallery, London, 1945, and
transferred to The Tate Gallery the same year

Exhibitions
The Works of Sir John E. Millais, Bart., R. A., Grosvenor
Gallery, London, 1886, no. 140
*Works of the Late Sir John Everett Millais, Bart.,
President of the Royal Academy,* Royal Academy,
London, 1898, no. 219
Millais: PRB: PRA, Royal Academy, London, and Walker
Art Gallery, Liverpool, 1967, no. 243

224
Study for "The Woodman's Daughter"
The Art Museum, Princeton University
Pencil; 8⅝ x 5⅝ in.
c. 1850-51

This drawing shows the identical subject as the picture which Millais exhibited at the Royal Academy in 1851 (Guildhall Art Gallery, London). It is based on Coventry Patmore's poem "The Tale of Poor Maud" which tells how Maud, the daughter of Gerald the woodman, accompanied her father as he worked in the park of the ancient manor. Millais quoted the following lines in the Academy catalogue:

> She went merely to think she helped;
>   And, whilst he hack'd and saw'd,
> The rich squire's son, a young boy then,
>   For whole days, as if awed,
> Stood by, and gazed alternately
>   At Gerald, and at Maud.

> He sometimes, in a sullen tone,
>   Would offer fruits, and she
> Always received his gifts with an air
>   So unreserved and free,
> That half-feign'd distance soon became
>   Familiarity

J. G. Millais dates no. 224, 1848, but this early date is most unlikely, as the background of the drawing is virtually identical with that of the painting which Millais painted in the summer of 1850 near Oxford.

At the request of the picture's owner, Millais in 1886 repainted the figure of the girl in the picture, much to its detriment; the signs of the repainting are clearly evident, and the girl in the painting has taken on the bland sweetness characteristic of the later Millais. No. 224 presumably shows the girl as she originally was in the painting, and there is consequently a tension between the two children, the "sullen tone" of Patmore's poem, which has disappeared from the painting as it now exists. Millais was frequently criticized for the inelegance

of the figures in his early Pre-Raphaelite pictures, an element of which can be seen in the drawing of the girl, and it was the later reiteration of this criticism which eventually led him to give her a more conventionally attractive appearance in the oil painting.
A.S.

Provenance
Frank Jewett Mather, Jr., Princeton (bequest to the Museum, 1942)

Exhibitions
Dante Gabriel Rossetti and His Circle, The University of Kansas Museum of Art, Lawrence, Kansas, 1958

References
J. G. Millais, I, ill. p. 92; II, 490

225
A Huguenot, on St. Bartholomew's Day, Refusing to Shield Himself from Danger by Wearing the Roman Catholic Badge
The Gallery of Modern Art, The Huntington Hartford Collection
Oil on canvas; 36⅞ x 25⅝ in., arched top
Inscribed: *J. Millais 1852* (monogram)

Millais and Holman Hunt spent the summer and autumn of 1851 at Worcester Park Farm near Ewell, in Surrey. Their purpose was to paint the backgrounds of their *Hireling Shepherd* and *Ophelia,* but while in the country each began to work on a second picture. Millais had a difficult time finding a suitable subject for his; on July 28 he wrote to his friend and patron Mrs. Thomas Combe in Oxford, "I am nightly working my brains for a subject." According to Hunt, he began the background of no. 225, intending to illustrate the line from Tennyson's poem "Circumstance," "Two lovers whispering by an orchard wall." Hunt objected to this as having no interest other than prurient intrusion on what should be private; he felt that the lovers should be actuated by some

225

generous thought of the larger world, rather than only by personal interest, and he proposed that they could be from opposite sides in the Wars of the Roses. This subject proved unsuitable because it had to be set on a castle rampart, and Millais's background of an ivy-covered wall was already too far along. Millais then suggested that the lovers be a Cavalier and a Puritan, but Hunt objected that the theme had already been worked to death. Finally Millais, remembering Meyerbeer's opera *The Huguenots,* decided upon a Catholic and a Protestant on the eve of St. Bartholomew's day. This decision apparently came on October 15, after the background was well under way; on October 16 Millais entered in his diary that he had sat up late the night before and discovered "a first rate story for my present picture." On November 22 he wrote to Mrs. Combe: "I am in high spirits about the subject, *as it is entirely my own,* and I think contains the highest moral. It will be very quiet, and but slightly suggest the horror of a massacre. The figures will be talking against a secret-looking garden wall, which I have painted here." When the picture appeared at the Royal Academy the following May, Millais accompanied it in the catalogue with a quotation from *The Protestant Reformation in France* by Anne Marsh-Caldwell, vol. II, p. 352: " 'When the clock of the Palais de Justice shall sound upon the great bell, at daybreak, then each good Catholic must bind a strip of white linen round his arm, and place a fair white cross in his cap.'—*The Order of the Duke of Guise.*" In the picture, Millais's Huguenot, putting faith above worldly love, prevents the girl from tying the white handkerchief around his arm. The nasturtiums in the foreground are symbols of suffering, and the ivy behind is an emblem of constancy.

Millais kept a diary from October 16, 1851 until he left Worcester Park Farm on December 6. In it he records daily work through the entire period on the wall and its covering of ivy, which he painted directly out-of-doors from an old brick wall at the foot of the farm's garden. During November it became very cold, and he built a straw hut from

which he could paint. The figures were painted in the studio after Millais's return to London. On January 9, 1852 he wrote to Mr. Combe that he had spent the day "drawing from two living creatures embracing each other," and on March 6 he reported that the man was nearly complete but that the girl was only sketched in. Arthur Lemprière, a friend of Millais's family, posed for the Huguenot, and Miss Ryan, a professional model, sat for the girl. J. G. Millais reproduced five drawings as purported sketches for the picture. However, four of these contain background figures and, as we know Millais thought of the subject after beginning the background and thus establishing a context for only two figures, it seems likely that they were intended for some other work. The fifth drawing (p. 138, now in Birmingham) shows just the two figures and the man in a costume similar to that in the picture. A drawing reproduced by Hunt (Liverpool City Libraries) is apparently a sketch for Millais's proposed picture of two lovers.

The Huguenot was Millais's first popular success. He sold it in March 1852, before sending it to the Academy, to the dealer D. T. White for £250. White immediately resold it to the collector B. G. Windus, who already owned Millais's *Lorenzo and Isabella.* The *Art Journal,* which had previously been violently hostile to the Pre-Raphaelites and still disliked Millais's *Ophelia,* proclaimed *The Huguenot* the best picture Millais had exhibited and predicted an illustrious future for the artist. The *Art Journal* and several other critics did find some faults: the man's right leg was invisible, and from lack of aerial perspective the figures did not stand out from their background. The latter criticism immediately drew fire in the third volume of *The Stones of Venice* from Ruskin, who denounced the whole concept of aerial perspective as a ridiculous convention. He assumed that the figures in no. 225 were standing about three feet from the wall and then calculated that the aerial perspective accurately given would have amounted to "less than the 15,000th part of the depth of any given colour." Ruskin referred to the picture on numerous other occasions as one of the most successful of Pre-Raphaelite works.

The popularity of no. 225 led Millais to repeat it in several replicas, among them an oil painting in an English private collection, a watercolor in Bedford, and another watercolor of only the heads in the Fogg Art Museum. He also repeated its emotional formula—lovers in the face of conflict with the woman being prettily heroic—three times in the 1850s: in *The Proscribed Royalist* (private collection, England), *The Order of Release* (Tate Gallery), and *The Black Brunswicker* (Port Sunlight). In these pictures' sentimental appeal lay the seeds of Millais's later art. No. 225 was also the prototype for a whole series of Pre-Raphaelite pictures of lovers huddling before foliate backgrounds such as Arthur Hughes's *April Love* (Tate Gallery) and *Long Engagement* (Birmingham). The close study of brick walls also became such a staple of Pre-Raphaelite painting, that one such structure, examined by an artist through binoculars, forms the central element of Florence Claxton's caricature of the movement *The Choice of Paris: An Idyll* (version, collection of Ralph Dutton, 1860).
A.S.

Provenance
D. T. White (dealer)
B. G. Windus, Tottenham, 1852
T. H. Miller, Preston, c. 1860
Thomas Pitt Miller, Preston, by descent (sale, Christie's, London, 26 April 1946, no. 88, bt. Agnew)
Huntington Hartford, New York

Exhibitions
Royal Academy, 1852, no. 478
Liverpool Academy, 1852, no. 49
The Works of Sir John E. Millais, Bart., R. A., Grosvenor Gallery, London, 1886, no. 6
Loan Collection of Pictures, Guildhall, London, 1897, no. 133
Works of the Late Sir John Everett Millais, Bart., President of the Royal Academy, Royal Academy, London, 1898, no. 61
Franco-British Exhibition, London, 1908, no. 101
Dante Gabriel Rossetti and His Circle, The University of Kansas Museum of Art, Lawrence, Kansas, 1958
The Pre-Raphaelites, Herron Museum of Art, Indianapolis, and Gallery of Modern Art, New York, 1964, no. 49
Millais: PRB: PRA, Royal Academy, London, and Walker Art Gallery, Liverpool, 1967, no. 35

References
Art Journal, 1852, p. 173
Ruskin, V, 127; XI, 59-60; XXXIV, 167
Spielmann, pp. 29-30, 103-04, 168, ill. p. 39
J. G. Millais, I, 115-16, 123-49, 155, 160-64, ill. p. 139; II, 468
W. Holman Hunt, *Pre-Raphaelitism and the Pre-Raphaelite Brotherhood,* London, 1905, I, 283-86, 289-90
W. E. Fredeman, "The Pre-Raphaelites in Caricature," *Burlington,* CII, 1960, pp. 523-29, cf. pl. 26
Allen Staley, "Radical Romantics," *Art News,* LXIII, May, 1964, pp. 33-34

Reproductions
Engraved by T. O. Barlow, 1856; G. Zobel, 1869; and R. B. Parkes, 1880

226
Retribution (The Man with Two Wives)
Miss Veronica MacEwen
Pen and sepia ink; 8 x 10⅜ in.
Inscribed: *JEM* (monogram) *1854*

This is one of a group of drawings made in 1853 and 1854 in which Millais shows scenes of passion in contemporary life. The time coincides with the joint trip to Scotland made by Millais and the Ruskins and the period following in which the Ruskin marriage was dissolved and Mrs. Ruskin became the wife of Millais. During all this Millais was under intense emotional strain (see Lutyens, *passim),* and these drawings would seem to reflect some of his preoccupations. One of them, *Married*

for Love, is known only through a copy made by Mrs. Ruskin in 1853; another, *Woman in Church Watching Her Former Lover Married,* was apparently begun by Millais in 1853 and finished by Mrs. Ruskin in 1854 (both collection of Raoul Millais); and it may be that all these drawings showing subjects of such timely interest were mutually conceived by the pair. Another drawing in the series, *The Ghost at the Wedding Ceremony* (Victoria and Albert Museum), has been interpreted by Miss Joan Evans as symbolizing Ruskin's wedding. No. 226, of course, does not represent the situation of the childless Ruskin, but its theme of the dishonesty of a husband towards his young bride corresponds to the grievance quite legitimately held against Ruskin: that he failed to reveal until after the wedding his inability or unwillingness to consummate the marriage.

J. G. Millais in the introduction to the 1901 exhibition of Millais's work wrote that his father's intention in this group of drawings had been to show "the various tragedies of sin and temptation which assail the lot of men." John Gere has suggested that there may be a connection between

no. 226 and Rossetti's *Found* (Wilmington) and
Holman Hunt's *Awakening Conscience* (collection
Sir Colin Anderson), but he points out that themes
of this sort were in the air among the
Pre-Raphaelite group. Millais's drawing style,
especially his exaggeration of the long lines of the
pipe-stem trousers, may owe something to Richard
Doyle, whose illustrations to Thackeray's *The
Newcomes* began to appear in September 1853.
A.S.

Provenance
Lady Millais, who gave it to her brother George Gray
Melville Gray (and family descent)

Exhibitions
*Pictures, Drawings, and Sketches for Pictures by Sir
J. E. Millais, P. R. A.,* Fine Art Society, London, 1901,
no. 77
Millais: PRB: PRA, Royal Academy, London, and Walker
Art Gallery, Liverpool, 1967, no. 334

References
J. G. Millais, I, ill. p. 227; II, 490 *(The Man with
Two Wives)*
Robin Ironside and John Gere, *Pre-Raphaelite Painters,*
London, 1948, pp. 32-33, 41, pl. 59
Joan Evans, "Millais' Drawings of 1853," *Burlington,*
XCII, 1950, pp. 198, 201

227
The Rescue
National Gallery of Victoria, Felton Bequest
Oil on canvas; 47¾ x 33 in.
Inscribed: *J. E. M.* (monogram)
1855

The two chief authorities give conflicting accounts
of the genesis of no. 227. According to Spielmann,
it was suggested by Millais's friend Mike Halliday,
who hurried him off to a raging fire and impressed
upon him the opportunities of the subject. J. G.
Millais says that it was inspired by a fire which
Millais and his brother saw when returning home
from a ball in Porchester Terrace. According to
this account, Millais announced: "soldiers and

227

sailors have been praised on canvas a thousand times. My next picture shall be of the fireman." J. G. Millais also quotes a letter from Arthur Hughes, to whom early in 1855 Millais described his next picture honoring "a set of men quietly doing a noble work." In January 1855 Millais also discussed the subject with Dickens, who sent him a relevant clipping from *Good Words,* and before beginning the picture he visited several big fires in London to study the light effects. The captain of the London fire brigade was a friend whom Millais and Halliday accompanied to at least one scene of nocturnal action.

Millais painted the picture in the studio of F. B. Barwell. A model named Baker posed for the fireman and Mrs. Nassau Senior for the mother. The effect of the glare was achieved by putting a sheet of colored glass between the window and the models. Millais spent much less time on no. 227 than on his previously exhibited pictures and he had to work night and day to complete it in time for the Royal Academy. Charles Collins sat up with him and painted the fire hose; the flaming timber in the picture was painted from a burning brand placed on a sheet of iron in the studio, which caused suffocating smoke.

According to Barwell, Millais made several rough pencil sketches for the composition and drew a full-sized cartoon from nature before starting the picture itself. His composition, although ultimately varied in details, seems to be based upon Mulready's scene of *The Fire,* engraved on p. 181 in the edition of *The Vicar of Wakefield* which Mulready illustrated in 1843. In this, the Vicar emerges out of the smoke carrying his two babies over his shoulders, while his wife on her knees before him reaches up toward the children. This was not the first time that Millais took a compositional hint from Mulready's illustrations; the juxtaposed heads of the figures at the table in *Lorenzo and Isabella* are anticipated in several of Mulready's scenes, particularly that of the *Dispute between Moses and Thornhill* on p. 43; the four-square composition and the old woman

leaning over the workbench in *Christ in the House of His Parents* recall the painted version of *Choosing the Wedding Gown,* which Mulready exhibited in 1846 (Victoria and Albert Museum).

At the Royal Academy, no. 227 was so badly hung that Millais threatened to resign unless it was moved, which was done. The critics found it impressive, but questioned many of the details; the *Art Journal,* for example, suggested that in such a fire the whole scene would be made invisible by smoke and that the fiery light which illuminates the clothes of the children should also affect the uniform of the fireman. In *Academy Notes* Ruskin, despite his personal conflicts with Millais, pronounced no. 227 as "the only *great* picture exhibited this year; but this is *very* great. The immortal element is in it to the full." Ruskin replied to the criticism of the fireman's uniform, saying that near black juxtaposed to a bright color always seems black, and when this assertion was challenged he plowed into the subject again in a supplement. He also remarked that the execution was remarkably bold and in some ways imperfect, but that, except for the face of the child kissing its mother, it probably could not be improved upon, "For there is a true sympathy between the impetuousness of execution and the haste of the action."

According to J. G. Millais, his father considered no. 227 his best work. It is certainly his most important picture of a contemporary subject. The subject and Millais's hobnobbing with firemen parallel Courbet's interest in painting a scene of fire fighting as a modern urban drama three years earlier.
A.S.

Provenance

Joseph Arden, London (sale, Christie's, London, 26 April 1879, no. 68, bt. Agnew)
Holbrook Gaskell, Woolton (sale, Christie's, London, 24 June 1909, no. 67, bt. Agnew)
Charles Fairfax Murray (sale, Christie's, London, 14 Dec. 1917, no. 59, bt. Cremetti)

Eugene Cremetti (sale, Christie's, London, 1 June 1923, no. 149)
W. W. Sampson, from whom it was bought by the National Gallery of Victoria, 1923

Exhibitions

Royal Academy, 1855, no. 282
Liverpool Academy, 1855, no. 224
The Works of Sir John E. Millais, Bart., R. A., Grosvenor Gallery, London, 1886, no. 92 (lent by Holbrook Gaskell)
International Exhibition, Glasgow, 1888, no. 164
Works of the Late Sir John Everett Millais, Bart., President of the Royal Academy, Royal Academy, London, 1898, no. 10
Irish International Exhibition, Dublin, 1907, no. 60
The Tate Gallery, London, 1923
Pre-Raphaelite Art, State Galleries of Australia, 1962, no. 50

References

Art Journal, 1855, p. 175
William Michael Rossetti, *Fine Art, Chiefly Contemporary: Notices Reprinted with Revisions,* London, 1867, pp. 214-17
"Mr. Joseph Arden's Collection," *The Times,* London, 28 April 1879 (reprinted in George Redford, *Art Sales,* London, 1888, I, 292-93)
F. G. Stephens, "The Private Collections of England: no. LXXIX: Allerton, Liverpool (Mr. Holbrook Gaskill)," *The Athenaeum,* 1884, p. 439
Spielmann, pp. 74-76
J. G. Millais, I, 247-58, ill. p. 301; II, 469
Ruskin, XIV, 22-23, 35-37
Daniel Thomas, "Pre-Raphaelite Works in the Collection," *Annual Bulletin of the National Gallery of Victoria,* II, 1960, p. 23

Reproductions

Engraved by Henry Linton, *National Magazine,* 1857, p. 193

John William Inchbold

1830-1888

Inchbold was born in Leeds, where his father owned a newspaper. In 1847 he entered the Royal Academy schools, and he began to exhibit at the Society of British Artists in 1849 and at the Royal Academy in 1851. His works of 1849 and 1850 are broadly painted, but in 1852 he exhibited a picture of a tree stump entitled *A Study,* which William Michael Rossetti cited in *The Spectator* as an example of the progress of Pre-Raphaelitism. Henceforth, Inchbold was generally regarded as the leading Pre-Raphaelite landscape painter. In 1854 Ruskin commended his work in a letter to *The Times* which was not printed, and in the following years he praised it in *Academy Notes.* In 1855, wanting to convert Charles Kingsley to Pre-Raphaelitism, Ruskin borrowed one of Inchbold's pictures to show him. Through 1856 all of Inchbold's exhibited works depicted English or Scottish subjects; then, in 1857 he exhibited a view of the Jungfrau at the Royal Academy. This change of subject was certainly due to Ruskin's influence. In each of the summers of 1856, 1857, and 1858, Ruskin and Inchbold were together for some time in Switzerland, and from Ruskin's correspondence we know that he tried to tell Inchbold how to paint. During this process Ruskin's admiration for Inchbold seems to have come to an end; he only passingly referred to his Swiss views in *Academy Notes* and did not mention the artist's work at all after 1857.

William Michael Rossetti described Inchbold as an unsuccessful man who, harassed by ill success, frittered away his abilities as an artist. There are a few shining moments, notably, a group of oil sketches from the neighborhood of Leeds done in 1866 and some watercolors of the surroundings of Lake Geneva done in the last years of Inchbold's life, but much of his later work is of depressingly low quality. A financial crisis struck in 1869, forcing him to give up his lodgings and live successively with several acquaintances. This inspired Rossetti's limerick:

> There is a mad artist named Inchbold
> With whom you must be at a pinch bold:
>   Or else you may score
>   The brass plate on your door
> With the name of J. W. Inchbold.

He apparently had a difficult personality, vacillating, in William Michael Rossetti's words, "between uneasy modesty and angular self-assertion, not promoting smoothness of intercourse." His closest associates seem to have been the Rossettis and Swinburne; the latter wrote a memorial ode upon his death. Inchbold himself published a volume of verse entitled *Annus Amoris* in 1876.

A.S.

Bibliography
Rosalie Mander, "Inchbold in Springtime," *Apollo,* LXXXV, 1967, pp. 62-63

228

228
The White Doe of Rylstone (At Bolton)
Leeds City Art Galleries
Oil on canvas; 27 x 20 in.
Inscribed: *I. W. INCHBOLD/1855*

In the catalogue of the Royal Academy exhibition of 1855, Inchbold accompanied no. 228 with seven lines from the first canto of Wordsworth's *White Doe of Rylstone:*

> And through yon gateway, where is found,
> Beneath the arch with ivy bound,
> Free entrance to the churchyard ground,
> Comes gliding in with lovely gleam,
> Comes gliding in serene and slow,

Soft and silent as a dream
A solitary *Doe!*

Inchbold's painting somewhat perverts the sense of the poem. The lines are extracted from a passage which describes a crowd of people filling the ruins of Bolton Priory. The doe wanders among them, and the poem records their reactions. In the picture there is no hint of any human presence, and the mood of solitude is enhanced by a rabbit, which is not mentioned in the poem, sitting on the ground to the left of the doe.

The ruins of Bolton Priory stand not far from Inchbold's native Leeds. In 1853 he had exhibited *The Chapel, Bolton* at the Royal Academy, also accompanying it with lines from *The White Doe of Rylstone:*

Nature, softening and concealing,
And busy with a hand of healing.

In both pictures, Inchbold emphasized the weathered, lichen- and ivy-covered condition of the ruin. In no. 228, the careful painting of walls with ivy growing over them is a variant of a standard Pre-Raphaelite type, of which Millais's *Huguenot* (no. 225) is the prime example. As in many Pre-Raphaelite figural paintings, most of the picture is limited to a shallow foreground space and a wall immediately beyond. This is complicated by the arches, through which are seen a further wall of the abbey and the lovely Yorkshire scenery in the distance, but essentially the effect of the picture is one of two-dimensional surface, and Inchbold's attention to details of weathered stone, lichens, and foliage serves to enrich this surface.

When the picture was exhibited, Ruskin called it "ineffective, but yet full of excellent work and right feeling." Inchbold obviously had difficulty with the doe, as *pentimenti* are visible all around it. The painting was apparently his first venture outside of pure landscape, and this probably accounts for his having to make alterations in the placing of the animal. The *pentimenti* are especially evident

because of the Pre-Raphaelite technique of painting over a wet white ground, which did not readily allow changes after the first painting. A.S.

Provenance
Ernest Inchbold (who presented the picture to Leeds in 1934)

Exhibitions
Royal Academy, 1855, no. 1075 *(At Bolton)*
Yorkshire Artists: 1600-1900 (Arts Council), 1946, no. 29
Twelve Yorkshire Artists of the Past (Arts Council), 1951, no. 32
Leeds Artists of the 19th Century, various Yorkshire galleries, 1965, no. 9

References
Ruskin, XIV, 22

Frederic Leighton, Baron Leighton of Stretton

1830-1896

Leighton's grandfather was court physician to the Czar in St. Petersburg, and his father also practiced medicine in St. Petersburg before deafness forced his retirement. Leighton was born in Scarborough but for much of his youth the family lived on the continent for the sake of Frederic's education and his mother's health. In 1844 his father asked Hiram Powers if he should make Frederic an artist and was told, "Sir, you cannot help yourself; nature has made him one already." Leighton thence entered the Accademia delle Belle Arti in Florence. He also studied in Brussels and Paris, but the most important part of his education was a three-year period from 1850 through 1852 spent in Frankfurt working under Edward von Steinle, a follower of the Nazarenes. From 1853 until 1855 he was in Rome, where he met Overbeck and Cornelius and the French artists Gérôme and Bouguereau. While in Rome he painted his large (87 by 205 in.) *Cimabue's Celebrated Madonna Being Carried in Procession Through the Streets of Florence,* with which he made his debut at the Royal Academy in 1855. It caused a sensation and was purchased by Queen Victoria. Although he continued to exhibit regularly at the Royal Academy, Leighton lived in Paris and Italy for most of the rest of the decade, settling permanently in London in 1859. He was elected A.R.A. in 1864, R.A. in 1869, and President of the Royal Academy in 1878, in which year he was knighted. He was created a baronet in 1886 and raised to the peerage, the only painter ever so honored, a few days before his death in January 1896. His home and studio in Holland Park Road subsequently became a museum.

Cimabue's Madonna and Leighton's following works were of immense importance for later Victorian painting. He was pushed by the Academy as a rival of the home-grown Pre-Raphaelites, and because of his cosmopolitan background he exerted a strong influence towards continental academicism. His later works reflect the decorative orientation of aestheticism, somewhat modified by a tendency to melodrama and conspicuous virtuosity of handling.
A.S.

Bibliography
Ernest Rhys, *Sir Frederic Leighton, Bart., P. R. A.: An Illustrated Chronicle with Prefatory Essay by F. G. Stephens,* London, 1895 (revised editions, without Stephens's essay, 1900 and 1902)
S. Pepys Cockerell, *Drawings in Pencil, Chalk and Other Mediums by Lord Leighton,* London, 1898
Mrs. Russell Barrington, *The Life, Letters and Work of Frederic Leighton,* 2 vols., London, 1906
William Gaunt, *Victorian Olympus,* London, 1952

229
Portrait of Walter Creyke
Trustees of The British Museum
Pencil; 8⁵⁄₁₆ x 7⅛ in.
Inscribed: *FL (monogram) 1855,* and *W. Creyke from his sincere friend/Fred Leighton*

Leighton was in Rome during the winter and spring of 1855, in England from May to September, and in Paris for the rest of the year. It would seem most likely that no. 229 was drawn in Paris, as Walter Creyke apparently had French connections, publishing in 1864 a translation of *Roman d'un Jeune Homme Pauvre* by Octave Feuillet. However, no. 229 belongs to a tradition of portrait drawings in pencil made by and for foreigners in Rome.

229

Those of Ingres, whom Leighton met in 1855, are the best-known examples, but there are also comparable drawings by German Nazarenes such as Carl Philipp Fohr and Julius Schnorr von Carolsfeld. Leighton probably knew Fohr's drawings from the collection in the possession of Johann David Passavant, who was curator of the Städelsches Kunstinstitut in Frankfurt when Leighton was a student there. No. 229 might also be compared to Watts's portrait drawings (cf. no. 205), which stem from the same Italy-based tradition.
A.S.

230
A Thistle
The Royal Borough of Kensington & Chelsea (Leighton House)
Pencil; 8½ x 7 in.
Inscribed: *thistle/banks of Tiber/ stalk. lt. wm. brown/ leaf. dk. cld. brown/ flow. dk. wm. brown/ grows in thick tufts/ Roma/ 56*

This is one of a group of drawings of plant forms dated 1856 which are preserved at Leighton House. Mrs. Barrington states that they were found among a mass of old papers and that they come from a dismembered sketchbook. Leighton made large numbers of such careful drawings all through the 1850s. In his journal of 1852 he praised minuteness as "the beautiful fruit of a refined love for nature," and in a letter to his mother in the same year, he wrote that he looked forward with delight to the studies he would make in the summer outside of Rome: "I long to find myself again face to face with Nature, to follow it, to watch it, and to copy it, closely, faithfully, ingenuously—as Ruskin suggests, 'choosing nothing, and rejecting nothing.'" This attitude seems to have motivated Leighton throughout the decade. In 1859 he made a large and elaborate drawing of *A Lemon Tree,* which he later compared to Pre-Raphaelite work and which he probably drew purposely to prove that he could outdo the Pre-Raphaelites at their own game. However, the earlier drawings, such as no. 230, which are slighter studies made simply for their own sake, probably owe nothing to the Pre-Raphaelite example, as at that time Leighton had had little contact with the group. On the other hand, he may well have been influenced by Nazarene drawings, such as the studies of withered leaves made by Friedrich Olivier and Julius Schnorr von Carolsfeld, and as the letter quoted above suggests, Leighton was encouraged in these pursuits by his reading of Ruskin.
A.S.

230

Exhibitions
Studies for Pictures, Designs and Sketches by the Late Lord Leighton, Fine Art Society, London, 1896, no. 26

References
Mrs. Barrington, I, 70, 109, 197-221 *passim;* II, 375-76

231
Pavona (Nanna)
The Royal Borough of Kensington & Chelsea
(Leighton House)
Oil on canvas; 24 x 20 in.
Inscribed: *L/59*

Leighton spent the winter of 1858-59 in Rome, where he painted three pictures of the same model to send to the Royal Academy exhibition of 1859. In his letters to his mother, reprinted by Mrs. Barrington, Leighton refers to all three pictures as *Nanna.* The title *Pavona* or *Pavonia* (Italian for peahen) was apparently only ascribed to no. 231 for the sake of differentiating it in the Academy catalogue from its two companions. Leighton was very pleased with the three paintings. He described them in his letters from Rome as his best works, and he showed them to many people, both "artists and Philistines," and found them to be universally admired. No. 231 had apparently been promised to George de Monbrison who, however, gave it up to the Prince of Wales. To assuage his disappointment Leighton proposed painting a copy, but this apparently was never done.

When the pictures were exhibited, *The Athenaeum* commented, "anything more feeling, commanding, or coldly beautiful, we have not seen for many a day" (quoted by Rhys). The phrase "coldly beautiful" best suggests that quality which Leighton introduced into English painting at the end of the 1850s and which would lie at the heart of English Aestheticism of the 1870s. Although Leighton himself turned in another direction, the detached calm of Whistler's *Mrs. Leyland* (Frick Collection) or Albert Moore's classically robed ladies is a later manifestation of the same spirit. The appearance of peacock feathers in the background of no. 231 also anticipates the fetishistic appeal which these exotic objects would hold for the Aesthetes.

Nanna Risi, the model, had one of the most painted faces of the 19th century. She is best known from the long series of portraits of her painted between 1860 and 1865 by the German artist Anselm Feuerbach, and there is distinct resemblance between Leighton's and Feuerbach's paintings. Although in Leighton's published correspondence there is no mention of Feuerbach, both were working in Rome at the same time, and it seems likely, due to Leighton's German background, that they would have been acquainted.   A.S.

231

Provenance
H. M. King Edward VII
Mrs. Russell Barrington, London
Kensington and Chelsea Borough Council, 1926

Exhibitions
Royal Academy, 1859, no. 32 *(Pavonia)*
International Exhibition, London, 1862, no. 429 *(Nanna,* lent by the Prince of Wales)
Leighton Memorial Exhibition, Royal Academy, London, 1897, no. 163 *(Nanna,* lent by the Prince of Wales)

References
Rhys (1902), pp. 17, 107-08, 122
Mrs. Barrington, II, 37-42, 48, 382
John Edgcumbe Staley, *The Makers of British Art: Lord Leighton of Stretton, P. R. A.,* London and New York, 1906, pp. 55-56

1830-1916

Although Wallis died only in 1916, his life is frustratingly obscure. He seems to have been looked upon as a black sheep in Pre-Raphaelite circles as a result of his running off with George Meredith's wife in 1858, an act which led the memoir writers readily to forget or ignore him. He was a native of London and studied at Cary's Academy and at the Royal Academy schools, but he also went to Paris, where he attended the École des Beaux-Arts and worked in the atelier of Gleyre, which slightly later was to be the meeting place of several of the impressionists. He first exhibited in London in 1854, and he created a mild sensation at the Royal Academy in 1856 with his *Death of Chatterton* (Tate Gallery). Two years later, he repeated his success with no. 232; then he eloped. Wallis's later works, with the exception of some handsome drawings in Birmingham and some rather slight landscapes, seem to have entirely disappeared. In his later years, he travelled extensively, he collected, and he wrote articles on oriental and Italian ceramics.

None of Wallis's few known works show any traces of his French training. Both *The Death of Chatterton* and no. 232 are fully in the Pre-Raphaelite manner. They are among the masterpieces of mid-19th-century British painting, but they exist in a curious vacuum due to the slimness of our knowledge of their creator.
A.S.

232

The Stonebreaker (Thou Wert Our Conscript)
Birmingham City Museum and Art Gallery
Oil on panel; 25¾ x 31 in.
Inscribed: *HW* (monogram) *1857*

The picture, which shows a stonebreaker who has died at his work, was accompanied in the Royal Academy catalogue with a quotation from Carlyle's *Sartor Resartus:* "Hardly-entreated Brother! For us was thy back so bent, for us were thy straight limbs and fingers so deformed: thou wert our Conscript, on whom the lot fell, and fighting our battles were so marred. For in thee too lay a god-created Form, but it was not to be unfolded; encrusted must it stand with the thick adhesions and defacements of Labour: and thy body, like thy soul, was not to know freedom."

Stonebreakers were popular subjects by mid-19th century. Courbet's well-known painting dates from 1849 (destroyed, formerly Dresden). There exist an oil painting by Landseer (Victoria and Albert Museum) and a watercolor by William Henry Hunt (private collection), and in the same Royal Academy exhibition in which no. 232 was shown, John Brett's *Stonebreaker* (Liverpool) also appeared. Although both Brett and Wallis were members of the Pre-Raphaelite circle, we do not know enough about their lives to say how aware either may have been of the other's picture before the exhibition. The two artists' visualizations of their subjects could hardly be less alike. While Brett shows a fresh-faced boy at work in a cheerful sun-filled landscape, a bird singing and his dog playing, Wallis's dead stonebreaker lies in a twilight stillness, which is disturbed only by the weasel at his foot. The picture is one of several Pre-Raphaelite works containing a large element of Carlylean social consciousness; the most important example is Ford Madox Brown's *Work* (Manchester), which even includes Carlyle's portrait as one of the brainworkers whose activities give meaning to the labors of others.

Wallis's two best-known pictures are both scenes of death, and in both his use of vibrant colors by contrast makes death seem even the quieter; in no. 232 the stonebreaker has succumbed before a landscape as resplendent in its way as the visionary world of Samuel Palmer. The sunset glow over the horizon seems to reflect that of Millais's *Autumn Leaves* of two years earlier (Manchester).

In his *Academy Notes* for 1858, Ruskin pronounced no. 232 "the picture of the year; and but narrowly missing being a first-rate of any year."
A.S.

Provenance
Temple Soames
Joseph Dixon, 1887
Given to the Birmingham City Museum and Art Gallery by Charles Aitken, 1936

Exhibitions
Royal Academy, 1858, no. 562 (accompanied by a quotation from Carlyle's *Sartor Resartus)*
Liverpool Academy, 1860, no. 54 (accompanied by a different quotation from *Sartor Resartus)*
Whitechapel Art Gallery, London, 1887, no. 197
The Pre-Raphaelite Brotherhood, City Art Gallery, Birmingham, 1947, no. 77
The Pre-Raphaelite Brotherhood, The Tate Gallery, London, 1948, no. 23
Victorian Paintings, Aldeburgh Festival, etc. (Arts Council), 1962, no. 64

References
Ruskin, XIV, 170
Catalogue of Paintings, City Museum and Art Gallery, Birmingham, 1960, p. 149
Graham Reynolds, *Victorian Painting,* London, 1966, pp. 68-69, 91-92, pl. 50

Brett was born in Surrey. He entered the Royal Academy schools in 1854 and first exhibited in 1856. He was an accomplished figural artist, as demonstrated by his *Lady with a Dove* of 1864 in the Tate Gallery, and his first exhibits at the Royal Academy were portraits. In 1857 he exhibited a painting named *Faces in the Fire* and no. 233, and subsequently his exhibited works were almost exclusively of landscapes and seascapes. Several early drawings, dated from 1850 to 1854, in the possession of the Brett family show no trace of Pre-Raphaelite influence. However, he exhibited in 1856 a portrait of Mrs. Coventry Patmore, whose husband was an intimate of the group, and who, herself, had been painted by Millais a few years earlier, so by then Brett did have some contact with Pre-Raphaelitism. He seems to have been a brusque person (William Michael Rossetti in his *Reminiscences* described Brett as a man of "downright self-centered tone"), and he apparently did not share the conviviality of the Rossetti circle.

In 1858 and 1859 Brett exhibited his two best-known pictures *The Stonebreaker* (Liverpool) and no. 234. These both drew long discussions in *Academy Notes* from Ruskin, who obviously considered Brett the new hope of English landscape painting and, in the case of no. 234, even tried to direct Brett's painting. It is sometimes asserted that Ruskin and Brett fell out over no. 234 and that after 1859 Brett's art rapidly declined. However, all Brett's pictures of the next few years have disappeared. In 1863 he sold a watercolor of the *Ponte Vecchio* to Ruskin's father, and his other

Italian views of this time are still of considerable interest. His friendship with Ruskin ended in 1865 because of scientific rather than artistic disagreement. After 1870 Brett's work consisted almost entirely of seascapes. Their bright prismatic colors and precise brushwork might be considered remnants of Pre-Raphaelitism, but they have a hard impersonal emptiness which robs them of appeal. In 1881 Brett was elected A.R.A., but he never became a full Academician.

Brett was an active scientist as well as a painter. He published papers on astronomy, participated in an expedition to Sicily to observe a solar eclipse, and was a Fellow of the Royal Astronomical Society. His scientific interests no doubt strengthened his association with Ruskin, who once described Brett as "one of my keenest-minded friends," and they also provided the basis for his highly individual approach to painting.
A.S.

Bibliography
H. H. T. [Herbert Hall Tunner], obituary, *Monthly Notices of the Royal Astronomical Society,* LXII, 1902, pp. 238-41

233
The Glacier of Rosenlaui
The Trustees of The Tate Gallery, London
Oil on canvas; 17½ x 16½ in.
Inscribed: *John Brett Aug. 23/56*

This is Brett's first exhibited landscape. Nothing is known about the trip to Switzerland which he must have made in 1856 in order to paint it. The picture shows clearly the influence of Ruskin both in subject and in treatment; the foreground rocks might be compared to those in numerous drawings by Ruskin. The trees on the cliff to the left suggest that Brett may also have looked at drawings by Dürer, such as the *Quarry* in The British Museum.

After exhibiting no. 233 at the Royal Academy, Brett sent it to America later in 1857, to the Liverpool Academy in 1858, and to another exhibition in 1859, but he only managed to sell it in 1860 through the good offices of Holman Hunt. His difficulty in finding a buyer is understandable; the composition is unconventional and Brett's minute handling makes the work look more like an elaborate drawing than a painting. Ruskin did not mention no. 233 in his *Academy Notes* when it was exhibited in 1857. However, William Michael Rossetti, in a letter in the Yale University Library explaining the works in the 1857 American exhibition, described Brett as "much admired by Ruskin (tho' he has not written about it)." Ruskin later criticized Brett for painting large studies by way of pictures, and a similar objection may have been the reason that he neglected to mention a picture which seems so close to his own interests.

Brett exhibited two other Alpine subjects at the Pre-Raphaelite exhibition in Russell Place of 1857. One of them was titled *The Engels Hörner and Glacier, from Rosenlaui.* As the Russell Place exhibition overlapped with the Royal Academy exhibition, there is no possibility that it is the same work. It is probable that the works in the Russell Place exhibition, as well as an Alpine view sent to the Liverpool Academy, were drawings; Brett obviously put so much labor into no. 233 that it seems unlikely that he would have been able to prepare another picture of any pretensions during the same period.
A.S.

Provenance
Sir Thomas Fairbairn, Manchester, 1860 (sale, Christie's, London, 7 May 1887, no. 144, bt. Watts)
The Nicholson Gallery, London
The Tate Gallery, 1946

Exhibitions
Royal Academy, 1857, no. 1124
American Exhibition of British Art, National Academy of Design, New York, 1857, no. 18; and Pennsylvania Academy of the Fine Arts, Philadelphia, 1858, no. 5

233

Liverpool Academy, 1858, no. 173
Winter Exhibition, 120 Pall Mall, London, 1859, no. 13

References
Ruskin, XXXVI, 441-42
T. S. R. Boase, "English Artists and the Val d'Aosta," *JWCI,* XIX, 1956, p. 292 n. 4

234
The Val d'Aosta
Sir William H. Cooper, Bt.
Oil on canvas; 34½ x 26¾ in.
Inscribed: *John Brett 1858*

Ruskin concluded his discussion of Brett's

Stonebreaker in his *Academy Notes* of 1858 with the comment that if Brett could paint such a lovely view of the inferior Surrey landscape, "what would he not make of the chestnut groves of the Val d'Aosta! I heartily wish him good-speed and long exile." This seems to refer to plans that had already been made, probably at the instigation of Ruskin. From the diary of Brett's sister we know that the artist set off to the Val d'Aosta on June 16, 1858. Ruskin soon followed, and from Turin he wrote to his father on August 26: "I mentioned that Mr. Brett was with me at La Tour. He has been here a week today. I sent for him at Villeneuve, Val d'Aosta, because I didn't like what he said in his letter about his present work, and thought he wanted some lecturing like Inchbold: besides that, he could give me some useful hints. He is much tougher and stronger than Inchbold, and takes more hammering; but I think he looks more miserable every day, and have good hope of making him completely wretched in a day or two more . . ."

The result of this hammering was the *tour-de-force* of clear-eyed precise vision which Brett exhibited in the following May. The painting was badly hung at the Royal Academy; the *Art Journal's* reviewer did not mention it at all; and Millais mentioned it in a letter to his wife in terms of absolute loathing. Ruskin, on the other hand, devoted a long review to it in *Academy Notes,* beginning "Yes, here we have it at last . . ." He proclaimed that for once an artist had devoted himself to a scene worth painting, and "for the first time in history, we have by help of art, the power of visiting a place, reasoning about it, and knowing it, just as if we were there." No. 234 represents the fulfillment of the approach to landscape for which Ruskin had proselytized in *Modern Painters* and towards which during the 1850s he had urged the Pre-Raphaelites. Nonetheless, Ruskin was disappointed; he found the picture strangely emotionless, without awe of the mountains or love of the chestnuts and the vines: "He has cared for nothing, except as it was more or less pretty in colour and form. I never saw the mirror so held up to Nature; but it is Mirror's work, not Man's."

234

This expression of disappointment is surprising, as the gist of Ruskin's writings for the previous fifteen years had been to encourage exactly such detached scientific observation. His dictum to young artists to go to nature, "selecting nothing, rejecting nothing," and even his personal geological bias seem embodied in no. 234. *The Val d'Aosta,* more than any painting by Turner, seems to be the kind of picture Ruskin describes over and over in *Modern Painters* when citing examples of Turner's keen observation. However, Brett by painting a vast Alpine landscape put himself in a position to be compared with Turner, and seen in contrast to the paintings which provided a visual equivalent for Ruskin's emotional responses to the mountains, Brett's detachment must have seemed disappointing. Previously Ruskin had argued that Turner and the Pre-Raphaelites were fundamentally akin, and even in his review of no. 234, he did not admit the possibility that the emotional level of a Turner and the load of factual information which he demanded of Brett might have been incompatible. Ruskin did buy no. 234, although not until after it returned unsold from the Liverpool Academy in the autumn of 1859, and there are two ambivalently admiring references to it in Ruskin's later writings. However, his disillusionment with the picture, to whose success he had publicly committed himself before it was begun, was apparently profound and probably a major factor in the redirection of Ruskin's interests away from contemporary art and the encouragement of young artists after 1859.

T. S. R. Boase has identified the exact view in no. 234. It is from the hill to the west of the castle of St. Pierre at Villeneuve, in which Brett stayed, and shows the Tête du Rutor and Mt. Paramount. Professor Boase notes that Brett must have gone out of his way not to include Chatel-Argent or the mountain La Grivola, the most arresting features of that part of the valley. Thus Brett seems intentionally to have avoided the kind of imagery that attracted Turner. His painting is in effect a detailed geographical statement, which shows not only the geology but also the cultivation and life of the valley, and it is close to the spirit of *Erdlebenbildkunst* embodied in the Alpine landscapes of Germanic artists such as Joseph Anton Koch. There is no evidence that Brett knew Koch's works, but it is likely that he had seen the Alpine views of the younger Austrian painter Ferdinand Waldmüller, who held an exhibition in London in 1856. However, if there is affinity, there is probably little actual influence, as what Brett and the Germans held in common, a concept of landscape as a means of giving certain knowledge, seems in Brett's case to come so obviously and directly out of the writings of Ruskin.
A.S.

Provenance
John Ruskin, Herne Hill, London, 1859 or 1860 (sale, Christie's, London, 15 April 1869, no. 47, bt. in; thence in Ruskin's possession until his death in 1900)
Sir R. P. Cooper, by 1908 (and by family descent)

Exhibitions
Royal Academy, 1859, no. 908
Liverpool Academy, 1859, no. 33
International Exhibition, London, 1862, no. 481
Pictures and Water-Colour Drawings, Douglas, Isle of Man, 1880 (with catalogue notes by Ruskin)
Art and Industrial Exhibition, Wolverhampton, 1902, no. 98
Ruskin, City Art Gallery, Manchester, 1904, no. 191
Franco-British Exhibition, London, 1908, no. 104
International Fine Arts Exhibition, Rome, 1911, no. 4
The Pre-Raphaelite Brotherhood, City Art Gallery, Birmingham, 1947, no. 2
Pre-Raphaelite Centenary Exhibition, Whitechapel Art Gallery, London, 1948, no. 2
The First Hundred Years of the Royal Academy: 1769-1868, Royal Academy, London, 1951-52, no. 283
Victorian Painting: 1837-1887, Thos. Agnew & Sons, London, 1961, no. 18
Ruskin and His Circle, Arts Council Gallery, London, 1964, no. 259

References
Ruskin, XIV, xxiii-xxiv, 22 n., 172, 234-38, 293, frontispiece
Robin Ironside and John Gere, *Pre-Raphaelite Painters,* London, 1948, pp. 45-46, pl. 79
T. S. R. Boase, "English Artists and the Val d'Aosta," *JWCI,* XIX, 1956, pp. 292-93, pl. 62, fig. c

Hughes was born in London. In 1846 he entered the Schools of Design at Somerset House, where he studied under Alfred Stevens, and in the following year he entered the Royal Academy schools. According to his own account, he was converted to Pre-Raphaelitism in 1850, largely by reading *The Germ.* During the 1850s he painted in the full Pre-Raphaelite manner. His best-known pictures *April Love* and *The Tryst* (Tate Gallery), *Home from Sea* (Ashmolean Museum), and *The Long Engagement* (Birmingham) stylistically depend on Millais, but they have a sensitive delicacy of mood which is Hughes's distinctive contribution. In 1857 he was one of the painters who joined Rossetti in decorating the Oxford Union with frescoes of the Arthurian legends. Around 1860 his painting began to lose all vigor, and the most important works of his long later life are his numerous book illustrations.

Hughes was an intimate member of the Pre-Raphaelite circle, although he was not a member of the Brotherhood. Otherwise he led such a retiring life that we know surprisingly little about him. Nonetheless, he was a considerable artist, and his best works are among the masterpieces of the Pre-Raphaelite movement.
A.S.

Bibliography
Robert Ross, "April Love, A Note," *Burlington,* XXVIII, 1916, p. 171 (see also the obituary by Ross, *ibid.,* pp. 204-07)
Memorial Exhibition of Arthur Hughes, Walker's

Galleries, London, 1916 (exhibition catalogue with introduction by Albert Goodwin)
Robin Ironside and John Gere, *Pre-Raphaelite Painters,* London, 1948, pp. 41-44

235
Ophelia
City of Manchester Art Galleries
Oil on canvas; 27 x 48¾ in., arched top
Inscribed: *Arthur Hughes*
c. 1852

Hughes's first picture of note was no. 235, which he exhibited at the Royal Academy in 1852. This was the year that Millais exhibited his *Ophelia* (Tate Gallery), but Hughes, although he had previously known Rossetti and Hunt, did not meet Millais until varnishing day of the 1852 exhibition, and he apparently was unaware of Millais's picture when preparing his own. After 1852 Hughes fell heavily under Millais's influence, as can be seen by comparing his *Long Engagement,* begun in 1853 (Birmingham), with Millais's *Ophelia* or *The Huguenot* (no. 225), also exhibited in 1852. Hughes's *Ophelia* is strikingly different from Millais's both in conception and style. The distraught maiden is not yet in the brook, but sits on its edge shredding flowers into the water. The flowers and a few of the foreground plants are precisely delineated, but the rest of the painting dissolves into un-Pre-Raphaelite vagueness and suggestion of deep space.

Hughes was only twenty years old when he exhibited this picture, and much about it is still tentative. There are evident *pentimenti,* and the modelling of the figure is reminiscent of the life class. But Hughes is remarkably effective in evoking mood. Ironically, while Hughes in the

235

following years was painting with the tightness of early Millais, Millais in *Autumn Leaves* (Royal Academy, 1856; also in Manchester) was broadening his background to achieve a suggestive effect comparable to that of no. 235. Hughes later, in the 1860s, painted another *Ophelia* (Toledo, Ohio) which has sometimes been confused with this picture. A smaller version of no. 235 belongs to Lord and Lady Northbourne, and was included in the 1948 Pre-Raphaelite exhibitions at Birmingham and the Whitechapel Art Gallery.
A.S.

Provenance
Francis McCracken, Belfast (sale, Christie's, London, 17 June 1854, [Addenda] no. 95, bt. Plint)
Thomas Plint, Leeds (sale, Christie's, London, 7-8 March 1867, no. 263, bt. Grindley)
John Bibby, Liverpool, by 1884
Anonymous sale, Christie's, London, 7 Nov. 1952 (bt. Dent)
J. Hingston, 1952
Manchester Art Galleries, 1955

Exhibitions
Royal Academy, 1852, no. 1247
Pre-Raphaelite exhibition, Russell Place, London, 1857, no. 34
American Exhibition of British Art, National Academy of Design, New York, 1857, no. 85 (apparently withdrawn before the exhibition moved to Philadelphia)
French Gallery, London, 1858, no. 68
Special Loan Collection of Modern Pictures, City Art

Gallery, Birmingham, 1891, no. 206 (lent by Bibby)
Shakespeare in Art, Nottingham University Art Gallery, 1961, no. 69
Shakespeare in Art, Arts Council Gallery, London, 1964, no. 63

References
F. G. Stephens, "The Private Collections of England: LXXVIII—Allerton, and Croxteth Drive, Liverpool," *Athenaeum,* 1884, p. 409
John Guille Millais, *The Life and Letters of Sir John Everett Millais,* London, 1899, I, 146
Mary Bennett, "A Check List of Pre-Raphaelite Pictures Exhibited at Liverpool, and some of their Northern Collectors," *Burlington,* CV, 1963, pp. 488-89, 495 n

Reproductions
Engraved by C. Cousen, *Art Journal,* 1865, p. 332

Listing catalogue numbers

Agasse, Jacques-Laurent, 1767-1849
103 The Nubian Giraffe

Barker, Thomas (Barker of Bath), 1769-1847
109 Interior of a Mill

Barry, James, 1741-1806
 61 Male Nude
 62 Satan Calling up His Legions
 63 Jupiter and Juno on Mount Ida
 64 Self Portrait

Bewick, Thomas, 1753-1828
 84 A Starling

Blake, William, 1757-1827
 92 Study of a Nude Male Model
 93 A Breach in a City the Morning After a Battle
 94 The Bard
 95 And Power was Given Him over all Kindreds
     and Tongues and Nations
 96 The Number of the Beast is 666
 97 Queen Katherine's Dream
 98 Illustration to Milton's *Paradise Lost: The Fall*
 99 Albion Compelling the Four Zoas to Their
     Proper Tasks

Bonington, Richard Parkes, 1802-1828
166 Two Parrots
167 Marly from the Terrace of St-Germain-en-Laye
168 Male Costume, 1580
169 The Doge's Palace, Venice
170 The Castelbarco Tomb, Verona
171 Four Studies of Cloud Effects

Brett, John, 1831-1902
233 The Glacier of Rosenlaui
234 The Val d'Aosta

Brown, Ford Madox, 1821-1893
210 The Body of Harold Brought Before William
    the Conqueror
211 Lear Curses Goneril's Infidelity
212 The Pretty Baa-Lambs
213 Carrying Corn

Brown, John, 1752-1787
78 The Basilica of Constantine and
   Maxentius, Rome, with a Scene of Murder
   in the Foreground
79 Three Roman Ladies, Seen from the Back
80 Unidentified Lady

Chinnery, George, 1774-1852
112 Design for a Title Page

Constable, John, 1776-1837
123 View in the Lake District
124 Fir Trees at Hampstead
125 A Cart and Horses
126 Study of Clouds and Trees
127 Landscape Study: Figures by a Clump of Trees
128 Study for "A Boat Passing a Lock"
129 Waterloo Bridge
130 View at Hampstead

Copley, John Singleton, 1738-1815
43 Study for Sir William Pepperell and His Family
44 Watson and the Shark
45 Lord Heathfield
46 Study for the Siege of Gibraltar
47 Thomas Lane and His Sister Harriot
48 A Hussar Officer on Horseback

Cosway, Richard, 1742-1821
73 Horace Beckford at the Age of Thirteen

Cotman, John Sell, 1782-1842
131 Greta Woods from Brignal Banks
132 Horses Drinking
133 A Spanish Arquebusier

Cox, David, 1783-1859
135 Greenwich Hospital
136 On the Sands

Cozens, Alexander, 1717-1786
4 A Clump of Trees
5 The Cloud

Cozens, John Robert, 1752-1797
82 Schwartze Lütschine and the Mettenburg
83 On the Strada Nomentana, Rome

Dadd, Richard, 1817-1886
202 The Ballad Monger
203 Mercy. David Spareth Saul's Life

Danby, Francis, 1793-1861
160 View of the Avon Gorge
161 Subject from the Revelations
162 Pagan Rites

Davis, William, 1812-1873
195 Old Mill and Pool at Ditton, Lancashire

Dyce, William, 1806-1864
188 Bacchus Nursed by the Nymphs of Nysa
189 The Attendant Spirit, from Milton's *Comus*
190 The Meeting of Jacob and Rachel
191 Welsh Landscape with Two Women Knitting

Egg, Augustus Leopold, 1816-1863
200 The Opera Mantle
201 Outward Bound

Etty, William, 1787-1849
150 Self Portrait
151 Reclining Male Nude Leaning on a Staff
152 Venus and Her Satellites

Flaxman, John, 1755-1826
85 Self Portrait
86 A Young Girl
87 Dante and Virgil in the Suicidal Wood
88 Penelope's Dream

Freebairn, Robert, 1765-1808
101 Neptune's Grotto: Tivoli

Frith, William Powell, 1819-1909
209 Derby Day

Fuseli, John Henry, 1741-1825
66 The Madhouse
67 Martha Hess
68 The Nightmare
69 Macbeth and the Witches
70 Roland at Roncesvalles

Gainsborough, Thomas, 1727-1788
19 Johann Christian Bach
20 Lady Anna Horatia Waldegrave
21 A Lady Walking in the Mall
22 The Harvest Wagon
23 Wooded Landscape with a Herdsman and Cow
24 The Woodman
25 Haymaker and Sleeping Girl

Gillray, James, 1756-1815
89 Study for Charon's Boat—or—the Ghosts of
   "All the Talents" Taking Their Last Voyage

Girtin, Thomas, 1775-1802
113 Lindisfarne Castle, Northumberland
114 Kirkstall Abbey

Grant, Sir Francis, 1803-1878
176 Mary Isabella Grant

Hamilton, Gavin, 1723-1798
10 William Hamilton of Bangour
11 Priam Pleading with Achilles for the Body
   of Hector

Hamilton, William, 1751-1801
77 Joan of Arc and the Furies

Haydon, Benjamin Robert, 1786-1846
145 Head of the Horse of Selene
146 George IV and the Duke of Wellington on the
    Field of Waterloo

Hodges, William, 1744-1797
74 A Crater in the Pacific

Holland, James, 1800-1870
165 Greenwich Hospital

Holst, Theodore Von, 1810-1844
194 Les Adieux

Hughes, Arthur, 1832-1915
235 Ophelia

Hunt, William Henry, 1790-1864
155 Farmer in a Barn
156 Hawthorne and Bird's Nest

Hunt, William Holman, 1827-1910
215 Rienzi Vowing to Obtain Justice for the Death
of His Younger Brother Slain in a Skirmish
between the Colonna and Orsini Factions
216 Strayed Sheep
217 Cairo—Sunset on the Gebel Mokattum

Inchbold, John William, 1830-1888
228 The White Doe of Rylstone

Jones, Thomas, 1742-1803
71 Penkerrig
72 House with a Verandah

Kauffmann, Angelica, 1741-1807
65 The Artist in the Character of Design Listening
to the Inspiration of Poetry

Landseer, Sir Edwin, 1802-1873
172 A Boar
173 Ptarmigan
174 Queen Victoria and the Duke of Wellington
Reviewing the Life Guard
175 The Challenge

Lawrence, Sir Thomas, 1769-1830
104 Arthur Atherley as an Etonian
105 Satan as a Fallen Angel with Beëlzebub
106 Miss Sarah Martha (Sally) Siddons
107 Benjamin West

108 Sir Richard Page Croft, Sixth Baronet

Lear, Edward, 1812-1888
196 Grey Cockatoo
197 The Quarries of Syracuse
198 Civitella di Subiaco, Sunrise
199 Corfu from near the Village of Virò

Leighton, Frederic, Baron Leighton of Stretton, 1830-1896
229 Portrait of Walter Creyke
230 A Thistle
231 Pavona

Leslie, Charles Robert, 1794-1859
163 Woman and Child under a Garden Trellis
164 Scene from Henry VIII—Act IV, Scene ii

Lewis, John Frederick, 1805-1876
117 Study for "The Proclamation of Don Carlos"
178 Two Camels
179 Life in the Harem

Linnell, John, 1792-1882
157 Southampton from the River near Netley Abbey
158 Portrait of Carlyle
159 Summer Evening, Boys Bathing, Harrow in
the Distance

Loutherbourg, Philip James de, 1740-1812
59 The Falls of the Rhine at Schaffhausen
60 A Midsummer's Afternoon, with a
Methodist Preacher

Maclise, Daniel, 1806-1870
192 The Debut of Paganini
193 The Spirit of Chivalry

Martin, John, 1789-1854
153 The Seventh Plague of Egypt
154 View of Shepherd's Bush and the Grounds
of Norlands

Master of the Giants
81 Scene with Four People and a Spider

Millais, Sir John Everett, 1829-1896
223 The Disentombment of Queen Matilda
224 Study for "The Woodman's Daughter"
225 A Huguenot, on St. Bartholomew's Day,
Refusing to Shield Himself from Danger by
Wearing the Roman Catholic Badge
226 Retribution
227 The Rescue

Morland, George, 1763-1804
100 Gypsy Encampment with Seated Man
Breaking Firewood

Mortimer, John Hamilton, 1740-1779
55 Fishermen Being Robbed of Their Catch
by Bandits
56 Head of Beatrice
57 Bandit Taking Up His Post
58 Fish Devouring Mussels

Mulready, William, 1786-1863
147 The Mall, Kensington Gravel Pits
148 The Sonnet
149 Seated Nude with Snake

Palmer, Samuel, 1805-1881
180 Oak Trees in Lullingstone Park
181 Pear Tree in a Walled Garden
182 Moonlit Landscape
183 The Harvest Moon
184 Portrait of the Artist as Christ
185 View of Tivoli
186 Study of Barley, Oats and Wheat

Prout, Samuel, 1783-1852
134 View in Ghent

Raeburn, Sir Henry, 1756-1823
90 Sir John and Lady Clerk

Reynolds, Sir Joshua, 1723-1792
6 Lady Sarah Bunbury Sacrificing to the Graces
7 Comedy
8 Portrait of Baretti
9 Bust of a Young Girl

Romney, George, 1734-1802
31 Study for the Viscountess Bulkeley as Hebe
32 A Sibyl
33 Medea Slaying a Child
34 Sidonian Recollections
35 Portrait of Lady Hamilton as Miranda
36 John Howard Visiting a Prison

Rossetti, Dante Gabriel, 1828-1882
218 Woman in a Bonnet
219 The Sleeper
220 Elizabeth Siddal
221 Passover in the Holy Family
222 The Tune of Seven Towers

Rowlandson, Thomas, 1756-1827
91 Dressing for a Masquerade

Runciman, Alexander, 1736-1785
40 The Landing of St. Margaret
41 Orestes Pursued by the Furies
42 Double Portrait of Brown and Runciman

Ruskin, John, 1819-1900
206 Landscape
207 Loggia of the Ducal Palace, Venice
208 St. Nicholas, Lake Lucerne

Samuel, George, died 1823
102 London from Greenwich Park

Sandby, Paul, 1725-1809
17 The Duke of Cumberland with a Gentleman,
   His Groom on Horseback, and Dogs
18 View of Windsor Castle from the Eton Shore

Scott, David, 1806-1849
187 Philoctetes Left in the Isle of Lemnos
   by the Greeks in Their Progress Towards Troy

Stubbs, George, 1724-1806
12 Rufus
13 Labourers: The Brick Cart
14 Lion Attacking a Horse
15 Ecorché of a Standing Male Figure
16 The Owl

Towne, Francis, 1739/40?-1816
54 Hyde Park, Study of a Tree on the Ground

Turner, Joseph Mallord William, 1775-1851
115 Fonthill Abbey
116 Cottage Destroyed by an Avalanche
117 The Church of SS. Giovanni and Paolo, Rome
118 Storm over St. Peter's
119 Berne
120 Burning of the Houses of Parliament
121 Fluelen, Lake of Lucerne
122 The Apse of the Church of St. Laurent, Eu

Wallis, Henry, 1830-1916
232 The Stonebreaker

Ward, James, 1769-1859
110 Lioness and Heron
111 Marengo, the Barb Charger

Watts, George Frederic, 1817-1904
204 The Irish Famine
205 Portrait of Emily, Lady Tennyson

West, Benjamin, 1738-1820
49 The Landing of Agrippina at Brundisium
   with the Ashes of Germanicus
50 The Blind Belisarius
51 King Lear
52 Cadmus Slaying the Dragon
53 General Kosciusko

Wheatley, Francis, 1747-1801
75 The Wilkinson Family
76 Julie and St. Preux at Meillerie

Wilkie, Sir David, 1785-1841
137 The Blind Fiddler
138 Study for the Letter of Introduction
139 Going to the Drawing-Room Holyrood House
140 A Greenwich Pensioner
141 Study for "The First Ear Ring"
142 The Orderly of Sir David Baird
   and Three Companions
143 Josephine and the Fortune Teller
144 Captain Leigh and His Dragoman

Wilson, Richard, 1713?-1782
1 Thomas Jenkins, the Roman Cicerone
   and Dealer, Seated to the Left
2 House of Pompey at Albano
3 Tivoli: Temple of the Sibyl and the Campagna

Windus, William Lindsay, 1822-1907
214 The Interview of the Apostate Shaxton,
   Bishop of Salisbury, with Anne Askew in Prison

Wright, Joseph (Wright of Derby), 1734-1797
26 Mrs. Sarah Clayton of Liverpool
27 Man in a Turban
28 An Iron Forge
29 The Old Man and Death
30 A Cavern: Morning

Zoffany, Johann, 1734/35-1810
37 Self Portrait
38 The Third Duke of Richmond
   out Shooting with His Servant
39 John Cuff with an Assistant

Book Design:
Murphy Levy Wurman, Architects

Type:
Helvetica, and Helvetica Medium set by
Typographic Service Inc.
Philadelphia, Pennsylvania

Printing:
Falcon Press

Cover:
The Duke of Cumberland with a Gentleman,
His Groom on Horseback, and Dogs
by Paul Sandby, reproduced by gracious
permission of Her Majesty Queen Elizabeth II

Under the Gracious Patronage of
Her Majesty Queen Elizabeth II
and the President of the United States
Lyndon Baines Johnson

most striking impression is absence of color. Constable's study for "A Boat Passing a Lock" (Phil) gives light impression initially, especially in the sky & tree (much energy) but it is essentially non-color. (Romanticism & Cézanne, = poy & form sensations, = at once linking to 1900 & 1700, SM causes much confusion, as it can be poy sensation while dull in form (also sentimentality issues). Drawing = letter the furnished poetry of B West / Romney Reynolds.